The Econometrics of Panel Data
Volume II

The International Library of Critical Writings in Econometrics

Series Editors: Mark Blaug
Professor Emeritus, University of London
Consultant Professor, University of Buckingham
Visiting Professor, University of Exeter
Adrian Darnell
Senior Lecturer in Economics, University of Durham

1. The Econometrics of Panel Data (Volumes I and II)
   G.S. Maddala

Future titles will include:

Macroeconometric Model-Building
Kenneth F. Wallis

Simultaneous Equation Estimates: Cowles Commission Approach
Carl F. Christ

Time Series
Andrew Harvey

General to Specific Modelling
Neil R. Ericsson

Selection Bias
James J. Heckman

Bayesian Inference
George C. Tiao and Nicholas Polson

The History of Econometrics
Adrian Darnell

Specification Problems

Non-Linear Models

Methodology of Econometrics

The Econometrics of Panel Data Volume II

Edited by

G.S. Maddala

Professor of Economics
University of Florida
and The Ohio State University

An Elgar Reference Collection

Published by
Edward Elgar Publishing Limited
Gower House
Croft Road
Aldershot
Hants GU11 3HR
England

Edward Elgar Publishing Company
Old Post Road
Brookfield
Vermont 05036
USA

A CIP catalogue record for this book is available from the British Library

Library of Congress Cataloguing in Publication Data
The Econometrics of panel data/edited by G.S. Maddala.
p. cm. – (The International library of critical writings in econometrics; 1) (An Elgar reference collection.)
Includes bibliographical references and index.
1. Econometrics. 2. Panel analysis. 3. Analysis of variance.
I. Maddala, G.S. II. Series. III. Series: An Elgar reference collection.
HB139.E318 1992
330'.01'5195–dc20

92–21369
CIP

ISBN 1 85278 585 3 (2 volume set)

Printed in Great Britain at the University Press, Cambridge

Contents

Acknowledgements

The editor and publishers wish to thank the following who have kindly given permission for the use of copyright material.

American Statistical Association for article: J.D. Kalbfleisch and J.F. Lawless (1985), 'The Analysis of Panel Data under a Markov Assumption', *Journal of the American Statistical Association*, **80** (392), 863–71.

Elsevier Science Publishers B.V. for article: Jacques Mairesse (1990), 'Time-Series and Cross-Sectional Estimates on Panel Data: Why are They Different and Why Should They be Equal?' in J. Hartog, G. Ridder and J. Theeuwes (eds), *Panel Data and Labor Market Studies*, 81–95.

Elsevier Sequoia S.A. for articles: Zvi Griliches and Jerry A. Hausman (1986), 'Errors in Variables in Panel Data', *Journal of Econometrics*, **31** (1), 93–118; Erik Biørn (1981), 'Estimating Economic Relations from Incomplete Cross-Section/Time-Series Data', *Journal of Econometrics*, **16** (2), 221–36; Tom Wansbeek and Arie Kapteyn (1989), 'Estimation of the Error-Components Model with Incomplete Panels', *Journal of Econometrics*, **41** (3), 341–61; Angus Deaton (1985), 'Panel Data from Time Series of Cross-Sections', *Journal of Econometrics*, **30** (1/2), 109–26; Suk Kang (1985), 'A Note on the Equivalence of Specification Tests in the Two-Factor Multivariate Variance Components Model', *Journal of Econometrics*, **28** (2), 193–203; Christopher Cornwell, Peter Schmidt and Robin C. Sickles (1990), 'Production Frontiers with Cross-Sectional and Time-Series Variation in Efficiency Levels', *Journal of Econometrics*, **46** (1/2), 185–200; James J. Heckman and Richard Robb, Jr. (1985), 'Alternative Methods for Evaluating the Impact of Interventions: An Overview', *Journal of Econometrics*, **30** (1/2), 239–67.

The Econometric Society for articles: J.A. Hausman (1978), 'Specification Tests in Econometrics', *Econometrica*, **46** (6), 1251–71; Marc Nerlove (1971), 'A Note on Error Components Models', *Econometrica*, **39** (2), 383–96; Yair Mundlak (1978), 'On the Pooling of Time Series and Cross Section Data', *Econometrica*, **46** (1), 69–85; Douglas Holtz-Eakin, Whitney Newey and Harvey S. Rosen (1988), 'Estimating Vector Autoregressions with Panel Data', *Econometrica*, **56** (6), 1371–95; J.S. Butler and Robert Moffitt (1982), 'A Computationally Efficient Quadrature Procedure for the One-Factor Multinomial Probit Model', *Econometrica*, **50** (3), 761–4, erratum; Robin C. Sickles and Paul Taubman (1986), 'An Analysis of the Health and Retirement Status of the Elderly', *Econometrica*, **54** (6), 1339–56; Jerry A. Hausman and David A. Wise (1979), 'Attrition Bias in Experimental and Panel Data: The Gary Income Maintenance Experiment', *Econometrica*, **47** (2), 455–73; Jerry Hausman, Bronwyn H. Hall and Zvi Griliches (1984), 'Econometric Models for Count Data with an Application to the Patents-R & D Relationship', *Econometrica*, **52** (4), 909–38.

International Economic Review for article: Robert B. Avery, Lars Peter Hansen and V. Joseph Hotz (1983), 'Multiperiod Probit Models and Orthogonality Condition Estimation', *International Economic Review*, **24** (1), 21–35.

Journal of Business & Economic Statistics for articles: Brent R. Moulton (1987), 'Diagnostics for Group Effects in Regression Analysis', *Journal of Business & Economic Statistics*, **5** (2), 275–82; Peter Schmidt and Robin C. Sickles (1984), 'Production Frontiers and Panel Data', *Journal of Business & Economic Statistics*, **2** (4), 367–74; Joshua D. Angrist and Whitney K. Newey (1991), 'Over-Identification Tests in Earnings Functions With Fixed Effects', *Journal of Business & Economic Statistics*, **9** (3), 317–23; Lawrence S. Mayer (1986), 'On Cross-Lagged Panel Models with Serially Correlated Errors', *Journal of Business & Economic Statistics*, **4** (3), 347–57.

Physica-Verlag, Heidelberg, Germany, for excerpt: D.M. Grether and G.S. Maddala (1982), 'A Time Series Model with Qualitative Variables' in M. Deistler, E. Fürst and G. Schwödiauer (eds), *Games, Economic Dynamics, and Time Series Analysis*, 291–305.

Review of Economic Studies Ltd for articles: Manuel Arellano and Stephen Bond (1991), 'Some Tests of Specification for Panel Data: Monte Carlo Evidence and an Application to Employment Equations', *Review of Economic Studies*, **58**, 277–97; Gary Chamberlain (1980), 'Analysis of Covariance with Qualitative Data', *Review of Economic Studies*, **XLVII**, 225–38.

University of Wisconsin Press for article: G.S. Maddala (1987), 'Limited Dependent Variable Models Using Panel Data', *Journal of Human Resources*, **XII** (3), 307–38.

Every effort has been made to trace all the copyright holders but if any have been inadvertently overlooked the publishers will be pleased to make the necessary arrangement at the first opportunity.

In addition the publishers wish to thank the library of the London School of Economics and Political Science and The Alfred Marshall Library, Cambridge University, and the Photographic Unit of the University of London library for their assistance in obtaining these articles.

Introduction

This volume covers the topics of errors in variables and incomplete data; specification tests; limited dependent variables; frontier production functions, and special problems of panel data. References only will be given to duration models, self-selection models and simulation based inference. The last topic was omitted because most of the relevant papers are still unpublished; the subject of self-selection models was not included because there is a separate volume in this area (edited by J.J. Heckman), while duration models were omitted due to lack of space.

Errors in Variables and Incomplete Data

In the topics covered in Volume I, the emphasis was on efficient estimation. With errors in variables we first have to worry about obtaining consistent estimates of the parameters. With time-series data, if we assume that the errors in the explanatory variables are serially uncorrelated, we can use lagged values of these variables as instruments. In panel data, because we assume correlated individual effects, we cannot use this procedure. Griliches and Hausman (1986) suggest eliminating the individual effects by differencing and then using lagged or future values of the explanatory variables as instruments. Since there are many differences to consider (for instance, $y_{it} - y_{i,t-1}$, $y_{it} - y_{i,t-2}$, etc.), we have to use a system method of estimation. Some extensions of the results reported in Griliches and Hausman can be found in Wansbeek and Koning (1991) and Wansbeek and Kapteyn (1992).

Biørn (Chapter 2) and Wansbeek and Kapteyn (Chapter 3) consider the problem of estimation from incomplete panels. In many of the commonly used panel data sets in the US, like PSID, NLS Young Men, NLS Youth, ASA-NBER forecasts, Compustat, IBES forecasts and so on, eliminating all individuals with missing data would leave only 10-20 per cent of all observations. Thus, the missing data problem is an important one. Blundell et al. (1992) provides an interesting application of estimation from incomplete panel data. Deaton (Chapter 4) argues that in many countries there are few or no panel data, whereas a series of independent cross-sections may exist. He suggests estimation methods for such data sets. Some extensions of Deaton's analysis can be found in Moffitt (1990) and Verbeek and Nijman (1992).

Specification Tests

A commonly used specification test in econometrics is the Hausman test (see Chapter 5) for fixed vs. random effects in panel data models. However, the test is based on a particular specification of random effects considered by Mundlak in Chapter 6 (see equation (5) in Introduction to Volume I). The null hypothesis H_0 tested is that the model is a random effects model. If H_0 is correct, then the GLS estimator from the random effects model is both consistent and efficient. But it is not consistent under the alternative hypothesis of a fixed effects model. On the other hand, the within group estimator $\hat{\beta}_w$ is consistent whether the null hypothesis is valid or not since all the time invariant effects are subtracted out. Thus, we can consider the difference $q = \hat{\beta}_w - \hat{\beta}_{GLS}$. Also $V(q) = V(\hat{\beta}_w) - V(\hat{\beta}_{GLS})$. Hence, we use $m = \hat{q}' \, [\hat{V}(\hat{q})]^{-1} \, \hat{q}$ as a χ^2 statistic with d.f. k where k is the dimensionality of β. Denoting the between group estimate of β by $\hat{\beta}_B$, one could also construct tests based on $\hat{\beta}_B - \hat{\beta}_{GLS}$ and $\hat{\beta}_B - \hat{\beta}_w$. Such tests have been suggested by Pudney (1978). Hausman and Taylor show that the χ^2 statistics for all the tests are numerically exactly identical (see Chapter 23 of Volume I, p. 397). See also Chapter 7 by Kang.

Chamberlain (Chapter 18 in Volume I and 1984) pointed out that the fixed effects model for panel data (in the case of qualitative dependent variables) imposes testable restrictions on coefficients from regressions of all leads and lags of dependent variables on all leads and lags of independent variables. Chamberlain suggested that estimation and testing be carried out by minimizing an optimally weighted quadratic form in the difference between unrestricted parameters and the restrictions implied by the fixed effects model. Angrist and Newey (Chapter 10) use this result to test the validity of the fixed effects model for human capital earnings functions based on the NLS Youth data but find the fixed effects model inappropriate.

Holz-Eakin, Newey and Rosen (Chapter 9) consider estimating VAR models from panel data. They allow for individual-specific effects and cross-section heteroskedasticity. Arrellano and Bond (Chapter 11) also consider estimation of dynamic models with panel data. They propose a test of serial correlation based on the GMM residuals and compare this with Sargan tests of over-identifying restrictions and Hausman specification tests.

Moulton (Chapter 8) discusses regression diagnostics for group effects in fixed and random effects models. He reviews several tests in the literature on panel data and illustrates them using housing price data.

Limited Dependent Variables

In the case of continuous variables and no autoregressions, the fixed effects model gives consistent estimates of the slope parameters. Chamberlain (Chapter 12) shows that this is not the case when the dependent variable y_{it} is observed only as a qualitative variable and when there are only a few time-series observations per individual. He demonstrates this for the logit model and suggests a conditional likelihood approach. However, the conditional likelihood approach is not possible for the probit model. Hence, for the analysis of fixed effects models, the logit model is appropriate, on the other hand, for the analysis of random effects models, the probit model is relevant. The first application of a random effects probit model was that of Heckman and Willis (1976). Butler and Moffitt (Chapter 13) provide an efficient computational algorithm for the ML estimation of the random effects probit model. Their procedure is much faster than the one used by Heckman and Willis.

Avery, Hansen and Hotz (Chapter 15) drop the equicorrelation assumption implied by the one-factor random effects model. They consider a model with a general correlation structure for errors and suggest using the method of moments estimators. Chamberlain (1984) also suggests an extension of the random effects probit model to include correlations between the random effects and the explanatory variables. Extensions of these models to the tobit case can be found in Heckman and MaCurdy (1980) for the fixed effects model, and in Hausman and Wise (1979) for the random effects model.

When it comes to an extension of the random effects probit model to more complicated situations like simultaneous equations models, the models by Avery, Hansen and Hotz (1983) and Chamberlain (1984) get very complicated. Sickles and Taubman (Chapter 17) consider a generalization of the one-factor probit model to simultaneous equations and estimate it using the Butler and Moffitt (1982) algorithm.

When we consider autoregressive models using limited dependent variables, we have to distinguish between lagged-index vs. lagged-dummy models. An example of the lagged index model is in Grether and Maddala (Chapter 14).

Maddala (Chapter 18) presents a survey of all the above mentioned models – logit, probit and tobit models with fixed and random effects. One useful paper in this area that does not appear to have received attention in the econometric literature is that of Kalbfleisch and Lawless (Chapter 16).

Frontier Production Functions

Frontier production functions is an important area of application of limited dependent variable models. Pitt and Lee (1981) is a first application of a random effects frontier production model using panel data. Schmidt and Sickles (Chapter 19) present a survey of this area, while Cornwell, Schmidt and Sickles (Chapter 20) offer some extensions of this model.

Special Problems with Panel Data

Hausman and Wise (Chapter 21) discuss attrition problems in panel data. They use a random effects tobit model with self-selection. Hausman, Hall and Griliches (Chapter 22) consider estimation of poisson models based on panel data. Heckman and Robb (Chapter 23) review a whole series of models that can be used for the evaluation of the impact of interventions. Mairesse (Chapter 25) identifies several practical problems that arise in the interpretation of time-series and cross-sectional estimates of the same parameters. The paper by Mayer (Chapter 24) discusses some panel data models that are current in the statistical literature.

Simulation Based Inference

The estimation methods by Avery, Hansen and Hotz (Chapter 15) and Chamberlain (1984) are not as efficient as ML, however, and their extensions to systems of equations is cumbersome. Recently, simulation based methods have been suggested to solve the problem of evaluation of multiple integrals that one encounters while estimating probit models with an arbitrary serial correlation structure. The method of simulated moments (MSM) suggested by McFadden (1989) and Pakes and Pollard (1989) has been extended by Keane (1990) to cover the case of panel data. Gourieroux and Monfort (1992) present a survey of simulation-based inference with special reference to panel data models. In the next few years simulation based methods will be standard techniques in the analysis of limited dependent variable models with panel data.

Duration Models

Since Lancaster's (1979) paper, duration models have become commonly used in econometrics. These are discussed in greater detail in Lancaster (1991). Kiefer (1988), Tuma (1982), Tuma and Hannan (1978), and Tuma, Hannan and Goenwald (1979) all provide non-technical introductions to this area. Heckman and Singer (1985, 1986) also present some surveys from the econometric point of view. The econometric literature emphasizes unobserved heterogeneity, whereas the statistical literature exemplified in Cox and Oakes (1984) uses non-parametric methods. Ahn and Hausman (1990) is an example of a combination of the two approaches.

References

Note: References to papers included in these two volumes are omitted here.

Ahn, A. and J.A. Hausman (1990), 'Flexible Parametric Estimation of Duration and Competing Risk Models', *Journal of Applied Econometrics*, **5**, 1–28.

Blundell, R., S. Bond, M. Devereux and F. Schiantarelli (1992), 'Investment and Tobins's Q: Evidence from Company Panel Data', *Journal of Econometrics*, **51**, 233–57.

Chamberlain, G. (1984), 'Panel Data' in Z. Griliches and M.D. Intrilligator (eds), *Handbook of Econometrics*, Vol. 2, Amsterdam: North Holland, 1248–318.

Cox, D.R. and D. Oakes (1984), *Analysis of Survival Data*, London: Chapman and Hall.

Gourieroux, C. and A. Monfort (1992), 'Simulation Based Inference: A Survey with Special Reference to Panel Data Models', forthcoming in *Journal of Econometrics*.

Heckman, J.J. and B.S. Singer (eds), (1985), *Longitudinal Analysis of Labor Market Data*, New York: Cambridge University Press.

Heckman, J.J. and B.S. Singer (1986), 'Econometric Analysis of Longitudinal Data' in Z. Griliches and M.D. Intrilligator (eds), *Handbook of Econometrics*, Vol. 3, Amsterdam, North Holland.

Heckman, J.J. and R. Willis (1976), 'Estimation of a Stochastic Model of Reproduction: An Econometric Approach' in N. Terleckyj (ed.), *Household Production and Consumption*, New York: National Bureau of Economic Research.

Heckman, J.J. and T.E. MaCurdy (1980), 'A Life-Cycle Model of Female Labor Supply', *Review of Economic Studies*, **47**, 47–74.

Keane, M.P. (1990), 'A Computationally Practical Simulation Estimator for Panel Data, with Applications to Estimating Temporal Dependence in Employment and Wages', Discussion Paper, University of Minnesota.

Kiefer, N. (1988), 'Economic Duration Data and Hazard Functions', *Journal of Economics Literature*, **26**, 646–79.

Lancaster, T. (1979), 'Econometric Methods for the Duration of Unemployment', *Econometrica*, **47**, 939–56.

Lancaster, T. (1991), *The Econometric Analysis of Transition Data*, New York: Cambridge University Press.

McFadden, D. (1989), 'A Method of Simulated Moments for Estimation of Discrete Response Models without Numerical Integration', *Econometrica*, **57**, 995–1026.

Moffitt, R. (1990), 'Estimating Dynamic Models with a Time Series of Repeated Cross Sections', mimeo, Providence, Rhode Island: Brown University.

Pakes, A. and D. Pollard (1989), 'Simulation and the Asymptotics of Optimization Estimators', *Econometrica*, **57**, 1027–57.
Pitt, M.M. and L.F. Lee (1981), 'The Measurement of Sources of Technical Inefficiency in the Indonesian Weaving Industry', *Journal of Development Economics*, **9**, 43–64.
Pudney, S.E. (1978), 'The Estimation and Testing of Some Error Components Models', mimeo, London School of Economics.
Tuma, N.B. (1982), 'Non-Parametric and Partially Parametric Approaches to Event-History Analysis', *Sociological Methodology*, 11–60.
Tuma, N.B. and M.T. Hannan (1978), 'Approaches to the Censoring Problem in Analysis of Event Histories', *Sociological Methodology*, 209–40.
Tuma, N.B., M.T. Hannan and L.P. Goenwald (1979), 'Dynamic Analysis of Event Histories', *American Journal of Sociology*, **84**, 820–54.
Verbeek, M. and T. Nijman (1992), 'Minimum MSE Estimation of a Regression Model with Fixed Effects from a Series of Cross Sections', Discussion Paper No. 9201, CENTER, Tilburg University.
Wansbeek, T.J. and A. Kapteyn (1992), 'Simple Estimators for Dynamic Panel Data Models with Errors in the Variables' in R. Bewley and Tran Van Hoa (eds), *Contributions to Consumer Demand and Econometrics*, London: MacMillan, 238–51.
Wansbeek, T.J. and R.H. Koning (1991), 'Measurement Error and Panel Data', *Statistica Neerlandica*, **45**, 85–92.

Part I
Errors in Variables and Incomplete Data

[1]

Journal of Econometrics 31 (1986) 93–118. North-Holland

ERRORS IN VARIABLES IN PANEL DATA

Zvi GRILICHES

Harvard University and NBER, Cambridge, MA 02138, USA

Jerry A. HAUSMAN

MIT and NBER, Cambridge, MA 02139, USA

Received May 1984, final version received November 1985

Panel data based studies in econometrics use the analysis of covariance approach to control for various 'individual effects' by estimating coefficients from the 'within' dimension of the data. Often, however, the results are unsatisfactory, with 'too low' and insignificant coefficients. Errors of measurement in the independent variables whose relative importance gets magnified in the within dimension are then blamed for this outcome.

Errors-in-variables models have not been used widely, in part because they seem to require extraneous information to be identified. We show how a variety of errors-in-variables models may be identifiable and estimable in panel data without the use of external instruments and apply it to a relatively simple but not uninteresting case: the estimation of 'labor demand' relationships, also known as the 'short-run increasing returns to scale' puzzle.

1. Introduction

Panel data based on various longitudinal surveys have become ubiquitous in economics in recent years. Their popularity stems in part from their ability to allow and control for various 'individual effects' and other relatively slowly changing left-out variables. Using the analysis of covariance approach, one can estimate the relevant relationships from the 'within' dimension of the data. Quite often, however the 'within' results are unsatisfactory, 'too low' and insignificant. The tendency is then to blame this unhappy outcome, among other things, on errors of measurement in the independent variables whose relative importance gets magnified in the within dimension.

That errors of measurement are important in micro data is well known but has had little influence on econometric practice.[1] The standard errors-in-

*We would like to thank the NSF and NBER for research support; Gary Chamberlain, Bronwyn H. Hall, Adrian Pagan, Ariel Pakes, Whitney Newey, William Nordhaus and the anonymous referees for a number of very helpful comments; and John Bound, Adam Jaffe and Bruce Meyer for excellent research assistance.

[1]Matters are somewhat better in sociology: see Griliches (1984) for general discussion, and Bielby, Hauser and Featherman (1977) for an applied example.

0304-4076/86/$3.50

variables model has not been applied widely, partly because in the usual context it requires extraneous information to identify the parameters of interest. It is rather obvious but does not appear to be widely known that in the panel data context a variety of errors-in-variables models may be identifiable and estimable without the use of external instruments.

It is clear that once one has a time series and one is willing to assume that errors of measurement are serially uncorrelated then one can use lagged values of the relevant variables as instruments. The problem in panel data is that because one is likely to assume the presence of correlated individual effects, lagged values are not valid instruments without further analysis. But, because the errors of measurement are assumed to have a particular time series structure (usually uncorrelated over time), different transformations of the data will induce different and deducible changes in the biases due to such errors which can be used then to identify the importance of these errors and recover the 'true' parameters. We exposit and develop this idea and illustrate its application in a relatively simple but not uninteresting case: the estimation of 'labor demand' relationships, also known as the 'short-run increasing returns to scale' puzzle; see Solow (1964) and Medoff and Fay (1985).

In the next four sections we first outline our approach in a very simple context; next we present the algebra for the more general case and discuss the different estimation strategies; we turn then to a description and discussion of our empirical example and conclude with recommendations for a particular empirical strategy which should be followed when analyzing such data.

2. The problem of errors in variables in panel data: An introduction

The following simple model will serve to illustrate our main ideas. Let the true equation be of the form

$$y_{it} = \alpha_i + \beta z_{it} + \eta_{it}, \tag{1}$$

where the α_i are unobserved individual effects which may be correlated with the true independent variable of interest, the z_{it}. The η_{it} are the standard 'best case' disturbances: i.i.d., with mean zero and variance σ_η^2. The z_{it} are not observed directly, however. Only their erroneous reflection, the x_{it},

$$x_{it} = z_{it} + v_{it}, \tag{2}$$

are observed, where v_{it} is an i.i.d. measurement error with variance σ_v^2. If OLS is applied to the observed variables, the equation to be estimated is

$$y_{it} = \bar{\alpha} + \beta x_{it} - \beta v_{it} + \eta_{it} + (\alpha_i - \bar{\alpha}), \tag{3}$$

and the resulting parameters will be biased for two distinct reasons: (1) because of the correlation of the x_{it} with the left-out individual effects (usually upward), and (2) downward because of the negative correlation between the observed x_{it} and the new composite disturbance term.

It is clear that in panel data one can eliminate the first source of bias by going 'within' by analyzing deviations around individual means. It is also reasonably well known that going within might exacerbate the second source of bias and make things worse rather than better.[2] What is less obvious is that there are different ways of eliminating the first source of bias, that they imply different consequences for the size of the second bias, and hence provide an opportunity for identifying its magnitude and recovering the 'true' coefficients.

An alternative to the 'within' estimator is a first difference estimator, which also sweeps out the individual effects. We shall show in the next section that assuming stationary and uncorrelated measurement errors the plims of the difference and within estimators are

$$\operatorname{plim} b_d = \beta\left(1 - \frac{2\sigma_v^2}{\operatorname{var}(\mathrm{d}x)}\right), \qquad \operatorname{plim} b_w = \beta\left(1 - \frac{T-1}{T}\frac{\sigma_v^2}{\operatorname{var}\tilde{x}}\right), \tag{4}$$

where

$$\mathrm{d}y_{it} = y_{it} - y_{it-1}, \qquad \tilde{y}_{it} = y_{it} - \bar{y}_i,$$

and similarly for the other variables.

For the most likely case in economics: positively serially correlated 'true' x's (z's) with a declining correlogram and, for $T > 2$,

$$\operatorname{var}(\mathrm{d}x) < \frac{2T}{T-1}\operatorname{var}\tilde{x}, \tag{5}$$

and hence $|\text{bias } b_d| > |\text{bias } b_w|$. That is, errors of measurement will usually bias the first difference estimators downward (toward zero) by more than they will bias the within estimators.

Note, however, that if we have estimated both b_d and b_w we have already computed $\operatorname{var}\mathrm{d}x$ and $\operatorname{var}\tilde{x}$ and hence have all the ingredients to solve out for the unknown σ_v^2 and β. In fact, consistent estimates can be had from

$$\beta = \left[2b_w/\operatorname{var}(\mathrm{d}x) - (T-1)b_d/T\operatorname{var}\tilde{x}\right] \\ /\left[2/\operatorname{var}\mathrm{d}x - (T-1)/T\operatorname{var}\tilde{x}\right], \tag{6}$$

$$\sigma_v^2 = (\beta - b_d)\operatorname{var}(\mathrm{d}x)/2\beta. \tag{7}$$

[2] See Griliches (1979) for a related discussion in the context of the analysis of sibling data and Freeman (1984) and Chowdhury and Nickell (1985) in the zero–one variable (impact of unionization) context.

The first difference and within estimators are not the only ones that can yield such implicit estimates of the bias. If we define $d^j = 1 - L^j$ as the difference operator 'j periods apart', where L is the lag operator, then $\mathrm{d}^j y_t = y_t - y_{t-j}$ (and similarly for $\mathrm{d}^j x_t$) and, for example, $\mathrm{d}^{T-1} y = y_T - y_1$ is the 'longest' difference possible in a particular panel. For $T > 2$ several more slope estimators can be computed based on 'different lengths' differences with

$$\operatorname{plim} b_j = \beta - 2\beta\sigma_v^2/\mathrm{var}(\mathrm{d}^j x), \tag{8}$$

implying additional estimates of β and σ_v^2. These take the form of

$$\tilde{\beta}_{jh} = (\omega_j - \omega_h)/(s_j^2 - s_h^2), \tag{9}$$

where ω_j is the covariance between $\mathrm{d}^j y$ and $\mathrm{d}^j x$ while s_j^2 is the comparable variance of $\mathrm{d}^j x$. Such estimates can be combined optimally to improve upon their individual efficiency.

It is worth noting that these 'contrast' or 'moments' estimators can be given a straightforward instrumental variables interpretation. Let us take as an example $\tilde{\beta}_{21}$, i.e., an estimate derived by solving the implied bias relationship from OLS estimates computed using differences two periods apart $(y_T - y_{T-2})$ and one period apart $(y_T - y_{T-1})$. The numerator of (9) can be rewritten as

$$x'F_2'F_2 y - x'F_1'F_1 y = x'[F_2'F_2 - F_1'F_1]y = x'Qy = w'y,$$

and similarly also for the denominator of (9), where F_2 and F_1 are appropriate 'differencing' matrices. In the simplest $T = 3$ case, where we are using three cross-sectional equations to estimate one β, these matrices take the $(-1\ 0\ 1)$ and $(0\ -1\ 1)$ form, respectively, and the resulting instrumental variable can be seen to equal $w = (x_1 - x_3\ \ x_3 - x_2\ \ x_2 - x_1)$.[3] If the measurement errors are stationary and uncorrelated ($\sigma_{vt}^2 = \sigma_v^2$, $\sigma_{v_t v_{t+h}} = 0$ for $h \neq 0$), then $\mathrm{E}w'x = w'z$ and w is a valid instrument for x.

The above results were derived assuming that the measurement errors were not serially correlated, while the true z's are. It is possible to allow for serial correlation in the measurement errors, the v's, provided that we are willing to make one of the following three types of assumptions:

(1) The correlation is of the moving average form of order k and the available sample is long enough in the time dimension, $T > k + 1$, to allow the use of more distant instruments.

[3] This is one of two such possible instruments. The other can be derived using the alternative $F_1 = (-1\ 1\ 0)$. A. Pagan suggested this simplification.

(2) The measurement errors are stationary while the true underlying variables (the z's) are not.[4] For example, $x_4 - x_1$ can be used as an instrument for $x_3 - x_2$ as long as $\mathrm{E}v_4v_3 = \mathrm{E}v_2v_1$ but $\operatorname{cov}(z_4, z_3) \neq \operatorname{cov}(z_2, z_1)$. We shall come back to this point in the next section.

(3) More generally, one can always allow for correlation in the measurement errors if its magnitude is know a priori. For example, if x is a gross capital stock measure based on a twenty-year life assumption and the i.i.d. measurement errors occur in the measurement of investment, then the first-order serial correlation of the errors in the capital stock is approximately $19/20 = 0.95$. The first difference bias formula now becomes

$$\operatorname{plim}(b_d - \beta) = \frac{-2\beta\sigma_v^2(1-\rho_\varepsilon)}{\operatorname{var} \mathrm{d}x} = \frac{-0.1\beta\sigma_v^2}{\operatorname{var} \mathrm{d}x}, \tag{10}$$

and a similar expression can be worked out for the bias of the within estimator. Other forms of serial dependence in the errors of measurement can be tested for and consistent estimators can be derived in their presence.

These results have been derived assuming only one independent variable. If there are more independent variables in the equation, but they are not subject to error, they can be swept out from all the other variables and the formulae reinterpreted in terms of the variances of residuals from regressions on these other variables. If some of them are also subject to measurement error, the formulae become more complex but can be similarly derived provided that these measurement errors are mutually uncorrelated (or correlated with a known correlation structure).

We now turn to the consideration of the general case and the formulation of optimal estimators for it.

3. Derivation of results

We now reconsider our basic model, eq. (1), and derive the relationship among the various estimators. The general specification of (1) for an observation on an individual unit (there are N such units or individuals) is

$$y = z\beta + l\alpha + \eta, \tag{11a}$$

$$x = z + v, \tag{11b}$$

$$y = x\beta + l\alpha + \eta - v'\beta = x\beta + l\alpha + \varepsilon, \tag{11c}$$

[4] This was suggested to us by A. Pakes.

with

$$V(\eta) = \Sigma, \qquad V(\upsilon) = \Omega,$$

where y, z, x, y and υ are $T \times 1$ vectors, l is a vector of ones, β is a constant, but α varies across the N units or individuals, while Σ and Ω are $T \times T$ symmetric matrices.

The within estimator and difference estimator can be seen to arise from the transformation of eq. (11c),

$$Ry = Rx\beta + R\alpha + R\varepsilon, \tag{12}$$

where each row of R must sum to zero to eliminate α. For instance, the R for the first difference estimator will be a bi-diagonal matrix with -1 on the diagonal and $+1$ on the superdiagonal. The within estimator has $R = I_T - J$ where J is $1/T$ times a matrix of all ones. We calculate for this class of estimators

$$\begin{aligned} \operatorname{plim}(\beta_T) &= [\mathrm{E}(x'R'Rx)]^{-1}\mathrm{E}(x'R'Ry) \\ &= [\mathrm{E}(z'Qz) + \mathrm{E}(\upsilon'Q\upsilon)]^{-1}\mathrm{E}[\upsilon'Q\upsilon]\beta, \end{aligned} \tag{13}$$

where

$$Q = R'R, \qquad \mathrm{E}(\upsilon'Q\upsilon) = \operatorname{tr}[Q\Omega],$$

and all plims in the paper are taken as $N \to \infty$. For ease in derivation of the results, we assume that all the random variables are jointly covariance stationary. For the present we also assume that both η_{it} and υ_{it} are not serially correlated and that Σ and Ω are both diagonal matrices. (We shall relax all of these assumptions below.) With these assumptions we calculate the probability limit of the first difference estimator as

$$\begin{aligned} \operatorname{plim} b_d - \beta &= [2\sigma_z^2(1-\rho_1) + 2\sigma_\upsilon^2]^{-1}(-2\sigma_\upsilon^2\beta) \\ &= -[\sigma_z^2(1-\rho_1) + \sigma_\upsilon^2]^{-1}\sigma_\upsilon^2\beta, \end{aligned} \tag{14}$$

where ρ_j is the jth serial correlation coefficient between the true regression variables z. Note that as expected the inconsistency increases as the correlation increases so long as it is positive. First differencing 'removes more of the signal' for given σ_z^2 and σ_υ^2 the higher is ρ_1, which exacerbates the errors in variables problem.

Table 1

Comparison of first difference and within estimator.

T	plim $b_d - \beta$	plim $b_w - \beta$	Conditions for $\|b_w\| - \|b_d\| > 0,\ \rho_i > 0$
2	$-(\sigma_x^2 - \sigma_z^2\rho_1)^{-1}\sigma_v^2\beta$	$-(\sigma_x^2 - \sigma_z^2\rho_1)^{-1}\sigma_v^2\beta$	Same
3	$-(\sigma_x^2 - \sigma_z^2\rho_1)^{-1}\sigma_v^2\beta$	$-(\sigma_x^2 - (\sigma_z^2/3)(2\rho_1 + \rho_2))^{-1}\sigma_v^2\beta$	$\frac{2}{3}\rho_1 + \frac{1}{3}\rho_2 < \rho_1$
4	$-(\sigma_x^2 - \sigma_z^2\rho_1)^{-1}\sigma_v^2\beta$	$-(\sigma_x^2 - (\sigma_z^2/6)(3\rho_1 + 2\rho_2 + \rho_3))^{-1}\sigma_v^2\beta$	$\frac{1}{2}\rho_1 + \frac{1}{3}\rho_2 + \frac{1}{6}\rho_3 < \rho_1$
$\vdots$			
$T \to \infty$	$-(\sigma_x^2 - \sigma_z^2\rho_1)^{-1}\sigma_v^2\beta$	$-(\sigma_x^2 - (2\sigma_z^2/(T-1))\Sigma((T-j)/T)\rho_j)^{-1}\sigma_v^2\beta$	$(2/T)(\rho_1 + \rho_2 + \cdots) < \rho_1$

For the within estimator, the probability limit is

$$\operatorname{plim} b_w - \beta = -\left[\sigma_x^2 - \frac{2\sigma_z^2}{T(T-1)} \sum (T-j)\rho_j\right]^{-1} \sigma_v^2\beta. \qquad (15)$$

The formula is the same as in the usual OLS with errors of measurement case, except for the term involving the serial correlation coefficients ρ_j for the z's which arises from the within transformation

$$\tilde{x}_{it} = x_{it} - \frac{1}{T}\sum x_{ij}.$$

To compare the inconsistencies between the first difference and within estimators note that plim b_d does not depend on T (as $N \to \infty$), but that plim b_w does depend on T because of the within transformation. The conditions which cause the within estimator to be less inconsistent, which we expect to be the usual case, are given in table 1.

For $T = 2$, the estimators give numerically identical results since the within transformation and first differences are related by the formula $\frac{1}{2}\,\mathrm{d}x = \tilde{x}$. For $T = 3$, the condition for b_w to be less biased than b_d is $\rho_1 > \rho_2$ which is assured with a declining correlogram. For $T = 4$, the required condition is $\rho_1 > \frac{2}{3}\rho_2 + \frac{1}{3}\rho_3$, which again follows from a declining correlogram. The general result follows by induction. This condition then is a sufficient condition for the within estimator to be less inconsistent. The steepness in the decline of the correlogram will determine the differences in magnitude, but in many cases we would expect a substantial difference.

The situation reverses if we difference the data more than one period apart. Then the probability limit of the least squares estimator based on differences j

periods apart is

$$\operatorname{plim} b_j - \beta = -\left(\sigma_z^2(1-\rho_j) + \sigma_v^2\right)^{-1}\sigma_v^2\beta. \tag{16}$$

For example, take $T = 3$ and $j = 2$. The inconsistency of b_2 is smaller than b_w so long as $\rho_1 > \rho_2$ for positive ρ_1. For $T = 4$ and $j = 3$, the condition is $5\rho_3 < 3\rho_1 + 2\rho_2$, which holds under the assumption of a declining correlogram. For $T = 4$ and $j = 2$, so that the 'longest' difference is not used, the condition is $4\rho_2 < 3\rho_1 + 1\rho_3$ so that a declining correlogram is not sufficient to assure that the inconsistency in b_2 is less than b_w. The general result is that for a given sample T, the estimator with $j = T - 1$ will be less inconsistent than b_w, but for intermediate $1 < j < T - 1$ no definite ordering can be made. Note that our comparison only involves the inconsistency in the estimators for the case $N \to \infty$. For moderate size N, the mean square error may be a better comparison criterion, and the estimator with $j = T - 1$ eliminates a non-negligible proportion $(T-2)/(T-1)$ of the observations.

In the more general case of serial correlation in the v's and η's, Σ and Ω are not diagonal anymore. For our two leading special cases,

$$\operatorname{tr}[Q\Omega \otimes I] = 2N(T-1)\sigma_v^2(1-r), \tag{17}$$

for first differences, and

$$\operatorname{tr}[Q\Omega \otimes I] = N\left[\frac{T-1}{T}\sigma_v^2 - \frac{2\sigma_v^2}{T^2}\sum_{j=1}^{T}(T-j)r_j\right],$$

for the within estimator, where r_j is the jth serial correlation in the measurement error v.

The inconsistency of the first difference estimator is therefore

$$\operatorname{plim} b_d - \beta = -\left[\sigma_z^2(1-\rho_1) + \sigma_v^2(1-r_1)\right]^{-1}\sigma_v^2(1-r_1)\beta. \tag{18}$$

The bias of the first difference estimation here as compared to eq. (12) is less if $r_1 > 0$. The more highly positively correlated the measurement error is, the more you eliminate using first differences. However, the presumption that $r_1 > 0$ seems less strong in economic data than the assumption we used before that $\rho_1 > 0$.

The inconsistency of the within estimator is

$$\operatorname{plim} b_w - \beta = -\left[\sigma_x^2 - \frac{2}{T(T-1)}\sum\left[\sigma_z^2(T-j)\rho_j + \sigma_v^2(T-j)r_j\right]\right]^{-1} \times\left[\sigma_v^2 - \frac{2\sigma_v^2}{T(T-1)}\sum_j(T-j)r_j\right]\beta. \tag{19}$$

As with first differences, the inconsistency in the within estimator decreases with respect to the uncorrelated case so long as all $r_j > 0$. Again this assumption is not as compelling as the analogous assumption about the ρ_j. To compare the bias of the first difference and within estimators, first note that, for $T = 2$, they are identical as before. For $T \geq 3$, it may be reasonable to assume that $\rho_j > r_j > 0$ for all j. That is, serial correlation is higher in the true variable than in the measurement error. Then, for the case $T = 3$, the within estimator is less biased than the first difference estimator if $(\rho_1 - \rho_2)/(r_1 - r_2) > (1 - \rho_1)/(1 - r_1)$ which holds if the serial correlation in the true variable decreases less slowly than the serial correlation in the measurement error.[5] This type of condition generalizes to values of T larger than 3. While the condition seems plausible that $\rho_j > r_j$ and that the decrease in the serial correlation of the z's be less than for the v's, it is not overwhelming. Counterexamples are easy to construct. The particular case under consideration would need to be examined.

The 'long' difference estimator is the same as in eq. (18) with ρ_1 and r_1 replaced by ρ_j and r_j, respectively. Note that the most favorable case need no longer be $j = T - 1$ because r_j decreases along with ρ_j. The j which minimizes the inconsistency maximizes the ratio $(1 - \rho_j)/(1 - r_j)$. For a positive and declining correlogram for both ρ_j and r_j the tradeoff is between removing too much signal and removing some of the noise. If both z and v follow AR1 processes with $\rho_1 > r_1$, then $j = T - 1$ will minimize the inconsistency. On the other hand, if z follows an AR1 process and v follows an MA1 process, then $j = 1$ can be optimal. The optimal choice depends on both the type of process as well as the particular correlation coefficients.

It would be interesting to know which combinations of estimators of the form $(X'Qx)^{-1}X'Qy$, used to eliminate α from eq. (11), have good properties with respect to errors of measurement. Even if we choose the minimization of the inconsistency as our criterion, the optimal combination will depend on the properties of Σ and Ω. In the uncorrelated case, diagonal Ω, with a declining correlogram for z, the long difference estimator, $j = T - 1$, minimizes minus the inconsistency. For the correlated case of non-diagonal Ω, the optimal estimator depends on both Σ and Ω. A potential topic for future research would be to characterize this dependence for interesting classes of stochastic processes determining Σ and Ω.[6]

We now turn to the question of consistent estimation. In the general correlated case, with Ω unrestricted, the problem remains unidentified. That is, external instruments uncorrelated with the measurement error are required for consistent estimation. While the assumption of stationarity of the measurement

[5] The necessary and sufficient condition is $(1 - \rho_1)/(1 - r_1) < (1 - \frac{2}{3}\rho_1 - \frac{1}{3}\rho_2)/(1 - \frac{2}{3}r_1 - \frac{1}{3}r_2)$.

[6] The inconsistency of the estimator may well constitute the major part of a criterion such as asymptotic mean square error given the quite large samples, in N, which are often present with panel data.

errors in combination with non-stationarity of the underlying true variables (the z's) does allow identification also in the correlated errors case, we do not find it especially compelling and focus first on the non-stationary z's and uncorrelated v's case. The procedures we develop can be used also in the 'partial' correlation case, e.g., if v follows the MA(m) process with $m < T$, and can be also extended to the stationary case. The strategy we propose here is to take advantage of the existence of alternative consistent estimators, i.e. over-identification, to test the assumption of no correlation in the v's and their stationarity. If the alternative estimates of β are mutually coherent, then the researcher can have some confidence that his assumptions hold true.

Our estimation strategy starts with the original eq. (11c),

$$y = x\beta + l\alpha + \varepsilon,$$

and looks for instrumental variables of the form

$$w = Px,$$

where the matrix P must satisfy three sets of conditions·

$$\begin{aligned} &l'P = 0, \\ &\mathrm{E}w'x = \mathrm{E}w'z, \quad \text{i.e.,} \quad \mathrm{E}x'P'v = 0 \rightarrow \operatorname{tr} \Omega P = 0, \qquad (20) \\ &\mathrm{E}x'P'x \neq 0. \end{aligned}$$

The first requirement assures the elimination of α, the individual effects, from (11). The second requirement allows the use of those x's and their combinations which are uncorrelated with the particular measurement error v_t. Its content will change depending on the assumptions made about the serial correlation structure of the v's. The final requirement is one of non-zero correlation between the instrument w and x.

The simplest and least restrictive set of assumptions to start with are (1) that the z's are non-stationary and (2) the v's are non-stationary and white (uncorrelated) to some order. Under these assumptions we need to *difference* the y's to get rid of the α's, and we can use non-corresponding adjacent x levels to instrument the x difference. Starting with the case of correlated errors we can either relax the restrictions further by allowing for serial correlation in the errors up to some order or restrict the model further by imposing the assumption of stationarity on the measurement errors. In the latter case additional combinations of differences in the x's become valid instruments.[7]

[7]If the z's were also stationary, there would be no gain in instruments here since the additional instruments would have zero variance. On the other hand, it is remarkable that under stationarity of (x_{it}, α_i) the original specification $y = X\beta + l\alpha + \eta$ can be estimated using differenced x's as instruments since, e.g., $\mathrm{E}[x_{i2} - x_{i1})\alpha_i] = 0$. This approach would allow an application of the Hausman–Taylor (1981) procedure where other right-hand-side variables are included, say D, and $(D - \bar{D}.)$ are used as additional instruments.

Table 2

Potential list of instruments for $T = 4$ under different assumptions about Ω; $y = z\beta + l\alpha + \eta$, $x = z + v$.

Equations to be estimated	Valid instruments[a]: Non-stationary v's, No correlation	Non-stationary v's, MA(1)	Stationary v's, No correlation	Stationary v's, MA(1)	Stationary v's, MA(2) & (3)
$(y_2 - y_1) = \beta(x_2 - x_1)$	x_4	x_4	$x_1 + x_2$, x_4	$x_1 + x_2, x_4$	$x_1 + x_2$
$(y_3 - y_2) = \beta(x_3 - x_2)$	x_1, x_4		$x_1, x_2 + x_3, x_4$	$x_2 + x_3$	$x_2 + x_3$
$(y_4 - y_3) = \beta(x_4 - x_3)$	x_1, x_2	x_1	x_1, $x_3 + x_4$	$x_1, x_3 + x_4$	$x_3 + x_4$
$(y_3 - y_1) = \beta(x_3 - x_1)$	x_2		x_2	x_2	x_2
$(y_4 - y_2) = \beta(x_4 - x_2)$	x_3		x_3	x_3	x_3
$(y_4 - y_1) = \beta(x_4 - x_1)$	x_2, x_3		x_2, x_3		
$\begin{pmatrix} y_3 - y_2 \\ y_4 - y_1 \end{pmatrix} = \beta \begin{pmatrix} x_3 - x_2 \\ x_4 - x_1 \end{pmatrix}$		$\begin{pmatrix} -x_1 \\ x_2 \end{pmatrix} \begin{pmatrix} -x_4 \\ x_3 \end{pmatrix}$		$\begin{pmatrix} -x_1 \\ x_2 \end{pmatrix} \begin{pmatrix} -x_4 \\ x_3 \end{pmatrix}$	$\begin{pmatrix} -x_1 \\ x_2 \end{pmatrix} \begin{pmatrix} -x_4 \\ x_3 \end{pmatrix}$
$\begin{pmatrix} y_2 - y_1 \\ y_4 - y_3 \end{pmatrix} = \beta \begin{pmatrix} x_2 - x_1 \\ x_4 - x_3 \end{pmatrix}$		$\begin{pmatrix} x_3 \\ x_2 \end{pmatrix}$		$\begin{pmatrix} x_3 \\ x_2 \end{pmatrix}$	$\begin{pmatrix} x_3 \\ x_2 \end{pmatrix} \begin{pmatrix} x_4 \\ x_1 \end{pmatrix}$
Total number of instruments	8	5	11	10	9

[a] Only one possible list of instruments which exhausts all available information is presented. For some equations, valid instruments are not listed. For example, x_3 is valid for the $y_2 - y_1$ difference in the no-correlation case. However, the information from this instrument is redundant. The information is already included in the instruments for the other equations.

To the extent that we have enough data (time periods) some versions of this model will be heavily overidentified and hence some of these restrictions are testable. We shall illustrate our approach and list the different possible sets of instruments for the $T=4$ case in table 2. Consider, for example, the second line of table 2. It corresponds to estimating β from the cross-sectional difference between y_3 and y_2. (Note that each such cross-section has N degrees of freedom.) For uncorrelated measurement errors, x_1 and x_4 are both valid instruments. If the errors are correlated according to a MA(1) or higher order scheme there are no valid instruments for this difference without imposing further restrictions. If we are willing to assume stationarity for the v's, we gain x_2+x_3 as an instrument. The quality or contribution of such an instrument is dubious, however, since it depends on $\text{var}(z_2)-\text{var}(z_3)\neq 0$ and non-negligible. As we relax the no-correlation assumption in the stationary v's case, we lose some instruments, but can form other 'combinations' of difference estimators which use all of the available information in the data. They are shown in the southeast corner of this table where the corner $\tilde{\beta}$ is given by $[x_3'(y_2-y_1)+x_2'(y_4-y_3)]/[x_3'(x_2-x_1)+x_2'(x_4-x_3)]$. A more general version of table 2 for arbitrary T is given in the appendix (co-authored with Bruce Meyer) with a discussion of the rules for constructing and finding the relevant number of such instruments.

The asymptotically efficient way of combining all the different $\tilde{\beta}$ estimators in table 2 is using a 'system' estimator where the estimated β's are constrained to be equal and the covariance of the stochastic disturbances Σ is taken into account in weighting them and in computing the variance of the resulting coefficient. It is important to note that a 3SLS or GLS type estimator is *inconsistent* because instruments from a given equation are not orthogonal to the disturbances in another equation unless they are also contained in the instrument set of that equation.

It is useful, as a start, to estimate each equation in table 2 separately by 2SLS using different instrumental variables in each equation. But to combine such estimators optimally we use the Generalized Method of Moments estimator, developed by Hansen (1982) and White (1982), and allow also for conditional heteroscedasticity. The estimator is

$$\beta^* = [\tilde{x}'\tilde{w}U^{-1}\tilde{w}'\tilde{x}]^{-1}\tilde{x}'\tilde{w}U^{-1}\tilde{w}'y \quad \text{with} \quad U=\frac{1}{N}\sum_i^N \tilde{w}_i'\tilde{\varepsilon}_i\tilde{\varepsilon}_i'\tilde{w}_i, \tag{21}$$

where $\tilde{\varepsilon}$ are the stacked $\mathrm{d}^j\varepsilon$'s and $\tilde{\varepsilon}$ is calculated from an initial consistent estimate of β, $\tilde{x}$ are the stacked $\mathrm{d}^j x$'s, $\tilde{y}$ are the stacked $\mathrm{d}^j y$'s, and $\tilde{w}$ is the matrix of instruments.[8] The asymptotic covariance matrices of the estimator is $V(\beta^*)=[\tilde{x}'\tilde{w}U^{-1}\tilde{w}'\tilde{x}]^{-1}$. This asymptotic covariance matrix is different from

[8]Note that w is a block-diagonal matrix.

a simple weighting of β_{IV} from 2SLS. Effectively we estimate each instrument equation combination (or orthogonality condition) separately, compute their associated estimated variance–covariance matrix, and then pool the individual β's using this matrix for weighting them.

We now turn to the question of whether the no-correlation assumption in the errors in measurement is valid. Some such assumption about the form of the process generating the measurement error is needed because the general correlated case is unidentified without the use of special stationarity assumptions or other extraneous variables as instruments. Note that if we applied least squares (OLS) to the equations in table 2, equation by equation, we would expect the estimates of β to differ according to our previous formulae. Similarly, it can be demonstrated that in the IV case with correlated errors in measurement different estimates of β will have different probability limits. Therefore, a testing procedure is to estimate a system of equations based on different d^j's in unrestricted form so that each equation is allowed to have its own β. A large sample χ^2 test with $m-1$ degrees of freedom for equality of the β_j's is equivalent to the implicit test in table 2 that all the β_j's are equal. An alternative specification test is to take an equation, say the first, and restrict the set of instruments. For $x_{it} - x_{it-1}$, instead of using all the other x's as instrumental variables we could restrict the list to those x's which are at least two time periods away. I.e., use only the instruments given in column 2 or 4 of table 2. The test statistic proposed by Hausman (1978) or Hausman and Taylor (1981) provides a large sample χ^2 test with one degree of freedom. Lastly, overidentification tests of the Sargan (1958) and Hansen (1982) type can also be used. Under stationarity assumptions these various tests are closely related but have different operating characteristics because they are based on different degrees of freedom. In the general case of non-stationarity of the x's they will differ, although Newey (1983) provides a partial guide to their comparability.

There is an alternative, asymptotically equivalent approach to estimation based on treating the y and x as jointly normally distributed and using maximum likelihood estimators to estimate the 'unobservables': Ω and the variance–covariance matrices of the z's. We can rewrite our original (11) model as

$$\begin{aligned} y_1 &= z_1\beta + l\alpha + \eta_1 = x_1\beta + l\alpha + \eta_1 - \beta v_1, \\ \mathrm{d}y &= (\mathrm{d}z)\beta + \mathrm{d}\eta, \\ x &= z + v, \end{aligned} \tag{22}$$

where $\mathrm{d}y$ and $\mathrm{d}z$ are now $(T-1)\times 1$ vectors. Since the relationship between α and z_1 is free, the y_1 equation is unconstrained and can be ignored in what follows. We consider then the $(2T-1)\times(2T-1)$ matrix of observable moments of all the data:

$$S=\begin{pmatrix}\mathrm{d}y\\ x\end{pmatrix}(\mathrm{d}y \quad x)=\begin{pmatrix}\mathrm{d}y\cdot\mathrm{d}y' & \mathrm{d}y\cdot x'\\ \mathrm{d}y'\cdot x & xx'\end{pmatrix},$$

whose expectation, given our model, is

$$M(\Theta)=\begin{pmatrix}\beta^2\mathrm{d}z\cdot\mathrm{d}z'+\tilde{\Sigma} & \beta\,\mathrm{d}z\cdot z'\\ \beta\,\mathrm{d}z'\cdot z & zz'+\Omega\end{pmatrix}, \tag{23}$$

where

$$\tilde{\Sigma}=\mathrm{E}\,\mathrm{d}\eta\cdot\mathrm{d}\eta'.$$

We leave $\tilde{\Sigma}$ unconstrained and hence the identification of β hinges on our assumptions about Ω and the order of zz'. For $T=4$ and Ω diagonal, the interesting right half of $M(\Theta)$ can be written as

$$\beta\begin{bmatrix} z_{21}-z_{11} & z_{22}-z_{12} & z_{23}-z_{13} & z_{24}-z_{14}\\ z_{31}-z_{21} & z_{32}-z_{22} & z_{33}-z_{23} & z_{34}-z_{24}\\ z_{41}-z_{31} & z_{42}-z_{32} & z_{43}-z_{33} & z_{44}-z_{34}\end{bmatrix}$$

$$\begin{bmatrix} z_{11}+\tau_1 & z_{12} & z_{13} & z_{14}\\ & z_{22}+\tau_2 & z_{23} & z_{24}\\ & & z_{33}+\tau_3 & z_{34}\\ & & & z_{44}+\tau_4\end{bmatrix}$$

where the z_{ii}'s are the appropriate second-order moments of the unobservable z's and the τ_t's are the diagonal elements of Ω. We have then the twenty-four distinct observable moments of the $\mathrm{d}y\cdot x'$ and $x\cdot x'$ variety and thirteen unknowns [ten components of zz', β, and four τ's, where $\tau_t=\sigma_v^2(t)$] and the model is heavily over-identified. It can be constrained further by assuming $\tau_t=\tau$, that the v's are stationary, and/or it can be relaxed by adding another set of τ_{ij} terms to allow for MA(1) or MA(2) correlation between these measurement errors.

More generally, under our assumptions, S is a sufficient statistic for $M(\Theta)$ and we can estimate the unknown parameter vector Θ by 'fitting' the model $M(\Theta)$ to the observed matrix of variances and covariances S using either the LISREL or MOMENTS statistical packages and different versions of the model can then be compared using likelihood ratio tests.[9]

[9]See Jöreskog and Sörbom (1981) and Hall (1979), respectively, and Aigner et al. (1984) and Griliches (1984) for additional discussions of such models. Note that fourth moments are not being used in either estimation or inference here.

4. An empirical example

The empirical example we consider is related to the old conundrum of 'short-run increasing returns to scale'. Let l = logarithm of employment and q = logarithm of output. The relationship between l and q depends on what is assumed about the production function, what is held constant, and what expectational assumptions are made about the relevant prices. If the production function is assumed to be Cobb–Douglas with a labor elasticity α, then one can derive two alternative relationships: the first based on inverting the production function and the second on solving the value of marginal productivity equals the wage condition:

$$l = \frac{1}{\alpha} q - \frac{1-\alpha}{\alpha} k, \tag{24a}$$

$$l = \log \alpha + q - w', \tag{24b}$$

where k is the logarithm of capital services and w' is logarithm of the real wage $\log w - \log P$, where P is the price of the product. In either form, the coefficient of q should be one or higher. In econometric practice one tends to get coefficients which are less than one, implying short-run increasing returns to labor alone [Brechling (1973), Sims (1974)]. Adding lags helps a little, but usually not enough. A reasonable interpretation of the data and one rationale for the introduction of lags is that labor is hired in anticipation of 'normal' or expected output, while actual output is subject to unanticipated 'transitory' fluctuations. Since this argument is isomorphic with the errors-in-variables model [see Friedman (1957), Maddala (1977)], we can apply our framework to it.

We shall use data on 1,242 U.S. manufacturing firms for the six years, 1972–1977, from the NBER R&D panel [Cummins, Hall and Laderman (1982)], and adopt the second interpretation of the equation to be estimated. In this model,

$$l_{it} = d_t + q_{it}^* + \{-w_{it}' + (\log \alpha_i - \log \bar{\alpha}) + \eta_{it}\}, \tag{25}$$

q_{it}^* is the expected or 'permanent' output level, d_t is a set of individual year constants (time dummies), and the bracketed term represents a composite 'disturbance' which consists of three terms: (1) a real wage term, which presumably differs in some consistent fashion across firms and moves, more or less in unison for all the firms, over time; specifically, we assume that

$$w_{it}' = \mu_i + \gamma_t + \tau_{it} \tag{26}$$

has a variance component structure with γ_t subsumed in the d_t and τ_{it}

assumed to be uncorrelated with q_{it}; (2) a term associated with the fact that the labor elasticities α_i might differ across firms; and (3) a pure i.i.d. disturbance term η_{it}. We do not observe the expected output variable q_{it}^* but only the actual output

$$q_{it} = q_{it}^* + v_{it}, \tag{27}$$

where v_{it} is an i.i.d. 'error' or transitory component in q_{it}. Note that v_{it} need not be an actual 'measurement' error. Observed q_{it} may be measured correctly but relatively to the conceptual variable desired in the model; q_{it} is erroneous![10] We can rewrite the model in terms of observables as

$$l_{it} = a_i + \beta q_{it} + d_t + (-\beta v_{it} - \tau_{it} + \eta_{it}), \tag{28}$$

where we expect $\beta = 1$ and the a_i are a set of individual firm effects incorporating both permanent real wage differences and differences in the labor elasticity across firms and hence likely to be correlated with the q_{it}.

To recapitulate the model, we assume that workers are hired in anticipation of actual demand, that actual demand is met primarily by unanticipated fluctuations in hours of work per man (which are unobservable in our data) and inventory fluctuations, and that we can subsume the real wage variable into the time dummies and the individual firm effects![11] Our focus then is on the estimation of β and σ_v^2, the variance of the 'error' (v) in q, its unanticipated component.

Table 3 presents the estimated β's for different cuts of the data, total, within, first differences, and 'long' differences, and the associated net variance of q (net of year and industry dummy variables). It also shows a set of parallel instrumental variable estimates of β, where data on capital are used as an external instrument for q. The validity of such external instruments depends on the lack of a firm-specific short-run movement in real wages, or the non-correlation of the capital measures with τ_{it}. Note that the OLS results behave as predicted, with the first difference estimator being lower than the within one. The long difference estimate is greater than both the first difference estimate and the within estimate as the derivations in section 3 predicted.

There are two ways of interpreting these results. The first would maintain the assumption that $\beta = 1$, ignore the potential presence of correlated individ-

[10] They need not be 'errors' as far as other variables are concerned. For example, both hours worked per man and materials used are likely to be related to such transitory output fluctuations.

[11] An alternative interpretation would divide l into two components, 'fixed' labor which changes only in response to permanent changes in q, and 'variable' labor which is related to v. We experimented also with the use of distributed lags in certain of our models. While lagged q is present when errors in variables are not accounted for, only current q has any statistical or 'economic' significance in the errors in variables models. Thus, 'costs of adjustment' do not seem important on an annual basis in our model once errors in variables are accounted for.

Table 3

Estimates of the employment–output relationship for 1,242 U.S. manufacturing firms, 1972–77; $l_{it} = \alpha_i + \beta q_{it} + d_t$.[a]

Estimation method and degrees of freedom	Net variance of q	β	MSE	Instrumental variables estimates β	MSE
(1) Total d.f. = 7,425	2.265	0.966 (0.003)	0.158	0.994 (0.003)	0.159
(2) Within d.f. = 6,203	0.0313	0.643 (0.008)	0.011	n.c.	
(3) First difference d.f. = 6,204	0.0246	0.480 (0.010)	0.015	0.868 (0.153)	0.019
(4) 'Long' difference d.f. = 1,240	0.1359	0.731 (0.016)	0.047	1.063 (0.039)	0.062

[a] The terms in parentheses are the estimated standard errors. Total regressions contain also five year and twenty-two industry dummy variables. The within and first difference regressions include also year dummies. The instrumental variables used are the logarithm of net plant, the first difference in log net plant and the long difference in log net plant, respectively.

ual effects, and accept the instrumental variable results as vindicating this position. There are difficulties with this view, however. The implied 'error' in variables variance of σ_v^2 is 0.038, which is larger than the variance of the first differences of q which should contain $2\sigma_v^2$, if the model were right! Also, it is unlikely that net investment which is the first difference in net plant is independent of the unmeasured fluctuations in real wage rates. Hence, the consistency of the external instrumental variable estimates is rather suspect.

We turn, therefore, to the estimation of β and σ_v^2 using only 'internal' instruments, i.e., adjacent 'non-corresponding' x's and their combinations. The results, based on the differenced form of our model, are summarized in table 4. The individual firm effects, the α_i, are eliminated by the differencing operation which eliminates the correlation between the individual firm effects and output. We list eleven such differences in this table: five first differences, four differences two periods apart, and two differences four periods apart. The remaining four possible differences (three three periods and one five periods apart) can be derived, in the non-stationary errors case, as linear combinations of the listed (IV) estimates.[12] In the first column we give the simple OLS results for all of these differences. They again yield quite low estimates of β, which rise significantly as the period of differencing is lengthened. Also, the data

[12] Even this system has redundancies as far as the total number of valid orthogonality conditions. It will suffice below to use a shortened list of instruments and to impose all of the twenty-four distinct orthogonality conditions. With $T = 6$, the no correlation of errors assumption yields twenty-five orthogonality conditions of which one is lost in the elimination of the α's. See the appendix for additional discussion of the 'right' number of instruments.

seems distinctly non-stationary, especially during the steep recession year of 1975. Column 2 gives the instrumental variable results under the assumption of no correlation in measurement error [labeled MA(0)]. Here, for example, the instrumental variables used for the second line, the difference between 1974 and 1973, are the levels of output in 1972, 1975, 1976 and 1977. Again, the 1975–74 difference gives a significantly lower estimate than do the other years, as does also the 1973–72 difference. But the latter has a much higher standard error due to the absence of good (early) instruments for it. In lines 12 and 13 we give two different restricted IV results where β is restricted to be the same across all the combination of years. The first is based on combining optimally the eleven different 2SLS estimates of β, using the estimated 2SLS residuals to form the appropriate weighting matrix which allows, also, for conditional heteroskedasticity. They are not fully efficient because they do not allow a free correlation structure between all the different possible instrumental variable estimators in such a set-up, and because of the redundancy in the list of instruments and equations. Line 14 gives the Generalized Method of Moments estimator which takes the individual single instruments as its 'elemental' set and uses the 2SLS residuals to form the appropriate weighting matrix (of larger dimension). The two different system estimators yield similar results. The null hypothesis of equality of β across these different combinations of years leads to a χ^2 variable with the number of distinct instruments minus one as its degree of freedom which is listed in line 14 of table 4. For the column 2, MA(0)–IV estimators, it is 80 with 10 degrees of freedom, and implies a rejection of the null hypothesis, although one should recognize that our rather large sample size makes rejection of most such hypotheses likely at the usual significance levels.

In column 3 of table 4, we relax the no correlation in measurement error assumption and allow for a MA(1) process. To do this, we use only instruments that are two or more years away from the years used to form the particular difference. First, note that the IV estimates rise for most of the differences (eight out of eleven). On the basis of a Hausman (1978) test, the difference is significant for eight out of the eleven estimates![13]

Also note that in five of the eleven equations the estimate of β exceeds one, although never by a statistically significant amount. However, the difference of 1975 minus 1974 is again much lower. Primarily because of this one equation, which has the lowest standard error, the restricted estimates give an almost identical estimate to the no correlation restricted estimate.

In the last column of table 4 we allow for a MA(2) process in the measurement error. Only four of the eleven equations remain individually

[13] Overidentifying restriction tests on sets of instruments can also be used here. They lead to χ^2 tests with higher degrees of freedom. See Newey (1983). For instance, for the five first difference estimates in column 2 of table 4, the test statistics are: 8, 14, 15, 28 and 14. All of these statistics are higher than conventional significance levels of a χ^2_3 variable.

Table 4

OLS, IV and GMM estimates of the employment–output relationship.[a]

Years for difference	Coefficient (standard error)			
		Consistent IV estimates		
	OLS	MA(0)	MA(1)	MA(2)
(1) 1973–2	0.481 (0.024)	0.276 (1.35)	0.465 (0.145)	0.635 (1.77)
(2) 1974–3	0.569 (0.029)	0.842 (0.038)	1.257 (0.292)	1.241 (0.289)
(3) 1974–4	0.395 (0.029)	0.512 (0.021)	0.647 (0.047)	
(4) 1976–5	0.506 (0.020)	0.748 (0.037)	1.454 (0.322)	3.557 (3.562)
(5) 1977–6	0.491 (0.023)	0.726 (0.165)	1.192 (0.249)	1.203 (0.254)
(6) 1974–2	0.599 (0.022)	1.003 (0.048)	−0.040 (0.340)	1.597 (0.996)
(7) 1975–3	0.581 (0.017)	0.716 (0.027)	0.791 (0.141)	
(8) 1976–4	0.587 (0.020)	0.666 (0.026)	3.135 (2.537)	
(9) 1977–5	0.617 (0.019)	0.695 (0.042)	1.327 (0.107)	3.068 (2.096)
(10) 1976–2	0.708 (0.017)	0.751 (0.019)	−41.795 (1572.56)	
(11) 1977–3	0.703 (0.017)	0.754 (0.020)	0.223 (0.247)	
(12) Restricted β OLS & W2SLS	0.567 (0.015)	0.727 (0.021)	0.670 (0.045)	0.916 (0.161)
(13) Wald test for equality of β's (d.f.)	189 (10)	89.0 (10)	25.0 (10)	6.0 (5)
(14) GMM		0.705 (0.021)	0.678 (0.038)	0.643 (0.115)
(15) Wald test for equality of β's (d.f.)		155.0 (23)	47.0 (18)	61.0 (14)
(16) Hausman test (using GMM)		Stationarity 5.7	MA(1) vs. MA(0) 0.7	MA(2) vs. MA(1) 0.1

[a] The MA(0) column uses all adjacent non-coinciding x levels as instruments. There are four such instruments per equation. The MA(1) and MA(2) columns use only those instruments which are one or two periods away, respectively.

In line 12 all eleven estimates are pooled using the estimated 2SLS residuals allowing for conditional heteroskedasticity. Line 14 is based on the pooling of the twenty-four individual (independent) orthogonality conditions [nineteen for MA(1), and fifteen for MA(2)]. The stationary MA(0) estimate alluded to in line 16, column 2, is computed by adding five additional instruments of the $x_t + x_{t+1}$ form. The resulting estimate is 0.66 (0.02).

identified, and in all cases the estimated β rises or remains the same, though the precision with which they are estimated declines precipitously. The restricted estimate rises to 0.92, but the GMM estimator falls to 0.64, and is not significantly different from the MA(1) one. The estimated coefficients are quite unstable at this point. A GMM estimator using a subset of five instruments yields $\beta = 1.2$ (0.2), implying that the relationship may not be stable over time (as is already indicated by the high χ^2 value for the pooling tests).

We can also test the hypothesis of stationarity of the error mechanism by using additional instruments to estimate the various models. In the MA(0) case it is rejected using the Hausman test (see line 16, column 1 of table 4). It is rather cumbersome, however, within the GMM framework to test similar hypotheses in the MA(1) and MA(2) context. Moreover, the Hausman tests may not be very powerful against such a hypothesis since they focus on the resulting changes in β rather than on the estimation of the correlation structure of the errors, which is of direct interest in this context. Maximum likelihood procedures are more convenient for this purpose since they yield explicit estimates of the various error variances and covariances.

Maximum likelihood estimates of this same range of models are given in table 5. The model given in (23) is estimated using the LISREL-V program. It differs from the GMM estimators by assuming joint normality for all of the variables and by not allowing for conditional heteroskedasticity explicitly. The latter fact explains why the computed standard errors are somewhat lower in this table. We show only the estimated β and the associated standard errors and χ^2 statistics. Because the 75–74 difference is an outlier in many respects, the residual from the fitted model being twice as large as for the other years and exceeding four times its estimated standard error, we present also results based only on using four differences (but all six x levels) in the bottom half of the table. Except for the final size of β, the results are similar to the system estimates in table 4. Here the stationarity of the v's is rejected resoundingly and so is also the no-correlation assumption. If 75–74 is eliminated from the system, the fit improves significantly and the MA(1) assumption appears to be adequate.[14] As we relax the various restrictions, the estimated β's rise towards one and beyond, though the precision with which they are estimated falls concomitantly.

Our empirical results are not easily summarized. First, we found that it is quite likely that correlation exists between firm effects and measured output. Second, traditional covariance techniques are subject to errors in variables which have a sizeable effect, in the predicted direction. Next, 2SLS and system-IV estimators reduce the magnitude of the bias. Correlation in measurement error seems present, although an MA(1) process seems adequate for our particular data set.[15]

[14] The estimated first-order correlation of the errors is positive and about 0.3.

[15] A MA(1) process in measurement error could well arise because of differences in fiscal years across firms and the change in fiscal years among many firms which took place in 1976.

Table 5

Maximum likelihood estimates of β in the employment–output relationship coefficients (standard errors) and model χ^2's.[a]

	Non-stationary v's β	Difference in χ^2's	Stationary v's β	Difference in χ^2's
(1) Full data 5 differences				
MA(0)	0.701 (0.015) 402		0.689 (0.014) 440	38 (5)
MA(1)	0.780 (0.028) 324	78 (5)	0.763 (0.020) 414	26 (1)
MA(2)	1.355 (0.220) 304	20 (4)	0.715 (0.022) 401	13 (1)
(2) Without 75–74				
MA(0)	0.789 (0.024) 199		0.739 (0.018) 261	62 (5)
MA(1)	1.274 (0.157) 123	76 (5)	0.906 (0.032) 215	46 (1)
MA(2)	1.356 (0.200) 117	6 (4)	0.885 (0.034) 213	2 (1)

[a]The numbers in the main columns are first the estimated coefficient β, its standard error (in parentheses) and the χ^2 statistic for the estimated model as a whole. The numbers in columns 2, 3 and 4 are the respective differences in the χ^2 and the associated degrees of freedom.

Lastly, we return to the puzzle: Is β really less than one? Apart from 1975–1974, the system-MA(1) results and the maximum likelihood estimates indicate that $\beta \simeq 1$, while the GMM estimates put it closer to 0.7, but the precision of these estimates is not very high. The following might be a possible interpretation. Approximately 0.006 of the variance of log of output is unanticipated.[16] This is less than 0.3% of the total variance in log output, but it accounts for close to 50% in the variance of its first differences.[17] Allowing for such errors raises the estimated β from about 0.5 to about 0.9, for most years,

[16]And unadjusted to as far as labor input is concerned. This same fluctuation may not be an 'error' as far as more flexible inputs such as materials or hours per man are concerned. In similar computations using data on French firms, Jacques Mairesse found that while the employment–output relationship behaves very similarly to what has been reported here, the materials–output relationship yields coefficients of 1 also in the within, first difference, and long difference versions. As far as material purchases are concerned, such fluctuations are not 'errors'!

[17]For the MA(1) version, the numbers are approximately 0.0095 for the variance and 0.0035 for the covariance of such errors. In the non-stationary case, these numbers vary significantly from year to year.

leaving us rather close to the expected unitary elasticity. A related interpretation of these results arises from the distinction between variable and overhead labor. If 'overhead' labor does not vary much over the horizon and range of our data and the size of shocks that we observe, our estimates would imply that it accounts for about 10 percent of manufacturing employment. Our results are also consistent with Sims (1974), whose final estimate of the 'total' β was about 0.8 for a specification which used the number of workers rather than manhours as the dependent variable.

5. A suggested research strategy

The general approach that we suggest can be summarized as follows:

(i) Estimate eq. (11) by GLS (variance components) and by the within estimator. Do a test for equality of the estimates using a Hausman (1978) or Hausman–Taylor (1981) type test.

(ii) If the hypothesis in (i) is rejected, calculate some differenced estimates (of different lengths) by OLS. If they differ significantly, errors in measurement may well be present.

(iii) Estimate the equations in table 2 or their equivalent by Instrumental Variables, Maximum Likelihood, or the Generalized Method of Moments. Then do a specification test(s) of the no-correlation assumption in the errors in measurement. If they do differ significantly, the specification of a correlated errors in measurement process, use of outside instruments, or respecification of the original model (11) seems to be called for.

6. Notes on the literature

For work on panel data, see Maddala (1971), Mundlak (1978), Hausman (1978), Hausman and Taylor (1981) and Chamberlain (1982). For the importance of errors in such contexts, see Griliches (1979, 1984) and Freeman (1984). For an earlier effort at identifying the error variance from the contrast between levels and first differences in a single series, see Karni and Weissman (1974). For a related attempt to derive consistent estimators in error-ridden panel data in the context of zero–one variables, see Chowdhury and Nickell (1985). For estimation methods in such contexts, see Aigner et al. (1984) and Hansen (1982).

Appendix on optimal instruments

by Z. Griliches, J. Hausman and Bruce Meyer

Consider the model (11):

$$y_{it} = z_{it}\beta + \alpha_i + \eta_{it}, \tag{A.1}$$

where α_i is potentially correlated with z_{it},

$$x_{it} = z_{it} + v_{it}, \tag{A.2}$$

$$y_{it} = x_{it}\beta + \alpha_i + \eta_{it} - v_{it}\beta, \qquad i = 1,\ldots, N, \quad t = 1,\ldots, T. \tag{A.3}$$

Stacking the observations for a given i we have

$$\begin{aligned} y_i &= x_i\beta + l\alpha_i + \eta_i - v_i\beta \\ &= x_i\beta + l\alpha_i + \varepsilon_i, \qquad i = 1,\ldots, N, \end{aligned} \tag{A.4}$$

where y_i, x_i, η_i, v_i and ε_i are all T-dimensional column vectors and l is the vector of 1's. Also let $\mathrm{var}(\eta_i) = \Sigma$ and $\mathrm{var}(v_i) = \Omega$, $i = 1,\ldots, N$. The model can be stacked once more to obtain

$$y = x\beta + \alpha + \eta - v\beta, \tag{A.5}$$

where y, x, α, η and v are $NT \times 1$ column vectors.

This appendix examines instrumental variables estimators of the form $\beta_{\mathrm{IV}} = (w'x)^{-1}w'y$, where $w = (I_N \otimes P)x$ for some $T \times T$ matrix P. Note that the various difference estimators as well as the within estimator can be written in this form. For w to be a valid instrument, P must satisfy three requirements. One needs

$$l'P = 0, \tag{A.6}$$

$$\operatorname*{plim}_{N\to\infty} \frac{1}{N} \sum_{i=1}^{N} x_i' P \varepsilon_i = 0, \tag{A.7}$$

$$\operatorname*{plim}_{N\to\infty} \frac{1}{N} \sum_{i=1}^{N} x_i' P x_i \neq 0. \tag{A.8}$$

An efficient estimate of β will use all non-redundant instruments w, satisfying (A.6)–(A.8). By non-redundant we mean that each instrument contains some information about x not included in the other instruments. I.e., in the multiple regression of x on the w's, the coefficients on the w's should all be identified and asymptotically non-zero. In general, this is a stronger condition than the w's being linearly independent. However, here the two conditions will be the same. After obtaining a complete set of instruments, the efficient β is calculated as a weighted average of the β's from each w. The inverse of the variance–covariance matrix of the β's is the appropriate weighting matrix.

The number of non-redundant instruments equals the number of linearly independent P matrices satisfying (A.6)–(A.8). In most cases (A.8) is not binding. In such cases the number of linearly independent P matrices equals T^2 minus the number of unique linear restrictions (A.6) and (A.7) impose on P.

Requirement (A.6),

$$l'P = 0,$$

assures the elimination of α, the fixed effects, by having the columns of P sum to zero. This imposes T linear restrictions. Requirement (A.7),

$$\operatorname{plim} \frac{1}{N} \sum_{i=1}^{N} x_i' P \varepsilon_i = 0,$$

is the usual requirement that an instrument be uncorrelated with the composite error term. Rewriting (A.7), we have

$$\operatorname{plim} \frac{1}{N} \sum_{i=1}^{N} (z_i + v_i)' P (\eta_i - v_i \beta)$$

or

$$\operatorname{plim} \frac{1}{N} \sum_{i=1}^{N} \sum_{t=1}^{T} \sum_{\tau=1}^{T} v_{it} v_{i\tau} P_{t\tau} = 0.$$

The implied restrictions on P depend on Ω, the covariance of v_i. For example, if the v_{it} are not stationary or serially correlated, then $p_{t\tau}$ must equal zero whenever $t = \tau$. This imposes T additional restrictions on P. If the v_{it} are stationary, then only the sum of the diagonal elements of P must equal zero. This imposes one linear restriction. Note that the additional restriction MA($T-1$) imposes vis-a-vis MA($T-2$) is redundant.

In certain circumstances (A.6) and (A.7) will imply that (A.8) is not satisfied. This occurs when T^2 minus the number of restrictions implied by (A.6) and (A.7) is less than or equal to $T(T-1)/2 - (T-1)$. $T(T-1)/2 - (T-1)$ is always the dimension of the space of P matrices satisfying (A.6) and (A.7), but *not* satisfying (A.8). To see this, note that when (A.8) is not satisfied, P is of the form

$$\begin{bmatrix} 0 & -A \\ A & 0 \end{bmatrix},$$

where A is any triangular array with $T(T-1)/2$ elements. (A.6) imposes $T-1$ independent linear restrictions on A or P, since one of the restrictions is redundant. The restrictions of (A.7) always hold when P has the above form.

Table 6 gives the number of non-redundant instruments. This equals also the number of P matrices satisfying (A.6) and (A.7) unless (A.8) is violated. Then

Table 6

The optimal number of instruments.[a]

(A) *$T=6$ case*	
1. Stationarity and no correlation	29
2. No stationarity and no correlation	24
3. Stationarity, MA(1)	28
4. Stationarity, MA(2)	27
5. Stationarity, MA(3)	26
6. Stationarity, MA(4)	25
7. Stationarity, MA(K), $K>4$	25
8. No stationarity, MA(1)	19
9. No stationarity, MA(2)	15
10. No stationarity, MA(3)	12
11. No stationarity, MA(K), $K \geq 4$	0[b]
(B) *Arbitrary T case*	
1. Stationarity and no correlation	$T^2-(T+1)$
2. No stationarity and no correlation	$T^2-(2T)$
3. Stationarity and MA(K), $K<T-2$	$T^2-(T+K+1)$
4. Stationarity and MA(K), $K \geq T-2$	$T^2-(T+T-1)$
5. No stationarity and MA(K)[c]	$T^2-[2T+(T-1)+\cdots+(T-K)]$

[a] The number of P matrices satisfying (A.6)–(A.7) and the number of valid instruments is the same as long as $[T-[2T+(T-1)+\cdots+(T-K)]] > (T-1)(T/2-1)$.

[b] The number of P matrices satisfying (A.6)–(A.7) is ten here, even though there are no valid instruments.

[c] 0 if $[T-[2T+(T-1)+\cdots+(T-K)]] \leq (T-1)(T/2-1)$. The number of P matrices is still $T^2-[2T+(T-1)+\cdots+(T-K)]$.

no valid instruments are available. Both the $T=6$ case and the arbitrary T case are presented.

In our framework, it is fairly easy to construct an optimal set of instruments under any assumptions about v. One lists linearly independent P matrices satisfying (A.6)–(A.8). Since a basis for this space can be written using P matrices with entries of 1, -1 and 0, it is fairly easy to check linear independence. As a given basis of a vector space is not unique, the set of instruments will not be either.

References

Aigner, D., C. Hsiao, A. Kapteyn and T. Wansbeek, 1984, Latent variable models in econometrics, in: Z. Griliches and M. Intriligator, eds., Handbook of econometrics, Vol. 2 (North-Holland, Amsterdam) 1321–1393.

Bhargava, A. and D. Sargan, 1983, Estimating dynamic random effects models from panel data covering short time periods, Econometrica 51, no. 6.

Bielby, W.T., R.M. Hauser and K.K. Featherman, 1977, Response errors of non-black males in models of the stratification process, in: A. Goldberger and D. Aigner, eds., Latent variables in socioeconomic models (North-Holland, Amsterdam) 227–251.

Brechling, F.P.R., 1965, The relationship between output and employment in British manufacturing industries, Review of Economic Studies 32, no. 3.

Chamberlain, G., 1982, Multivariate regression models for panel data, Journal of Econometrics 18, no. 1.

Chamberlain, G. and Z. Griliches, 1975, Unobservables with a variance-components structure: Ability, schooling and the economic success of brothers, International Economic Review 16, no. 2.

Chowdhury, G. and S. Nickell, 1985, Hourly earnings in the U.S.: Another look at unionization, schooling, sickness and unemployment using PSID data, Journal of Labor Economics 3, 38–69.

Cummins, C., B.H. Hall and E.S. Laderman, 1982, The R&D master file: Documentation, Unpublished (Harvard University and NBER, Cambridge, MA).

Fay, J.A. and J.L. Medoff, 1985, Labor and output over the business cycle: Some direct evidence, American Economic Review 76, no. 4.

Freeman, R.B., 1984, Longitudinal analyses of the effects of trade unions, Journal of Labor Economics 2, 1–26.

Friedman, M., 1957, A theory of the consumption function, NBER general series 63 (NBER, New York).

Griliches, Z., 1979, Sibling models and data in economics: Beginnings of a survey, Journal of Political Economy 78, no. 5, part 2.

Griliches, Z., 1984, Data problems in econometrics, in: Z. Griliches and M. Intriligator, eds., Handbook of econometrics, Vol. 3 (North-Holland, Amsterdam) forthcoming.

Hall, B. H., 1979, MOMENTS: The moment matrix processor user manual (Stanford, CA).

Hansen, L., 1982, Large sample properties of generalized methods of moments, Econometrica 50, no. 4.

Hausman, J., 1978, Specification tests in econometrics, Econometrica 46, no. 6.

Hausman, J. and W. Taylor, 1981, Panel data and unobservable individual effects, Econometrica 49, no. 6.

Jöreskog, K.G. and D. Sörbom, 1981, LISRELV: Analysis of linear structural relationships by maximum likelihood and least squares method (National Education Resources, Chicago, IL).

Karni, E. and I. Weissman, 1974, A consistent estimator of the slope in a regression model with errors in variables, Journal of the American Statistical Association 69.

Maddala, G. S., 1971, The use of variance components models in pooling cross-section and time series data, Econometrica 39, no. 2.

Maddala, G. S., 1977, Econometrics (McGraw-Hill, New York).

Mundlak, Y., 1978, On the pooling of time series and cross section data, Econometrica 46, no. 1.

Newey, W., 1983, Specification testing and estimation using a generalized method of moments, Ph.D. thesis (MIT, Cambridge, MA).

Sargan, J. D., 1958, The estimation of economic relationships using instrumental variables, Econometrica 26, no. 3.

Sims, C. A., 1974, Output and labor input in manufacturing, Brookings Papers on Economic Activity no. 3.

Solow, R., 1964, Draft of presidential address on the short-run relation of employment and output, Unpublished draft.

White, H., 1982, Instrumental variables regression with independent observations, Econometrica 50, no. 2.

[2]

Journal of Econometrics 16 (1981) 221–236. North-Holland Publishing Company

ESTIMATING ECONOMIC RELATIONS FROM INCOMPLETE CROSS-SECTION/TIME-SERIES DATA

Erik BIØRN*

Central Bureau of Statistics, Oslo, Norway

Received January 1979, final version received February 1981

Authors dealing with combined cross-section/time-series data usually assume that complete time-series exist for all units under observation. In the context of micro data, however, this may be a very restrictive assumption. The paper is concerned with problems of model specification and estimation when the data at hand are incomplete time-series from a sample of micro units. Particular attention is paid to a situation where the sample of micro units 'rotates' over time. The main results are compared with those derived by Nerlove and others for the standard specification with complete cross-section/time-series data. Some illustrative examples based on data from Norwegian household budget surveys are also given.

1. Introduction

During the last 10–15 years, problems of model specification and estimation related to combined cross-section/time-series (CS/TS) data have received increasing attention from econometricians. However, almost all efforts have been devoted to the case where *complete* time-series exist for all units under observation [see, e.g. Balestra and Nerlove (1966), Chetty (1968), Wallace and Hussain (1969), Maddala (1971), Nerlove (1971), Johnson and Lyon (1973), Avery (1977), and Mundlak (1978)]. Analytical convenience may partly account for this.[1] Another reason may be the fact that in many practical applications of the CS/TS approach, the units of observation are some sorts of aggregates, for instance geographic regions. In such cases, complete time-series are readily available.

On the other hand, if the data are collected by *sampling* from a population of genuine micro units, e.g. households, complete CS/TS data rarely occur. In some cases, of course, the econometrician has access to panel data (longitudinal data), but this seems to be the exception rather than the rule.

*I am indebted to Yoel Haitovsky for his very helpful suggestions to improve the formal presentation of the model. Comments from Petter Frenger, Eilev S. Jansen, and an anonymous referee are also gratefully acknowledged. Remaining errors and shortcomings are, of course, my own.

[1]Mention must, however, be made of the recent literature on 'selectivity bias' problems in panel data; see e.g. Hausman and Wise (1977). Such problems will not be dealt with in the present paper.

In practice, the data-collecting agency can hardly force, nor persuade, randomly selected individuals to report more than once or twice, at least if detailed and time-consuming reporting is required. Thus, in the context of micro data, the *practising* econometrician will find models based on *incomplete* CS/TS data more appropriate and interesting than the standard model assuming complete data sets.

In this paper, we shall explore some of the problems of specification and estimation which arise when using incomplete time-series of cross-section data in connection with single equation *disturbance components* (error components) models. Section 2 gives a brief general description of the model and the sampling scheme. In section 3, we derive a general expression for the disturbance covariance matrix. This is a preliminary to section 4, dealing with estimation. We develop an iterative Maximum Likelihood estimation procedure for a situation with rotating (partly overlapping) samples to be compared, in section 5, with the estimation procedure for the standard model based on complete CS/TS data. An application is discussed in section 6. Section 7 briefly summarizes the results.

2. Model and sampling scheme

Consider the structural equation

$$y_{it}=f(x_{it};\,\beta)+e_{it}, \tag{1}$$

where β is the vector of coefficients, and y_{it}, x_{it}, and e_{it} denote, respectively, the values of the endogenous variable, the vector of exogenous (non-stochastic) variables, and the disturbance relating to individual (micro unit) i in time period t. At this stage, we assume that i and t can be any positive integer, i.e., the model applies to all individuals in the population at all points of time. We decompose, in the usual way, e_{it} into an individual, a time specific and a combined component,

$$e_{it}=u_i+v_t+w_{it}, \tag{2}$$

where the three components are independently distributed with zero expectations. We also assume $E(u_iu_k)=\delta_{ik}\sigma_u^2$, $E(v_tv_s)=\delta_{ts}\sigma_v^2$, $E(w_{it}w_{ks})=\delta_{ik}\delta_{ts}\sigma_w^2$ for all values of i, k, t and s, where the δ's are 'Kronecker deltas'. Then

$$E(e_{it})=0, \tag{3}$$

$$
\begin{aligned}
E(e_{it}e_{ks}) &= \sigma^2 \quad \text{for} \quad k=i, \quad s=t, \\
&= \rho\sigma^2 \quad \text{for} \quad k=i, \quad s\neq t, \\
&= \omega\sigma^2 \quad \text{for} \quad k\neq i, \quad s=t, \\
&= 0 \quad \text{for} \quad k\neq i, \quad s\neq t,
\end{aligned}
\tag{4}
$$

where $\sigma^2 = \sigma_u^2 + \sigma_v^2 + \sigma_w^2$ is the total variance, $\rho = \sigma_u^2/\sigma^2$ is the individual part and $\omega = \sigma_v^2/\sigma^2$ is the time specific part of this total. [Cf. e.g. Nerlove (1971, pp. 384–385).][2]

The individuals are selected according to the following *sampling plan*: Let all individuals in the population be numbered consecutively, and let the sample in period 1 consist of individuals $1, 2, \ldots, N$. In period 2, individuals $1, 2, \ldots, m$ $(0 \leqq m \leqq N)$ are replaced by individuals $N+1, N+2, \ldots, N+m$. This procedure — dropping the first m individuals from the sample selected in the previous period and augmenting it by drawing m individuals from the population so that the sample size remains the same — continues in all the following periods until period T. In general, the sample in period t consists of the individuals with numbers $(t-1)m+1$, $(t-1)m+2, \ldots,$ $(t-1)m+N$ $(t = 1, 2, \ldots, T)$. The total number of individuals observed is then

$$
H = (T-1)m + N,
\tag{5}
$$

and the total number of observations is TN.

The situation with *completely overlapping samples* studied by Balestra–Nerlove et al. is the special case with $m=0$, i.e. $H=N$. At the other extreme, $m=N$, i.e. $H=TN$, corresponds to a sampling design with *non-overlapping samples*; all individuals are observed only once. If $0<m<N$, we have a situation with *rotating* (*partly overlapping*) *samples*. Our main attention in this paper will be devoted to the latter sort of sampling design. If $m \geqq N/2$, no individual is observed more than twice; this is perhaps the most interesting situation in practice.

3. The disturbance covariance matrix

Before considering estimation problems, we derive an analytical expression for the covariance matrix of the disturbances of the TN observations. By utilizing (4), giving the variances and covariances of the 'population disturbances' e_{it}, in combination with suitably defined selection matrices, this is straightforward.

[2]Of course, the x vector can be similarly decomposed, i.e., $x_{it} = (q_i, s_t, z_{it})$, where q_i is the (vector of) individual, time invariant variables, s_t is the time specific, individual invariant variables, and z_{it} contains the variables varying across individuals as well as over time.

If individuals $1, 2, \ldots, H$ were observed in all the T periods under consideration, the disturbance vector in period t would be

$$e_t = (e_{1t} e_{2t} \ldots e_{Ht})', \qquad t = 1, 2, \ldots, T. \tag{6}$$

A subset of N individuals is actually selected. Let ε_{it} be the disturbance of the ith of these individuals [its number in the population is $(i-1)m+i$], and define

$$\varepsilon_t = (\varepsilon_{1t} \varepsilon_{2t} \ldots \varepsilon_{Nt})', \qquad t = 1, 2, \ldots, T. \tag{7}$$

We then have

$$\varepsilon_t = D_t e_t, \qquad t = 1, 2, \ldots, T, \tag{8}$$

where D_t is a sample design (selection) matrix of dimension $N \times H$ defined as follows:

$$D_t = (0_{N,(t-1)m} \vdots I_N \vdots 0_{N,(T-t)m}), \qquad t = 1, 2, \ldots, T, \tag{9}$$

$0_{N,n}$ denoting the $N \times n$ zero matrix and I_N the $N \times N$ identity matrix. An entry of 1 in position (i, j) of D_t means that the jth individual in the population is the ith individual in the sample in period t. In completely overlapping samples we obviously have

$$D_t = I_N \quad \text{for all } t.$$

Non-overlapping samples correspond to

$$D_t = (0_{1,t-1}\ 1\ 0_{1,T-t}) \otimes I_N,$$

where $\otimes$ is the Kronecker product operator.

From (4) and (6) we obtain

$$\begin{aligned} E(e_t e_s') &= \sigma^2\{(1-\omega)I_H + \omega E_H\} && \text{for} \quad s = t, \\ &= \sigma^2 \rho I_H && \text{for} \quad s \neq t, \end{aligned} \qquad s, t = 1, 2, \ldots, T, \tag{10}$$

where E_H is the $H \times H$ matrix with all elements equal to one. Since $D_t D_t' = I_N$

and $D_t E_H D_t' = E_N$ for all t, regardless of the sampling design, (8) and (10) imply

$$E(\varepsilon_t \varepsilon_s') = D_t E(e_t e_s') D_s' = \sigma^2 \Omega_{ts}$$

$$= \sigma^2 \{(1-\omega) I_N + \omega E_N)\} \quad \text{for} \quad s=t,$$

$$s, t = 1, 2, \ldots, T, \qquad (11)$$

$$= \sigma^2 \rho D_t D_s' \qquad \text{for} \quad s \neq t,$$

where Ω_{ts} is defined by the last equality. From this equation we directly observe that ρ, the part of the total disturbance variance which is due to individual differences, is not identifiable unless $D_t D_s' \neq 0_{N,N}$ for at least one $s \neq t$, i.e., unless at least two of the T samples in our data set overlap. The general expression for the covariance matrix of the complete $TN \times 1$ disturbance vector,

$$\varepsilon = (\varepsilon_1' \varepsilon_2' \ldots \varepsilon_T')', \qquad (12)$$

can then be written as

$$E(\varepsilon\varepsilon') = \sigma^2 \Omega = \sigma^2 \{ I_T \otimes [(1-\omega) I_N + \omega E_N] + \rho [DD' - I_T \otimes I_N] \}$$

$$= \sigma^2 \{(1-\rho-\omega) I_T \otimes I_N + \omega (I_T \otimes E_N) + \rho DD' \}, \qquad (13)$$

where $\Omega = (\Omega_{ts})$ and

$$D = (D_1' D_2' \ldots D_T')'. \qquad (14)$$

In the special case with completely overlapping samples ($m=0$), we have $D = 1_T \otimes I_N$, where 1_T is the $T \times 1$ vector with all elements equal to one, and consequently $DD' = (1_T 1_T') \otimes I_N = E_T \otimes I_N$. Inserting this into (13), we obtain

$$\Omega = (1-\rho-\omega) I_T \otimes I_N + \omega (I_T \otimes E_N) + \rho (E_T \otimes I_N). \qquad (13a)$$

This formula is, apart from the difference in notation, identical with the one derived by Nerlove (1971, eq. (1.7)). (Recall that we have ordered the elements of the disturbance vector first by period, second by individual, whereas Nerlove has chosen the reverse ordering.) At the other extreme, in the special case with non-overlapping samples ($m=N$), i.e. $D = I_T \otimes I_N$, (13) degenerates to

$$\Omega = (1-\omega) I_T \otimes I_N + \omega (I_T \otimes E_N), \qquad (13b)$$

irrespective of the value of ρ.

4. Estimation

Let y denote the $TN \times 1$ vector of y_{it}'s ordered in the same way as ε, and let $f(x;\beta)$ be the corresponding vector representation of $f(x_{it};\beta)$. Provided that all disturbances are normally distributed, the log-likelihood function of y can be written as

$$L = L(y, x; \beta, \Omega, \sigma^2)$$

$$= -\frac{TN}{2}\log(2\pi) - \frac{TN}{2}\log\sigma^2 - \tfrac{1}{2}\log|\Omega| - \tfrac{1}{2}\sigma^{-2}\varepsilon'\Omega^{-1}\varepsilon, \tag{15}$$

using ε as a shorthand notation for $y - f(x;\beta)$. Here the matrix Ω is known if ρ and ω are known, since D is known once the sampling scheme is specified, cf. (13).

Maximum Likelihood (ML) estimation of β, ρ, ω and σ can, *in principle*, be solved by iteratively switching between the following two subproblems:[3]

(i) Minimize $Q = \varepsilon'\Omega^{-1}\varepsilon$ with respect to β, conditionally on ρ and ω.

(ii) Minimize $TN\log\sigma^2 + \log|\Omega| + \sigma^{-2}\varepsilon'\Omega^{-1}\varepsilon$ with respect to ρ, ω and σ, conditionally on β.

To start this algorithm, initial values have to be assigned to ρ and ω. A convenient choice is $\rho = \omega = 0$, i.e. $\Omega = I_{TN}$, so that the first stage degenerates to ordinary least squares estimation of β.

We shall not elaborate the details of this algorithm in the general case,[4] but confine our attention to an interesting special case: We assume that $N = 2m$, i.e., exactly one half of the individuals observed in any period 'rotates' to the next one, and set $\omega = 0$, i.e., we disregard the time specific disturbance component. In practice, this component seems to be of less importance than the individual one — at least when T is small and the data employed are genuine micro data.

When $N = 2m$, we find from (9) that

$$D_t = (0_{2,t-1} \vdots I_2 \vdots 0_{2,T-t}) \otimes I_m. \tag{16}$$

[3]Cf. Oberhofer and Kmenta (1974).

[4]This would require analytical expressions for Ω^{-1} and $|\Omega|$, which in practice would involve calculation of all the eigenvalues of Ω. Confer the procedure adopted by Nerlove (1971, sect. 2) for the special case with completely overlapping samples.

Inserting this into (11) with $\omega=0$, we obtain

$$\begin{aligned}\Omega_{ts} &= I_2 \otimes I_m && \text{for} \quad s=t, \\ &= \rho \begin{pmatrix} 0 & 0 \\ 1 & 0 \end{pmatrix} \otimes I_m && \text{for} \quad s=t+1, \qquad t=1,2,\dots,T. \\ &= 0_{2m,2m} && \text{for} \quad s \geqq t+2,\end{aligned}$$

Hence,

$$\Omega = \begin{pmatrix} 1 & 0 & 0 \\ 0 & I_{T-1} \otimes B_2 & 0 \\ 0 & 0 & 1 \end{pmatrix} \otimes I_m, \tag{17}$$

where

$$B_2 = \begin{pmatrix} 1 & \rho \\ \rho & 1 \end{pmatrix},$$

and consequently,

$$\Omega^{-1} = \begin{pmatrix} 1 & 0 & 0 \\ 0 & I_{T-1} \otimes B_2^{-1} & 0 \\ 0 & 0 & 1 \end{pmatrix} \otimes I_m, \tag{18}$$

and

$$|\Omega| = |B_2|^{m(T-1)} = (1-\rho^2)^{m(T-1)}. \tag{19}$$

The quadratic form Q to be minimized in *subproblem* (i) can now be written in a simple form. Since the individuals observed in period t have population numbers $(t-1)m+1$, $(t-1)m+2, \dots, (t+1)m$, the following decomposition of the vector ε_t is convenient:

$$\varepsilon_t = \begin{pmatrix} \varepsilon_{tA} \\ \varepsilon_{tB} \end{pmatrix}, \qquad t=1,2,\dots,T, \tag{20}$$

where

$$\varepsilon_{tA} = (\varepsilon_{1t}, \varepsilon_{2t}, \ldots, \varepsilon_{mt})'$$

$$= (e_{(t-1)m+1,t}, e_{(t-1)m+2,t}, \ldots, e_{tm,t})',$$

$$\varepsilon_{tB} = (\varepsilon_{m+1,t}, \varepsilon_{m+2,t}, \ldots, \varepsilon_{2m,t})'$$

$$= (e_{tm+1,t}, e_{tm+2,t}, \ldots, e_{(t+1)m,t})',$$

i.e., ε_{tA} contains the disturbances in period t of the individuals observed in periods $t-1$ and t ($t=2,\ldots,T$), and ε_{tB} contains the disturbances in period t of those observed in periods t and $t+1$ ($t=1,\ldots,T-1$). The subvectors ε_{1A} and ε_{TB} represent the individuals observed only once. Combining (12), (18) and (20), we obtain

$$Q = \varepsilon_{1A}'\varepsilon_{1A} + \sum_{t=2}^{T} (\varepsilon_{t-1,B}'\varepsilon_{tA}')(B_2^{-1} \otimes I_m)\begin{pmatrix} \varepsilon_{t-1,B} \\ \varepsilon_{tA} \end{pmatrix} + \varepsilon_{TB}'\varepsilon_{TB}. \tag{21}$$

From the fact that $I_k - E_k/k$ and E_k/k are both idempotent for $k=2,3,\ldots,$ it is easy to show that the inverse of the matrix

$$B_k = (1-\rho)I_k + \rho E_k = (1-\rho)(I_k - E_k/k) + [1+(k-1)\rho]E_k/k, \tag{22}$$

can be written as

$$B_k^{-1} = (1-\rho)^{-1}\{I_k - (1-\alpha_k^2)E_k/k\} = (1-\rho)^{-1}F_k'F_k, \tag{23}$$

where

$$\alpha_k = \{(1-\rho)/(1+(k-1)\rho)\}^{\frac{1}{2}}, \tag{24}$$

$$F_k = I_k - (1-\alpha_k)E_k/k. \tag{25}$$

Hence,

$$Q = \varepsilon_{1A}'\varepsilon_{1A} + (1-\rho)^{-1}\sum_{t=2}^{T}\left[(F_2 \otimes I_m)\begin{pmatrix} \varepsilon_{t-1,B} \\ \varepsilon_{tA} \end{pmatrix}\right]'\left[(F_2 \otimes I_m)\begin{pmatrix} \varepsilon_{t-1,B} \\ \varepsilon_{tA} \end{pmatrix}\right]$$

$$+ \varepsilon_{TB}'\varepsilon_{TB}$$

$$= \frac{1}{1-\rho}\left\{(1-\rho)\varepsilon_{1A}'\varepsilon_{1A} + \sum_{t=2}^{T}(\varepsilon_{t-1,B}^{*\prime}\varepsilon_{t-1,B}^{*} + \varepsilon_{tA}^{*\prime}\varepsilon_{tA}^{*}) + (1-\rho)\varepsilon_{TB}'\varepsilon_{TB}\right\},$$

where

$$\varepsilon^*_{t-1,B} = \varepsilon_{t-1,B} - (1-\alpha_2)(\varepsilon_{t-1,B} + \varepsilon_{tA})/2,$$

$$\varepsilon^*_{tA} = \varepsilon_{t,A} - (1-\alpha_2)(\varepsilon_{t-1,B} + \varepsilon_{tA})/2.$$

The algorithm for solving subproblem (i) of iterative ML estimation thus becomes:

Multiply the disturbances from individuals observed only once by $(1-\rho)^{\frac{1}{2}}$, *replace the disturbances from individuals observed twice by the original disturbance minus* $1-\alpha_2 = 1-\{(1-\rho)/(1+\rho)\}^{\frac{1}{2}}$ *times the corresponding individual average,*[5] *and minimize the resulting sum of squares.*

We see that $1-\alpha_2$, the fraction of the individual average to be subtracted, increases from 0 to 1 as ρ increases from 0 to 1. A transformation to that effect is intuitively very reasonable when we recall that ρ represents the coefficient of correlation between the first and the second disturbance of the individuals observed twice.

The algorithm above can be generalized in a straightforward way to situations where some individuals are observed more than twice. Assume that the data set includes individuals observed $k=1,2,\ldots,K$ times. It can then be shown that minimization of the quadratic form in the log-likelihood function can be carried out as follows:

Multiply the disturbances from individuals observed only once by $\alpha_1 = (1-\rho)^{\frac{1}{2}}$, *subtract from the disturbances of all individuals observed k times a fraction* $1-\alpha_k = 1-\{(1-\rho)/(1+(k-1)\rho)\}^{\frac{1}{2}}$ *of the corresponding individdividual average* $(k=2,2,\ldots,K)$, *and minimize the resulting sum of squares.*

We then turn to *subproblem* (ii). Utilizing (23) and (24), we note that (21) can be written as

$$Q = \frac{1}{1-\rho^2}(Q_1 - 2\rho Q_2 - \rho^2 Q_3),$$

where

$$Q_1 = \sum_{t=1}^{T} (\varepsilon'_{tA}\varepsilon_{tA} + \varepsilon'_{tB}\varepsilon_{tB}) = \sum_{t=1}^{T} \varepsilon'_t\varepsilon_t,$$

$$Q_2 = \sum_{t=2}^{T} \varepsilon'_{t-1,B}\varepsilon_{tA},$$

$$Q_3 = \varepsilon'_{1A}\varepsilon_{1A} + \varepsilon'_{TB}\varepsilon_{TB}.$$

[5]Recall that the m elements in the subvectors $\varepsilon_{t-1,B}$ and ε_{tA} represent the same m individuals.

The log-likelihood function (15) then becomes

$$L = -\frac{2Tm}{2}\log(2\pi) - \tfrac{1}{2}\{2Tm\log\sigma^2 + m(T-1)\log(1-\rho^2)\}$$

$$-\frac{1}{2\sigma^2(1-\rho^2)}(Q_1 - 2\rho Q_2 - \rho^2 Q_3), \qquad (26)$$

after inserting (19). Partial maximization of L with respect to σ^2 gives the following conditional estimator:

$$\hat{\sigma}^2 = \frac{1}{2Tm(1-\rho^2)}(Q_1 - 2\rho Q_2 - \rho^2 Q_3). \qquad (27)$$

Inserting this into (26) yields the concentrated log-likelihood function

$$L^* = \text{constant} - \tfrac{1}{2}\{2Tm\log(Q_1 - 2\rho Q_2 - \rho^2 Q_3)$$

$$-(T+1)m\log(1-\rho^2)\}.$$

We find, after some algebra, that partial maximization of L^* with respect to ρ, with β fixed, implies solution of the following cubic equation:

$$(T-1)Q_3\rho^3 - 2Q_2\rho^2 + \{(T+1)Q_1 - 2TQ_3\}\rho - 2TQ_2 = 0. \qquad (28)$$

By utilizing the fact that Q_3/Q_1 is of order $1/T$, an approximate solution can be found. Setting $Q_3 = Q_1/T$, (28) reduces to

$$\left(\frac{1}{T}\rho^2 + 1\right)\{(T-1)Q_1\rho - 2TQ_2\} = 0,$$

which has

$$\hat{\rho} = \frac{2T}{T-1}\frac{Q_2}{Q_1} = \frac{2T}{T-1}\left(\sum_{t=2}^{T}\hat{\varepsilon}'_{t-1,B}\hat{\varepsilon}_{tA} \Big/ \sum_{t=1}^{T}(\hat{\varepsilon}'_{tA}\hat{\varepsilon}_{tA} + \hat{\varepsilon}'_{tB}\hat{\varepsilon}_{tB})\right) \qquad (29)$$

as its only real solution.[6] Substituting $\rho = \hat{\rho}$ back into (29) and letting once again $Q_3 = Q_1/T$, the variance estimator can be written as

$$\hat{\sigma}^2 = \frac{Q_1}{2Tm} = \frac{1}{2Tm}\sum_{t=1}^{T}(\hat{\varepsilon}'_{tA}\hat{\varepsilon}_{tA} + \hat{\varepsilon}'_{tB}\hat{\varepsilon}_{tB}). \qquad (30)$$

[6]The 'hats' indicate residuals calculated from the (conditionally) estimated equation.

The estimators $\hat{\rho}$ and $\hat{\sigma}^2$ are *approximations* to the conditional estimators of ρ and σ^2 in subproblem (ii) of iterative ML estimation. Our difficulties in finding the exact solution are due to the fact that the m first and the m last individuals are observed only once. It can be shown that if these individuals were deleted from the ε vector, and Ω redefined accordingly, i.e. $\Omega = I_{T-1} \otimes B_2 \otimes I_m$, then we would get the following *exact* solution to subproblem (ii):[7]

$$\tilde{\rho} = \left(2 \sum_{t=2}^{T} \hat{\varepsilon}'_{t-1,B} \hat{\varepsilon}_{tA}\right) \Big/ \left(\sum_{t=2}^{T} \hat{\varepsilon}'_{tA} \hat{\varepsilon}_{tA} + \sum_{t=1}^{T-1} \hat{\varepsilon}'_{tB} \hat{\varepsilon}_{tB}\right), \tag{29'}$$

$$\tilde{\sigma}^2 = \frac{1}{2m(T-1)} \left\{\sum_{t=2}^{T} \hat{\varepsilon}'_{tA} \hat{\varepsilon}_{tA} + \sum_{t=1}^{T-1} \hat{\varepsilon}'_{tB} \hat{\varepsilon}_{tB}\right\}. \tag{30'}$$

5. Comparison with the estimators based on completely overlapping samples (complete CS/TS data)

It is illuminating to compare our results above with those obtained in the standard case with completely overlapping samples. When $\omega = 0$, the disturbance covariance matrix is equal to [cf. (13a)]

$$\Omega = \Omega_C = (1-\rho) I_T \otimes I_N + \rho (E_T \otimes I_N) = B_T \otimes I_N,$$

with the corresponding quadratic form [cf. (23)–(25)]

$$Q = Q_C = \varepsilon' \Omega_C^{-1} \varepsilon = (1-\rho)^{-1} \{(F_T \otimes I_N)\varepsilon\}' \{(F_T \otimes I_N)\varepsilon\}$$

$$= \frac{1}{1-\rho} \sum_{i=1}^{N} \sum_{t=1}^{T} \varepsilon_{it}^{*2},$$

where

$$\varepsilon_{it}^{*} = \varepsilon_{it} - \frac{1-\alpha_T}{T} \sum_{s=1}^{T} \varepsilon_{is}.$$

Thus *subproblem* (i), conditional minimization of Q with respect to β, can be solved by *minimizing the sum of squares of disturbances after having made the following data transformation: Original observation minus* $1-\alpha_T$ *times the*

[7] We are not ensured that $\hat{\rho}$ (or $\tilde{\rho}$) is positive, as it should be to have the interpretation of an estimate of a variance ratio. As noted by Berzeg (1979), with reference to the Balestra–Nerlove (1966) model, this problem can be solved if we relax the assumption of zero correlation between the individual disturbance component u_i and the remainder w_{it} and re-interpret ρ accordingly. The same solution can be applied in our case.

individual average. The analogy to the corresponding algorithm for partly overlapping samples is quite obvious.

Subproblem (ii), conditional estimation of ρ and σ^2 given β, is solved by inserting $Q=Q_C$ and

$$|\Omega|=|\Omega_C|=|B_T|^N=(1-\rho)^{(T-1)N}\{1+(T-1)\rho\}^N$$

into the log-likelihood function (15), and maximizing the resulting expression,

$$L=L_C=-\frac{TN}{2}\log(2\pi)$$

$$-\tfrac{1}{2}\{TN\log\sigma^2+(T-1)N\log(1-\rho)+N\log(1+(T-1)\rho)\}$$

$$-\tfrac{1}{2}\sigma^{-2}Q_C,$$

partially with respect to ρ and σ^2. After some algebra, we obtain the following estimators:[8]

$$\hat{\rho}_C=\frac{1}{T-1}\frac{\sum_{i=1}^{N}\left\{\left(\sum_{t=1}^{T}\hat{\varepsilon}_{it}\right)^2-\sum_{t=1}^{T}\hat{\varepsilon}_{it}^2\right\}}{\sum_{t=1}^{T}\sum_{i=1}^{N}\hat{\varepsilon}_{it}^2}$$

$$=\frac{1}{T-1}\frac{\sum_{t=1}^{T}\sum_{i=1}^{N}\sum_{s=1\neq t}^{T}\hat{\varepsilon}_{it}\hat{\varepsilon}_{is}}{\sum_{t=1}^{T}\sum_{i=1}^{N}\hat{\varepsilon}_{it}^2},$$

$$\hat{\sigma}_C^2=\frac{1}{TN}\sum_{t=1}^{T}\sum_{i=1}^{N}\hat{\varepsilon}_{it}^2.$$

The variance estimator $\hat{\sigma}_C^2$ is, apart from the difference in notation, identical with $\hat{\sigma}^2$, given in (30). We also find a striking similarity between the expressions for $\hat{\rho}_C$ and $\hat{\rho}$. In both cases we (1) form *all possible* cross-products of residuals relating to *different* observations from each individual i, (2) sum all such terms across periods and individuals, (3) divide this sum by the overall sum of squares of residuals, and finally, (4) adjust for the different number of terms in the numerator and the denominator.

[8]Cf. e.g. Balestra and Nerlove (1966, eq. (35)).

6. An application[9]

The estimation procedure developed in section 4 has been utilized to estimate household expenditure functions by means of data from the *Norwegian Surveys of Consumer Expenditure.* Since 1973 these sampling surveys have been performed annually and give data in the incomplete CS/TS format.[10]

The model is

$$y_{it}=\beta_0+\beta_1 n_{it}+\beta_2 a_{it}+(\beta_3+\beta_4 n_{it}+\beta_5 a_{it})\frac{\log x_{it}}{x_{it}}$$

$$+(\beta_6+\beta_7 n_{it}+\beta_8 a_{it})\frac{1}{x_{it}}+\varepsilon_{it},$$

where y is the budget share of the commodity considered, x is total expenditure divided by the price index of total consumption, n is the number of persons in the household, and a is the age of its head. The subscripts i and t have the same interpretation as before. The 'background variables' n and a represent in a compact way 'type of household'. This specification implies, *inter alia*, that expenditure, in value terms, is a composite linear and semi-logarithmic function of the value of total expenditure. The expenditure function is transformed to budget shares in order to compensate for heteroscedasticity of disturbances.

The estimation is based on reports from 418 households, of which one half has been observed in 1975 and 1976, and the other half in 1976 and 1977, i.e. $T=3$, $m=209$. The disturbance vector corresponding to this data set is[11]

$$\varepsilon=\begin{pmatrix}\varepsilon_{1B}\\ \varepsilon_{2A}\\ \varepsilon_{2B}\\ \varepsilon_{3A}\end{pmatrix},$$

[9]The results discussed in this section are taken from Biørn and Jansen (1980b, sect. VI). The author is grateful to Eilev Jansen for permission to include this material in the present paper.

[10]For an extensive discussion of this data source, see Biørn and Jansen (1980a).

[11]Since households observed only once are excluded from the data set, the estimation of ρ and σ^2 is based on eqs. (29′) and (30′).

where

ε_{1B} = vector in 1975 of the households observed in 1975 and 1976,

ε_{2A} = vector in 1976 of the same households,

ε_{2B} = vector in 1976 of the households observed in 1976 and 1977,

ε_{3A} = vector in 1977 of the same households.

Table 1

Maximum Likelihood estimates of expenditure functions based on data from 418 households observed twice.[a]

	Dairy products			Tobacco		
	Alt. A	Alt. B	Alt. C	Alt. A	Alt. B	Alt. C
$\tilde{\beta}_0 \cdot 10^2$	−2.156	0.914	0.911	−5.439	0.473	0.475
$\tilde{\beta}_1 \cdot 10^2$	−0.319	−0.515	—	0.639	0.153	—
$\tilde{\beta}_2 \cdot 10^4$	4.588	—	—	8.014	—	—
$\tilde{\beta}_3 \cdot 10^2$	6.058	−1.575	2.366	15.89	1.983	1.247
$\tilde{\beta}_4 \cdot 10^2$	1.686	2.205	—	−2.275	−0.978	—
$\tilde{\beta}_5 \cdot 10^4$	−10.38	—	—	−19.08	—	—
$\tilde{\beta}_6 \cdot 10^2$	2.185	3.227	5.886	12.91	1.021	2.503
$\tilde{\beta}_7 \cdot 10^2$	1.892	1.874	—	0.288	0.862	—
$\tilde{\beta}_8 \cdot 10^4$	1.049	—	—	−17.19	—	—
$\tilde{\rho}$	0.369	0.393	0.473	0.707	0.710	0.720
$\tilde{\sigma} \cdot 10^2$	2.102	2.160	2.427	2.536	2.617	2.654
$\tilde{\sigma}_w \cdot 10^2 = \tilde{\sigma}\sqrt{1-\tilde{\rho}} \cdot 10^2$	1.670	1.683	1.762	1.373	1.409	1.404
No. of iterations	3	3	3	3	3	3

[a]The alternatives considered are: *Alt. A* (two background variables, family size and age of household's head, included), *Alt. B* (one background variable, family size, included), *Alt. C* (no background variables included).

Maximum Likelihood estimates of the β's and corresponding estimates of ρ and σ^2 for two selected commodity groups, Dairy Products and Tobacco, and with three different specifications of background variables, are given in table 1. Using $\rho=0$ as starting value for ρ, convergence was obtained after only 3 iterations in all cases. The results indicate that our disturbance component specification has been successful: a substantial part of the total disturbance variance can be ascribed to individual differences in 'tastes', 'habits' and other unobserved (or unobservable) factors affecting consumption.

For Tobacco, the consumption of which is commonly thought to have a strong element of habit formation, the estimate exceeds 70 percent. We also note that for both commodities inclusion of n and a among the structural variables of the model leads to a reduction of the estimate of ρ. However, even with these background variables included, there are significant individual factors left; in both cases $\tilde{\rho}$ is significantly positive, according to a 1 percent likelihood ratio test.

7. Concluding remarks

In this paper, we have been concerned with problems of specification and estimation of disturbance components models when data are incomplete times series of observations from micro units. We have found a striking similarity between our estimation formulae for partly overlapping samples and those derived by Nerlove et al. for completely overlapping samples, but also notable differences.

In principle, our approach can be extended to seemingly unrelated regression models by a generalization similar to that discussed by Avery (1977) and Baltagi (1980) for models assuming completely overlapping samples. Some work remains to be done, however, to obtain general estimation formulae in situations where time-specific disturbance components are taken into account along with the individual ones.

References

Avery, R.B., 1977, Error components and seemingly unrelated regressions, Econometrica 45, 199-209.

Balestra, P. and M. Nerlove, 1966, Pooling cross section and time series data in the estimation of a dynamic model: The demand for natural gas, Econometrica 34, 585-612.

Baltagi, B.H., 1980, On seemingly unrelated regressions with error components, Econometrica 48, 1547–1551.

Berzeg, K., 1979, The error components model: Conditions for the existence of the maximum likelihood estimates, Journal of Econometrics 10, 99–102.

Biørn, E. and E.S. Jansen, 1980a, Consumer demand in Norwegian households 1973–1977: A data base for micro-econometrics, Report no. 80/4 (Central Bureau of Statistics of Norway, Oslo).

Biørn, E. and E.S. Jansen, 1980b, Econometrics of incomplete cross-section/time-series data: Consumer demand in Norwegian households 1975–1977, Paper presented at the 4th World Congress of the Econometric Society, Aix-en-Provence.

Chetty, V.K., 1968, Pooling of time series and cross section data, Econometrica 36, 279–290.

Hausman, J.A. and D.A. Wise, 1977, Social experimentation, truncated distributions, and efficient estimation, Econometrica 45, 919–938.

Johnson, K.H. and H.L. Lyon, 1973, Experimental evidence on combining cross section and time series information, Review of Economics and Statistics 55, 465-474.

Maddala, G.S., 1971, The use of variance components models in pooling cross section and time series data, Econometrica 39, 341–358.

Mundlak, Y., 1978, On the pooling of time series and cross section data, Econometrica 46, 69-85.

Nerlove, M., 1971, A note on error components models, Econometrica 39, 383–396.
Oberhofer, W. and J. Kmenta, 1974, A general procedure for obtaining maximum likelihood estimates in generalized regression models, Econometrica 42, 579–590.
Wallace, T.D. and A. Hussain, 1969, The use of error components models in combining cross section with time series data, Econometrica 37, 55–72.

[3]

Journal of Econometrics 41 (1989) 341–361. North-Holland

ESTIMATION OF THE ERROR-COMPONENTS MODEL WITH INCOMPLETE PANELS*

Tom WANSBEEK

Groningen University, Groningen, The Netherlands

Arie KAPTEYN

Tilburg University, Tilburg, The Netherlands

Received March 1986, final version received September 1988

The error-components model (ECM) is probably the most frequently used approach to analyze panel data in econometrics. When the panel is incomplete, which is the rule rather than the exception when the data come from large-scale surveys, standard estimation methods cannot be applied. We first discuss estimation in the fixed-effects analogue of the ECM, and then present two estimators (quadratic unbiased and maximum likelihood) for the ECM. Some simulation results are given to assess finite-sample properties and computational burden of the various methods.

1. Introduction

Analysis of panel data (i.e., time series of cross-sections) by means of the error-components model (ECM) has attracted a lot of attention in econometrics; see, e.g., Balestra and Nerlove (1966), Wallace and Hussain (1969), Nerlove (1971a, b), Mazodier (1972), Fuller and Battese (1974), Taylor (1977), Mazodier (1978), Baltagi (1981), Wansbeek and Kapteyn (1982), and Dielman (1983). The recent monograph by Hsiao (1986) presents an excellent overview. A problem that often occurs in practice, but which is by and large ignored in the literature, is the phenomenon of missing observations, i.e., not all cross-sectional units are observed during all time periods. If that occurs, we have what we will call an *incomplete panel* or *incomplete data*. Note that we use the word 'incomplete' to denote the absence of *all* information for a certain cross-section unit for a certain time period, and not to be the absence of information on some variables only.

*Detailed and helpful comments from two anonymous referees are gratefully acknowledged. We thank Anton Markink and Paul Flapper for their expert programming support, Brent Moulton and Theo Nijman for their comments on an earlier version, and Jaap Verhees for checking the many algebraic manipulations.

In their pioneering study, Balestra and Nerlove (1966) analyzed panel data where the cross-section units were states of the USA, the time periods being years. The data set was constructed by the authors from existing sources and in such a context incompleteness in the above sense will not be a major concern. However, with the growing attention for micro-data in econometrics, data are increasingly obtained from large-scale surveys and there incompleteness will be the rule rather than the exception. For example, individuals may disappear from a panel after a few waves because they refuse to cooperate any longer, because they leave the household that is participating in the panel, or by death. Moreover, incompleteness may in fact be part of a sample design in which part of a panel is replaced by new units in each wave (rotating panels). The advantage of such a design is that it eases the task of respondents, thereby reducing attrition from the panel. Since attrition generally causes selection bias [see, e.g., Hausman and Wise (1977)], which can only be remedied by means of fairly elaborate and computationally costly models, a sample design which minimizes attrition is of practical interest.

The absence of some observations makes most of the results obtained in the error-components literature inapplicable. A solution was suggested by Fuller and Battese (1974), in which a dummy exogenous variable is added to the set of regressors for each missing observation. After this amendment of the data set, the usual methods can be applied. In many practical cases, however, this means that hundreds of regressors have to be added. This is clearly computationally impractical and an alternative is called for.

Biørn (1981) seems to be the first to discuss error-components models with missing observations. He discusses maximum-likelihood (ML) estimation in the case where a fixed proportion of the sample is replaced with each new wave, and does not allow for observations that may be missing randomly. He writes down the likelihood of this model, but then observes that it involves both the inverse and the determinant of the error-covariance matrix. Given the size of this matrix in practice, ML estimation without further provisions does not seem to be of practical value. Hence, he concentrates on the special case where at each wave exactly half of the sample is replaced and where there is no time-specific effect. Then, the inverse and the determinant can be worked out rather easily. Baltagi (1985) studies some aspects of the error-covariance matrix for a general 'missing pattern' in a model without time-specific effects.

In this paper we will first consider the relatively simple case where the effects (pertaining to the cross-section units and to the time periods) are fixed rather than random, as in the ECM. This case is dealt with in section 2. These results are of interest in themselves and are used, after section 3 where some basic aspects of the random-effects model are discussed, in section 4 as a starting point for deriving quadratic unbiased estimators in the (random-effects) ECM. Section 5 discusses ML estimation of the ECM. Section 6 contains some simulation results, and section 7 concludes. Some of the more technical points are relegated to appendices; the subject of incomplete panels is closely related to the topic of 'unbalanced data' in the ANOVA literature, from which it is well-known that the results are invariably rather messy.

For clarity, it must be emphasized that some interesting problems lie outside the scope of the present paper. We only consider the single-equation model, and do not look at SUR-type or simultaneous equations. The only role that 'time' plays in the ECM is via the (supposedly independent) time-specific effects and we do not look at lagged endogenous variables or a more sophisticated modelling of the time component in the error structure; nor do we go into the problems caused by selective nonresponse. For all these extensions, we first need the basic apparatus given in the present paper.

2. The fixed-effects model

Consider the following regression model:

$$y_{ht} = \alpha_h + \gamma_t + x'_{ht}\beta + u_{ht}, \tag{2.1}$$

where h $(h = 1, \ldots, H)$ denotes, say, households, and t $(t = 1, \ldots, T)$, say, years; x_{ht} is a k-vector of explanatory variables; and β a k-vector of parameters. The error term u_{ht} has the usual 'classical' properties: its variance is σ^2; α_h and γ_t are fixed constants. Therefore, we will sometimes refer to this model as the 'fixed-effects' (FE) model. When we have a *complete* panel, i.e., all households h are observed for all years t, it is well-known that OLS in (2.1) is equivalent to OLS in the transformed model

$$y_{ht} - y_{h.} - y_{.t} + y_{..} = (x_{ht} - x_{h.} - x_{.t} + x_{..})'\beta + e_{ht}, \tag{2.2}$$

where a dot in the place of an index denotes the average over that index. A way to prove this result is to first write (2.1) in vector format,

$$y = (\iota_T \otimes I_H)\alpha + (I_T \otimes \iota_H)\gamma + X\beta + u. \tag{2.3}$$

Note that we have ordered the observations such that the data on the H households are ordered in T consecutive sets; the index t 'runs slowly' and the index h 'runs fast'. In (2.3), it is simple to show that the projector perpendicular to the regressors corresponding to the household and time effects, viz. $(\iota_T \otimes I_H,\ I_T \otimes \iota_H)$, is given by $E_T \otimes E_H$, where $E_T \equiv I_T - \iota_T\iota'_T/T$ and E_H is defined analogously. Moreover, it is rather straightforward to see that application of this projector to both sides of (2.1) effectuates the transformation shown in (2.2).

When we have incomplete data, these simple projection and transformation results no longer hold. We will now derive the corresponding more general results for the incomplete case.

Let N_t ($N_t \leq H$) be the number of observed households in year t. Let $N \equiv \sum_t N_t$. Let D_t be the ($N_t \times H$) matrix obtained from the ($H \times H$) identity matrix from which rows corresponding to households *not* observed in year t have been omitted, and consider

$$Z \equiv \Big(\underset{N \times H}{Z_1}, \underset{N \times T}{Z_2} \Big) \equiv \begin{bmatrix} D_1 & D_1\iota_H & & \\ \vdots & & \ddots & \\ D_T & & & D_T\iota_H \end{bmatrix}. \tag{2.4}$$

The matrix Z gives the dummy-variable structure for the incomplete-data model. (For complete data, $Z_1 = \iota_T \otimes I_H$, $Z_2 = I_T \otimes \iota_H$.)

Next, let

$$\Delta_H \equiv Z_1'Z_1, \qquad \Delta_T \equiv Z_2'Z_2, \qquad A \equiv Z_2'Z_1, \tag{2.5}$$

where Δ_H is the diagonal ($H \times H$) matrix with hth element indicating the number of years for which the hth household has been observed; Δ_T is the diagonal ($T \times T$) matrix with tth element the number of observations in year t; and A is the ($T \times H$) matrix of zeros and ones indicating the absence or presence of a household in a certain year. (For complete data, $\Delta_H = T I_H$, $\Delta_T = H I_T$, and $A = \iota_T \iota_H'$.) Further define

$$\bar{Z} \equiv Z_2 - Z_1 \Delta_H^{-1} A' \quad \left[= \left(I_N - Z_1(Z_1'Z_1)^{-1}Z_1' \right) Z_2 \right], \tag{2.6}$$

$$Q \equiv \Delta_T - A \Delta_H^{-1} A' \quad \left[= Z_2'\bar{Z} \right]. \tag{2.7}$$

In the complete data case, $Q = H E_T$. In the incomplete data case, Q has no specific structure. If each household is observed at least twice (and $H \geq T$), rank(Q) = $T - 1$. In order to avoid unnecessary complications, we assume in this section that this condition holds. (If a certain household is observed only once, it conveys no useful information as we then have the case of a single observation with its own dummy variable.)

Now consider the following matrix:

$$P \equiv P_1 - P_2 \equiv \left(I_N - Z_1 \Delta_H^{-1} Z_1' \right) - \bar{Z} Q^- \bar{Z}'. \tag{2.8}$$

Lemma. *P is the projection matrix onto the null-space of Z.*

Proof. The proof is in three steps:

(i) P is idempotent: $Z_1'\bar{Z} = 0$ [clear from (2.6)], $\bar{Z}'\bar{Z} = Z_2'\bar{Z} = Q$. As $\bar{Z}Q^-Q = \bar{Z}$, $P_2^2 = \bar{Z}Q^-QQ^-\bar{Z}' = \bar{Z}Q^-\bar{Z}' = P_2$. Also, $P_1^2 = P_1$ and $P_1P_2 = P_2P_1 = P_2$. So $P^2 = P_1^2 + P_2^2 - P_1P_2 - P_2P_1 = P_1 - P_2 = P$.

(ii) $PZ = 0$: $PZ = P_1(Z_1, Z_2) - P_2(Z_1, Z_2) = (0, \bar{Z}) - (0, \bar{Z}Q^-Q) = 0.$

(iii) $\text{rank}(P) + \text{rank}(Z) = N$: $\text{rank}(P) = \text{tr}(P) = \text{tr}(P_1) - \text{tr}(P_2) = (N - H) - \text{tr}(Q^-\bar{Z}'\bar{Z}) = (N - H) - \text{tr}(Q^-Q) = (N - H) - (T - 1)$; $\text{rank}(Z) = H + T - 1$.

Together, (i), (ii), and (iii) prove the lemma [e.g., Balestra (1973, lemma 9)]. Q.E.D.

So, P generalizes the expression $E_T \otimes E_H$ to the incomplete-data model. Note that there is an asymmetry in the way that we deal with both dimensions (households and years): P contains the generalized inverse of the $(T \times T)$ matrix Q for which no closed-form expression is available in general. Alternatively, we could have derived an expression for P that contains the inverse of an analogous $(H \times H)$ matrix, but as $H \gg T$ in most practical situations, our choice is the most favorable one from the point of view of computation. The asymmetry and its inherent lack of elegance is the kind of uncomeliness that one has to face when dealing with incomplete or unbalanced data.

How to use P? We will give the generalization of the transformation given in (2.2). Let $v(N \times 1)$ denote a vector of variables occurring in the regression equation; in (2.3), $v = y$ or v is a column of X. We are interested in the form of Pv. Let

$$\phi_1 \equiv Z_1'v \quad (H \times 1) \tag{2.9}$$

and

$$\phi_2 \equiv Z_2'v \quad (T \times 1) \tag{2.10}$$

denote the sum of elements of v over years and households, respectively, and let

$$\bar{\phi} \equiv Q^-\bar{Z}v = Q^-\left(\phi_2 - A\Delta_H^{-1}\phi_1\right). \tag{2.11}$$

(The choice of generalized inverse is arbitrary.) Now

$$Pv = v - Z_1\Delta_H^{-1}Z_1'v - \bar{Z}Q^-\bar{Z}'v = v - Z_1\Delta_H^{-1}\phi_1 - \overline{Z\phi}. \tag{2.12}$$

In scalar format this reads as

$$(Pv)_{th} = v_{th} - \frac{1}{\delta_h}\phi_{1h} + \frac{1}{\delta_h}a_h'\bar{\phi} - \bar{\phi}_t, \tag{2.13}$$

with a_h the hth column of A and δ_h the hth diagonal element of Δ_H. So, OLS on data from an incomplete panel with fixed year and household effects amounts to OLS in a model without these effects when the variables have been transformed according to (2.13). Then using a standard regression package for the transformed data one should not forget to adjust the standard errors and the R^2 printed by the program for the loss of degrees of freedom. When there are k 'true' regressors (apart from the dummies), the printed standard errors should be multiplied by $\{(N-k)/(N-H-T+1-k)\}^{\frac{1}{2}}$. Analogously, the OLS residual variance estimate printed by the program should be multiplied by $(N-k)/(N-H-T+1-k)$ to obtain an unbiased estimate of σ^2.

3. The random-effects model

In the usual ECM formulation the α_h and γ_t in (2.1) are i.i.d. random variables with mean zero, mutually independent and independent of the x_{ht} and u_{ht}. Let σ^2 be the variance of u_{ht}, then the covariance matrix of the composite error term $\varepsilon_{ht} \equiv u_{ht} + \alpha_h + \gamma_t$ is

$$\Omega = \sigma^2 I_N + \sigma_1^2 Z_1 Z_1' + \sigma_2^2 Z_2 Z_2', \tag{3.1}$$

with

$$\sigma_1^2 \equiv \operatorname{var}(\alpha_h), \qquad \sigma_2^2 \equiv \operatorname{var}(\gamma_t).$$

For any sort of efficient estimation of the parameter vector β we need an expression for the inverse of Ω. This is given by the following:

Lemma.

$$\sigma^2 \Omega^{-1} = V - V Z_2 \tilde{Q}^{-1} Z_2' V, \tag{3.2}$$

where

$$V \equiv I_N - Z_1 \tilde{\Delta}_H^{-1} Z_1' \qquad (N \times N), \tag{3.3}$$

$$\tilde{Q} \equiv \tilde{\Delta}_T - A \tilde{\Delta}_H^{-1} A' \qquad (T \times T), \tag{3.4}$$

$$\tilde{\Delta}_H \equiv \Delta_H + \frac{\sigma^2}{\sigma_1^2} I_H \qquad (H \times H), \tag{3.5}$$

$$\tilde{\Delta}_T \equiv \Delta_T + \frac{\sigma^2}{\sigma_2^2} I_T \qquad (T \times T). \tag{3.6}$$

Proof.

$$Z_2'VZ_2 = \Delta_T - A\tilde{\Delta}_H^{-1}A' = \tilde{Q} - \frac{\sigma^2}{\sigma_2^2} I_T, \tag{3.7}$$

so

$$\tilde{Q} - Z_2'VZ_2 = \frac{\sigma^2}{\sigma_2^2} I_T. \tag{3.8}$$

From (3.3),

$$\begin{aligned} V^{-1} &= I_N + Z_1\left(\tilde{\Delta}_H - Z_1'Z_1\right)^{-1} Z_1' \\ &= I_N + Z_1\left(\tilde{\Delta}_H - \Delta_H\right)^{-1} Z_1' \\ &= I_N + \frac{\sigma_1^2}{\sigma^2} Z_1 Z_1', \end{aligned} \tag{3.9}$$

so inverting the expression in (3.2) yields

$$\begin{aligned} \left(V - VZ_2\tilde{Q}^{-1}Z_2'V\right)^{-1} &= V^{-1} + Z_2\left(\tilde{Q} - Z_2'VZ_2\right)^{-1} Z_2' \\ &= I_N + \frac{\sigma_1^2}{\sigma^2} Z_1 Z_1' + \frac{\sigma_2^2}{\sigma^2} Z_2 Z_2' \\ &= \sigma^{-2}\Omega. \qquad \text{Q.E.D.} \end{aligned} \tag{3.10}$$

The expression for Ω^{-1} is somewhat messy and is asymmetric in households and years. In contrast with the complete-data case, no closed-form expression for Ω^{-1} (or for the eigenvalues and eigenvectors) can be given in general. This is only possible for some very specific and 'neat' patterns of missing data. However, for practical purposes the expression for Ω^{-1} is quite useful as compared to the situation where Ω is inverted numerically. The aspect of main interest is the *computational complexity*, i.e., the number of computations, and hence the computing time, as a function of the number of observations. In our case, where T typically is a small number and N and H are large, we are interested in the computing time of the GLS estimator of the regression coefficients in terms of N and H, and take T to be a constant.

We can make the following observations. The computation of $\hat{\beta}$ involves a constant number of evaluations of the type $f'\Omega^{-1}g$, with f and g being

N-vectors (f and g may be one of the various regressors or the regressand). This, in its turn, involves a constant number of evaluations of the type $f'Vg$ [cf. (3.2)], where f and g now also comprise the columns of Z_2. Now, $f'Vg = f'g - f'Z_1\tilde{\Delta}_H^{-1}Z_1'g$; $f'g$ can be computed in $O(N)$ time and $f'Z_1\tilde{\Delta}_H^{-1}Z_1'g$ in $O(H)$ time [at least, when the elements of f and g are displayed in a $(T \times H)$ matrix, then $f'Z_1$ and $Z_1'g$ are simply the H-vector of column totals, computable in $O(H)$ time]. If the structure of Ω would not have been exploited, Ω would have to be inverted numerically, which requires in principle $O(H^3)$ time. (The latter statement neglects recent developments in complexity theory, which allow for a reduction of the exponent 3 to a somewhat lower figure. Up until now, this development has theoretical significance only.)

The implication of the above is that the expressions used in inverting Ω may look a little deterring, but that they enable efficient computation (viz. computing time linear in H) of the GLS estimator of the regression coefficients.

4. Quadratic estimators of the variance components

Statistically efficient estimation of the ECM can take place along two lines. One is to use ML (see section 5). The other is to estimate the variance components (σ^2, σ_1^2, and σ_2^2) by a quadratic unbiased estimation method (QUE; below the E in QUE can also stand for estimator) and to estimate the regression coefficients by GLS with these estimates inserted in Ω. In this section we derive QUE's for σ_1^2 and σ_2^2. The estimator for σ^2 from the FE model is unbiased under RE assumptions as well, so we concentrate on σ_1^2 and σ_2^2.

An intuitively appealing approach to derive QUE's for σ_1^2 and σ_2^2 is to estimate the (FE) model and to use the FE residuals, averaged over households or averaged over years, as the basic ingredients. By residuals we mean in the present context the residuals with respect to the X-part of the FE model, not those with respect to all regressors (X *and* Z); the latter are not informative about σ_1^2 and σ_2^2 as the variation of interest is projected out.

We first assume that X does not contain a vector of ones. Let e be the N-vector of FE residuals, i.e., $e \equiv y - Xb$ with b the FE estimate of β, and let

$$q_H \equiv e'Z_2\Delta_T^{-1}Z_2'e, \tag{4.1}$$

$$q_T \equiv e'Z_1\Delta_H^{-1}Z_1'e, \tag{4.2}$$

$$k_H \equiv \operatorname{tr}(X'PX)^{-1}X'Z_2\Delta_T^{-1}Z_2'X, \tag{4.3}$$

$$k_T \equiv \operatorname{tr}(X'PX)^{-1}X'Z_1\Delta_H^{-1}Z_1'X. \tag{4.4}$$

Lemma.

$$\mathrm{E}(q_H) = (T + k_H)\sigma^2 + T\sigma_1^2 + N\sigma_2^2, \tag{4.5}$$

$$\mathrm{E}(q_T) = (H + k_T)\sigma^2 + N\sigma_1^2 + H\sigma_2^2. \tag{4.6}$$

Proof. We first prove (4.5). Let

$$M \equiv I_N - X(X'PX)^{-1}X'P, \tag{4.7}$$

then by definition $e = My = M\varepsilon$. As $PZ_1 = 0$ and $PZ_2 = 0$, $P\Omega = \sigma^2 P$, so

$$M\Omega = \Omega - \sigma^2 X(X'PX)^{-1}X'P, \tag{4.8}$$

$$M\Omega M' = \Omega - \sigma^2 X(X'PX)^{-1}X'P - \sigma^2 PX(X'PX)^{-1}X' + \sigma^2 X(X'PX)^{-1}X', \tag{4.9}$$

$$\begin{aligned} Z_2'M\Omega M'Z_2 &= Z_2'\Omega Z_2 + \sigma^2 Z_2'X(X'PX)^{-1}X'Z_2 \\ &= \sigma^2\Delta_T + \sigma_1^2 AA' + \sigma_2^2\Delta_T^2 + \sigma^2 Z_2'X(X'PX)^{-1}X'Z_2. \end{aligned} \tag{4.10}$$

Using (4.10) and $\mathrm{tr}(\Delta_T^{-1}AA') = T$,

$$\begin{aligned} \mathrm{E}(q_H) &= \mathrm{E}(e'Z_2\Delta_T^{-1}Z_2'e) \\ &= \mathrm{tr}\,\mathrm{E}(\Delta_T^{-1}Z_2'M\varepsilon\varepsilon'M'Z_2) \\ &= \mathrm{tr}(\Delta_T^{-1}Z_2'M\Omega M'Z_2) \\ &= \mathrm{tr}(\sigma^2 I_T + \sigma_1^2\Delta_T^{-1}AA' + \sigma_2^2\Delta_T + \sigma^2\Delta_T^{-1}Z_2'X(X'PX)^{-1}X'Z_2) \\ &= (T + k_H)\sigma^2 + T\sigma_1^2 + N\sigma_2^2. \end{aligned} \tag{4.11}$$

The proof of (4.6) is analogous. Q.E.D.

We obtain QUE's for σ_1^2 and σ_2^2 when solving (4.5) and (4.6) for σ_1^2 and σ_2^2 and using an unbiased estimator for σ^2. The latter may be based on

$$\mathrm{E}(e'Pe) = \sigma^2(N - T - H + 1 - k), \tag{4.12}$$

i.e., the estimator of σ^2 in the FE model.

So far, we have assumed that X does not contain a vector of ones. When, in addition to X, there is an intercept δ in the regression, we have

$$e = My = M\iota_N\delta + M\varepsilon = \iota_N\delta + \varepsilon \tag{4.13}$$

[cf. the line below (4.7)], so in that case we will use the centered residuals $f \equiv E_N e$ rather than e. Computing the expectation of the redefined q_H and q_T (with f substituted for e) is essentially the same but is more complicated. See appendix A for results.

When the effects α_h and γ_t are normally distributed, explicit expressions for the variance of the QUE's of σ_1^2 and σ_2^2 can be derived. This is indicated in appendix B.

5. ML estimation and the information matrix

For complete data, ML estimation in error-components models has been studied by Amemiya (1971). Applying the general results obtained by Magnus (1978), the first-order conditions for ML estimation of β and the parameters in Ω are

$$\hat{\beta} = \left(X'\hat{\Omega}^{-1}X\right)^{-1}X'\hat{\Omega}^{-1}y, \tag{5.1}$$

$$\mathrm{tr}\left(\hat{\Omega}_\theta^{-1}\Omega\right) = e'\hat{\Omega}_\theta^{-1}e, \qquad \theta = \sigma^2,\ \sigma_1^2, \text{ or } \sigma_2^2, \tag{5.2}$$

with $e \equiv y - X\hat{\beta}$ and Ω_θ^{-1} being the derivative of Ω^{-1} with respect to θ. In appendix C, it is shown that

$$\Omega_{\sigma^2}^{-1} = \sigma^{-2}\left\{-\Omega^{-1} + \sigma_1^{-2}R\tilde{\Delta}_H^{-2}R' + \sigma_2^{-2}VZ_2\tilde{Q}^{-2}Z_2'V\right\}, \tag{5.3}$$

$$\Omega_{\sigma_1^2}^{-1} = -\sigma_1^{-4}R\tilde{\Delta}_H^{-2}R', \tag{5.4}$$

$$\Omega_{\sigma_2^2}^{-1} = -\sigma_2^{-4}VZ_2\tilde{Q}^{-2}Z_2'V, \tag{5.5}$$

with

$$R \equiv \left(I_N - VZ_2\tilde{Q}^{-1}Z_2'\right)Z_1, \tag{5.6}$$

and that

$$\mathrm{tr}\left(\Omega_{\sigma^2}^{-1}\Omega\right) = \sigma^{-2}\{-N + p_1 + p_2\}, \tag{5.7}$$

$$\mathrm{tr}\left(\Omega_{\sigma_i^2}^{-1}\Omega\right) = -\sigma_i^{-2}p_i, \qquad i = 1,2, \tag{5.8}$$

where

$$p_1 \equiv H - \frac{\sigma^2}{\sigma_1^2}\,\mathrm{tr}\left(\tilde{\Delta}_H^{-1} + \tilde{\Delta}_H^{-1}A'\tilde{Q}^{-1}A\tilde{\Delta}_H^{-1}\right), \tag{5.9}$$

$$p_2 \equiv T - \frac{\sigma^2}{\sigma_2^2}\,\mathrm{tr}\,\tilde{Q}^{-1}. \tag{5.10}$$

A few comments on these results are in order. When complete data are available, there do not exist closed-form expressions for the MLE's of the variance components, and this holds true a fortiori for the incomplete-data case.

Again, the formulae do not look particularly attractive. Yet it is simple to see that all expressions of interest can be computed in O(H) time. [Since the number of iterations is unknown, this does of course not guarantee that the computation of the MLE's until convergence also can be done in O(H) time.]

Both for the purpose of computing asymptotic standard errors of the ML estimators and to test hypotheses it is useful to compute the information matrix. The information matrix is derived in appendix C to be

$$\begin{bmatrix} X'\Omega^{-1}X & 0 \\ 0 & \frac{1}{2}\psi \end{bmatrix} \quad [(k+3)\times(k+3)], \tag{5.11}$$

with

$$\psi \equiv \begin{bmatrix} \psi_{00} & \psi_{01} & \psi_{02} \\ \psi_{10} & \psi_{11} & \psi_{12} \\ \psi_{20} & \psi_{21} & \psi_{22} \end{bmatrix}, \tag{5.12}$$

and

$$\psi_{00} \equiv \sigma^{-4}\{N + q_{11} + q_{22} - 2(p_1 + p_2 - q_{12})\}, \tag{5.13}$$

$$\psi_{0i} = \psi_{i0} \equiv \sigma^{-2}\sigma_i^{-2}(p_i - q_{ii} - q_{12}), \quad i = 1,2, \tag{5.14}$$

$$\psi_{ij} = \sigma_i^{-2}\sigma_j^{-2}q_{ij}, \qquad i, j = 1,2, \tag{5.15}$$

$$q_{11} \equiv \operatorname{tr}\left(I_H - \frac{\sigma^2}{\sigma_1^2}\left(\tilde{\Delta}_H^{-1} + \tilde{\Delta}_H^{-1}A'\tilde{Q}^{-1}A\tilde{\Delta}_H^{-1}\right)\right)^2, \tag{5.16}$$

$$q_{22} \equiv \operatorname{tr}\left(I_T - \frac{\sigma^2}{\sigma_2^2}\tilde{Q}^{-1}\right)^2, \tag{5.17}$$

$$q_{21} = q_{12} \equiv \frac{\sigma^4}{\sigma_1^2\sigma_2^2}\operatorname{tr}\left(\tilde{\Delta}_H^{-1}A'\tilde{Q}^{-2}A\tilde{\Delta}_H^{-1}\right). \tag{5.18}$$

All these expressions can be computed in O(H) time.

The problem of estimation with incomplete panels can be considered as a 'missing-observations' problem. By 'missing' we mean that for some (h,t) pairs both y_{ht} and x_{ht} are not observed. In the context of missing observations, the EM algorithm for obtaining ML estimates has attracted a lot of attention, recently also in econometrics. Fair's treatment of the Tobit model is possibly the best-known example [Fair (1977)]. In our context the EM approach suggests the following. Choose starting values for the model parameters, and compute the distribution of the 'missing' y_{ht} (with $x_{ht}=0$ without loss of generality) conditioned on the observed data and the starting values. Next write down the likelihood function for the complete panel (with its nicely structured Ω), take its expectation with respect to the missing 'y_{ht}', and maximize it to obtain new parameter values, etc. As far as we know, the EM algorithm has not yet been elaborated for the ECM with incomplete observations. It could offer a useful alternative to our approach, but a preliminary inspection suggests that working out the EM approach produces a lot of messy algebra, much of the same type as with our approach. This apparently is inherent to the problem at hand.

6. Some simulation results

We consider the following simple version of model (2.1): $\sigma_1^2=\text{var}(\alpha_h)=400$, $\sigma_2^2=\text{var}(\gamma_t)=25$, $\sigma^2=\text{var}(u_{ht})=25$, $x_{ht}=(1,\tilde{x}'_{ht})'$, $\beta=(\beta_0,\beta_1)'=(25,2)'$, $H=100$, $T=5$. The scalars x_{ht} were generated according to the scheme introduced by Nerlove (1971a, p. 367) and subsequently used by, e.g., Arora (1973), Baltagi (1981), and Heckman (1981):

$$x_{ht}=0.1t+0.5x_{h,t-1}+\omega_{ht}, \tag{6.1}$$

with the ω_{ht} uniform $[-\frac{1}{2},\frac{1}{2}]$ and $x_{h0}=5+10\omega_{h0}$. Three cases are considered:

1. No observations are missing: 'complete data'.
2. Each period 20% of the households left in the panel is removed randomly: 'random attrition'.
3. In period 1 we start with 40 households. In period 2, 20 new households are added. In period 3, 20 households remaining from period 1 are removed and 20 new households are added. In period 4, the 20 households still remaining from period 1 are removed and 20 new households are added, etc.: 'rotating panel'.

The x values have been drawn once and are used in all experiments. Given the x values we generated values of y_{ht} according to model (2.1) in each new simulation run. For each case 50 runs are made, all using the same pattern of

Table 1

Computational burden of different estimation methods.[a]

Set up	OLS	GLS	ML
Complete data	100	414	2026
Random attrition	68	333	3296
Rotating panel	53	297	3663

[a] In CPU seconds relative to OLS on the complete data. The computing time for ML includes the time required to generate starting values by means of the GLS procedure.

'missings' in the 'random attrition' case. For the ML estimation we always use the estimates of the two-step GLS procedure as starting values.

Table 1 gives an indication of the average computing time required by the two estimation methods for each case (GLS and ML), plus OLS. It is quite obvious that GLS is a lot cheaper than ML. Furthermore, computation time for GLS *de*creases if more observations are missing, whereas computation time for ML *in*creases. For complete data (100 households each period) ML requires about 5 times more CPU seconds than GLS. In the rotating panel case (40 or 60 households each period), ML takes about 12 times more CPU seconds than GLS. Of course, the precise magnitude of these figures depend on the particular design matrix chosen.

Table 2 presents means and variances of various estimates obtained in the 50 simulation runs. After each figure, its variance over the 50 runs is given. As to the regression coefficients, it appears that OLS, though unbiased conditional on the x_{ht}, performs badly, and that GLS and ML give nearly identical results, both in terms of point estimates and of sampling variances. The latter are somewhat smaller than those obtained with FE. The sampling variances of β_1 increase over the three cases, which are ordered by a decreasing number of observations, and go markedly up when moving to the 'rotating panel' case with its short time series.

Regarding the estimation of the variance components, it is striking that on average the unbiased QUE's are in all cases at least as close to the true value as the MLE's, and in a majority of cases much better. If one is interested in the values of the variance components, the results suggest a preference for the QUE's – iteration does not seem to pay off.

The column 'variance of GLS estimate' gives the means of the estimates of the variance of the estimates of σ_1^2, σ_2^2, and σ^2, respectively. Although the variance formulae indicated in appendix B are exact, the estimates actually used are not unbiased, because we have to plug in estimates of σ^2, σ_1^2, and σ_2^2. The 'variance of the ML estimate' is based on the information matrix. It turns out that the variance estimates for GLS and ML show some agreement, both between the two and with the corresponding sampling variances, but there are some striking exceptions – variances of variances can be volatile.

Table 2

Simulation results.[a]

Parameter	True value	OLS estimate	FE estimate	GLS estimate	Variance of GLS estimate	ML estimate	Variance of ML estimate
				Complete data			
β_0	25	27.5 (139)	0 (0)	26.0 (90.1)		26.0 (90.1)	
β_1	2	0.973 (24.2)	1.97 (0.122)	1.95 (0.109)		1.95 (0.109)	
σ_1^2	400			389 (109000)	130000 (1.37×10^{11})	311 (69800)	66800 (3.61×10^{10})
σ_2^2	25			25.3 (15.1)	3.00 (199)	25.3 (14.9)	18.9 (22.7)
σ^2	25			24.8 (2.57)	3.12 (0.162)	24.8 (2.57)	3.12 (0.162)
				Random attrition (20%)			
β_0	25	26.9 (135)	0 (0)	26.0 (91.8)		26.0 (92.1)	
β_1	2	1.12 (22.2)	1.96 (0.264)	1.93 (0.160)		1.94 (0.168)	
σ_1^2	400			386 (119000)	144000 (2.25×10^{11})	311 (70100)	66800 (3.66×10^{10})
σ_2^2	25			23.5 (290)	643 (4.27×10^{6})	21.6 (94.7)	21.7 (88.2)
σ^2	25			24.9 (4.63)	5.34 (0.869)	28.3 (75.5)	7.26 (25.7)
				Rotating panel			
β_0	25	27.6 (167)	0 (0)	26.1 (89.1)		26.2 (89.6)	
β_1	2	0.851 (27.6)	1.94 (0.587)	1.88 (0.415)		1.88 (0.407)	
σ_1^2	400			390 (108000)	134000 (1.44×10^{11})	312 (70100)	67100 (3.52×10^{10})
σ_2^2	25			22.3 (419)	5750 (2.55×10^{8})	17.7 (136)	21.7 (64.4)
σ^2	25			24.9 (7.74)	7.97 (3.16)	31.7 (139)	14.5 (123)

[a] Entries are means over 50 simulation runs; numbers in parentheses are corresponding variances.

7. Concluding remarks

Altogether, missing observations lead to less elegant expressions for estimators, and computer programs are accordingly more complicated. Yet, in terms of computational complexity missing observations do not constitute major problems. In view of the large difference in computational cost, GLS is to be preferred over ML in the ECM. Statistically, ML and GLS do not seem to behave very differently in finite samples. In the ECM, the FE estimator is also a viable alternative. It has a somewhat larger sampling variance, but one has not to make the assumption that the random effects are independent from the regressors, which may be troublesome in many applications.

Appendix A: QUE's in a model with an intercept

When an intercept term is present, we develop the QUE's starting from quadratic functions of the centered residuals:

$$q'_H \equiv f'Z_2\Delta_T^{-1}Z_2'f, \tag{A.1}$$

$$q'_T \equiv f'Z_1\Delta_H^{-1}Z_1'f. \tag{A.2}$$

In this appendix we evaluate the expectation of q'_H, which makes clear how unbiased estimators of σ_1^2 and σ_2^2 can be constructed. As $f \equiv E_N e = E_N M\varepsilon$,

$$q'_H = \varepsilon' M' E_N Z_2 \Delta_T^{-1} Z_2' E_N M\varepsilon \tag{A.3}$$

and, by elaborating E_N,

$$\begin{aligned} \mathrm{E}(q'_H) &= \mathrm{E}(q_H) + \iota_N' Z_2 \Delta_T^{-1} Z_2' \iota_N \iota_N' M \Omega M' \iota_N / N^2 \\ &\quad - 2\iota_N' M\Omega M' Z_2 \Delta_T^{-1} Z_2' \iota_N / N. \end{aligned} \tag{A.4}$$

As $Z_2\Delta_T^{-1}Z_2'\iota_N = \iota_N$, this carries over into

$$\begin{aligned} \mathrm{E}(q'_H) &= \mathrm{E}(q_H) - \iota_N' M\Omega M' \iota_N / N \\ &= \mathrm{E}(q_H) - \left\{ \iota_N' \Omega \iota_N + \sigma^2 \iota_N' X (X'PX)^{-1} X' \iota_N \right\} / N \\ &= \mathrm{E}(q_H) - \sigma^2(1 + k_0) - \left(\sigma_1^2 \lambda_1 + \sigma_2^2 \lambda_2 \right) / N, \end{aligned} \tag{A.5}$$

where the second equality is based on (4.9) and $Z_1\Delta_T^{-1}Z_1'\iota_N = \iota_N$ and where in the last step the following definitions have been used:

$$k_0 \equiv \iota_N' X(X'PX)^{-1} X' \iota_N / N, \tag{A.6}$$

$$\lambda_1 \equiv \iota_N' Z_1 Z_1' \iota_N \equiv \sum_{h=1}^{H} m_h^2, \tag{A.7}$$

$$\lambda_2 \equiv \iota_N' Z_2 Z_2' \iota_N \equiv \sum_{t=1}^{T} n_t^2. \tag{A.8}$$

The interpretation of m_h is that it is the number of times $(2 \leq m_h \leq T)$ that household h was in the panel, whereas n_t $(2 \leq n_t \leq H)$ denotes the number of households in the panel at time t.

So the presence of an intercept term introduces an adjustment of $\mathrm{E}(q_H)$; see the last line of (A.5). The same adjustment has to be made to $\mathrm{E}(q_T)$.

Appendix B: On the variances of the QUE's

Let again θ denote any one of the variance components σ^2, σ_1^2, or σ_2^2. Their QUE's can be written as

$$\hat{\theta} = \varepsilon' M E_N W E_N M' \varepsilon = f' W f, \tag{B.1}$$

with

$$W = aP + bZ_1 \Delta_H^{-1} Z_1' + cZ_2 \Delta_T^{-1} Z_2'. \tag{B.2}$$

Here a, b, and c are constants that can be chosen such that (B.1)–(B.2) generate the QUE's. According to multivariate normal theory,

$$\mathrm{var}(\hat{\theta}) = 2\,\mathrm{tr}(M E_N W E_N M' \Omega)^2. \tag{B.3}$$

Elaborating (B.3) is a tedious affair but is in principle straightforward. We have elaborated and programmed (B.3) to compute the variances of the QUE's in the simulations reported in section 6. Since the formulae for the variances are ugly and do not yield any insights, they are not given here. The formulae are available from the authors on request.

Appendix C: Derivation of results on ML

Let θ denote any one of the parameters σ^2, σ_1^2, or σ_2^2. Then

$$\begin{aligned} \Omega_\theta^{-1} &= \sigma^{-2}\{-\sigma_\theta^2 \Omega^{-1} + (V - VZ_2 \tilde{Q}^{-1} Z_2' V)_\theta\} \\ &= \sigma^{-2}\{-\sigma_\theta^2 \Omega^{-1} + V_\theta - V_\theta Z_2 \tilde{Q}^{-1} Z_2' V \\ &\quad + VZ_2 \tilde{Q}^{-1} \tilde{Q}_\theta \tilde{Q}^{-1} Z_2' V - VZ_2 \tilde{Q}^{-1} Z_2' V_\theta\}. \end{aligned} \tag{C.1}$$

There holds

$$\tilde{Q}_\theta = \tilde{\Delta}_{T\theta} + A\tilde{\Delta}_H^{-1}\tilde{\Delta}_{H\theta}\tilde{\Delta}_H^{-1}A' = \tilde{\Delta}_{T\theta} + Z_2'V_\theta Z_2, \tag{C.2}$$

so

$$VZ_2\tilde{Q}^{-1}\tilde{Q}_\theta\tilde{Q}^{-1}Z_2'V = VZ_2\tilde{Q}^{-1}\tilde{\Delta}_{T\theta}\tilde{Q}^{-1}Z_2'V + VZ_2\tilde{Q}^{-1}Z_2'V_\theta Z_2\tilde{Q}^{-1}Z_2'V. \tag{C.3}$$

Substitution of (C.3) into (C.1) yields

$$\Omega_\theta^{-1} = \sigma^{-2}\{-\sigma_\theta^2\Omega^{-1} + (I_N - VZ_2\tilde{Q}^{-1}Z_2')V_\theta(I_N - Z_2\tilde{Q}^{-1}Z_2'V) + VZ_2\tilde{Q}^{-1}\tilde{\Delta}_{T\theta}\tilde{Q}^{-1}Z_2'V\}. \tag{C.4}$$

In view of the definition of V [see (3.3)], there holds

$$V_\theta = Z_1\tilde{\Delta}_H^{-1}\tilde{\Delta}_{H\theta}\tilde{\Delta}_H^{-1}Z_1'. \tag{C.5}$$

This expression and the definition of R [see (5.6)] allow for writing (C.4) as

$$\Omega_\theta^{-1} = \sigma^{-2}\{-\sigma_\theta^2\Omega^{-1} + R\tilde{\Delta}_H^{-1}\tilde{\Delta}_{H\theta}\tilde{\Delta}_H^{-1}R' + VZ_2\tilde{Q}^{-1}\tilde{\Delta}_T\tilde{Q}^{-1}Z_2'V\}. \tag{C.6}$$

It remains to substitute for σ_θ^2, $\tilde{\Delta}_{T\theta}$, and $\tilde{\Delta}_{H\theta}$ in order to establish (5.3)–(5.5). There holds

$$\tilde{\Delta}_{T\sigma^2} = \sigma_2^{-2}I_T, \qquad \tilde{\Delta}_{T\sigma_1^2} = 0, \qquad \tilde{\Delta}_{T\sigma_2^2} = -\frac{\sigma^2}{\sigma_2^4}I_T, \tag{C.7}$$

$$\tilde{\Delta}_{H\sigma^2} = \sigma_1^{-2}I_H, \qquad \tilde{\Delta}_{H\sigma_1^2} = -\frac{\sigma^2}{\sigma_1^4}I_H, \qquad \tilde{\Delta}_{H\sigma_2^2} = 0, \tag{C.8}$$

and this leads to (5.3)–(5.5) directly.

For further results, we need an expression for $\Omega_\theta^{-1}\Omega$. In view of (C.6), this means that we first have to consider $R'\Omega$ and $Z_2'V\Omega$. Now, since

$V^{-1} = I_N + (\sigma_1/\sigma)^2 Z_1 Z_1'$, $\Omega = \sigma^2 V^{-1} + \sigma_2^2 Z_2 Z_2'$. Hence

$$\begin{aligned} Z_2' V \Omega &= Z_2' V\left(\sigma^2 V^{-1} + \sigma_2^2 Z_2 Z_2'\right) \\ &= \sigma^2 Z_2' + \sigma_2^2 Z_2' V Z_2 Z_2' \\ &= \sigma^2 Z_2' + \sigma_2^2 \left(\tilde{Q} - \frac{\sigma^2}{\sigma_2^2} I_T \right) Z_2' \\ &= \sigma^2 Z_2' + \sigma_2^2 \tilde{Q} Z_2' - \sigma^2 Z_2' \\ &= \sigma_2^2 \tilde{Q} Z_2' \end{aligned} \tag{C.9}$$

and

$$\begin{aligned} R'\Omega &= Z_1'\left(I_N - Z_2 Q^{-1} Z_2' V \right)\Omega \\ &= Z_1'\Omega - Z_1' Z_2 \tilde{Q}^{-1} Z_2' V \Omega \\ &= Z_1'\Omega - \sigma_2^2 Z_1' Z_2 \tilde{Q}^{-1} \tilde{Q} Z_2' \\ &= \sigma^2 Z_1' + \sigma_2^2 Z_1' Z_2 Z_2' + \sigma_1^2 Z_1' Z_1 Z_1' - \sigma_2^2 Z_1' Z_2 Z_2' \\ &= \sigma^2 Z_1' + \sigma_1^2 \left(\tilde{\Delta}_H - \frac{\sigma^2}{\sigma_1^2} I_H \right) Z_1' \\ &= \sigma_1^2 \tilde{\Delta}_H Z_1'. \end{aligned} \tag{C.10}$$

These expressions, with (5.3)–(5.5), yield

$$\left(\partial \Omega^{-1}/\partial \sigma^2\right)\Omega = \sigma^{-2}\left\{ -I_N + R\tilde{\Delta}_H^{-1} Z_1' + V Z_2 \tilde{Q}^{-1} Z_2' \right\}, \tag{C.11}$$

$$\left(\partial \Omega^{-1}/\partial \sigma_1^2\right)\Omega = -\sigma_1^{-2} R \tilde{\Delta}_H^{-1} Z_1', \tag{C.12}$$

$$\left(\partial \Omega^{-1}/\partial \sigma_2^2\right)\Omega = -\sigma_2^2 V Z_2 \tilde{Q}^{-1} Z_2'. \tag{C.13}$$

To verify (5.7) and (5.8) we have to take traces of these expressions. We use the following facts:

$$\operatorname{tr}\left(R\tilde{\Delta}_H^{-1}Z_1'\right) = \operatorname{tr}\left(Z_1'R\tilde{\Delta}_H^{-1}\right)$$

$$= \operatorname{tr} Z_1'\left(I_N - VZ_2\tilde{Q}^{-1}Z_2'\right)Z_1\tilde{\Delta}_H^{-1}$$

$$= \operatorname{tr}\left(Z_1'Z_1 - Z_1'VZ_2\tilde{Q}^{-1}A\right)\tilde{\Delta}_H^{-1}$$

$$= \operatorname{tr}\left(Z_1'Z_1 - \frac{\sigma^2}{\sigma_1^2}\tilde{\Delta}_H^{-1}A'\tilde{Q}^{-1}A\right)\tilde{\Delta}_H^{-1} \tag{C.14}$$

$$= \operatorname{tr}\left(\tilde{\Delta}_H - \frac{\sigma^2}{\sigma_1^2}I_H - \frac{\sigma^2}{\sigma_1^2}\tilde{\Delta}_H^{-1}A'\tilde{Q}^{-1}A\right)\tilde{\Delta}_H^{-1}$$

$$= H - \frac{\sigma^2}{\sigma_1^2}\operatorname{tr}\left(\tilde{\Delta}_H^{-1} + \tilde{\Delta}_H^{-1}A'\tilde{Q}^{-1}A\tilde{\Delta}_H^{-1}\right)$$

$$= p_1 \quad [\text{cf. } (5.9)].$$

$$\operatorname{tr}\left(VZ_2\tilde{Q}^{-1}Z_2'\right) = \operatorname{tr}\left(Z_2'VZ_2\tilde{Q}^{-1}\right)$$

$$= \operatorname{tr}\left(\tilde{Q} - \frac{\sigma^2}{\sigma_2^2}I_T\right)\tilde{Q}^{-1} \tag{C.15}$$

$$= T - \frac{\sigma^2}{\sigma_2^2}\operatorname{tr}\tilde{Q}^{-1}$$

$$= p_2 \quad [\text{cf. } (5.10)].$$

This establishes (5.7) and (5.8).

We finally derive the elements of the information matrix (5.12). The element of ψ [cf. (5.12)] corresponding with parameters θ and θ', say, is $\operatorname{tr}(\Omega_\theta^{-1}\Omega\Omega_{\theta'}^{-1}\Omega)$, and is hence obtained by taking the trace of the product of any two right-hand sides of (C.11)–(C.13). The following facts are used

$$\operatorname{tr}\left(R\tilde{\Delta}_H^{-1}Z_1'R\tilde{\Delta}_H^{-1}Z_1'\right) = \operatorname{tr}\left(I_H - \frac{\sigma^2}{\sigma_1^2}\left(\tilde{\Delta}_H^{-1} + \tilde{\Delta}_H^{-1}A'\tilde{Q}^{-1}A\tilde{\Delta}_H^{-1}\right)\right)^2$$

$$= q_{11} \quad [\text{cf. } (5.16)], \tag{C.16}$$

$$\operatorname{tr}\left(VZ_2\tilde{Q}^{-1}Z_2'VZ_2\tilde{Q}^{-1}Z_2'\right) = \operatorname{tr}\left(Z_2'VZ_2\tilde{Q}^{-1}\right)^2$$

$$= \operatorname{tr}\left(I_T - \frac{\sigma^2}{\sigma_2^2}\tilde{Q}^{-1}\right)^2 \tag{C.17}$$

$$= q_{22} \quad [\text{cf. } (5.17)],$$

$$\operatorname{tr}\left(VZ_2\tilde{Q}^{-1}Z_2'R\tilde{\Delta}_H^{-1}Z_1'\right) = \operatorname{tr}\left(Z_1'VZ_2\tilde{Q}^{-1}Z_2'R\tilde{\Delta}_H^{-1}\right)$$

$$= \frac{\sigma^4}{\sigma_1^2\sigma_2^2}\operatorname{tr}\left(\tilde{\Delta}_H^{-1}A'\tilde{Q}^{-2}A\tilde{\Delta}_H^{-1}\right) \tag{C.18}$$

$$= q_{12} \quad [\text{cf. } (5.18)],$$

where the second equality sign in (C.18) is based on

$$Z_2'R = Z_2'\left(I_N - VZ_2\tilde{Q}^{-1}Z_2'\right)Z_1$$

$$= A - Z_2'VZ_2\tilde{Q}^{-1}A$$

$$= \left(I_T - \left(\tilde{Q} - \frac{\sigma^2}{\sigma_2^2}I_T\right)\tilde{Q}^{-1}\right)A \tag{C.19}$$

$$= \frac{\sigma^2}{\sigma_2^2}\tilde{Q}^{-1}A.$$

With the aid of (C.16)–(C.18), the elements of the information matrix follow directly.

References

Amemiya, T., 1971, The estimation of the variances in a variance-components model, International Economic Review 12, 1–13.

Arora, S., 1973, Error components regression models and their applications, Annals of Economic and Social Measurement 2, 451–462.

Balestra, P., 1973, Best quadratic unbiased estimators of the variance–covariance matrix in normal regression, Journal of Econometrics 1, 17–28.

Balestra, P. and M. Nerlove, 1966, Pooling cross section and time series data in the estimation of a dynamic model: The demand for natural gas, Econometrica 34, 585–612.

Baltagi, B.H., 1981, Pooling: An experimental study of alternative testing and estimation procedures in a two-way error component model, Journal of Econometrics 17, 21–49.

Baltagi, B.H., 1985, Pooling cross-sections with unequal time-series lengths, Economics Letters 18, 133–136.

Biørn, E., 1981, Estimating economic relations from incomplete cross-section/time-series data, Journal of Econometrics 16, 221–236.

Dielman, T.E., 1983, Pooled cross-sectional and time series data: A survey of current statistical methodology, The American Statistician 37, 111–122.

Fair, R.C., 1977, A note on the computation of the Tobit estimator, Econometrica 45, 1723–1728.

Fuller, W.A. and G.E. Battese, 1974, Estimation of linear functions with crossed-error structure, Journal of Econometrics 2, 67–78.

Hausman, J.A. and D.A. Wise, 1977, Social experimentation, truncated distributions, and efficient estimation, Econometrica 45, 919–938.

Heckman, J.J., 1981, The incidental parameters problem and the problem of initial conditions in estimating a discrete time-discrete data stochastic process, in: C. Manski and D. McFadden, eds., Structural analysis of discrete data with econometric applications (MIT Press, Cambridge, MA).

Hsiao, C., 1986, Analysis of panel data (Cambridge University Press, Cambridge).

Magnus, J.R., 1978, Maximum likelihood estimation of the GLS model with unknown parameters in the disturbance covariance matrix, Journal of Econometrics 7, 281–312.

Mazodier, P., 1972, l'Estimation des modèles à erreurs composées, Annales de l'INSEE 7, 43–72.

Mazodier, P., ed., 1978, The econometrics of panel data, Special Edition of Annales de l'INSEE, 30–31.

Nerlove, M., 1971a, Further evidence on the estimation of dynamic economic relations from a time series of cross sections, Econometrica 39, 359–382.

Nerlove, M., 1971b, A note on error components models, Econometrica 39, 383–396.

Taylor, W.E., 1977, Small sample properties of a class of two stage Aitken estimators, Econometrica 45, 497–508.

Wallace, T.D. and A. Hussain, 1969, The use of error component models in combining cross section with time series data, Econometrica 37, 55–72.

Wansbeek, T.J. and A. Kapteyn, 1982, A class of decompositions of the variance covariance matrix of a generalized error components model, Econometrica 50, 713–724.

[4]

Journal of Econometrics 30 (1985) 109–126. North-Holland

PANEL DATA FROM TIME SERIES OF CROSS-SECTIONS

Angus DEATON*

Woodrow Wilson School, Princeton University, Princeton, NJ 08544, USA

In many countries, there are few or no panel data, but there exists a series of independent cross-sections. For example, in the United Kingdom, there are no panel data on consumers' expenditure or on household labor supply, but there are several large household surveys carried out every year. Samples for these surveys are drawn anew each year, so that it is impossible to track individual households over time. This paper considers the possibility of tracking 'cohorts' through such data. A 'cohort' is defined as a group with fixed membership, individuals of which can be identified as they show up in the surveys. The most obvious example is an age cohort, e.g. all males born between 1945 and 1950, but there are other possibilities (Korean war veterans or founding members of the Econometric Society). Consider any economic relationship of interest that is linear in parameters (but not necessarily in variables). Corresponding to individual behavior, there will exist a cohort version of the relationship of the same form, but with cohort means replacing individual observations. If there are additive individual fixed effects, there will be corresponding additive cohort fixed effects. Further, the sample cohort means from the surveys are consistent but error-ridden estimates of the true cohort means. Hence, provided errors-in-variables techniques are used (and error variances and covariances can be estimated from the surveys), the sample cohort means can be used as panel data for estimating the relationship. Such data are immune to attrition bias and can be extended for long time periods. There is also evidence to suggest that the errors in variables problems may be just as severe for genuine panel data; in the created panels considered here, the problem is controllable. The paper discusses appropriate errors in variables estimators, with and without fixed effects.

1. Introduction

In many countries, there are few or no panel data, but there exists a series of independent cross-sections. For example, in the United Kingdom, there are no panel data on consumers' expenditure or on household labor supply, but there are several large household surveys that are carried out every year. Samples for these surveys are drawn anew each year, so that *individual* households cannot be traced over time. This paper is concerned with the possibility of tracking 'cohorts' through such data. A 'cohort' is defined as a group with fixed membership, individuals of which can be identified as they show up in the surveys. The most obvious example is an age cohort, for example, all males born between 1945 and 1950, but there are many other possibilities; consider Korean war veterans, or founder members of the Econometric Society. For

*I am grateful to Badi Baltagi, Bill Barnett, Martin Browning, Margaret Irish, Whitney Newey, and an anonymous referee for help and comments.

large enough cohorts, or large enough samples, successive surveys will generate successive random samples of individuals from each of the cohorts. Summary statistics from these random samples generate a time series that can be used to infer behavioral relationships for the cohort as a whole just as if panel data were available. Procedures for constructing such cohorts and for estimation using the resulting data are discussed in this paper.

I consider economic relationships that are linear in parameters, though not necessarily in data, and that may or may not contain individual fixed effects. Corresponding to these individual relationships, there will exist averaged versions of the same form for the cohort population, but with unobservable data points. If there are additive individual fixed effects, there will be corresponding additive cohort fixed effects for the cohort population. Furthermore, the *sample* cohort means from the surveys are consistent but error-ridden estimates of the unobservable cohort populations means. Since the micro data are used to construct the means, they can also be used to construct estimates of the variances and covariances of the sample means. It is therefore possible to use errors-in-variable estimators to estimate consistently the population relationships. Sections 3 and 4 of this paper derive appropriate estimators in the absence and in the presence of individual fixed effects.

Section 2, below, presents some of the models for which the technique is designed with particular emphasis on models of consumption and labor supply. I suggest that the estimation procedures discussed here may shed light on some long-standing puzzles in empirical demand analysis, and that they are likely to be useful for the estimation of life-cycle models in the absence of panel data.

Although the methods discussed here are primarily formulated as a response to the absence of panel data, it is not necessarily the case that they will give inferior results. The attrition problem that effectively curtails the useful length of much panel data is absent here. Because new samples are drawn each year, representativeness is constantly maintained. Indeed, to the extent that long-running panels replace respondents that drop out by 'look alikes', the resulting data will have many of the features discussed here. Of course, the errors-in-variables nature of the current methodology is absent in genuine panel studies, but I suspect that the difference is more apparent than real. Survey statisticians who collect panel data are in little doubt as to the magnitude of response error, particularly in the differenced data for individual respondents. And as Ashenfelter (1983) has shown, it is extremely difficult to interpret the diversity of labor supply elasticities obtainable from the Michigan PSID data (certainly the most heavily used panel data set among American economists), without assigning a central role to large and persistent errors of measurement. The technique discussed here has the advantage of recognizing measurement error from the outset and explicitly controlling for it.

2. Model formation

The models discussed in this section are of substantive interest in their own right and form the basis for current research using the methods discussed below. The main purpose in presenting them here, however, is to motivate the methodological discussion in the following sections. Further, the provision of concrete economic examples will justify some of the specific issues of estimation that are dealt with later.

In all of this work, my ultimate aim has been to bring to bear the methodology of panel data on problems of consumer demand analysis. Even in the United States, there is little panel information on the details of consumer expenditure, and a few isolated examples apart, the same is true of the rest of the world. For cross-sectional consumer expenditure surveys, however, most countries of the world are better supplied than is the United States. For example, the British Family Expenditure Survey is in continuous operation and surveys some 7000 households annually; questions on income, labor supply, and a very detailed disaggregation of consumers' expenditure provide a mass of high-quality data. There are also many excellent series of household surveys from LDC's; India's National Sample Survey Office has run some twenty nationwide household expenditure surveys since independence, and both Indonesia and Sri Lanka have closely comparable household surveys for two or more separate years. There is therefore a large potential for any method that can 'convert' these data sets into panel data.

To illustrate some of the more important issues, consider the Engel curve model,

$$q_{iht} = f_{ih}(x_{ht}, \boldsymbol{a}_{ht}), \tag{1}$$

for quantity purchased of good (or leisure) i by household h in period t, household total outlay x_{ht}, and vector of socio-economic or demographic characteristics $\boldsymbol{a}_{ht}$. A convenient functional form is provided by taking the budget share $w_{iht} = p_{it}q_{iht}/x_{ht}$ as dependent variable and writing

$$w_{iht} = \alpha_i + \beta_i \log x_{ht} + \sum^{J} \gamma_{ij} a_{jht} + \varepsilon_{iht}, \tag{2}$$

where there are J socio-economic characteristics, α, β and γ are parameters, and ε_{iht} represents an error term. Eq. (2) is typically estimated in one of two derived forms. In the first, using a single cross-section, the t subscript is dropped, and systems of Engel curves are estimated. In the second, the equation is aggregated over h to give, for example,

$$\tilde{w}_{it} = \alpha_i + \beta_i \log \tilde{x}_t + \sum \gamma_{ij} \tilde{a}_{jt} + \tilde{\varepsilon}_{it}, \tag{3}$$

where $\tilde{w}_{it}$, $\tilde{a}_{jt}$ and $\tilde{\varepsilon}_{it}$ are weighted averages using $x_h/\sum x_h$ as weights, and $\tilde{x}_t$ is a representative budget level defined by the aggregation procedure [see Deaton and Muellbauer (1980) for a full discussion of the model]. The weighting procedure guarantees that $\tilde{w}_{it}$ is the share of good i in the total of consumers expenditures, and, provided the distribution over households of x does not change over time (as measured by Theil's entropy measure of inequality), $\tilde{x}_t$ can be replaced by $\bar{x}_t$. Consequently, apart from the substitution of demographics for prices, neither of which explains very much in aggregate, (3) is a conventional aggregate demand system.

The point I want to emphasize is that the values of β_i estimated from cross-sections tend to differ substantially from those estimated using time series. Such contradictions were first extensively documented by Kuznets (1962), not only for aggregate consumption, but also for the components of consumption. It is widely known that savings ratios rise more in cross-sections that in aggregate time series. It is less well-known that it is generally true that total expenditure elasticities for many commodities and groups of commodities are further dispersed from unity when estimated on cross-sections than when estimated on time series. For example, the food share in England in 1955 was almost identical to its value a century earlier in spite of a manyfold increase in real income and in spite of the repeated confirmation of Engel's law in every household survey during that century; see Deaton (1975), Stone and Rowe (1966) and Clark (1957) for further details. The presence of such phenomena also poses problems for *forecasting* demands in those situations where only cross-sectional data are available.

In terms of the foregoing model, goods are necessities if $\beta_i < 0$, luxuries if $\beta_i > 0$, and neither if $\beta_i = 0$. The Kuznets' finding, so stylized, is that β_i is closer to zero in time series than in cross-sections. Presumably, the problem lies in inadequate statistical control. Expenditure differences between poor and rich consumers are not likely to be replicated by making a poor man rich unless the poor and rich consumers are otherwise identical. Controlling for even a long list of socio-economic characteristics is not satisfactory compared with the opportunity yielded only by panel data to use individuals as their own controls. Recognizing this, write (2) as

$$w_{iht} = \alpha_i + \beta_i \log x_{ht} + \sum \gamma_{ij} a_{jht} + \theta_{ih} + \varepsilon_{iht}, \tag{4}$$

for individual fixed effect θ_{ih}. Since, in general, θ_{ih} will be correlated with the other explanatory variables, such an equation can only be consistently estimated from panel data. Consider, however, the case where h is a member of a well-defined cohort group that can be tracked via its (randomly chosen) representatives through successive surveys. Let h belong to a cohort c, and take simple *population* averages of (4) over all h belonging to c to obtain

$$w_{ict}^{*} = \alpha_i + \beta_i(\log x_{ct})^{*} + \sum \gamma_{ij} a_{jct}^{*} + \theta_{ic}^{*} + \varepsilon_{ict}^{*}, \tag{5}$$

where asterisks denote population (i.e., cohort population) means. If it were possible to observe the true cohort means, eq. (5) would hold for each cohort in each time period rather than for each household in each time period, and could be directly estimated using cohort dummy variables for the cohort fixed effects θ_{ic}^{*}. This would be feasible since each cohort appears in each time period; it is of course *in*feasible on the individual model (4) since each individual household appears only once. In practice, the other starred variables can only be proxied by cohort means from the *sample*; these will contain sampling errors and if used without appropriate correction will generally lead to inconsistent estimates since the model is effectively one of errors in variables with *all* variables (except dummies) subject to error. However, the sample can be used in the standard way to derive estimates of sampling variances and covariances and these estimates can be used to derive consistent estimators using more or less standard errors in variables procedures; see sections 3 and 4 below.

Two other features of eq. (5) should be noted. First, the total outlay variable is the mean of the logarithms, not the logarithm of the means. There is no need in this context to fudge the issue since the sample can be used just as easily to estimate the mean of a non-linear function as to estimate the non-linear function of the mean. Second, it is usually possible to select cohorts that are more or less broadly defined. Ultimately, the cohort that is all inclusive is the total population and (5) becomes a macroeconomic aggregate time-series model. In consequence, selection of cohort size allows us to move by degrees from micro to macro data; this is ideal for detecting the roots of a contradiction between micro and macro results.

In the foregoing example, the formation of cohorts can be thought of as an instrumentation procedure that removes the inconsistencies associated with the fixed effects. In my second example, the cohort structure arises naturally out of the formulation of the problem. Consider an individual household choosing consumption and labor supply in an intertemporal setting to maximize the expectation

$$\mathrm{E}_t\left\{\sum_{\tau=t}^{L} u_\tau(q_\tau)\right\}, \tag{6}$$

subject to an evolving and uncertain budget constraint

$$W_{t+1} = (1 + i_{t+1})\{W_t + y_t - p_t \cdot q_t\}, \tag{7}$$

where, as before, q_τ includes leisure demands, u_τ is period τ's utility function, W_t is assets at t, y_t is income, and i_{t+1} is the money interest rate from t to $t+1$.

In Browning, Deaton and Irish (1985), it is shown that the solution to this problem can be straightforwardly characterized in terms of Frisch demand/supply functions

$$q_{it} = f_{it}(r_t, p_t), \tag{8}$$

the vector of which is the gradient with respect to p_{it} of a period t 'profit function' $\pi_t(r_t, p_t)$, a convex linearly homogeneous function. The quantity r_t, the period t price of utility, evolves stochastically according to

$$\mathrm{E}_t\{(1+i_{t+1})/r_{t+1}\} = 1/r_t. \tag{9}$$

Once again, the discussion is more useful given a specific functional form. Browning, Deaton and Irish show that the following is consistent with the theory:

$$q_{it} = \alpha_{it} + \beta_i \log p_{it} + \sum_{j\neq i} \theta_{ij}\{p_{jt}/p_{it}\}^{1/2} - \beta_i \log r_t. \tag{10}$$

This model is correct both under certainty and under uncertainty. In the former case, (9) holds without the expectation operator so that r_t is simply proportional to a discount factor $\Pi(1+i_\tau)$ relative to some arbitrary date. Re-introducing the household subscript h, the certainty version of (10) is therefore

$$q_{iht} = \alpha_{iht} + \beta_i \log \tilde{p}_{it} + \sum_{j\neq i} \theta_{ij}(p_{jt}/p_{it})^{1/2} - \beta_i \log r_{0h}, \tag{11}$$

where r_{0h} is independent both of time and the commodity under consideration and $\tilde{p}_{it}$ is p_{it} discounted back to the arbitrary data 0. It is therefore an individual fixed effect which is essentially a sufficient statistic for the influence of current and future values of assets, prices, interest rates, and wages; see MaCurdy (1981). Since r_{0h} is the price of life-time utility to h, it is an increasing function of life-time real wealth given concavity of (6). Consequently r_{0h} will vary with h and thus with cohorts in the cohort version of (11). Moreover, since younger cohorts are on average wealthier than older ones, we should expect the cohort dummy variables to be monotonically related to cohort age. The cohort structure here not only has the advantage of linking micro with macro, but also explicitly recognizes the life-cycle nature of consumption and labor supply. Indeed cohort methods have been widely used in work with life-cycle models; see e.g. Ghez and Becker (1975) and Smith (1977), though these authors work with single cross-sections which lack the panel element introduced here.

Under uncertainty, (9) can be written approximately as

$$\Delta \log r_{t+1} = \log(1 + i_{t+1}) + v_{t+1}, \tag{12}$$

where $E_t(v_{t+1}) = 0$. Taking differences of (10) and substituting

$$\Delta q_{iht} = \Delta\alpha_{iht} - \beta_i \log(1 + \rho_{it}) + \sum\theta_{ij}\Delta(p_{jt}/p_{it})^{1/2} + v_{th}, \tag{13}$$

where ρ_{it} is the real commodity i rate of interest. Note that in this case, even if the shocks to the system, v_t, are stationary, $\log r_t$ will be non-stationary, so that differencing is required to obtain consistent estimates. In general, the v_t can only be guaranteed to be mean stationary, and further assumptions will be required for the consistency of techniques applied to (13). Even so, the differenced version is likely to be a better starting point for estimation than the original version in levels once uncertainty is taken into account. Once again, the aggregation to cohorts provides the repeated observations necessary for differencing, while the microdata provide the estimates of cohort means together with their sampling errors. The differenced versions will have a different measurement error structure than the levels models, and this is discussed below in sections 3 and 4. Note also that in (13), to the extent that the current prices and interest rates contain relevant new information, the innovation v_{th} will be correlated with the explanatory variables necessitating an estimator than can deal with both errors of measurement and simultaneity.

3. Estimation of models in levels

Before presenting the estimator to be discussed, consider an alternative, and perhaps more obvious approach to the estimation of an equation like (4) of section 2. To unify notation, rewrite this in standard form as

$$y_{ht} = x_{ht} \cdot \beta + \theta_h + \varepsilon_{ht}, \tag{14}$$

where the i subscript is no longer required, y_{ht} is the dependent variable for individual h at t, x_{ht} is a vector of explanatory variables, and θ_h is the fixed effect. Aggregate first over those h belonging to cohort c that happen to be observed in the survey taken at t. We then get *observed sample* cohort means which satisfy the relationship

$$\bar{y}_{ct} = \bar{x}_{ct} \cdot \beta + \bar{\theta}_{ct} + \bar{\varepsilon}_{ct}. \tag{15}$$

Note that $\bar{\theta}_{ct}$ is the average of the fixed effects for those members of c that show up in the survey; unlike the unobserved fixed effect for the cohort population mean, θ_c, say, $\bar{\theta}_{ct}$ is *not* constant over time. Furthermore, $\bar{\theta}_{ct}$ is unobserved and, in general, is correlated with the $\bar{x}_{ct}$. Hence, although (15) may be useful for 'signing' the bias in regressing $\bar{y}_{ct}$ on $\bar{x}_{ct}$, it is not an appropriate basis for consistent estimation any more than is (14), unless the cohort sample sizes are so large that $\bar{\theta}_{ct}$ is a very good approximation for θ_c. In this case, (15) can be estimated by replacing $\bar{\theta}_{ct}$ by dummy variables, one for each cohort.

Consider, instead of (15), the cohort *population* version of (14). I write this

$$y^*_{ct} = x^*_{ct} \cdot \beta + \theta_c + \varepsilon_{ct}, \tag{16}$$

where y^*_{ct} and x^*_{ct} are the unobservable cohort population means, and θ_c is the cohort fixed effect. Since the population belonging to the cohort is assumed to be fixed through time, θ_c is a constant for each c and can be replaced in (16) by cohort dummies. The y^*_{ct} and x^*_{ct} cannot be observed, but the cohort sample means $\bar{y}_{ct}$ and $\bar{x}_{ct}$ are error-ridden estimators, with variances that can also be estimated from the micro survey data. Eq. (16) can then be estimated by errors in variables techniques where *all* variables, except the dummies, are measured subject to error.

Eq. (16) can now be written in convenient standard form

$$y^*_t = x^*_t \cdot \beta + \varepsilon_t, \tag{17}$$

where the cohorts and surveys have been 'stacked' into a single index t, running from 1 to T where T is the product of the number of surveys and the number of cohorts. The cohort dummies θ_c have been absorbed into the x^*_t's; there is no loss of generality since the dummies can be thought of as being measured with an error that has zero mean and variance. To fix ideas, take the British Family Expenditure Survey as an illustration. Currently, there are about ten years of data available, with about 7000 observations per year. In Browning, Deaton and Irish's (1985) work on consumption and labor supply, various selection criteria (which are always likely to be present in one form or another) reduce this to between 2500 and 3000 observations, which were formed into sixteen cohorts of five-year age bands. Hence, $T = 80$, but the cohorts, with a maximum size of 300, are not large enough for us to ignore the sampling errors in estimating y^*_t and x^*_t by $\bar{y}_t$ and $\bar{x}_t$. Since, in this context (and in many others) there is a new survey every year, it is sensible to construct estimators that are consistent as T tends to infinity; with sixteen cohorts $T \to \infty$ sixteen times faster than annual, and four times as fast as quarterly time series data. The cohort size, however, is held fixed as T becomes large.

The error ε_t in (17) is assumed to be normal, independent over t, and homoskedastic; if the cohorts are very different in size, this will require that each observation be weighted by the square root of the cohort size. I shall assume this has been done as necessary. The model is completed by adding to (17) the assumed measurement structure. The cohort means, $\bar{y}_t$ and $\bar{x}_t$ are observed; dropping the overbars – from now on these are the basic data – I assume

$$\begin{pmatrix} \bar{y}_t \\ \bar{x}_t \end{pmatrix} \sim \mathrm{N}\begin{pmatrix} y_t^* ; & \sigma_{00} & \boldsymbol{\sigma}' \\ \boldsymbol{x}_t^* & \boldsymbol{\sigma} & \Sigma \end{pmatrix}. \tag{18}$$

Given the sampling structure, the normality does not seem to be an implausible assumption. However, the error variances σ_{ij} will in general have to be estimated by their sample counterparts s_{ij} based on the micro survey data. Note that, in estimating the σ_{ij}'s, all T observations can be pooled, so that, if there are n_c observations in each cohort, the sampling variance of s_{ij} diminishes in proportion to $(Tn_c)^{-1}$ and that of $\bar{y}_t$ and $\bar{x}_t$ as $(n_c)^{-1}$. The former is (a) smaller, and (b) tends to zero as $T \to \infty$ instead of remaining fixed, so that it may be reasonable to assume that the σ's are known in carrying out the estimation. Nevertheless, I shall derive formulae for both cases, when σ_{00}, $\boldsymbol{\sigma}$ and Σ are known, and when they are estimated by s_{00}, $\boldsymbol{s}$ and S.

The model is now in the form in which I can apply the results of Fuller (1975, 1981); indeed, in the rest of this section, I essentially repeat Fuller's (1975) formulae in the current context and notation. The interested reader is referred to that paper for further details.

Assume that means have been removed from all data and let the sample moments and cross-product matrices of X and y be M_{xx}, $\boldsymbol{m}_{xy}$ and m_{yy} in an obvious notation. Write σ_ε^2 for the variance of ε_t and Ω for the moment matrix of the unobservable x_t^*'s. Hence

$$\mathrm{E}(M_{xx}) = \Omega + \Sigma = \Sigma_{xx}, \quad \text{say,} \tag{19}$$

$$\mathrm{E}(\boldsymbol{m}_{xy}) = \Omega\boldsymbol{\beta} + \boldsymbol{\sigma} = \boldsymbol{\sigma}_{xy}, \quad \text{say,} \tag{20}$$

$$\mathrm{E}(m_{yy}) = \boldsymbol{\beta}'\Omega\boldsymbol{\beta} + \sigma_{00} + \sigma_\varepsilon^2 = \sigma_{yy}, \quad \text{say.} \tag{21}$$

The estimator $\tilde{\boldsymbol{\beta}}$ is then clearly consistent as $T \to \infty$, where

$$\tilde{\boldsymbol{\beta}} = (M_{xx} - \Sigma)^{-1}(\boldsymbol{m}_{xy} - \boldsymbol{\sigma}) \tag{22}$$

$$= (X'X - T\Sigma)^{-1}(X'y - T\boldsymbol{\sigma}), \tag{23}$$

and, provided $(X'X - T\Sigma)$ is positive definite, will be a MLE under the normality assumptions on x_t^* that are sometimes made in errors in variables models. I shall not assume normality of x_t^* here. Note that if Σ and σ are replaced by estimators S and s, $\tilde{\beta}$ is replaced by

$$\beta^* = (M_{xx} - S)^{-1}(m_{xy} - s) = (X'X - TS)^{-1}(X'y - Ts). \tag{24}$$

The formula for the variances are derived first for the case where Σ, σ and σ_{00} are known, i.e., for $\tilde{\beta}$. Expanding (22) yields

$$\tilde{\beta} - \beta = \Omega^{-1}(m_{xy} - \sigma_{xy}) - \Omega^{-1}(M_{xx} - \Sigma_{xx})\Omega^{-1}(\sigma_{xy} - \sigma) + O_p(T^{-1}), \tag{25}$$

But, from (20), $\Omega^{-1}(\sigma_{xy} - \sigma) = \beta$, so that

$$\tilde{\beta} - \beta = \Omega^{-1}\left[(m_{xy} - M_{xx}\beta) - (\sigma_{xy} - \Sigma_{xx}\beta)\right] + O_p(T^{-1}). \tag{26}$$

The variance of $\tilde{\beta}$ thus depends asymptotically on the variance–covariance matrix of $m_{xy} - M_{xx}\beta$. But

$$\{m_{xy} - M_{xx}\beta\}_i = \frac{1}{T}\sum_t x_{ti}\Big(y_t - \sum_k x_{tk}\beta_k\Big) \tag{27}$$

$$= \frac{1}{T}\sum_t (x_{ti}^* + u_{ti})\Big(\varepsilon_t + u_{t0} - \sum_k u_{tk}\beta_k\Big), \tag{28}$$

where

$$u_{t0} = y_{t0} - y_{t0}^* \quad \text{and} \quad u_{ti} = x_{ti} - x_{ti}^*.$$

Treating the x_{ti}^* as fixed but unknown constants, and using the standard properties of the normal distribution yields

$$TV\{m_{xy} - M_{xx}\beta\} = \Sigma_{xx}(\sigma_\varepsilon^2 + \sigma_{00} + \beta'\Sigma\beta - 2\sigma'\beta) + (\sigma - \Sigma\beta)(\sigma - \Sigma\beta)'. \tag{29}$$

Hence the asymptotic variance–covariance matrix of $\tilde{\beta}$ is given by

$$TV(\tilde{\beta}) = \Omega^{-1}\left[\Sigma_{xx}\omega^2 + (\sigma - \Sigma\beta)(\sigma - \Sigma\beta)'\right]\Omega^{-1}, \tag{30}$$

where

$$\omega^2 = \sigma_\varepsilon^2 + \sigma_{00} + \beta'\Sigma\beta - 2\sigma'\beta. \tag{31}$$

An estimate of (30) is straightforwardly derived from the observable moment matrices. From (19) to (21)

$$\tilde{\Omega} = M_{xx} - \Sigma, \tag{32}$$

$$\tilde{\sigma}_{\varepsilon}^2 = m_{yy} - \sigma_{00} - \tilde{\beta}'\tilde{\Omega}\tilde{\beta}. \tag{33}$$

Substitution in (31) yields an estimate of ω^2, i.e.,

$$\tilde{\omega}^2 = \frac{1}{T}(y - X\tilde{\beta})'(y - X\tilde{\beta}) = \frac{1}{T}e'e, \tag{34}$$

where

$$e = y - X\tilde{\beta}. \tag{35}$$

But

$$\Sigma\tilde{\beta} - \sigma = (\Sigma\tilde{\beta} + \Omega\tilde{\beta}) - (\sigma + \Omega\tilde{\beta}) \tag{36}$$

$$= M_{xx}\tilde{\beta} - \sigma_{xy} = \frac{1}{T}X'e. \tag{37}$$

Hence, the estimated variance–covariance matrix is given by

$$T\tilde{V}(\tilde{\beta}) = \tilde{\Omega}^{-1}\left[T^{-1}M_{xx}e'e + T^{-2}X'ee'X\right]\tilde{\Omega}^{-1}, \tag{38}$$

which is straightforwardly evaluated in practice.

The derivation of the variance–covariance matrix of β^*, the estimator using the *estimated* error variances, requires only minor modification of the above. I assume that the estimates s_{ij} of σ_{ij}, $i, j = 0, 1, \ldots, K$, the dimension of x, are based on νT degrees of freedom. If all cohorts are pooled in estimating the s_{ij}'s, $\nu = n_c$, the number of observations per cohort, but clearly other schemes are possible. Some estimate of the variances and covariances of the s_{ij} is also required; to focus attention I shall use that derived from sampling under normality. Hence, I assume that s_{ij} is consistent for σ_{ij}, and that asymptotically,

$$(\nu T)\mathrm{E}\{(s_{ij} - \sigma_{ij})(s_{kl} - \sigma_{kl})\} = \sigma_{ik}\sigma_{jl} + \sigma_{il}\sigma_{jk}. \tag{39}$$

The derivation proceeds as before except that the expansion (25) has an additional term corresponding to the stochastic variation in S and s. Hence,

(26) becomes

$$\beta^* - \beta = \Omega^{-1}\left[(m_{xy} - M_{xx}\beta) - (\sigma_{xy} - \Sigma_{xx}\beta)\right]$$
$$- \Omega^{-1}[(s - S\beta) - (\sigma - \Sigma\beta)] + O_p(T^{-1}). \tag{40}$$

By the properties of sampling under normality, the first and second terms are independent, so that, asymptotically

$$TV(\beta^*) = \Omega^{-1}\left[\Sigma_{xx}\omega^2 + (\sigma - \Sigma\beta)(\sigma - \Sigma\beta)'\right]\Omega^{-1}$$
$$+ \nu^{-1}\Omega^{-1}V(s - S\beta)\Omega^{-1}. \tag{41}$$

Elementary manipulation yields

$$V(s - S\beta) = \Sigma(\sigma_{00} - 2\sigma'\beta + \beta'\Sigma\beta) + (\sigma - \Sigma\beta)(\sigma - \Sigma\beta)'. \tag{42}$$

Note that if ν is large, (41) reduces to (30), the case of known variances; this latter is likely to be a formula that would normally be adequate in practice.

Eqs. (23), (24), (38) and (41) are the basic results of this section. I conclude with four issues of practical importance. First, the error variances σ_{00}, σ and Σ will generally vary from survey to survey and cohort to cohort. Write σ_{00}^t, σ^t and Σ^t for the values at observation t, so that (19) and (20) become

$$\mathrm{E}(M_{xx}) = \Omega + \bar{\Sigma}, \tag{19'}$$

$$\mathrm{E}(m_{xy}) = \Omega\beta + \bar{\sigma}, \tag{20'}$$

where $\bar{\Sigma}, \bar{\sigma}$ are the mean values over the t observations. The analysis then goes through with σ_{00}, σ and Σ (or s_{00}, s and S in the case of estimated variances) replaced by their means. Given the nature of the variation with t, an appropriate variance–covariance matrix for the $\bar{S}_{ij}$'s can be derived and substituted for $V(s - S\beta)$ in (41). Second, it is necessary to allow for the presence of some x variables that are measured without errors. For example, relationships like (5) of section 2 contain cohort dummies that are clearly error-free. Other variables may not be drawn from the surveys but from other data sources; macroeconomic variables that are the same for all cohorts but vary with time (prices) are the obvious examples, and, exceptionally, there may be other relevant data on the cohorts themselves. One way to proceed is to introduce additional error-free variables to the right-hand side of (14) and to track them through the analysis. This turns out to be equivalent to the simpler (and intuitive) procedure of setting the appropriate elements of σ and rows and columns of Σ to zero; the formulae for $\tilde{\beta}, \beta^*$ and their asymptotic variances then remain unchanged. Third, for the reasons discussed in section 2, it may be necessary to recognize contemporaneous correlations between some of the x_t^*'s and ε_t. Instrumental variables will typically be available; in the example of section 2, in the form of lagged cohort wages or prices. On the assumption that the instrument vector w_t is constructed from a survey prior to that used for x_t so that their errors of measurement are uncorrelated, the appropriate instrumental variable estimator is

$$\tilde{\beta}_{\mathrm{IV}} = \left[W'X(W'W - T\Sigma_w)^{-1}X'W\right]^{-1}\left[W'X(W'W - T\Sigma_w)^{-1}W'y\right], \tag{43}$$

with a variance matrix calculable by the methods given above. If measurement errors in W and X are correlated, the obvious additional corrections can be made. Fourth, and finally, note that there will typically be some flexibility in constructing cohorts. If cohorts are constructed by age, the age bands can be taken broad or narrow (e.g., a five-year window versus a one-year window), and other qualifying characteristics can be left unspecified or tightly defined. Clearly, the construction of cohorts with members that are distinct from one another and internally homogeneous will minimize the errors in variable problem and enhance precision. Beyond that, it is possible to use trial cohorts to estimate $\tilde{\beta}$ and its variance, and to use these consistent estimates to gauge the consequences of combining or separating cohorts.

4. Estimation of models in differences

In this section, I develop the estimators appropriate for the case where the model, like the second model of section 2, requires differencing prior to estimation. The previous results do not go through directly because the measurement errors induced by the sampling scheme now have a MA(1) structure relative to the unobservable true first differences.

I now write the model in the form

$$\Delta y_t^* = \Delta x_t^* \cdot \beta + \varepsilon_t, \tag{44}$$

for the true unobservable first differences. Corresponding to (18), the measurement structure is

$$\Delta y_t = \Delta y_t^* + v_{t0}, \tag{45}$$

$$\Delta x_t = \Delta x_t^* + v_t, \tag{46}$$

and

$$y_{t0} = u_{t0} - u_{t-10}, \tag{47}$$

$$v_{ti} = u_{ti} - u_{t-1i}, \tag{48}$$

with u_{t0} and u_{ti} the original measurement errors on the y_t and x_{ti} variables respectively. The relationship between Δy_t and $\Delta \boldsymbol{x}_t$ is therefore given by

$$\Delta y_t = \boldsymbol{\beta} \cdot \Delta \boldsymbol{x}_t + (\varepsilon_t + v_{t0} - \boldsymbol{\beta} \cdot \boldsymbol{v}_t). \tag{49}$$

In passing note a tempting but ineffective possible route to estimation. Consider $Nx_t = x_t + x_{t-1}$, the moving average, as a possible instrument for Δx_t, the first-difference, and for simplicity, assume x_t is scalar. Since $Nx_t = Nx_t^* + u_t + u_{t-1}$, and since $u_t + u_{t-1}$ is independent of $v_t = u_t - u_{t-1}$, Nx_t is orthogonal to the compound error in (49). However, in large samples Nx_t is also orthogonal to the regressor Δx_t; $\mathrm{E}(Nx_t \cdot \Delta x_t) = x_t^{*2} - x_{t-1}^{*2}$, so that $\mathrm{E}(T^{-1}\Sigma Nx_t \cdot \Delta x_t) = T^{-1}(x_T^{*2} - x_0^{*2})$ with a limit as $T \to \infty$ of zero. In consequence, instrumental variables estimation of this type will not work. It is therefore necessary to follow through a scheme similar to that of section 3.

To ease notation, write $n_t \equiv \Delta y_t$ and $z_t \equiv \Delta \boldsymbol{x}_t$ so that, corresponding to (19) to (21) the moment matrices are now

$$\mathrm{E}(M_{zz}) = W + 2\Sigma = \Sigma_{zz}, \quad \text{say}, \tag{50}$$

$$\mathrm{E}(\boldsymbol{m}_{zn}) = W\boldsymbol{\beta} + 2\boldsymbol{\sigma} = \boldsymbol{\sigma}_{zn}, \quad \text{say}, \tag{51}$$

$$\mathrm{E}(\boldsymbol{m}_{nn}) = \boldsymbol{\beta}'W\boldsymbol{\beta} + \sigma_\varepsilon^2 + 2\sigma_{00} = \sigma_{nn}, \quad \text{say}, \tag{52}$$

where W is the sample moment matrix of the $\Delta \boldsymbol{x}_t^* \equiv z_t^*$ variables. The doubled role of measurement error comes from the moving average errors in (47) and (48). The first-difference estimator, $\tilde{\boldsymbol{\beta}}_\Delta$, is immediately given as

$$\tilde{\boldsymbol{\beta}}_\Delta = (M_{zz} - 2\Sigma)^{-1}(\boldsymbol{m}_{zn} - 2\boldsymbol{\sigma}), \tag{53}$$

or equivalently

$$\tilde{\boldsymbol{\beta}}_\Delta = (Z'Z - 2T\Sigma)^{-1}(Z'\boldsymbol{n} - 2T\boldsymbol{\sigma}). \tag{54}$$

Expansion, as in section 3, yields

$$\tilde{\boldsymbol{\beta}}_\Delta - \boldsymbol{\beta} = (\Sigma_{zz} - 2\Sigma)^{-1}\{(m_{zn} - M_{zz}\boldsymbol{\beta}) - (\sigma_{zn} - \Sigma_{zz}\boldsymbol{\beta})\} + \mathrm{O}_p(T^{-1}), \tag{55}$$

so that if C is the variance–covariance matrix of $m_{zn} - M_{zz}\beta$, the asymptotic variance of $\tilde{\beta}_\Delta$ is given by

$$TV(\tilde{\beta}_\Delta) = (\Sigma_{zz} - 2\Sigma)^{-1}C(\Sigma_{zz} - 2\Sigma)^{-1}. \tag{56}$$

Now

$$(m_{zn} - M_{zz}\beta)_i = \frac{1}{T}\sum z_{ti}(n_t - \beta \cdot z_t),$$

so that

$$(m_{zn} - M_{zz}\beta)_i = \frac{1}{T}\sum(z^*_{ti} + v_{ti})\Big(\varepsilon_t + v_{t0} - \sum_k \beta_k v_{tk}\Big). \tag{57}$$

The variance of this is tedious to calculate, particularly given the MA structure (47) and (48). In the appendix it is shown that

$$C = (W + 2\Sigma)(\sigma_\varepsilon^2 + 2\sigma_A^2) - \sigma_A^2(W^+ + W^- - \Sigma)$$
$$+ 14(\sigma - \Sigma\beta)(\sigma - \Sigma\beta)', \tag{58}$$

where

$$\sigma_A^2 = \sigma_{00}^2 - 2\sigma \cdot \beta + \beta'\Sigma\beta, \tag{59}$$

and

$$W^+ = \frac{1}{T}\sum z_t^* z_{t-1}^{*\prime}, \tag{60}$$

$$W^- = \frac{1}{T}\sum z_{t-1}^* z_t^{*\prime}. \tag{61}$$

The presence of W^+ and W^- reflects the autocorrelation in the measurement error. Comparing with (29), and taking the case where $W^+ = W^- = 0$, the measurement errors now play a much larger role in determining the variance. Put differently, given the same amount of variance in the true unobservables under levels and differences, estimation precision will be lower in the latter case. This result, which is not surprising, can be enhanced or modified by positive or negative autocorrelation in the true z_t^* series.

The asymptotic variance covariance matrix of $\tilde{\beta}_\Delta$ is obtained by substituting (58) into (56). In practice, an estimation formula can be obtained by noting that, from (52),

$$\tilde{\sigma}_\varepsilon^2 = m_{nn} - 2\sigma_{00} - \tilde{\beta}_\Delta' \tilde{W} \tilde{\beta}_\Delta. \tag{62}$$

Hence, from (59),

$$\tilde{\sigma}_\varepsilon^2 + 2\sigma_A^2 = m_{nn} - 2\tilde{\beta}_\Delta'(2\sigma + \tilde{W}\tilde{\beta}_\Delta) + \tilde{\beta}_\Delta'(\tilde{W} + 2\Sigma)\tilde{\beta}_\Delta \tag{63}$$

$$= m_{nn} - 2\tilde{\beta}_\Delta' \boldsymbol{m}_{zn} + \tilde{\beta}_\Delta' M_{zz} \tilde{\beta}_\Delta \tag{64}$$

$$= T^{-1}\boldsymbol{e}'\boldsymbol{e}, \tag{65}$$

where

$$\boldsymbol{e} = \boldsymbol{n} - Z \cdot \tilde{\beta}_\Delta = \Delta y - \Delta X \cdot \tilde{\beta}_\Delta. \tag{66}$$

Similarly,

$$\begin{aligned} 2\Sigma\tilde{\beta}_\Delta - 2\sigma &= 2\Sigma\tilde{\beta}_\Delta + \tilde{W}\tilde{\beta}_\Delta - \tilde{W}\tilde{\beta}_\Delta - 2\sigma \\ &= M_{zz}\tilde{\beta}_\Delta - \boldsymbol{m}_{zn} = T^{-1}Z'\boldsymbol{e}. \end{aligned} \tag{67}$$

Finally, therefore, writing M_{zz}^+ for $T^{-1}\Sigma z_t z_{t-1}$ and M_{zz}^- similarly, the estimated variance matrix of $\tilde{\beta}_\Delta$ is given by

$$T\hat{V}(\tilde{\beta}_\Delta) = \tilde{W}^{-1}\left[M_{zz}\frac{1}{T}\boldsymbol{e}'\boldsymbol{e} - \tilde{\sigma}_A^2(M_{zz}^+ + M_{zz}^-) + \frac{7}{2T^2}Z'\boldsymbol{e}\boldsymbol{e}'Z\right]\tilde{W}^{-1}, \tag{68}$$

$$\tilde{\sigma}_A^2 = \sigma_{00}^2 - 2\sigma \cdot \tilde{\beta}_\Delta + \tilde{\beta}_\Delta' \Sigma \tilde{\beta}_\Delta. \tag{69}$$

The modification of these formulae for the case where σ_{00}, σ and Σ are replaced by estimates is straightforward and is left to the reader.

Appendix: Derivation of the variance for the differenced case

Starting from eq. (57), define

$$\theta_i = (\boldsymbol{m}_{zn} - M_{zz}\boldsymbol{\beta})_i, \tag{A.1}$$

$$\xi_t = \varepsilon_t + v_{t0} - \sum_k \beta_k v_{tk}, \tag{A.2}$$

so that

$$\theta_i = \frac{1}{T}\sum(z^*_{ti} + v_{ti})\xi_t. \tag{A.3}$$

To obtain the variance–covariance matrix of θ_i, start from

$$\mathrm{E}(\theta_i\theta_j) = \mathrm{E}\left\{T^{-2}\sum_t\sum_s(z^*_{ti} + v_{ti})\xi_t(z^*_{sj} + v_{sj})\xi_s\right\} \tag{A.4}$$

$$= \mathrm{E}\left\{T^{-2}\sum_t\sum_s(z^*_{ti}z^*_{sj}\xi_t\xi_s + v_{ti}\xi_t v_{sj}\xi_s)\right\}, \tag{A.5}$$

since ξ_t and v_t are jointly normal with zero third moments. By the MA(1) structure of the v's,

$$\begin{aligned}\mathrm{E}(\theta_i\theta_j) = T^{-1}\{&\mathrm{E}(z^*_{ti}z^*_{tj}\xi^2_t) + \mathrm{E}(z^*_{ti}z^*_{t+1j}\xi_t\xi_{t+1})\\ &+\mathrm{E}(z^*_{t+1i}z^*_{tj}\xi_{t+1}\xi_t) + \mathrm{E}(v_{ti}\xi_t v_{tj}\xi_t)\\ &+2\mathrm{E}(v_{ti}\xi_t v_{t+1j}\xi_{t+1})\},\end{aligned} \tag{A.6}$$

Now

$$\mathrm{E}(\xi^2_t) = \sigma^2_\varepsilon + 2\sigma^2_{00} + 2\beta'\Sigma\beta - 4\beta'\sigma = \sigma^2_\varepsilon + 2\sigma^2_A, \quad \text{say,} \tag{A.7}$$

$$\mathrm{E}(\xi_t\xi_{t+1}) = -\sigma_{00} + 2\beta'\sigma - \beta'\Sigma\beta = -\sigma^2_A. \tag{A.8}$$

Hence, evaluating (A.6) term by term using, where necessary, the standard formulae for fourth movements of normals, gives

$$\mathrm{E}(z^*_{ti}z^*_{tj}\xi^2_t) = w_{ij}(\sigma^2_\varepsilon + 2\sigma^2_A), \tag{A.9}$$

$$\mathrm{E}(z^*_{ti}z^*_{t+1j}\xi_t\xi_{t+1}) = -w^+_{ij}\sigma^2_A, \tag{A.10}$$

with a similar expression for its transpose,

$$\begin{aligned}\mathrm{E}(v_{ti}v_{tj}\xi^2_t) &= 2\sigma_{ij}(\sigma^2_\varepsilon + 2\sigma^2_A) + 2\left\{2\sigma_i - 2\sum_k\beta_k\sigma_{ik}\right\}\left\{2\sigma_j - 2\sum_k\beta_k\sigma_{jk}\right\}\\ &= 2\sigma_{ij}(\sigma^2_\varepsilon + 2\sigma^2_A) + 8(\sigma - \Sigma\beta)_i(\sigma - \Sigma\beta)_j.\end{aligned} \tag{A.11}$$

$$\mathrm{E}(v_{ti}\xi_t v_{t+1j}\xi_{t+1}) = \sigma_{ij}\sigma^2_A + 5(\sigma - \Sigma\beta)_i(\sigma - \Sigma\beta)_j. \tag{A.12}$$

Hence, collecting terms and subtracting $\mathrm{E}(\theta_i)\mathrm{E}(\theta_j) = 4(\boldsymbol{\sigma} - \Sigma\boldsymbol{\beta})_i(\sigma - \Sigma\boldsymbol{\beta})_j$ yields

$$V(\boldsymbol{\theta}) = (W + 2\Sigma)(\sigma_r^2 + 2\sigma_A^2) - \sigma_A^2(W^+ + W^- - \Sigma)$$

$$+ 14(\boldsymbol{\sigma} - \Sigma\boldsymbol{\beta})(\boldsymbol{\sigma} - \Sigma\boldsymbol{\beta}), \qquad \text{(A.13)}$$

which is eq. (58) of the main text.

References

Ashenfelter, O., 1983, Macroeconomic analyses of labor supply and microeconomic analyses of labor supply, Presented to Carnegie–Rochester Conference, Bal Harbor, FL, Nov. 1983.

Browning, M., A. Deaton and M. Irish, 1985, A profitable approach to labor supply and commodity demands over the life-cycle, Econometrica 53, 503–543.

Clark, C., 1957, The conditions of economic progress (Macmillan, London).

Deaton, A., 1975, The structure of demand 1920–1970, in: C.M. Cipolla, ed., The Fontana economic history of Europe (Collins-Fontana, London).

Deaton, A. and J. Muellbauer, 1980, An almost ideal demand system, American Economic Review 70, 312–326.

Fuller, W.A., 1975, Regression analysis for sample survey, Sankhya: The Indian Journal of Statistics C37, 117–132.

Fuller, W.A., 1981, Measurement error models (Department of Statistics, Iowa State University, Ames, IA).

Ghez, G.R. and G.S. Becker, 1975, The allocation of time and goods over the life-cycle (NBER, New York).

Kuznets, S., 1962, Quantitative aspects of the economic growth of nations: VII, The share and structure of consumption, Economic Development and Cultural Change 10, 1–92.

MaCurdy, T.E., 1981, An empirical model of labor supply in a life-cycle setting, Journal of Political Economy 89, 1059–1085.

Smith, J., 1977, Family labor supply over the life-cycle, Explorations in Research 4, 205–276.

Stone, R. and D.A. Rowe, 1966, The measurement of consumers' expenditures and behavior in the United Kingdom 1920–1938, Vol. II (Cambridge University Press, Cambridge).

Part II
Specification Tests

ECONOMETRICA

VOLUME 46 NOVEMBER, 1978 NUMBER 6

SPECIFICATION TESTS IN ECONOMETRICS

BY J. A. HAUSMAN[1]

Using the result that under the null hypothesis of no misspecification an asymptotically efficient estimator must have zero asymptotic covariance with its difference from a consistent but asymptotically inefficient estimator, specification tests are devised for a number of model specifications in econometrics. Local power is calculated for small departures from the null hypothesis. An instrumental variable test as well as tests for a time series cross section model and the simultaneous equation model are presented. An empirical model provides evidence that unobserved individual factors are present which are not orthogonal to the included right-hand-side variable in a common econometric specification of an individual wage equation.

1. INTRODUCTION

SPECIFICATION TESTS FORM ONE of the most important areas for research in econometrics. In the standard regression framework, $y = X\beta + \varepsilon$, the two stochastic specifications are first that the conditional expectation of ε given X be zero (or for fixed X, ε have expectation zero) and that ε have a spherical covariance matrix

(1.1a) $E(\varepsilon|X)=0$ or in large samples $\operatorname{plim}\frac{1}{T}X'\varepsilon = 0,$

(1.1b) $V(\varepsilon|X)=\sigma^2 I.$

Failure of the first assumption, sometimes called the orthogonality assumption, leads to biased estimates while failure of the second assumption, sometimes called the sphericality assumption, leads to loss of efficiency although the central tendency of the estimator is still correct. While in many problems the payoff to detecting failure of assumption (1.1a) is presumably greater than detecting failure of assumption (1.1b), most of the attention in the econometric literature has been paid to devising tests for the latter assumption. Ramsey **[16]** and Wu **[25]** are among the few references to specification tests. Yet, the problem is so important that increased attention should be paid, especially since efficient estimators under assumption (1.1) are now available in almost all situations; and these estimators are often quite sensitive to failures of the first assumption.

In this paper a general form of specification test is proposed which attempts to provide powerful tests of assumption (1.1a) and presents a unified approach to specification error tests. Thus, an ad hoc test would not need to be devised for each specific situation, but the general scheme presented here could be applied

[1] I would like to thank T. Amemiya, D. W. Carlton, G. Chamberlain, G. Chow, F. M. Fisher, Z. Griliches, R. H. Gordon, R. E. Hall, T. J. Rothenberg, H. L. White, and A. Zellner for helpful discussions. A. S. Kelso and E. R. Rosenthal provided research assistance. Research support has been provided by the NSF. An editor and referee of *Econometrica* provided very helpful comments. The views expressed in this paper are the author's sole responsibility and do not reflect those of the Department of Economics, the Massachusetts Institute of Technology, or the National Science Foundation.

to specific situations. A main stumbling block to specification tests has been a lack of precisely specified alternative hypotheses. Here, I point out that in many situations, including time series-cross section specifications, errors in variables specifications, and simultaneous equation specifications, the alternative hypothesis that assumption (1.1a) fails may be tested in an expanded regression framework. The basic idea follows from the existence of an alternative estimator which is consistent under both null and alternative hypotheses. By comparing the estimates from this estimator with the efficient estimator (under assumption 1.1a) and noting that their difference is uncorrelated with the efficient estimator when the null hypothesis is true, easily used tests may be devised from the regression

$$y = X\beta + \tilde{X}\alpha + v \tag{1.2}$$

where $\tilde{X}$ is a suitably transformed version of X. The specification tests are performed by constructing a test of the hypothesis H_0: $\alpha = 0$. Also local power considerations are discussed, and the distribution of the power function under the alternative hypothesis is derived.

In Section 2 the basic lemma regarding these types of specification tests is proven. The test is applied to an errors in variables problem and equation (1.2) is derived. The following two sections discuss two new specification tests for the time series-cross section model and for the simultaneous equation model. Both tests are always available (unlike the errors in variables test which requires an instrumental variable) and should be used for these two important model specifications. Lastly, an example is provided. The example is interesting since a widely used time series-cross section specification, the random effects model, is found not to be consistent with the alternative specification. The general principle of this paper can be applied in additional problems not considered here. Therefore the tests should be useful to the applied econometrician.

2. THEORY AND A TEST OF ERRORS IN VARIABLES

The theory underlying the proposed specification tests rests on one fundamental idea. Under the (null) hypothesis of no misspecification, there will exist a consistent, asymptotically normal and asymptotically efficient estimator, where efficiency means attaining the asymptotic Cramer–Rao bound.[2] Under the alternative hypothesis of misspecification, however, this estimator will be biased and inconsistent. To construct a test of misspecification, it is necessary to find another estimator which is not adversely affected by the misspecification; but this estimator will not be asymptotically efficient under the null hypothesis. A consideration of the difference between the two estimates, $\hat{q} = \hat{\beta}_1 - \hat{\beta}_0$ where $\hat{\beta}_0$

[2] This paper will concentrate on the large sample case since in each test one or both of the estimators has a normal distribution only asymptotically. Most econometric estimators, except for least squares, have this property. A discussion of the notion of asymptotic efficiency may be found in Rothenberg [**18**, Ch. 2]. Henceforth, efficient will stand for asymptotically efficient and likewise for bias, while variance means variance of the asymptotic distribution. Analogous finite sample results hold true under appropriate conditions.

is the efficient estimate under H_0 and $\hat{\beta}_1$ is a consistent estimator under H_1, will then lead to a specification test. If no misspecification is present, the probability limit of $\hat{q}$ is zero. With misspecification plim $\hat{q}$ will differ from zero; and if the power of the test is high, $\hat{q}$ will be large in absolute value relative to its asymptotic standard error. Hopefully, this procedure will lead to powerful tests in important cases because the misspecification is apt to be serious only when the two estimates differ substantially.

In constructing tests based on $\hat{q}$, an immediate problem comes to mind. To develop tests not only is the probability limit of $\hat{q}$ required, but the variance of the asymptotic distribution of $\sqrt{T}\hat{q}$, $V(\hat{q})$, must also be determined. Since $\hat{\beta}_0$ and $\hat{\beta}_1$ use the same data, they will be correlated which could lead to a messy calculation for the variance of $\sqrt{T}\hat{q}$. Luckily, this problem is resolved easily and, in fact, $V(\hat{q}) = V(\hat{\beta}_1) - V(\hat{\beta}_0) = V_1 - V_0$ under the null hypothesis of no misspecification. Thus, the construction of specification error tests is simplified, since the estimators may be considered separately because the variance of the difference $\sqrt{T}\hat{q} = \sqrt{T}(\hat{\beta}_1 - \hat{\beta}_0)$ is the difference of the respective variances. The intuitive reasoning behind this result is simple although it appears to have remained generally unnoticed in constructing tests in econometrics. The idea rests on the fact that the efficient estimator, $\hat{\beta}_0$, must have zero asymptotic covariance with $\hat{q}$ under the null hypothesis for any other consistent, asymptotically normal estimator $\hat{\beta}_1$. If this were not the case, a linear combination of $\hat{\beta}_0$ and $\hat{q}$ could be taken which would lead to a consistent estimator $\hat{\beta}_*$ which would have smaller asymptotic variance than $\hat{\beta}_0$ which is assumed asymptotically efficient. To prove the result formally, consider the following lemma:

LEMMA 2.1: *Consider two estimators $\hat{\beta}_0$, $\hat{\beta}_1$ which are both consistent and asymptotically normally distributed with $\hat{\beta}_0$ attaining the asymptotic Cramer–Rao bound so $\sqrt{T}(\hat{\beta}_0 - \beta) \overset{A}{\sim} N(0, V_0)$ and $\sqrt{T}(\hat{\beta}_1 - \beta) \overset{A}{\sim} N(0, V_1)$ where V_0 is the inverse of Fisher's information matrix. Consider $\hat{q} = \hat{\beta}_1 - \hat{\beta}_0$. Then the limiting distributions of $\sqrt{T}(\hat{\beta}_0 - \beta)$ and $\sqrt{T}\hat{q}$ have zero covariance, $C(\hat{\beta}_0, \hat{q}) = 0$, a zero matrix.*[3,4]

PROOF: Suppose $\hat{\beta}_0$ and $\hat{q}$ are not orthogonal. Since plim $\hat{q} = 0$ define a new estimator $\hat{\beta}_2 = \hat{\beta}_0 + rA\hat{q}$ where r is a scalar and A is an arbitrary matrix to be chosen. The new estimator is consistent and asymptotically normal with asymptotic variance

$$V(\hat{\beta}_2) = V(\hat{\beta}_0) + rAC(\hat{\beta}_0, \hat{q}) + rC'(\hat{\beta}_0, \hat{q})A' + r^2AV(\hat{q})A'. \tag{2.2}$$

Now consider the difference between the asymptotic variance of the new

[3] Besides consistency and asymptotic normality, uniform convergence is also required to rule out superefficiency. However, it is not difficult to demonstrate that standard econometric estimators converge uniformly. A sufficient condition which leads to a straightforward proof is to assume that the parameter space is compact. T. Amemiya and T. Rothenberg have helped in resolving this issue.

[4] A statement of this lemma in the finite sample case for one parameter is contained in a paper by R. A. Fisher [**8**], a reference supplied by W. Taylor. It is clearly related to an asymptotic version of the Rao-Blackwell theorem (Rao [**17**]).

estimator and the old asymptotically efficient estimator

$$F(r) = V(\hat{\beta}_2) - V(\hat{\beta}_0) = rAC + rC'A' + r^2AV(\hat{q})A'. \tag{2.3}$$

Taking derivatives with respect to r yields

$$F'(r) = AC + C'A' + 2rAV(\hat{q})A'. \tag{2.4}$$

Then choose $A = -C'$ and note that C is symmetric, which leads to

$$F'(r) = -2C'C + 2rC'V(\hat{q})C. \tag{2.5}$$

Therefore at $r = 0$, $F'(0) = -2C'C \leq 0$ in the sense of being nonpositive definite. But $F(0) = 0$ so for r small $F(r) < 0$ and there is a contradiction unless $C = C(\hat{\beta}_0, \hat{q}) = 0$ since $\hat{\beta}_0$ is asymptotically efficient implies $F(r) \geq 0$.

Once it has been shown that the efficient estimator is uncorrelated with $\hat{q}$, the asymptotic variance of $\hat{q}$ is easily calculated.

COROLLARY 2.6: $V(\hat{q}) = V(\hat{\beta}_1) - V(\hat{\beta}_0) \geq 0$ *in the sense of being nonnegative definite.*

PROOF: Since $\hat{q} + \hat{\beta}_0 = \hat{\beta}_1$, $V(\hat{q}) + V(\hat{\beta}_0) = V(\hat{\beta}_1)$. Furthermore, $\hat{\beta}_0$ attains the asymptotic CR bound. Given the above result a general misspecification test can be specified by considering the statistic

$$m = T\hat{q}'\hat{V}(\hat{q})^{-1}\hat{q} \tag{2.7}$$

where $\hat{V}(\hat{q})$ is a consistent estimate of $V(\hat{q})$. This statistic will be shown to be distributed asymptotically as central χ^2_K under the null hypothesis where K is the number of unknown parameters in β when no misspecification is present. In what follows, it is sometimes easier to work with $\hat{q}$ rather than $\sqrt{T}\hat{q}$ so define $M_0 = (1/T)V_0$, $M_1 = (1/T)V_1$, and $M(\hat{q}) = (1/T)V(\hat{q})$. In terms of the M's, the statistic is $m = \hat{q}'\hat{M}(\hat{q})^{-1}\hat{q}$.

The statistic m in equation (2.7) specifies the distribution of the difference of the two estimators when no misspecification is present. The other operating characteristic of a test is its power. Unfortunately, power considerations have not been paid much attention in econometrics, probably due to the imprecise-ness of alternative hypotheses and the complexity of deriving distributions of power functions. The power of our specification test depends on the nonnull distribution of the statistic in equation (2.7). In most applications I will show that the power can be approximated in large samples, for alternatives close to the null hypothesis, by the noncentral χ^2 distribution with noncentrality parameter

$$\delta^2 = \bar{q}'M(\hat{q})^{-1}\bar{q}, \tag{2.8}$$

where $\bar{q} = \text{plim}\,(\hat{\beta}_1 - \hat{\beta}_0)$ the probability limit of the difference between the two estimates.[5]

[5] The discussion of local power which follows is due to the extremely helpful guidance of T. J. Rothenberg. A good reference is Cox and Hinkley [6, Ch. 9].

Power considerations are important because they give the probability of rejecting the null hypothesis when it is false. In many empirical investigations $\hat{\beta}_0$ and $\hat{\beta}_1$ seem to be far apart yet the null hypothesis that $q=0$ is not rejected. If the probability of rejection is small for a difference of say q_A where q_A is large enough to be important, then not much information has been provided by the test. Now deriving the large sample distributions of test statistics under the alternative hypothesis is a difficult matter especially under a wide range of alternative hypotheses which are being considered here. Therefore, I will only be able to derive the asymptotic distributions of the power function of a sequence of models under local conditions where the sequence of alternatives $\bar{q}$ is of order $a/\sqrt{T}$ where a is a constant vector. Only alternatives close to the null hypothesis can be investigated in this manner but they hopefully provide a guide to a broader range of cases. The necessity of this limitation can be best shown by a simple example. Consider a two equation triangular system

(2.9a) $\quad y_1 = x_1\gamma + u_1,$

(2.9b) $\quad y_2 = \beta y_1 + u_2.$

If u_1 and u_2 have zero covariance, least squares on equation (2.9b) is the (asymptotically) efficient estimator of β while with nonzero covariance it is inconsistent. Then, an instrumental variable estimator (say two stage least squares) is consistent. The test statistic m from equation (2.7) is asymptotically equivalent to a test that $\sigma_{12}=0$ where the estimated covariance is formed from the residuals of the 2SLS estimate of equation (2.9b), $\hat{u}_2$, and the residuals of the OLS estimate of equation (2.9a), $\hat{u}_1$. Under the alternative hypothesis assume that the true covariance is σ_{12}, and I want to construct a test based on the fact that $\sqrt{T}(\hat{\sigma}_{12}-\sigma_{12}) \overset{A}{\sim} N(0, v_{12})$. Assume a consistent estimate $\hat{v}_{12}$ is used for v_{12} and let $v_{12}^{\frac{1}{2}} = w$ while $\hat{v}_{12}^{\frac{1}{2}} = \hat{w}$. Tests will be usually formed from the statistic $\sqrt{T}[(\hat{\sigma}_{12}-\sigma_{12}^0)/\hat{w}]$ where σ_{12}^0 is the hypothesized value of σ_{12}; here $\sigma_{12}^0=0$. Adding and subtracting the true σ_{12} leads to the expression

$$(2.10) \quad \sqrt{T}\left(\frac{\hat{\sigma}_{12}-\sigma_{12}}{\hat{w}}\right) - \sqrt{T}\left(\frac{\sigma_{12}^0-\sigma_{12}}{\hat{w}}\right).$$

Under the null hypothesis only the first term is present since $\sigma_{12}=\sigma_{12}^0=0$ so asymptotically normal or central χ^2 distributions are derived for tests of $\hat{\sigma}_{12}=\sigma_{12}^0$. When $\sigma_{12}\neq\sigma_{12}^0$ under the alternative hypothesis, the second term remains finite only when a sequence of models is considered so that $\sqrt{T}(\sigma_{12}-\sigma_{12}^0)$ converges to a finite constant since $\hat{w}$ is a consistent estimate of w. Otherwise the second term explodes and large sample power functions cannot be derived unless further approximations are made. However, the explosion of this term insures a consistent test. The analysis of the case where σ_{12} converges to σ_{12}^0 at rate $\sqrt{T}$ corresponds to the idea of local power: the distribution of the test statistic under the alternative hypothesis is considered for cases close to the null hypothesis.

To return from the simple example to our more general case I will consider a sequence of models corresponding to the concept of local power. Thus as before under H_0, I assume both estimates are consistent, that $\sqrt{T}(\hat{\beta}_0-\beta)\overset{A}{\sim}N(0, V_0)$, and that $\sqrt{T}(\hat{\beta}_1-\beta)\overset{A}{\sim}N(0, V_1)$. I assume that under H_1, $\sqrt{T}(\hat{\beta}_0-\text{plim}\,\hat{\beta}_0)$ and $\sqrt{T}(\hat{\beta}_1-\beta)$ are asymptotically normal with covariance matrices that are continuous functions of the true β.

THEOREM 2.1: *Under H_0, the test statistic $m = T\hat{q}'\hat{V}(\hat{q})^{-1}\hat{q}\overset{A}{\sim}\chi^2_K$ where $\hat{V}(\hat{q})$ is a consistent estimate (under H_0), of $V(\hat{q})$ using $\hat{\beta}_1$ and $\hat{\beta}_0$.*[6]

PROOF: Let $\sqrt{T}\hat{q}=\sqrt{T}(\hat{\beta}_1-\hat{\beta}_0)\overset{A}{\sim}N(0, V(\hat{q}))$ using the corollary. Then $T\hat{q}'\hat{V}(\hat{q})^{-1}q$ is distributed asymptotically as central χ^2_K since it has the same asymptotic distribution as $T\hat{q}'V(\hat{q})^{-1}\hat{q}$.

As an approximation for practical use, the statistic $\hat{q}'\hat{M}(\hat{q})^{-1}\hat{q}$ can be used in place of m.

To derive the asymptotic distribution of the test statistic under the alternative hypothesis, consider local alternatives. That is, consider a sequence of models such that the sequence of alternatives $\bar{q}$ is of order $(1/\sqrt{T})$. Then I can show that as long as $\hat{V}(\hat{q})$ approaches $V(\hat{q})$ the asymptotic distribution of the test statistic is non-central χ^2.

THEOREM 2.2: *Under H_1 consider a sequence of models represented by a sequence of parameters $q/\sqrt{T}(q\neq 0)$ so that $g_T=\text{plim}\,\hat{\beta}_{0T}-\beta=\breve{\beta}_T-\beta$ such that $\lim_{T\to\infty}\sqrt{T}g_T=a<\infty$. Then as $T\to\infty$ along the chosen path $m_T=T\hat{q}'_T\hat{V}_T(\hat{q})^{-1}\hat{q}_T$ is distributed asymptotically as noncentral χ^2 with k degrees of freedom and noncentrality parameter $\delta^2=\lim_{T\to\infty}Tg'_TV(\hat{q})^{-1}g_T$ which is approximately $\bar{q}'M(\hat{q})^{-1}\bar{q}$ so long as $\hat{V}_T(\hat{q})$ is a consistent estimate of $V(\hat{q})$ under H_1.*

PROOF: Because the asymptotic covariance matrices of $\hat{\beta}_0$ and $\hat{\beta}_1$ are continuous functions of β, along the sequence of local departures of the model as $T\to\infty$, their covariance matrices approach V_0 and V_1, respectively. For each local departure from the null hypothesis in the sequence, $\{g_T\}$, $\hat{\beta}_{0T}$ is inconsistent. However, since the departures are only local, it can be shown (Cox and Hinkley [**6**, pp. 317–18]) that asymptotically $\sqrt{T}(\hat{\beta}_{0T}-\breve{\beta}_T)\overset{A}{\sim}N(0, V_0)$. Thus although the mean of the asymptotic distribution of $\hat{\beta}_0$ has changed from the true β to $\breve{\beta}_T$, the asymptotic variance remains the same. Furthermore $\hat{V}_T(\hat{q})$, the estimate of $V(\hat{q})$ is still consistent. Therefore, since asymptotically $\sqrt{T}\hat{q}_T\overset{A}{\sim}N(a, V(\hat{q}))$ the test statistic m_T is distributed approximately as noncentral χ^2 with degrees of freedom k and noncentrality parameter δ^2.

To make this argument more concrete, return to the example of equations (2.9). Define $K_T=(1/T)\gamma'x'_{1T}x_{1T}\gamma$ and assume it approaches a finite limit K.

[6] Any consistent estimate of $V(\hat{q})$ under H_0 is sufficient to cause Theorem 2.1 to hold. Power considerations under H_1 may lead to a specific choice of an estimate. These considerations are discussed for a specific example following equation (2.11).

Now under H_1 let $\sigma_{12} \neq 0$ and then the inconsistency in $\hat{\beta}_0$ is $\operatorname{plim} \hat{\beta}_0 - \beta = \sigma_{12}/(K + \sigma_{22})$. To determine the limiting distribution of $\hat{\beta}_0$ it is convenient to assume that u_1 and u_2 have a bivariate normal distribution. Then Rothenberg [19] has shown that

$$(2.11)\qquad \sqrt{T}\left[\hat{\beta} - \beta - \frac{\sigma_{12}}{K_T + \sigma_{22}}\right] \overset{A}{\sim} N\left[0, \frac{\sigma_{11}}{K + \sigma_{22}} - \frac{\sigma_{12}^2}{(K + \sigma_{22})^2} - \frac{2\sigma_{12}^2 K^2}{(K + \sigma_{22})^4}\right]$$

where $\lim \sqrt{T}[\sigma_{12}/(K + \sigma_{22})]$ is the a of Theorem 2.2. However $V_0 = \sigma_{11}/(K + \sigma_{22})$ so it needs to be shown that for local departures from the null hypothesis the last two terms in the asymptotic variance disappear as $T \to \infty$. But since by assumption $\sqrt{T}\sigma_{12}$ converges to a (finite) constant the terms involving σ_{12}^2 converge to zero so long as $(K + \sigma_{22})$ is nonzero. Thus, for local departures in large samples V_0 gives a correct approximation and a noncentral χ^2 distribution may be used.[7,8]

For a given size of test the power increases with δ^2 which in turn depends on how far the plim of the biased and inconsistent estimator $\hat{\beta}_0$ is from the plim of the consistent estimator $\hat{\beta}_1$ when misspecification is present. Thus, the comparison estimator $\hat{\beta}_1$ should be chosen so that if a certain type of misspecification is feared to be present, $\hat{q}$, which is the difference of the estimates, is expected to be large. The other consideration in equation (2.8) is to keep $V(\hat{q})$ small so that a large departure between $\hat{\beta}_0$ and $\hat{\beta}$ will not arise by chance. This requirement means that $\hat{\beta}_1$ should be relatively efficient but at the same time sensitive to departures from the model specification. To highlight the power considerations the specification test of equation (2.7) will be reformulated in a statistically equivalent form. Also, the reformulated test may be easier to use with available econometrics computer programs. To demonstrate this reformulated test, an errors in variables example is considered.

An errors in variables test attempts to determine if stochastic regressors and the disturbances in a regression are independent. In the simplest case consider the model

$$(2.12)\qquad y_i = \beta x_i + \varepsilon_{1i} \qquad (i = 1, \ldots, T)$$

where ε_{1i} is iid with mean zero and distributed normally. Under the null

[7] Wu's [25] derivation of the (nonlocal) limiting distribution of the test statistic under the alternative hypothesis in equation (3.12) of his paper seems incorrect since application of the central limit theorem on p. 748 requires the sum of random variables with zero mean. Thus his variable e_1 does not have a limiting distribution. Interpreted locally Wu's results seem valid since only the usual least squares variance term V_0 is needed.

[8] A referee points out that in general there may exist many estimates of $V(\hat{q})$ which are consistent under H_0 so that Theorem 2.1 holds. However, the estimate which provides the greatest power under H_1 is preferable to use. If one considers a class of estimators such that $\operatorname{plim} \hat{V}(\hat{q}) = cV(\hat{q})$ where c is a constant, Wu's [25] results (interpreted locally) lead to the conclusion that one should use the estimator associated with the smallest c. Therefore for the instrumental variable test, s_0^2, the least squares estimate of σ^2, seems appropriate to use for this example. For Theorem 2.2 to hold in general, consistent estimates of the nuisance parameters are required.

hypothesis x_i and ε_1 are orthogonal in large samples:

$$(2.13)\quad \operatorname{plim} \frac{1}{T} x'\varepsilon_1 = 0,$$

while under the alternative hypothesis the plim is nonzero.

The efficient estimator under the null hypothesis is, of course, least squares. Under the alternative hypothesis least squares is biased and inconsistent with H_1: plim $\hat{\beta}_0 = \beta(m_x^2 - \sigma_{\varepsilon_2}^2)/m_x^2$ where the observed $x_i = x_i^* + \varepsilon_{2i}$ is the sum of the "true" regressor and a normal random variable with mean zero which is assumed independent of ε_{1i} while $m_x^2 = \operatorname{plim}(1/T)x'x$. The comparison estimator $\hat{\beta}_1$ will be an instrumental variable (IV) estimator based on the instrument z with properties

$$(2.14)\quad \operatorname{plim} \frac{1}{T} z'\eta = 0, \qquad \operatorname{plim} \frac{1}{T} z'x \neq 0, \qquad \text{for } \eta_i = \varepsilon_{1i} - \beta\varepsilon_{2i}.$$

Then the IV estimator is

$$(2.15)\quad \hat{\beta}_1 = (z'x)^{-1}z'y.$$

To form the test statistic under the null hypothesis using Corollary 2.6

$$(2.16)\quad \sqrt{T}\hat{q} = \sqrt{T}(\hat{\beta}_1 - \hat{\beta}_0) \overset{A}{\sim} N(0, D)$$

with $D = V(\hat{q}) = \sigma^2[\operatorname{plim}((1/T)\hat{x}'\hat{x})^{-1} - \operatorname{plim}((1/T)x'x)^{-1}]$ where $\hat{x} = z(z'z)^{-1}z'x$. Again using the corollary, $T\hat{q}'D^{-1}q$ is distributed as χ_1^2 under the null hypothesis. Then the test of misspecification using s_1^2, the IV estimator of σ^2, to form $\hat{B}$, becomes:

$$(2.17)\quad m = \hat{q}'\hat{B}^{-1}\hat{q} \overset{A}{\sim} \chi_1^2$$

where $(1/T)B$ is our finite sample approximation to D, $B = \sigma^2[(\hat{x}'\hat{x})^{-1} - (x'x)^{-1}]$. Under H_1, the probability limit of q, $\bar{q} = \beta \cdot \sigma_{\varepsilon_2}^2/m_x^2$ so the asymptotic distribution of m for local departures depends on the magnitude of the two coefficients and the correlation of the right hand side variable with the disturbance. To compute the power as a function of β, equation (2.8) can be used. The IV estimates, $\hat{\beta}_{IV}$ and s_1^2, are consistent under both the null and alternative hypotheses.

A consistent estimate of m_x^2 follows from the data, and an estimate of $\sigma_{\varepsilon_2}^2$ is derived from the equation $\hat{\sigma}_{\varepsilon_2}^2 = (1 - \hat{\beta}_{OLS}/\hat{\beta}_{IV})\hat{m}_x^2$. Then an estimate of $\bar{q}$ may be calculated for any choice of β and the non-centrality parameter δ^2 is a quadratic function around $\beta = 0$, $\delta^2 = (\beta^2\sigma_{\varepsilon_2}^4/m_x^4(\hat{q}))$. Note that the asymptotic variance of the IV estimator enters the denominator as expected, so that IV estimates with large variance decrease the power of the test. The tables of the noncentral χ^2 test in Scheffé [**21**] can be consulted to find the probability of the null hypothesis being rejected for a given value of β if the alternative hypothesis is true conditional on the estimates of the incidental parameters of the problem. This type of IV (instrumental variable) test for errors in variables was first proposed by Liviatan [**12**]. Wu [**25**] considers tests with different estimates of the nuisance parameter σ^2 to derive a finite sample F test under a stronger hypothesis about the stochastic properties of x.[9]

The IV test for errors in variables is known in the literature, but an alternative formulation of the test leads to easier implementation.[10] Partition the vector x into two orthogonal components, $x = \hat{x} + v$, which is the sum of the instrument and that part of x orthogonal to z. Then the least squares regression specification of equation (2.12) can be rewritten as

$$(2.18) \qquad y = \beta x + \varepsilon_1 = \beta \hat{x} + \beta v + \varepsilon_1.$$

Now consider running this regression to compare the two estimates of β.

The variable $\hat{x}$ is asymptotically orthogonal to ε_1 under both the null and alternative hypothesis and is orthogonal to v by construction. Therefore the least squares regression coefficient of $\hat{x}$ is consistent under both hypotheses, being the IV estimate $\hat{\beta}_1$. The estimate of β corresponding to the variable v, however, should only have the same plim as $\hat{\beta}_1$ under the null hypothesis when v is orthogonal to ε_1. Thus, we might test whether the two estimates are equal. Since under the alternative hypothesis the plim of the second coefficient is no longer β, I will refer to it as γ and then rewrite equation (2.15) after adding and subtracting βv to make the test of equality easier:

$$(2.19) \qquad y = \beta \hat{x} + \gamma v + \varepsilon_1 = \beta(\hat{x} + v) + (\gamma - \beta) v + \varepsilon_1 = \beta x + \alpha v + \varepsilon_1.$$

Thus for $\alpha = \gamma - \beta$, the proposed test is a large sample test on the hypothesis that $\alpha = 0$. One last minor simplification can be made by noting that an equivalent regression to equation (2.19) is

$$(2.20) \qquad y = \beta x + \alpha \hat{x} + \varepsilon_1$$

since $\hat{\alpha} = (v'Q_x v)^{-1} v'Q_x y = -(\hat{x}'Q_x\hat{x})^{-1}\hat{x}'Q_x y$ where $Q_x = I - x(x'x)^{-1}x'$. A test of $\alpha = 0$ from equation (2.20) under the null hypothesis is then based on the statistic $\sigma^2\chi^2 = \hat{\alpha}'(\hat{x}'Q_x\hat{x})\hat{\alpha}$. But $(1/\sigma^2)(\hat{x}'Q_x\hat{x})^{-1} = (\hat{x}'\hat{x})^{-1}B^{-1}(\hat{x}'\hat{x})^{-1}$ and $\hat{\alpha} = (\hat{x}'Q_x\hat{x})^{-1}(\hat{x}'\hat{x})\hat{q}$. Thus, this formulation is equivalent to the IV test of equation (2.17) since

$$(2.21) \qquad \frac{1}{\sigma^2}\hat{\alpha}'(\hat{x}'Q_x\hat{x})\hat{\alpha} = \frac{1}{\sigma^2}\hat{q}'(\hat{x}'\hat{x})(\hat{x}'Q_x\hat{x})^{-1}(\hat{x}'\hat{x})\hat{q}$$
$$= \hat{q}'\hat{B}^{-1}\hat{q}.$$

[9] The instrumental variable test can also be considered a formalization and an improvement of a suggestion by Sargan [**20**] who recommended checking whether the least squares estimates lie outside the confidence regions of the IV estimates. For individual coefficients the procedure used here is to see whether the least squares estimate lies outside the confidence regions centered at the IV estimate and with length formed from the square root of the *difference* of the IV variance minus the OLS variance. Thus shorter confidence intervals follow from the current procedure than from Sargan's suggestion. The joint χ^2 test on all the coefficients in equation (2.14) if there are more than one, however, is the preferred test of the null hypothesis rather than separate consideration of each confidence interval.

[10] Presentation of this alternative method of testing has been improved from an earlier version of the paper using a suggestion of Z. Griliches.

A simple large sample normal test of $\alpha = 0$ based on the OLS estimate $\hat{\alpha}$ from equation (2.15) yields a test on whether errors in variables is present and is equivalent asymptotically to the test of equation (2.17) using s_0^2, the least squares estimate of σ^2, under the null hypothesis.[11] Besides ease of computation another advantage may be present. Three outcomes of the test will be encountered leading to simple approximate power interpretations which may not be as evident using the previous formulation of the test. First, $\hat{\alpha}$ may be large relative to its standard error. This result points to rejection of the hypothesis of no misspecification. The other clear cut case is a small $\hat{\alpha}$ with a small standard error which presents little evidence against H_0. The last result is a large standard error relative to the size of $\hat{\alpha}$. This finding indicates a lack of power which will be very evident to the user since he will not have a precise estimate of α.

Two immediate generalizations of the errors in variables specification test can be made. The test can be used to test any potential failure of assumption (1.1a) that additional right-hand-side variables are orthogonal to the error term so long as instrumental variables are available. First, additional right-hand-side variables can be present:

$$(2.22) \qquad y = X_1\beta_1 + X_2\beta_2 + \varepsilon,$$

where the X_1 variables are possibly correlated with ε while the X_2 variables are known to be uncorrelated. Given a matrix of variables Z (which should include X_2), $\hat{q}$ will again be the difference between the IV estimator and the efficient OLS estimator. Letting $\hat{X}_1 = P_Z X_1$ where $P_z = Z(Z'Z)^{-1}Z'$ leads to the regression

$$(2.23) \qquad y = X_1\beta_1 + X_2\beta_2 + \hat{X}_1\alpha + v$$

where a test of H_0: $\alpha = 0$ is a test for errors in variables.[12] The last orthogonality test involves a lagged endogenous variable which may be correlated with the disturbance. In this case, however, if the specification of the error process is known such as first order serial correlation, a more powerful test may be available.[13]

In this section the general nature of the misspecification problem has been discussed when there exists an alternative estimator which provides consistent estimates under misspecification. By demonstrating that the efficient estimator has zero asymptotic covariance with the difference between the consistent estimator $\hat{\beta}_1$ and the asymptotically efficient estimator (under H_0) $\hat{\beta}_0$, a simple expression for the variance of $(\hat{\beta}_0 - \hat{\beta}_1)$ test is found. Then by applying it to the

[11] Using s_0^2 to estimate σ^2 corresponds to the Lagrange multiplier form of the test while using s_1, the IV estimate, corresponds to using the Wald form of the test. The tests differ under the alternative hypothesis depending on the estimate of the nuisance parameter σ^2 which is used. Silvey **[23]** discusses the large sample relationship of the tests.

[12] For $V(\hat{q})$ to be nonsingular here, it is necessary that enough instruments be available to insure that $X_1 - \hat{X}_1$ has rank q.

[13] For the true regression problem (no lagged endogenous variables) under both the null hypothesis of no serial correlation and the alternative hypothesis $\hat{\beta}_0$, the OLS estimator, is unbiased and consistent since only assumption (1.1b) is violated. Therefore, if the null hypothesis of serial correlation is tested with an autoregressive estimator $\hat{\beta}_1$, plim $\hat{q} = \bar{q} = 0$ under *both* hypotheses. If $\hat{q}$ is large relative to its standard error, misspecification is likely to be present.

errors in variables problem, an easy method to apply the test is demonstrated which also makes power considerations clearer. The usefulness of this test is unfortunately decreased by the lack of a valid instrument in some situations. The next misspecification test, however, always can be done since the necessary data is available. It is a test of the random effects model which has been widely used in econometrics.

3. TIME SERIES-CROSS SECTION MODELS

Time series-cross section models have become increasingly important in econometrics. Many surveys, rather than being limited to a single cross section, now follow a panel of individuals over time. These surveys lead to a rich body of data given the wide variability between individuals coupled with much less variability for a given individual over time. Another important use of these models is to estimate demand across states over a period of time. Since for many goods (e.g., energy) considerable price variation exists across states while aggregate price indices move smoothly over time, time series-cross section models allow disentanglement of income and substitution effects which is often difficult to do with aggregate data.

The simplest time series-cross section model is specified as

$$y_{it} = X_{it}\beta + \mu_i + \varepsilon_{it} \qquad (i = 1, N; t = 1, T), \tag{3.1}$$

where μ_i is the individual effect. The two alternative specifications of the model differ in their treatment of the individual effect. The so-called fixed effects model treats μ_i as a fixed but unknown constant differing across individuals. Therefore, least squares on equation (3.1) is the correct estimator. To estimate the slope coefficients, deviation from means are used leading to the transformed observations $\tilde{y}_{it} = y_{it} - \bar{y}_i$, $\tilde{X}_{it} = X_{it} - \bar{X}_i$, $\tilde{\varepsilon}_{it} = \varepsilon_{it} - \bar{\varepsilon}_i$, and the regression specification,[14]

$$\tilde{y}_{it} = \tilde{X}_{it}\beta + \tilde{\varepsilon}_{it}. \tag{3.2}$$

An equivalent way of writing equation (3.2) is to let e be a T column vector of ones so that $e = (1, 1, \ldots, 1)'$ and to let $P_e = e(e'e)^{-1}e' = (1/T)ee' = (1/T)J_T$ with $Q_e = I \otimes (I - P_e)$. Then the fixed effects specification on the stacked model is

$$Q_e y = Q_e X\beta + Q_e\alpha + Q_e\varepsilon = \tilde{X}\beta + \tilde{\varepsilon} \tag{3.3}$$

which is identical to equation (3.2) since $Q_e\alpha = 0$.

The alternative specification for the time series-cross section model is known as the random effects or variance components model. Instead of treating μ_i as a fixed constant, this specification assumes that μ_i is drawn from an idd distribution, $\mu_i \sim N(0, \sigma_\mu^2)$, and is uncorrelated both with the ε_i and with the X_{it}. The specification then becomes

$$y_{it} = X_{it}\beta + \eta_{it}, \quad \eta_{it} = \mu_i + \varepsilon_{it}, \tag{3.4}$$

[14] Analysis of variance notation is being used, e.g., $\bar{y}_i = (1/T)\Sigma_{t=1}^{T} y_{it}$.

so that $E\eta = 0$ and the covariance matrix is block diagonal:

$$\Omega = V(\eta) = \begin{bmatrix} \sigma_\mu^2 J_T + \sigma_\varepsilon^2 I_T & & 0 \\ & \sigma_\mu^2 J_T + \sigma_\varepsilon^2 I_T & \\ 0 & & \sigma_\mu^2 J_T + \sigma_\varepsilon^2 I_T \end{bmatrix}. \tag{3.5}$$

Here the appropriate estimator is generalized least squares $\hat{\beta}_{GLS} = (X'\Omega^{-1}X)^{-1}X'\Omega^{-1}y$ which can be expressed in least squares form by transforming the variables by $\check{y}_{it} = y_{it} - \gamma\bar{y}_i$, $\check{X}_{it} = X_{it} - \gamma\bar{X}_i$ and then running ordinary least squares where

$$\gamma = 1 - \left(\frac{\sigma_\varepsilon^2}{\sigma_\varepsilon^2 + T\sigma_\mu^2}\right)^{\frac{1}{2}}. \tag{3.6}$$ [15]

Usually the variances, σ_μ^2 and σ_ε^2, are not known, so consistent estimates are derived from initial least squares estimates to form $\hat{\gamma}$ (see Wallace and Hussain [**24**]. This estimator is asymptotically efficient; and, if iterated to convergence, it yields the maximum likelihood estimates.

The choice of specification seems to rest on two considerations, one logical and the other statistical. The logical consideration is whether the μ_i can be considered random and drawn from an iid distribution. Both Scheffé [**21**] and Searle [**22**] contain excellent discussions of this question within an analysis of variance framework. Another way to consider the problem, suggested by Gary Chamberlain, is to decide whether the μ_i's satisfy di Finnetti's exchangeability criterion which is both necessary and sufficient for random sampling. Briefly, the criterion is to consider the sample $\boldsymbol{\mu} = (\mu_1, \ldots, \mu_N)$ and to see whether we can exchange μ_i and μ_j (e.g., the constant for Rhode Island and California) while maintaining the same subjective distribution. If this logical criterion is satisfied, as it might well be for models of individuals like an earnings function, then the random effects specification seems appropriate. A statistical consideration is then to compare the bias and efficiency of the two estimators in estimating β, the slope coefficients.[16] Wallace and Hussain [**24**], Maddala [**13**], and Nerlove [**15**] have recently discussed this issue, all pointing out that the estimators become identical as T becomes large in the appropriate way as can be seen by the definition of γ in equation (3.6). Since the case in econometrics is usually that N is large relative to T, differences between the two estimators are an important problem.

[15] This method of estimating the random effects models seems to have gone unnoticed in the literature. It requires less computation than the usual GLS method or the matrix weighted average of two estimates.

[16] In other words, even if one decides that the random effects specification is appropriate on logical grounds, he may decide to use the fixed effects *estimator* which conditions on the particular sample of μ_i, thus treating them as fixed in the sample.

Under the random effects specification $\hat{\beta}_{GLS}$ is the asymptotically efficient estimator while the fixed effects estimator $\hat{\beta}_{FE}$ is unbiased and consistent but not efficient.[17] However, an important issue of specification arises which was pointed out by Maddala [**13**, p. 357] and has been further emphasized by Mundlak [**14**]. The specification issue is whether the conditional mean of the μ_i can be regarded as independent of the X_{it}'s, i.e., whether $E(\mu_i|X_{it})=0$.[18] If this assumption is violated, the random effects estimator is biased and inconsistent while the fixed effects estimator is not affected by this failure of orthogonality. Consider an individual earnings equation over time. If an unobserved variable, "spunk", affects education and has an additional effect on earnings, then the assumption of independent μ_i's will be violated. Thus, a natural test of the null hypothesis of independent μ_i's is to consider the difference between the two estimators, $\hat{q}=\hat{\beta}_{FE}-\hat{\beta}_{GLS}$. If no misspecification is present, then $\hat{q}$ should be near zero. Using the lemma, $V(\hat{q})=V(\hat{\beta}_{FE})-V(\hat{\beta}_{GLS})$ so a specification test follows from $m=\hat{q}'\hat{M}(\hat{q})^{-1}\hat{q}$ where $\hat{M}(\hat{q})=(X'Q_eX)^{-1}-(X'\hat{\Omega}^{-1}X)^{-1}$. If the random effects specification is correct the two estimates should be near each other, rather than differing widely as has been reported sometimes in the literature as a virtue of the random effects specification. Therefore, while Maddala [**13**, p. 343] demonstrates that $\hat{\beta}_{GLS}$ is a matrix weighted average of $\hat{\beta}_{FE}$ (the within group estimator) and the between group estimator, if the specification is correct then plim $\hat{q}=0$ so $\hat{\beta}_{GLS}$ and $\hat{\beta}_{FE}$ should be almost the same within sampling error. When the econometrician finds his estimates $\hat{\beta}_{FE}$ to be unsatisfactory, this evidence is a finding against his specification, not his choice of estimator. However, he should not necessarily accept the fixed effects estimates as correct but should reconsider the specification because errors in variables problems may be present which invalidate the fixed effects estimates.[19]

The equivalent test in the regression format is to test $\alpha=0$ from doing least squares on

$$(3.7)\qquad \check{y}=\check{X}\hat{\beta}+\tilde{X}\alpha+v$$

where $\check{y}$ and $\check{X}$ are the γ transformed random effects variables while $\tilde{X}$ are the deviations from means variables from the fixed effects specification. The tests can be shown to be equivalent using the methods of the previous section and the fact that $Q_e\check{y}=Q_ey$. This test is easy to perform since $\check{X}$ and $\tilde{X}$ differ only in the choice of γ from equation (4.6) while $\tilde{X}$ has $\gamma=1$.

[17] A potentially important problem for the fixed effects estimator is its sensitivity to errors in variables. Since much variation is removed in forming deviations from individual means, the amount of inconsistency would be greater for the fixed effects estimates if errors in variables are present.

[18] If the regression specification of equation (3.1) is expanded to include a lagged endogenous variable, this variable is correlated by definition with the μ_i. Nerlove [**15**] discusses methods to estimate this specification. The test presented here would then be used to ascertain whether the μ_i are uncorrelated with the exogenous variables.

[19] Another possible test is to consider the difference of $\hat{\beta}_{FE}$, the within group estimator, from the between group estimator. Since the estimators are based on orthogonal projections, the variance of the difference equals the sum of the variances. However, this test seems less powerful than the test proposed here since our test statistic subtracts off the GLS variance from the fixed effects variance rather than adding on the between groups variance. The difference arises because our test uses the efficient estimator to form the comparison with the fixed effects estimator.

If $\hat{\gamma}$ is near unity the two estimators will give similar results and $\hat{q}$ will be near zero. It will often be the case in econometrics that $\hat{\gamma}$ will not be near unity. In many applications σ_{μ}^2 is small relative to σ_{ε}^2; and the problem sometimes arises that when σ_{μ}^2 is estimated from the data it may turn out to be negative. For a panel followed over time the X_{it} are often constant so that some of the parameters of interest will be absorbed into the individual constant when the fixed effects estimator is used. However, it seems preferable to have alternative estimates of the remaining slope coefficients to try to sort out possible interaction of the individual constants with the included right-hand-side variables. The misspecification test from equation (3.7) thus seems a desirable test of the random effects specification.[20]

In this section a test of the implicit assumption behind the random effects specification has been considered. This test should follow the logical specification of whether the μ_i are truly random. Thus, the situation is very similar to simultaneous equation estimation which follows the logical question of identification. In the next section, the specification of simultaneous equation systems is considered, and a test is developed for correct system specification.

4. SPECIFICATION OF SIMULTANEOUS EQUATION SYSTEMS

Most estimation associated with simultaneous equation models has used single equation, limited information estimators. Thus, two stage least sequares (2SLS) is by far the most widely used estimator. If a simultaneous equation system is estimated equation by equation, no check on the "internal consistency" of the entire specification is made. An important potential source of information on misspecification is thus neglected. This neglect is not total; one class of tests compares estimates of the unrestricted reduced form model with the derived reduced form estimates from the structural model as a test of the overidentifying restrictions.[21] Unfortunately, this type of test has not been widely used. Perhaps the reason has been the inconvenience of calculating the likelihood value or the nonlinear expansions which are required to perform the statistical comparison. In this section a test of system specification is proposed within a more simple framework. The test rests on a comparison of 2SLS to 3SLS estimates. Thus, the econometrician is comparing two different estimates of the structural parameters rather than the reduced form parameters. Usually, he has more knowledge about what comprises a "significant difference" with respect to the structural parameters. Under the null hypothesis of correct specification, 3SLS is efficient

[20] As previously mentioned, as T becomes large, γ in equation (3.6) approaches one and the two estimators approach each other. Thus both the numerator and denominator of the test statistic approach zero. The test appears to remain valid so long as γ does not exactly equal one and N increases faster than T; however, numerical problems of inverting a near singular matrix may arise.

[21] Within the single equation context this test has been proposed by Anderson and Rubin [**1**], Basmann [**2**], and Koopmans and Hood [**11**]. Within the full information context the likelihood ratio (LR) test has been used. Recently, Byron [**4, 5**] has simplified this test by advocating use of the Lagrange multiplier test or the Wald test both of which are asymptotically equivalent to the LR test under the null hypothesis. For further details see Silvey [**23**, Ch. 7].

but yields inconsistent estimates of all equations if any equation is misspecified. 2SLS is not as efficient as 3SLS, but only the incorrectly specified equation is inconsistently estimated if misspecification is present in the system. Thus, instead of comparing reduced form parameter estimates about which the econometrician often has little knowledge, the test compares estimates of the structural form parameters which he should have a better feeling for since they are derived from economic theory and are reported in estimates of other structural models.

Consider the standard linear simultaneous equation model

$$YB + Z\Gamma = U \tag{4.1}$$

where Y is the $T\times M$ matrix of jointly dependent variables, Z is the $T\times K$ matrix of predetermined variables, and U is a $T\times M$ matrix of structural disturbances of the system. Full column rank of Z, nonsingularity of B, nonsingular probability limits of second order moment matrices, and the rank condition for identification are all assumed to hold. The structural disturbances are multivariate normal $U\sim N(0, \Sigma\otimes I_T)$. After a choice of normalization and imposition of zero restrictions each equation is written

$$y_i = X_i\delta_i + U_i \quad \text{where} \quad X_i = [Y_i Z_i] \quad \text{and} \quad \delta_i = \begin{bmatrix}\beta_i\\ \gamma_i\end{bmatrix}, \tag{4.2}$$

where β_i has r_i elements and γ_i has σ_i elements which correspond to the variables in X_i whose coefficients are not known a priori to be zero. It is convenient to stack the M equations into a system

$$y = X\delta + U \quad \text{where} \tag{4.3}$$

$$y = \begin{bmatrix} y_1\\ \vdots \\ y_M\end{bmatrix}, \quad X = \begin{bmatrix} X_1 & & 0\\ & \ddots & \\ 0 & & X_M\end{bmatrix}, \quad \delta = \begin{bmatrix}\delta_1\\ \vdots\\ \delta_M\end{bmatrix}, \quad U = \begin{bmatrix} U_1\\ \vdots\\ U_M\end{bmatrix}.$$

The two stage least squares estimator when used on each equation of the system can conveniently be written in stacked form as $\hat{\delta}_2 = (X'\tilde{P}_Z X)^{-1}X'\tilde{P}_Z y$ where $\tilde{P}_Z = I_M \otimes Z(Z'Z)^{-1}Z'$. To simplify notation rewrite the estimator as $\hat{\delta}_2 = (\hat{X}'\hat{X})^{-1}\hat{X}'y$. Three stage least squares uses full information and links together all equations of the system through the estimate of the covariance matrix $\hat{\Sigma}$. Letting $\tilde{P}_{\Sigma Z} = \hat{\Sigma}^{-1}\otimes Z(Z'Z)^{-1}Z'$, the 3SLS estimator is $\hat{\delta}_3 = (X'\tilde{P}_{\Sigma Z}X)^{-1}X'\tilde{P}_{\Sigma Z}y$ which is simplified to $\hat{\delta}_3 = (\tilde{X}'\tilde{X})^{-1}\tilde{X}'y$.[22] Now 3SLS transmits misspecificiation throughout the entire system, affecting the estimates of all coefficients since $\hat{\delta}_3 - \delta = (\tilde{X}'\tilde{X})^{-1}\tilde{X}'U$. Thus, if the jth equation is misspecified plim $(1/T)\hat{X}_i'U_j \neq 0$, and so assuming probability limits exist with $\hat{\Sigma}$

[22] If $T \leq K$ so 2SLS and 3SLS cannot be used, asymptotically equivalent instrumental variable estimators are discussed in Brundy and Jorgenson [3], Dhrymes [7], and Hausman [10]. Thus, the current misspecification test can be applied when the full information likelihood ratio test is not possible because unrestricted estimates of the reduced form cannot be made due to sample size limitations.

being the probability limit of the inconsistent estimate of Σ with $\tilde{\sigma}^{ij}$ the element of its inverse, the inconsistency is calculated from plim $(\hat{\delta}_3 - \delta) =$ plim $((1/T)\hat{X}'\tilde{X})^{-1} \cdot$ plim $((1/T)\hat{X}'U)$. Looking at the crucial last term more closely, consider the unknown elements from the first equation δ_1. The last term takes the form

$$\text{(4.4)} \qquad \text{plim} \frac{1}{T} \sum_{m=1}^{M} \tilde{\sigma}^{1m} \hat{X}_1' U_m$$

so that the amount of inconsistency for the first equation due to misspecification in the jth equation depends both on the lack of orthogonality between $\hat{X}_1$ and U_j, and also on the size of $\tilde{\sigma}^{1j}$.

Lemma 2.1 leads us to consider the specification test based on the difference between the two estimators $\sqrt{T}\hat{q} = \sqrt{T}(\hat{\delta}_2 - \hat{\delta}_3)$ which has large sample variance $V(\hat{q}) = V(\hat{\delta}_2) - V(\hat{\delta}_3)$. However, an alternative procedure is to consider the regression on the stacked system

$$\text{(4.5)} \qquad y = \hat{X}\tilde{\delta} + \tilde{X}\alpha + V$$

and to test whether $\alpha = 0$. Since $\hat{X}$ and $\tilde{X}$ are computed by programs which have 2SLS and 3SLS estimators, the regression of equation (5.5) should not be difficult to perform.

The noncentrality parameter of the local noncentral χ^2 distribution will be proportional to plim $(1/T)\hat{X}_i'U_i$ for any equation which is misspecified and also the magnitude of the covariance elements $\tilde{\sigma}^{ij}$. If the inverse covariance elements are large, then $\hat{X}$ and $\tilde{X}$ will not be highly correlated so that the test will be powerful for a given size of inconsistency. As the $\tilde{\sigma}^{ij}$'s go to zero, then 3SLS approaches 2SLS and the test will have little power. Since the misspecification represented by the alternative hypothesis is not specific, the appropriate action to take in the case of rejection of H_0 is not clear. One only knows that misspecification is present somewhere in the system. If one is confident that one or more equations are correctly specified, then the specification of other equations could be checked by using them, say one at a time, to form a 3SLS type estimator. That is, if equation 1 is correct and equation 2 is to be tested, then 2SLS on equation 1 could be compared to 3SLS on equation 1 where $\hat{\sigma}_{ij}$ is set to zero for $i \neq j$ except for $i = 1, j = 2$ and vice-versa in the 3SLS estimator. Using this method the misspecification might be isolated; but, unfortunately, the size of the test is too complicated to calculate when done on a sequence of equations.[23]

The simultaneous equations specification test is the last to be presented although the same principle may be applied to further cases such as aggregation. I now turn to an empirical example of the specification test to demonstrate its potential usefulness.

[23] If one attempts to check the specification of the entire system by comparing the 2SLS and 3SLS estimates, the χ^2 test of Theorem 2.1 is appropriate under H_0. However, under H_1 the non-central χ^2 distribution is no longer appropriate since the 2SLS estimates are also inconsistent.

5. EMPIRICAL EXAMPLE

Comparing two alternative estimators as a means of constructing misspecification tests has been applied to a number of situations in the preceding sections. In this section an empirical example is presented. The example is the time series-cross section specification test discussion in Section 4. This type of data set is becoming increasingly common for econometric studies such as individuals' earnings, education, and labor supply. However, added interest in this test comes from the fact that it also implicitly tests much cross section analysis of similar specifications. Cross section analysis can allow for no individual constant but must assume, as does random effect analysis, that the right hand side variables are orthogonal to the residual: If the random effect specification is rejected serious doubt may be cast therefore on much similar cross section analysis.

For the time-series-cross-section specification test a wage equation is estimated for male high school graduates in the Michigan income dynamics study.[24] The sample consists of 629 individuals for whom all six years of observations are present. A wage equation has been chosen due to its importance in "human capital" analysis. The specification used follows from equation (3.1). The right hand side variables include a piecewise linear representation of age, the presence of unemployment or poor health in the previous year, and dummy variables for self-employment, living in the South, or in a rural area. The fixed effects estimates, $\hat{\beta}_{FE}$, are calculated from equation (3.3). They include an individual constant for each person and are consistent under both the null hypothesis of no misspecification and the alternative hypothesis. The random effects estimates, $\hat{\beta}_{GLS}$, are calculated from equations (3.4)–(3.6). The estimate of $\hat{\gamma}$ from equation (3.6) is .72736 which follows from least squares estimates of the individual variance $\hat{\sigma}_\mu^2 = .12594$ and the residual variance $\hat{\sigma}_\varepsilon^2 = .06068$. Under the null hypothesis the GLS estimate is asymptotically efficient, but under the alternative hypothesis it is inconsistent. The specification test consists of seeing how large the difference in estimates is, $\hat{q} = \hat{\beta}_{FE} - \hat{\beta}_{GLS}$, in relation to its variance $M(\hat{q}) = M(\hat{\beta}_{FE}) - M(\hat{\beta}_{GLS})$ which follows from Lemma (2.1). In comparing the estimates in column 1 and column 2 of Table I it is apparent that substantial differences are present in the two sets of estimates relative to their standard errors which are presented in column 3.[25] The effects of unemployment, self-employment, and geographical location differ widely in the two models. The geographical differences may be explained by the implicitly different way that migration is handled in the two specifications since the fixed effects coefficient specification coefficients only represent changes during the sample period. Unobserved individual characteristics might well be correlated with geographical location. Also, the effect of unemployment in the previous year is seen to be much less

[24] The specification used is based on research by Gordon [9] who also kindly helped me construct this example.

[25] Note that the elements of $\hat{q}$ and its standard errors are simply calculated given the estimates of $\hat{\beta}_{FE}$ and $\hat{\beta}_{GLS}$ and their standard errors, making sure to adjust to use the fixed effects estimate of σ_ε^2. The main computational burden involves forming and inverting $M(\hat{q})$.

TABLE I

DEPENDENT VARIABLE—LOG WAGE[a]

Variable	Fixed Effects	Random Effects	$\hat{q}$	$\hat{\alpha}$
1. Age 1 (20–35)	.0557	.0393	.0164	.0291
	(.0042)	(.0033)	(.0030)	(.0060)
2. Age 2 (35–45)	.0351	.0092	.0259	.0015
	(.0051)	(.0036)	(.0039)	(.0070)
3. Age 3 (45–55)	.0209	−.0007	.0216	.0058
	(.0055)	(.0042)	(.0040)	(.0083)
4. Age 4 (55–65)	.0209	−.0097	.0306	−.0308
	(.0078)	(.0060)	(.0050)	(.0112)
5. Age 5 (65–)	−.0171	−.0423	.0252	−.0380
	(.0155)	(.0121)	(.0110)	(.0199)
6. Unemployed$_{-1}$	−.0042	−.0277	.0235	−.3290
	(.0153)	(.0151)	(.0069)	(.0914)
7. Poor Health$_{-1}$	−.0204	−.0250	.0046	−.1716
	(.0221)	(.0215)	(.0105)	(.0762)
8. Self-Employment	−.2190	−.2670	.0480	−.3110
	(.0297)	(.0263)	(.0178)	(.0558)
9. South	−.1569	−.0324	−.1245	.0001
	(.0656)	(.0333)	(.0583)	(.0382)
10. Rural	−.0101	−.1215	.1114	−.2531
	(.0317)	(.0237)	(.0234)	(.0352)
11. Constant	—	.8499	—	—
	—	(.0433)	—	—
s^2	.0567	.0694		.0669
degrees of freedom	3135	3763		3753

[a] 3774 observations. Standard errors are in parentheses.

important in affecting the wage in the fixed effects specification. Thus, unemployment has a more limited and transitory effect once permanent individual differences are accounted for. The test of misspecification which follows from Lemma 2.1 is

$$(5.1) \qquad m = \hat{q}'\hat{M}(\hat{q})^{-1}\hat{q} = 129.9.$$

Since m is distributed asymptotically as χ^2_{10} which has a critical value of 23.2 at the 1 per cent level, very strong evidence of misspecification in the random effects model is present. The right hand side variables X_{it} are not orthogonal to the individual constant μ_i so that the null hypothesis is decisively rejected. Considerable doubt about previous cross section work on wage equations may arise from this example.

The reason for this doubt about previous cross section estimation is that ordinary least squares on a cross section of one year will have the same expectation as $\hat{\beta}_{GLS}$, the random effects estimate, on the time series-cross section data. For example, cross section estimates of the wage equation have no individual constants and make assumption (1.1a) that the residual is uncorrelated with the right-hand-side variables. However, this example demonstrates that in the Michigan survey important individual effects are present which are *not* uncorrelated with the right-hand variables. Since the random effects estimates seem significantly biased with high probability, it may well be important to take account of permanent unobserved differences across individuals. This problem can only be resolved within a time series-cross section framework using a specification which allows testing of an important maintained hypothesis of much cross section estimation in econometrics. Thus, the importance of this type of data is emphasized which permits us to test previously maintained hypotheses.

An equivalent formulation of the specification test is provided by the regression framework of equation (3.7). Instead of having to manipulate 10×10 matrices, $\check{y}$ is regressed on both $\check{X}$ and $\tilde{X}$. The test of the null hypothesis is then whether $\hat{\alpha}=0$. As is apparent from column 4 of Table I many of the elements of $\hat{\alpha}$ are well over twice their standard error so that misspecification is clearly present. The misspecification test follows easily from comparing s^2, the estimated variance from the random effects specification, to s^2 from the augmented specification

$$(5.2)\qquad m=\frac{.06938-.06689}{.06689}\cdot 3754=139.7.$$

Again m well exceeds the approximate critical χ^2 value of 23.2. Since this form of the test is so easy to implement when using a random effects specification as only one additional weighted least squares regression is required, hopefully applied econometricians will find it a useful device for testing specification.

The empirical example presented in this section illustrates use of the misspecification test. The example rejects an application of the random effects specification. I feel that this finding may well be quite general, and that the uncorrelated random effects model is not well suited to many econometric applications. The two requirements of exchangeability and orthogonality are not likely to be met in many applied problems. Certainly, the random effects estimates should be compared with the fixed effects estimates to see if significant differences occur. If they do, the specification of the equation should be reconsidered to either explain the difference or to try a different specification which corrects the problem.

6. EXTENSIONS AND CONCLUSION

Another possible application of the methodology presented here arises when one wants to test whether only a limited part of a model specification differs. For instance, consider two different model specifications, where the difference arises because the second specification has additional parameters which are restricted in the first specification, e.g., sample selection specifications. One could do maximum likelihood on each specification and then perform a likelihood ratio test thus comparing the different specifications. However, if interest of the model centers on a particular parameter which is unrestricted in both specifications, the traditional methodology yields no way to test for a significant difference only in that parameter. Lemma 2.1 applies so this paper provides a simple method of testing the hypothesis of a significant difference in that particular parameter since the unrestricted model is inefficient under the null hypothesis while it is consistent under both the null and alternative hypotheses.

By using the result that under the null hypothesis of no misspecification, an asymptotically efficient estimator must have zero covariance with its difference from a consistent, but asymptotically inefficient estimator, specification tests are devised from a number of important model specifications in econometrics. New tests for the cross section-time series model and for the simultaneous equation model are presented. Lastly, an empirical example is provided. The example provides strong evidence that unobserved individual factors are present which are not orthogonal to included right-hand-side variables in a common econometric specification.

Massachusetts Institute of Technology

Manuscript received August, 1976; final revision received April, 1978.

REFERENCES

[1] ANDERSON, T. W., AND H. RUBIN: "Estimation of the Parameters of a Single Stochastic Equation in a Complete System of Stochastic Equations," *Annals of Mathematical Statistics*, 20 (1949), 46–63.

[2] BASMANN, R. L.: "A Generalized Classical Method of Linear Estimation of Coefficients in a Structural Equation," *Econometrica*, 25 (1957), 77–83.

[3] BRUNDY J., AND D. W. JORGENSON: "Efficient Estimation of Simultaneous Equation Systems by Instrumental Variables," *Review of Economics and Statistics*, 53 (1971), 207–224.

[4] BYRON, R. P.: "Testing for Misspecification in Econometric Systems Using Full Information," *International Economic Review*, 13 (1972), 745–756.

[5] ———: "Testing Structural Specification Using the Unrestricted Reduced Form," *Econometrica*, 42 (1974), 869–883.

[6] COX, D. R., AND D. V. HINKLEY: *Theoretical Statistics*. London: Chapman and Hall, 1974.

[7] DHRYMES, P. J.: "A Simplified Structural Estimator for Large-Scale Econometric Models," *Australian Journal of Statistics*, 13 (1971), 168–175.

[8] FISHER, R. A.: "Theory of Statistical Estimation," *Cambridge Philosophical Society Proceedings*, 22 (1925), 700–725.

[9] GORDON, R.: "Essays on the Causes and Equitable Treatment of Differences in Earnings and Ability," Massachusetts Institute of Technology Ph.D. Thesis, June, 1976.

[10] HAUSMAN, J.: "An Instrumental Variable Approach to Full-Information Estimators for Linear and Certain Nonlinear Econometric Models," *Econometrica*, 43 (1975), 727–738.

[11] KOOPMANS, T. C., AND W. HOOD: "The Estimation of Simultaneous Economic Relationships," in *Studies in Econometric Method*, ed. by W. Hood and T. C. Koopmans. New Haven: Yale University Press, 1953, pp. 113–199.

[12] LIVIATAN, N.: "Tests of the Permanent Income Hypothesis Based on a Re-interview Savings Study," in *Measurement in Economics*, ed. by C. Christ. Stanford: Stanford University Press, 1963, pp. 29–59.

[13] MADDALA, G. S.: "The Use of Variance Components Models in Pooling Cross Section and Time Series Data," *Econometrica*, 39 (1971), 341–358.

[14] MUNDLAK, Y.: "On the Pooling of Time Series and Cross Section Data," 1976, mimeo.

[15] NERLOVE, M.: "A Note on Error Component Models," *Econometrica*, 39 (1971), 383–396.

[16] RAMSEY, J. B.: "Classical Model Selection through Specification Error Tests," in *Frontiers of Econometrics*, ed. by P. Zarembka. New York: Academic Press, 1974.

[17] RAE, C. R.: *Linear Statistical Inference*. New York: Wiley, 1973.

[18] ROTHENBERG, T. J.: *Efficient Estimation With A Priori Information*. New Haven: Yale University Press, 1973.

[19] ROTHENBERG, T. J.: "The Asymptotic Distribution of the Least Squares Estimator in the Errors in Variables Model," mimeo, 1972.

[20] SARGAN, J. D.: "The Estimation of Economic Relationships Using Instrumental Variables," *Econometrica*, 26 (1958), 393–415.

[21] SCHEFFÉ, H.: *Analysis of Variance*. New York: Wiley, 1959.

[22] SEARLE, P.: *Linear Models*. New York: Wiley, 1971.

[23] SILVEY, S. D.: *Statistical Inference*. Harmondsworth: Penguin Press, 1970.

[24] WALLACE, T. D., AND A. HUSSAIN: "The Use of Error Components Models in Combining Cross Section with Time Series Data," *Econometrica*, 37 (1969), 57–72.

[25] WU, D.: "Alternative Tests of Independence Between Stochastic Regressors and Disturbances," *Econometrica*, 41 (1973), 733–750.

[6]

Econometrica, Vol. 46, No. 1 (January, 1978)

ON THE POOLING OF TIME SERIES AND CROSS SECTION DATA[1]

BY YAIR MUNDLAK

In empirical analysis of data consisting of repeated observations on economic units (time series on a cross section) it is often assumed that the coefficients of the quantitiative variables (slopes) are the same, whereas the coefficients of the qualitative variables (intercepts or effects) vary over units or periods. This is the constant-slope variable-intercept framework. In such an analysis an explicit account should be taken of the statistical dependence that exists between the quantitative variables and the effects. It is shown that when this is done, the random effect approach and the fixed effect approach yield the same estimate for the slopes, the "within" estimate. Any matrix combination of the "within" and "between" estimates is generally biased. When the "within" estimate is subject to a relatively large error a minimum mean square error can be applied, as is generally done in regression analysis. Such an estimator is developed here from a somewhat different point of departure.

1. INTRODUCTION

The use of a sample consisting of time series observations on a cross section constitutes an important problem of empirical research in economics. A simple version of this problem is concerned with the estimation of a vector of parameters $\underset{\sim}{\beta}$ in the relation.

$$(1.1)\qquad \underset{\sim}{Y} = X\underset{\sim}{\beta} + \underset{\sim}{\varepsilon}$$

where $\underset{\sim}{Y}$ and $\underset{\sim}{\varepsilon}$ are n-vectors, X is a $n \times k$ matrix of full rank and $\underset{\sim}{\beta}$ is a k vector of parameters to be estimated. The error term is decomposed into:

$$(1.2)\qquad \varepsilon_{it} = m_i + s_t + u_{it}$$

where m_i and s_t are the systematic components, or effects, associated with the ith economic unit and the tth period (year) respectively; $i = 1, \dots, N$; $t = 1, \dots, T$ and $n = NT$. Thus, it is recognized that $X\underset{\sim}{\beta}$ does not account for all the systematic variations in $\underset{\sim}{Y}$.

The question is what effect should the decomposition (1.2) have on the method of estimation. Basically, two alternative approaches have been suggested, the "fixed effects" (FE) and the "random effects" (RE) of the analysis of variance. Each of the two models has been associated with a different estimator, the FE has resulted in the "within" estimator of covariance analysis [**14**] whereas the RE has led to a GLSE [**2, 23**]. Knowing the variances in question, it is generally true that the GLSE is BLUE and therefore the current thinking among some writers has been to prefer this estimator. Furthermore, it has been explained that the gain in efficiency results from the utilization of the "between" estimator in addition to the within estimator. Since the GLSE is associated with the RE, its use had to be

[1] This is a revised and shorter version of [**17**]. At points, reference is made to [**17**] for more details. This work has been supported by an NSF Grant #SOC73-05374AO1. I have greatly benefited from the insight of Gary Chamberlain in discussions of the model. This, as well as the helpful comments of Zvi Griliches are reflected in the paper.

justified by arguing that economic effects are indeed random and not fixed. This position is well presented by Maddala **[11]**.

The present state of thinking is unsatisfactory for two major reasons: first, the suggested rules for deciding whether an effect is fixed or random are at best inadequate. Second, the proposed GLSE approach has completely neglected the consequences of the correlation which may exist between the effects and the explanatory variables. Such a correlation leads to a biased estimator and it is the elimination of this bias that has originally led to the use of the covariance analysis estimator **[14]**.

This paper proposes to remedy the situation by first indicating that the whole approach which calls for a decision on the nature of the effect, whether it is random or fixed, is both, arbitrary and unnecessary. Without a loss in generality, it can be assumed from the outset that the effects are random and view the FE inference as a conditional inference, that is, conditional on the effects that are in the sample. It is up to the user of the statistics to decide whether he wants inference with respect to the population of all effects or only with respect to the effects that are in the sample.[2] This view unifies the two approaches in a well defined form and eliminates any arbitrariness in deciding about "nature," in a way which is influenced by the subsequent choice of a "desirable" estimator.

If the foregoing approach is accepted the question is why would a uniform approach lead to two competing estimators for β, the coefficients which do not vary over individuals. That brings us to the second point which can be stated very simply: when the model is properly specified, the GLSE is identical to the "within" estimator. Thus there is only one estimator. The whole literature which has been based on an imaginary difference between the two estimators, starting with Balestra and Nerlove **[2]** is based on an incorrect specification which ignores the correlation between the effects and the explanatory variables.

It is thus argued that there is a uniform approach and a unique estimator. Furthermore, to obtain the correct GLSE of β, it is not necessary to know the components of variance. If this is the case, the old question of what to do if the within estimator has a large variance still remains but it is not different in nature from the question of having too many variables in a regression. One way to deal with this question is to use a mean square error estimator (MSEE). This is not a new idea but it is integrated into the discussion here.

The foregoing comments summarize the main points of the paper. In the remainder of this section we outline the plan of the paper and give some more detailed results. The model is outlined in Section 2. The formulation takes an explicit account of the relationships between the effects and the explanatory variables. Section 3 evaluates the performance of the alternative estimators under the RE set up. It is shown that the GLSE of β is the within estimator. Furthermore, when the effects are not correlated with the explanatory variables, the within and the between estimators are the same and therefore any weighted matrix combination thereof will be the same. What has been known in the literature as the GLSE for the error component model is actually a restricted

[2] The move to the unconditional inference requires that the sample be randomly drawn.

estimator, and when the restriction does not hold it is a biased estimator. A similar analysis is conducted under the FE model in Section 4.

The MSE estimator is introduced and discussed in Section 5. Basically, this estimator minimizes the MSE of the estimate of any linear combination of β. It requires a two stage procedure. The whole motivation for introducing the GLSE has been to gain efficiency. The question of efficiency is particularly important in small samples. The variance of the within estimator declines with the size of the sample as determined by increasing either the number of observations per unit or the number of units. Thus, any alternative estimator which increases the precision in small samples at the expense of unbiasedness should have the property of converging to the within estimator or simply be consistent. As shown in Section 6, the restricted GLS estimator is inconsistent and asymptotically biased when the sample increases by increasing the number of units rather than the number of observations per unit. This is of course the relevant process for increasing the sample size in economics. In contrast, the MSE estimator converges to the within estimator when the sample increases either by increasing the number of units or the number of observations per unit.

Section 7 outlines the analysis for a two way layout where "time effects" are added to individual effects. Section 8 outlines the estimation of the variance components which are necessary for statistical inference and the computation of the restricted GLS as well as the MSE estimators.

2. THE MODEL

Let us rewrite the basic equation to be estimated:

$$(2.1) \qquad \underset{\sim}{Y} = X\underset{\sim}{\beta} + Z\underset{\sim}{\alpha} + \underset{\sim}{u}$$

and assume

$$(2.2) \qquad \underset{\sim}{u} = (\underset{\sim}{0}, \sigma^2 I_n), \qquad E(\underset{\sim}{u}'X) = E(\underset{\sim}{u}'Z\underset{\sim}{\alpha}) = 0,$$

where $\underset{\sim}{Z}$ is a matrix of qualitative variables, or dummies, and $\underset{\sim}{\alpha}$ is a vector of effects. We now proceed under the assumption that there is no time effect and therefore we can write $Z = I_N \otimes \underset{\sim}{e}_T$ where $\underset{\sim}{e}_T$ is a T-vector on ones. However some of the discussion is not restricted to qualitative Z and it applies as well to quantitative Z. To simplify the discussion at this point, it is assumed that the X's are deviations from their sample means and the matrix (X, Z) is of full rank. A more general formulation is taken up in Section 7 below.

The properties of the various estimators to be considered depend on the existence and extent of the relations between the X's and the effects. In order to take an explicit account of such relationships we introduce the auxiliary regression:[3]

$$(2.3) \qquad \alpha_i = \underset{\sim}{X}_{it}\underset{\sim}{\pi} + w_{it};$$

averaging over t for a given i:

$$(2.4) \qquad \alpha_i = \underset{\sim}{X}_{i\cdot}\underset{\sim}{\pi} + w_{i\cdot}$$

[3] $(E\alpha_i|X)$ need not be linear. However, only the linear expression is pertinent for the present analysis.

It is assumed that

(2.5) $w_{i\cdot} \sim (0, \omega_1^2)$.

Clearly, $\underline{\pi} = \underline{0}$ if and only if the explanatory variables are uncorrelated with the effects. Let the projection matrix on the column space of Z be denoted as $K(Z) = Z(Z'Z)^{-1}Z'$ and its orthogonal complement by $M(Z) = I - K(Z)$. For the present definition of Z, $K(Z) \equiv K = I_N \otimes \bar{J}_T$ where $\bar{J}_T = (1/T)\underline{e}_T\underline{e}'_T$. Equation (2.4) can now be written as an NT vector:

(2.6) $Z\underline{\alpha} = K(X\underline{\pi} + \underline{W})$

where $\underline{W}$ is the NT-vector of w_{it}.

Combining (2.6) and (2.1) yields:

(2.7) $\underline{Y} = X\beta + K(X\underline{\pi} + \underline{W}) + \underline{U}$,

(2.8) $\underline{\varepsilon} \equiv \underline{U} + K\underline{W} \sim (\underline{0}, \sigma^2 I_{NT} + T\omega_1^2 K)$.[4]

We are now in a position to differentiate between the two models. Under the random effects we are concerned with the expectation of Y conditional on X and the grouping, to be denoted by Z. This is given by the systematic part of (2.7):

(2.9) $E(Y|\cdot) = X(\beta + K\pi)$

where $E(Y|\cdot) \equiv E(Y|X, Z)$. On the other hand, the FE model calls for the expectation of Y conditional on X and the effects to be denoted by $Z\underline{\alpha}$. This is given by the systematic part of (2.1):

(2.10) $E(Y|\cdot\cdot) = X\beta + Z\underline{\alpha}$

where $E(Y|\cdot\cdot) = E(Y|X, Z\underline{\alpha})$.

This is the framework for the subsequent analysis. In the following two sections we show that the within estimator is the GLS estimator for both models. At the same time we evaluate the moments of alternative estimators. The various estimators can all be generated by the expression:[5]

(2.11) $\underline{b}_F = A(F)\underline{Y}, A(F) = (X'FX)^{-1}X'F$.

In what follows we consider the following estimators:

Notation	Name	F
$\underline{b}_o$	OLS	I_{NT}
$\underline{b}_b$	Between	K
$\underline{b}_w$	Within	M
$\underline{b}_g$	GLS	Σ^{-1}

[4] A more general version of assumption (2.5) would call for a decomposition of w_{it} into systematic and random components with respect to the ith unit. Consequently, var $\underline{w} = \omega_0^2 I_{NT_2} + \omega_1^2 K$. For a given T, the two components are non-distinguishable and ω_0^2 can be ignored without affecting the analysis. However, a comparison of samples with different T may reveal such a decomposed variance structure.

[5] Unless otherwise indicated, it is assumed that rank $F \geqslant$ rank $X = k$. When this assumption is violated, a GI should replace the inverse in (2.11).

Σ is the variance of the error term and will be explicitly specified for each of the cases under consideration. In addition, the estimators will be differentiated by the restrictions which are imposed on the coefficients.

3. ESTIMATION UNDER THE RE MODEL (CONDITIONAL ON X AND Z)

Under the RE model $\underline{\beta}$ has to be estimated from equation (2.7). Starting with the GLSE, the relevant variance is given in (2.8). Consequently

$$\begin{aligned} &\Sigma^{-1}=\gamma_2 I_{NT}+\gamma_1 TK, \\ (3.1)\quad & \\ &\gamma_1=-\omega_1^2/\sigma^2(\sigma^2+T\omega_1^2), \qquad \gamma_2=1/\sigma^2. \end{aligned}$$

Then the GLSE of $\underline{\beta}$and $\underline{\pi}$ in (2.7) is given by:

$$(3.2)\qquad \begin{bmatrix} \underline{b}_g \\ \hat{\underline{\pi}}_g \end{bmatrix} = \left[\begin{pmatrix} X' \\ X'K \end{pmatrix}\Sigma^{-1}(X, KX)\right]^{-1}\Sigma^{-1}(X, KX)\underline{Y}.$$

Utilizing (3.1) and the expression for the inverse of a partitioned matrix, we can obtain after some simplications:

$$\begin{aligned} &\underline{b}_g=\underline{b}_w, \\ (3.3)\quad & \\ &\hat{\underline{\pi}}_g=\underline{b}_b-\underline{b}_w, \end{aligned}$$

where $\underline{b}_b$ and $\underline{b}_w$ are defined in Section 2. Thus, the GLSE is the within estimator and as such it does not depend on the knowledge of the variance components; in the present framework it is invariably BLUE.

The present analysis differs from previous discussions on the subject in that $KX\underline{\pi}$ appears in (2.7). The question is how is this estimator affected by when $\underline{\pi}=0$ and conversely what happens to estimators which restrict $\pi = 0$ when such restriction is violated. Starting with the first question, if $\underline{\pi}=0$, $\underline{b}_b$ and $\underline{b}_w$ have the same expectation and, therefore, their difference will only reflect sampling errors. Consequently, any matrix combination of them will also have the same expectation, a point of subsequent pertinence. The term $KX\underline{\pi}$ can also vanish when $KX=0$ which implies that there are no between individuals variations in the X's (recall that the X's are measured from their sample means). In this case, no between regression can be calculated.

We turn now to the second question, the consequence of imposing $\underline{\pi}=0$. We refer to such estimates as restricted estimates. We start with the restricted GLSE (RGLSE):

$$(3.4)\qquad \underline{b}_{rg}=(X'\Sigma^{-1}X)^{-1}X'\Sigma^{-1}\underline{Y}.$$

This is the Balestra-Nerlove estimator.

Utilizing (3.1) we obtain, as shown in [3],

$$(3.5)\qquad \underline{b}_{rg}=\underline{\lambda}_{rg}\underline{b}_b+(I-\underline{\lambda}_{rg})\underline{b}_w$$

where $\lambda_{rg}=(X'KX+(1/\sigma^2(\gamma_1+\gamma_2))X'MX)^{-1}X'KX$. Thus when $\underline{b}_b=\underline{b}_w$, $\underline{b}_{rg}=\underline{b}_w$, but in general:

(3.6) $E(\underline{b}_b|\cdot)=\underline{\beta}+\underline{\pi}$

and therefore, by (3.5) and (3.6),

(3.7) $E(\underline{b}_{rg}|\cdot)=\underline{\beta}+\lambda_{rg}\underline{\pi}$.

Thus the estimator is biased.

Another restricted estimator to be considered is the restricted LSE (RLSE), to be denoted as $\underline{b}_{ro}$:

(3.8) $\underline{b}_{ro}=(X'X)^{-1}X\underline{Y}$.

It can be written as a matrix weighted combination of the between and within estimators and it is therefore generally biased. Let $\lambda_0=(X'X)^{-1}X'KX$; then $E(\underline{b}_{ro}|\cdot)=\underline{\beta}+\lambda_{ro}\underline{\pi}$.

The reason for considering the restricted estimators is that restrictions are likely to decrease the variance of the estimators. As we have seen, the price for such possible reduction is the bias. There is therefore a trade off between bias and variance and the choice of an estimator depends on the weights to be assigned to the two components. In Table I we summarize the variances and MSE of the alternative estimators.

TABLE I

RE—VARIANCES AND MEAN SQUARE ERRORS OF ALTERNATIVE ESTIMATORS, CONDITIONAL ON (X, Z)

Estimator	Variance	MSE
	Unrestricted Estimators	
$\underline{b}_w, \underline{b}_g, \underline{b}_0$	$V_w\equiv\sigma^2(X'MX)^{-1}$	V_w
$\underline{b}_b$	$V_b=(\sigma^2+T\omega_1^2)(X'KX)^{-1}$	$M_b=V_b+\underline{\pi}\underline{\pi}'$
	Restricted Estimators	
$\underline{b}_{ro}$	$V_{ro}=\lambda_{ro}V_b\lambda'_{ro}+(I-\lambda_{ro})V_w(I-\lambda_{ro})'$	$M_{ro}=\lambda_{ro}M_b\lambda'_{ro}+(I-\lambda_{ro})V_w(I-\lambda_{ro})'$
$\underline{b}_{rg}$	$V_{rg}\equiv\lambda_{rg}V_b\lambda'_{rg}+(I-\lambda_{rg})V_w(I-\lambda_{rg})'$	$M_{rg}=\lambda_{rg}M_b\lambda'_{rg}+(I-\lambda_{rg})V_w(I-\lambda_{rg})'$

Clearly, none of the terms in the last column of Table I dominates the others for all possible values V_w, V_b, and $\underline{\pi}$. By dominance it is meant that any quadratic form in the difference between two M's will be uniquely signed for all admissible values of the matrices in question. We return to this question below.

4. ESTIMATOR UNDER THE FE MODEL (CONDITIONAL ON X AND $Z\alpha$)

The FE model can be viewed as an end by itself so that the conditional inference, given the particular effects which appear in the sample, is all that matters. In that case equation (2.3) simply represents the design of the experiment. On the other hand, if the sample is a random sample, the conditional inference can be also considered as a step in deriving the unconditional inference.

Under the FE, β is to be estimated from (2.1). The conditional variance is given in (2.2) and clearly the GLSE of (2.1) is identical to the OLSE. The OLSE of β in (2.1) is simply the within estimator. This remark concludes the statement about the BLUE. We now turn to examine properties of some of the restricted estimators.

The RLSE is obtained by omitting $Z\underset{\sim}{\alpha}$ from (2.1), and it is the same as (3.8). The moments are:

$$(4.1) \qquad E(\underset{\sim}{b}_{ro}|\cdot\cdot) = \underset{\sim}{\beta} + \hat{\underset{\sim}{\pi}}_{ro}$$

where $E(\underset{\sim}{b}_{ro}|\cdot\cdot)$ represents conditional expectation given X and $Z\underset{\sim}{\alpha}$,

$$(4.2) \qquad \hat{\underset{\sim}{\pi}}_{ro} = A(I)Z\underset{\sim}{\alpha},$$

$$(4.3) \qquad V(\underset{\sim}{b}_{ro}) = \sigma^2(X'X)^{-1}.$$

Again, the restriction is likely to decrease the variance of the estimator. This however is done at the expense of obtaining a biased estimator, which may have a larger MSE than that of the unrestricted estimator. To compare the MSE of the restricted and unrestricted estimator we write:[6]

$$(4.4) \qquad M(\underset{\sim}{b}_w|\cdot\cdot) - M(\underset{\sim}{b}_{ro}|\cdot\cdot) = A(I)Z(V_{\hat{\alpha}} - \underset{\sim}{\alpha}\underset{\sim}{\alpha}')Z'A(I)'$$

where $V_{\hat{\alpha}}$ is the variance of the unrestricted L.S. estimator of $\underset{\sim}{\alpha}$. Equation (4.4) constitutes a special case of a result obtained by Toro–Vizcarondo and Wallace [**22**] who also show that (4.4) is positive semidefinite if and only if $\underset{\sim}{\alpha}'V_{\hat{\alpha}}^{-1}\alpha \leq 1$.[7] Thus, when effects exist and the variance of their estimate is not excessively large the unrestricted L.S. dominates the restricted L.S. in MSE. This result is repeated here in order to emphasize that the omission of the variables is not priceless. We return to this point below.

As in Section 3, RLSE can be written as a matrix weighted sum of the between and within estimators. In a more general form this expression can be written as

$$(4.5) \qquad \underset{\sim}{b}_p = \lambda_p \underset{\sim}{b}_b + (I - \lambda_p)\underset{\sim}{b}_w,$$

$$(4.6) \qquad \lambda_p = [(X'KX) + \theta(X'MX)]^{-1}X'KX.$$

When $\theta = 1$ the estimator in (4.5) becomes the RLSE. Thus, (4.5) has a general appearance and it looks like a GLSE. But as noted above, in view of (2.2) the GLSE is the within estimator. We therefore refer to (4.5) as a pseudo GLSE (PGLSE). In Section 5 we deal with the optimal selection of weights such as λ_p so as to minimize the variance of the resulting estimator. It turns out that $\underset{\sim}{b}_p$ has a minimum variance when $\theta = 1$ and for that value $\underset{\sim}{b}_p = \underset{\sim}{b}_{ro}$. Thus, the scope for the PGLS is rather limited.

We are left with the two estimators whose MSE are compared in (4.4). It is possible to dominate these estimators in a MSE sense by deliberately selecting an estimator to do it. We outline the derivation of such an estimator from two points of view. However, it should be indicated that such an estimator requires

[6] Referring to $(\underset{\sim}{b}_w)$, we can write a symmetric expression: $\hat{\alpha} = (Z'M(X)Z)^{-1}Z'M(X)\underset{\sim}{Y}$ and $V_\alpha = \sigma^2(Z'M(X)Z)^{-1}$. Using $(X'X)^{-1} + A(I)Z(Z'M(X)Z)^{-1}Z'A(I) = (X'M(Z)X)^{-1}$ leads to (4.4).

[7] Feldstein [5] obtained a similar result for the case of a simple regression with one left out variable.

knowledge of σ^2 and $\underset{\sim}{\alpha}$ and therefore, in practical applications it can only be computed in two stages in the same spirit as the RGLSE. In fact, we start the presentation by deriving a GLS-like estimator the weights of which are obtained not from the variance of the error term but rather from its MSE. Let $\underset{\sim}{m} \equiv Z\underset{\sim}{\alpha}$,

(4.7) $\tilde{\Sigma} \equiv E\{(\underset{\sim}{Y} - X\underset{\sim}{\beta})(\underset{\sim}{Y} - X\underset{\sim}{\beta})' | X, \underset{\sim}{m}\} = \underset{\sim}{m}\underset{\sim}{m}' + \sigma^2 I_{NT}$,

and obtain

(4.8) $\underset{\sim}{b}_m = (X'\tilde{\Sigma}^{-1}X)^{-1}X'\tilde{\Sigma}^{-1}\underset{\sim}{Y}$.

It can be shown that[8]

(4.9) $E(\underset{\sim}{b}_m | \cdot\cdot) = \underset{\sim}{\beta} + \hat{\underset{\sim}{\pi}}_{r0}(1 - \tilde{\rho})$

where $1 - \tilde{\rho} = \sigma^2(\sigma^2 + \hat{\underset{\sim}{w}}'\hat{\underset{\sim}{w}})^{-1}$, $\underset{\sim}{w} = M(X)\underset{\sim}{m}$,

(4.10) $M(b_m | \cdot\cdot) = \sigma^2(X'X)^{-1} + \hat{\underset{\sim}{\pi}}_{r0}\hat{\underset{\sim}{\pi}}'_{r0}(1 - \tilde{\rho}) \equiv M_m$.

This estimator dominates $\underset{\sim}{b}_{r0}$ since

(4.11) $M_{r0} - M_m = \tilde{\rho}\hat{\underset{\sim}{\pi}}_0\hat{\underset{\sim}{\pi}}'_0$

and (4.11) is positive semidefinite. Thus, we conclude that if some variables are omitted and their coefficients are known, it would be better to add the omitted part to the error term and use a GLS-like estimator rather than restricted LS. This is a general result and it is not limited to qualitative variables.

A comparison of $\underset{\sim}{b}_m$ with $\underset{\sim}{b}_w$ indicates that it also dominates the within estimator. This can be seen by comparing (4.10) and V_w using the result of footnote 6:

(4.12) $M(\underset{\sim}{b}_w | \cdot\cdot) - M(\underset{\sim}{b}_m | \cdot\cdot) = A(I)Z[V_{\hat{\alpha}} - \underset{\sim}{\alpha}\underset{\sim}{\alpha}'(1 - \tilde{\rho})]Z'A(I)'$

where (4.12) is a positive semidefinite matrix.[9] The implication is that if $\underset{\sim}{m}$ is known, then it need not be estimated and it could be used in deriving a MSE estimator.

The main purpose of introducing this MSE estimator is suggestive. It cannot be used as such since $\underset{\sim}{m}$ is not known. If it were known, it could be used for deriving a modified LS estimator which dominates all the others:

(4.13) $\underset{\sim}{b}_f = A(I)(\underset{\sim}{Y} - \underset{\sim}{m}) \sim (\underset{\sim}{\beta}, \sigma^2(X'X)^{-1})$.

An alternative approach to the construction of the MSE estimator is discussed in the next section.

5. AN ALTERNATIVE VIEW OF THE VARIOUS ESTIMATORS

In introducing the MSEE it is helpful first to consider the GLSE from a different point of view. Assume that we want to estimate a linear function in $\underset{\sim}{\beta}$, $\psi = \underset{\sim}{c}'\underset{\sim}{\beta}$, with

[8] Note that for large samples $1 - \hat{\rho}$ is close to zero.

[9] (4.12) is positive semidefinite if and only if $\underset{\sim}{\alpha}'V_{\hat{\alpha}}^{-1}\underset{\sim}{\alpha} < 1/(1 - \tilde{\rho})$. Using the definitions, $\underset{\sim}{\alpha}'V_{\hat{\alpha}}^{-1}\underset{\sim}{\alpha} = \sigma^{-2}\underset{\sim}{w}'\underset{\sim}{w} = \tilde{\rho}/(1 - \tilde{\rho}) \leq 1/(1 - \tilde{\rho})$.

$\underset{\sim}{c}$ given. The problem is to select λ so as to minimize $V(\hat{\psi}_g) \equiv \text{var}\,(\underset{\sim}{c}'\underset{\sim}{b}_g)$. Since $\text{cov}\,(\underset{\sim}{b}_b, \underset{\sim}{b}_w) = 0$, we can write $V_g = \lambda V_b \lambda' + (I - \lambda) V_w (I - \lambda)'$ where $V_g = \text{var}\,\underset{\sim}{b}_g$, etc. The result is given by:

$$(5.1) \qquad \lambda = V_w(V_b + V_w)^{-1} = (V_b^{-1} + V_w^{-1})^{-1} V_b^{-1}.$$

The resultant value of λ is the same as that obtained by GLS. We can therefore consider the GLS as the estimator which combines the various orthogonal estimators of $\underset{\sim}{\beta}$ so as to minimize the variance of $\hat{\psi}$. The proof is obtained by considering an alternative estimator, $b_H = H\underset{\sim}{b}_b + (I - H)\underset{\sim}{b}_w$ to be used in $\hat{\psi}_H = \underset{\sim}{c}'b_H$. Comparing the variances of the two estimators, we obtain after some simplifications:

$$(5.2) \qquad V(\hat{\psi}_H) - V(\hat{\psi}_g) = \underset{\sim}{c}'\{(H - \lambda)(V_b + V_w)(H - \lambda)' - 2(H - \lambda)[V_w - (V_b + V_w)\lambda']\}\underset{\sim}{c}.$$

Selecting λ according to (5.1) annihilates the second term on the right-hand side and makes (5.2) nonnegative for any H and $\underset{\sim}{c}$.

In a similar way it is possible to construct a minimum MSE estimator. The problem can be formulated as follows:

Select λ_m such that the MSE of $\hat{\psi}_m = \underset{\sim}{c}'\underset{\sim}{b}_m$ as an estimator of $\underset{\sim}{c}'\underset{\sim}{\beta}$ is minimized for any $\underset{\sim}{c}$ and where

$$(5.3) \qquad \underset{\sim}{b}_m = \lambda_m \underset{\sim}{b}_b + (I - \lambda_m)\underset{\sim}{b}_w.$$ [10]

The result is:

$$(5.4) \qquad \lambda_m = (M_b^{-1} + M_w^{-1})^{-1} M_b^{-1} = M_w(M_b + M_w)^{-1}.$$

To apply (5.4) in the model under consideration, assuming the RE, Table I and other results of Section 3 are used. It can then be shown that:

$$(5.5) \qquad E(b_m) = \underset{\sim}{\beta} + \lambda_m \underset{\sim}{\pi},$$

$$(5.6) \qquad V_m = (M_b^{-1} + V_w^{-1})^{-1}(M_b^{-1} V_b M_b^{-1} + V_w^{-1})(M_b^{-1} + V_w^{-1})^{-1}.$$

By writing M_b explicitly and simplifying it can be shown that:

$$(5.7) \qquad \underset{\sim}{c}'(M_{rg} - M_m)\underset{\sim}{c} \geq 0$$

and the superiority of $\underset{\sim}{b}_m$ in the MSE sense is demonstrated.

The estimator $\underset{\sim}{b}_m$ cannot be utilized directly since the variances and biases in question are not known . However, it is possible to follow the two stage procedure as used also in obtaining the RGLS estimator. In addition to the estimators of the variance we need also an estimate of $\underset{\sim}{\pi}$. Such an estimate can be obtained from:

$$(5.8) \qquad \hat{\underset{\sim}{\pi}} = \underset{\sim}{b}_b - \underset{\sim}{b}_w$$

and the weight for the MSE estimator is derived from:

$$(5.9) \qquad \hat{\lambda}_m = \hat{V}_w(\hat{M}_b + \hat{V}_w)^{-1}$$

[10] Cf. Feldstein [5].

where $\hat{\_}$ indicates an estimator and:[11]

$$(5.10) \qquad \hat{M}_b = \hat{V}_b + \hat{\pi}\hat{\pi}'.$$

We do not deal here with the distribution of this two stage estimator. However its limiting value is considered in the next section.

The RGLS and the MSE estimators can be considered as parts of a more general framework. Suppose, we have r estimators b_j of β, $j = 1, \ldots, r$. Let b be the rk vector of such estimators. Then, $E(b)$ can be written as

$$(5.11) \qquad E(b) = A_1\beta + A_2\pi.$$

The variance of b is denoted by Σ_b, a square nonsingular matrix of order kr. The problem is how to combine the components of b in order to obtain a final estimator. Assuming first a knowledge of Σ_b, we can derive the maximum likelihood estimator (ML):

$$(5.12) \qquad \begin{matrix}\hat{\beta} \\ \hat{\pi}\end{matrix} = (A'\Sigma_b^{-1}A)^{-1}A'\Sigma_b^{-1}b.$$

This estimator is unbiased as can be verified immediately in view of (5.11). Consequently, we already know from the foregoing discussion that it is not necessarily the most efficient MSE estimator.

In the problem under consideration we have $A_1 = e_2 \otimes I_k$ and $A_2 = \binom{I}{0}k)$ and

$$(5.13) \qquad \hat{\beta} = b_w, \qquad \hat{\pi} = b_b - b_w,$$

and we are back with the within estimator.

The present formulation of the problem allows us to utilize the discussion in Section 4 above. Since we are mainly interested in estimating β, we can omit $A_2\pi$ to gain precision and obtain

$$(5.14) \qquad \hat{\beta} = (A_1'\Sigma_b^{-1}A_1)^{-1}A_1'\Sigma_b^{-1}b.$$

With $A_1 = e_r \otimes I_k$, (5.14) is the RGLS estimator. From the discussion in Section 4 we also know that the MSE can be reduced by adding the omitted term $A_2\pi$ to the error and replacing Σ_b in (5.14) by M_b:

$$(5.15) \qquad \hat{\beta} = (A_1'M_b^{-1}A_1)^{-1}A_1'M_b^{-1}b$$

where $M_b = \Sigma_b + A_2\pi\pi'A_2'$. The estimator in (5.15) is simply our MSE estimator.

We have thus produced a framework which yields the three estimators, the within, as a ML, the RGLS and the MSE as special cases. This approach can be further generalized as it is shown in [**17**, Section 6].

6. INCREASING THE SIZE OF THE SAMPLE

We now examine the properties of the estimators as the size of the sample increases. In so doing, we differentiate between an increase in the number of observations, T, taken on each individual, and the increase in the number of

[11] $\hat{\pi}$ can be used to correct b_{rg} so as to make it unbiased; the result is b_w.

individuals, N. It is assumed that the design matrices are bounded and their limits exist:

$$\text{(6.1)}\quad \begin{aligned} &\lim_{T\to\infty}\left(\frac{1}{T}X'KX\right)=\bar{B}_N, \qquad \lim_{T\to\infty}\left(\frac{1}{T}X'MX\right)=\bar{W}_N,\\ &\lim_{N\to\infty}\left(\frac{1}{N}X'KX\right)=\bar{B}_T, \qquad \lim_{N\to\infty}\left(\frac{1}{N}X'MX\right)=\bar{W}_T, \end{aligned}$$

where all the limits are positive definite matrices. We can now obtain:

$$\text{(6.2)}\quad \lim_{T\to\infty} V(\underset{\sim}{b}_b|\cdot)=\omega_1^2\bar{B}_N^{-1},$$

$$\text{(6.3)}\quad \lim_{N\to\infty} V(\underset{\sim}{b}_b|\cdot)=0.$$

Consequently, the between variance can be reduced only by increasing the number of individuals and not by increasing the number of observations per individual. Referring to (3.6) it is seen that $\underset{\sim}{b}_b$ is asymptotically biased and from (6.3), $P_{N\to\infty}\lim \underset{\sim}{b}_b=\underset{\sim}{\beta}+\underset{\sim}{\pi}$. Consequently

$$\lim_{T\to\infty} M(\underset{\sim}{b}_b|\cdot)=\omega_1^2\bar{B}_N^{-1}+\underset{\sim}{\pi}\underset{\sim}{\pi}',$$

$$\lim_{N\to\infty} M(\underset{\sim}{b}_b|\cdot)=\underset{\sim}{\pi}\underset{\sim}{\pi}'.$$

The variance of the within estimator decreases with either T or N:

$$\text{(6.4)}\quad \lim_{T\to\infty} V(\underset{\sim}{b}_w|\cdot)=0=\lim_{N\to\infty} V(\underset{\sim}{b}_w|\cdot).$$

Therefore $\underset{\sim}{b}_w$ is asymptotically unbiased and consistent.

These results make it possible to evaluate the plim of the other estimators which are expressed as weighted combination of the within and between estimators. The following comments can be made, omitting the technical details.

1. The weight λ_0 of the RLSE has a limit. Therefore $\text{plim}_{N\to\infty}\underset{\sim}{b}_{r0}\neq\underset{\sim}{\beta}$ if $\text{plim}_{N\to\infty}\underset{\sim}{b}_b\neq\underset{\sim}{\beta}$. On the other hand, $\underset{\sim}{b}_{r0}$ does not converge with T.

2. The RGLSE estimator converges to $\underset{\sim}{b}_w$ with T since $\lim_{T\to\infty}\lambda_{rg}=0$. On the other hand, $\lim_{N\to\infty}\lambda_{rg}\neq 0$ and therefore $\text{plim}_{N\to\infty}\underset{\sim}{b}_{rg}\neq\underset{\sim}{\beta}$ if $\text{plim}\,\underset{\sim}{b}_b\neq\underset{\sim}{\beta}$.

3. The MSE converges to $\underset{\sim}{b}_w[\text{plim}\,(\underset{\sim}{b}_m-\underset{\sim}{b}_w)=0]$ with both N and T since in both cases $\lim\lambda_m=0$.

Of the two limits considered, the one generated by increasing N is by far more important for two reasons. First, in general, the number of observations per individual (T) is limited and relatively small, and second, if it were not small then it would be inappropriate to assume that the effects α_i remain constant. Since the observations are periods, usually a year, it would not be reasonable to assume that individuals do not change. In fact, a more realistic approach would be to assume that individuals constantly change but when observed for short time intervals such changes could be neglected **[16]**. However, it is in this process that the RGLSE fails and the MLSE survives. They are both biased for finite samples, but by increasing N the bias of the MLSE approaches zero whereas that of the RGLSE does not.

A similar evaluation can now follow conditional on the FE. However in this case it does not make sense to trace the effect of $N \to \infty$. If N becomes very large, one would be interested not in the specific effect of each individual but rather in the characteristics of the population and will therefore carry the analysis within the RE framework.

Increasing T results in the decline of both variances:

$$(6.5) \qquad \lim_{T\to\infty} V(\underset{\sim}{b}_b | \cdot\cdot) = 0, \qquad \lim_{T\to\infty} V(\underset{\sim}{b}_w | \cdot\cdot) = 0.$$

It is therefore concluded that the between estimator is asymptotically biased and inconsistent. Similar properties are attributed to $\underset{\sim}{b}_{r0}$ and the pseudo-GLS estimator $\underset{\sim}{b}_p$ defined in (4.5) and (4.6) since the weights are invariant to the sample size. Different results are obtained for the MSE estimator $\underset{\sim}{b}_m$. Since $\lim_{T\to\infty}(1-\tilde{\rho}) = 0$, we have

$$(6.6) \qquad \lim_{T\to\infty} V(b_m | \cdot\cdot) = 0 \quad \text{and} \quad \lim_{T\to\infty} E(b_m | \cdot\cdot) = \underset{\sim}{\beta}$$

and the estimator is consistent and asymptotically unbiased.

7. INTRODUCING TIME EFFECT

The introduction of time effects does not introduce conceptual problems and this is primarily due to the fact that time will only represent here another "lay out." It is introduced here briefly in order to give a complete technical framework which is utilized in the next section for estimating the components of variance.

The basic equation is still given by (2.1) except that we now decompose $Z\underset{\sim}{\alpha} = Z_1\underset{\sim}{\alpha}_1 + Z_2\underset{\sim}{\alpha}_2$ where $\underset{\sim}{m} \equiv Z_1\underset{\sim}{\alpha}_1$ and $\underset{\sim}{s} \equiv Z_2\underset{\sim}{\alpha}_2$ are the vectors representing unit and time effects respectively. The observations are arranged by units, beginning with the T readings on the first unit, etc.

Then $Z_1 = I_N \otimes \underset{\sim}{e}_T$, $Z_2 = \underset{\sim}{e}_N \otimes I_T$. We now have to be more specific about the intercept. Let $Z_0 = \underset{\sim}{e}_{NT}$ and rank $X = k-1$.[12] The projecting matrices on the vector spaces generated by the columns of Z_1, Z_2, and Z_0 respectively are:

$$(7.1) \qquad K_1 + K_0 = I_N \otimes \bar{J}_T, \qquad K_2 + K_0 = \bar{J}_N \otimes I_T, \qquad K_0 = \bar{J}_{NT}.$$

Note that $K_1 + K_0$ is the same as K in the previous sections. Also

$$(7.2) \qquad K_1K_2 = K_1K_0 = K_2K_0 = 0$$

and therefore

$$(7.3) \qquad K_1Z_2 = K_1Z_0 = K_2Z_1 = K_2Z_0 = 0.$$

[12] There are $k-1$ columns in X and the requirement of zero means is eliminated.

Rewrite the basic equations:

(7.4) $\underline{Y} = X\beta + Z_0\alpha_0 + Z_1\underline{\alpha}_1 + Z_2\underline{\alpha}_2 + \underline{u}, \qquad \underline{u} \sim (\underline{0}, \sigma^2 I_{NT}),$

(7.5) $\underline{m} \equiv Z_1\underline{\alpha}_1 = (K_1 + K_0)X\underline{\pi}_1 + (K_1 + K_0)\underline{w}_1, \qquad \underline{w}_1 \sim [\underline{0}, T\omega_1^2(K_1 + K_0)],$

(7.6) $\underline{s} \equiv Z_2\underline{\alpha}_2 = (K_2 + K_0)X\underline{\pi}_2 + (K_2 + K_0)\underline{w}_2, \qquad \underline{w}_2 \sim [\underline{0}, N\omega_2^2(K_2 + K_0)],$

where we have used $(K_j + K_0)Z_j = Z_j$, $j = 1, 2$. We also assume that the error components $\underline{u}$, $\underline{w}_1$, and $\underline{w}_2$ are independent for all i and t.

Combining (7.4) and (7.6) and following the procedure of Section 3 we can derive Table II for the RE model.

TABLE II

BIAS AND VARIANCE CONDITIONAL ON X AND Z OF VARIOUS WITHIN AND BETWEEN ESTIMATORS[a]

Estimator	F	Bias	Variance
(1) $\underline{b}_w^{it}$	M_{12}	0	$\sigma^2(X'M_{12}X)^{-1}$
(2) $\underline{b}_b^i$	K_1	$\underline{\pi}_1$	$(\sigma^2 + T\omega_1^2)(X'K_1X)^{-1}$
(3) $\underline{b}_b^t$	K_2	$\underline{\pi}_2$	$(\sigma^2 + N\omega_2^2)(X'K_2X)^{-1}$
(4) $\underline{b}_w^i$	M_1	$A(M)_1K_2X\underline{\pi}_2$	$(X'M_1X)^{-1}[\sigma^2(X'M_1X) + N\omega_2^2(X'K_2X)](X'M_1X)^{-1}$
(5) $\underline{b}_w^t$	M_2	$A(M)_2K_1X\underline{\pi}_1$	$(X'M_2X)^{-1}[\sigma^2(X'M_2X) + T\omega_1^2(X'K_1X)](X'M_2X)^{-1}$
(6) $\underline{b}_0$	M_0	$A(I)(K_1X\underline{\pi}_1 + K_2X\underline{\pi}_2)$	$(XM_0X)^{-1}X'M_0[\sigma^2 I_{NT} + T\omega_1^2K_1 + N\omega_2^2K_2]M_0X(X'M_0X)^{-1}$

[a] $M_0 = I_{NT} - K_0$, $M_1 = I_{NT} - K_1 - K_0$, $M_2 = I_{NT} - K_2 - K_0$, $M_{12} = I_{NT} - K_1 - K_2 - K_0$; when rank $F < k - 1$, the particular estimator is ignored.

A similar evaluation now follows for the FE. This is done by applying F to (7.4), recalling (7.2). The results are summarized in Table III.

TABLE III

BIAS AND VARIANCE CONDITIONAL ON X, $\underline{m}$ AND $\underline{s}$ OF VARIOUS WITHIN AND BETWEEN ESTIMATORS

Estimator	F	Bias	Variance
b_w^{it}	M_{12}	0	$\sigma^2(X'M_{12}X)^{-1}$
b_b^i	K_1	$A\,(K_1)\underline{m}$	$\sigma^2(X'K_1X)^{-1}$
b_b^t	K_2	$A\,(K_2)\underline{s}$	$\sigma^2(X'K_2X)^{-1}$
b_w^i	M_1	$A\,(M_1)\underline{s}$	$\sigma^2(X'M_1X)^{-1}$
b_w^t	M_2	$A\,(M_2)\underline{m}$	$\sigma^2(X'M_2X)^{-1}$
b_0	M_0	$A\,(M_0)(\underline{m} + \underline{s})$	$\sigma^2(X'M_0X)^{-1}$

See footnote to Table II.

The MSE examination can now be written as a matrix weighted combination of the alternative estimators. Assuming $T, N > k - 1$, then:

(7.7) $\underline{b}_m = \lambda_1\underline{b}_b^i + \lambda_2\underline{b}_b^t + (I - \lambda)\underline{b}_w^{it}$

where according to [**17**, Section 6] we have

$$(7.8) \qquad (\lambda_1 \lambda_2) = (V_w V_w) \begin{bmatrix} M_{11} + V_w M_{12} + V_w \\ M_{12} + V_w M_{22} + V_w \end{bmatrix}^{-1}$$

where $M_{11} = M(\underline{b}_b^i)$, $M_{22} = M(\underline{b}_b^t)$, $V_w = V(\underline{b}_w^{it})$, and $M_{12} = \underline{\pi}_1 \underline{\pi}_2'$. Note that we utilize the fact that the three estimators are orthogonal and that the within estimator is also unbiased.

If $\underline{b}_b^t$ cannot be computed we can use $\underline{b}_w^i$ instead. However, $\underline{b}_w^i$ is orthogonal to $\underline{b}_b^i$ but not to $\underline{b}_w^{it}$; consequently the simple form (7.8) cannot be used and the weight matrixes will have to be computed from a somewhat more detailed form [**17**].

The examination of the behavior of the estimators as the sample size increases follows directly the analysis of Section 6. Assuming the limits exist, the following remarks can be made. The RGLS estimator based on the first three estimators in Table II does not converge in distribution to the within estimator unless both T and $N \to \infty$. Since it is unlikely to have a large T, $\underline{b}_{rg}$ will be inconsistent. On the other hand, the MSEE tends to the within estimator in large samples, regardless of whether the increase is in N or T.[13]

As indicated in Section 6, it is not particularly relevant to consider the limits under the FE since as the size of the sample increases in a particular dimension, interest would shift toward characterization of the propulation in terms of a fewer parameters.

The discussion has been conducted for the FE and RE models. It is also possible to consider mixed models where some effects are random whereas others are fixed. Such a specification simply dictates the conditional variables and as such the foregoing results are immediately applicable.

Finally when t stands for time and T is sufficiently large, it would be unrealistic to assume that the individuals do not change in a differential way as the model assumes. As indicated in the previous section, it is more realistic to assume that individuals do change differentially but at a pace that can be ignored for short time intervals. Under this assumption, it would be desirable to allow for interaction between i and t. Such interaction introduces too many parameters and a simplifying form has to be used. A possible formulation for the effects, i and t, is:

$$\mu_{it} = \gamma_{0i} + \gamma_{1i} t.$$

Such a formulation was used empirically in Mundlak [**16**] and Evenson and Kislev [**4**, Ch. 5].

[13] Nerlove [**18**, p. 395] raises the question why treating the effects as fixed rather than random should become asymptotically unimportant. "After all as N, $T \to \infty$ there are infinite number of such parameters, their number increases just as fast as the number of pieces of new information available as the sample size increases. The solution to the puzzle is in fact that we are not estimating them but only β..." It is not quite clear what is meant here by pieces of information. However it should be noted that under the FE there are $T-1$ degrees of freedom in estimating α_i and $N-1$ degrees of freedom in estimating α_τ. Obviously those increase with N and T. The degree of freedom in estimating β increase with the product $(N-1)(T-1)$. The reason why $\text{plim}_{N,T\to\infty} (\underline{b}_{rg} - \underline{b}_w^{it}) = 0$ under the assumption of $\underline{\pi}_1 = \underline{\pi}_2 = 0$, which corresponds to the model examined by Nerlove, is that b_w^{it}, b_b^i, b_b^t are all unbiased and converge in quadratic mean to $\underline{\beta}$.

8. ESTIMATING THE VARIANCE COMPONENTS

In order to make statistical reference in the RE model it is necessary to estimate the components of variance. Such estimators are also required for obtaining the RGLSE and the MSEE.[14] In what follows we present unbiased estimators based on the residuals of the various regressions.

To derive those, let $F\hat{\underline{Y}} = FX\underline{b}_F$, and the residual is

$$V_F = F(\underline{Y} - \hat{\underline{Y}}) = M(FX)F\underline{Y} \tag{8.1}$$

where $M(FX) = I_{NT} - FX(X'FX)^{-1}X'F$. Under the RE,

$$V_F = M(FX)F\underline{\varepsilon} \tag{8.2}$$

where $\underline{\varepsilon}$ is the combined error term. Then

$$E(V_F'V_F) = E(\underline{\varepsilon}'FM(FX)F\underline{\varepsilon}) = \operatorname{tr} M(FX)F\Sigma_\varepsilon. \tag{8.3}$$

The degrees of freedom in each case are given by $\operatorname{tr} M(FX)F = \operatorname{tr} F - (k-1)$, assuming of course that $\operatorname{tr} F \geq k$. The results are presented in Table IV. The last column of the Table gives the expected value of the error mean square, denoted by s_F^2.

TABLE IV

ESTIMATORS FOR COMPONENTS OF VARIANCE[a]

	F	$\operatorname{tr} F$	$E\left[s_F^2 = \dfrac{V_F'V_F}{\operatorname{tr} F - (k-1)}\right]$
(1)	M_{12}	$(N-1)(T-1)$	σ^2
(2)	K_1	$N-1$	$\sigma^2 + T\omega_1^2$
(3)	K_2	$T-1$	$\sigma^2 + N\omega_2^2$
(4)	M_1	$N(T-1)$	$\sigma^2 + \dfrac{N}{N(T-1)-(k-1)}[(T-1) - \operatorname{tr}(X'M_1X)^{-1}(X'K_2X)]\omega_2^2$
(5)	M_2	$T(N-1)$	$\sigma^2 + \dfrac{T}{T(N-1)-k-1}[(N-1) - \operatorname{tr}(X'M_2X)^{-1}(X'K_1X)]\omega_1^2$
(6)	M_0	$NT-1$	$\sigma^2 + \dfrac{1}{NT-k}\{[(N-1) - \operatorname{tr}(X'M_0X)^{-1}(X'K_1X)]T\omega_1^2 + [(T-1) - \operatorname{tr}(X'M_0X)^{-1}(X'K_2X)]N\omega_2^2\}$

[a] In cases where $\operatorname{tr} F < k$, ignore the corresponding line in the table.

For $N > k$, ω_1^2 is estimable from lines (1) and (2) of the table. Such an estimate is independent of ω_2^2 and holds true also when $\omega_2^2 = 0$. Consequently, it is also the appropriate estimator for the one way layout with no time effect. Similarly, if $T \geq k$, ω_2^2 is estimable from lines (3) and (1). If however T is small, ω_2^2 can be estimated from lines (4) and (1).

[14] Alternative estimators exist for estimating the variance components. Maddala and Mount [**12**] examine the effect of using alternative estimators of the components on the MSE of the resulting GLS estimator, using the Monte Carlo technique. They find the results in general to be insensitive to most of the alternatives.

The results of Table IV are basically the analysis of variance results modified for the model under consideration. This modification has an important implication. Note that we estimate ω_i^2 rather than the unconditional variance $\sigma_{\alpha_i}^2$. The difference reflects the true correlation coefficients of equations (7.5) and (7.6). Let for instance $1-\alpha_1^2=\omega_1^2$. When the systematic component of (7.5) constitutes an important role, $1-\rho_1^2$, and therefore ω_1^2 will be relatively small. Thus, the estimate based on lines (1) and (2):

$$\text{(8.4)} \qquad \hat{\omega}_1=\frac{1}{T}(s_{K_1}^2-s_{M_{1,2}}^2)$$

is an unbiased estimator of a small number and the probability of such a number to be negative increases with ρ_1^2. This finding bears on the negative values that are sometimes obtained for estimators like (8.4). To avoid this problem Nerlove [**19**] used as an estimator of the between variance component the $\Sigma\hat{\alpha}_1^2$ where $\hat{\alpha}_i$ is the LS estimate of α_i, or simply the estimate of the fixed effects α_i. Such an estimate constitutes an upper limit for est ω_1^2 and, aside from some correction factor, it is appropriate only for the case of $\rho_1^2=0$, that is when there is no auxiliary regression. The relative importance of the auxiliary regression in the total variance of σ_α^2 was computed for a specific problem in Mundlak [**14**, p. 53; **15**, p. 76]. The results vary depending on the estimator, between 0.4 to 0.5.

It is of some interest to obtain $E(S_F^2|X, \underset{\sim}{m}, \underset{\sim}{s})$, that is under the FE structure. The result has the following structure:

$$\text{(8.5)} \qquad E(S_F^2 X, \underset{\sim}{m}, s)=\sigma^2+\frac{(\underset{\sim}{\alpha}'Z')F'M(FX)F(Z\underset{\sim}{\alpha})}{\operatorname{tr} F-(k-1)}.$$

For $F=K_1$ and K_2 the second term on the right-hand side of (8.5) has a simple interpretation; it is equal to the sum of the computed residuals from the particular auxiliary regression. For instance,

$$\text{(8.6)} \qquad \underset{\sim}{m}'K_1M(K_1X)K_1\underset{\sim}{m}=T\sum_{i=1}^{N}\hat{w}_i^2$$

and we can then write

$$\text{(8.7)} \qquad T\tilde{\omega}_1^2=\frac{T\Sigma_{=1}^{N}\hat{w}_i^2}{N-k}$$

and a similar expression can be obtained for $N\omega_2^2$ by letting $F=K_2$. Of course, when $F=M_{12}$, the second term on the right-hand side of (8.5) vanishes. (8.7) can be considered as an estimate of $T\omega_1^2$ only if α_i were random.

Hebrew University of Jerusalem

Manuscript received February, 1976; final revision received March, 1977.

REFERENCES

[1] AMEMIYA, TAKESHI: "The Estimation of the Variance in a Variance-Component Model," *International Economic Review*, 12 (1971), 1–13.

[2] BALESTRA, P., AND M. NERLOVE: "Pooling Cross-Section and Time Series Data in the Estimation of a Dynamic Model: The Demand for Natural Gas," *Econometrica*, 34 (1966), 585–612.

[3] CHAMBERLAIN, GARY: *Unobservables in Econometric Models*, unpublished Ph.D. dissertation, Harvard University, Cambridge, Ma., 1975.

[4] EVENSON, ROBERT E., AND YOAV KISLEV: *Agricultural Research and Productivity*. New Haven: Yale University Press, 1975.

[5] FELDSTEIN, MARTIN S: "Multicollinearity and the Mean Square Error of Alternative Estimators," *Econometrica*, 41 (1973), 337–346.

[6] FRIEDMAN, MILTON: *Theory of Consumption Function*. Princeton, N.J.: Princeton University Press, 1957.

[7] GRILICHES, ZVI: "Specification Bias in Estimates of Production Functions," *Journal of Farm Economics*, 39 (1957), 8–20.

[8] ———: "Estimating the Returns to Schooling," Harvard Institute of Economic Research, Discussion Paper #433, 1975.

[9] HENDERSON, CHARLES R., JR.: "Comment on the Use of Error Components Models in Combining Cross Section With Time Series Data," *Econometrica*, 39 (1971), 397–401.

[10] KUH, EDWIN: "The Validity of Cross Sectionally Estimated Behavior Equations in Time Series Applications," *Econometrica*, 27 (1959), 197–214.

[11] MADDALA, G. S.: "The Use of Variance Components Models in Pooling Cross Section and Time Series Data," *Econometrica*, 39 (1971), 341–358.

[12] MADDALA, G. S., AND T. D. MOUNT: "A Comparative Study of Alternative Estimators for Variance Components Models Use in Econometric Applications," *Journal of the American Statistical Association*, 68 (1973), 324–328.

[13] MCELROY, F. W.: "A Necessary and Sufficient Condition that Ordinary Least Squares Estimators be Best Unbiased," *Journal of the American Statistical Association*, 62 (1967), 1302–1304.

[14] MUNDLAK, YAIR: "Empirical Production Function Free of Management Bias," *Journal of Farm Economics*, 43 (1961), 44–56.

[15] ———: *An Economic Analysis of Established Family Farms in Israel*. Jerusalem: Falk Project for Economic Research in Israel, 1964.

[16] ———: "Empirical Production Functions with a Variable Firm Effect," Working Paper #7005, The Center for Agricultural Economic Research, Rehovot, Israel, 1970.

[17] ———: "On the Pooling of Time Series and Cross Section Data," Harvard Institute of Economic Research, Discussion Paper #457, 1976.

[18] NERLOVE, M.: "A Note on Error Components Models," *Econometrica*, 39 (1971), 383–396.

[19] ———: "Further Evidence on the Estimation of Dynamic Economic Relations From a Time Series of Cross Section Data," *Econometrica*, 39 (1971), 359–382.

[20] RAO, R. C., AND S. K. MITRA: *Generalized Inverse of Matrices and its Applications*. New York: John Wiley & Sons, Inc., 1971.

[21] THEIL, H.: "Specification Errors and the Estimation of Economic Relationships," *Review of International Statistical Institute*, 25 (1957), 41–51.

[22] TORO-VIZCARONDO, CARLOS, AND T. D. WALLACE: "A Test of The Mean Square Error Criterion for Restrictions in Linear Regression," *Journal of the American Statistical Association*, 63 (1968), 558–572.

[23] WALLACE, T. D., AND ASHIQ HUSSAIN: "The Use of Error Components Models in Combining Cross Section With Time Series Data," *Econometrica*, 37 (1969), 55–68.

[24] ZYSKIND, GEORGE: "Parametric Augmentation and Error Structures Under Which Certain Simple Least Squares and Analysis of Variance Procedures Are Also Best," *Journal of the American Statistical Association*, 64 (1969), 1353–1368.

Journal of Econometrics 28 (1985) 193–203. North-Holland

A NOTE ON THE EQUIVALENCE OF SPECIFICATION TESTS IN THE TWO-FACTOR MULTIVARIATE VARIANCE COMPONENTS MODEL

Suk KANG*

Ohio State University, Columbus, OH 43210-1090, USA

Received February 1984, final version received December 1984

This note offers a generalization of Hausman and Taylor's equivalence of specification tests in the single-equation variance (error) components model to the two-factor multivariate variance components case. The relationship between the specification tests and the hypothesis tests in the model proposed by Mundlak is also discussed.

1. Introduction

In this note we prove an equivalence for specification tests in the two-factor multivariate variance components model, which is a generalization of Hausman and Taylor's (1981) result in the single-equation one-factor model. Hausman and Taylor have shown that the chi-square statistics for testing for correlation between variance components and the explanatory variables are numerically identical when we compare the GLS estimator and the within estimator, the GLS estimator and the between estimator, and the within estimator and the between estimator. Hausman and Taylor's result is derived from the fact that the efficient GLS estimator is a matrix weighted average of the within and between estimators which are, by themselves, inefficient. In a two-factor model, however, the GLS estimator is a matrix weighted average of three estimators. We propose five specification tests in the two-factor model under the combination of fixed and random assumptions and derive the equivalence for those tests. The relationship between the specification test and the classical test in the variance components model considered by Mundlak (1978) is also discussed.

2. The multivariate variance components model and its GLS estimator

In this part we introduce the multivariate variance components model and its GLS estimator, as proposed by Baltagi (1980).

*I would like to thank Professor Gary Chamberlain and anonymous referees for helpful comments and suggestions.

0304-4076/85/$3.30

Let us consider the set of M equations,

$$y_i = X_i\beta_i + u_i, \qquad i = 1,\ldots, M, \tag{1}$$

where y_i is $NT \times 1$, X_i is $NT \times k_i$ and β_i is $k_i \times 1$.

We may, for example, interpret N as the number of individuals and T as the number of time periods. Also, the data are ordered in such a way that the first T elements are observations from individual 1, in time periods 1 through T.

We assume that the disturbance term u_i has additive error components,

$$u_i = (I_N \otimes \mathbf{1}_T)\mu_i + (\mathbf{1}_N \otimes I_T)\lambda_i + v_i, \tag{2}$$

where $\mathbf{1}_m$ is a $m \times 1$ vector whose elements are all 1, and

$$\mu_i = (\mu_{i1},\ldots,\mu_{iN})',$$

$$\lambda_i = (\lambda_{i1},\ldots,\lambda_{iT})',$$

$$v_i = (v_{i11}, v_{i12},\ldots, v_{iNT})', \qquad i = 1,\ldots, M.$$

μ_i is a vector of individual-specific effects which do not change over time, λ_i is a vector of time-specific effects which uniformly affect all the individuals at time t, and v_i is a vector of residual random factors.

We assume the expected values of μ_i, λ_i and v_i conditional on $X_1,\ldots, X_M$ are all zero and, that

$$\mathrm{E}\left[\begin{bmatrix}\mu_i\\ \lambda_i\\ v_i\end{bmatrix}\begin{bmatrix}\mu_j\\ \lambda_j\\ v_j\end{bmatrix}' \middle| X_1,\ldots, X_M\right]$$

$$= \begin{bmatrix}\sigma_{\mu ij}I_N & 0 & 0\\ 0 & \sigma_{\lambda ij}I_T & 0\\ 0 & 0 & \sigma_{v ij}I_{NT}\end{bmatrix}, \qquad i, j = 1,\ldots, M. \tag{3}$$

Stacking the M equations in (1) we obtain

$$y = X\beta + u. \tag{4}$$

where

$$X = \operatorname{diag}\{X_1, \dots, X_M\}$$

$$y = (y_1', \dots, y_M')',$$

$$\beta = (\beta_1', \dots, \beta_M')'$$

$$u = (u_1', \dots, u_M')'.$$

The variance of u is given by

$$\operatorname{var}(u) = \Sigma = \Sigma_\mu \otimes A + \Sigma_\lambda \otimes B + \Sigma_\upsilon \otimes I_{NT},^{1} \tag{5}$$

where

$$\Sigma_\mu = (\sigma_{\mu ij}), \quad \Sigma_\lambda = (\sigma_{\lambda ij}), \quad \Sigma_\upsilon = (\sigma_{\upsilon ij}), \qquad i, j = 1, \dots, M,$$

and

$$A = I_N \otimes 1_T 1_T', \qquad B = 1_N 1_N' \otimes I_T.$$

Σ can be rewritten as

$$\Sigma = \Sigma_3 \otimes J^* + \Sigma_1 \otimes A^* + \Sigma_2 \otimes B^* + \Sigma_\upsilon \otimes Q, \tag{6}$$

where

$$J^* = 1_{NT} 1_{NT}'/NT,$$

$$A^* = A/T - J^*,$$

$$B^* = B/N - J^*,$$

$$Q = I_{NT} - A^* - B^* + J^*,$$

and

$$\Sigma_1 = \Sigma_\upsilon + T\Sigma_\mu, \quad \Sigma_2 = \Sigma_\upsilon + N\Sigma_\lambda, \quad \Sigma_3 = \Sigma_\upsilon + N\Sigma_\lambda + T\Sigma_\mu.$$

It is easily verified that J^*, A^*, B^* and Q are all idempotent, mutually orthogonal and add up to the unit matrix I_{NT}. The inverse of Σ is

$$\Sigma^{-1} = \Sigma_3^{-1} \otimes J^* + \Sigma_1^{-1} \otimes A^* + \Sigma_2^{-1} \otimes B^* + \Sigma_\upsilon^{-1} \otimes Q.^{2} \tag{7}$$

[1] We assume Σ is known and Σ_υ is non-singular. See Baltagi (1980) and Prucha (1984) for the feasible GLS estimators.

[2] See Baltagi (1980).

In the discussion of specification tests without loss of generality, we assume that all the variables are measured as deviations from their means.[3] Then from (4) and (7) the GLS estimator of $\boldsymbol{\beta}$ is given by

$$b_{GLS} = \left[X'\left(\Sigma_1^{-1} \otimes A^* + \Sigma_2^{-1} \otimes B^* + \Sigma_v^{-1} \otimes Q\right)X\right]^{-1}$$
$$\times X'\left(\Sigma_1^{-1} \otimes A^* + \Sigma_2^{-1} \otimes B^* + \Sigma_v^{-1} \otimes Q\right)y, \tag{8}$$

The GLS estimator is efficient if individual effects, $\boldsymbol{\mu}$, and time effects, $\boldsymbol{\lambda}$, are uncorrelated with the explanatory variables, X. However, if these effects are correlated with the explanatory variables the GLS estimator is inconsistent. Hausman (1978) proposed a specification test for correlation between the unobserved effects ($\boldsymbol{\mu}$ and $\boldsymbol{\lambda}$) and the explanatory variables. The test statistic is given by

$$(\hat{\beta}_1 - \hat{\beta}_0)' \operatorname{var}(\hat{\beta}_1 - \hat{\beta}_0)^{-1}(\hat{\beta}_1 - \hat{\beta}_0),$$

which asymptotically follows the chi-square distribution with k degrees of freedom, where $\hat{\beta}_1$ is a consistent but not efficient estimator, $\hat{\beta}_0$ is the efficient estimator, and k is the order of $\boldsymbol{\beta}$.

3. Equivalence of specification tests in the two-factor model

We shall show that the GLS estimator, b_{GLS}, is a matrix weighted sum of the three estimators of $\boldsymbol{\beta}$. They are the between individual estimator, the between time estimator, and the within individual and time estimator. The question which we address is whether specification tests based on the comparisons of b_{GLS} and the between individual estimator, b_{GLS} and the between time estimator, and b_{GLS} and the within individual and time estimator are equivalent. While we find that these specification tests are not equivalent, we do find a different type of equivalence in the two-factor model, which is a generalization of Hausman and Taylor's result.

In the framework of the two-factor model we examine possible specifications of the unobservable effects. We define the random and fixed effects by the following:

$\boldsymbol{\mu}(\boldsymbol{\lambda})$ *is random*: $\mathrm{E}(\boldsymbol{\mu}|X)=\boldsymbol{0}$, $\operatorname{Var}(\boldsymbol{\mu}|X)=\Sigma_\mu \otimes I_N$,
$(\mathrm{E}(\boldsymbol{\lambda}|X)=\boldsymbol{0}$, $\operatorname{Var}(\boldsymbol{\lambda}|X)=\Sigma_\lambda \otimes I_T)$.

$\boldsymbol{\mu}(\boldsymbol{\lambda})$ *is fixed*: $\mathrm{E}(\boldsymbol{\mu}|X)\neq \boldsymbol{0}$, $(\mathrm{E}(\boldsymbol{\lambda}|\boldsymbol{X})\neq 0)$.

[3]Alternatively, we can assume that $\boldsymbol{\beta}$ consists of slope parameters only.

Under the random specification, the model is parameterized in terms of the covariance matrix of the individual and/or time effects. Under the fixed specification λ and/or μ are treated as parameters of the model.[4]

Before proceeding to our result in the two-factor model, let us describe procedures for the specification tests under alternative assumptions about the structure of the variance components. There are five possible tests for correlation between individual and/or time effects and explanatory variables. They are:

Test 1. Assume that individual effects are fixed, and test for correlation between time effects and the explanatory variables.

Test 2. Assume that individual effects are random, and test for correlation between time effects and the explanatory variables.

Test 3. Assume that time effects are fixed, and test for correlation between individual effects and the explanatory variables.

Test 4. Assume that time effects are random, and test for correlation between individual effects and the explanatory variables.

Test 5. Compare two estimators, one which assumes that both individual and time effects are fixed, and the other which assumes that both are random and uncorrelated with the explanatory variables.

Test statistics corresponding to the above five tests can be constructed by the following procedure: Define

$$V_C = X'(\Sigma_1^{-1} \otimes A^*)X,$$

$$V_T = X'(\Sigma_2^{-1} \otimes B^*)X,$$

$$V_Q = X'(\Sigma_v^{-1} \otimes Q)X,$$

$$V = V_C + V_T + V_Q. \tag{9}$$

We define the within individual and time estimator, $\boldsymbol{b}_Q$, the between time estimator, $\boldsymbol{b}_T$, and the between individual estimator, $\boldsymbol{b}_C$, by formulas (10) through (12).

The within (individual and time) estimator

$$\boldsymbol{b}_Q = V_Q^{-1}X'(\Sigma_v^{-1} \otimes Q)y, \tag{10}$$

[4]A mixed model of the fixed and random effects is considered first by Hussain (1969).

The between time estimator

$$b_T = V_T^{-1} X' (\Sigma_2^{-1} \otimes B^*) y, \tag{11}$$

The between individual estimator

$$b_C = V_C^{-1} X' (\Sigma_1^{-1} \otimes A^*) y. \tag{12}$$

Hereafter we call the estimator in (10), *the within estimator*.

Using (10)–(12) we can rewrite the GLS estimator in (8) as

$$b_{\mathrm{GLS}} = V^{-1}(V_T b_T + V_C b_C + V_Q b_Q). \tag{13}$$

In (13) the GLS estimator in the two-factor model is expressed as a matrix weighted sum of three estimators, b_T, b_C and b_Q.

Next, we define two more estimators by the following formulas:

$$b_{\mathrm{PGLS1}} = (V_T + V_Q)^{-1}(V_T b_T + V_Q b_Q), \tag{14}$$

$$b_{\mathrm{PGLS2}} = (V_C + V_Q)^{-1}(V_C b_C + V_Q b_Q). \tag{15}$$

b_{PGLS1} corresponds to the estimator which treats individual effects as fixed and applies GLS to the within data and the between time data. PGLS refers to the 'partial' GLS in this sense. Also, b_{PGLS2} corresponds to the estimator which treats time effects as fixed and applies GLS to the within data and the between individual data.

We note that b_{PGLS1} and b_{PGLS2} are each formed by the matrix weighted sum of two estimators. In particular, b_{PGLS1} is formed from b_T and b_Q, and b_{PGLS2} is formed from b_C and b_Q. We may also look at a third estimator, which is formed by the matrix weighted sum of b_T and b_C. We will call this estimator b_{PGLS3}:

$$b_{\mathrm{PGLS3}} = (V_T + V_C)^{-1}(V_T b_T + V_C b_C). \tag{16}$$

We may interpret b_{PGLS3} as the GLS estimator applied to the between individual and the between time data.

Table 1 shows the estimators used in the tests 1 through 5. The equivalence of the specification tests in the two-factor model is stated in the following proposition.

Table 1

Specification tests in the multivariate variance components model.[a]

	Efficient estimator under H_0	Consistent estimator under H_0 and H_1	Test for correlation between X and
Test 1	PGLS1	within	time effects
Test 2	GLS	PGLS2	time effects
Test 3	PGLS2	within	individual effects
Test 4	GLS	PGLS1	individual effects
Test 5	GLS	within	individual and time effects

[a] H_0 assumes that correlations between the individual and/or time effects and the explanatory variables are zero, while H_1 assumes that the correlations are non-zero.

Proposition. *The specification tests comparing the within* ($\boldsymbol{b}_Q$) *and between time* ($\boldsymbol{b}_T$) *estimators, the between time* ($\boldsymbol{b}_T$) *and GLS* ($\boldsymbol{b}_{\text{GLS}}$) *estimators, and* $\boldsymbol{b}_{\text{PGLS3}}$ *and the within estimator* ($\boldsymbol{b}_Q$) *are equivalent to tests 1, 2 and 5, respectively. Furthermore, tests 1, 2 and 5 are equivalent to the tests comparing* $\boldsymbol{b}_T$ *and* $\boldsymbol{b}_{\text{PGLS1}}$, $\boldsymbol{b}_T$ *and* $\boldsymbol{b}_{\text{PGLS2}}$, *and* $\boldsymbol{b}_{\text{PGLS3}}$ *and* $\boldsymbol{b}_{\text{GLS}}$, *respectively.*

Proof. We prove the equivalence for test 2. The test statistic in test 2, m_2, is given by

$$m_2 = (\boldsymbol{b}_{\text{GLS}} - \boldsymbol{b}_{\text{PGLS2}})' \operatorname{var}(\boldsymbol{b}_{\text{GLS}} - \boldsymbol{b}_{\text{PGLS2}})^{-1} (\boldsymbol{b}_{\text{GLS}} - \boldsymbol{b}_{\text{PGLS2}}). \tag{17}$$

Note that the equivalence holds if $\boldsymbol{b}_{\text{GLS}} - \boldsymbol{b}_{\text{PGLS2}}$, $\boldsymbol{b}_{\text{GLS}} - \boldsymbol{b}_T$ and $\boldsymbol{b}_{\text{PGLS2}} - \boldsymbol{b}_T$ are non-singular transformations of each other.

Premultiplying $\boldsymbol{b}_{\text{GLS}} - \boldsymbol{b}_{\text{PGLS2}}$ by V we obtain

$$\begin{aligned} V(\boldsymbol{b}_{\text{GLS}} - \boldsymbol{b}_{\text{PGLS2}}) &= V_T\left[\boldsymbol{b}_T - (V_C + V_Q)^{-1}(V_C \boldsymbol{b}_C + V_Q \boldsymbol{b}_Q)\right] \\ &= V_T(\boldsymbol{b}_T - \boldsymbol{b}_{\text{PGLS2}}). \end{aligned} \tag{18}$$

So, $\boldsymbol{b}_{\text{GLS}} - \boldsymbol{b}_{\text{PGLS2}}$ is a non-singular transformation of $\boldsymbol{b}_T - \boldsymbol{b}_{\text{PGLS2}}$. This proves the second part of the equivalence. Next, premultiply $\boldsymbol{b}_{\text{GLS}} - \boldsymbol{b}_T$ by $(V_C + V_Q)^{-1}V$. The result is

$$(V_C + V_Q)^{-1} V(\boldsymbol{b}_{\text{GLS}} - \boldsymbol{b}_T) = \boldsymbol{b}_{\text{PGLS2}} - \boldsymbol{b}_T. \tag{19}$$

This proves the first part of the proposition. Equivalences for tests 1 and 5 can be shown in the same manner. Q.E.D.

Table 2
Equivalence of the specification tests.

	Specification test	Equivalent tests
Test 1	PGLS1 vs within	within *vs* between time PGLS1 *vs* between time
Test 2	GLS vs PGLS2	GLS *vs* between time PGLS2 *vs* between time
Test 3	PGLS2 vs within	within *vs* between individual PGLS2 *vs* between individual
Test 4	GLS vs PGLS1	GLS *vs* between individual PGLS1 *vs* between individual
Test 5	GLS vs within	PGLS3 *vs* within GLS *vs* PGLS3

The symmetry of the individual and the time effects leads to the following corrolary:

Corrolary. *The specification test 3 is equivalent to the comparisons of* $\boldsymbol{b}_Q$ *and* $\boldsymbol{b}_C$, *and* $\boldsymbol{b}_C$ *and* $\boldsymbol{b}_{\mathrm{PGLS2}}$. *The specification test 4 is equivalent to the comparisons of* $\boldsymbol{b}_C$ *and* $\boldsymbol{b}_{\mathrm{GLS}}$, *and* $\boldsymbol{b}_C$ *and* $\boldsymbol{b}_{\mathrm{PGLS1}}$.

Table 2 gives a summary of our results.

Remark 1. The results in the proposition and corrolary can be derived as special cases of Ruud's (forthcoming) factorization theorem which has shown a general condition for the equivalence.

Remark 2. The above results do not depend upon the shape of the X matrix. Previously, we specified X as a block-diagonal matrix, but in the derivation of the proposition the results are obtained without invoking the special form of X. This implies that the results are valid even in the presence of linear cross-equation restrictions on the parameters.

4. Generalized Mundlak model

In this section we consider a generalization of the variance components model considered by Mundlak (1978) and describe the relationship between the specification tests and the hypothesis tests in Mundlak's model. Mundlak considered the model in which each individual disturbance is a linear combination of the individual means and a random term,

$$\mu_{ij} = X'_{ij.}\pi + \tilde{\mu}_{ij}, \qquad i=1,\dots,M, \quad j=1,\dots,N, \tag{20}$$

where $X_{ij.}$ is the vector of individual means of the explanatory variables for the ith equation. A generalization of Mundlak's model in the two-factor model may be obtained by specifying each time effect as a linear function of the time means and a random term,

$$\lambda_{it} = X'_{i.t}\tau + \tilde{\lambda}_{it}, \qquad i=1,\dots,M, \quad t=1,\dots,T, \tag{21}$$

where $X_{i.t}$ is the vector of time means of the explanatory variables for the ith equation.

In vector notation the model is written as

$$y = X\beta + (I_M \otimes A/T)X\pi + (I_M \otimes B/N)X\tau + u. \tag{22}$$

The variance of the disturbance term u has the same structure as (5). Eq. (22) is rewritten as

$$y = (I_M \otimes Q)X\beta + (I_M \otimes A^*)X\alpha + (I_M \otimes B^*)X\delta + u, \tag{23}$$

where

$$\alpha = \beta + \pi \quad \text{and} \quad \delta = \beta + \tau.$$

The GLS estimators for β, α and δ are *the within*, *the between individual* and *the between time* estimators respectively,

$$\hat{\beta}_{\text{GLS}} = b_Q, \qquad \hat{\alpha}_{\text{GLS}} = b_C, \qquad \hat{\delta}_{\text{GLS}} = b_T. \tag{24}$$

It is easy to see that the test statistics for the classical test $\beta = \delta$ ($\tau = 0$) is identical to test 1. Test 1 is testing $\beta = \alpha$ under the maintained hypothesis that $\pi = 0$. On the other hand, if π is restricted to be zero then the GLS estimators for β and δ are given by b_{PGLS1} and b_C. It follows that the classical test $\beta = \delta$ ($\tau = 0$) under the maintained hypothesis that $\pi = 0$ is identical to test 2. Also, the symmetry of the individual and time effects implies that test 3 is equivalent to the hypothesis test that $\beta = \alpha$ under the maintained hypothesis that $\tau = 0$, and test 4 is equivalent to the test $\beta = \alpha$ given the restriction that $\tau = 0$. The joint test of $\beta = \delta$ and $\beta = \alpha$ against $\beta \neq \delta$ and $\beta \neq \alpha$, however, is not identical to test 5. The joint test statistic is given by

$$\begin{pmatrix} b_Q - b_T \\ b_Q - b_C \end{pmatrix}' \operatorname{var}\begin{pmatrix} b_Q - b_T \\ b_Q - b_C \end{pmatrix}^{-1} \begin{pmatrix} b_Q - b_T \\ b_Q - b_C \end{pmatrix}.$$

The test statistic is the 'joint' test of test 1 and test 3 and has a chi-square distribution with $2k$ degrees of freedom.

Appendix

In this appendix we prove the claims presented in table 1. The proof is given for test 4 only, but the same procedure will give the results in table 1 for the other tests.

In test 4 the maintained hypothesis is that time effects are random, and the specification is tested for correlation between the individual effects and the explanatory variables. To prove the claim it is sufficient to show $\boldsymbol{b}_{\mathrm{PGLS1}}$ is efficient when the individual effects are fixed.

The model is written as

$$y = X\beta + (I_M \otimes I_N \otimes \boldsymbol{1}_T)\boldsymbol{\mu} + \boldsymbol{u}. \tag{A.1}$$

The second term in (A.1) is the set of individual dummies. The variance of $\boldsymbol{u}$ is

$$\operatorname{var}(\boldsymbol{u}) = \Sigma_v \otimes (I - B/N) + \Sigma_2 \otimes B/N = \Sigma_B. \tag{A.2}$$

In (A.1) $\boldsymbol{\mu}$ is treated as a parameter of the model. We know the following three steps will yield the GLS estimator for $\boldsymbol{\beta}$.

Step 1. Transform the system by premultiplying by $\Sigma_B^{-\frac{1}{2}}$.

Step 2. Run an auxiliary regression of transformed y and X on transformed individual dummies.

Step 3. Regress the residuals for y on the residuals for X which are obtained in step 2.

Schmidt (1982) has pointed out that in the fixed effects model the GLS estimator can be obtained by exchanging the order of steps 1 and 2. Schmidt derived his result in the framework of the single-equation fixed time effects model with arbitrary across individual covariance. In our model the general cross-equation covariance corresponds to Schmidt's individual covariance, and our model is slightly more general than Schmidt's by permitting a free time covariance. Still, it can be shown that Schmidt's result is valid in deriving the GLS estimator for the model considered in this appendix.

The auxiliary regression on individual dummies gives

$$I_M \otimes (I - A/T)y = (I_M \otimes (I - A/T))X\beta + (I_M \otimes (I - A/T))\boldsymbol{u}. \tag{A.3}$$

The GLS estimator for $\boldsymbol{\beta}$ is then written as

$$\hat{\boldsymbol{\beta}}_{GLS} = [X'WX]^{-1}X'Wy, \tag{A.4}$$

where W is given by

$$\begin{aligned} W &= \left(I_M \otimes \left(I - \frac{A}{T}\right)\right)\left[\Sigma_v^{-1} \otimes \left(I - \frac{B}{N}\right) + \Sigma_2^{-1} \otimes \frac{B}{N}\right]\left(I_M \otimes \left(I - \frac{A}{T}\right)\right) \\ &= \Sigma_v^{-1} \otimes Q + \Sigma_2^{-1} \otimes B^*. \end{aligned} \tag{A.5}$$

Substitution of W into (A.4) yields the desired result:

$$\hat{\boldsymbol{\beta}}_{\mathrm{GLS}} = \boldsymbol{b}_{\mathrm{PGLS1}} = (V_Q + V_T)^{-1}(V_Q \boldsymbol{b}_Q + V_T \boldsymbol{b}_T). \tag{A.6}$$

References

Baltagi, B.H., 1980, On seemingly unrelated regression with error components, Econometrica 48, 1547–1551.

Hausman, J.A., 1978, Specification tests in econometrics, Econometrica 46, 1251–1271.

Hausman, J.A. and W.E. Taylor, 1981, Panel data and unobservable individual effects, Econometrica 49, 1377–1398.

Hussain, A., 1969, A mixed model for regressions, Biometrica 56, 327–336.

Mundlak, Y., 1978, On the pooling of time series and cross section data, Econometrica 46, 69–85.

Prucha, I.R., 1984, On the asymptotic efficiency of feasible Aitken estimators for seemingly unrelated regression models with error components, Econometrica 52, 203–207.

Ruud, P.A., forthcoming, Tests of specification in econometrics, Econometric Reviews.

Schmidt, P., 1983, A note on a fixed effect model with arbitrary interpersonal covariance, Journal of Econometrics 22, 391–393.

[8]

Journal of Business & Economic Statistics, April 1987, Vol. 5, No. 2

Diagnostics for Group Effects in Regression Analysis

Brent R. Moulton
Division of Price and Index Number Research, U.S. Bureau of Labor Statistics, Room 3306, 600 E Street, N.W., Washington, DC 20212

The diagnostic tools examined in this article are applicable to regressions estimated with panel data or cross-sectional data drawn from a population with grouped structure. The diagnostic tools considered include (a) tests for the existence of group effects under both fixed and random effects models, (b) checks for outlying groups, and (c) specification tests for comparing the fixed and random effects models. A group-specific counterpart to the studentized residual is introduced. The methods are illustrated using a hedonic housing price regression.

KEY WORDS: Regression diagnostics; Variance components; Grouped populations; Studentized residuals; Hedonic prices; Specification tests.

1. INTRODUCTION

Models for data grouping are now used extensively by economists in regression analysis of panel data (Dielman 1983). The grouping factors are typically the individual and time, and the group-specific effects are treated as either fixed parameters or as random variables drawn from a distribution. The analyst is often interested in choosing between alternative models, estimating realized individual or time effects, or checking for an outlying individual or time period.

Recently, increased attention has been given to the use of group effects models in regression analysis of large cross-sectional data sets (Pfeffermann and Smith 1985). Data in surveys are often drawn from populations with well-defined groups, such as geographical region, industry, or level of education, and a sample may include many observations from each group. Special econometric methods are usually needed to take account of group effects in the design and stochastic specification of the regression model. Failure to incorporate group effects can have serious consequences including inefficient coefficient estimation and large downward bias in the standard errors, especially when estimation of the coefficients of interest relies on between-group variation (Moulton 1986).

This article examines diagnostic tests in regression models under both fixed and random effects assumptions. Tests for outlying or unusual group effects are also considered, and I develop group-specific statistics that are analogous to studentized residuals in ordinary regression. Criteria for choosing between the fixed and random effects models are examined. These methods are applicable in both the panel and cross-sectional data contexts, although the application to cross-sectional grouped populations will be emphasized. The techniques are illustrated with an application using the Harrison and Rubinfeld (1978) hedonic housing price data.

2. MODELS

2.1 Alternative Models

The Harrison and Rubinfeld (1978) study, like many others, used a regression model without specific group effects for the geographical groups (towns) in their sample. They included several town-specific variables in an attempt to model the differences between towns, however. The regression model without group effects can be written as

$$y = X\beta + u, \tag{1}$$

where X is an $n \times k$ matrix of regressors of rank k, β is a k vector of parameters including the parameters of interest, and u is an n vector of iid errors. Ordinary least squares (OLS) is the standard estimation method, and the OLS estimator of β will be denoted by $\hat{\beta}^0$.

Alternatively, the fixed effects model assumes that each group has its own intercept. [Models in which slope parameters vary between groups are not considered here, although they were discussed by Moulton (1986).] Let W be an $n \times r$ matrix of 0–1 indicators of group membership for each of the r groups in the population. Partition $X = (X_1, X_2)$, where X_2 contains the k_2 variables that are a linear combination of the indicator variables for group membership, generally those variables that do not vary within the groups. The k_1 variables in X_1 all exhibit within-group variation and rank $(X, W) = k_1 + r$. Partition $\beta' = (\beta_1', \beta_2')$ conformably. Note that β_2 will generally include the constant.

The fixed effects model is

$$y = X_1\beta_1 + X_2\beta_2 + W\gamma + u, \tag{2}$$

where γ is an r vector of parameters. Note that β_2 and γ are not estimable, although β_1 and the error variance could be estimated using software that allows non-full-rank models. If full-rank software is used, the data in

X_1 can be transformed to deviations around group means, and OLS can be applied to estimate β_1. The standard error of the regression would then be multiplied by $[(n - k_1)/(n - k_1 - r)]^{1/2}$ to obtain the usual degrees-of-freedom adjustment. This estimator of β_1 will be referred to as the least squares with dummy variables (LSDV) estimator, or $\hat{\beta}_1^L$. Note that any estimated fixed effects represent certain linear combinations of parameters in γ and β_2.

Another model assumes the group effects to be random in a variance components model. This model is written as

$$y = X\beta + Wd + u, \tag{3}$$

where d is an r vector of random variables with mean 0 and variance $D = \sigma_d^2 I_r$. Let $\text{var}(u) = R = \sigma_u^2 I_n$; then $E(y) = X\beta$ and $\text{var}(y) = V = WDW' + R$.

I will use Henderson's (1953) method of fitting constants to estimate the variance components, σ_d^2 and σ_u^2, then estimate β with the feasible generalized least squares (GLS) estimator, denoted by $\hat{\beta}^G$. The fitting-of-constants estimators are

$$\tilde{\sigma}_u^2 = M_u$$

$$\tilde{\sigma}_d^2 = \frac{(M_d - M_u)}{\{\text{tr}[W'W - W'X(X'X)^{-1}X'W]/(r - k_2)\}}, \tag{4}$$

where M_u and M_d are the mean squares of u and d in a preliminary analysis of variance. The GLS estimator is then obtained by letting $\tilde{V} = \tilde{\sigma}_d^2 WW' + \tilde{\sigma}_u^2 I_n$ and

$$\hat{\beta}^G = (X'\tilde{V}^{-1}X)^{-1}X'\tilde{V}^{-1}y. \tag{5}$$

Simple methods of computing $\hat{\beta}^G$ using OLS software were given by Fuller and Battese (1973) and Harville (1986), and Fuller and Battese derived properties of the GLS estimator.

2.2 Choice Between Models

Observe that β_2 remains estimable under the random effects model, an important consideration in model selection for studies in which β_2 includes parameters of interest to the analyst. Moreover, when the assumptions underlying the random effects model are correct, $\hat{\beta}_1^G$ is efficient whereas $\hat{\beta}_1^L$ is not.

The model without group effects (1) is nested in (2) and (3), so standard tests are available to compare (1) with (2) or (3). Inappropriate use of OLS when the data are generated by the random effects model can lead to substantial bias in standard errors, particularly for $\hat{\beta}_2^0$, as shown in Moulton (1986). The choice between the fixed effects model (2) and the random effects model (3) has traditionally been based on whether the group effects can be considered random draws from an iid distribution (Searle 1971). Moreover, note that GLS reduces to LSDV as $\sigma_u^2/\sigma_d^2 \to 0$ (Henderson 1971).

An important specification issue when X is treated as stochastic was raised by Mundlak (1978). The issue is whether the assumption $E(d \mid X) = 0$ is warranted. When this assumption is violated, the GLS estimator is biased and inconsistent, but the LSDV estimator remains consistent because it conditions on the group effects. The natural interpretation of the group effects in most applications is that they represent the effects of omitted variables with grouped structure, so the assumption of exogeneity of the regressors with respect to the group effects may be difficult to justify a priori.

Hausman (1978) suggested the following test of the specification $E(d \mid X) = 0$. Under the hypothesis of exogeneity, the LSDV estimates of β_1, $\hat{\beta}_1^L$, should be close to the GLS estimates, $\hat{\beta}_1^G$. Define asymptotic variance matrices $V(\hat{\beta}_1^L)$ and $V(\hat{\beta}_1^G)$ and the difference of the coefficient estimates $\hat{q} = \hat{\beta}_1^L - \hat{\beta}_1^G$. Then Hausman showed that in large samples the test statistic

$$m = \hat{q}'[V(\hat{\beta}_1^L) - V(\hat{\beta}_1^G)]^{-1}\hat{q} \tag{6}$$

is approximately distributed as $\chi^2_{k_1}$ under the null hypothesis. Hausman and Taylor (1981) studied identification and estimation of the model when d is correlated with X.

3. DIAGNOSTICS

3.1 Fixed Effects Diagnostics

With normal errors, models (1) and (2) can be estimated using least squares, and standard finite sample tests can be used to choose between them. Define the sum-of-squares error (SSE) for model (1) without group effects as

$$\text{SSE}_1 = y'[I - X(X'X)^{-1}X']y.$$

Let $Q = (X, W)$. For model (2), the SSE is

$$\text{SSE}_2 = y'[I - Q(Q'Q)^{-}Q']y$$
$$= \dot{y}'[I - \dot{X}_1(\dot{X}_1'\dot{X}_1)^{-1}\dot{X}_1']\dot{y},$$

where $(\ )^{-}$ represents a generalized inverse, and $\dot{y}$ and $\dot{X}_1$ are deviations around group means. If model (1), the regression without the group effects, is correct, the following test statistic will be distributed as $F_{r-k_2, n-k_1-r}$:

$$\frac{(\text{SSE}_1 - \text{SSE}_2)/(r - k_2)}{\text{SSE}_2/(n - k_1 - r)}. \tag{7}$$

In some cases, the group effects may be caused by one or a few unusual or outlying groups. If this is the case, the investigator may wish to examine the outlying groups in more detail and possibly maintain the model without group effects for the remaining groups. Estimated fixed effects are not useful as diagnostics because they include the effects of $X_2\beta_2$ as well as γ. The group mean residual (GMR) and the studentized group mean residual (SGMR) are proposed as useful diagnostics for checking for outlying groups, omitted variables, and other functional form misspecification.

First, rewrite (1) using notation for the individual

observation

$$y_{ij} = x_{ij}'\beta + u_{ij}, \tag{8}$$

where y_{ij} is observation j in group i, x_{ij} is the vector of regressor data, and u_{ij} is the error. Define the OLS residual as

$$\hat{u}_{ij} = y_{ij} - x_{ij}'\hat{\beta}^0.$$

Now define the GMR as

$$\bar{u}_i = (1/m_i)\sum_j \hat{u}_{ij}, \tag{9}$$

where m_i is the number of observations in group i. Under the maintained assumption of independent normal errors, the distribution of $\bar{u}_i$ is given by

$$\bar{u}_i \sim N(0, \sigma^2 H_i),$$

where $H_i = (1/m_i)(1 - e'X_i(X'X)^{-1}X_i'e/m_i)$, X_i is the submatrix of X containing observations for group i, and e is an m_i vector of ones. $\bar{u}_i$ provides a measure of the average deviation of the group's residuals from the regression line in units of the dependent variable, and it is helpful in inferring the absolute size of the group effects.

The $\bar{u}_i$ can be plotted against variables in X_2 as checks for functional form misspecification. They can be used in conjunction with the F test (7) to check for lack of fit for the underlying regression model, particularly when the model without group effects seems plausible a priori. Such a use of the F test as a lack-of-fit test was illustrated for a wage equation by Doran and Kmenta (1986), who found that the model without group effects was rejected until a quadratic term for one of the variables was added to the specification. [Their lack-of-fit test is a special case of (7) in which $X = X_2$.]

It may also be useful to analyze group mean residuals relative to their standard deviation—that is, $\bar{u}_i/(\sigma H_i^{1/2})$. Since σ is unknown, an estimate will be substituted. Use of S, the standard error of the regression, is not recommended because it is correlated with $\bar{u}_i$. Instead, one can use S_i^*, the standard error of the regression estimated from a regression of y on X and a dummy variable for observations in the ith group. This is the SGMR:

$$\bar{u}_i^* = \bar{u}_i/S_i^* H_i^{1/2}. \tag{10}$$

In Appendix A, I demonstrate that $\bar{u}_i^*$ is the t statistic for testing the hypothesis that $\alpha_i = 0$, where α_i is the coefficient of a dummy variable for observations in group i. This is a test statistic for a single group effect, in contrast with the F test of (7), which is a joint test for all of the estimable group effects. Standard regression programs can be used to compute the $\bar{u}_i^*$ by forming dummy variables, and only a single pass through the data is necessary.

The use of the SGMR's for formal testing of hypotheses is complicated by the fact that they are not independent of each other. Nonetheless they, together with GMR's, can provide useful summary information to the data analyst on the existence, magnitude, and patterns of group effects and may help the analyst in identifying possible omitted variables or functional form misspecifications. Note that these group-specific measures differ in intent from the multiple-row diagnostics of Belsley, Kuh, and Welsch (1980) in that prior information is assumed about the relevant grouping pattern and a common shock within the group.

3.2 Random Effects Diagnostics

In this section, I discuss a Lagrange multiplier (LM) test for choosing between the OLS model without group effects (1) and the random effects model (3). Estimation of realized random effects under the latter model is then discussed.

Breusch and Pagan (1980) derived an LM test for the variance components regression model that is easy to implement because it can be computed using OLS residuals from the model without group effects. Honda (1985) and King and Evans (1986) subsequently observed that a one-sided LM test has more power than the two-sided test originally proposed by Breusch and Pagan. Comparing models (1) and (3), the hypothesis to be tested is H_0: $\sigma_d^2 = 0$, versus the alternative, H_1: $\sigma_d^2 > 0$. The one-sided LM or score statistic is given by

$$\mathrm{LM} = \frac{\sum (m_i\bar{u}_i)^2 - \sum\sum \hat{u}_{ij}^2}{\hat{\sigma}^2[2(\sum m_i^2 - n)]^{1/2}}, \tag{11}$$

where $\hat{\sigma}^2 = \sum\sum \hat{u}_{ij}^2/n$. The one-sided LM statistic has a standard normal asymptotic distribution under the null hypothesis.

If the null hypothesis is rejected, then the GLS estimator will be used to estimate β. It is interesting to estimate realized or sample values of d, which will be denoted by δ. Conditional on the estimates of the variance components, $\bar{\sigma}_w^2$ and $\bar{\sigma}_u^2$, a generalized Gauss–Markov theorem produces estimates of the realized random effects, $\hat{\delta}$:

$$\hat{\delta} = \bar{D}W'\bar{V}^{-1}(y - X\hat{\beta}^G). \tag{12}$$

[See Harville (1976) and Henderson (1963, 1975). The estimator would be minimum variance linear unbiased if the true values of the variance components were known.] Here $\bar{D}$ and $\bar{V}$ are evaluated at the estimates of the variance components, and $\hat{\beta}^G$ is the estimate of the coefficients. Note that

$$V^{-1} = R^{-1} - R^{-1}WD(I + W'R^{-1}WD)^{-1}W'R^{-1}.$$

An approximate variance–covariance matrix of $\hat{\delta}$ is given by

$$\mathrm{var}(\hat{\delta}) = \bar{D}W'\bar{V}^{-1}W\bar{D} - \bar{D}W'\bar{V}^{-1}X(X'\bar{V}^{-1}X)^{-1}X'\bar{V}^{-1}W\bar{D}. \tag{13}$$

[For alternative approximations, see Kackar and Harville (1984).] The estimated random effects can be calculated or plotted to provide insight into problems such as choice of functional form or existence of outlying groups. Thus, analysis of estimated random effect realizations in studying group effects is analogous to the examination of regression residuals in the basic regression model.

4. APPLICATION

4.1 Harrison–Rubinfeld Model

The diagnostic tools are illustrated using a data set developed by Harrison and Rubinfeld (1978) for a study of hedonic housing prices and the willingness to pay for clean air. Robust regression methods have been used to analyze these data by Belsley et al. (1980) and Krasker, Kuh, and Welsch (1983). A hedonic price index is estimated for the log of the median value of owner-occupied homes using observations on 506 census tracts in the Boston Standard Metropolitan Statistical Area in 1970. These census tracts are located in 92 towns identified by Belsley et al. (1980, p. 230), who also listed the data (pp. 244–261). The model estimated by Harrison and Rubinfeld (1978) is

$$\begin{aligned} \text{LMV}_{ij} = {} & \beta_1 + \beta_2\,\text{CRIM}_{ij} + \beta_3\,\text{ZN}_i \\ & + \beta_4\,\text{INDUS}_i + \beta_5\,\text{CHAS}_{ij} \\ & + \beta_6\,\text{NOXSQ}_{ij} + \beta_7\,\text{RM}_{ij} \\ & + \beta_8\,\text{AGE}_{ij} + \beta_9\,\text{DIS}_{ij} + \beta_{10}\,\text{RAD}_i \\ & + \beta_{11}\,\text{TAX}_i + \beta_{12}\,\text{PTRATIO}_i + \beta_{13}B_{ij} \\ & + \beta_{14}\,\text{LSTAT}_{ij} + u_{ij}. \end{aligned} \tag{14}$$

A brief definition of each variable is given in Appendix B, and details were provided by Harrison and Rubinfeld (1978). The error term for census tract j in town i is u_{ij}, which was assumed to be iid in the original study. The variable of primary interest to them was NOXSQ, a measure of pollution, and the estimate of β_6 was used in computing the willingness to pay for automobile emission controls. Besides the intercept, five other variables—ZN, INDUS, RAD, TAX, and PTRATIO—are measured at the town level and do not exhibit within-town variation. (NOXSQ nearly falls into this category, having within-town variation in only 11 of the 92 towns.) Since the value of housing is likely to be influenced by omitted town-specific variables, a town-specific constant or error component seems quite natural.

For census tract j in town i, the fixed effects model adds a fixed parameter γ_i, but the random effects model adds a random variable d_i to the specification.

Belsley et al. (1980) observed that repeated large studentized residuals within a town indicated possible neighborhood effects not allowed in the basic multiple regression model, but they did not explicitly model these effects. Their principal concern was with the nonnormality or heavy-tailed distribution of the regression errors, an issue that is only discussed briefly in this article.

4.2 Fixed Effects Estimation

Harrison and Rubinfeld (1978) estimated (14) using OLS and assuming iid errors. These estimates are reported in column 2 of Table 1. Note that the OLS standard errors are biased downward if there is actually within-town correlation in the errors. In applying the F test (7), $r = 92$, $k_1 = 8$, $k_2 = 6$, and $n = 506$. The $F_{86,406}$ statistic is 6.45, which exceeds the 1% critical value of 1.45. The model without group effects is inconsistent with the data.

Next, I examined the grouped residuals from the basic OLS regression for unusual patterns or outliers. Table 2 lists the GMR and SGMR for each of the 12 largest (in absolute value) in each category from the Harrison–Rubinfeld data. Eight of the SGMR's exceed 3 in absolute value, and one is as large as −9.5. A pattern that emerges from these data is that the group-specific effects appear to be larger in Boston than in the suburbs. Only 15 of the 92 towns in the study are located within Boston, but 9 of the 12 largest $|\bar{u}_i^*|$ and 6 of the 12 largest $|\bar{u}_i|$ are in Boston. This result indicates the possibility of different models for the central city and the suburbs. At least two towns (Beacon Hill and South Boston) could be considered as unusual or outlying. Since 10 of 92 towns have SGMR's greater

Table 1. Fixed Effects Estimates for the Harrison–Rubinfeld Hedonic Housing Price Equation

Variable	OLS: no group effect	LSDV: entire sample	LSDV: Boston	LSDV: suburbs
Intercept	9.76	—	—	—
	(.15)			
CRIM × 10^{-2}	−1.19	−.63	−.62	−4.0
	(.12)	(.10)	(.14)	(2.0)
ZN × 10^{-3}	.08	—	—	—
	(.51)			
INDUS × 10^{-2}	.02	—	—	—
	(.24)			
CHAS × 10^{-1}	.94	−.46	−1.03	−.06
	(.34)	(.31)	(.97)	(.24)
NOXSQ × 10^{-2}	−.64	−.56	−1.06	−.51
	(.11)	(.14)	(.53)	(.10)
RM × 10^{-2}	.63	.93	−.03	1.70
	(.13)	(.12)	(.28)	(.11)
AGE × 10^{-2}	.09	−1.41	.6	−2.54
	(.53)	(.49)	(2.0)	(.38)
DIS × 10^{-1}	−1.91	.80	4.5	.12
	(.33)	(.71)	(2.1)	(.57)
RAD × 10^{-1}	.96	—	—	—
	(.19)			
TAX × 10^{-3}	−.42	—	—	—
	(.12)			
PTRATIO × 10^{-2}	−3.11	—	—	—
	(.50)			
B	.36	.66	.56	.71
	(.10)	(.10)	(.17)	(.15)
LSTAT × 10^{-1}	−3.71	−2.45	−4.62	−1.15
	(.25)	(.26)	(.70)	(.22)
S^2	.033	.017	.030	.0083
R^2	.806	.918	.877	.935
n	506	506	132	374

NOTE: Standard errors are in parentheses. Standard errors for OLS estimates are not adjusted for intragroup correlation in errors. Variable definitions are given in Appendix B.

Table 2. Group Mean Residuals and Studentized Group Mean Residuals From the Harrison–Rubinfeld Hedonic Housing Model Data

Town	No. of observations	$\bar{u}_i$	$\bar{u}_i^*$
Boston			
Allston-Brighton	8	.18	3.2
Back Bay	6	.24	3.6
Beacon Hill	3	.56	5.9
North End	2	.20	1.6
East Boston	11	−.12	−2.4
South Boston	13	−.39	−9.5
Downtown	8	.33	5.7
Roxbury	19	−.10	−3.3
Dorchester	11	.14	2.7
Mattapan	6	.20	2.8
Suburban			
Middleton	1	.24	1.4
Manchester	1	.34	1.9
Belmont	8	.19	3.2
Waltham	11	.17	3.3
Medfield	1	.29	1.6
Norfolk	1	.20	1.1
Sharon	3	−.19	−1.9
Chelsea	5	−.17	−2.4

NOTE: The criteria for inclusion were the 12 largest values of $|\bar{u}_i|$ and $|\bar{u}_i^*|$.

than 2.7 in absolute value, however, it appears appropriate to assume a general fixed or random model of group effects.

The LSDV estimates for the entire sample appear in column (3) of Table 1. Comparing the LSDV estimates, which include town-specific intercepts, with the OLS estimates of the basic model in column 2, I note important differences in several of the estimated coefficients. The estimated coefficient of DIS, a measure of distance from employment centers, is -1.9 ($t = 5.7$) without controlling for town effects, but it is positive and insignificant for the within-town equation. Other coefficient estimates showing large differences include CRIM, CHAS, and AGE.

As suggested earlier, the sample was divided between the central city and suburban observations, with coefficient estimates reported in columns 4 and 5 of Table 1, respectively. Again, important differences are apparent between estimates for the two sets of data. The coefficient of CRIM, a measure of the crime rate, is $-.62$ for the central city but -4.0 for the suburban model. Large differences are also apparent for RM, AGE, DIS, and LSTAT. The overall fit of the suburban equation is much tighter, with $S^2 = .0083$ for the suburbs and $S^2 = .030$ for Boston.

A formal test of the equality of coefficients between the suburban and Boston equations was performed. Since the error variances differ between the two groups, the Chow-type F test is inappropriate. A Wald test statistic for the equality of the Boston and suburban coefficients, $\beta_{1_B} = \beta_{1_S}$, is

$$W = (\hat{\beta}^L_{1_B} - \hat{\beta}^L_{1_S})' \times [\hat{\sigma}^2_B(X'_{1_B}X_{1_B})^{-1} + \hat{\sigma}^2_S(X'_{1_S}X_{1_S})^{-1}](\hat{\beta}^L_{1_B} - \hat{\beta}^L_{1_S}),$$

which is asymptotically $\chi^2_{k_1}$ under the null hypothesis, where $\hat{\sigma}^2_B$ and $\hat{\sigma}^2_S$ are maximum likelihood estimates of the error variances. For the data, $W = 73.9 > \chi^2_8(.01) = 20.1$, so equality of coefficients is rejected.

As Belsley et al. (1980) observed, the normality assumption may be inappropriate for these data because the residuals have a heavy-tailed distribution. Analysis of the residuals obtained after splitting the sample between central city and suburban observations indicates that some, but not all, of the nonnormality was due to combining of disparate observations from the two populations.

4.3 Random Effects Estimation

The one-sided LM test (11) for the variance components specification was performed using the residuals from the basic regression model (14). The LM statistic was 15.6, which compares with the 1% critical value of 2.33. Again, the evidence against the model without group effects is compelling.

In column 3 of Table 3, the GLS estimates for the variance components model estimated over the entire sample are reported. As was the case for the fixed effects model, taking account of group effects results in changes for several of the parameter estimates. The estimates for the coefficient of AGE, a measure of the

Table 3. Random Effects Estimates for the Harrison–Rubinfeld Hedonic Housing Price Equation

Variable	OLS: no group effect	Variance components: entire sample	Variance components: Boston	Variance components: suburbs
Intercept	9.76	9.67	9.07	9.80
	(.15)	(.21)	(.31)	(.15)
CRIM × 10^{-2}	−1.19	−.71	−.73	−2.0
	(.12)	(.10)	(.14)	(1.8)
ZN × 10^{-3}	.08	.01	—	.05
	(.51)	(.71)		(.41)
INDUS × 10^{-2}	.02	.24	—	.08
	(.24)	(.45)		(.25)
CHAS × 10^{-1}	.94	−.14	−.29	.04
	(.34)	(.29)	(.92)	(.22)
NOXSQ × 10^{-2}	−.64	−.59	−1.02	−.493
	(.11)	(.12)	(.43)	(.095)
RM × 10^{-2}	.63	.92	−.11	1.79
	(.13)	(.12)	(.26)	(.11)
AGE × 10^{-3}	.09	−.97	.7	−2.05
	(.53)	(.46)	(1.9)	(.34)
DIS × 10^{-1}	−1.91	−1.25	.4	−1.45
	(.33)	(.46)	(1.5)	(.32)
RAD × 10^{-1}	.96	.97	—	.62
	(.19)	(.29)		(.18)
TAX × 10^{-3}	−.42	−.37	—	−.69
	(.12)	(.20)		(.13)
PTRATIO × 10^{-2}	−3.11	−3.0	—	−2.57
	(.50)	(1.0)		(.55)
B	.36	.582	.44	.64
	(.10)	(.099)	(.16)	(.15)
LSTAT × 10^{-1}	3.71	2.82	5.44	1.31
	(.25)	(.24)	(.62)	(.20)
$\hat{\sigma}^2_u$	.033	.017	.030	.0083
$\hat{\sigma}^2_a$		.019	.041	.0045
n	506	506	132	374

NOTE: Standard errors are in parentheses. Standard errors for OLS estimates are not adjusted for intragroup correlation in errors. Standard errors for variance components estimates are approximate. Variable definitions are given in Appendix B. Variance component models were estimated by the method of fitting constants.

Table 4. Estimates of Realized Random Effects for 15 Boston Towns in the Variance Components Model

Town	$\hat{\delta}_i$	Approximate standard error
Allston-Brighton	.15	.17
Back Bay	.09	.17
Beacon Hill	.45	.16
North End	.18	.16
Charlestown	−.07	.18
East Boston	−.14	.19
South Boston	−.40	.19
Downtown	.23	.18
Roxbury	−.14	.19
Savin Hill	−.01	.19
Dorchester	.03	.18
Mattapan	.01	.18
Forest Hills	−.06	.18
West Roxbury	−.20	.17
Hyde Park	−.11	.17

NOTE: $\hat{\delta}_i$ is the estimate of realized random effect for town i, conditioned on estimates of the variance components.

age of the housing stock, are .09 in the basic OLS estimates and −.97 under the variance components model. Large differences are also observed for CRIM and CHAS. In contrast to the fixed effects results, however, the estimated coefficient of DIS remains negative and significant. The standard errors of several estimates, especially for variables that do not have within-town variation such as INDUS, TAX, and PTRATIO, appear to be substantially larger. The difference results from the downward bias in the unadjusted OLS standard errors, an issue investigated in more detail by Moulton (1986).

Repeating the estimation for Boston and suburban subsamples again results in large differences between the estimates, as seen in columns 4 and 5 of Table 3. The variance estimates are smaller for the suburbs than the city, and the estimates of within-group correlation, $\bar{\rho} = \bar{\sigma}_d^2/(\bar{\sigma}_u^2 + \bar{\sigma}_d^2)$, are .35 for the suburbs and .58 for Boston. The coefficient estimate of DIS remains strongly negative in the suburban equation.

Estimates of the realized random effects for the Boston equation are presented in Table 4. Equations (12) and (13) were used to compute the estimates and their standard errors. The town of Beacon Hill appears to be an outlier under the variance components model. Identification of outlying groups may permit the investigator to identify missing variables that may help to explain the aberrant groups. Lacking such data, the investigator may wish to treat the group effects for outlying groups as fixed or use a robust estimation method such as that proposed by Fellner (1986).

4.4 Specification Test

Recall that Hausman's (1978) specification test (6) treats the group effects and X as random and tests the hypothesis H_0: $E(d \mid X) = 0$. The test is implemented by comparing the LSDV and GLS estimates of β_1. Thus, rejection of the null hypothesis occurs when the fixed effects and random effects models yield significantly different estimates.

For the Boston equations, the estimates being compared are those reported in the fourth columns of Tables 1 and 3, and the Hausman test statistic is 18.4, but the 1% critical value for χ_8^2 is 20.1. Thus the test fails to reject H_0 for Boston. For the suburban equations the test statistic is 32.2, leading to rejection of H_0.

Faced with rejection of H_0 using Hausman's test, the investigator has several options available. The investigator may wish to use the LSDV estimates from the fixed effects model, drawing inferences conditional on the effects in the sample. Alternatively, Hausman and Taylor (1981) suggested identifying assumptions and estimation methods that yield estimates of all of the parameters even when some of the X variables are correlated with d. Another approach, suggested by Mundlak (1978), is to add explanatory variables in an auxiliary model of the group effects:

$$d_i = \bar{x}_{1i}'\pi + \varepsilon_i,$$

where $\bar{x}_{1i} = (1/m_i) \sum_j x_{1ij}$, π is a vector of between-group parameters, and ε_i is a group random effect.

In interpreting the Hausman test, the issue of errors in variables also should be addressed. The fixed effects LSDV estimator is very sensitive to errors in variables because it, in effect, removes all between-group variation in X. The Hausman test statistic is a measure of the difference between the LSDV and variance components model estimates. Rejection could be due to either correlation between X and the group effects, invalidating the variance components model, or bias from errors in variables intensified under the LSDV model.

Consider the estimates of the coefficient of DIS in the suburban equation. DIS is a weighted average of distances from five employment centers, intended as a proxy for transportation costs from a given census tract. Although it is probably a reasonably good proxy when comparing different towns, the measure is likely to be a poor measure of differences in transportation costs between census tracts in a given town. The intraclass correlation for DIS is very high, .92, so little variation occurs within towns (see Table 5). For the suburbs the

Table 5. Intraclass Correlations of Independent Variables

Variable	Entire sample	Boston	Suburbs
CRIM	.48	.14	.77
ZN	1.00	—	1.00
INDUS	1.00	—	1.00
CHAS	.20	.36	.17
NOXSQ	.70	.72	.66
RM	.32	.20	.33
AGE	.62	.35	.60
DIS	.93	.81	.92
RAD	1.00	—	1.00
TAX	1.00	—	1.00
PTRATIO	1.00	—	1.00
B	.51	.42	.22
LSTAT	.43	.42	.27

random effects estimate of its coefficient is − 1.45 (standard error = .32), a reasonable value given a priori considerations, but the fixed effects estimate of .12 (standard error = .57) is not in conformity with theory and seems to indicate substantial measurement error. Thus one should not be hasty in accepting the fixed effects model when the Hausman test statistic is large. (The Hausman test statistic excluding the coefficient of DIS is 26.7, which remains significant at the .01 significance level.)

Pakes (1983) suggested a method of consistent estimation for group effects models when the group effects are correlated with the regressors and the regressors are subject to errors in variables. The method relies on information obtained from subgroups within the major groups. Since subgrouping information was not available for the Harrison–Rubinfeld data, the method was not used in this example. Additional prior information is required to identify and estimate the model when both correlated group effects and errors in variables are present.

5. CONCLUSIONS

This article discussed regression diagnostics for group effects in fixed and random effects models. These diagnostics include the F test for linear models, group mean and studentized group mean residuals, the LM test, estimation of realized random effects, and the Hausman specification test for comparing and reconciling the fixed and random effects estimates. The methods were illustrated using the Harrison and Rubinfeld (1978) housing price data.

The implications of the diagnostics for the Harrison–Rubinfeld model are fairly negative. The coefficients in the suburbs were found to be quite different from the coefficients in the city. This result indicates important differences between suburban and city housing markets either in the behavior of economic agents or in the influence of possible omitted variables. Significant differences were found between the fixed effects and random effects estimates for the suburban equation, which may result from correlation between the group effects and the explanatory variables or from errors in explanatory variables. It may be of some interest, however, that the coefficient estimates of the variable of primary interest to the original investigators, NOXSQ, were fairly consistent across specifications.

ACKNOWLEDGMENTS

I thank James Duggan, Dennis Fixler, Thesia Garner, John Greenlees, Raj Jain, William Randolph, Arnold Zellner, Kimberly Zieschang, and the referees for helpful comments and suggestions. I also thank Anna Sanders for skillfully typing the manuscript. The views expressed are mine and do not reflect the policies of the U.S. Bureau of Labor Statistics (BLS) or the views of other BLS staff members.

APPENDIX A: COMPUTING THE STUDENTIZED GROUP MEAN RESIDUALS

I wish to demonstrate that $\bar{u}_i^*$ is equal to the t statistic for $\alpha_i = 0$, where α_i is the coefficient for a group dummy variable, w_i, in the regression of y on X and w_i. The coefficient estimates are given by

$$\begin{pmatrix} \hat{\beta}^* \\ \hat{\alpha}_i \end{pmatrix} = \begin{bmatrix} X'X & X'w_i \\ w_i'X & w_i'w_i \end{bmatrix}^{-1} \begin{bmatrix} X'y \\ w_i'y \end{bmatrix},$$

where $\hat{\beta}^*$ is the estimate of β from regression with the dummy variable. Using formulas for partitioned matrix inversion and the facts that $w_i'X = e'X_i$ and $w_i'(y - X\hat{\beta}^*) = m_i\bar{u}_i$, I obtain, after some algebra, $\hat{\alpha}_i = \bar{u}_i/(m_iH_i)$. Letting S_i^* be the standard error of the regression for the dummy variable regression and noting that the standard error for the estimated coefficient of the dummy variable is $S_{\hat{\alpha}_i} = S_i^*/[m_i(H_i)^{1/2}]$, I obtain

$$\hat{\alpha}_i/S_{\hat{\alpha}_i} = \bar{u}_i/(S_i^*H_i^{1/2}) = \bar{u}_i^*.$$

APPENDIX B: DEFINITIONS OF VARIABLES FOR THE HARRISON–RUBINFELD HEDONIC HOUSING PRICE INDEX MODEL

LMV—logarithm of the median value of owner-occupied homes
CRIM—per capita crime rate by town
ZN—proportion of a town's residential land zoned for lots greater than 25,000 square feet
INDUS—proportion of nonretail business acres per town
CHAS—Charles River dummy variable with value 1 if the tract bounds on the Charles River
NOXSQ—nitrogen oxide concentration (parts per hundred million) squared
RM—average number of rooms squared
AGE—proportion of owner-occupied units built prior to 1940
DIS—logarithm of the weighted distances to five employment centers in the Boston region
RAD—logarithm of index of accessibility to radial highways
TAX—full-value property-tax rate (per $10,000)
PTRATIO—pupil–teacher ratio by town
B—$(Bk - .63)^2$, where Bk is the proportion of blacks in the population
LSTAT—logarithm of the proportion of the population that is lower status

[*Received November 1985. Revised August 1986.*]

REFERENCES

Belsley, D. A., Kuh, E., and Welsch, R. E. (1980), *Regression Diagnostics: Identifying Influential Data and Sources of Collinearity*, New York: John Wiley.

Breusch, T. S., and Pagan, A. R. (1980), "The Lagrange Multiplier Test and Its Applications to Model Specification in Econometrics," *Review of Economic Studies*, 47, 239–253.

Dielman, T. E. (1983), "Pooled Cross-Sectional and Time Series Data: A Survey of Current Statistical Methodology," *The American Statistician*, 37, 111–122.

Doran, H. E., and Kmenta, J. (1986), "A Lack-of-Fit Test for Econometric Applications to Cross-Section Data," *Review of Economics and Statistics*, 68, 346–350.

Fellner, W. H. (1986), "Robust Estimation of Variance Components," *Technometrics*, 28, 51–60.

Fuller, W. A., and Battese, G. E. (1973), "Transformations for Estimation of Linear Models With Nested-Error Structure," *Journal of the American Statistical Association*, 68, 626–632.

Harrison, D., and Rubinfeld, D. L. (1978), "Hedonic Housing Prices and the Demand for Clean Air," *Journal of Environmental Economics and Management*, 5, 81–102.

Harville, D. (1976), "Extension of the Gauss–Markov Theorem to Include the Estimation of Random Effects," *The Annals of Statistics*, 4, 384–395.

——— (1986), "Using Ordinary Least Squares Software to Compute Combined Intra-Interblock Estimates of Treatment Contrasts," *The American Statistician*, 40, 153–157.

Hausman, J. A. (1978), "Specification Tests in Econometrics," *Econometrica*, 46, 1251–1271.

Hausman, J. A., and Taylor, W. E. (1981), "Panel Data and Unobservable Individual Effects," *Econometrica*, 49, 1377–1398.

Henderson, C. R. (1953), "Estimation of Variance and Covariance Components," *Biometrics*, 9, 226–252.

——— (1963), "Selection Index and Expected Genetic Advance," in *Statistical Genetics and Plant Breeding*, eds. W. D. Hanson and H. F. Robinson, Washington, DC: National Academy of Sciences—National Research Council, pp. 141–163.

——— (1975), "Best Linear Unbiased Estimation and Prediction Under a Selection Model," *Biometrics*, 31, 423–447.

Henderson, C. R., Jr. (1971), "Comment on 'The Use of Error Components Models in Combining Cross Section With Time Series Data,'" *Econometrica*, 39, 397–401.

Honda, Y. (1985), "Testing the Error Components Model With Non-Normal Disturbances," *Review of Economic Studies*, 52, 681–690.

Kackar, R. N., and Harville, D. A. (1984), "Approximations for Standard Errors of Estimators of Fixed and Random Effects in Mixed Linear Models," *Journal of the American Statistical Association*, 79, 853–862.

King, M. L., and Evans, M. E. (1986), "Testing for Block Effects in Regression Models Based on Survey Data," *Journal of the American Statistical Association*, 81, 677–679.

Krasker, W. S., Kuh, E., and Welsch, R. E. (1983), "Estimation for Dirty Data and Flawed Models," in *Handbook of Econometrics* (Vol. 1), eds. Z. Griliches and M. D. Intriligator, Amsterdam: North-Holland, pp. 651–698.

Moulton, B. R. (1986), "Random Group Effects and the Precision of Regression Estimates," *Journal of Econometrics*, 32, 385–397.

Mundlak, Y. (1978), "On the Pooling of Time Series and Cross Section Data," *Econometrica*, 46, 69–85.

Pakes, A. (1983), "On Group Effects and Errors in Variables in Aggregation," *Review of Economics and Statistics*, 65, 168–173.

Pfeffermann, D., and Smith, T. M. F. (1985), "Regression Models for Grouped Populations in Cross-Section Surveys," *International Statistical Review*, 53, 37–59.

Searle, S. R. (1971), *Linear Models*, New York: John Wiley.

Econometrica, Vol. 56, No. 6 (November, 1988), 1371–1395

ESTIMATING VECTOR AUTOREGRESSIONS WITH PANEL DATA

BY DOUGLAS HOLTZ-EAKIN, WHITNEY NEWEY, AND HARVEY S. ROSEN[1]

This paper considers estimation and testing of vector autoregression coefficients in panel data, and applies the techniques to analyze the dynamic relationships between wages and hours worked in two samples of American males. The model allows for nonstationary individual effects, and is estimated by applying instrumental variables to the quasi-differenced autoregressive equations. Particular attention is paid to specifying lag lengths, forming convenient test statistics, and testing for the presence of measurement error. The empirical results suggest the absence of lagged hours in the wage forecasting equation. Our results also show that lagged hours is important in the hours equation, which is consistent with alternatives to the simple labor supply model that allow for costly hours adjustment or preferences that are not time separable.

KEYWORDS: Vector autoregression, panel data, causality tests, labor supply.

1. INTRODUCTION

VECTOR AUTOREGRESSIONS are now a standard part of the applied econometrician's tool kit. Although their interpretation in terms of causal relationships is controversial, most researchers would agree that vector autoregressions are a parsimonious and useful means of summarizing time series "facts."

To date, vector autoregressive techniques have been used mostly to analyze macroeconomic time series where there are dozens of observations. (See, e.g., Taylor (1980), or Ashenfelter and Card (1982).) In principle, these techniques should apply equally well to disaggregate data. For example, a vector autoregression can be used to summarize the dynamic relationship between an individual's hours of work and wages (see below) or the dynamic relationship between a government's revenues and expenditures (see Holtz-Eakin, Newey, Rosen (forthcoming)). Unlike macroeconomic applications, however, the available time series on micro units are typically quite short. Many of the popular panel data sets, for example, have no more than ten or twelve years of observations for each unit.[2] Also, it is possible that individual heterogeneity is an important feature of disaggregate data. For these reasons, it is inappropriate to apply standard techniques for estimating vector autoregressions to panel data.

The purpose of this paper is to formulate a coherent set of procedures for estimating and testing vector autoregressions in panel data. Section 2 presents the basic model, which builds upon Chamberlain (1983). Section 3 discusses identification and gives methods of parameter estimation and testing. The estimation

[1] This research was supported in part by NSF Grants SES-8419238 and SES-8410249. We are grateful to Joseph Altonji, the Editors, and three referees for useful comments. Joseph Altonji and David Card graciously provided us with the data used in the empirical analysis.

[2] Nevertheless, our techniques are appropriate for more "traditional" macroeconomic applications. For example, Taylor (1980) examined and compared the time series properties of several key macroeconomic variables for a number of European countries. Our methods could be used to execute formal tests of similarity between them.

method is similar in spirit to that of Anderson and Hsiao (1982). Section 4 applies the methods to an example from labor economics; we investigate the dynamic relationships between wages and hours worked. Section 5 provides a brief summary and conclusion.

2. THE MODEL

In the usual time series context, equations of a bivariate autoregression typically take the form

$$y_t = \alpha_0 + \sum_{l=1}^{m} \alpha_l y_{t-l} + \sum_{l=1}^{m} \delta_l x_{t-l} + u_t, \tag{2.1}$$

where the α's and δ's are the coefficients of the linear projection of y_t onto a constant and past values of y_t and x_t, and the lag length m is sufficiently large to ensure that u_t is a white noise error term. While it is not essential that the lag lengths for y and x are equal, we follow typical practice by assuming that they are identical.

Consistent estimation of the parameters of equation (2.1) requires many observations of x and y values. In time series applications these observations typically are obtained from a record of x and y over a long period of time. In contrast, panel data usually have a relatively small number of time series observations. Instead, there often are a great number of cross-sectional units, with only a few years of data on each unit. To estimate the parameters of equation (2.1) one must pool data from different units, a procedure which imposes the constraint that the underlying structure is the same for each cross-sectional unit.

The constraint that the time series relationship of x and y is the same for each cross-sectional unit is likely to be violated in practice, so that it is desirable to be able to relax this restriction. One way to relax the pooling constraint is to allow for an "individual effect," which translates in practice into an individual specific intercept in equation (2.1). Changes in the intercept of a stationary vector autoregression correspond to changes in the means of the variables, so that allowing for an individual effect allows for individual heterogeneity in the levels of x and y. A second way to allow for individual heterogeneity is to allow the variance of the innovation in equation (2.1) to vary with the cross-section unit. Changes in the innovation variance of a vector autoregression correspond to changes in the variance of the variables, so that allowing for cross-section heteroskedasticity in the innovation variance allows for individual heterogeneity in the variability of x and y. In what follows we allow for both an individual effect and cross-section heteroskedasticity in the variance of the innovation.

It is likely that the level and variability of the variables are important sources of individual heterogeneity, but it would also be nice to allow for individual heterogeneity in the time series correlation pattern of x and y. In this context, allowing for such heterogeneity is difficult because the variables on the right-hand side of the equation are lagged endogenous variables. Here it is impossible to interpret the α's and δ's as means of parameters that vary randomly across individual cross-section units, although this interpretation of regression parameters is possible when the right-hand side variables are exogenous. (See Pakes and Griliches (1984).)

On the other hand, pooling cross-sectional units does have certain advantages. First, the assumption of time stationarity can be relaxed. The presence of a large number of cross-sectional units makes it possible to allow for lag coefficients that vary over time. Second, the asymptotic distribution theory for a large number of cross-sectional units does not require the vector autoregression to satisfy the usual conditions that rule out unit and explosive roots. Of course, the presence of an explosive process may lead to difficulties in interpreting the model. Nevertheless, it is still possible, for example, to use standard asymptotic distribution theory to formulate valid tests for explosive behavior.[3]

A model with individual effects that relaxes the time stationarity assumption can be obtained by modifying a model presented by Chamberlain (1983). Assume that there are N cross-sectional units observed over T periods. Let i index the cross-sectional observations and t the time periods. A model that is analogous to equation (2.1), but allows for individual effects and nonstationarities across time is

$$y_{it} = \alpha_{0t} + \sum_{l=1}^{m} \alpha_{lt} y_{it-l} + \sum_{l=1}^{m} \delta_{lt} x_{it-l} + \Psi_t f_i + u_{it} \qquad (i = 1, \ldots, N;\ t = 1, \ldots, T), \tag{2.2}$$

where f_i is an unobserved individual effect and the coefficients α_{0t}, $\alpha_{1t}, \ldots, \alpha_{mt}, \delta_{1t}, \ldots, \delta_{mt}, \Psi_t$ are the coefficients of the linear projection of y_{it} on a constant, past values of y_{it} and x_{it}, and the individual effect f_i.

The model of equation (2.2) is different than that of Chamberlain (1983, p. 1263) in that Chamberlain avoids restricting the lag length by assuming that the first period of observation corresponds to the first period of the life of the individual unit. This assumption implies that the projection of y_{it} on all the observed past values for y_{it} and x_{it} (i.e. $\{y_{it-1}, \ldots, y_{i1}, x_{it-1}, \ldots, x_{i1}\}$) is equal to the projection on the entire past. That is, the lag length m in equation (2.2) varies with t according to the relation $m(t) = t - 1$. In practice, the entire history of each economic unit is not usually observed and some assumptions must be imposed to identify the time series relationship of x and y using the observed data.[4] Our method takes this fact into account. The assumption embodied in equation (2.2) is that for each observed time period t the projection of y_{it} on the

[3] The asymptotic theory does require that various moments of the data exist. Existence of moments in models with unit or explosive roots requires an assumption concerning the initial conditions of the data such as the assumption that the first point in the life of the individual units is a constant.

[4] Pakes and Griliches (1984) have considered a similar identification issue in the context of distributed lag models with exogenous regressors.

entire past depends only on the past m observations. In the next section we will discuss identification, estimation, and inference under this assumption on lag length, as well as ways of testing restrictions on the parameters of equation (2.2).

3. STATISTICAL INFERENCE

A. Identification

The specification of equation (2.2) as a projection equation implies that the error term u_{it} satisfies the orthogonality condition

$$(3.1)\qquad E[y_{is}u_{it}] = E[x_{is}u_{it}] = E[f_i u_{it}] = 0, \quad (s < t).$$

These orthogonality conditions imply that lagged values of x and y qualify as instrumental variables for equation (2.2). Our analysis of identification will be restricted to use of these orthogonality conditions.[5] Of course, if other restrictions are imposed on equation (2.2), such as absence of cross-section heteroskedasticity in the forecast error u_{it}, then it will be easier to identify the parameters.[6] Such extra restrictions will often take the form of imposing additional cross-section or time-series homogeneity in the relationship of x and y, so that restricting attention to the orthogonality conditions (3.1) is consistent with allowing as much heterogeneity as possible.

In order to use the orthogonality conditions (3.1) to identify the parameters of equation (2.2), the investigator must deal with the presence of the unobserved individual effect, f_i. It is well known that in models with lagged dependent variables it is inappropriate to treat individual effects as constants to be estimated.[7] Instead, we can transform equation (2.2) to eliminate the individual effect. Let $r_t = \Psi_t/\Psi_{t-1}$, and consider multiplying equation (2.2) for time period $t-1$ by r_t and subtracting the result from the equation for period t. Collecting all x and y terms dated $t-1$ or before on the right-hand side yields

$$(3.2)\qquad y_{it} = a_t + \sum_{l=1}^{m+1} c_{lt} y_{it-l} + \sum_{l=1}^{m+1} d_{lt} x_{it-l} + v_{it} \qquad (t = (m+2), \ldots, T),$$

[5] Note that it would be valid to use nonlinear functions of lagged values of x and y as instruments only if equation (2.2) could be interpreted as a conditional expectation rather than a linear projection. We choose to work with a linear projection specification because specification of the form of the conditional expectation of y_{it} given lagged values of x and y is difficult. It seems likely that this conditional expectation would involve nonlinear functions of lagged values of x and y.

[6] If the first and second moments of the data are the same for different cross-section units, then the minimum distance methods of MaCurdy (1981a) and Chamberlain (1983) could be used to estimate the parameters from cross-section moments. In this case it will be easier to identify the parameters, because the orthogonality conditions (3.1) do not involve all the cross-section moments.

[7] One common technique is to compute the difference between each variable and its time mean (by cross-section unit) to eliminate the individual effect. See, e.g., Lundberg (1985). In the current context, this procedure will yield inconsistent estimates, even when the parameters are stationary, because of the presence of lagged endogenous variables. See Nickell (1981).

where

$$
\begin{aligned}
(3.3)\qquad & a_t = \alpha_{0t} - r_t\alpha_{0t-1}, \\
& c_{1t} = r_t + \alpha_{1t}, \\
& c_{lt} = \alpha_{lt} - r_t\alpha_{l-1,t-1} \qquad (l = 2, \dots, m), \\
& c_{m+1,t} = -r_t\alpha_{m,t-1}, \\
& d_{1t} = \delta_{1t}, \\
& d_{lt} = \delta_{lt} - r_t\delta_{l-1,t-1} \qquad (l = 2, \dots, m), \\
& d_{m+1,t} = -r_t\delta_{m,t-1}, \\
& v_{it} = u_{it} - r_t u_{i,t-1}.
\end{aligned}
$$

Note that in the special case of $r_t = 1$ for each t, then this transformation is simple differencing of equation (2.2). This has been suggested for use in estimation of univariate autoregressive models in panel data by Anderson and Hsiao (1982). More generally, this transformation is a quasi-differencing transformation that has been suggested by Chamberlain (1983). We will proceed by first discussing identification of the parameters of the transformed equation (3.2), and then discussing identification of the original parameters of equation (2.2) from (3.2).

The orthogonality conditions of equation (3.1) imply that the error term of the transformed equation (3.2) satisfies the orthogonality condition

$$(3.4)\qquad E[y_{is}v_{it}] = E[x_{is}v_{it}] = 0 \qquad (s < (t-1)).$$

Thus, the vector of instrumental variables that is available to identify the parameters of equation (3.2) is

$$Z_{it} = [1, y_{it-2}, \dots, y_{i1}, x_{it-2}, \dots, x_{i1}].$$

Using the orthogonality conditions (3.4), a necessary condition for identification is that there are at least as many instrumental variables as right-hand side variables.[8] Since there are a total of $2m+3$ right-hand variables in equation (3.2) and the dimension of Z_{it} is $2t-3$, this order condition reduces to $t \geqslant m+3$. Thus, we must have $T \geqslant m+3$ in order to estimate the parameters of equation (3.2) for any t.

Consider the identification of the original parameters. Note first that the parameters of equation (3.2) involve only the ratio r_t of the coefficients of the individual effect. This is to be expected. Since changes in the level of these coefficients correspond to changes in the scale of the individual effect, the level of these coefficients is not identified. The original coefficients that can be identified are therefore the lag coefficients and the ratios of the coefficients of the individual

[8] See Fisher (1966). A sufficient condition for identification is that in the limit, the cross-product matrix between the instruments and the right-hand side variables have rank equal to the number of right-hand side variables.

effect. We will ignore identification of the constant terms (i.e., the α_{0t}'s) since they are usually considered nuisance parameters.

To identify the original parameters there must be at least as many parameters in the transformed equation as in the original equation. Note that it is possible to estimate the parameters of (3.2) for a total of $T-m-2$ time periods. Ignoring the constant terms, there is a total of $(T-m-2)2(m+1)$ parameters in the transformed equation, which involve a total of $(T-m-2)+(T-m-1)2m$ original parameters. Thus, it will not be possible to identify the original parameters unless $T-m-2 \geqslant 2m$, i.e., the number of estimable time periods is at least as large as twice the lag length. Also, because many of the parameters of the transformed equation consist of nonlinear functions of the original parameters with complicated interactions across time periods, for some values of the parameters it may not be possible to recover the original parameters, even when $T \geqslant 3m+2$.

Importantly, there is no need to recover the original parameters to test certain interesting hypotheses. For example, the hypothesis that x does not (Granger) cause y conditional on the individual effect restricts $\delta_{lt}=0$ for each l and t. Since this further implies that $d_{lt}=0$ for each l and t, this noncausality hypothesis can be tested by testing for zero coefficients for the lagged x variables in the transformed equation.

It is also useful to note that additional restrictions on the original parameters can aid their identification. When the restriction $r_t=1$ for each t is imposed, the parameters of the estimable transformed equations involve only $(T-m-1)2m$ original parameters. There will be at least as many parameters in the estimable time periods for the transformed equation as original parameters when $T-m-2 \geqslant m$. Thus, when $r_t=1$ and the number of estimable time periods is at least as large as the lag length, recovery of the original parameters from the transformed parameters is possible and, as is apparent from equation (3.3), straightforward.

Identification of the original parameters is easiest when the individual effect coefficients and the lag coefficients are stationary. In this case the transformed equation (3.2) can be written:

$$(3.5) \qquad y_{it}-y_{it-1}=a_t+\sum_{l=1}^{m}\alpha_l(y_{it-l}-y_{it-l-1})+\sum_{l=1}^{m}\delta_l(x_{it-l}-x_{it-l-1})+v_{it}.$$

Here there are only $2m+1$ right-hand side variables, so that there are enough instruments to identify the parameters if $t \geqslant m+2$. In the stationary case it is possible to obtain estimates of the lag parameters when $T \geqslant m+2$.

A final case that is of interest occurs when measurement error is present. Suppose that x_{it} and y_{it} are unobserved, and that instead we observe

$$(3.6) \qquad \tilde{x}_{it}=x_{it}+e_{it}^{x}, \qquad \tilde{y}_{it}=y_{it}+e_{it}^{y},$$

where e_{it}^{x} and e_{it}^{y} are measurement errors that are uncorrelated with all x and y observations and are uncorrelated across time. For simplicity we consider the implications of such measurement error for the stationary case. Substitution of

x_{it} and y_{it} from equation (3.6) in equation (3.5) yields

$$\tilde{y}_{it} - \tilde{y}_{it-1} = a_t + \sum_{l=1}^{m} \alpha_l (\tilde{y}_{it-l} - \tilde{y}_{it-l-1}) + \sum_{l=1}^{m} \delta_l (\tilde{x}_{it-l} - \tilde{x}_{it-l-1}) + \tilde{v}_{it}, \tag{3.7}$$

where

$$\tilde{v}_{it} = v_{it} + e_{it}^{y} - e_{it-1}^{y} - \sum_{l=1}^{m} \alpha_l (e_{it-l}^{y} - e_{it-l-1}^{y}) - \sum_{l=1}^{m} \delta_l (e_{it-l}^{x} - e_{it-l-1}^{x}). \tag{3.8}$$

By the assumption that the measurement errors are uncorrelated across time, the vector

$$\tilde{Z}_{it} = [1, \tilde{y}_{it-m-2}, \ldots, \tilde{y}_{i1}, \tilde{x}_{it-m-2}, \ldots, \tilde{x}_{i1}]$$

will be uncorrelated with $\tilde{v}_{it}$ and thus qualify as the vector of instrumental variables for equation (3.7).[9] Here there are only $2(t - m - 2) + 1$ instrumental variables, so that the requirement that there are at least as many instrumental variables as right-hand side variables becomes $t \geqslant 2m + 2$. Thus, it will only be possible to estimate the lag parameters in the stationary case with uncorrelated measurement error when $T \geqslant 2m + 2$.

B. *Estimation*

The presentation requires some additional notation. Let

$$Y_t = [y_{1t}, \ldots, y_{Nt}]' \quad \text{and} \quad X_t = [x_{1t}, \ldots, x_{Nt}]'$$

be $N \times 1$ vectors of observations on units for a given time period. Let

$$W_t = [e, Y_{t-1}, \ldots, Y_{t-m-1}, X_{t-1}, \ldots, X_{t-m-1}]$$

be the $N \times (2m + 3)$ vector of right-hand side variables for equations (3.2), where e is an $N \times 1$ vector of ones. Let

$$V_t = [v_{1t}, \ldots, v_{Nt}]'$$

be the $N \times 1$ vector of transformed disturbance terms, and let

$$B_t = \left[a_t, c_{1t}, \ldots, c_{m+1,t}, d_{1t}, \ldots, d_{m+1,t}\right]'$$

be the $(2m + 3) \times 1$ vector of coefficients for the equations. Then we can write equations (3.2) as[10]

$$Y_t = W_t B_t + V_t \qquad (t = (m+3), \ldots, T). \tag{3.9}$$

[9] The autoregressive structure of equation (3.7) will result in $\tilde{Z}_{it}$ being correlated with the right-hand side variables. The use of instrumental variables to identify equation (3.7) under measurement error is similar to the methods for identification of panel data models with measurement error that have been suggested by Griliches and Hausman (1984).

[10] Observe that we exclude $t \leqslant (m + 2)$ because these equations are not identified. See the discussion above.

To combine all the observations for each time period, we can "stack" equations (3.5). Let

$$Y = [Y'_{m+3}, \ldots, Y'_t]', \quad ((T-m-2)N \times 1)$$

$$B = [B'_{m+3}, \ldots, B'_T]', \quad ((T-m-2)(2m+3) \times 1)$$

$$V = [V'_{m+3}, \ldots, V'_T]', \quad ((T-m-2)N \times 1)$$

$$W = \text{diag}[W'_{m+3}, \ldots, W'_T], \quad ((T-m-2)N \times (T-m-2)(2m+3))$$

where diag[ ] denotes a block diagonal matrix with the given entries along the diagonal. With this, the observations for equations (3.2) can be written:

$$(3.10) \qquad Y = WB + V.$$

So far the discussion is quite similar to that of a classical simultaneous equations system where the equations are indexed by t and the observations by i. However, here the instrumental variables are different for different equations. The matrix of variables which qualify for use as instrumental variables in period t is

$$Z_t = [e, Y_{t-2}, \ldots, Y_1, X_{t-2}, \ldots, X_1]$$

which changes with T. Consider the matrix Z defined as

$$Z = \text{diag}[Z_{m+3}, \ldots, Z_T].$$

The orthogonality conditions ensure that

$$\operatorname*{plim}_{N\to\infty} (Z'V)/N = \operatorname*{plim}_{N\to\infty} \begin{bmatrix} (Z'_{m+3}V_{m+3})/N \\ \vdots \\ (Z'_T V_T)/N \end{bmatrix} = 0.$$

It follows directly that Z is the appropriate choice of instrumental variables for (3.10).[11]

To estimate B, premultiply (3.10) by Z' to obtain:

$$(3.11) \qquad Z'Y = Z'WB + Z'V.$$

We can then form a consistent instrumental variables estimator by applying GLS to this equation. As usual, such an estimator requires knowledge of the covariance matrix of the (transformed) disturbances, $Z'V$. This covariance matrix, Ω, is

[11] Limits are taken as $N \to \infty$, with T fixed.

given by

$$\Omega = E\{Z'VV'Z\}.$$

Ω is not known and therefore must be estimated. To do so, let $\tilde{B}_t$ be the preliminary consistent estimator of B_t formed by estimating the coefficients of the equation for time period t using two-stage least squares (2SLS) on the equation for each time period alone—using the correct list of instrumental variables.[12] Using these preliminary estimates, form the vector of residuals for period t: $\tilde{V}_t = Y_t - W_t\tilde{B}_t$. A consistent estimator of (Ω/N) is then formed by[13]

$$(3.12) \qquad (\tilde{\Omega}/N)_{rs} = \sum_{i=1}^{N} (v_{ir}v_{is}Z_{ir}'Z_{is})/N$$

where v_{it} $(t = r, s)$ is the ith element of V_t and Z_{it} is the ith row of Z_t. Finally, $\tilde{\Omega}$ is used to form a GLS estimator of the entire parameter vector, $\hat{B}$, using all the available observations:

$$(3.13) \qquad \hat{B} = \left[W'Z(\tilde{\Omega})^{-1}Z'W\right]^{-1} W'Z(\tilde{\Omega})^{-1}Z'Y.$$

(i) Imposing Linear Constraints

Stationarity of the individual effect and of the lag coefficients requires estimating B subject to linear constraints. The hypothesis that x does not cause y also imposes linear constraints on B. A simple way to formulate such constraints is to specify that

$$(3.14) \qquad B = H\gamma + G$$

where γ is a $k \times 1$ vector of parameters, H is a constant matrix with dimensions $((T - m - 2)(2m + 3) \times k)$, and G is a constant vector of the same dimension as B.[14] Since γ is the restricted parameter vector, it has dimension smaller than B.

Replacing B by $H\gamma + G$ and subtracting WG from both sides of (3.10) gives

$$(3.15) \qquad \tilde{Y} = Y - WG = WH\gamma + V = \tilde{W}\gamma + V.$$

This equation has exactly the same form as (3.10). Thus, we can estimate γ as before—using the data matrices transformed by G and H.

[12] That is:

$$\tilde{B}_t = \left[W_t'Z_t(Z_t'Z_t)^{-1}Z_t'W_t\right]^{-1} W_t'Z_t(Z_t'Z_t)^{-1}Z_t'Y_t.$$

[13] This procedure is an extension of White's (1980) heteroskedasticity consistent covariance matrix estimator. It is appropriate if $E\{v_{ir}v_{js}\} = 0$ for i, j, r, s such that $i \neq j$, that is, error terms for different units are uncorrelated. Note that common factors are controlled by inclusion of time dummy variables in the estimating equations.

[14] The rank of H must be k for the restrictions to be unique.

(ii) Efficiency

Several comments concerning the efficiency of $\hat{B}$ are in order. First, $\hat{B}$ is efficient in the class of instrumental variable estimators which use linear combinations of the instrumental variables. This follows directly from the results of Hansen (1982). (See also White (1982).) However, just as 3SLS on an entire system of equations may be more efficient than 3SLS on a subset of the equations, it may be possible to improve the efficiency by jointly estimating both the equation for y_{it} given past values of y and x *and* the equation for x_{it} given the history of x and y.

Second, recall that our procedure involves dropping the equations for the first $m+2$ time periods. When the parameters are nonstationary this procedure involves no loss in efficiency. Although the equations that are dropped may be correlated with the remaining equations, there are no cross equation restrictions, and they are underidentified. When the parameters are stationary, dropping the first $m+2$ periods may involve some loss in efficiency. Because there are cross-equation restrictions, efficiency can be improved by adding back $t=m+2$ and $t=m+1$ period equations, both of which have observable lags. Also, if there is no heteroskedasticity (across time or individuals) in the innovation variance for y_{it} and x_{it}, then all of the parameters for the joint y_{it} and x_{it} process can be estimated without the earliest cross-section moments, so that it may be possible to further improve efficiency by using these moments. Cross-section moment based estimation of moving average (but not autoregressive) time series models in panel data has been considered by MaCurdy (1981a).

C. Hypothesis Testing

In this section we discuss the computation of statistics to test the hypotheses that x does not cause y, that the parameters are stationary, that m is the correct lag length, and other possible hypotheses. In each case, the test statistic revolves around the sum of squared residuals, resulting in tests with chi-square distribution in large samples. Further, we consider two additional topics: tests when parameters are not identified under the alternative hypothesis and sequences of tests.

We consider only tests of linear restrictions on the estimated parameters, B. Consider the null hypothesis:

$$(3.16)\qquad H_0\colon B = H\gamma + G$$

where the notation is as before. As we have shown, it is straightforward to impose this restriction during estimation. Let

$$(3.17)\qquad Q = (Y - W\hat{B})'Z(\tilde{\Omega})^{-1}Z'(Y - W\hat{B})/N,$$

$$Q_R = \left(Y - \tilde{W}_{\hat{\gamma}}\right)'Z(\tilde{\Omega})^{-1}Z'\left(Y - \tilde{W}_{\hat{\gamma}}\right)/N.$$

Q is the unrestricted sum of squared residuals and Q_R is the restricted sum of squared residuals. Q and Q_R each have a chi-square distribution as N grows.[15] By analogy with the F statistic in the standard linear model, an appropriate test statistic is

$$(3.18) \qquad L = Q_R - Q.$$

L has the form of the numerator of the F statistic. By construction, the covariance matrix of the transformed disturbances is an identity matrix. As a result, L has a chi-squared distribution with degrees of freedom equal to the degrees of freedom of Q_R minus the degrees of freedom of Q. When all of the parameters are identified under both the null and the alternative hypotheses, the degrees of freedom of Q is equal to the number of instrumental variables (the number of rows of $Z'V$ in (3.11)) minus the number of parameters, i.e., the dimension of B. Similarly, Q_R has degrees of freedom equal to the dimension of B minus the dimension of γ.[16]

So far we have restricted our discussion to testing linear hypotheses concerning the coefficients of a single equation of a vector autoregression. In some contexts hypotheses that involve the coefficients of more than one equation and/or are nonlinear may be of interest. The case of linear hypotheses on the coefficients of more than one equation can be handled by simply stacking together the time periods for the several equations and proceeding in the manner we have discussed. The case of nonlinear restrictions can be handled by formulating the constraints as $B = H(\gamma)$, estimating γ by nonlinear GLS on equation (3.11), with $H(\gamma)$ in place of B, and forming the test statistic as before.

(*i*) *Unidentified Parameters*

When executing the tests, it is often the case that some parameters are not identified under the alternative hypothesis. For example, under the null hypothesis that x does not cause y, lagged x's can be used as instrumental variables for lagged y's. This is because lagged x's will be correlated with lagged y's via the individual effect. Use of these instruments permits us to identify the parameters in (3.11). Under the alternative hypothesis, the greater number of parameters means that not all of the parameters are identified. Nonetheless, a test of the null

[15] To see this, let P be the matrix such that $PP = \Omega^{-1}$. Then premultiplying (3.11) by P results in

$$PZ'Y/\sqrt{N} = (PZ'W/\sqrt{N})B + (PZ'V/\sqrt{N}).$$

Note that asymptotically, the disturbance $P'Z'V/\sqrt{N}$ is normally distributed with a covariance matrix equal to the identity matrix. As usual, sums of these squared residuals will have a chi-square distribution.

[16] L can be thought of as the extension of the Gallant and Jorgenson (1979) test statistic for 3SLS to this application. Of course, we could use other asymptotically equivalent test statistics to test the null hypothesis. In fact, the well known Wald test is numerically equivalent to our L. Newey and West (1987) discuss the relationship between L and other test statistics, including regularity conditions.

hypothesis is still possible. The method is analogous to conducting a Chow test with insufficient observations.[17] (See Fisher (1966).)

In more general notation, suppose that the parameters of the equation

$$Y_s = W_s B_s + V_s$$

are not identified (in the absence of the restrictions imposed by the null hypothesis) for time period s, i.e. Z_s has fewer elements than B_s (and, hence fewer than W_s). That is, in the equation

$$Z_s' Y_s = Z_s' W_s B_s + Z_s' V_s \tag{3.19}$$

the number of rows in $Z_s' Y_s$ is fewer than the number of parameters in B_s.

The appropriate test statistic once again uses the difference between the restricted and unrestricted sum of squared residuals, but care must be taken in constructing the covariance matrix Ω. Since the same covariance matrix must be used when computing both the restricted and unrestricted sum of squared residuals, the following procedure is appropriate.

First obtain the restricted sum of squares, incorporating the fact that B_s is identified under the null hypothesis by adding equation (3.19) to the list of equations to be estimated. Let $B^* = [B', B_s']'$ be the coefficients for the equations for all time periods. The parameters B are identified under either hypothesis, but those for time period s are not. Consider the null hypothesis

$$H_0\colon B^* = H\gamma + G \tag{3.20}$$

where the elements of γ are identified. Using similar notation, let

$$V^* = [V', V_s']', \qquad Y^* = [Y', Y_s'].$$

$$W^* = \operatorname{diag}[W, W_s], \qquad Z^* = \operatorname{diag}[Z, Z_s].$$

Under the null hypothesis, we may add equation (3.19) to equation (3.11) as:

$$Z^{*\prime}\tilde{Y}^* = Z^{*\prime}\tilde{W}^*\gamma + Z^{*\prime}v^*, \tag{3.21}$$

where $\tilde{Y}^* = Y^* - W^*G$ and $\tilde{W}^* = W^*H$.

Next estimate the parameters, B^*, and covariance matrix, Ω, using the procedure described above.

To obtain the unrestricted sum of squares and the appropriate test statistic. only those equations identified under the alternative hypothesis are employed. Accordingly, the appropriate estimate of the covariance matrix, Ω, is a submatrix of the covariance matrix estimated under the null hypothesis. The desired submatrix is that for equations identified under the alternative hypothesis.[18]

[17] The analogy is not exact because we consider more general hypotheses than simply hypotheses which impose equality across equations and because the joint covariance matrix across (3.11), above, and (3.19), below, is not diagonal.

[18] Importantly, the submatrix must be obtained from the estimated covariance matrix, Ω, *prior* to inverting the matrix and constructing the unrestricted sum of squares.

As before, $Q_R' - Q$ will have a chi-square distribution in large samples. In this instance, the degrees of freedom is given by:

$$\text{(3.22)} \qquad [\dim(Z^{*\prime}v^*) - \dim(\gamma)] - [\dim(Z'v) - \dim(B)].$$

(ii) Sequences of Tests

Two important questions in this framework are whether the data are consistent with a lag of length m and whether x causes y. It seems natural to nest the hypothesis of noncausality within the hypothesis about the lag length. That is, it makes sense to think of testing for noncausality conditional upon the outcome of a test for the lag length. When hypotheses are nested in this manner, we can construct a sequence of test statistics which will be (asymptotically) statistically independent. This permits us to isolate the reason for the rejection of the joint hypothesis.

To see how such a sequence is constructed, consider the two hypotheses

$$H_1\colon B = H\gamma + G,$$

and the second hypothesis, nested within H_1,

$$H_2\colon \gamma = \bar{H}\bar{\gamma} + \bar{G}.$$

Let Q be the unrestricted sum of squares, Q_{R1} the restricted sum of squares from imposing H_1, and Q_{R2} the sum of squares from imposing both H_1 and H_2, i.e., the restriction

$$B = H\bar{H}\gamma + (\bar{H}G + G).$$

Then $Q_{R1} - Q$ is the appropriate test statistic for testing H_1 and $Q_{R2} - Q_{R1}$ is the appropriate statistic for testing H_2 conditional upon H_1 being true. Furthermore, it is the case that the two statistics are asymptotically independently distributed.[19]

The significance of a joint test of H_1 and H_2 may be determined. Suppose that the test consists of rejecting H_1 and H_2 if either statistic is too large. Let the first test have significance level a_1 and the second a_2. The significance of the joint test is:

$$a_1 + a_2 - a_1 a_2.$$[20]

Notice that, if H_1 is accepted, we can infer the correctness of H_2 from whether or not the test statistic for H_2 is too large. However, if H_1 is rejected we can say nothing about H_2 because it is nested within H_1.

[19] This result is a simple extension of similar results for the likelihood ratio test for maximum likelihood.

[20] A similar procedure based upon Wald tests is discussed by Sargan (1980) in the closely related context of testing for dynamic specification of time series models.

IV. AN EXAMPLE

In this section we demonstrate the techniques described above in a dynamic analysis of the relationship between annual hours worked and hourly earnings.

A. The Issues

The conventional approach to analyzing the relationship between hours worked and the wage rate is to specify and estimate a model in which hours worked in a given period depend upon that period's wage rate. Implicitly, past hours and wages are assumed to have no impact on current hours. Similarly, the possibility that the past history of wages and hours affects the current wage is ruled out.

However, on theoretical grounds it is quite plausible to expect intertemporal relationships between wages and hours worked. For example, maximization of utility in some life cycle models leads to labor supply functions which depend on wages in other periods. (See, e.g., MaCurdy (1983).) Moreover, if there are costs to adjusting hours of work in response to changes in wages, one might expect that past hours of work would help predict current hours of work. At the same time, some human capital accumulation models suggest that present wage rates depend on past hours of work. (As hours increase, so does expertise on the job, leading to a higher subsequent wage.) Alternatively, one can imagine incentive schemes that link a worker's current wage rate to his past hours of work. (Hamilton (1986) argues that such schemes may help explain the behavior of medical interns, associates in law firms, and assistant professors.)

To fix ideas, consider the equation pair

$$h_{it} = \alpha_t^h + \beta w_{it} + \mu_i^h + \varepsilon_{it}^h, \tag{4.1a}$$

$$w_{it} = \alpha_t^w + \delta_1 w_{it-1} + \cdots + \delta_l w_{it-l} + \mu_i^w + \varepsilon_{it}^w, \tag{4.1b}$$

where

$$\begin{aligned} 0 &= E\left[\varepsilon_{it}^h \middle| \mu_i^h, \mu_i^w, h_{it-1}, h_{it-2}, \ldots, w_{it}, w_{it-1}, \ldots\right] \\ &= E\left[\varepsilon_{it}^w \middle| \mu_i^h, \mu_i^w, h_{it-1}, h_{it-2}, \ldots, w_{it-1}, w_{it-2}, \ldots\right] \end{aligned} \tag{4.2}$$

and h_{it} is the natural log of hours worked for individual i in period t, w_{it} is the natural log of the wage of individual i in period t, and μ_i^h and μ_i^w are unobserved individual effects. Equation (4.1a) is similar to a life cycle labor supply equation derived by MaCurdy (1981b) for a particular specification of preferences. In this equation μ_i^h represents the marginal utility of lifetime income (see also Heckman and MacCurdy (1980) and Browning, Deaton, and Irish (1985)), plus other individual specific variables. Unlike MaCurdy's (1981b) model, this equation imposes the strong restriction that ε_{it} is serially uncorrelated. Of course, variables which are a sum of a function of t and a function of i, such as experience, are allowed for, since they would be absorbed by the time specific term α_t^h and the individual specific term μ_i^h.

Equation (4.1b) is a wage forecasting equation. An important feature of this equation is that lagged hours are excluded. If lagged hours were of use in predicting wages, as might be the case in some of the scenarios previously discussed, then the individual would take into account the effect of today's choice of hours on tomorrow's wages, and the labor supply equation would take a different form.

Substituting w_{it} from equation (4.1b) into equation (4.1a) gives

$$(4.3) \qquad h_{it} = (\alpha_t^h + \beta\alpha_t^w) + \beta\delta_1 w_{it-1} + \cdots + \beta\delta_l w_{it-l} + (\mu_i^h + \beta\mu_i^w) + (\varepsilon_{it}^h + \beta\varepsilon_{it}^w),$$

which together with equation (4.1b) gives a VAR of the form considered in Section 2. Note that lagged hours is excluded from equation (4.1a) and (4.3) and that cross-equation restrictions are present. Evidence of the presence of lagged hours in either equation might therefore be interpreted as evidence against this specification. The presence of lagged hours in the wage equation might be interpreted as presence of the kind of human capital or incentive effects previously mentioned, while the presence of lagged hours in the hours equations might occur because of preferences that are not time separable or costs of adjusting hours. Of course, the presence of lagged hours in the hours equation could also be due to the omission of relevant variables or the violation of the assumption of no serial correlation in ε_{it}^h. Since serial correlation is often thought to be present in such models, this perhaps reduces the substantive implications of the finding that lagged hours appears in the hours equation.

The important point here is that this model and similar models imply the presence of dynamic interrelationships between wages and hours, and these interrelationships can be investigated using panel data on wages and hours. This fact, of course, has been recognized by earlier investigators. Lundberg (1985) used panel data to test whether hours Granger-cause wages. However, her estimation procedure involved taking deviations from means to account for the presence of individual effects. As we argued in Section II, such a procedure leads to inconsistent estimates. Abowd and Card (1986) analyzed the time series properties of the first differences in hours and earnings. Like MaCurdy (1981b) and Lundberg, they assumed that the individual effect was stationary. Moreover, although it would be possible to work backward from their estimates to learn about the time series properties of the *levels*, this would be extremely cumbersome, and they made no attempt to do so. In contrast, the procedures developed in Section 3 allow us to obtain consistent estimates of the time series properties of the *levels* of wages and hours without having to impose stationary individual effects, and without having to employ difficult nonlinear methods.

B. The Data

We estimate equations for wages and hours using a sample of 898 males from the Panel Study of Income Dynamics (PSID) covering the years 1968 to 1981.[21]

[21] Our data include the Survey of Economic Opportunity (SEO) subsample, which oversamples low income households. We performed all of the tests reported in the next section deleting the SEO subsample. The results, which are available upon request, do not in general differ substantially from those presented below. For the one exception, see footnote 22.

We study two variables for each individual. First is the log of the individual's annual hours of work ("hours", denoted h_t), and second is the log of his annual average hourly earnings ("wages", denoted w_t). (For a complete description of the data, see Altonji and Paxson (1986).) As discussed below, we also check some of our results using data from the National Longitudinal Survey of Men 45–59.

The wage variable in both data sets is constructed by dividing total earnings by hours worked. As a result, to the extent that measurement errors are present, they will be correlated across variables. While this presents a problem for full-information methods, the single equation techniques used here are unaffected by this correlation. Finally, to the extent that measurement error induces a serial correlation in the composite error terms of the autoregression, this problem will reveal itself as a correlation between instrumental variables and the transformed errors.

C. *Estimation and Testing*

Using the PSID data, we estimate two equations, one for hours and one for wages. On the right side of each are lags of both wages and hours. We conduct tests for parameter stationarity, minimum lag length, and causality or exclusion restrictions.

While in principle it is desirable to begin by specifying an arbitrarily long initial lag length, this poses a problem in practice. As additional lags are specified, the block structure of the matrix of instrumental variables causes the size of the weighting matrix (Ω in equation (3.12) above) to grow rapidly. For such large matrices, standard numerical procedures for inversion may yield unsatisfactory results. Therefore we initially assume a lag length $m = 3$, leading to four lags in the quasi-differenced reduced form. The wage and hours equations are estimated for the years 1977 to 1981.

(*i*) *Wage Equation*

Results for the wage equation are presented in Table I. The first step is to test for parameter stationarity; i.e., both the individual effects and the lag parameters in the equation are the same for each year. As the second line of the table shows, the chi-square statistic for this test (26.22) indicates that one cannot reject this hypothesis at any level of significance less than roughly 80%. Thus, the appropriate specification of the wage equation is a first-differenced form containing at least three lags each of wages and hours.

Column (1) of Table II shows estimates of the wage equation assuming parameter stationarity, but with no other constraints imposed. The only parameter that is statistically significant is that of the first lagged wage. Not only are the other coefficients insignificant, they are relatively small in absolute value as well. None of the other coefficients is more than about one-third the coefficient on the first lagged wage, in absolute value. While suggestive, these observations do not tell us which lag length is most consistent with the data. It is necessary to use the

TABLE I

WAGE EQUATION

	Q	L	DF	P
(i) $m = 3$	0.00	—	0	—
(ii) All Parameters Stationary	26.22	26.22	34	0.828
(iii) $m = 2$	27.14	0.92	2	0.631
(iv) $m = 1$	29.31	2.17	2	0.338
(v) $m = 0$	43.40	14.09	2	0.001
(vi) Exclude Hours $m = 1$	29.94	0.63	1	0.427

TABLE II

UNCONSTRAINED PARAMETER ESTIMATES[a]

	(1) Wage Equation	(2) Hours Equation
Δh_{t-1}	0.0623	0.145
	(0.0476)	(0.0262)
Δw_{t-1}	0.183	0.00116
	(0.0631)	(0.0385)
Δh_{t-2}	0.0189	−0.00489
	(0.0276)	(0.0158)
Δw_{t-2}	0.0359	−0.0455
	(0.0320)	(0.0190)
Δh_{t-3}	0.0200	0.0158
	(0.0234)	(0.0202)
Δw_{t-3}	−0.00328	−0.00185
	(0.0245)	(0.0168)

[a] Figures in parentheses are standard errors.

methods of Section III.C to conduct the appropriate tests. The lag length results are recorded in lines (iii) through (v) of Table I, which show the results for the sequence $m = 2$, $m = 1$, and $m = 0$, respectively. The results provide no evidence that the wage equation contains more than a single lag of hours and wages.

Finally, we conduct a test of the hypothesis that hours do not cause wages. Line (vi) of Table I shows that one cannot reject the hypothesis that lagged hours may be excluded from the wage equation. The estimate of this single autoregressive parameter is shown in column (1) of Table III. Note that the exclusion of lagged hours from the wage equation rejects the notion that past hours of work affect the current wage. To the extent that workers face a market locus of hours and wages, it contains at most contemporaneous tradeoffs between hours and wages.

(*ii*) *Hours Equation*

To complete the investigation, we perform a symmetric set of tests for the specification of the hours equation. The results are reported in Table IV. As was

TABLE III

CONSTRAINED PARAMETER ESTIMATES[a]

	(1) Wage Eq.	(2) Hours Eq.	(3) Hours Eq.
		$(m=2)$	$(m=1)$
Δh_{t-1}	—	0.156	0.156
	—	(0.0206)	(0.0175)
Δh_{t-2}	—	0.002	—
	—	(0.0181)	—
Δw_{t-1}	0.135	−0.001	—
	(0.0368)	(0.05)	—
	—	−0.045	—
Δw_{t-2}	—	(0.0174)	—

[a] Figures in parentheses are standard errors.

TABLE IV

HOURS EQUATION

	Q	L	DF	P
(i) $m=3$	0.00	—	—	—
(ii) Parameters Stationary	26.69	26.69	34	0.810
(iii) $m=2$	27.33	0.64	2	0.726
(iv) $m=1$	34.09	6.76	2	0.034
(v) Exclude Wages, $m=2$	37.47	10.14	2	0.006
(vi) Exclude Wages, $m=1$	37.62	3.53	1	0.060

the case with the wage equation, we cannot reject the hypothesis that the appropriate specification is a first-differenced equation with constant lag parameters (see line (ii)). The unconstrained parameter estimates for this specification are presented in column (2) of Table II. As in the wage equation, the strongest effect both from the point of view of the absolute value of the coefficient and statistical significance, is the own first lag. However, while in the wage equation nothing else seems to "matter," in the hours equation, the second lag on wages is statistically significant.[22] Indeed, as in Table IV one cannot reject the hypothesis that $m=2$ (see line iii). Further restrictions depend, however, on the chosen level of significance. As line (iv) indicates, one cannot reject the hypothesis that $m=1$ at the 1% level. However, this conclusion is reversed using a 5% significance level.

Therefore, we test the hypothesis that lagged wages do not cause hours conditional on both $m=1$ and $m=2$. Using $m=2$ (and, thus, adopting a 5% significance level) one can reject the hypothesis that lagged wages may be excluded from the equation for hours (line (v)). The parameter estimates for this AR(2) model are shown in column (2) of Table III. Using the 1% level of

[22] When the SEO subsample was excluded, the data did not reject the hypothesis that lagged wages could be excluded from the hours equation.

significance leads to different results. As shown in line (vi) of Table IV, one cannot reject the hypothesis that lagged wages may be excluded from the AR(1) specification of the hours equation at a 5% significance level. The resulting parameter estimate is shown in column (3) of Table III.

Thus, using a 1% significance level, one is left with a parsimonious representation of the dynamic behavior of hours and wages. Both variables may be represented as autonomous autoregressive processes with a single lag. The robustness of this result is examined below.

(*iii*) *Deviations from Time Means*

It is interesting to determine whether an inappropriate statistical technique would lead to substantively different results. Recall that Lundberg tested for intertemporal relationships between wages and hours by conducting F-tests for exclusion of wages and hours from a VAR in which individual effects are removed by measuring all variables as deviations from individual time means. We applied this method to the PSID data. Specifically, we estimated a VAR with constant parameters and three lags of wages and hours, measuring all variables as deviations from time means. In direct contrast to the results presented above, this procedure indicates that hours Granger-cause wages and wages Granger-cause hours. The F statistic for the former test is 11.4 and for the latter 4.0. Both are significant at the 1% level. In short, in this context using an inappropriate estimation technique can lead to serious errors.

(*iv*) *Measurement Error*

The estimation procedure used in the wage and hours equations makes no special allowance for the possibility of measurement error. Altonji (1986) has estimated that a large part of the yearly variation in PSID data is due to measurement error. As noted in Section 3, the estimation procedure may be modified to accommodate measurement error by simply using a different set of instrumental variables.

We examine the effect of measurement error on our results by re-estimating the final form of both the wage and hours equations. In order to isolate the effect of measurement error, we focus on the correlation between the composite error term and the instrumental variables. For the AR(1) specification, measurement error will produce a correlation between instrumental variables dated $t-2$ and the composite error. In the absence of measurement error, no such correlation will be present. (See equation (3.8).) We estimate the equation for wages using two different sets of instrumental variables: (i) lagged wages dated both $t-2$ and $t-3$ and (ii) lagged wages dated $t-3$.[23] We estimate the hours equation using the corresponding sets of instrumental variables. One can formally test the null hypothesis of no correlation between the instrumental variables dated $t-2$ and

[23] Note that this set of instruments is more restrictive than that used in our previous estimations. This change is an attempt to increase the power of the test for measurement error.

TABLE V
MEASUREMENT ERROR CORRECTION[a]

	Wage Equation	Hours Equation
(i) Δh_{t-1}	—	0.169 (0.0279)
Δw_{t-1}	0.179 (0.050)	—
(ii) Δh_{t-1}	—	0.170 (0.224)
Δw_{t-1}	0.460 (0.172)	—
(iii) $\chi^2(5)$	6.23 ($p = 0.284$)	1.427 ($p = 0.921$)

[a] Figures in parentheses are standard errors. Estimates in part (i) of the table use variables dated $t-2$ and $t-3$ as instrumental variables; the estimates in part (ii) use only variables dated $t-3$. Part (iii) contains the test statistic for a test of the null hypothesis of no correlation.

the error terms—and thus no measurement error—using a generalized method of moments test. (See Holtz-Eakin (forthcoming).)

The results are presented in Table V. Part (i) of the table shows the parameter estimates using instrumental variables lagged $t-2$ and $t-3$. Part (ii) gives the alternative parameter estimates using only variables dated $t-3$ as instrumental variables. Part (iii) contains the test statistic for a test of the null hypothesis of no correlation. The statistic is distributed as a chi-square with five degrees of freedom. The significance level of the test is shown in parentheses.

As the p-value indicates, the test of the null hypothesis of no correlation fails to reject at conventional significance levels.[24] It is important to note, however, that the estimated autoregressive parameter in the wage equation changes substantially with the measurement error correction. It increases from 0.179 to 0.460 when wages dated $t-2$ are excluded.

Turning to the hours equation, we find that the estimate of the autoregressive parameter for hours does not vary with the measurement error correction, although the precision of the estimate is affected. Not surprisingly, the null hypothesis of no measurement error in the hours equation cannot be rejected.

In sum, our attempt to correct for measurement error produces mixed signals. On one hand, changing the set of instrumental variables to allow for measurement error can have an important effect on the parameter estimates. On the other, the formal test suggests that this difference is not statistically significant. This suggests that the test may have low power in this particular application.

(v) *Evidence from the NLS*

As another check of the robustness of these results, we examine data on wages and hours from the National Longitudinal Survey of Men 45–59 (NLS). The

[24] A Hausman test on the difference between the two coefficients also fails to reject the hypothesis, although the p value of about 0.10 provides somewhat stronger evidence against the null hypothesis.

TABLE VI
NLS RESULTS

	Q	L	DF	P
Hours Equation				
$m = 1$, All Parameters				
Stationary	21.21	—	16	0.170
Exclude wages	21.36	0.15	1	0.699
Wage Equation				
$m = 1$, All Parameters				
Stationary	25.95	—	16	0.055
Exclude Hours	26.00	0.05	1	0.823

NLS sample consists of 1446 men who had positive earnings and hours in each of the survey years 1966, 1967, 1969, 1971, 1973, and 1975. (See Abowd and Card (1986) for details on the construction of the sample.) As in the PSID, we use two data series: the log of annual hours of work and the log of average hourly earnings. The latter is constructed as the difference between the log of annual earnings and the log of annual hours.

Use of the NLS is complicated by the above-noted fact that the data are not available for consecutive years. For the simple AR(1) model

$$y_{it} = f_i + \alpha_1 y_{it-1} + u_{it}, \tag{4.4}$$

the problem of missing years can be circumvented by successive substitution to yield a relationship between two-year differences:

$$y_{it} - y_{it-2} = \alpha_1^2(y_{it-2} - y_{it-4}) + u_{it} + \alpha_1 u_{it-1} - u_{it-2} - \alpha_1 u_{it-3}. \tag{4.5}$$

Equation (4.5) is estimable using our methods. However, for an AR(2) (or longer lag), successive substitution gives an infinite order lag specification that is not estimable using our methods. Fortunately, the results from the PSID discussed above indicate (using the 1% significance level) that equation (4.4) may be an adequate representation of both wages and hours. For these reasons, we concentrate on the estimation of AR(1) models. We test the assumption of excludability and the overidentifying restrictions implied by the initial assumptions on stationarity and lag length.

The test results are contained in Table VI. For both wages and hours, we cannot reject the initial assumptions of stationarity and lag length; although the test for wages is borderline at the 5% level.[25] Under the identification restriction that both own lag coefficients are nonzero and have the same sign, we can test for causality by testing whether the wage is significant in the hours equation, and whether hours is significant in the wage equation. The result of these tests is that one cannot reject the hypotheses that hours do not cause wages and wages do not

[25] Note that we only identify the square of the matrix of autoregressive coefficients from the biannual data. These restrictions allow us to solve for the original matrix in terms of its square.

TABLE VII

NLS PARAMETER ESTIMATES[a]

	Wage Equation	Hours Equation
Δh_{t-2}	—	0.0263
	—	(0.0410)
Δw_{t-2}	0.0492	—
	(0.0259)	—

TRANSFORMED NLS PARAMETER ESTIMATES[a]

	Wage Equation	Hours Equation
Δh_{t-1}	—	0.162
	—	(0.127)
Δw_{t-1}	0.222	—
	(0.0584)	—

[a] Figures in parentheses are standard errors.

cause hours. The result in both cases is an equation of the form specified in (4.5). Thus, neither the PSID nor NLS data lend support to the notion that the current wage rate depends upon past hours of work.

The parameter estimates are shown in Table VII. Of course, because of the presence of the α_1^2 in equation (4.5), these parameters do not correspond directly to those we obtained using PSID data. To make the estimates comparable, we take square roots, imposing an identifying assumption that the underlying coefficients are positive. These transformed estimates (and their standard errors) are shown at the bottom of Table VII.

The correspondence between these point estimates and those in Table III is striking. This is particularly compelling when one considers that the two data sets cover different years and contain different types of individuals: the PSID has only hourly employees, while the NLS has only relatively old workers. With respect to the statistical significance of the estimates, in both data sets the lagged wage is significant at conventional levels. There is some disagreement with respect to lagged hours, however. For the PSID the t statistic for the coefficient of lagged hours in the hours equation is 8.90; for the NLS it is 1.28. While this evidence is mixed it does suggest that it is potentially dangerous to exclude lagged hours from the autoregressive hours equation. Whether this fact has consequences for the appropriate specification of the structural hours equation is unclear; it depends on whether the presence of lagged hours is due to serial correlation.[26]

[26] Using PSID data, we tested for the presence of first order serial correlation in ε_{it}^h of equation (4.1a) using a Wald test of the common factor restriction that the coefficient of H_{t-1} times the coefficient of w_{t-1} is equal to the negative of the coefficient of w_{t-2}. (This test is valid under the assumption that only w_{t-1} appears in the wage equation.) The test indicated that one can reject the hypothesis of first order autocorrelation at a 3 percent significance level. Of course, testing for other patterns of serial correlation might produce a different result. Hence, while this test is suggestive that the presence of lagged hours is indeed due to "structural" considerations, it is not conclusive.

TABLE VIII

NLS MEASUREMENT ERROR CORRECTION[a]

	Wage Equation	Hours Equation
(i) Δh_{t-2}	—	-0.092
	—	(0.0597)
Δw_{t-2}	0.063	—
	(0.0312)	—
(ii) Δh_{t-2}	—	-0.224
	—	(0.35)
Δw_{t-2}	0.420	—
	(0.154)	—
(iii) $\chi^2(3)$	10.913	2.295
	($p = 0.017$)	($p = 0.513$)

[a] Figures in parentheses are standard errors. Estimates in part (i) of the table use variables dated $t-2$ and $t-4$ as instrumental variables; the estimates in part (ii) use only variables dated $t-4$. Part (iii) contains the test statistic for a test of the null hypothesis of no correlation.

Finally, in the same fashion as for the PSID we check for the importance of measurement error by re-estimating the equations using alternative sets of instrumental variables. The results for the untransformed parameter estimates are shown in Table VIII. Comparing these results to those in the top of Table VII, we see that much like the results from the PSID, the most seriously affected coefficient is that in the wage equation. Here, however, the formal test for the wage equation supports the hypothesis of measurement error at close to the 1% level.[27] As before, for the hours equation, the hypothesis of measurement error is not supported.

5. CONCLUSION

We have presented a simple method of estimating vector autoregression equations using panel data. The key to its simplicity is the fact that estimation and testing have straightforward GLS interpretations—no nonlinear optimization is required.

We applied our estimation procedure to the study of dynamic relationships between wages and hours. Our empirical results are consistent with the absence of lagged hours in the wage forecasting equation, and thus with the absence of certain human capital or dynamic incentive effects. Our results also show that lagged hours is important in the hours equation, which is consistent with alternatives to the simple labor supply model that allow for costly hours adjustment or preferences that are not time separable. As usual, of course, these results might be due to serial correlation in the error term or to a functional form misspecification. However, we find it encouraging that broadly similar results are obtained from two different data sets.

[27] A Hausman test also supports the measurement error hypothesis for the wage equation; the p value is about 0.02.

More generally, our empirical example demonstrates the importance of testing for the appropriate lag length prior to causality testing, an issue of considerable importance in short panels. In the absence of such tests, no inferences concerning causal relationships can be drawn. The example also demonstrates that use of inappropriate methods to deal with individual effects in the VAR context can lead to highly misleading results.

Columbia University, New York City, New York, U.S.A.
and
Princeton University, Princeton, NJ, U.S.A.

Manuscript received June, 1985; final revision received October, 1987.

REFERENCES

ABOWD, JOHN M., AND DAVID CARD (1986): "On the Covariance Structure of Earnings and Hours Changes," mimeo, Princeton University, October, 1986.

ALTONJI, J. (1986): "Intertemporal Substitution in Labor Supply: Evidence from Micro Data," *Journal of Political Economy*, 94, S176–S215.

ALTONJI, J., AND C. PAXSON (1986): "Job Characteristics and Hours of Work," *Research in Labor Economics*.

ANDERSON, T. W., AND C. HSIAO (1982): "Formulation and Estimation of Dynamic Models Using Panel Data," *Journal of Econometrics*, 18, 47–82.

ASHENFELTER, ORLEY, AND D. CARD (1982): "Time Series Representations of Economic Variables and Alternative Models of the Labour Market," *Review of Economic Studies*, 49, 761–782.

BROWNING, M. J., A. S. DEATON, AND M. IRISH (1985): "A Profitable Approach to Labor Supply and Commodity Demands Over the Life-Cycle," *Econometrica*, 53, 503–544.

CHAMBERLAIN, GARY (1983): "Panel Data," Chapter 22 in *The Handbook of Econometrics Volume II*, ed. by Z. Griliches and M. Intrilligator. Amsterdam: North-Holland Publishing Company.

FISHER, FRANKLIN (1966): *The Identification Problem in Econometrics*. Huntington, N.Y.: Krieger Publishing Company.

GALLANT, RONALD, AND D. JORGENSON (1979): "Statistical Inference for a System of Nonlinear, Implicit Equations in the Context of Instrumental Variables Estimation," *Journal of Econometrics*, 11, 275–302.

GRILICHES, ZVI, AND J. HAUSMAN (1984): "Errors in Variables in Panel Data," National Bureau of Economic Research Technical Working Paper No. 37, May, 1984.

HAMILTON, BRUCE (1986): "Merit Pay Increases and the Supply of Labor," mimeo, Johns Hopkins University, November, 1986.

HANSEN, LARS (1982): "Large Sample Properties of Generalized Method of Moments Estimators," *Econometrica*, 50, 1029–1054.

HECKMAN, J. J., AND T. E. MACURDY (1980): "A Life Cycle Model of Female Labor Supply," *Review of Economic Studies*, 47, 47–74.

HOLTZ-EAKIN, D. (FORTHCOMING): "Testing for Individual Effects in Autoregressive Models," forthcoming in *Journal of Econometrics*.

HOLTZ-EAKIN, D., W. NEWEY, AND H. ROSEN (FORTHCOMING): "The Revenues-Expenditures Nexus: Evidence from Local Government Data," forthcoming in *International Economic Review*.

LUNDBERG, S. (1985): "Tied Wage-Hours Offers and the Endogeneity of Wages," *Review of Economics and Statistics*, 67, 405–410.

MACURDY, T. (1981a): "Time Series Models Applied to Panel Data," mimeo, Stanford University.

——— (1981b): "An Empirical Model of Labor Supply in a Life Cycle Setting," *Journal of Political Economy*, 89, 1059–1086.

——— (1983): "A Simple Scheme for Estimating an Intertemporal Model of Labor Supply and Consumption in the Presence of Taxes and Uncertainty," *International Economic Review*, 24, 265–289.

NEWEY, WHITNEY, AND K. WEST (1987): "Hypothesis Testing with Efficient Method of Moment Estimation," *International Economic Review*, 28, 777–787.

NICKELL, STEPHEN (1981): "Biases in Dynamic Models with Fixed Effects," *Econometrica*, 49, 1417–1426.

PAKES, ARIEL, AND ZVI GRILICHES (1984): "Estimating Distributed Lags in Short Panels with an Application to the Specification of Depreciation Patterns and Capital Stock Constructs," *Review of Economic Studies*, 51, 243–262.

SARGAN, J. D. (1980): "Some Tests of Dynamic Specification for a Single Equation," *Econometrica*, 48, 879–898.

TAYLOR, JOHN (1980): "Output and Price Stability—An International Comparison," *Journal of Economic Dynamics and Control*, 2, 109–132.

WHITE, HALBERT (1980): "A Heteroskedasticity-Consistent Covariance Matrix Estimator and a Direct Test for Heteroskedasticity," *Econometrica*, 48, 817–838.

——— (1982): "Instrumental Variables Regression with Independent Observations," *Econometrica*, 50, 483–500.

[10]

Journal of Business & Economic Statistics, July 1991, Vol. 9, No. 3

Over-Identification Tests in Earnings Functions With Fixed Effects

Joshua D. Angrist
Department of Economics, Harvard University, Cambridge, MA 02138

Whitney K. Newey
Department of Economics, Massachusetts Institute of Technology, Cambridge, MA 02139

The fixed-effects model for panel data imposes restrictions on coefficients from regressions of all leads and lags of the dependent variable on all leads and lags of right-side variables. In the standard fixed-effects model, the omnibus goodness-of-fit statistic is shown to simplify to the degrees of freedom times the R^2 from a regression of analysis of covariance residuals on all leads and lags of right-side variables. This result is applied to test models for the union-wage effect using data from the National Longitudinal Survey of Youth (NLSY). Identification and estimation of the return to schooling in models with fixed effects is also discussed. Although schooling is often treated as time-invariant, schooling increases over a five-year period for nearly 20% of continuously employed men in the NLSY. The analysis of covariance estimate of the returns to schooling is precisely estimated and roughly twice as large as the ordinary least squares estimate. Unlike in the union-wage effects equation, however, the omnibus goodness-of-fit test suggests that the fixed-effects assumption may be inappropriate for human capital earnings functions.

KEY WORDS: Panel data; Specification testing.

In two influential articles, Chamberlain (1982, 1984) developed the theory of multivariate regression models for panel data. An important contribution of this work was to point out that the fixed-effects specification imposes testable restrictions on coefficients from regressions of all leads and lags of dependent variables on all leads and lags of independent variables. Chamberlain suggested that estimation and testing be carried out by minimizing an optimally weighted quadratic form in the difference between unrestricted parameters and the restrictions implied by the fixed-effects model. In the simultaneous equations context, Rothenberg (1973) referred to this as minimum chi-square (MCS) because the estimation minimand is a chi-squared goodness-of-fit statistic for restrictions on reduced-form coefficients.

In addition to MCS procedures, Chamberlain also considered a generalization of three-stage least squares (3SLS), demonstrating that there are 3SLS estimators asymptotically equivalent to MCS. In the first part of this article, we show that the over-identification test statistics associated with 3SLS equivalents of MCS are identical to the MCS test statistic. Furthermore, in the standard fixed-effects model in which the time-varying error component has a scalar covariance matrix, the 3SLS over-identification test statistic is simply the degrees of freedom times the R^2 from a regression of analysis of covariance (deviations from mean) residuals on all leads and lags of right-side variables. Thus the form of the test statistic is the same as that of standard orthogonality test statistics in homoscedastic regression models (Hausman 1984). Moreover, this version of the test statistic highlights a useful interpretation of the identifying information in fixed-effects models: Untransformed regressors are valid instrumental variables for equations in deviations from means form, and vice versa.

The relationship between MCS and 3SLS test statistics leads to considerable computational simplification in exploratory specification analysis. We illustrate this by estimating and testing a number of models for the union-wage effect using data from the National Longitudinal Survey of Youth (NLSY). Our empirical work begins by replicating Chamberlain's (1984) estimates from the earlier National Longitudinal Survey of Young Men (NLSYM).

Following the estimates of union-wage effects, we consider the identification and estimation of the returns to schooling in fixed-effects models. In Chamberlain's equation for union-wage effects, schooling is included as a time-invariant regressor with a time-varying coefficient. This specification identifies differences in the returns to schooling over time, although the actual return to time-invariant schooling in fixed-effect models is not identified without additional assumptions. As an empirical matter, however, schooling increases by roughly one-third of a year for continuously employed men in our five-year panel, and almost 20% of the sample experiences some increase in schooling. We show that these changes are enough to produce remarkably precise estimates of the return to schooling. The analysis of covariance estimates are roughly twice as large as the ordinary least squares (OLS) estimates. In contrast to the union-wage-effects equation, however, the omnibus goodness-of-fit tests suggest that the fixed-effects assumption may be inappropriate for human capital earnings functions.

1. MCS AND 3SLS IN FIXED-EFFECTS MODELS

The fixed-effects model for panel data is

$$y_{it} = x_{it}\beta + \alpha_i + u_{it}$$
$$\alpha_i = x_{i1}\lambda_1 + \cdots + x_{iT}\lambda_T + \varepsilon_i, \quad (1)$$

where $t = 1, \ldots, T$ indexes time, $i = 1, \ldots, N$ indexes individuals, x_{it} is a $1 \times k$ row vector of regressors, and β and the λ's are $k \times 1$ column vectors of coefficients. Correlation between x_{it} and the unobserved individual effect α_i is described by the linear combination in the second line of (1). The error term u_{it} is assumed uncorrelated with $x_{i2}, \ldots, x_{it}$, and ε_{it} is uncorrelated with $x_{i1}, \ldots, x_{iT}$ by construction. Because of correlation between α_i and x_{it}, the OLS regression of y_{it} on x_{it} will not produce a consistent estimate of β. Writing $\bar{y}_i$ and $\bar{x}_i$ for the time means of y_{it} and x_{it}, however, the OLS estimate of β in

$$y_{it} - \bar{y}_i = (x_{it} - \bar{x}_i)\beta + (u_{it} - \bar{u}_i) \quad (2)$$

will be consistent. Least squares estimation of Equation (2) is sometimes known as *analysis of covariance* (ANACOVA).

The specification that justifies ANACOVA implies many testable restrictions. For example, data from any pair of time periods may be differenced and the differenced equation consistently estimated by OLS. Differenced equations that are more than two periods apart should yield estimates of β that are not statistically different from estimates based on adjacent differences. Griliches and Hausman (1986) used this property of fixed-effects models to develop tests for measurement error in panel data. In a related article, Holtz-Eakin, Newey, and Rosen (1988) discussed tests for misspecification in panel-data vector autoregressions with fixed effects.

Chamberlain's MCS procedure for estimation of β and λ is based on the unrestricted regression of all leads and lags of y_{it} on all leads and lags of x_{it} and provides an "omnibus test" of all the restrictions implied by the fixed effects model. Let $y_i = [y_{i1}, \ldots, y_{iT}]$ and $x_i = [x_{i1}, \ldots, x_{iT}]$, and denote the "reduced form" regression of y_i on x_i by $y_i = x_i\Pi + v_i$. Writing $\Pi(\beta, \lambda)$ for the relationship between reduced form and structural parameters, (1) implies that

$$\Pi(\beta, \lambda) = (I_T \otimes \beta) + \lambda l', \quad (3)$$

where $l' \equiv [1, \ldots, 1]$ is of dimension $1 \times T$ and $\lambda' = [\lambda_1', \ldots, \lambda_T']$. For example, when $T = 2$ and $k = 1$,

$$\Pi = \begin{pmatrix} \beta + \lambda_1 & \lambda_1 \\ \lambda_2 & \beta + \lambda_2 \end{pmatrix}.$$

Let $\hat{\Pi}$ be a consistent estimate of Π. MCS estimates of β and λ are computed by minimizing

$$h(\beta, \lambda) = N * \text{vec}[\hat{\Pi} - \Pi(\beta, \lambda)]'\hat{\Omega}^{-1} \times \text{vec}[\hat{\Pi} - \Pi(\beta, \lambda)], \quad (4)$$

where $\hat{\Omega}$ is a consistent estimate of the asymptotic variance of $\sqrt{N}[\text{vec}(\hat{\Pi} - \Pi)]$. When (1) is the true model, the minimized value of $h(\beta, \lambda)$ has a chi-squared distribution with $kT^2 - (Tk + k)$ df because there are Tk λ's and k elements of β to infer from the kT^2 elements of Π.

The MCS procedure has a number of 3SLS equivalents, the simplest of which is based on the original model transformed to differences from the Tth observation:

$$y_{i1} - y_{iT} = (x_{i1} - x_{iT})\beta + (u_{i1} - u_{iT})$$
$$y_{iT-1} - y_{iT} = (x_{iT-1} - x_{iT})\beta + (u_{iT-1} - u_{iT})$$
$$y_{iT} = x_{iT}(\beta + \lambda_T) + x_{i1}\lambda_1 + \cdots + x_{iT-1}\lambda_{T-1} + \varepsilon_i + u_{iT}, \quad (5)$$

or

$$[y_{i1}, \ldots, y_{iT}]\begin{pmatrix} 1 & 0 & . & . & 0 \\ 0 & 1 & . & . & 0 \\ . & . & . & . & . \\ -1 & -1 & . & . & 1 \end{pmatrix} - [x_{i1}, \ldots, x_{iT}]\begin{pmatrix} \beta & 0 & . & . & \lambda_1 \\ 0 & \beta & . & . & \lambda_2 \\ . & . & . & . & . \\ -\beta & -\beta & . & . & \lambda_T + \beta \end{pmatrix} = [u_{i1} - u_{iT}, \ldots, u_{iT-1} - u_{iT}, \varepsilon_i + u_{iT}].$$

Define $e_i = [u_{i1} + \varepsilon_i, \ldots, u_{iT} + \varepsilon_i]$, so that (5) can be written compactly as

$$y_i\Gamma - x_iB = e_i\Gamma = v_i. \quad (5')$$

Let y, x, and v denote data matrices corresponding to y_i, x_i, and v_i. Then 3SLS estimates of system (5′) minimize

$$m(\beta, \lambda) = N^{-1} * \text{vec}[X'(Y\Gamma - XB)]'\hat{\Psi}^{-1} \times \text{vec}[X'(Y\Gamma - XB)],$$

where $\hat{\Psi}$ is a consistent estimate of the asymptotic variance of $\text{vec}[X'v/\sqrt{N}]$. In conventional 3SLS, where v_i is homoscedastic, $\hat{\Psi}$ is estimated by $[v'v\,N \otimes [X'X/N]$. Evaluated at the parameter estimates, $m(\beta, \lambda)$ is a generalized method of moments (GMM) over-identification test statistic of the type considered by Newey (1985).

The 3SLS test statistic $m(\hat{\beta}, \hat{\lambda})$ and the MCS test statistic $h(\hat{\beta}, \hat{\lambda})$ are the same. To see this, note that any 3SLS minimand such as $m(\beta, \lambda)$ is asymptotically the same as

$$N * \text{vec}[\hat{\Pi} - B\Gamma^{-1}]'\hat{\Omega}^{-1}\,\text{vec}[\hat{\Pi} - B\Gamma^{-1}], \quad (6)$$

where $\hat{\Pi} = (X'X)^{-1}X'Y$ and $\hat{\Omega}$ is again a consistent estimate of the variance of $\hat{\Pi}$ (Chamberlain 1982, pp. 26–27). In this case, $B\Gamma^{-1}$ is easily verified to be $(I_T \otimes \beta) + \lambda l'$ so that (6) is also the MCS minimand for fixed-effects models. Moreover, because MCS and 3SLS estimators minimize asymptotically equivalent quadratic forms with unique minima (if the parameters are identified), the resulting estimators are asymptotically equivalent as well. Finally, because (1) imposes linear restrictions on a linear model, the MCS and 3SLS estimators and test statistics will be numerically identical unless different residual variance estimators are used in the MCS and 3SLS quadratic forms (e.g., see Newey and West 1987).

As a practical matter, it is easy to confirm that $m(\hat{\beta}, \hat{\lambda})$ and $h(\hat{\beta}, \hat{\lambda})$ have distributions with equal degrees of freedom. There are $T - 1$ over-identified equations in (5), and each over-identified equation has $k(T - 1)$ over-identifying orthogonality restrictions (using the columns of X as instruments). In addition, there are $k(T - 2)$ equality restrictions on the β's; $k(T - 1)^2 + k(T - 2)$ is indeed equal to $kT^2 - (kT + k)$, the degrees of freedom for $h(\beta, \lambda)$.

ANACOVA and the 3SLS Orthogonality Test Statistic

In the standard fixed-effects model, $Eu_i'u_i = \sigma^2 I_T$ for all i. In this case, it is well known that the ANACOVA estimator is the normal maximum likelihood estimator of β (e.g., see Mundlak 1978). This fact serves to establish that any 3SLS equivalent of the fully efficient MCS estimator reduces to ANACOVA in the scalar covariance case. For an algebraic proof, see Angrist and Newey (1989).

The over-identification test statistic associated with the MCS estimator (and any 3SLS equivalent) also simplifies in the scalar covariance case. This is easiest to show by working with deviations from means:

$$y_{i1} - \bar{y}_i = (x_{i1} - \bar{x}_i)\beta + (u_{i1} - \bar{u}_i)$$

$$\vdots$$

$$y_{iT-1} - \bar{y}_i = (x_{iT-1} - \bar{x}_i)\beta + (u_{iT-1} - \bar{u}_i)$$

$$y_{iT} = x_{iT}(\beta + \lambda_T) + x_{i1}\lambda_1 + \cdots + x_{iT-1}\lambda_{T-1} + \varepsilon_i + u_{iT}. \quad (7)$$

Systems (7) and (5) are equivalent because they are related by a nonsingular transformation (and therefore have the same reduced form).

The Tth equation in System (7) is just-identified, so 3SLS estimates of the first $T - 1$ equations are unaffected by dropping the Tth equation [Theil (1971); see the appendix to Chamberlain (1984) for the heteroscedastic case]. Let $\hat{\upsilon}_t$ be the vector of ANACOVA residuals in period t; each element of $\hat{\upsilon}_t$ is $\hat{\upsilon}_{it} = (y_{it} - \bar{y}_i) - (x_{it} - \bar{x}_i)\hat{\beta}$. When $Eu_i'u_i = \sigma^2 I_T$, the 3SLS minimand for the $T - 1$ over-identified equations in System (7) can be written

$$(q - W\hat{\beta})'[(F'F)^{-1} \otimes P_x](q - W\hat{\beta})/\sigma^2 = \hat{\upsilon}'[(F'F)^{-1} \otimes P_x]\hat{\upsilon}/\sigma^2, \quad (8)$$

where $P_x = X(X'X)^{-1}X'$, F is the $T \times (T - 1)$ matrix that transforms a $1 \times T$ vector to $1 \times (T - 1)$ deviations from means by postmultiplication, W is the stacked vector of regressors in deviations from means form (the stacked submatrices of $X[F \otimes I_k]$ for each period), $q = \text{vec}(YF)$, and $\hat{\upsilon} = \text{vec}[\hat{\upsilon}_1 \ldots \hat{\upsilon}_{t-1}]$. Using the fact that $(F'F)^{-1} = [I_{T-1} + l_{T-1}l_{T-1}']$ and that the sum of $T - 1$ deviations from means is equal to minus the Tth deviation from means, it is easy to show that (8) reduces to

$$(1/\sigma^2) \sum_{t=1}^{T} \hat{\upsilon}_t' P_x \hat{\upsilon}_t.$$

Each term in this sum is simply the degrees of freedom times the R^2 from a regression of the ANACOVA residuals for a particular period on all leads and lags of the right-side variables. The R^2 from a regression of residuals on instruments is also the basis of orthogonality test statistics in conventional homoscedastic models with endogenous regressors (Hausman 1984).

2. UNION–WAGE EFFECTS

We illustrate alternative procedures for the estimation and testing of fixed-effects models using NLSY data to replicate Chamberlain's (1984) NLSYM estimates of union-wage effects. The equation we estimate is

$$w_{it} = \delta_t + Z_i\gamma_t + X_{it}\beta + \alpha_i + u_{it}, \quad (9)$$

where w_{it} is the log of the hourly rate of pay on the main job; δ_t is a period-specific intercept; Z_i is a vector of time-invariant covariates that includes a nonwhite dummy, completed years of schooling in 1983, potential experience in 1983 (age − schooling − 6) and its square; and X_{it} is a vector of time-varying covariates that includes union status, urban, and South dummies. The coefficients on the time-varying covariates β are fixed. The coefficients on the time-invariant covariates γ_t are time-varying so that time-invariant regressors are not eliminated by the deviations from means transformation.

The sample is selected from the NLSY random subsample containing 3,003 men age 18–26 in 1983. Although the NLSY began in 1979, we use only data from 1983 to 1987. Roughly 500 men who were listed on the employment status recode in any year as enrolled in school were excluded from the sample, and an additional 1,000 with no wage and salary earnings in one of the five sample years were also excluded. Of the 1,500 who were not enrolled and were continuously employed, roughly 400 had no hourly wage data or were missing data on one of the other covariates. Also discarded were 8 men with negative potential experience in at least one year and 59 men whose schooling either decreased in any year or increased by more than two years between two interviews. The final sample includes 1,045 men.

Descriptive statistics for the sample are shown in Table 1. Seventeen percent of the sample is nonwhite, and the average age in 1983 was 22. Roughly 20% had their wages set by a collective-bargaining agreement, most lived in cities, and a third lived in the South. In spite of the fact that the sample contains men with large labor-force attachment, schooling rose by roughly one-third of a year in the five-year panel, and figures not shown in the table indicate that schooling increased for around 19% of the sample.

Table 2 reports OLS, ANACOVA, and 3SLS estimates of coefficients on the time-varying covariates in Equation (9). Columns 1, 3, 5, and 7 report results from equations that include as time-varying covariates union status, urban, and South dummies. Columns 2, 4, 6, and 8 report results from equations in which union status is the only time-varying covariate. The OLS estimate of the effects of union status is around .23, falling to .13 when estimated by ANACOVA. The urban coefficient also falls, and the South coefficient becomes positive, although insignificant.

The test statistic in columns 3 and 4 is calculated by regressing the ANACOVA residuals from each period on all leads and lags of the time-varying regressors and the time-invariant regressors. The test statistic equals the degrees of freedom per equation times the sum of the R^2's from each residuals regression times a degrees-of-freedom correction to account for the deviations from means transformation. A simple and asymptotically correct degrees-of-freedom correction is to multiply the test statistic times $(T - 1)/T$. The standard errors printed by regression software should be divided by the square root of this number. Thus the degrees-of-freedom correction adjusts for the fact that ANACOVA appears to use data from T periods, whereas the 3SLS estimator is computed using only $T - 1$ equations (one equation is dropped because the residual covariance matrix of T deviations from means has rank $T - 1$.) The test statistic in column 3 is 87, but the 5% critical value of a χ^2 (57) is 76. The test statistic in column 4 is 38, which exceeds the χ^2 (19) 5% critical value of 33.

Columns 5 and 6 report the results of estimating Equation (9) by 3SLS for the first four years of the sample. The 3SLS estimates in this case are algebraically the same as estimates derived from seemingly unrelated regressions (SUR) estimates of the Chamberlain Π-matrix (because 3SLS estimates of the structure and SUR estimates of the reduced form use the same estimated residual covariance matrix when Γ consists of known constants). The 3SLS coefficient estimates are similar to the ANACOVA estimates reported in columns 3 and 4. [Chamberlain's MCS estimates and standard errors from the same specification are union .121 (.013), urban .050 (.050), South −.085 (.040)]. Estimates of the effect of union status are not affected by the presence of the urban and South dummies. The test statistics in columns 5 and 6 can be calculated in Π-matrix estimation from the F statistic for linear restrictions in linear models or as a 3SLS orthogonality test statistic. In the latter approach, the test statistic is the sample size times the system-weighted R^2 from SUR regressions of 3SLS residuals on all leads and lags of the time-varying covariates and the time-invariant covariates. The test statistic is 80 for the model that includes urban and South dummies and 35 for the model that includes only union status. Both of these values are close to a marginal significance level of 2.5%.

If the residuals v_i are heteroscedastic, the efficient 3SLS estimator is Chamberlain's (1982) generalization of White's (1982) instrumental-variables procedure. This estimator substitutes $(1/N)\Sigma(\hat{v}_i'\hat{v}_i \otimes x_i'x_i)$ for $\hat{\Psi}$ in the 3SLS weighting matrix, where the $\hat{v}_i$ are consistent estimates of the true residuals. We used conventional 3SLS residuals for $\hat{v}_i$ and computed the efficient 3SLS estimator and test statistic with software for matrix manip-

Table 1. Descriptive Statistics

Variable	1983	1984	1985	1986	1987
Nonwhite	.165				
Age	21.8				
	(2.25)				
Grade	12.35	12.49	12.57	12.63	12.68
	(1.79)	(1.87)	(1.92)	(1.96)	(2.01)
Wages set by collective bargaining on main job	.201	.204	.206	.189	.239
Urban	.761	.768	.767	.770	.764
South	.293	.297	.276	.302	.300
Log hourly wage on main job	6.31	6.40	6.50	6.61	6.73
	(.47)	(.49)	(.47)	(.47)	(.50)

NOTE: Data are from the NLSY random subsample of civilian men. The sample was selected to include men not listed as enrolled on the employment status recode, with nonnegative potential experience and positive earnings each year and with hourly wage data for the main job each year. The sample excludes men with other missing covariates and any annual schooling increment less than 0 or greater than 2. Sample size = 1,045. Standard deviations are in parentheses.

Table 2. Coefficients on Time-Varying Regressors

	OLS		ANACOVA		3SLS/SUR II		White 3SLS/SUR π matrix	
Coefficient	1	2	3	4	5	6	7	8
Union	.233	.232	.136	.136	.127	.128	.137	.145
	(.015)	(.015)	(.018)	(.018)	(.016)	(.016)	(.017)	(.018)
Urban	.142		.077		.067		.015	
	(.014)		(.033)		(.031)		(.027)	
South	−.016		.090		.085		.012	
	(.013)		(.058)		(.051)		(.056)	
Test statistic			87(57)	38(19)	80(57)	35(19)	74(57)	26(19)

NOTE: Estimates are from equations that include year dummies, potential experience in 1983 and its square, a nonwhite dummy, and schooling in 1983. Coefficients on these regressors were free to vary by year. Time-varying regressors (union, urban, and South) were entered with coefficients restricted to be equal across years. Analysis of covariances standard errors and test statistics were corrected for the loss of degrees of freedom due to the deviations from means transformation. Standard errors are in parentheses.

ulation. The estimates, reported in columns 7 and 8, differ little from the conventional 3SLS estimates. [Chamberlain's efficient MCS estimates from the same specification are union .107 (.016), urban .056 (.020), South −.082 (.045).] The test statistics, however, now fall to 74.2 in column 7 and 25.6 in column 8. Both of these fail to reject the fixed-effects specification at the 5% level, and the statistic reported in column 8 fails to reject at the 10% level.

3. THE RETURNS TO SCHOOLING

We turn next to fixed-effects estimates of the return to schooling in a conventional human capital earnings function. The equation estimated is

$$w_{it} = \delta_t + Z_i\gamma_t + c_{it}\phi + x_{it}\beta_0 + x_{it}^2\beta_1 + e_{it}\rho + \alpha_i + u_{it}, \quad (10)$$

where Z_i now includes only a nonwhite dummy, c_{it} indicates wages set by collective bargaining, x_{it} is potential experience, and e_{it} is the highest grade completed. It might appear that Equation (10) cannot be estimated by ANACOVA because schooling is often thought of as a time-invariant covariate that is absorbed by the fixed effect (e.g., Hausman and Taylor 1981). We have seen, however, that even for continuously employed men in the NLSY, schooling rises over time.

A second problem arises because of the definition of potential experience, x_{it}. Denote i's age at t by a_{it}, and note that since $x_{it} = a_{it} - e_{it} - 6$, $x_{it} - \bar{x}_i = \kappa + t - (e_{it} - \bar{e}_i)$, where κ is a constant. The linear trend in $x_{it} - \bar{x}_i$ is absorbed by the unrestricted period effects δ_t, and $e_{it} - \bar{e}_i$ appears as a separate regressor with coefficient ρ. Therefore, the effect of schooling conditional on potential experience is not identified by ANACOVA. The overall effect of schooling is identified, however. To see this, expand the quadratic terms in (10):

$$w_{it} = \delta_t + Z_i\gamma_t + c_{it}\phi + \pi_0 + a_{it}\pi_1 + a_{it}^2\pi_2 + e_{it}\pi_3 + e_{it}^2\pi_4 + a_{it}e_{it}\pi_5 + \alpha_i + u_{it}, \quad (11)$$

where

$$\pi_0 = [-6\beta_0 + 36\beta_1], \qquad \pi_1 = [\beta_0 - 12\beta_1]$$
$$\pi_2 = \beta_1, \qquad \pi_3 = [\rho + 12\beta_1 - \beta_0]$$
$$\pi_4 = \beta_1, \qquad \pi_5 = -2\beta_1. \quad (12)$$

Thus the quadratic potential experience model parameterizes the reduced-form effect of schooling as linear in schooling and age: $\partial w_{it}/\partial e_{it} = \pi_3 + 2e_{it}\pi_4 + a_{it}\pi_5$. The only coefficient that is not identified in ANACOVA estimation of (11) is π_1, the coefficient on linear age. Therefore, $\partial w_{it}/\partial e_{it}$ is identified. Note also that (12) puts two restrictions on the coefficients in (11), $\pi_2 = \pi_4$ and $\pi_4 = -\pi_5/2$.

Column 1 of Table 3 reports OLS estimates of the unrestricted reduced-form equation (11). Column 2 reports the results of imposing the quadratic potential experience model on the OLS etimates. Column 3 reports estimates of a regression that excludes grade squared and the age/grade interaction so that the equation includes only a quadratic in age and a linear schooling term. A chi-squared test for the restrictions in column 2 has value 6.4, with a marginal significance level between 5.0% and 2.5%. The restrictions in the specification reported in column 3, however, are strongly rejected with a χ^2 (2) value of 78. In columns 1 and 2, the reduced-form schooling effect, $\partial w_{it}/\partial e_{it}$, is evaluated at 12 years of schooling and age 24. In spite of the test results, the estimated effect of schooling varies remarkably little across the three specifications, ranging from .034 to .039.

Columns 4–6 and columns 7–9 report results from ANACOVA and 3SLS estimation of the specifications reported in columns 1–3. ANACOVA estimates of the reduced-form schooling effect are substantially larger than the OLS estimates, ranging from .07 to .089. The ANACOVA and OLS numbers are also significantly different in a Hausman test. But the specification test statistic now provides fairly strong evidence that the fixed-effects restrictions are not satisfied for this model.

Table 3. Estimates of the Return to Schooling

	Method											
	OLS			*ANACOVA*			*3SLS/SUR Π-matrix*			*White 3SLS/SUR Π-matrix*		
Coefficient	*RF* 1	*X* 2	*A* 3	*RF* 4	*X* 5	*A* 6	*RF* 7	*X* 8	*A* 9	*RF* 10	*X* 11	*A* 12
Grade π_3	−.173	−.095	.036	−.219	−.036	.080	−.269	−.035	.074	−.272	.076	.080
	(.037)	(.013)	(.003)	(.111)	(.023)	(.015)	(.111)	(.023)	(.015)	(.096)	(.014)	(.016)
Grade^2 π_4	−.003	−.0056		.0005	−.0052		.0024	−.0051		.0001	.0001	
	(.001)	(.0005)		(.0013)	(.0007)		(.0042)	(.0007)		(.0037)	(.0003)	
Age π_1	.207	.194	.263									
	(.036)	(.013)	(.036)									
Age^2 π_2	−.006		−.0042	−.005		−.0031	−.005		−.0029	−.0022		−.00003
	(.001)		(.0017)	(.0008)		(.0087)	(.0008)		(.0008)	(.0004)		(.00027)
Grade * age π_5	.012			.012			.011			.013		
	(.011)			(.002)			(.002)			(.002)		
Reduced form schooling effect (at age = 24, grade = 12)	.034	.039	.036	.070	.089	.080	.062	.087	.074	.052	.073	.080
	(.004)	(.003)	(.003)	(.022)	(.015)	(.015)	(.022)	(.015)	(.015)	(.014)	(.013)	(.016)
Union	.235	.230	.236	.133	.133	.135	.125	.126	.126	.138	.152	.143
	(.015)	(.015)	(.015)	(.018)	(.018)	(.018)	(.016)	(.016)	(.016)	(.016)	(.016)	(.017)
Test statistic χ^2 (df)		6.4(2)	78.5(2)	151(83)	156(85)	140(45)	142(83)	148(85)	123(45)	112(83)	199(85)	91(45)

NOTE: Columns labeled *RF* show estimates from an unrestricted regression on grade, grade^2, age, age^2, and the interaction of grade and age. Columns labeled *X* show results from imposition of restrictions implied by a quadratic potential experience (= age − grade − 6) model. These restrictions are that the coefficient on grade^2 = coefficient on age^2 = (−½ * coefficient on the age/grade interaction). Columns labeled *A* show results from an unrestricted regression on grade and quadratic age. Each equation also includes a period-specific intercept and a period-specific race dummy. The reduced-form schooling effect $\partial w_{it}/\partial e_{it} = \pi_3 + 2e_{it}\pi_4 + a_{it}\pi_5$, calculated using unrounded coefficient estimates. Standard errors are in parentheses.

The value of 151 in Column 4 is well above the 2.5% critical value of 107 for a chi-squared distribution with 83 df. On the other hand, the difference in the chi-squared statistics between columns 4 and 5 suggests that imposition of the quadratic experience model does not lead to a serious deterioration in fit. The poorest fitting specification is that including only a quadratic in age and a linear schooling term, reported in column 6.

The 3SLS estimates in columns 7–9 are similar to the ANACOVA estimates. The specification test statistics here are somewhat lower but still well beyond conventional critical values. The efficient 3SLS estimates in columns 10–12 are also similar to the ANACOVA estimates. The test statistic for efficient 3SLS estimation of the unrestricted reduced form in column 10 falls to 112 and is close to a marginal significance level of 2.5%. But the test statistic in column 8, which reports the results of imposing the quadratic potential-experience model on the reduced form, is now considerably larger than the test statistic for the same specification in conventional 3SLS estimation. As before, the specification that includes only a quadratic in age and a linear schooling term provides the poorest fit.

4. SUMMARY AND CONCLUSIONS

This article shows that the omnibus goodness-of-fit statistic for fixed-effects models in which the time-varying error component has a scalar covariance matrix can be written as the degrees of freedom times the R^2 from a regression of ANACOVA residuals on regressors. This is a useful simplifying result, which also serves to highlight the instrumental-variables interpretation of the identifying information in fixed-effects models. The R^2 form of the omnibus specification test is also the formula used to calculate orthogonality test statistics in conventional homoscedastic regression models with endogenous regressors.

Estimating union-wage effects using five years of data from the NLSY, we find results similar to those found by Chamberlain, although our evidence from the omnibus specification test is somewhat more equivocal. Overall, however, our findings do not suggest that the assumption of a fixed effect in an equation for union-wage effects is strongly at odds with the data.

Fixed-effects estimates of a standard human capital earnings function in which log earnings are regressed on a quadratic in potential experience and a linear schooling term are also presented. In spite of the fact that schooling is often viewed as a time-invariant covariate, we observe substantial changes in schooling in our sample of young men. The effect of schooling conditional on potential experience is not identified in fixed-effects estimation because the deviations from means of schooling and potential experience are linearly related. But changes in schooling can be used to identify a reduced-form schooling effect that is derived from the potential experience specification.

Fixed-effects estimates of the return to schooling in the NLSY are roughly twice as large as OLS estimates, although our specification tests suggest that the fixed-effects assumption may be inappropriate for human capital earnings functions. Moreover, an increase in the return to schooling after controlling for time-invariant unobservables contradicts the notion that positive correlation between schooling and error components such as "ability" causes OLS estimates of the returns to schooling to overstate the true return (Willis 1986). But our findings are broadly consistent with a wide range of empirical studies that find that correcting for omitted variables *raises* the estimated returns to schooling. Examples include Hausman and Taylor (1981), Griliches (1977), and Angrist and Krueger (1990), each of which found that the estimated return to schooling goes up when fixed-effects or instrumental-variables strategies are used to control for unobserved covariates.

Griliches (1977) showed that negative bias in OLS schooling coefficients can be theoretically justified if schooling and ability are substitutes instead of complements. A useful agenda for future research is to ascertain whether the larger estimates of the return to schooling in endogenous schooling models reflect schooling-ability substitution or are merely an artifact of statistical problems in the estimation strategy. For example, individuals with unexpectedly low earnings may subsequently return to school. In this case, negative correlation between schooling and lagged earnings residuals could lead to upward bias in ANACOVA estimates.

ACKNOWLEDGMENTS

Angrist thanks the Harvard Institute for Economic Research and the National Science Foundation (Grant SES-9012149) for financial support. Newey thanks the Sloan Foundation, the National Science Foundation (Grant SES-8810049), and Bell Communications Research. The authors also thank Marc McClellan for research assistance and Gary Chamberlain for helpful comments.

[*Received February 1990. Revised November 1990.*]

REFERENCES

Angrist, J. D., and Krueger, A. (1990), "Does Compulsory School Attendance Affect Schooling and Earnings?" Working Paper 273, Princeton Industrial Relations Section.

Angrist, J. D., and Newey, W. K. (1989), "Minimum Chi-Square and Three-Stage Least Squares in Fixed Effects Models," Working Paper 246, Princeton University Industrial Relations Section.

Chamberlain, G. (1982), "Multivariate Regression Models for Panel Data," *Journal of Econometrics,* 18, 5–46.

——— (1984), "Panel Data," in *Handbook of Econometrics,* eds. Z. Griliches and M. Intriligator, Amsterdam: North-Holland, pp. 1248–1318.

Griliches, Z. (1977), "Estimating the Returns to Schooling—Some Econometric Solutions," *Econometrica,* 45, 1–22.

Griliches, Z., and Hausman, J. A. (1986), "Errors in Variables in Panel Data," *Journal of Econometrics,* 31, 93–118.

Hausman, J. A. (1984), "Specification and Estimation of Simultaneous Equation Models," in *Handbook of Econometrics,* eds. Z. Griliches and M. Intriligator, Amsterdam: North-Holland, pp. 391–448.

Hausman, J. A., and Taylor, W. E. (1981), "Panel Data and Unobservable Individual Effects," *Econometrica,* 49, 1377–1398.

Holtz-Eakin, D., Newey, W. K., and Rosen, H. (1988), "Estimating Vector Auto-Regressions in Panel Data," *Econometrica,* 56, 1371–1398.

Mundlak, Y. (1978), "On the Pooling of Times Series and Cross Section Data," *Econometrica,* 46, 69–85.

Newey, W. K. (1985), "Generalized Method of Moments Estimation and Testing," *Journal of Econometrics,* 29, 229–256.

Newey, W. K. and West, K. (1987), "Hypothesis Testing With Efficient Method of Moments Estimation," *International Economic Review,* 3, 777–787.

Rothenberg, T. J. (1973), *Efficient Estimation With A Priori Information,* New Haven: Yale University Press.

Theil, H. (1971), *Principles of Econometrics,* New York: John Wiley.

White, H. (1982), "Instrumental Variables With Independent Observations," *Econometrica,* 50, 483–501.

Willis, R. J. (1986), "Wage Determinants: A Survey and Reinterpretation of Human Capital Earnings Functions," in *Handbook of Labor Economics* (Vol. 1), eds. O. Ashenfelter and R. Layard, Amsterdam: Elsevier, pp. 525–602.

[11]

Review of Economic Studies (1991) **58**, 277-297
0034-6527/91/00180277$02.00

Some Tests of Specification for Panel Data: Monte Carlo Evidence and an Application to Employment Equations

MANUEL ARELLANO
London School of Economics

and

STEPHEN BOND
University of Oxford

First version received May 1988; final version accepted July 1990 (Eds.)

This paper presents specification tests that are applicable after estimating a dynamic model from panel data by the generalized method of moments (GMM), and studies the practical performance of these procedures using both generated and real data. Our GMM estimator optimally exploits all the linear moment restrictions that follow from the assumption of no serial correlation in the errors, in an equation which contains individual effects, lagged dependent variables and no strictly exogenous variables. We propose a test of serial correlation based on the GMM residuals and compare this with Sargan tests of over-identifying restrictions and Hausman specification tests.

1. INTRODUCTION

The purpose of this paper is to present specification tests that are applicable after estimating a dynamic model from panel data by the generalized method of moments (GMM) and to study the practical performance of these procedures using both generated and real data.

Previous work concerning dynamic equations from panel data (e.g. Chamberlain (1984), Bhargava and Sargan (1983)) has emphasized the case where the model with an arbitrary intertemporal covariance matrix of the errors is identified. The fundamental identification condition for this model is the strict exogeneity of some of the explanatory variables (or the availability of strictly exogenous instrumental variables) conditional on the unobservable individual effects. In practice, this allows one to use past, present and future values of the strictly exogenous variables to construct instruments for the lagged dependent variables and other non-exogenous variables once the permanent effects have been differenced out. Bhargava and Sargan (1983) and Arellano (1990) considered estimation and inference imposing restrictions on the autocovariances, but the assumption that the model with unrestricted covariance matrix is identified was never removed.

However, sometimes one is less willing to assume the strict exogeneity of an explanatory variable than to restrict the serial correlation structure of the errors, in which case different identification arrangements become available. Uncorrelated errors arise in a number of environments. These include rational expectations models where the disturbance is a surprise term, error-correction models and vector autoregressions. Moreover, if there are a priori reasons to expect autoregressive errors in a regression model, these can be represented as a dynamic regression with non-linear common factor restrictions and uncorrelated disturbances (e.g. Sargan (1980)). In these cases and also in models with moving-average errors, lagged values of the dependent variable itself become valid instruments in the differenced equations corresponding to later periods. Simple estimators of this type were first proposed by Anderson and Hsiao (1981, 1982). Griliches and Hausman (1986) have developed estimators for errors-in-variables models whose identification relies on assumptions of lack of (or limited) serial correlation in the measurement errors. Holtz-Eakin, Newey and Rosen (1988) have also considered estimators of this type for vector autoregressions which are similar to the ones we employ in this paper.

An estimator that uses lags as instruments under the assumption of white noise errors would lose its consistency if in fact the errors were serially correlated. It is therefore essential to satisfy oneself that this is not the case by reporting test statistics of the validity of the instrumental variables (i.e. tests of lack of serial correlation) together with the parameter estimates. In this paper we consider three such tests: a direct test on the second-order residual serial correlation coefficient, a Sargan test of over-identifying restrictions and a Hausman specification test. The operating characteristics of these tests are different as well as their number of degrees of freedom. In addition, depending on alternative auxiliary distributional assumptions concerning stationarity and heterogeneity, different forms of each of the tests are available. These alternative versions of a given test are asymptotically equivalent under the less general set of auxiliary assumptions but they still may perform quite differently in finite samples. We have therefore produced a number of Monte Carlo experiments to investigate the relative performance of the various tests. Finally, as an empirical illustration we report some estimated employment equations using the Datastream panel of quoted U.K. companies.

The paper is organized as follows. Section 2 presents the model and the estimators. For a fixed number of time periods in the sample, the model specifies a finite number of moment restrictions and therefore an asymptotically efficient GMM estimator is readily available. The discussion is kept as simple as possible by concentrating initially on a first-order autoregression with a fixed effect. Exogenous variables and unbalanced panel considerations are subsequently introduced. Section 3 presents the various tests of serial correlation and their asymptotic distributions. Section 4 reports the simulation results. Section 5 contains the application to employment equations and Section 6 concludes.

2. ESTIMATION

The simplest model without strictly exogenous variables is an autoregressive specification of the form

$$y_{it} = \alpha y_{i(t-1)} + \eta_i + v_{it}, \qquad |\alpha| < 1. \tag{1}$$

We assume that a random sample of N individual time series $(y_{i1}, \ldots, y_{iT})$ is available. T is small and N is large. The v_{it} are assumed to have finite moments and in particular $E(v_{it}) = E(v_{it}v_{is}) = 0$ for $t \neq s$. That is, we assume lack of serial correlation but not necessarily independence over time. With these assumptions, values of y lagged two periods or more are valid instruments in the equations in first differences. Namely, for

$T \geqq 3$ the model implies the following $m = (T-2)(T-1)/2$ linear moment restrictions

$$E[(\bar{y}_{it} - \alpha\bar{y}_{i(t-1)})y_{i(t-j)}] = 0 \qquad (j = 2, \ldots, (t-1);\ t = 3, \ldots, T) \tag{2}$$

where for simplicity $\bar{y}_{it} = y_{it} - y_{i(t-1)}$. We wish to obtain the optimal estimator of α as $N \to \infty$ for fixed T on the basis of these moment restrictions alone. That is, in the absence of any other knowledge concerning initial conditions or the distributions of the v_{it} and the η_i. Note that our assumptions also imply quadratic moment restrictions, for example $E(\bar{v}_{it}\bar{v}_{i(t-2)}) = 0$, which however we shall not exploit in order to avoid iterative procedures.

This estimation problem is an example of those analyzed by Hansen (1982) and White (1982), and an optimal GMM or two-stage instrumental variables estimator should be available. The moment equations in (2) can be conveniently written in vector form as $E(Z_i'\bar{v}_i) = 0$ where $\bar{v}_i = (\bar{v}_{i3} \cdots \bar{v}_{iT})'$ and Z_i is a $(T-2) \times m$ block diagonal matrix whose sth block is given by $(y_{i1} \cdots y_{is})$.[1]

The GMM estimator $\hat{\alpha}$ is based on the sample moments $N^{-1}\sum_{i=1}^{N} Z_i'\bar{v}_i = N^{-1}Z'\bar{v}$ where $\bar{v} = \bar{y} - \alpha\bar{y}_{-1} = (\bar{v}_1', \ldots, \bar{v}_N')'$ is a $N(T-2) \times 1$ vector and $Z = (Z_1', \ldots, Z_N')'$ is a $N(T-2) \times m$ matrix. $\hat{\alpha}$ is given by

$$\hat{\alpha} = \operatorname{argmin}_{\alpha}\, (\bar{v}'Z)A_N(Z'\bar{v}) = \frac{\bar{y}_{-1}'ZA_NZ'\bar{y}}{\bar{y}_{-1}'ZA_NZ'\bar{y}_{-1}}. \tag{3}$$

Multivariate standard CLT implies that $\bar{V}_N^{-1/2}N^{-1/2}Z'\bar{v}$ is asymptotically standard normal where $\bar{V}_N = N^{-1}\sum_i E(Z_i'\bar{v}_i\bar{v}_i'Z_i)$ is the average covariance matrix of $Z_i'\bar{v}_i$. Under our assumptions, $\bar{V}_N$ can be replaced by $\hat{V}_N = N^{-1}\sum_i Z_i'\hat{\bar{v}}_i\hat{\bar{v}}_i'Z_i$ where the $\bar{v}_i$ are residuals from a preliminary consistent estimator $\hat{\alpha}_1$. The one-step estimator $\hat{\alpha}_1$ is obtained by setting $A_N = (N^{-1}\sum_i Z_i'HZ_i)^{-1}$ where H is a $(T-2)$ square matrix which has twos in the main diagonal, minus ones in the first subdiagonals and zeroes otherwise. A consistent estimate of avar $(\hat{\alpha})$ for arbitrary A_N is given by

$$\widehat{\text{avar}}(\hat{\alpha}) = N\frac{\bar{y}_{-1}'ZA_N\hat{V}_NA_NZ'\bar{y}_{-1}}{(\bar{y}_{-1}'ZA_NZ'\bar{y}_{-1})^2}. \tag{4}$$

The optimal choice for A_N is $\hat{V}_N^{-1}$ (e.g. see Hansen (1982)) which produces a two-step estimator $\hat{\alpha}_2$.[2] $\hat{\alpha}_1$ and $\hat{\alpha}_2$ will be asymptotically equivalent if the v_{it} are independent and homoskedastic both across units and over time.

It is useful to relate these estimators to the Anderson–Hsiao (AH) estimator which is commonly used in practice. Anderson and Hsiao (1981) proposed to estimate α by regressing $\bar{y}$ on $\bar{y}_{-1}$ using either $\bar{y}_{-2}$ or y_{-2} as instruments. Since both $\bar{y}_{-2}$ and y_{-2} are linear combinations of Z the resulting estimators will be inefficient. Note that under stationarity, namely when $E(y_{it}y_{i(t-k)}) = c_{ik}$ for all t, the estimator that uses $Z_i^{\dagger} = \text{diag}\,(y_{it})$ $(t = 1, \ldots, T-2)$ is asymptotically equivalent to the one based on the stacked vector y_{-2}, whose computation is much simpler (since A_N becomes irrelevant). However neither of the two is asymptotically equivalent to $\hat{\alpha}_1$ or $\hat{\alpha}_2$, not even under stationarity.

The extension of the previous results to the case where a limited amount of serial correlation is allowed in the v_{it} is straightforward. Suppose that v_{it} is MA (q) in the

1. In this paper we represent this type of matrix by $Z_i = \text{diag}\,(y_{i1}, \ldots, y_{is})$, $(s = 1, \ldots, T-2)$.

2. An alternative choice of A_N is $(N^{-1}\sum_i Z_i'\hat{\Omega}Z_i)^{-1}$ with $\hat{\Omega} = N^{-1}\sum_i \hat{\bar{v}}_i\hat{\bar{v}}_i'$. The resulting estimator does not depend on the data fourth-order moments and is asymptotically equivalent to $\hat{\alpha}_2$ provided the v_{it} are serially independent. Note that in this case $E(Z_i'\bar{v}_i\bar{v}_i'Z_i) = E(Z_i'\Omega_iZ_i)$ and $\lim_{N\to\infty} N^{-1}\sum_i E[Z_i'(\Omega_i - \bar{\Omega}_N)Z_i] = 0$ (see White (1982), p. 492).

sense that $E(v_{it}v_{i(t-k)}) \neq 0$ for $k \leq q$ and zero otherwise. In this case α is just identified with $T = q+3$ and there are $m_q = (T-q-2)(T-q-1)/2$ restrictions available.

Models with exogenous variables

We now turn to consider an extended version of equation (1) where $(k-1)$ independent explanatory variables have been included

$$y_{it} = \alpha y_{i(t-1)} + \beta' x_{it}^* + \eta_i + v_{it} = \delta' x_{it} + \eta_i + v_{it} \tag{5}$$

where $x_{it} = (y_{i(t-1)}\, x_{it}^{*\prime})'$ is $k \times 1$ and the v_{it} are not serially correlated. Suppose initially that the x_{it}^* are all correlated with η_i. In this context the form of the optimal matrix of instruments depends on whether the x_{it}^* are predetermined or strictly exogenous variables. If the x_{it}^* are predetermined, in the sense that $E(x_{it}^* v_{is}) \neq 0$ for $s < t$ and zero otherwise, then only $x_{i1}^*, \ldots, x_{i(s-1)}^*$ are valid instruments in the differenced equation for period s so that the optimal Z_i is a $(T-2) \times (T-2)[(k-1)(T+1)+(T-1)]/2$ matrix of the form $Z_i = \text{diag}\,(y_{i1} \cdots y_{is} x_{i1}^{*\prime} \cdots x_{i(s+1)}^{*\prime})$, $(s = 1, \ldots, T-2)$. On the other hand, if the x_{it}^* are strictly exogenous, i.e. $E(x_{it}^* v_{is}) = 0$ for all t, s, then all the x^*'s are valid instruments for all the equations and Z_i takes the form $Z_i = \text{diag}\,(y_{i1} \cdots y_{is}\, x_{i1}^{*\prime} \cdots x_{iT}^{*\prime})$, $(s = 1, \ldots, T-2)$. Clearly, x_{it}^* may also include a combination of both predetermined and strictly exogenous variables. In either case, the form of the GMM estimator of the $k \times 1$ coefficient vector δ is

$$\hat{\delta} = (\bar{X}' Z A_N Z' \bar{X})^{-1} \bar{X}' Z A_N Z' \bar{y} \tag{6}$$

where $\bar{X}$ is a stacked $(T-2)N \times k$ matrix of observations on $\bar{x}_{it}$, and $\bar{y}$ and Z are as above for the appropriate choice of Z_i. As before, alternative choices of A_N will produce one-step or two-step estimators.[3]

Turning now to the case where x_{it}^* can be partitioned into $(x_{1it}^* x_{2it}^*)$ and x_{1it}^* is uncorrelated with η_i, additional moment restrictions exploiting this lack of correlation in the levels equations become available. For example, if x_{1it}^* is predetermined and letting $u_{it} = \eta_i + v_{it}$, we have T extra restrictions. Namely, $E(u_{i2} x_{1i1}^*) = 0$ and $E(u_{it} x_{1it}^*) = 0$, $(t = 2, \ldots, T)$. Note that all remaining restrictions from the levels equations are redundant given those previously exploited for the equations in first differences. Define $u_i = (u_{i2} \cdots u_{iT})'$, let v_i^+ be the $[(T-2)+(T-1)] \times 1$ vector $v_i^+ = (\bar{v}_i' u_i')'$ and let $v^+ = (v_1^{+\prime} \cdots v_N^{+\prime})' = y^+ - X^+ \delta$. The optimal matrix of instruments Z_i^+ is block diagonal and consists of two blocks: Z_i which is as in the predetermined x_{it}^* case above (assuming that x_{2it}^* is also predetermined), and Z_i^a which is itself block diagonal with $(x_{1i1}^{*\prime} x_{1i2}^{*\prime})$ in the first block and $x_{1is}^{*\prime}$, $s = 3, \ldots, T$ in the remaining blocks. The two-step estimator is of the same form as (6) with X^+, y^+ and Z^+ replacing $\bar{X}, \bar{y}$ and Z respectively, and $A_N = [N^{-1} \sum_i Z_i^+ \hat{v}_i^+ \hat{v}_i^{+\prime} Z_i^+]^{-1}$. On the other hand, if x_{1it}^* is strictly exogenous, the observations for all periods become valid instruments in the levels equations. However, given those previously exploited in first differences we only have T extra restrictions which in this case can be conveniently expressed as $E(T^{-1} \sum_{s=1}^{T} u_{is} x_{1it}^*) = 0$ $(t = 1, \ldots, T)$. Thus, the two-step estimator would just combine the $(T-1)$ first difference equations and the average level equation.[4]

3. Note that if $E(v_i v_i')$ is unrestricted (i.e. v_{it} is $MA(q)$ with $T < q+3$) but x_{it}^* is strictly exogenous, the model is identified with $Z_i = \text{diag}\,(x_{i1}^{*\prime} \cdots x_{iT}^{*\prime})$, $(s = 1, \ldots, T-2)$, in which case the two-step estimator coincides with the generalized three-stage least squares estimator proposed by Chamberlain (1984).

4. Note that when x_{1it}^* variables are available it may be possible to identify and estimate coefficients for time-invariant variables on the lines suggested by Hausman and Taylor (1981), Bhargava and Sargan (1983) and Amemiya and MaCurdy (1986).

Models from unbalanced panel data

By unbalanced panel data we refer to a sample in which consecutive observations on individual units are available, but the number of time periods available may vary from unit to unit as well as the historical points to which the observations correspond. This type of sample is very common particularly with firm data which is the context of the application reported below. Aside from often allowing one to exploit a much larger sample or to pool more than one panel, the use of unbalanced panels may lessen the impact of self selection of firms in the sample. In fact nothing fundamental changes in the econometric methods provided a minimal number of continuous time periods are available on each unit, and one assumes that if period-specific parameters are present the number of observations on these periods tend to infinity. Of course, the essential assumption is that the observations in the initial cross-section are independently distributed and that subsequent additions and deletions take place at random (see Hsiao (1986), Chapter 8).

The previous notation can accommodate unbalanced panels with minor changes. We now have T_i time-series observations on the ith unit, and there are N individual units in the sample. The matrices $\bar{X}$ and Z, and the vectors $\bar{y}$ and $\bar{v}$ are made of N row-blocks, the ith block containing (T_i-2) rows. Note that now the number of non-zero columns in each Z_i may vary across units. For example, in the first-order autoregressive specification above, the number of columns in Z_i is $p=(\tau-2)(\tau-1)/2$ where τ is the total number of periods on which observations are available for some individuals in the sample, and $Z_i = \mathrm{diag}\,(y_{i1}, \ldots, y_{is})$, $(s=1, \ldots, \tau-2)$, only if τ observations are available on i. For individuals with $T_i<\tau$, the rows of $\mathrm{diag}\,(y_{i1}, \ldots, y_{is})$ corresponding to the missing equations are deleted and the missing values of y_{it} in the remaining rows are replaced by zeroes. The two-step GMM estimator of α for this choice of instruments[5] is the same as in (3) using $A_N=(N^{-1}\sum_i Z_i'\hat{\bar{v}}_i\hat{\bar{v}}_i'Z_i)^{-1}$ where Z_i is $(T_i-2)\times p$ and $\hat{\bar{v}}_i$ is $(T_i-2)\times 1$.

3. TESTING THE SPECIFICATION

In order to keep the notation simple we now drop the bars from variables in first differences, so that the first-difference equation for the unbalanced panel is now

$$\underset{n\times 1}{y} = \underset{n\times k}{X}\ \underset{k\times 1}{\delta} + \underset{n\times 1}{v} \tag{7}$$

where $n=\sum_i (T_i-2)$. We also assume that the x_{it}^* are all potentially correlated with η_i. The $n\times 1$ vector of residuals is given by

$$\hat{v} = y - X\hat{\delta} = v - X(\hat{\delta}-\delta)$$

where $\hat{\delta}$ can be any estimator of the form (6) for a particular choice of Z and A_N. Let $\hat{v}_{-2}$ be the vector of residuals lagged twice, of order $q=\sum_i (T_i-4)$ and let v_* be a $q\times 1$ vector of trimmed v to match v_{-2} and similarly for X_*. Since the v_{it} are first differences of serially uncorrelated errors, $E(v_{it}v_{i(t-1)})$ need not be zero, but the consistency of the GMM estimators above hinges heavily upon the assumption that $E(v_{it}v_{i(t-2)})=0$. In an

5. This is the optimal choice amongst the estimators that can be obtained by stacking the equations for all periods and individuals. An alternative estimator would minimize the sum of the GMM criteria for each of the balanced sub-panels in the sample. Although the latter is strictly more efficient when the number of units in all sub-samples tend to infinity, it may have a poorer finite-sample performance when the various sub-sample sizes are not sufficiently large.

unbalanced panel $(\tau - 4)$ such covariances can be estimated in total, in principle with varying number of sample observations to estimate each of the covariances. Provided one assumes that all sub-samples tend to infinity, a $(\tau - 4)$ degrees of freedom test can be constructed of the hypothesis that the second-order autocovariances for all periods in the sample are zero. However, a considerably simpler procedure will look at the average covariances $\phi_i = v'_{i(-2)} v_{i*}$. These averages are independent random variables across units with zero mean under the null although with unequal variances in general. So a straight-forward one degree of freedom test statistic can be constructed to test whether $E(\phi_i)$ is zero or not.

The test statistic for second-order serial correlation based on residuals from the first-difference equation takes the form

$$m_2 = \frac{\hat{v}'_{-2}\hat{v}_*}{\hat{v}^{1/2}} \tilde{a}\, N(0, 1) \tag{8}$$

under $E(v_{it} v_{i(t-2)}) = 0$, where $\hat{v}$ is given by

$$\hat{v} = \textstyle\sum_{i=1}^{N} v'_{i(-2)} \hat{v}_{i*} v'_{i*} \hat{v}_{i(-2)} - 2\hat{v}'_{-2} X_* (X'ZA_N Z'X)^{-1} X'ZA_N (\textstyle\sum_{i=1}^{N} Z'_i \hat{v}_i \hat{v}'_{i*} \hat{v}_{i(-2)})$$
$$+ \hat{v}'_{-2} X_* \,\text{av}\hat{\text{a}}\text{r}\,(\hat{\delta}) X'_* \hat{v}_{-2}. \tag{9}$$

Note that m_2 is only defined if min $T_i \geqq 5$. A proof of the asymptotic normality result is sketched in the Appendix.

It is interesting to notice that the m_2 criterion is rather flexible, in that it can be defined in terms of any consistent GMM estimator, not necessarily in terms of efficient estimators, either in the sense of using optimal Z or A_N or both. However, the asymptotic power of the m_2 test will depend on the efficiency of the estimators used.

The m_2 statistic tests for lack of second-order serial correlation in the first-difference residuals. This will certainly be the case if the errors in the model in levels are not serially correlated, but also if the errors in levels follow a random-walk process. One may attempt to discriminate between the two situations by calculating an m_1 statistic, on the same lines as m_2, to test for lack of first-order serial correlation in the differenced residuals. Alternatively, notice that if the errors in levels follow a random walk, then both OLS and GMM estimates in the first-difference model are consistent which suggests a Hausman test based on the difference between the two estimators.

We now turn to consider two other tests of specification which are applicable in the same context. One is a Sargan test of over-identifying restrictions (cf. Sargan (1958, 1988), Hansen (1982)) given by

$$s = \hat{v}'Z(\textstyle\sum_{i=1}^{N} Z'_i \hat{v}_i \hat{v}'_i Z_i)^{-1} Z'\hat{v}\, \tilde{a}\, \chi^2_{p-k} \tag{10}$$

where $\hat{v} = y - X\hat{\delta}$, and $\hat{\delta}$ is a two-step estimator of δ for a given Z. Notice that Z need not be the optimal set of instruments; here p just refers to the number of columns in Z provided $p > k$. Also notice that while we are able to produce a version of the serial correlation test based upon a one-step estimator of δ which remained asymptotically normal on the null under the more general distributional assumptions, no robust chi-square Sargan test based on one-step estimates is available. Under the null a statistic of the form

$$s_1 = \frac{1}{\hat{\sigma}^2} \tilde{v}'Z(\textstyle\sum_{i=1}^{N} Z'_i H_i Z_i)^{-1} Z'\tilde{v}$$

where $\tilde{v}$ are one-step residuals, will only have a limiting chi-square distribution if the errors are indeed i.i.d. over time and individuals. In general, the asymptotic distribution of s_1 is a quadratic form in standard normal variables. Critical values can still be calculated by numerical integration but this clearly leads to a burdensome test procedure.

On the other hand, there may be circumstances where the serial correlation test is not defined while the Sargan test can still be computed. As a simple example, take the first-order autoregressive equation at the beginning of Section 2 with $T=4$; in this case the Sargan statistic tests two linear combinations of the three moment restrictions available, namely $E(\bar{v}_{i3}y_{i1}) = E(\bar{v}_{i4}y_{i1}) = E(\bar{v}_{i4}y_{i2}) = 0$, but no differenced residuals two periods apart are available to construct an m_2 test.

A further possibility is to use Sargan difference tests to discriminate between nested hypotheses concerning serial correlation in a sequential way. For example, let Z_l be a $n \times p_l$ matrix containing the columns of Z which remain valid instrumental variables when the errors in levels are first-order moving average, and let $\hat{\delta}_l$ be a two-step estimator of δ based on Z_l with associated residuals $\hat{v}_l$, then

$$s_l = \hat{v}_l Z_l \left(\textstyle\sum_{i=1}^{N} Z'_{li}\hat{v}_{li}\hat{v}'_{li}Z_{li}\right)^{-1} Z'_l \hat{v}_l \;\tilde{a}\; \chi^2_{p_l - k}$$

if the errors in levels are MA (0) or MA (1). In addition

$$ds = s - s_l \;\tilde{a}\; \chi^2_{p-p_l} \tag{11}$$

if the errors in levels are not serially correlated. Moreover ds is asymptotically independent of s_l (see Appendix).

A closely related alternative is to construct a Hausman test based on the difference $(\hat{\delta}_l - \hat{\delta})$ (cf. Hausman (1978) and Hausman and Taylor (1981)). This type of test has been proposed by Griliches and Hausman (1986) in the context of moving-average measurement errors. A test is based on the statistic

$$h = (\hat{\delta}_l - \hat{\delta})'[\hat{\text{avar}}(\hat{\delta}_l) - \hat{\text{avar}}(\hat{\delta})]^{-}(\hat{\delta}_l - \hat{\delta}) \;\tilde{a}\; \chi^2_r \tag{12}$$

where $r = \text{rank avar}(\hat{\delta}_l - \hat{\delta})$ and $(\;)^{-}$ indicates a generalized inverse. The value of r will depend on the number of columns of X which are maintained to be strictly exogenous. In particular, if the only non-exogenous variable is the lagged dependent variable then $r = 1$.

4. EXPERIMENTAL EVIDENCE

A limited simulation was carried out to study the performance of the estimation and testing procedures discussed above in samples of a size likely to be encountered in practice. In all the experiments the dependent variable y_{it} was generated from a model of the form

$$y_{it} = \alpha y_{i(t-1)} + \beta x_{it} + \eta_i + v_{it}, \qquad (i = 1, \ldots, N;\; t = 1, \ldots, T+10)$$

$$v_{it} = \sigma_{it}(\xi_{it} + \phi\xi_{i(t-1)}), \qquad \sigma^2_{it} = \theta_0 + \theta_1 x^2_{it} \tag{13}$$

where $\eta_i \sim$ i.i.d. $N(0, \sigma^2_\eta)$, $\xi_{it} \sim$ i.i.d. $N(0, 1)$ and $y_{i0} = 0$. The first ten cross-sections were discarded so that the actual samples contain NT observations.

With regard to x_{it}, we considered the following generating equation

$$x_{it} = \rho x_{i(t-1)} + \varepsilon_{it} \tag{14}$$

with $\varepsilon_{it} \sim$ i.i.d. $N(0, \sigma^2_\varepsilon)$ independent of η_i and v_{is} for all t, s and kept the observations on x_{it} fixed over replications. As an alternative choice of regressors we used total sales from a sample of quoted U.K. firms where large variations across units and outliers are likely to be present. In both cases, x_{it} is strictly exogenous and uncorrelated with the individual effects. However, since we are interested in the performance of estimators that rely on lags of y_{it} for the identification of α and β, the over-identifying restrictions arising from the strict exogeneity of x_{it} and the lack of correlation with η_i were not used in the simulated GMM estimator. Thus, we chose[6]

$$Z_i = [\text{diag}(y_{i1} \cdots y_{is}) \vdots (\bar{x}_{i3} \cdots \bar{x}_{iT})'] \qquad (s = 1, \ldots, T-2)$$

which is a valid instrument set provided $\phi = 0$.

In the base design, the sample size is $N = 100$ and $T = 7$, the v_{it} are independent over time and homoskedastic: $\theta_1 = \phi = 0$, $\theta_0 = \sigma^2 = 1$, $\sigma_\eta^2 = 1$, $\beta = 1$, $\rho = 0{\cdot}8$ and $\sigma_\varepsilon^2 = 0{\cdot}9$. Tables 1 and 2 summarize the results for $\alpha = 0{\cdot}2$, $0{\cdot}5$, $0{\cdot}8$ obtained from 100 replications. Results for other variants of this design were calculated ($N = 200$, $T = 6$, $\sigma^2 = 2$, 5, $\sigma_\eta^2 = 0$, $\rho = 0$], and are available from the authors on request. However the conclusions are the same as for the results reported here.

Table 1 reports sample means and standard deviations for one-step and two-step GMM estimators (GMM1 and GMM2 respectively), OLS in levels, within-groups, and

TABLE 1

Biases in the estimates

	GMM1	GMM2	OLS	Within-groups	AHd	AHl	One-step ASE	Robust One-step ASE	Two-step ASE
				$\alpha = 0{\cdot}5, \beta = 1$					
Coefficient: α									
Mean	0·4884	0·4920	0·7216	0·3954	−2·4753	0·5075	0·0683	0·0677	0·0604
St. Dev.	0·0671	0·0739	0·0216	0·0272	45·9859	0·0821	0·0096	0·0120	0·0106
Coefficient: β									
Mean	1·0053	0·9976	0·7002	1·0409	0·1625	0·9996	0·0612	0·0607	0·0548
St. Dev.	0·0631	0·0668	0·0484	0·0480	9·8406	0·0650	0·0031	0·0055	0·0052
				$\alpha = 0{\cdot}2, \beta = 1$					
Coefficient: α									
Mean	0·1937	0·1979	0·5108	0·0957	0·2025	0·2044	0·0610	0·0602	0·0533
St. Dev.	0·0597	0·0670	0·0340	0·0309	0·1973	0·0661	0·0045	0·0066	0·0060
Coefficient: β									
Mean	1·0048	0·9960	0·7030	1·0430	0·9973	0·9991	0·0620	0·0615	0·0553
St. Dev.	0·0630	0·0687	0·0526	0·0476	0·0818	0·0654	0·0028	0·0058	0·0052
				$\alpha = 0{\cdot}8, \beta = 1$					
Coefficient: α									
Mean	0·7827	0·7810	0·8997	0·7160	0·8103	0·8038	0·0529	0·0527	0·0470
St. Dev.	0·0582	0·0609	0·0090	0·0206	0·1313	0·2677	0·0069	0·0082	0·0075
Coefficient: β									
Mean	1·0001	0·9926	0·7754	1·0137	1·0000	0·9980	0·0609	0·0601	0·0544
St. Dev.	0·0622	0·0671	0·0423	0·0461	0·0789	0·0893	0·0035	0·0056	0·0056

Notes.

(i) $N = 100$, $T = 7$, 100 replications, $\sigma^2 = \sigma_\eta^2 = 1$.

(ii) Exogenous variable is first order autoregressive with $\rho = 0{\cdot}8$ and $\sigma_\varepsilon^2 = 0{\cdot}9$.

(iii) GMM1 and GMM2 are respectively one step and two step difference—IV estimators of the type described in Section 2. Both GMM use $Z_i = [\text{diag}(y_{i1} \cdots y_{is}) : (\bar{x}_{i3} \cdots \bar{x}_{iT})']$ $(s = 1, \ldots, T-2)$.

(iv) AHd and AHl are the Anderson-Hsiao stacked—IV estimators of the equation in first differences that use $\Delta y_{i(t-2)}$ and $y_{i(t-2)}$ as an instrument for $\Delta y_{i(t-1)}$ respectively.

(v) One Step ASE and Robust One Step ASE are estimates of the asymptotic standard errors of GMM1. The former are only valid for i.i.d. errors while the latter are robust to general heteroskedasticity over individuals and over time. Two step ASE is a robust estimate of the asymptotic standard errors of GMM2.

6. The optimal instrument set for the system of first difference equations would be $z_i = \text{diag}(y_{i1} \cdots y_{is}, x_{i1}, \ldots, x_{iT})$.

two AH estimators. The AHd estimator is given by

$$\begin{pmatrix} \hat{\alpha} \\ \hat{\beta} \end{pmatrix}_{\mathrm{AHd}} = \left(\sum_i^N \sum_{t=4}^T \Delta z_{it} \Delta w'_{it}\right)^{-1} \sum_i^N \sum_{t=4}^T \Delta z_{it} \, \Delta y_{it} \tag{15}$$

where $w_{it} = (y_{i(t-1)}, x_{it})'$ and $z_{it} = (y_{i(t-2)}, x_{it})'$. The AHl estimator replaces Δz_{it} with $(y_{i(t-2)}, \Delta x_{it})'$ and the summation goes from $t = 3$ to T. The next two columns report sample means and standard deviations for two alternative estimates of the asymptotic standard errors of the one step GMM estimator. The first one is only valid for i.i.d. errors while the second is robust to heteroskedasticity of arbitrary form. The last column corresponds to estimates of the asymptotic standard errors of the two-step GMM estimator.

The tabulated results show a small downward finite-sample bias in the GMM estimators of α (of about 2 to 3%). Not surprisingly, the OLS and the within-group (WG) estimators of α exhibit large biases in opposite directions (i.e. upward bias in OLS whose size depends on σ_η^2; downward bias in WG whose size depends on T). The behaviour of the AH estimators is more surprising. Concerning AHd, there is evidence of lack of identification for $\alpha = 0{\cdot}5$ and negligible biases, though coupled with large variances, for $\alpha = 0{\cdot}2$ and $0{\cdot}8$. On the other hand, the standard deviation of AHl is small for $\alpha = 0{\cdot}2$ and $\alpha = 0{\cdot}5$ but it more than doubles that of AHd for $\alpha = 0{\cdot}8$. These results are consistent with the calculations of asymptotic variance matrices for the AH estimators reported elsewhere (cf. Arellano (1989)). As explained in that note, in a model containing an exogenous variable in addition to the lagged dependent variable, there are values of α and ρ between 0 and 1 for which there is no correlation between $\Delta y_{i(t-1)}$ and $\Delta y_{i(t-2)}$, in which case $\Delta y_{i(t-2)}$ is not a valid instrument and AHd is not identified. In our first experiment, AHd is close to such a singularity which explains the result. In contrast, AHl has no singularities for stationary values of α and ρ but can nevertheless be even less precise than AHd for large values of α.

An interesting result is that the standard deviation of the GMM estimators of α is about three times smaller than that of AHd for $\alpha = 0{\cdot}2$ and $0{\cdot}8$ and between four and five times smaller than that of AHl for $\alpha = 0{\cdot}8$ (although the standard deviation of AHl for $\alpha = 0{\cdot}2$ and $\alpha = 0{\cdot}5$ is of a similar magnitude as for the GMM estimators). This suggests that there may be significant efficiency gains in practice by using GMM as opposed to AH, aside from overcoming potential singularities as in our first experiment.

Concerning GMM1, the two alternative estimators of their asymptotic standard errors behave in a similar way, although the robust alternatives always have a bigger standard deviation. Their sample mean is always very close to the finite-sample standard deviation in column one, suggesting that the asymptotic approximation is quite accurate for the simulated designs. On the other hand, the estimator of the asymptotic standard errors of GMM2 in the last column shows a downward bias of around 20 percent relative to the finite-sample standard deviations reported in the second column.

Table 2 reports the number of rejections together with sample means and variances for the test statistics discussed in Section 3. The first three columns contain two alternative versions of the one step m_2 statistic and the two step m_2 statistic (see the notes to the table). The Sargan tests are tests of the over-identifying restrictions based on minimized criteria of the GMM estimators of Table 1. The difference-Sargan tests are based on the difference between the minimized GMM criteria and the restricted versions of these that remain valid when the errors are MA (1). The Hausman statistics test the distance between the GMM and the restricted GMM estimates of α.

With only 100 replications we cannot hope to provide accurate estimates of the tail probabilities associated with the test statistics; our results can only be suggestive. The

TABLE 2

Sizes of the Test Statistics, Number of rejections out of 100 cases

	One-step m_2	Robust one-step m_2	Two-step m_2	One-step Sargan (df = 14)	Two-step Sargan (df = 14)	One-step difference-Sargan (df = 5)	Two-step difference-Sargan (df = 5)	One-step Hausman (df = 1)	Two-step Hausman (df = 1)
					$\alpha = 0{\cdot}5$				
10	12	15	14	11	7	13	12	13	20
5	5	5	6	6	4	6	6	9	12
1	1	1	1	0	0	0	2	2	3
Mean	0·013	0·003	0·002	13·622	13·844	5·195	5·209	1·135	1·487
Variance	1·049	1·071	1·063	28·004	23·092	10·889	10·788	3·547	4·693
					$\alpha = 0{\cdot}2$				
10	12	13	13	8	6	12	9	11	17
5	4	5	4	4	3	8	6	7	13
1	2	1	1	0	0	1	1	2	3
Mean	−0·002	−0·010	−0·018	13·519	13·691	5·043	5·004	1·047	1·528
Variance	1·127	1·146	1·124	24·471	22·092	10·928	10·806	2·612	5·003
					$\alpha = 0{\cdot}8$				
10	12	15	15	9	10	7	12	11	12
5	5	6	6	7	4	4	9	5	8
1	1	0	0	1	2	1	2	0	4
Mean	0·047	0·037	0·036	13·423	13·883	4·917	5·199	0·928	1·239
Variance	1·004	1·029	1·028	31·492	28·854	8·916	11·333	1·648	4·325

Notes.

(i) $N = 100$, $T = 7$, 100 replications, $\sigma^2 = \sigma_\eta^2 = 1$, $\beta = 1$.

(ii) Exogenous variable is first order autoregressive with $\rho = 0{\cdot}8$ and $\sigma_\varepsilon^2 = 0{\cdot}9$.

(iii) All tests are based on the one- and two-step GMM estimates reported in Table 1 as well as on restricted versions of those which only use the columns of Z_i that remain valid instruments when the errors are MA (1). The one-step m_2 statistic is described in the Appendix.

(iv) Results on an extended set of experiments are available from the authors on request.

TABLE 3

Power of the Test Statistics, Number of rejections out of 100 cases

	One-step m_2	Robust one-step m_2	Two-step m_2	One-step Sargan (df = 14)	Two-step Sargan (df = 14)	One-step difference-Sargan (df = 5)	Two-step difference-Sargan (df = 5)	One-step Hausman (df = 1)	Two-step Hausman (df = 1)
				Serial correlation: Corr $(v_t v_{t-1}) = 0{\cdot}2$					
10	54	53	53	47	33	60	46	27	25
5	45	46	46	33	20	53	34	15	20
1	24	25	25	22	2	29	9	8	11
Mean	−1·833	−1·823	−1·823	20·673	17·988	11·307	9·151	2·076	2·431
Variance	1·079	0·987	0·988	70·881	34·447	40·017	20·773	8·855	12·496
				Serial correlation: Corr $(v_t v_{t-1}) = 0{\cdot}3$					
10	95	96	96	78	71	91	86	29	33
5	91	92	92	72	47	86	70	20	22
1	78	77	78	57	30	69	51	11	11
Mean	−3·293	−3·118	−3·121	32·057	24·180	22·112	15·314	2·537	2·707
Variance	1·033	0·695	0·705	135·543	40·127	94·261	30·339	12·430	13·640
				Heteroskedasticity: Var $(v_{it}) = x_{it}^2$, x_{it} AR (1) data					
10	23	9	10	43	8	35	7	24	25
5	15	2	2	35	0	24	4	16	16
1	3	0	0	13	0	15	0	8	5
Mean	0·029	−0·023	−0·038	20·967	14·495	9·104	5·216	2·158	1·938
Variance	1·708	1·005	0·991	70·077	17·194	36·410	8·737	13·954	6·355
				Heteroskedasticity: Var $(v_{it}) = x_{it}^2$, x_{it}: U.K. Sales					
10	71	6	7	100	0	93	13	74	81
5	68	3	2	100	0	92	3	69	76
1	54	0	0	100	0	88	1	62	72
Mean	−0·870	−0·225	−0·301	207·789	14·940	63·389	5·611	43·241	154·452
Variance	15·022	1·126	1·014	5863·623	5·405	2659·712	9·095	12059·642	339856·703

Notes.

(i) $N = 100$, $T = 7$, 100 replications, $\alpha = 0{\cdot}5$, $\beta = 1$, $\sigma_\eta^2 = 0$.

(ii) In the serial correlation designs v_{it} has been generated as MA (1) with standard normal random errors.

(iii) In the first three designs x_{it} is AR (1) with $\rho = 0{\cdot}8$ and $\sigma_\varepsilon^2 = 0{\cdot}9$.

(iv) In the fourth design, x_{it} are total sales from a sample of quoted U.K. companies scaled to have Var $(\Delta x_{it}) = 1$. x_{it} behaves as a random walk process with large differences in mean and variance across firms.

(v) In the heteroskedastic designs there is no serial correlation in the v_{it}.

robust m_2 statistics, which depend on the fourth-order moments of the data, both tend to reject too often at the 10% level, suggesting that they have a slower convergence to normality by comparison with the other test, but they are still to be recommended when heteroskedasticity is suspected. Overall all three m_2 tests seem to be quite well approximated by their asymptotic distributions under the null, with no obvious indications of the need for systematic finite-sample size corrections. The same is true for the Sargan, difference-Sargan and one step Hausman tests. However, the two-step Hausman statistic appears to over-reject consistently in these experiments.

Table 3 repeats the exercise for two models with MA (1) serial correlation ($\phi = 0{\cdot}209$ and $0{\cdot}333$) and two other experiments with heteroskedastic errors. The m_2 statistic will reject the null more than half the time at the 10 per cent level when the correlation between v_{it} and $v_{i(t-1)}$ is only 0·2. However when the autocorrelation rises to 0·3, the null will be rejected in 95% of cases. The Hausman test has considerably less power than the difference-Sargan test or the m_2 statistics, and with increasing autocorrelation the difference in power becomes wider.

The last two panels of Table 3 investigate the effects of departures from homoskedasticity of the error distribution on the probabilities of rejection of the tests. Both experiments have $\theta_0 = 0$ and $\theta_1 = 1$. In the first, the x_{it} are generated AR (1) data as in the previous experiments, while in the second the x_{it} are U.K. sales data. This has a dramatic effect on the one-step tests which are not robust to heteroskedasticity. On the other hand, the robust m_2 statistics and the two-step difference-Sargan test show no serious departures from their nominal size. The two-step Sargan test tends to under-reject and the two-step Hausman test over-rejects, especially in the last experiment where the variance of x_{it} is much greater. We suspect that the two-step Hausman statistic is very sensitive to the presence of outliers.

5. AN APPLICATION TO EMPLOYMENT EQUATIONS

In this section we apply the strategy for estimation and testing outlined earlier to a model of employment, using panel data for a sample of U.K. companies. We consider a dynamic employment equation of the form

$$n_{it} = \alpha_1 n_{i(t-1)} + \alpha_2 n_{i(t-2)} + \beta'(L)x_{it} + \lambda_t + \eta_i + v_{it}. \qquad (16)$$

Here n_{it} is the logarithm of U.K. employment in company i at the end of year t,[7] the vector x_{it} contains a set of explanatory variables and $\beta(L)$ is a vector of polynomials in the lag operator. The specification also contains a time effect λ_t that is common to all companies,[8] a permanent but unobservable firm-specific effect η_i and an error term v_{it}.

Equation (16) will admit more than one theoretical interpretation. Suppose first that, in the absence of adjustment costs, a price-setting firm facing a constant elasticity demand curve would choose to set employment according to a log-linear labour demand equation (see, for example, Layard and Nickell (1986))

$$n^*_{it} = \gamma_0 + \gamma_1 w_{it} + \gamma_2 k_{it} + \gamma_3 \sigma^e_{it} + \eta'_i \qquad (17)$$

where $\gamma_1 < 0$, $\gamma_2 > 0$ and $\gamma_3 \geqq 0$. Here w_{it} is the log of the real product wage, k_{it} is the log

7. Note that the time period is taken to be the 12-month period covered in the company's accounts ("accounting year") and so differs across companies in the sample.

8. These time effects relate to calendar years and a company's accounting year is allocated to the calendar year in which it ends.

of gross capital, σ^e_{it} is a measure of expected demand for the firm's product relative to potential output, and the intercept may contain a firm-specific component η'_i. If employment adjustment is costly then actual employment will deviate from n^*_{it} in the short run. This suggests a dynamic labour demand model of the form of (16), where x_{it} contains k_{it}, w_{it} and σ^2_{it}, and unrestricted lag structures are included to model this sluggish adjustment. We include the log of industry output (ys_{it}) to capture industry demand shocks, and aggregate demand shocks are also included through the time dummies. The resulting employment equation is a skeleton version of those estimated on U.K. time series data by Layard and Nickell (1986) and on micro data by Nickell and Wadhwani (1989). The short-run dynamics will compound influences from adjustment costs, expectations formation and decision processes.

Alternatively, if adjustment costs take the standard additively-separable quadratic form $(1/2a)(N_{it}-N_{i(t-1)})^2$, where N_{it} denotes the level rather than the logarithm of company employment, then Dolado (1987), following Nickell (1984), derives a log-linear approximation to the Euler equation for a firm maximising the present discounted value of profits as

$$E_{t-1}(n_{it}) = \delta_0 + (2+r)n_{i(t-1)} - (1+r)n_{i(t-2)} + a(1+r)[n_{i(t-1)} - n^*_{i(t-1)}]. \qquad (18)$$

Here r is a real discount rate, assumed constant, and n^*_{it} is given by (17). Replacing the conditional expectation by its realisation and introducing an expectational error v_{it} yields a model with the form of (16), though with strong restrictions on the dynamic structure in this case. In particular the rational expectations hypothesis suggests a theoretical motivation for the assumption of serially-uncorrelated errors in this kind of model.

The principal data source used is the published accounts of 140 quoted companies whose main activity is manufacturing and for which we have seven or more continuous observations during the period 1976–1984. The panel is unbalanced both in the sense that we have more observations on some firms than on others, and because these observations correspond to different points in historical time. We allocate each of our companies to one of nine broad sub-sectors of manufacturing according to their main product by sales, and use value-added in that sector as our measure of industry output. Our wage variable is a measure of average remuneration per employee in the company, which we deflate using a value-added price deflator at the industry level. Finally we use an inflation-adjusted estimate of the company's gross capital stock. More information about the sample and the construction of these variables is provided in the Data Appendix.

In Table 4 we report GMM estimates of these dynamic employment equations.[9] We begin by including current-dated variables and unrestricted lag structures. Columns (a1) and (a2) present the one-step and two-step results respectively for the most general dynamic specification that we considered. Three cross-sections are lost in constructing lags and taking first differences, so that the estimation period is 1979–1984, with 611 useable observations. Here all variables other than the lagged dependent variables are assumed to be strictly exogenous, although none of the over-identifying restrictions that follow from this assumption are exploited.

Comparing columns (a1) and (a2) shows that the estimated coefficients are quite similar in all cases. Both models are well determined and have sensible long-run properties for a labour demand equation. However the asymptotic standard errors associated with the two-step estimates are generally around 30% lower than those associated with the

9. Estimation was performed using the DPD program written in GAUSS, described in Arellano and Bond (1988a) and available from the authors on request.

TABLE 4

Employment equations

GMM estimates (all variables in first differences)

Dependent variable: ln (Employment)$_{it}$ Sample Period: 1979–1984 (140 companies)

Independent variables	(a1)	(a2)	(b)	Instrumenting wages and capital* (c)	(d)
$n_{i(t-1)}$	0·686 (0·145)	0·629 (0·090)	0·474 (0·085)	0·800 (0.048)	0·825 (0.056)
$n_{i(t-2)}$	−0·085 (0·056)	−0·065 (0·027)	−0·053 (0·027)	−0·116 (0·021)	−0·074 (0·020)
w_{it}	−0·608 (0·178)	−0·526 (0·054)	−0·513 (0·049)	−0·640 (0·054)	—
$w_{i(t-1)}$	0·393 (0·168)	0·311 (0·094)	0·225 (0·080)	0·564 (0·066)	0·431 (0·076)
k_{it}	0·357 (0·059)	0·278 (0·045)	0·293 (0·039)	0·220 (0·051)	—
$k_{i(t-1)}$	−0·058 (0·073)	0·014 (0·053)	—	—	−0·077 (0·045)
$k_{i(t-2)}$	0·020 (0·033)	0·040 (0·026)	—	—	—
ys_{it}	0·608 (0.172)	0·592 (0·116)	0·610 (0·109)	0·890 (0·098)	—
$ys_{i(t-1)}$	−0·711 (0·232)	−0·566 (0·140)	−0·446 (0·125)	−0·875 (0·105)	−0·115(0·100)
$ys_{i(t-2)}$	0·106 (0·141)	0·101 (0·113)	—	—	0·096 (0·092)
m_2	−0·516	−0·434	−0·327	−0·610	−1·259
Sargan test	65·8 (25)	31·4 (25)	30·1 (25)	63·0 (50)	68·3 (51)
Difference-Sargan	41·9 (6)	15·4 (6)	10·0 (6)	28·6 (20)	31·6 (20)
Hausman	5·8 (1)	14·4 (1)	13·4 (1)	2·0 (1)	2·9 (1)
Wald test	408·3 (10)	667·0 (10)	372·0 (7)	779·3 (7)	623·9 (6)
No. of observations	611	611	611	611	611

* A subset of valid moment restrictions involving lagged wages and capital are exploited—see note (vi). Additional instruments used are the stacked levels and first differences of (firm real sales)$_{(t-2)}$ and (firm real stocks)$_{(t-2)}$.

Notes

(i) Time dummies are included in all equations.

(ii) Asymptotic standard errors robust to general cross-section and time series heteroskedasticity are reported in parentheses.

(iii) The GMM estimates reported are all two step except column (a1).

(iv) The m_2, Sargan, difference-Sargan and Hausman statistics are all two step versions of these tests except in column (a1). In column (a1) the m_2 and Hausman statistics are asymptotically robust to general heteroskedasticity, whilst the Sargan and difference-Sargan tests are only valid in the case of i.i.d. errors. All Hausman statistics test only the coefficient on $n_{i(t-1)}$. Degrees of freedom for χ^2 statistics are reported in parentheses.

(v) The Wald statistic is a test of the joint significance of the independent variables asymptotically distributed as χ^2_k under the null of no relationship, where k is the number of coefficients estimated (excluding time dummies).

(vi) The basic instrument set used in columns (a1), (a2) and (b) is of the form

$$Z_i \begin{bmatrix} n_{i1} & n_{i2} & 0 & 0 & 0 & \cdots & 0 & \cdots & 0 & \vdots & \Delta x'_{i4} \\ 0 & 0 & n_{i1} & n_{i2} & n_{i3} & & 0 & & 0 & \vdots & \Delta x'_{i5} \\ \vdots & & & & & \ddots & & & & & \\ 0 & 0 & 0 & 0 & 0 & \cdots & n_{i1} & \cdots & n_{i7} & . & \Delta x'_{i9} \end{bmatrix} \begin{matrix} 1979 \\ 1980 \\ \\ 1984 \end{matrix}$$

where x_{it} is the vector of exogenous variables included in the equation. For example, the equation for 1979 in first differences can be written as

$$\Delta n_{i4} = \alpha_1 \Delta n_{i3} + \alpha_2 \Delta n_{i2} + \Delta x'_{i4}\beta + \Delta v_{i4}$$

For companies on which less than 9 observations are available, the rows of Z_i corresponding to the missing equations are deleted and the missing values of n in the remaining rows are replaced by zeroes.

In columns (c) and (d) Z_i is modified to take the form

$$Z_i = [\text{diag}\,(n_{i1} \cdots n_{is} w_{i(s-1)} w_{is} k_{i(s-1)} k_{is}) \vdots (\Delta x'_{i4} \cdots \Delta x'_{i9})'] \qquad (s = 2, \ldots, 7)$$

where x_{it} is now the vector of explanatory variables excluding wages and capital but including stacked lagged sales and stocks.

one-step estimates, with the discrepancy being even larger in some cases. We suspect that most of this apparent gain in precision may reflect a downward finite-sample bias in the estimates of the two-step standard errors as indicated by the simulation results in Table 1, suggesting that caution would be advisable in making inferences based on the two-step estimator alone in samples of this size.

Turning to the test statistics, neither of the robust m_2 statistics nor the two-step Sargan test provide evidence to suggest that the assumption of serially uncorrelated errors is inappropriate in this example. The one-step Sargan and difference-Sargan statistics do reject the overidentifying restrictions but our simulation results showed a strong tendency for those tests to reject too often in the presence of heteroskedasticity. The two-step difference-Sargan test is more marginal but does reject at the 5 per cent significance level. Both Hausman tests also reject but these too show a tendency to over-reject in our simulation experiments. One possibility is that this instability across different instrument sets reflects the failure of the strict exogeneity assumption for wages and capital, rather than serial correlation per se.

In Table 5 we present some alternative estimates of this same model for comparison. Columns (e) and (f) report two instrumental variable estimates of the differenced equation using simpler instrument sets of the AH type. In column (e) we use the difference $\Delta n_{i(t-3)}$ to instrument $\Delta n_{i(t-1)}$, losing one further cross-section, whilst in column (f) we use the level $n_{i(t-3)}$ as the instrument. In both cases the coefficient estimates are poorly determined, indicating a massive loss in efficiency compared to either GMM estimator in this application. Using both $\Delta n_{i(t-3)}$ and $n_{i(t-3)}$ as instruments (not reported) helped a little, but the estimates remained very imprecise. In column (g) we report OLS estimates of the employment equation in levels. In this case the 1978 cross-section is available and the longer estimation period has been used here. Compared to the GMM estimates there is a serious upward bias on the lagged dependent variable, which suggests the presence of firm-specific effects. Column (h) reports the within-groups estimates, which are close to GMM in this example. In fact the WG estimate of the first-order autoregressive coefficient is bigger than the corresponding GMM estimates, although the comparison between WG and GMM in this case is obscured by the likely endogeneity of wages and capital.

Returning to the GMM estimates in Table 4, column (b) omits insignificant dynamics with little change in the long-run properties of the previous model. In columns (b)–(d) we report only the two-step estimates though the one-step coefficient estimates were invariably similar. In column (b) the two-step difference-Sargan test now marginally accepts the hypothesis of no serial correlation, but the two-step Hausman statistic remains an outlier. In column (c) we relax the assumption that the real wage and capital stock are strictly exogenous and instead treat them as being endogenous. We therefore use lags of w and k dated $(t-2)$ and earlier as instruments for w_{it}, $w_{i(t-1)}$ and k_{it}. We also use lagged values of the company's real sales and real stocks as additional instruments. Given the size of our sample, not all the available moment restrictions were used. The precise form of the instrument matrix is described in note (vi) to Table 4. The results in column (c) suggest that it is inappropriate to treat wages and capital as strictly exogenous in this model. In this case none of the test statistics indicate the presence of misspecification.

The coefficient estimates for our preferred specification in column (c) suggest a long-run wage elasticity of $-0{\cdot}24$ (standard error $= 0{\cdot}28$) and a long-run elasticity with respect to capital of $0{\cdot}7$ (S.E. $= 0{\cdot}14$). There is a strong suggestion that industry output enters the model in changes rather than levels, which is appealing since σ^e_{it} in (17) measures demand shocks relative to potential output. Layard and Nickell (1986) interpret

TABLE 5

Employment equations

Alternative estimates

Dependent variable: ln (Employment)$_{it}$

Independent variables	(e) AHd	(f) AHI	(g) OLS	(h) Within-groups
$n_{i(t-1)}$	1·423	2·308	1·045	0·734
	(1·001)	(1·055)	(0·051)	(0·058)
$n_{i(t-2)}$	−0·165	−0·224	−0·077	−0·141
	(0·128)	(0·117)	(0·048)	(0·077)
w_{it}	−0·752	−0·810	−0·524	−0·557
	(0·230)	(0·283)	(0·172)	(0·155)
$w_{i(t-1)}$	0·963	1·422	0·477	0·326
	(0·768)	(0·851)	(0·169)	(0·143)
k_{it}	0·322	0·253	0·343	0·385
	(0·105)	(0·110)	(0·048)	(0·056)
$k_{i(t-1)}$	−0·325	−0·552	−0·202	−0·084
	(0·386)	(0·357)	(0·064)	(0·053)
$k_{i(t-2)}$	−0·095	−0·213	−0·116	−0·025
	(0·123)	(0·145)	(0·035)	(0·042)
ys_{it}	0·766	0·991	0·433	0·521
	(0·311)	(0·338)	(0·176)	(0·193)
$ys_{i(t-1)}$	−1·362	−1·938	−0·768	−0·659
	(0·881)	(0·992)	(0·248)	(0·208)
$ys_{i(t-2)}$	0·321	0·487	0·312	0·001
	(0·416)	(0·425)	(0·130)	(0·139)
m_2	−0·781	−0·919	−1·029	
Wald test	199·3 (10)	101·1 (10)		
R^2			0·994	0·689
Number of observations	471	611	751	751

Notes.

(i) Time dummies are included in all equations.

(ii) Asymptotic standard errors robust to general cross-section and time series heteroskedasticity are reported in parentheses.

(iii) The m_2 and Wald tests are asymptotically robust to general heteroskedasticity.

(iv) Columns (e) and (f) report Anderson–Hsiao-type estimates of the equation in first differences: $\Delta n_{i(t-1)}$ is treated as endogenous and the additional instruments used are $\Delta n_{i(t-3)}$ in (e), and $n_{i(t-3)}$ in (f), so that one further cross-section is lost in (e) and the effective sample period becomes 1980–84.

(v) Column (g) reports OLS estimates of the equation in levels, where the effective sample period becomes 1978–1984.

(vi) Column (h) reports within-groups estimates. These are OLS estimates of the equation in deviations from time means.

the short-run effect of product demand fluctuations on labour demand as reflecting the practice of normal cost pricing.

Finally in column (d) we report estimates of the Euler equation model given in (18). Here again we treat wages and capital as endogenous variables. Although the tests for serial correlation remain below their critical values, the coefficient estimates are not favourable to the Euler equation interpretation. The coefficients on capital and industry output are poorly determined, whilst those on the lagged dependent variable imply a real discount rate of around −100%. Very similar results were obtained for versions of the Euler equation model allowing for an MA (1) error process and estimating in levels as opposed to logs. It appears that the process of employment adjustment is not well described by this model.

The results of this empirical application are generally in agreement with those of our Monte Carlo simulations. The GMM estimator offers significant efficiency gains compared to simpler IV alternatives, and produces estimates that are well-determined in dynamic panel data models. The tendency for non-robust test statistics to over-reject is confirmed. The robust m_2 statistics perform satisfactorily as do the two-step Sargan and difference-Sargan tests, but the two-step Hausman test must be considered suspect in samples of this size.

6. CONCLUSION

In this paper we have discussed the estimation of dynamic panel data models by the generalized method of moments. The estimators we consider exploit optimally all the linear moment restrictions that follow from particular specifications, and are extended to cover the case of unbalanced panel data. We focus on models with predetermined but not strictly exogenous explanatory variables in which identification results from lack of serial correlation in the errors. A test of serial correlation based on the GMM residuals is proposed and compared with Sargan tests of over-identifying restrictions and Hausman specification tests.

To study the practical performance of these procedures we performed a Monte Carlo simulation for 100 units, seven time-periods and two parameters. The results indicate negligible finite sample biases in the GMM estimators and substantially smaller variances than those associated with simpler IV estimators of the kind introduced by Anderson and Hsiao (1981). We also find that the distributions of the serial-correlation tests are well-approximated by their asymptotic counterparts.

We applied these methods to estimate employment equations using an unbalanced panel of 140 quoted U.K. companies for the period 1979–1984. The GMM estimators and the serial correlation tests performed well in this application. A potentially serious problem, suggested by both the experimental evidence and the application, concerns the estimates of the standard errors for the two-step GMM estimator which we find to be downward biased in our samples. Further results on alternative estimators of these standard errors would be very useful.

APPENDIX

A. The asymptotic normality of the m_2 statistic

Following the notation of Section 3, under the assumption that $(X'_{-2}v_*/N) = o_p(1)$ we have

$$N^{-1/2}\hat{v}'_{-2}\hat{v}_* = N^{-1/2}v'_{-2}v_* - (v'_{-2}X_*/N)N^{1/2}(\hat{\delta}-\delta) + o_p(1) \quad \text{as } N \to \infty$$

and also

$$N^{-1/2}\hat{v}'_{-2}\hat{v}_* = N^{-1/2}v'_{-2}v_* - g'_N N^{-1/2}Z'v + o_p(1),$$

where

$$g'_N = v'_{-2}X_*(X'ZA_NZ'X)^{-1}X'ZA_N.$$

Then a multivariate central limit theorem for independent observations ensures

$$\bar{W}_N^{1/2} N^{-1/2}\begin{pmatrix} v'_{-2}v_* \\ Z'v \end{pmatrix} \to^d N(0, I_{p+1}),$$

where $\bar{W}_N$ is the average covariance matrix of $(\phi_i, \xi_i')'$:

$$\bar{W}_N = \frac{1}{N}\sum_{i=1}^{N} E\begin{pmatrix} \phi_i^2 & \phi_i\xi_i' \\ \phi_i\xi_i & \xi_i\xi_i' \end{pmatrix} = \begin{pmatrix} \bar{\omega}_N & \bar{\psi}'_N \\ \bar{\psi}_N & \bar{V}_N \end{pmatrix},$$

and $\xi_i = Z_i' v_i$. Therefore

$$\bar{v}_N^{-1/2} N^{-1/2} \hat{v}'_{-2} v_* \to^d N(0, 1) \qquad \text{(A1)}$$

where

$$\bar{v}_N = \bar{\omega}_N - 2g'_N \bar{\psi}_N + g'_N \bar{V}_N g_N$$

or

$$\bar{v}_N = \frac{1}{N}[\sum_{i=1}^{N} E(v'_{i(-2)} v_{i*} v'_{i*} v_{i(-2)}) - 2(v'_{-2}X_*)(X'ZA_NZ'X)^{-1}X'ZA_N\sum_{i=1}^{N} E(Z_i'v_iv'_{i*}v_{i(-2)})$$
$$+ (v'_{-2}X_*)\text{ avar }(\hat{\delta})(X'_*v_{-2})]$$

with

$$\text{avar }(\hat{\delta}) = N(X'ZA_NZ'X)^{-1}(X'ZA_N\bar{V}_NA_NZ'X)(X'ZA_NZ'X)^{-1}.$$

A consistent estimate of $\bar{v}_N$ can be obtained by replacing population average expectations of errors by sample averages of residuals. Finally, noticing that under our assumptions (A1) remains valid after this replacement, the result follows.

For a one-step $\hat{\delta}$, we can also consider an alternative m_2 criterion ("one step m_2") which relies on more restrictive auxiliary distributional assumptions. Assuming that the errors in the model in levels are independent and identically distributed across individuals and time, we have

$$\bar{\omega}_N = \frac{1}{N}\sigma^2\sum_{i=1}^{N} E(v'_{i(-2)}H_{i*}v_{i(-2)})$$

where H_{i*} is a $(T_i - 4)$ square matrix which has twos in the main diagonal, minus ones in the first subdiagonals and zeros otherwise. Moreover

$$\bar{\psi}_N = \frac{1}{N}\sigma^2\sum_{i=1}^{N} E(Z_i'H_{i\dagger}v_{i(-2)})$$

where $H_{i\dagger}$ is a $(T_i - 2) \times (T_i - 4)$ matrix with

$$H_{i\dagger} = \begin{pmatrix} H_{i**} \\ H_{i*} \end{pmatrix}$$

and H_{i**} is a $2 \times (T_i - 4)$ matrix with minus one in the (2, 1) position and zeroes elsewhere. Under such conditions $\hat{v}$ can be replaced by

$$\hat{v} = \hat{\sigma}^2\sum_{i=1}^{N} \hat{v}'_{i(-2)}H_{i*}\hat{v}'_{-2}X_*(X'ZA_NZ'X)^{-1}X'ZA_N\left(\sum_{i=1}^{N} Z_i'H_{i\dagger}\hat{v}_{i(-2)}\right)\hat{\sigma}^2$$
$$+ \hat{v}'_{-2}X_*\text{ av}\hat{\text{a}}\text{r }(\hat{\delta})X'_*\hat{v}_{-2}$$

where $\hat{\sigma}^2$ is an estimate of σ^2.

B. The Sargan difference test

Note that s in (10) can be re-written as

$$s = \frac{\hat{v}'Z^*}{\sqrt{N}}\left(\frac{1}{N}\sum_{i=1}^{N} Z_i^{*\prime}\hat{v}_i\hat{v}_i'Z_i^*\right)^{-1}\frac{Z^{*\prime}\hat{v}}{\sqrt{N}},$$

where $Z^* = ZH$ and H is a $p \times p$ linear transformation matrix such that

$$Z^* = (Z_I \mid Z_{II})$$

with

$$\frac{1}{N}\sum_{i=1}^{N} Z'_{Ii}\hat{v}_i\hat{v}_i'Z_{IIi} \to^p 0.$$

Letting

$$\left(\frac{1}{N}\Sigma_{i=1}^{N} Z_i^{*\prime}\hat{v}_i\hat{v}_i' Z_i^*\right)^{-1} = C_N C_N'$$

where C_N is $p \times p$ nonsingular, and noting that

$$\frac{Z^{*\prime}\hat{v}}{\sqrt{N}} = \left\{I_p - \frac{Z^{*\prime}X}{N}\left[\frac{X'Z^*}{N} C_N C_N' \frac{Z^{*\prime}X}{N}\right]^{-1}\frac{X'Z^*}{N} C_N C_N'\right\}\frac{Z^{*\prime}v}{\sqrt{N}},$$

we have

$$s = \frac{v'Z^*}{\sqrt{N}} C_N[I_p - G(G'G)^{-1}G']C_N' \frac{Z^{*\prime}v}{\sqrt{N}}$$

where

$$G = C_N'\left(\frac{Z^{*\prime}X}{N}\right).$$

Following the usual argument one can show that $s \rightarrow^d \varepsilon' M\varepsilon \sim \chi^2_{p-k}$, where $\varepsilon \sim N(0, I_p)$ and M is of the form $I_p - D(D'D)^{-1}D'$ with rank $p-k$. O On the same lines we can write

$$s_l = \frac{v'Z_l}{\sqrt{N}} C_{lN}[I_{p_l} - G_l(G_l'G_l)^{-1}G_l']C_{lN}' \frac{Z_l'v}{\sqrt{N}},$$

where

$$G_l = C_{lN}'\left(\frac{Z_l'X}{N}\right)$$

and

$$\left(\frac{1}{N}\Sigma_{i=1}^{N} Z_{li}'\hat{v}_{li}\hat{v}_{li}' Z_{li}\right)^{-1} = C_{lN}C_{lN}'.$$

Let G^* contain the top p_l rows of G. Notice that $G^* - G_l \rightarrow^p 0$.

Therefore

$$ds = s - s_l \rightarrow^d \varepsilon' M\varepsilon - \varepsilon'\begin{pmatrix} M_l & 0 \\ 0 & 0 \end{pmatrix}\varepsilon$$

where $M_l = I_{p_l} - D_l(D_l'D_l)^{-1}D_l'$ and rank $(M_l) = p_l - k$ with $D' = (D_l' \mid D_{ll}')$.
Finally notice that

$$\left[M - \begin{pmatrix} M_l & 0 \\ 0 & 0 \end{pmatrix}\right]$$

is symmetric and idempotent with rank $p - p_l$ and also

$$\left[M - \begin{pmatrix} M_l & 0 \\ 0 & 0 \end{pmatrix}\right]\begin{pmatrix} M_l & 0 \\ 0 & 0 \end{pmatrix} = 0,$$

from which (11) follows.

DATA APPENDIX

(a) Sample

The principal data source used is company accounts from Datastream International which provide accounts records of employment and remuneration (i.e. wage bill) for all U.K. quoted companies from 1976 onwards. We have used a sample of 140 companies with operations mainly in the U.K., whose main activity is manufacturing and for which we have at least 7 continuous observations during the period 1976–1984. Where more than 7 observations are available we have exploited this additional information, so that our sample has the unbalanced structure described in Table A1.

TABLE A1

Number of records on each company	Number of companies
7	103
8	23
9	14

As well as requiring at least 7 continuous observations, companies were excluded from our sample for a number of reasons. We required complete records on a set of accounting variables including gross fixed assets, investment, inventories and sales as well as employment and remuneration. Companies that changed the date of their accounting year end by more than a few days were excluded, so that our data all refer to 12 month periods. We also excluded companies where either employment or one of our constructed measures of real wages, real capital, real inventories or real sales jumped by more than a factor of 3 from one year to the next. This filter will remove both those companies where data has been recorded erroneously and those companies that have experienced major mergers. Finally we restricted our attention to companies that we could allocate to one of 9 broad sub-sectors of manufacturing industry using Datastream's breakdown of total sales by product available from 1980 onwards.

(*b*) *Variables*

Employment

Number of U.K. employees (Datastream variable 216)

Real Wage

A measure of average annual remuneration per employee was constructed by dividing U.K. remuneration (Datastream variable 214) by the number of U.K. employees. This was adjusted to take into account changes in average weekly hours worked in manufacturing industries (manual and non-manual employees, 18 years and over, male and female, all occupations—source: Department of Employment Gazette, various issues). A measure of real average hourly remuneration was then obtained by deflating using an implicit value-added price deflator. These implicit price deflators were calculated for each of our sub-sectors of manufacturing industry, using the current price and constant price GDP data published in various Blue Books.

Gross Capital Stock

Denoting the historic cost book value of gross fixed assets (Datastream variable 330) by HCK_t, we obtain an estimate of the inflation-adjusted (or replacement cost) value of gross fixed assets (RCK_t) using the formula

$$\mathrm{RCK}_t = \mathrm{HCK}_t \times \left(\frac{P_t^I}{P_{t-A}^I}\right),$$

where P^I is a price index for investment goods and A is an estimate of the average age of gross fixed assets. An implicit price deflator for gross fixed investment by manufacturing industry was calculated using the current price and constant price gross fixed investment data published in Economic Trends Annual Supplement (1986, p. 56). For the purpose of this exercise a value of A of 6 years was assumed. Our estimates of the gross capital stock at replacement cost are then expressed in constant prices using our investment goods deflator.

Industry Output

An index of value-added output at constant factor cost was constructed for each of our 9 sub-sectors of manufacturing industry, using data published in the Blue Book (1986, Table 2.4). The 15 sub-sectors of manufacturing for which this data is reported were combined into 9 using the weights given in the Blue Book.

Further details on this data set can be found in Arellano and Bond (1988b).

Acknowledgement. We are grateful to Charlie Bean, Richard Blundell, Olympia Bover, Michael Devereux, Zvi Griliches, David Hendry, Grayham Mizon, John Muellbauer, Steve Nickell, Alain Trognon, Sushil Wadhwani and two anonymous referees for helpful comments on this work. All remaining errors are our own. We thank the Institute for Fiscal Studies for their assistance and the ESRC for financial support under grant B00232207.

REFERENCES

AMEMIYA, T. and MACURDY, T. E. (1986), "Instrumental-Variable Estimation of an Error-Components Model", *Econometrica*, **54**, 869–881.

ANDERSON, T. W. and HSIAO, C. (1981), "Estimation of Dynamic Models with Error Components", *Journal of the American Statistical Association*, **76**, 598–606.

ANDERSON, T. W. and HSIAO, C. (1982), "Formulation and Estimation of Dynamic Models Using Panel Data", *Journal of Econometrics*, **18**, 47–82.

ARELLANO, M. (1989), "A Note on the Anderson–Hsiao Estimator for Panel Data", *Economics Letters*, **31**, 337–341.

ARELLANO, M. (1990), "Testing for Autocorrelation in Dynamic Random Effects Models", *Review of Economic Studies*, **57**, 127–134.

ARELLANO, M. and BOND, S. R. (1988a), "Dynamic Panel Data Estimation Using DPD—A Guide for Users" (Institute for Fiscal Studies, Working Paper 88/15, London).

ARELLANO, M. and BOND, S. R. (1988b), "Some Tests of Specification for Panel Data: Monte Carlo Evidence and an Application to Employment Equations" (Institute for Fiscal Studies, Working Paper 88/4, London).

BHARGAVA, A. and SARGAN, J. D. (1983), "Estimating Dynamic Random Effects Models from Panel Data Covering Short Time Periods", *Econometrica*, **51**, 1635–1659.

CHAMBERLAIN, G. (1984), "Panel Data", in Griliches, Z. and Intriligator, M. D. (eds.), *Handbook of Econometrics, Volume II*. (Amsterdam: Elsevier Science Publishers.)

DOLADO, J. J. (1987), "Intertemporal Employment and Pricing Decision Rules in UK Manufacturing" (University of Oxford, Applied Economics Discussion Paper 18).

GRILICHES, Z. AND HAUSMAN, J. A. (1986), "Errors in Variables in Panel Data", *Journal of Econometrics*, **31**, 93–118.

HANSEN, L. P. (1982), "Large Sample Properties of Generalized Method of Moments Estimators", *Econometrica*, **50**, 1029–1054.

HAUSMAN, J. A. (1978), "Specification Tests in Econometrics", *Econometrica*, **46**, 1251–1272.

HAUSMAN, J. A. and TAYLOR, W. E. (1981), "Panel Data and Unobservable Individual Effects", *Econometrica*, **49**, 1377–1398.

HOLTZ-EAKIN, D., NEWEY, W. and ROSEN, H. (1988), "Estimating Vector Autoregressions with Panel Data", *Econometrica*, **56**, 1371–1395.

HSIAO, C. (1986) *Analysis of Panel Data* (Cambridge: Cambridge University Press).

LAYARD, R. and NICKELL, S. J. (1986), "Unemployment in Britain", *Economica*, **53**, Supplement, 5121–5169.

NICKELL, S. J. (1984), "An Investigation of the Determinants of Manufacturing Employment in the United Kingdom", *Review of Economic Studies*, **51**, 529–557.

NICKELL, S. J. and WADHWANI, S. (1989), "Employment Determination in British Industry: Investigations Using Micro-Data" (Centre for Economic Policy Research Discussion Paper 320, London).

SARGAN, J. D. (1958), "The Estimation of Economic Relationships Using Instrumental Variables", *Econometrica*, **26**, 393–415.

SARGAN, J. D. (1980), "Some Tests of Dynamic Specification for a Single Equation", *Econometrica*, **48**, 879–897.

SARGAN, J. D. (1988), "Testing for Misspecification after Estimating Using Instrumental Variables", in Maasoumi, E. (ed.), *Contributions to Econometrics: John Denis Sargan, Vol.* 1 (Cambridge: Cambridge University Press).

WHITE, H. (1982), "Instrumental Variables Regression with Independent Observations", *Econometrica*, **50**, 483–499.

Part III
Limited Dependent Variables

[12]

Review of Economic Studies (1980) XLVII, 225-238
0034-6527/80/00100225$02.00

Analysis of Covariance with Qualitative Data

GARY CHAMBERLAIN
University of Wisconsin—Madison

1. INTRODUCTION

This paper deals with data that has a group structure. A simple example in the context of a linear regression model is

$$E(y_{it}|\mathbf{x}, \boldsymbol{\beta}, \boldsymbol{\alpha}) = \boldsymbol{\beta}'\mathbf{x}_{it} + \alpha_i \qquad (i = 1, \ldots, N; t = 1, \ldots, T),$$

where there are T observations within each of N groups. The α_i are group specific parameters. Our primary concern is with the estimation of $\boldsymbol{\beta}$, a parameter vector common to all groups. The role of the α_i is to control for group specific effects; i.e. for omitted variables that are constant within a group. The regression function that does not condition on the group will not in general identify $\boldsymbol{\beta}$:

$$E(y_{it}|\mathbf{x}, \boldsymbol{\beta}) \neq \boldsymbol{\beta}'\mathbf{x}_{it}.$$

In this case there is an omitted variable bias.

An important application is generated by longitudinal or panel data, in which there are two or more observations on each individual. Then the group is the individual, and the α_i capture individual differences. If these person effects are correlated with $\mathbf{x}$, then a regression function that fails to control for them will not identify $\boldsymbol{\beta}$. In another important application the group is a family, with observations on two or more siblings within the family. Then the α_i capture omitted variables that are family specific, and they give a concrete representation to family background.

We shall assume that observations from different groups are independent. Then the α_i are incidental parameters (Neyman and Scott (1948)), and $\boldsymbol{\beta}$, which is common to the independent sampling units, is a vector of structural parameters. In the application to sibling data, T is small, typically $T = 2$, whereas there may be a large number of families. Small T and large N are also characteristic of many of the currently available longitudinal data sets. So a basic statistical issue is to develop an estimator for $\boldsymbol{\beta}$ that has good properties in this case. In particular, the estimator ought to be consistent as $N \rightarrow \infty$ for fixed T.

It is well-known that analysis of covariance in the linear regression model does have this consistency property. The problem of finding consistent estimators in other models is non-trivial, however, since the number of incidental parameters is increasing with sample size. We shall work with the following probability model: y_{it} is a binary variable with

$$\text{prob}\,(y_{it} = 1|\mathbf{x}, \boldsymbol{\beta}, \boldsymbol{\alpha}) = F(\boldsymbol{\beta}'\mathbf{x}_{it} + \alpha_i),$$

where $F(\ )$ is a cumulative distribution function such as a unit normal or a logistic. For example, y may indicate labour force participation, unemployment, job change, marital status, health status, or a college degree. Section 2 considers maximum likelihood (ML) estimation of the fixed effects version of this model. A simple algorithm is available which involves a weighted analysis of covariance at each iteration. The ML estimator of $\boldsymbol{\beta}$ is not consistent (for fixed T), however, and we present a simple example with $T=2$ in which the ML estimator of $\boldsymbol{\beta}$ converges to $2\boldsymbol{\beta}$.

Section 3 presents one solution to this problem by working with a conditional likelihood function that conditions on sufficient statistics for the incidental parameters. This likelihood function does not depend upon the incidental parameters, and hence standard asymptotic theory for maximum likelihood estimation applies. This approach is applied to a multinomial logit model for grouped data and to the multivariate log-linear probability model. Section 4 develops an alternative approach, based on a random effects model in which the incidental parameters are assumed to follow a distribution. The important point here is that the distribution of the α_i is not assumed to be independent of $\boldsymbol{x}$; otherwise the problem of omitted variable bias would be assumed away from the beginning. Throughout the paper we shall use the familiar linear regression case to guide the exposition.

2. FIXED EFFECTS: MAXIMIZATION OF THE JOINT LIKELIHOOD FUNCTION

We shall begin with a brief review of the linear regression case. Let

$$y_{it}=\boldsymbol{\beta}'\boldsymbol{x}_{it}+\alpha_i+\varepsilon_{it},$$

where ε_{it} is i.i.d. $N(0,\sigma^2)$. So in addition to assuming independence across the groups, we are assuming that observations within a group are independent as well, conditional on the group effects. The dependence of different observations within a group is assumed to be due to their common dependence on the group specific α_i. More general forms of dependence are, of course, possible; for example, there could be serial correlation in addition to the α_i in the longitudinal case.

Maximum likelihood for this model is simply a multiple regression of y on $\boldsymbol{x}$ and a set of group indicator dummy variables. A useful computational simplification is that the ML estimator of $\boldsymbol{\beta}$ can be obtained from a regression of $y_{it}-\bar{y}_i$ on $\boldsymbol{x}_{it}-\bar{\boldsymbol{x}}_i$, where $\bar{y}_i$ and $\bar{\boldsymbol{x}}_i$ are group means ($\bar{y}_i=\sum_t y_{it}/T$). In the case of $T=2$, this is equivalent to a regression of $y_{i2}-y_{i1}$ on $\boldsymbol{x}_{i2}-\boldsymbol{x}_{i1}$. Since we have

$$y_{i2}-y_{i1}=\boldsymbol{\beta}'(\boldsymbol{x}_{i2}-\boldsymbol{x}_{i1})+\varepsilon_{i2}-\varepsilon_{i1},$$

with the ε's independent of $\boldsymbol{x}$, it is clear this provides a consistent estimator of $\boldsymbol{\beta}$ as $N\to\infty$ (provided that there is sufficient variation in $\boldsymbol{x}_2-\boldsymbol{x}_1$).

There is a comparable computational simplification for the probability models. We shall discuss ML estimation using either a Newton–Raphson or a scoring algorithm, and shall show that each iteration reduces to a weighted analysis of covariance. The binary y_{it} are assumed to be independent (conditional on $\boldsymbol{x}$, $\boldsymbol{\beta}$, and $\boldsymbol{\alpha}$) both between and within groups, with prob $(y_{it}=1|\boldsymbol{x},\boldsymbol{\beta},\boldsymbol{\alpha})=F(\boldsymbol{\beta}'\boldsymbol{x}_{it}+\alpha_i)$. Let $\boldsymbol{\theta}'\boldsymbol{z}_{it}=\boldsymbol{\beta}'\boldsymbol{x}_{it}+\alpha_i$. Then the log-likelihood function is

$$L=\textstyle\sum_{i,t}\{y_{it}\ln F(\boldsymbol{\theta}'\boldsymbol{z}_{it})+(1-y_{it})\ln[1-F(\boldsymbol{\theta}'\boldsymbol{z}_{it})]\}.$$

Note that if $y_{it}=1$ for all t then the ML estimate of α_i is ∞, and if $y_{it}=0$ for all t then the ML estimate of α_i is $-\infty$. Hence the observations on such groups do not affect the ML estimate of $\boldsymbol{\beta}$, and we can simplify by only including in L the groups within which y varies.

We have the following score vector and Hessian:

$$\frac{\partial L}{\partial\boldsymbol{\theta}}=\textstyle\sum_{i,t}\left(\frac{y_{it}}{F}-\frac{1-y_{it}}{1-F}\right)F'\boldsymbol{z}_{it}\qquad\frac{\partial^2L}{\partial\boldsymbol{\theta}\,\partial\boldsymbol{\theta}'}=\sum_{i,t}h_{it}\boldsymbol{z}_{it}\boldsymbol{z}'_{it},$$

where F and its derivatives are evaluated at $\boldsymbol{\theta}' z_{it}$, and

$$h_{it} = -\left[\frac{y_{it}}{F^2} + \frac{1-y_{it}}{(1-F)^2}\right](F')^2 + \left(\frac{y_{it}}{F} - \frac{1-y_{it}}{1-F}\right)F''.$$

It is well-known that L is concave for probit $[F(u) = \int_{-\infty}^{u} e^{-r^2/2} dr/\sqrt{(2\pi)}]$ or for logit $[F(u) = e^u/(1+e^u)]$. Hence a Newton–Raphson algorithm is expected to be effective:

$$\Delta\boldsymbol{\theta} = -\left(\frac{\partial^2 L}{\partial\boldsymbol{\theta}\,\partial\boldsymbol{\theta}'}\right)^{-1}\frac{\partial L}{\partial\boldsymbol{\theta}}.$$

Also of interest is a scoring algorithm which replaces $\partial^2 L/\partial\boldsymbol{\theta}\,\partial\boldsymbol{\theta}'$ by its expectation:[1]

$$E\left(\frac{\partial^2 L}{\partial\boldsymbol{\theta}\,\partial\boldsymbol{\theta}'}\right) = \sum_{i,t} E(h_{it}) z_{it} z'_{it},$$

where

$$E(h_{it}) = -\frac{(F')^2}{F(1-F)}.$$

In either case the computational burden at each iteration comes from inverting $\sum_{i,t} s_{it} z_{it} z'_{it}$, where s_{it} is either h_{it} or $E(h_{it})$. Simplifying the partitioned inverse gives the following formulas for up-dating $\boldsymbol{\beta}$ and α_i:

$$\Delta\boldsymbol{\beta} = \left(\sum_{i,t} s_{it} \boldsymbol{x}_{it} \boldsymbol{x}'_{it} - \sum_i s_i \bar{\boldsymbol{x}}_i^* \bar{\boldsymbol{x}}_i'^*\right)^{-1}\left(\sum_{i,t} s_{it} \boldsymbol{x}_{it} \psi_{it} - \sum_i s_i \bar{\boldsymbol{x}}_i^* \bar{\psi}_i^*\right)$$

$$\Delta\alpha_i = \bar{\psi}_i^* - (\Delta\boldsymbol{\beta})' \bar{\boldsymbol{x}}_i^* \qquad (i = 1, \ldots, N),$$

where

$$\psi_{it} = (y_{it} - F)/F'$$

$$s_i = \sum_t s_{it}, \qquad \bar{\boldsymbol{x}}_i^* = \frac{1}{s_i}\sum_t s_{it} \boldsymbol{x}_{it}, \qquad \bar{\psi}_i^* = \frac{1}{s_i}\sum_t s_{it} \psi_{it}.$$

At each iteration, F and its derivatives are evaluated at the current values for $\boldsymbol{\beta}' \boldsymbol{x}_{it} + \alpha_i$.

This iterated, weighted analysis of covariance algorithm is computationally effective.[2] Unfortunately, the consistency property (for fixed T) of the ML estimator of $\boldsymbol{\beta}$ in the linear regression model does not carry over to this case. That maximum likelihood need not be consistent in the presence of incidental parameters can be illustrated in the linear regression model. The ML estimator of σ^2 does not adjust for degrees of freedom, and hence

$$\operatorname{plim}_{N\to\infty} \hat{\sigma}^2 = \frac{T-1}{T}\sigma^2.$$

For $T = 2$, the ML estimator is inconsistent by a factor of two.[3]

Another example is an autoregression:

$$y_{it} = \beta y_{i,t-1} + \alpha_i + \varepsilon_{it}.$$

We shall condition on y_{i0}. In that case the likelihood function with ε_{it} i.i.d. $N(0, \sigma^2)$ is formally identical to the previous case. The log-likelihood function is quadratic in β and $\boldsymbol{\alpha}$ (given σ^2), and the ML estimator of β is analysis of covariance. With $T = 2$, it can be obtained from a least squares regression of $y_{i2} - y_{i1}$ on $y_{i1} - y_{i0}$. Given that the log-likelihood function is quadratic, it is rather surprising that the ML estimator for β is not consistent. The inconsistency follows immediately since

$$y_{i2} - y_{i1} = \beta(y_{i1} - y_{i0}) + \varepsilon_{i2} - \varepsilon_{i1},$$

and ε_1 is correlated with y_1. If the joint distribution of (y_0, y_1, y_2) is stationary, then the estimator converges to $(\beta-1)/2$ as $N\to\infty$.

As an example of the inconsistency of maximum likelihood in the probability models, consider the following logit model: $F(u)=e^u/(1+e^u)$, $T=2$, $x_{i1}=0$, $x_{i2}=1$, $i=1,\ldots,N$. So the "treatment" is administered only to the second observation in the group. Assume that the sequence of α_i's is such that the following limits exist:

$$\lim_{N\to\infty}\frac{1}{N}\sum_i E[y_{i1}(1-y_{i2})|\alpha_i]=m_1$$

$$\lim_{N\to\infty}\frac{1}{N}\sum_i E[(1-y_{i1})y_{i2}|\alpha_i]=m_2,$$

where $E[y_{i1}(1-y_{i2})|\alpha_i]=F(\alpha_i)F(-\alpha_i-\beta)$ and $E[(1-y_{i1})y_{i2}|\alpha_i]=F(-\alpha_i)F(\alpha_i+\beta)$. Then Andersen (1973, p. 66) shows that the ML estimator of β almost surely satisfies

$$\hat{\beta}=2\beta$$

as $N\to\infty$. A simple extension of his argument shows that if F is a distribution function corresponding to a symmetric, continuous, non-zero probability density, then

$$\hat{\beta}=2F^{-1}\left(\frac{m_2}{m_1+m_2}\right)$$

almost surely as $N\to\infty$. The logit case is special in that $m_2/m_1=e^\beta$, independently of the sequence of α_i's. In general the limiting $\hat{\beta}$ depends on this sequence; but if all of the $\alpha_i=0$, then once again we obtain $\hat{\beta}=2\beta$ almost surely as $N\to\infty$.

We conclude that the linear regression model is very special. The consistency of the ML estimator of $\boldsymbol{\beta}$ does not carry over to other models. The next section interprets this result by introducing a conditional likelihood function that conditions on sufficient statistics for the incidental parameters. In the linear regression case, the conditional ML estimator of $\boldsymbol{\beta}$ is identical to the ML estimator based on the original joint likelihood function. Then we show that the idea of using such a conditional likelihood function can be applied to other models.

3. FIXED EFFECTS: THE CONDITIONAL LIKELIHOOD FUNCTION

We have seen that maximization of the fixed effects likelihood function can give seriously inconsistent estimators if there are only a small number of observations per group. This section will develop an alternative approach using a conditional likelihood function. The key idea is to base the likelihood function on the conditional distribution of the data, conditioning on a set of sufficient statistics for the incidental parameters.[4]

We shall begin by applying this idea to the familiar linear regression case. Let

$$y_{it}=\boldsymbol{\beta}'\mathbf{x}_{it}+\alpha_i+\varepsilon_{it},$$

with ε_{it} i.i.d. $N(0,\sigma^2)$. Then a sufficient statistic for α_i is $\sum_t y_{it}$. It is straightforward to check that the conditional density for $y_{i1},\ldots,y_{iT}$, conditional on $\sum_t y_{it}$, is

$$f(y_{i1},\ldots,y_{iT}|\textstyle\sum_t y_{it})=\sqrt{T}(2\pi)^{-(T-1)/2}\sigma^{-(T-1)}\exp\left\{-\dfrac{1}{2\sigma^2}\sum_t[(y_{it}-\bar{y}_i)-\boldsymbol{\beta}'(\mathbf{x}_{it}-\bar{\mathbf{x}}_i)]^2\right\}.$$

Note that this conditional density does not depend upon α_i. Hence the conditional log-likelihood function depends only upon $\boldsymbol{\beta}$ and σ:

$$L=-N(T-1)\ln\sigma-\frac{1}{2\sigma^2}\sum_{i,t}[(y_{it}-\bar{y}_i)-\boldsymbol{\beta}'(\mathbf{x}_{it}-\bar{\mathbf{x}}_i)]^2;$$

there is no incidental parameter problem, and so maximum likelihood will give consistent estimators provided that the usual regularity conditions are satisfied. The conditional ML estimator of $\boldsymbol{\beta}$ is the analysis of covariance estimator that results from maximization of the joint likelihood function. Hence the consistency of that estimator, which was surprising given the incidental parameter problem, follows immediately from the coincidence of the joint and the conditional ML estimators.

The advantage of the conditional likelihood approach can be seen in the conditional ML estimator for σ^2:

$$\hat{\sigma}^2 = \frac{1}{N(T-1)} \sum_{i,t} [(y_{it} - \bar{y}_i) - \hat{\boldsymbol{\beta}}'(\boldsymbol{x}_{it} - \bar{\boldsymbol{x}}_i)]^2.$$

Unlike the joint ML estimator, here there is a correction for degrees of freedom which ensures that $\hat{\sigma}^2$ is a consistent estimator of σ^2.

The conditional likelihood approach can be applied directly to the fixed effects logit probability model, since $\sum_t y_{it}$ is again a sufficient statistic for α_i.[5] Consider first the case of $T = 2$. If $y_{i1} + y_{i2} = 0$ or 2, then y_{i1} and y_{i2} are both determined given their sum. So the only case of interest is $y_{i1} + y_{i2} = 1$. Then the two possibilities are $w_i = 1$ if $(y_{i1}, y_{i2}) = (0, 1)$ and $w_i = 0$ if $(y_{i1}, y_{i2}) = (1, 0)$. The conditional density is

$$\begin{aligned} \text{prob}\,(w_i = 1 | y_{i1} + y_{i2} = 1) &= \text{prob}\,(w_i = 1)/[\text{prob}\,(w_i = 0) + \text{prob}\,(w_i = 1)] \\ &= \frac{e^{\boldsymbol{\beta}'(\boldsymbol{x}_{i2} - \boldsymbol{x}_{i1})}}{1 + e^{\boldsymbol{\beta}'(\boldsymbol{x}_{i2} - \boldsymbol{x}_{i1})}} = F[\boldsymbol{\beta}'(\boldsymbol{x}_{i2} - \boldsymbol{x}_{i1})], \end{aligned}$$

which does not depend upon α_i. The conditional log-likelihood function is

$$L = \sum_{i \in I_1} \{w_i \ln F[\boldsymbol{\beta}'(\boldsymbol{x}_{i2} - \boldsymbol{x}_{i1})] + (1 - w_i) \ln F[-\boldsymbol{\beta}'(\boldsymbol{x}_{i2} - \boldsymbol{x}_{i1})]\},$$

where

$$I_1 = \{i | y_{i1} + y_{i2} = 1\}.$$

This conditional likelihood function does not depend upon the incidental parameters. In fact, it is in the form of a binary logit likelihood function in which the two outcomes are (0, 1) and (1, 0) with explanatory variables $\boldsymbol{x}_2 - \boldsymbol{x}_1$. This is the analog of differencing in the two period regression model. The conditional ML estimate of $\boldsymbol{\beta}$ can be obtained simply from a standard ML binary logit programme.

The conditional ML estimator of $\boldsymbol{\beta}$ is consistent provided that the conditional likelihood function satisfies regularity conditions, which impose mild restrictions on the α_i. These restrictions, which constrain the rate at which the sequence of α_i's is allowed to become unbounded, are discussed in Andersen (1970), (1971*a*). Furthermore, the inverse of the information matrix based on the conditional likelihood function provides an asymptotic (as $N \to \infty$) covariance matrix for the conditional ML estimator of $\boldsymbol{\beta}$.[6] In deriving this information matrix, one must be careful to note that I_1 is a random set of indices. This can be made more explicit by defining $d_i = 1$ if $y_{i1} + y_{i2} = 1$ and $d_i = 0$ otherwise. Then we have

$$\frac{\partial^2 L}{\partial \boldsymbol{\beta}\, \partial \boldsymbol{\beta}'} = -\sum_i d_i F(1 - F)(\boldsymbol{x}_{i2} - \boldsymbol{x}_{i1})(\boldsymbol{x}_{i2} - \boldsymbol{x}_{i1})',$$

where F and its derivatives are evaluated at $\boldsymbol{\beta}'(\boldsymbol{x}_{i2} - \boldsymbol{x}_{i1})$. The information matrix is

$$\boldsymbol{J} = \sum_i P_i F(1 - F)(\boldsymbol{x}_{i2} - \boldsymbol{x}_{i1})(\boldsymbol{x}_{i2} - \boldsymbol{x}_{i1})',$$

where

$$P_i = E(d_i | \alpha_i) = F(\alpha_i + \boldsymbol{\beta}'\boldsymbol{x}_{i1})F(-\alpha_i - \boldsymbol{\beta}'\boldsymbol{x}_{i2}) + F(-\alpha_i - \boldsymbol{\beta}'\boldsymbol{x}_{i1})F(\alpha_i + \boldsymbol{\beta}'\boldsymbol{x}_{i2}).$$

This information matrix is difficult to evaluate since we do not have a consistent estimator for α_i, which appears in P_i. Moreover, a standard ML binary logit programme will be evaluating

$$J_d = -E\left(\frac{\partial^2 L}{\partial \boldsymbol{\beta}\, \partial \boldsymbol{\beta}'}\bigg| \boldsymbol{d}\right) = -\frac{\partial^2 L}{\partial \boldsymbol{\beta}\, \partial \boldsymbol{\beta}'}$$

(since the Hessian of the logit log-likelihood function is non-stochastic), which depends only upon $\boldsymbol{\beta}$ (given $\boldsymbol{d}$). In fact, J_d^{-1} is an appropriate asymptotic covariance matrix for the conditional ML estimator of $\boldsymbol{\beta}$, since we can apply the strong law of large numbers to establish that

$$\frac{1}{N}J_d - \frac{1}{N}J \quad \text{almost surely} \to 0 \text{ as } N \to \infty \text{ if } \textstyle\sum_i m_i m_i'/i^2 < \infty,$$

where m_i replaces each element of $(x_{i2} - x_{i1})$ by its square. This follows since the d_i are independent with $Ed_i = P_i$, and both F and the variance of d_i are uniformly bounded. The condition for convergence clearly holds if the x_{it} are uniformly bounded.[7]

For general T, conditioning on $\sum_t y_{it}$, $i = 1, \ldots, N$, gives the following conditional log-likelihood function:

$$L = \textstyle\sum_i \ln \left[\exp\left(\boldsymbol{\beta}' \sum_t x_{it} y_{it}\right) / \sum_{d \in B_i} \exp\left(\boldsymbol{\beta}' \sum_t x_{it} d_t\right)\right],$$

where

$$B_i = \{\boldsymbol{d} = (d_1, \ldots, d_T) | d_t = 0 \text{ or } 1 \text{ and } \textstyle\sum_t d_t = \sum_t y_{it}\}.$$

L is in conditional logit form with the alternative set (B_i) varying across the observations.[8] There are $T+1$ distinct alternative sets corresponding to $\sum_t y_{it} = 0, 1, \ldots, T$. Groups for which $\sum_t y_{it} = 0$ or T contribute zero to L, however, and so only $T-1$ alternative sets are relevant. The alternative set for groups with $\sum_t y_{it} = s$ has $\binom{T}{s}$ elements, corresponding to the distinct sequences of T trials with s successes. For example, with $T = 3$ and $s = 1$ there are three alternatives with the following conditional probabilities:

$$\text{prob}\,(1, 0, 0 | \textstyle\sum_t y_{it} = 1) = \dfrac{e^{\boldsymbol{\beta}'(x_{i1} - x_{i3})}}{D}$$

$$\text{prob}\,(0, 1, 0 | \textstyle\sum_t y_{it} = 1) = \dfrac{e^{\boldsymbol{\beta}'(x_{i2} - x_{i3})}}{D}$$

$$\text{prob}\,(0, 0, 1 | \textstyle\sum_t y_{it} = 1) = \dfrac{1}{D}, \qquad D = e^{\boldsymbol{\beta}'(x_{i1} - x_{i3})} + e^{\boldsymbol{\beta}'(x_{i2} - x_{i3})} + 1.$$

Since L is in the form of a conditional logit log-likelihood function, it can be maximized by standard programmes. The information matrix evaluated by such a programme will implicitly condition on the alternative sets, which are random in our problem. So the programme will evaluate $J_B = -E(\partial^2 L / \partial \boldsymbol{\beta} \partial \boldsymbol{\beta}' | B)$. Since the Hessian of the log-likelihood function in conditional logit is non-stochastic, we have $J_B = -\partial^2 L / \partial \boldsymbol{\beta} \partial \boldsymbol{\beta}'$. Hence J_B^{-1} is an appropriate asymptotic covariance matrix for the conditional ML estimator of $\boldsymbol{\beta}$ provided that J_B/N converges to its expectation. This will follow from the strong law of large numbers if, for example, the x_{it} are uniformly bounded.

In the remainder of this section we shall first extend our conditional likelihood approach from the binary to the multinomial case; then we shall apply our approach to the multivariate log-linear probability model, thereby relaxing the assumption that the observations within a group are independent.

3.1. *Multinomial Logit for Grouped Data*

Say that y_{it} can take on three values: a, b, c. Then we have

$$\text{prob}\,(y_{it}=j)=\frac{e^{\alpha_{ij}+\beta' x_{itj}}}{\sum_j e^{\alpha_{ij}+\beta' x_{itj}}},\qquad (j=a,b,c).$$

We assume that the y's are independent both within and between groups. We shall condition on the number of occurrences within the ith group of each of the three events.

If $T=2$, then the only cases of interest are those in which two of the three events each occurs once, for otherwise there is no stochastic variation. Conditioning on a and b each occurring once gives (suppressing the i subscript):

$$\text{prob}\,[(a,b)|(a,b)\text{ or }(b,a)]=\frac{e^{\beta' z}}{1+e^{\beta' z}},$$

where $z=(x_{2b}-x_{2a})-(x_{1b}-x_{1a})$. Hence we have a binary logit problem with (a,b) and (b,a) as the two alternatives and with z as the explanatory variables. The incidental parameters do not appear in this conditional probability. There is a similar result when we condition on a and c each occurring once, and also when b and c each occur once.

In the general case of T independent observations on each group with y_{it} taking on J values, we define $w_{itj}=1$ if $y_{it}=j$ and $w_{itj}=0$ otherwise. We condition on $s_{ij}=\sum_t w_{itj}$, $j=1,\dots,J$. This gives the following conditional log-likelihood function:

$$L=\textstyle\sum_i \ln\,[\exp\,(\beta'\sum_{t,j} x_{itj}w_{itj})/\sum_{d\in B_i}\exp\,(\beta'\sum_{t,j} x_{itj}d_{tj})],$$

where

$$B_i=\{d=(d_{11},\dots,d_{TJ})|d_{tj}=0\text{ or }1,\quad \textstyle\sum_j d_{tj}=1,\quad \sum_t d_{tj}=s_{ij},\quad j=1,\dots,J\}.$$

This is in the form of a conditional logit log-likelihood function and can be maximized by standard programmes.

3.2. *The Log-Linear Probability Model*

We shall relax the assumption that the y_{it} are independent within a group by extending the conditional likelihood approach to the general log-linear model.[9] We begin by illustrating the log-linear model for the binary case ($y_{it}=0$ or 1) with $T=3$ (the i subscripts are suppressed):

$$\ln\text{prob}\,(y_1,y_2,y_3)=\mu+\gamma_1 y_1^*+\gamma_2 y_2^*+\gamma_3 y_3^*+\gamma_{12}y_1^*y_2^*+\gamma_{13}y_1^*y_3^*+\gamma_{23}y_2^*y_3^*$$
$$+\gamma_{123}y_1^*y_2^*y_3^*,$$

where $y^*=1$ if $y=1$ and $y^*=-1$ if $y=0$. This is a saturated model since there are $2^3-1=7$ independent probabilities, and there are seven free parameters with μ determined by the constraint that the probabilities sum to one.

A common way to impose structure on this model is to specify the main effects in terms of a set of explanatory variables: $\gamma_{it}=\beta' x_{it}$, and to assume that the interaction terms are constant: $\gamma_{ist}=\gamma_{st}$, for $s,t=1,2,3$, and $\gamma_{i123}=\gamma_{123}$. Additional structure can be imposed by specifying that the interaction terms beyond some order are zero; for example, that $\gamma_{123}=0$.

We shall introduce group specific effects by letting $\gamma_{it}=\alpha_i+\beta' x_{it}$. It is straightforward to check that

$$\ln\frac{\text{prob}\,(y_{i1}=1|y_{i2},y_{i3})}{1-\text{prob}\,(y_{i1}=1|y_{i2},y_{i3})}=2\alpha_i+2\beta' x_{i1}+2\gamma_{12}y_{i2}^*+2\gamma_{13}y_{i3}^*+2\gamma_{123}y_{i2}^*y_{i3}^*.$$

So if the interaction terms $\gamma_{12} = \gamma_{13} = \gamma_{123} = 0$, then y_1 is independent of y_2 and y_3, and the probability of $y_1 = 1$ takes the logistic form that we have been using (except for a scale factor of 2).

For the general case of T binary variables we have (suppressing the i subscripts):

$$\ln \text{prob}\,(y_1, \ldots, y_T) = \mu + \textstyle\sum_{k=1}^{T} \sum_{t \in M_k} \gamma_t y^*_{t_1} \cdots y^*_{t_k},$$

where $M_k = \{(t_1, \ldots, t_k)\}$ is the set consisting of the $\binom{T}{k}$ groups of k integers that can be formed from the integers $1, \ldots, T$. We shall specify the first order terms as $\gamma_{it} = \alpha_i + \boldsymbol{\beta}' \boldsymbol{x}_{it}$. The interaction terms may depend upon $\boldsymbol{x}$ but with coefficients that do not vary in i, so that the incidental parameters are confined to the first order terms.

Since $\sum_t y_{it}$ is a sufficient statistic for α_i, we form the following conditional density:

$$\begin{aligned} \text{prob}\,(y_{i1}, \ldots, y_{iT} | \textstyle\sum_t y_{it}) &= \frac{\exp\,[\sum_t (\alpha_i + \boldsymbol{\beta}' \boldsymbol{x}_{it}) y^*_{it} + g(\boldsymbol{y}_i)]}{\sum_{\boldsymbol{d} \in B_i} \exp\,[\sum_t (\alpha_i + \boldsymbol{\beta}' \boldsymbol{x}_{it}) d^*_t + g(\boldsymbol{d})]} \\ &= \frac{\exp\,[\boldsymbol{\beta}' \sum_t \boldsymbol{x}_{it} y^*_{it} + g(\boldsymbol{y}_i)]}{\sum_{\boldsymbol{d} \in B_i} \exp\,[\boldsymbol{\beta}' \sum_t \boldsymbol{x}_{it} d^*_t + g(\boldsymbol{d})]}, \end{aligned}$$

where

$$B_i = \{\boldsymbol{d} = (d_1, \ldots, d_T) | d_t = 0 \text{ or } 1 \text{ and } \textstyle\sum_t d_t = \sum_t y_{it}\},\ \boldsymbol{y}_i = (y_{i1}, \ldots, y_{iT}),$$

and $g(\ )$ does not depend upon α_i.

We see that the conditional density does not depend upon α_i. The corresponding log-likelihood function differs from the one for independent y's only in the $g(\ )$ terms. For example, with $T = 3$ and $\sum_t y_{it} = 1$ we have $g(1, 0, 0) = -\gamma_{12} - \gamma_{13} + \gamma_{23} + \gamma_{123}$; $g(0, 1, 0) = -\gamma_{12} + \gamma_{13} - \gamma_{23} + \gamma_{123}$; $g(0, 0, 1) = \gamma_{12} - \gamma_{13} - \gamma_{23} + \gamma_{123}$. Rescaling all the coefficients by one-half, we can write the conditional probabilities as

$$\text{prob}\,(1, 0, 0 | \textstyle\sum_t y_{it} = 1) = \frac{1}{D} \exp\,[\boldsymbol{\beta}'(\boldsymbol{x}_{i1} - \boldsymbol{x}_{i3}) + \gamma_{23} - \gamma_{12}]$$

$$\text{prob}\,(0, 1, 0 | \textstyle\sum_t y_{it} = 1) = \frac{1}{D} \exp\,[\boldsymbol{\beta}'(\boldsymbol{x}_{i2} - \boldsymbol{x}_{i3}) + \gamma_{13} - \gamma_{12}]$$

$$\text{prob}\,(0, 0, 1 | \textstyle\sum_t y_{it} = 1) = \frac{1}{D},$$

with D determined so that the probabilities sum to one. So this differs from the independence case by introducing alternative specific constants into the conditional probabilities.

We have seen that it is fruitful to base the likelihood function on a conditional distribution that conditions on sufficient statistics for the incidental parameters. It is not always possible, however, to find a sufficient statistic for α_i such that the conditional distribution is sufficiently informative about $\boldsymbol{\beta}$.[10] The next section examines a random effects model in which a consistent estimator for $\boldsymbol{\beta}$ can be obtained without relying upon sufficient statistics for the α_i.

4. RANDOM EFFECTS: THE MARGINAL LIKELIHOOD FUNCTION

An alternative approach is to assume that the incidental parameters follow a distribution. Then the likelihood function can be based on the density for $\boldsymbol{y}$, given $\boldsymbol{x}$, $\boldsymbol{\beta}$, and G, the distribution function for $\boldsymbol{\alpha}$. If we specify a parametric family for G, indexed by a finite parameter vector $\boldsymbol{\tau}$, then we have the following log-likelihood function for $\boldsymbol{\beta}$, $\boldsymbol{\tau}$:

$$L = \ln \int f(\boldsymbol{y} | \boldsymbol{x}, \boldsymbol{\beta}, \boldsymbol{\alpha})\, dG(\boldsymbol{\alpha} | \boldsymbol{x}, \boldsymbol{\tau}).$$

So the density function for y conditional on $\boldsymbol{\alpha}$ has been replaced by a density function that is marginal on $\boldsymbol{\alpha}$.[11] The maximization of this likelihood function will, under weak regularity conditions, give consistent (as $N \rightarrow \infty$) estimators for $\boldsymbol{\beta}$ and $\boldsymbol{\tau}$.[12]

This approach introduces additional information and is most naturally formulated in Bayesian terms. A potentially appealing prior distribution specifies that the α's are independent and identically distributed. This can often be justified by de Finetti's (1937) exchangeability criterion. If (for arbitrary N) the distribution of the α_i's is not affected by permuting them, so that the subscript is purely a labelling device with no substantive content, then the joint distribution of the α's must be expressable as random sampling from a univariate distribution. This criterion will often be satisfied when i indexes individuals (longitudinal data) or families (sibling data).

The main point I want to make here is that the random sampling specification is appropriate only as a marginal distribution for $\boldsymbol{\alpha}$. We must, however, specify a distribution for $\boldsymbol{\alpha}$ conditional on $\boldsymbol{x}$. The conventional random effects model assumes that $\boldsymbol{\alpha}$ is independent of $\boldsymbol{x}$. But our interest in introducing the incidental parameters was motivated by missing variables that are correlated with $\boldsymbol{x}$. If one mistakenly models $\boldsymbol{\alpha}$ as independent of $\boldsymbol{x}$, then the omitted variable bias is not eliminated. So we want to specify a conditional distribution for $\boldsymbol{\alpha}$ given $\boldsymbol{x}$ that allows for dependence.[13] A convenient possibility is to assume that the dependence is only via a linear regression function: $\alpha_i = \boldsymbol{\pi}'\boldsymbol{x}_i + v_i$, with $\boldsymbol{x}_i' = (\boldsymbol{x}_{i1}', \ldots, \boldsymbol{x}_{iT}')$, and where v_i is independent of $\boldsymbol{x}$. We assume that the v_i are independent and identically distributed. A restriction on the regression function that may be appropriate is $\boldsymbol{\pi}'\boldsymbol{x}_i = \boldsymbol{\delta}'\bar{\boldsymbol{x}}_i$.

We shall illustrate this approach with a production function example that leads to a linear regression model.[14] Say that a farmer is producing a product under the following Cobb–Douglas technology: $Y = L^{\beta}Q^{\gamma}e^{\varepsilon}$, where Y is output, L is a variable factor (labour), Q is a fixed factor (soil quality), ε is stochastic (rainfall), and $0 < \beta < 1$. Assume that ε is distributed independently of Q; persistent differences in average rainfall can be incorporated into Q. We assume that the farmer knows the product price (P) and the factor price (W), which do not depend on his decisions, and that he knows Q. The factor input decision, however, is made before knowing ε, and we assume that L is chosen to maximize expected profit: $E(PY - WL|P, W, Q)$.

There are observations on $i = 1, \ldots, N$ farms in each of $t = 1, \ldots, T$ periods. Assume that Q is constant over the period of the sample and that the distribution of ε conditional on Q, W, and P is ε_{it} i.i.d. $N(0, \sigma^2)$. Then we have the following production and factor demand functions:

$$y_{it} = \beta x_{it} + \alpha_i + \varepsilon_{it}$$

$$x_{it} = \mu + \frac{1}{1-\beta}(z_{it} + \alpha_i) + u_{it},$$

where $y = \ln Y$, $x = \ln L$, $\alpha = \gamma \ln Q$, $\mu = (\ln \beta + \frac{1}{2}\sigma^2)/(1-\beta)$, $z = \ln (P/W)$, and u is a random term, reflecting optimization and other errors, which is independent of α and ε. Although Q is known to the farmer and affects his factor demand decisions, we assume that it is not observed by the econometrician; α_i is included in order to capture this omitted variable. The example is useful in showing explicitly how a correlation between x and α might arise.

We shall focus on estimating the production function without using whatever price data is available. A pooled least squares regression of y on x, which does not allow for farm effects, is inconsistent. If α is independent of z, then as $N \rightarrow \infty$ this estimator converges to

$$\beta + \frac{\sigma_\alpha^2}{(1-\beta)(V_W + V_B)},$$

where

$$V_W = \text{plim}_{N\to\infty} \frac{1}{NT} \sum_{i,t} (x_{it} - \bar{x}_i)^2, \qquad V_B = \text{plim}_{N\to\infty} \frac{1}{N} \sum_i (\bar{x}_i - \bar{x})^2,$$

and σ_α^2 is the marginal variance of α. Now consider a random effects approach, α_i i.i.d. $N(\psi, \sigma_\alpha^2)$, that incorrectly assumes that α is independent of x. Then the ML estimator of β, conditional on $\lambda = \sigma_\alpha^2/\sigma^2$, is generalized least squares. This is equivalent to ordinary least squares using deviations from fractional means: regress $y_{it} - \gamma\bar{y}_i$ on $x_{it} - \gamma\bar{x}_i$, where $\gamma = 1-(1+\lambda T)^{-\frac{1}{2}}$. This estimator converges, as $N\to\infty$, to

$$\beta + \frac{(1-\gamma)^2\sigma_\alpha^2}{(1-\beta)[V_W + (1-\gamma)^2 V_B]}.$$

Hence it is consistent only as $T\to\infty$.

So it is essential to allow for a dependence between α and x. Let $w_{it} = z_{it}/(1-\beta) + u_{it}$ and assume that $\boldsymbol{w}_i$ is i.i.d. $N(\boldsymbol{m}, \boldsymbol{\Sigma})$. Then the distribution of α conditional on x is given by $\alpha_i = \kappa + \boldsymbol{\pi}'\boldsymbol{x}_i + v_i$, where

$$\boldsymbol{\pi} = \frac{\sigma_\alpha^2}{1-\beta}\left[\frac{\sigma_\alpha^2}{(1-\beta)^2} \boldsymbol{l}\boldsymbol{l}' + \boldsymbol{\Sigma}\right]^{-1} \boldsymbol{l},$$

$\boldsymbol{l}$ is a $T\times 1$ vector of ones, and v is independent of x with v_i i.i.d. $N(0, \sigma_v^2)$. Note that assuming a stationary $\boldsymbol{\Sigma}$ does not imply that $\boldsymbol{\pi}'\boldsymbol{x}_i = \delta\bar{x}_i$ if $T>2$. A sufficient condition is that $\boldsymbol{\Sigma}$ is equicorrelated: $\boldsymbol{\Sigma} = \rho_1 \boldsymbol{I} + \rho_2 \boldsymbol{l}\boldsymbol{l}'$.

The ML estimator of $(\boldsymbol{\beta}, \boldsymbol{\pi})$, allowing for several variables in $\boldsymbol{x}_{it}$ and given $\lambda = \sigma_v^2/\sigma^2$, can be obtained from the regression of $y_{it} - \gamma\bar{y}_i$ on $\boldsymbol{x}_{it} - \gamma\bar{\boldsymbol{x}}_i$ and $(1-\gamma)\boldsymbol{x}_i$. The resulting estimator for $\boldsymbol{\beta}$ can be obtained from the regression of $y_{it} - \gamma\bar{y}_i$ on the residual from the regression of $\boldsymbol{x}_{it} - \gamma\bar{\boldsymbol{x}}_i$ on $\boldsymbol{x}_i$. This residual is $\boldsymbol{x}_{it} - \bar{\boldsymbol{x}}_i$; but the regression of $y_{it} - \gamma\bar{y}_i$ on $\boldsymbol{x}_{it} - \bar{\boldsymbol{x}}_i$ is equivalent to the regression of $y_{it} - \bar{y}_i$ on $\boldsymbol{x}_{it} - \bar{\boldsymbol{x}}_i$.

We have obtained the interesting result that a random effects specification can give a ML estimator of $\boldsymbol{\beta}$ that is identical to the fixed effects estimator, if we allow the distribution of the incidental parameters to depend upon $\boldsymbol{x}$.[15] Of course the linear regression case is special, since the fixed effects estimator is consistent. This is not true for the (joint) ML estimator of $\boldsymbol{\beta}$ in the linear autoregressive model or in the probability models. So the random effects specification leads to new estimators in those cases.

In the autoregressive case, let

$$y_{i1} = \beta y_{i0} + \alpha_i + \varepsilon_{i1}$$

$$y_{i2} = \beta y_{i1} + \alpha_i + \varepsilon_{i2},$$

where, conditional on y_{i0} and α_i, we have $(\varepsilon_{i1}, \varepsilon_{i2})$ i.i.d. from a normal distribution with mean $\boldsymbol{0}$ and diagonal covariance matrix: diag $\{\sigma_1^2, \sigma_2^2\}$. Let $\alpha_i = \pi y_{i0} + v_i$, where, conditional on y_{i0}, we have v_i i.i.d. $N(0, \sigma_v^2)$. Then

$$(y_{i1}, y_{i2}) = (\delta_1, \delta_2) y_{i0} + (u_{i1}, u_{i2}),$$

where

$$\delta_1 = \beta + \pi,\ \delta_2 = \beta\delta_1 + \pi, \text{ and } \boldsymbol{u}_i \text{ is i.i.d. } N(\boldsymbol{0}, \boldsymbol{\Sigma}).$$

This is a multivariate regression model in which the ML estimator of $\boldsymbol{\delta}$ is obtained from the least squares regressions of y_1 and y_2 on y_0. Then we can solve for the ML estimator of β from $\hat{\beta} = (\hat{\delta}_2 - \hat{\delta}_1)/(\hat{\delta}_1 - 1)$. This estimator is consistent if the y_{i0} have sufficient variation and if $\beta + \pi \neq 1$. It is equivalent to taking first differences, $y_{i2} - y_{i1} = \beta(y_{i1} - y_{i0}) + \varepsilon_{i2} - \varepsilon_{i1}$, and using y_{i0} as an instrumental variable for $y_{i1} - y_{i0}$. If we add the assumption that $\sigma_1 = \sigma_2$, then an additional consistent estimator of β can be obtained from a consistent estimator of $\boldsymbol{\Sigma}$. Now the ML estimator of β will combine the estimator obtained from the regression coefficients with the estimator obtained from the residual covariance matrix.

The likelihood function for the joint distribution of (y_0, y_1, y_2) is obtained by multiplying the likelihood conditional on y_0 by the marginal density of y_0. If the parameters of this marginal density are left unconstrained, then the ML estimator of β is unaffected. Imposing stationarity on the joint distribution will, however, imply constraints. If y_{i0} is i.i.d. normal with variance ρ, then stationarity implies that $\rho = \sigma_v^2/[(1-\delta_1)\pi]$.

In the binary data case, let prob $(y_{it} = 1|\boldsymbol{x}, \boldsymbol{\beta}, \boldsymbol{\alpha}) = F(\boldsymbol{\beta}'\boldsymbol{x}_{it} + \alpha_i)$. Then the log-likelihood function under our random effects specification is

$$L = \sum_i \ln \int \Pi_t F(\boldsymbol{\beta}'\boldsymbol{x}_{it} + \boldsymbol{\pi}'\boldsymbol{x}_i + v)^{y_{it}}[1 - F(\boldsymbol{\beta}'\boldsymbol{x}_{it} + \boldsymbol{\pi}'\boldsymbol{x}_i + v)]^{1-y_{it}} dH(v|\boldsymbol{\psi}),$$

where H is a family of univariate distribution functions indexed by the parameter vector $\boldsymbol{\psi}$. For example, if F is a unit normal distribution function and we choose H to be the distribution function of a $N(0, \sigma_v^2)$ random variable, then our specification gives a multivariate probit model:

$$y_{it} = 1 \text{ if } \boldsymbol{\beta}'\boldsymbol{x}_{it} + \boldsymbol{\pi}'\boldsymbol{x}_i + u_{it} > 0$$

$$\boldsymbol{u}_i \text{ i.i.d. } N(\boldsymbol{0}, \sigma_v^2 \boldsymbol{l}_T \boldsymbol{l}_T' + \boldsymbol{I}_T),$$

where $\boldsymbol{l}_T$ is a $T \times 1$ vector of ones. The novel feature of this model is the inclusion of the term $\boldsymbol{\pi}'\boldsymbol{x}_i$ to capture the dependence between the incidental parameters and $\boldsymbol{x}$.

For example, consider estimating the effect of ability on the probability of attending college, controlling for family background. There is a sample of N families with test scores (x) for each of $T = 2$ brothers per family. The family effect α_i is intended to capture omitted variables such as family wealth and parents' schooling. Under this interpretation, α is likely to be correlated with x. Our procedure in the probit case is to fit a (constrained) bivariate probit model for y_{i1} and y_{i2} on x_{i1} and x_{i2}. This provides estimates of

$$\begin{bmatrix} \beta + \pi_1 & \pi_2 \\ \pi_1 & \beta + \pi_2 \end{bmatrix},$$

from which we obtain an estimate of β by taking the coefficient of sib 1's test score in sib 1's equation minus the coefficient of sib 1's test score in sib 2's equation. We can do the same with sib 2's test score and hence the constraint on the matrix of probit coefficients.

From the symmetry of this example (ignoring birth order effects), it is appropriate to set $\pi_1 = \pi_2$. Then β can be consistently estimated by taking the coefficient of sib 1's test score in sib 1's equation minus the coefficient of sib 2's test score in sib 1's equation. Hence we only require y for one of the sibs provided that we have x for both. For example, the Michigan Panel Study of Income Dynamics (1972) has extensive information on the respondent and much less complete information on his siblings. There is schooling data for the respondent and his oldest brother, but earnings and occupation data only for the respondent. Nevertheless, we can control for family background in assessing the relationship between schooling and earnings by including the schooling of sib 2 in a regression of sib 1's earnings on his schooling. Then β is estimated by the excess of sib 1's schooling coefficient over that of his brother. A probit example could arise in studying the relationship between schooling and occupation, where occupations are classified into two groups corresponding to production and non-production workers.

5. CONCLUSION

The paper has discussed three approaches to the analysis of grouped data: the joint likelihood function, the conditional likelihood function, and the marginal likelihood function. Throughout the paper, our concern has been with the parameters $(\boldsymbol{\beta})$ that are common to all of the groups; the incidental parameters (α_i) are intended to capture group effects whose omission would result in biased estimates of $\boldsymbol{\beta}$. The objective has been to obtain estimators that converge to $\boldsymbol{\beta}$ as the number of groups (N) increases, even if the number of observations per group (T) is small. Important applications include longitudinal data, in which there are two or more observations on each individual, and the α_i capture person effects; and sibling data, in which the α_i capture family effects, such as omitted family background variables.

We have illustrated the inconsistency of the joint ML estimator in the fixed effects probability models. One solution, within the fixed effects model, is to maximize a conditional likelihood function that conditions on sufficient statistics for the incidental parameters. This conditional likelihood function does not depend upon the incidental parameters, and so standard asymptotic theory can be applied. In the (normal-theory) linear regression model, the consistency of the joint ML estimator of $\boldsymbol{\beta}$ corresponds to the coincidence of the joint and the conditional ML estimators. In the logit case, however, the conditional ML estimator of $\boldsymbol{\beta}$ is consistent whereas the joint ML estimator is not (for fixed T). The conditional ML estimator for the logit case can be implemented with a standard conditional logit programme, which allows the alternative set to vary across the observations.

Finally, we discussed random effects models which impose a (prior) distribution on the incidental parameters. Then the likelihood function is based on the distribution for y that is marginal on the incidental parameters. The important point here is that the specification of the conditional distribution for α_i given $\boldsymbol{x}$ should allow for dependence; the common assumption that α_i is independent of $\boldsymbol{x}$ assumes away omitted variable bias. In the linear regression model, the ML estimator for $\boldsymbol{\beta}$ under our random effects specification is once again analysis of covariance. So in this special case, all three of our approaches give identical estimators for $\boldsymbol{\beta}$. In the probability models, however, the marginal likelihood specification leads to new estimators.

The marginal likelihood approach has the advantage of not requiring simple sufficient statistics for the incidental parameters. Furthermore, it imposes (stochastic) restrictions on the fixed effects model, which will lead to more precise estimators if the restrictions are valid. The disadvantage is that in order to specify that the α_i are independent of each other (conditional on $\boldsymbol{x}$), our approach requires a particular parametric class of conditional distributions for α_i given $\boldsymbol{x}$. Hence some sensitivity analysis is called for. The fixed effects model allows for a very general relationship between the incidental parameters and the explanatory variables.

Financial support was provided by the National Science Foundation Grant No. SOC77-15624.

NOTES

1. In the logit case the Hessian does not depend upon y, and so scoring is identical to the Newton–Raphson algorithm.

2. A programme to implement this algorithm is described in Hall (1978), along with an example of the computational efficiency of the programme. A labour force participation application of a fixed effects probit model is presented in Heckman (1978).

3. This example is discussed in Neyman and Scott (1948).

4. The use of conditional likelihood functions for incidental parameter problems is discussed in Bartlett (1936*a*), (1936*b*), (1937), Andersen (1970), (1973), Kalbfleisch and Sprott (1970), and Barndorff-Nielsen (1978).

5. The conditional likelihood approach in the logit case is closely related to R. A. Fisher's (1935) exact test for independence in a 2×2 table. This exact significance test has been extended by Cox (1970) and others to the case of several contingency tables. Additional references are in Cox (1970) and in Bishop *et al.* (1975). A conditional likelihood approach was used by Rasch (1960), (1961) in his model for intelligence tests. The probability that person i gives a correct answer to item number t is $\exp(\alpha_i + \beta_t)/[1 + \exp(\alpha_i + \beta_t)]$; this is a special case in which x_{it} is a set of dummy indicator variables. An algorithm for conditional maximum likelihood estimation in this model is described in Andersen (1972).

6. The efficiency of the conditional ML estimator is maximized by conditioning on minimal sufficient statistics for the incidental parameters. $\sum_t y_{it}$ is a minimal sufficient statistic for α_i both in the linear regression model and in the logit model. Even so the conditional ML estimator need not attain the asymptotic Cramer–Rao bound as $N \to \infty$ for fixed T. It does in the linear regression case but not in the logit model. However, I doubt whether there is another consistent estimator that has smaller asymptotic variance in the fixed effects logit model. The random effects model of Section 4, which introduces additional (stochastic) restrictions, can lead to a more efficient estimator of $\boldsymbol{\beta}$.

7. An alternative justification for the use of $-E(\partial^2 L/\partial\boldsymbol{\beta}\partial\boldsymbol{\beta}'|\boldsymbol{d})$ can be based on stating the limiting distribution properties in terms of the conditional distribution, in which the observed values of the sufficient statistics are treated as parameters. This approach is pursued in Andersen (1971*b*).

8. The conditional logit model is developed in McFadden (1974).

9. The log-linear model is developed in Goodman (1970), (1972), Haberman (1974), and Nerlove and Press (1976). Additional references are in Bishop *et al.* (1975).

10. In the probit model, for example, there does not appear to be such a sufficient statistic.

11. Kalbfleisch and Sprott (1970) call this an integrated likelihood function. A marginal likelihood function can also be useful in a fixed effects approach, in which we consider the distribution of some function of $\boldsymbol{y}_i$, conditional on α_i. For example, in the linear regression case with $T = 2$, the distribution of $y_{i2} - y_{i1}$ does not depend upon α_i. Hence maximizing the associated likelihood function gives consistent (as $N \to \infty$) estimators of $\boldsymbol{\beta}$ and σ. Once again the ML estimator of $\boldsymbol{\beta}$ is the standard analysis of covariance estimator.

12. Note that the original Kiefer and Wolfowitz (1956) results were not limited to the parametric case.

13. Note that the empirical work by Chamberlain and Griliches (1975), (1977) and Chamberlain (1978) does allow the random effects to be correlated with the explanatory variables. Also in the original Balestra and Nerlove (1966) model, the autoregressive component is correlated with the random effects.

14. This example is discussed in Mundlak (1961), (1963).

15. This result is discussed in Mundlak (1978) for the case $\boldsymbol{\pi}'\boldsymbol{x}_i = \boldsymbol{\delta}'\bar{\boldsymbol{x}}_i$.

REFERENCES

ANDERSEN, E. B. (1970), "Asymptotic Properties of Conditional Maximum Likelihood Estimators", *Journal of the Royal Statistical Society*, Series *B*, **32**, 283–301.

ANDERSEN, E. B. (1971*a*) "Asymptotic Properties of Conditional Likelihood Ratio Tests", *Journal of the American Statistical Association*, **66**, 630–633.

ANDERSEN, E. B. (1971*b*), "A Strictly Conditional Approach in Estimation Theory", *Skandinavisk Aktuarietidskrift*, 39–49.

ANDERSEN, E. B. (1972), "The Numerical Solution of a Set of Conditional Estimation Equations", *Journal of the Royal Statistical Society*, Series B, **34**, 42–54.

ANDERSEN, E. B. (1973) *Conditional Inference and Models for Measuring* (Copenhagen: Mentalhygiejnisk Forlag).

BALESTRA, P. and NERLOVE, M. (1966), "Pooling Cross Section and Time Series Data in the Estimation of a Dynamic Model: The Demand for Natural Gas", *Econometrica*, **34**, 585–612.

BARNDORFF-NIELSEN, O. (1978) *Information and Exponential Families in Statistical Theory* (New York: Wiley).

BARTLETT, M. S. (1936*a*), "The Information Available in Small Samples", *Proceedings of the Cambridge Philosophical Society*, **32**, 560–566.

BARTLETT, M. S. (1936*b*), "Statistical Information and Properties of Sufficiency", *Proceedings of the Royal Society*, Series A, **154**, 124–137.

BARTLETT, M. S. (1937), "Properties of Sufficiency and Statistical Tests", *Proceedings of the Royal Society*, Series A, **160**, 268–282.

BISHOP, Y. M. M., FIENBERG, S. E. and HOLLAND, P. W. (1975) *Discrete Multivariate Analysis: Theory and Practice* (Cambridge, Mass.: M.I.T. Press).

CHAMBERLAIN, G. (1978), "Omitted Variable Bias in Panel Data: Estimating the Returns to Schooling", *Annales de l'INSEE*, **30-31**, 49–82.

CHAMBERLAIN, G. and GRILICHES, Z. (1975), "Unobservables with a Variance-Components Structure: Ability, Schooling, and the Economic Success of Brothers", *International Economic Review*, **16**, 422–449.

CHAMBERLAIN, G. and GRILICHES, Z. (1977), "More on Brothers" in Taubman, P. (ed.) *Kinometrics: The Determinants of Socio-economic Success Within and Between Families* (Amsterdam: North Holland Publishing Company).

COX, D. R. (1970) *Analysis of Binary Data* (London: Methuen).

DE FINETTI, B. (1937), "La Prévision: Les Lois Logiques, ses Sources Subjectives", *Annales de l'Institut Henri Poincaré*, **7**. English translation in Kyburg, H. E. and Smokler, H. E. (eds.) *Studies in Subjective Probability* (New York: Wiley).

FISHER, R. A. (1935), "The Logic of Inductive Inference", *Journal of the Royal Statistical Society*, Series B, **98**, 39–54.

GOODMAN, L. (1970), "The Multivariate Analysis of Qualitative Data: Interactions Among Multiple Classifications", *Journal of the American Stastistical Association*, **65**, 226–256.

GOODMAN, L. (1972), "A Modified Multiple Regression Approach to the Analysis of Dichotomous Variables", *American Sociological Review*, **37**, 28–46.

HABERMAN, S. J. (1974) *The Analysis of Frequency Data* (Chicago: University of Chicago Press).

HALL, B. H. (1978), "A General Framework for Time Series–Cross Section Estimation", *Annales de l'INSEE*, **30–31**, 177–202.

HECKMAN, J. J. (1978), "Statistical Models for Discrete Panel Data", (University of Chicago).

KALBFLEISCH, J. D. and SPROTT, D. A. (1970), "Application of Likelihood Methods to Models Involving Large Numbers of Parameters", *Journal of the Royal Statistical Society*, Series B, **32**, 175–208.

KIEFER, J. and WOLFOWITZ, J. (1956), "Consistency of the Maximum Likelihood Estimator in the Presence of Infinitely Many Incidental Parameters", *Annals of Mathematical Statistics*, **27**, 887–906.

MCFADDEN, D. (1974), "Conditional Logit Analysis of Qualitative Choice Behavior" in Zarembka, P. (ed.) *Frontiers in Econometrics* (New York: Academic Press.).

MORGAN, J. N. *et al.* (1972) *A Panel Study of Income Dynamics* (Ann Arbor: Institute for Social Research).

MUNDLAK, Y. (1961), "Empirical Production Function Free of Management Bias", *Journal of Farm Economics*, **43**, 44–56.

MUNDLAK, Y. (1963), "Estimation of Production and Behavioral Functions from a Combination of Cross-Section and Time-Series Data" in Christ, C. *et al. Measurement in Economics* (Stanford University Press).

MUNDLAK, Y. (1978), "On the Pooling of Time Series and Cross Section Data", *Econometrica*, **46**, 69–85.

NERLOVE, M. and PRESS, S. J. (1976), "Multivariate Log-Linear Probability Models for the Analysis of Qualitative Data", *Center for Statistics and Probability Discussion Paper*, No. 1 (Northwestern University).

NEYMAN, J. and SCOTT, E. L. (1948), "Consistent Estimates Based on Partially Consistent Observations", *Econometrica*, **16**, 1–32.

RASCH, G. (1960) *Probabilistic Models for Some Intelligence and Attainment Tests* (Copenhagen: Danmarks Paedagogiske Institut).

RASCH, G. (1961), "On General Laws and the Meaning of Measurement in Psychology", *Proceedings of the Fourth Berkeley Symposium on Mathematical Statistics and Probability*,**4**, 321–333.

[13]

Econometrica, Vol. 50, No. 3 (May, 1982)

NOTES AND COMMENTS

A COMPUTATIONALLY EFFICIENT QUADRATURE PROCEDURE FOR THE ONE-FACTOR MULTINOMIAL PROBIT MODEL

BY J. S. BUTLER AND ROBERT MOFFITT[1]

A PROBLEM OF ESTIMATION that has long confronted many economists is the difficulty of estimating the parameters of equations with limited dependent variables on cross-section time-series (i.e., panel) data. While there are widely available packaged computer programs for estimating either (a) cross-section probit and Tobit models or (b) simple permanent-transitory, random-effects panel models with continuous dependent variables, there are no available computationally feasible methods of combining these two models. This is because the likelihood function that arises in such a combined model contains multivariate normal integrals whose evaluation is quite difficult, if not impossible, with conventional approximation methods. There is a widespread feeling among those working in the area that one possible method of evaluation, the use of quadrature techniques, is in principle possible but is in practice computationally too burdensome to consider (e.g., Albright et al. [**2**, p. 13]; Hausman and Wise [**6**, p. 12]). In this note we point out that this is true only of standard quadrature techniques such as trapezoidal integration or its improved variants; Gaussian quadrature, on the other hand, is extremely efficient and is well within the bounds of computational feasibility on modern computers. In what follows, we state the nature of the integrals that need to be evaluated, provide a brief exposition of Gaussian quadrature, and provide a numerical illustration of its use in estimating a one-factor multinomial probit model.

Assume we have the following panel probit model:

$$Y_{it}^* = X_{it}\beta + \epsilon_{it} \qquad (i = 1, \dots, N;\ t = 1, \dots, T),$$

$$Y_{it} = \begin{cases} 1 & \text{if } Y_{it}^* \geq 0, \\ 0 & \text{otherwise,} \end{cases}$$

where i indexes individuals, t indexes time periods, X is a vector of independent variables, and β is a vector of corresponding coefficients. Assume that the disturbances are generated by the permanent-transitory process $\epsilon_{it} = \mu_i + \nu_{it}$, where $\epsilon_{it} \sim N(0, \sigma^2)$ and ρ is the correlation between successive disturbances for the same individual. The log-likelihood function for the problem is $L = \sum_{i=1}^{N} \log[\text{prob}(Y_{i1}, \dots, Y_{iT})]$, where

$$\text{(1)} \qquad \text{prob}(Y_{i1}, \dots, Y_{iT}) = \int_{a_{i1}}^{b_{i1}} \cdots \int f(\epsilon_{i1}, \dots, \epsilon_{iT})\, d\epsilon_{iT} \dots d\epsilon_{i1}$$

and $a_{it} = -X_{it}\beta$ and $b_{it} = \infty$ if $Y_{it} = 1$, and $a_{it} = -\infty$ and $b_{it} = -X_{it}\beta$ if $Y_{it} = 0$, and $f(.)$ is the normal density function. The standard difficulty in this problem is the evaluation of the T-fold integrals in equation (1). Since the random components are independent conditional upon the permanent component, the integral can be simplified by condition-

[1]The authors would like to thank Mathematica Policy Research for subsidizing the research reported herein. Comments from Randall Brown and Timothy Carr as well as from two anonymous referees are much appreciated.

ing on the permanent component:

$$\text{(2)}\qquad \text{prob}(Y_{i1},\ldots,Y_{iT})\text{prob}(Y_{i1},\ldots,Y_{iT})$$
$$=\int_{a_{i1}}^{b_{i1}}\cdots\int_{a_{iT}}^{b_{iT}}\int_{-\infty}^{\infty} f(v_{i1}\mid\mu_i)f(\mu_i)\,d\mu_i\,dv_{iT}\cdots dv_{i1}$$
$$=\int_{-\infty}^{\infty} f(\mu_i)\prod_{t=1}^{T}\left[F(b_{it}\mid\mu_i)-F(a_{it}\mid\mu_i)\right]d\mu_i$$

where $F(\ )$ is the normal cumulative distribution function (cdf).[2] Thus, the expression can be reduced to a single integral whose integrand is a product of one normal density and T differences of normal cdf's for which highly accurate approximations are available. Nevertheless, even the evaluation of the single integral in equation (2) is extremely burdensome using conventional quadrature procedures such as trapezoidal integration or its variants such as Romberg integration.[3] Gaussian quadrature, on the other hand, is a much more sophisticated procedure that requires the evaluation of the integrand at many fewer points in the domain of μ, thus achieving gains in computational efficiency of several orders of magnitude. The formula for the evaluation of the necessary integral is the Hermite integration formula $\int_{-\infty}^{\infty} e^{-Z^2}g(Z)\,dZ=\sum_{j=1}^{G} w_j g(Z_j)$, where G is the number of evaluation points, w_j is the weight given to the jth evaluation point, and $g(Z_j)$ is $g(Z)$ evaluated at the jth point of Z.[4] This formula is appropriate to our problem because the normal density f in equation (2) contains a term of the form $\exp(-Z^2)$, and the function $g(Z)$ is, in our case, the product of T univariate cdf's.

The key question for computational feasibility is the number of points at which the integrand must be evaluated for accurate approximation. Several evaluations of the integral using four periods of arbitrary values of the data and coefficients on six right-hand-side variables showed us that even two-point integration is highly accurate.[5] Table I provides estimates of a fertility equation (dependent variable = 1 if a birth in year t, 0 if not) on a sample of 1550 women with a maximum of 11 periods each, drawn from the Young Women's cohort of the National Longitudinal Survey. The algorithm of Berndt et al. [3] was used for maximization of the likelihood function.[6] As the table shows, some

[2]This factorization is "periodically and independently rediscovered" according to Gupta [5, p. 800] and has recently been discussed by Heckman [7]. See Heckman's paper for an explicit representation of the conditional cdf's equation (2).

[3]For example, Heckman and Willis [8] used the extremely expensive trapezoidal technique. These methods approximate integrals such as that in (2) by a polynomial in the integrand evaluated at several equally spaced intervals in the domain of the integrating variable μ, which is quite expensive because the integrand must generally be evaluated at many points for the approximation to be of acceptable accuracy. See Pennington [10, 247–251] for a discussion.

[4]See Stroud and Secrest [11, p. 22] and Pennington [10, p. 260]. Hermite integration can evaluate the integral $\int_{-\infty}^{\infty} e^{-Z^2}g(Z)\,dZ$ exactly with P points if $g(Z)$ is a polynomial of degree less than $2P-1$. Romberg integration requires 2^P-1 points to attain the same degree of accuracy.

[5]Using synthetic data and arbitrary coefficients, and with $X\beta$ ranging from .60 to .75 in four periods of hypothetical data, the value of the integral for 2, 3, 4, and 5 evaluation points was .31735585, .31734161, .31734174, and .31734174, respectively. The points and weights for the calculations are available from several easily accessible sources: Stroud and Secrest [11], Abramowitz and Stegun [1, p. 924]. We also included an Appendix table in an earlier version of this paper giving the points and weights for two-point to five-point integrations. This is available upon request.

[6]The starting values used were obtained by estimating the equation on only five periods of data, but using the approximation of Clark [4] for the evaluation of the integrals. Probit starting values could also have been used. The Clark approximation was tested on the eleven-period data and was found to be extremely inaccurate, even for the one-factor error structure assumed here. For example, the area under the 11-fold surface summed to 1.9 instead of 1.0. The inaccuracy was reduced the fewer the number of periods; for 5 the Clark approximation appeared to be reasonably accurate in the present problem.

TABLE I

COEFFICIENT ESTIMATES OF A MULTINOMIAL PROBIT FERTILITY EQUATION USING GAUSSIAN QUADRATURE MAXIMUM LIKELIHOOD

	Number of Evaluation Points			
Variables[a]	2	3	4	5
Constant	0.198006 (0.531493)	0.579574 (0.636880)	0.681029 (0.739860)	0.895984 (0.739124)
Race	0.435691* (0.048866)	0.391777* (0.062498)	0.372754* (0.066584)	0.399289* (0.067595)
Education	− 0.087276* (0.011250)	− 0.104133* (0.013863)	− 0.101742* (0.016208)	− 0.107280* (0.016285)
Coh	− 0.023634* (0.009520)	− 0.028942* (0.011232)	− 0.030927* (0.012773)	− 0.034811* (0.012805)
Wealth	− 0.031125 (0.049793)	0.058309 (0.061394)	0.020812 (0.064974)	0.041226 (0.066930)
Oths	0.028244 (0.024087)	0.043871** (0.026354)	0.048919** (0.027525)	0.049346** (0.027569)
Time	0.607854* (0.028321)	0.612613* (0.029532)	0.609026* (0.029249)	0.614247* (0.029550)
Time Squared	− 0.040195* (0.002711)	− 0.040179* (0.002856)	− 0.039651* (0.002817)	− 0.040261* (0.002850)
Rho	0.298808* (0.011360)	0.322650* (0.015322)	0.326820* (0.015920)	0.339101* (0.016491)
CPU time (seconds)[b]	81.8	114.4	116.8	169.6

NOTE: Standard errors in parentheses.
* Significant at the 5 per cent level of confidence.
** Significant at the 10 per cent level of confidence.
[a] Race = 1 if nonwhite, 0 if not; Education = years of schooling; Coh = year of birth (e.g., "48" for 1948); Wealth = discounted present value of lifetime family income other than wife's earnings (1967 dollars); Oth = number of adults in family other than husband and wife; Time = duration of marriage in years. Taken from Moffitt [9].
[b] Hermite points are symmetric about zero and include zero if there is an odd number of them. For purposes of calculation, then, $2k-1$ and $2k$ evaluation points are virtually equivalent, having k different absolute values. CPU times mainly rise in going from 2 to 3, 4 to 5, etc., evaluation points.

coefficients change substantially, the more accurate the approximation of the likelihood function. However, those that change much at all are insignificant even at the lowest, two-point integration; no hypothesis test at the 5 per cent level of confidence would come out differently at the four-point evaluation and at the two-point evaluation. Going from 2 to 3 point integration changes the "significant" coefficients (those on "Oths" and the six with t values above 2) an average of 16.2 per cent; going from 3 to 4 changes them an average of 4.1 per cent; and going from 4 to 5 changes them an average of 3.6 per cent.[7]

[7] The average change in going from 3 to 5 points is 6.1 per cent. The likelihood function and its derivatives are being estimated more accurately with more points, but there is no simple link between this accuracy and the direction of change in the estimated coefficients. Four, six, and eight Hermite points replace 15, 31, and 127 trapezoids.

Thus, those coefficients significant at the two-point evaluation are changed very little by the increase in accuracy. Therefore, the evidence shows clearly that a two-point evaluation is quite satisfactory for hypothesis testing, and probably also for significant coefficient values. The CPU times (for an IBM 370) shown at the bottom are well within financial feasibility at most academic and nonacademic institutions.

We conclude with several points. First, in the context of a maximization algorithm, accuracy could be increased and costs reduced by raising the number of evaluation points as the likelihood function approaches its optimum. Second, a more general point is that the technique is clearly applicable to other limited-dependent-variable models such as single-bound Tobit, double-bound Tobit, and others that are currently proliferating. The modification required in each case is to replace the cdf's in equation (2) with whatever the appropriate cross-section analogue is (e.g., simple probability density functions for Tobit observations above the limit). Third, though we have not tested it ourselves, two-fold-integration by Gaussian methods may also be within the bounds of feasibility; this would allow the estimation of two-factor models as well. Fourth, the technique is applicable to the cross-section multiple-indicator model as well. That the dependent variables are limited in these models is usually ignored.[8]

Mathematica Policy Research, Inc., Princeton, New Jersey

and

Rutgers University and Mathematica Policy Research, Inc., Princeton, New Jersey

Manuscript received November, 1980; revision received June, 1981.

[8] A copy of the deck used to estimate the equations in Table I is available from the authors at reproduction cost for two years from the date of publication.

REFERENCES

[1] Abramowitz, M., and I. Stegun: *Handbook of Mathematical Functions with Formulas, Graphs, and Mathematical Tables*. National Bureau of Standards Applied Mathematics Series No. 55. Washington, D.C.: U.S. Government Printing Office, 1964.

[2] Albright, R., S. Lerman, and C. Manski: "Report on the Development of an Estimation Program for Mutinomial Probit Model," Report prepared for the Federal Highway Administration, 1977.

[3] Berndt, E., B. Hall, R. Hall, and J. Hausman: "Estimation and Inference in Nonlinear Structural Models," *Annals of Economic and Social Measurement*, 3(1974), 653–665.

[4] Clark, C: "The Greatest of a Finite Set of Random Variables," *Operations Research*, 9(1964), 145–162.

[5] Gupta, S.: "Probability Integrals of Multivariate Normal and Multivariate *t*," *Annals of Mathematical Statistics*, 34(1963), 792–838.

[6] Hausman, J., and D. Wise: "AFDC Participation: Measured Variables or Unobserved Characteristics, Permanent or Transitory," mimeographed, Department of Economics, M.I.T., 1979.

[7] Heckman, J.: "Statistical Models for Discrete Panel Data," in *The Econometrics of Panel Data*, ed. by D. McFadden and C. Manski. Cambridge: MIT Press, 1981.

[8] Heckman, J., and R. Willis: "Estimation of a Stochastic Model of Reproduction," in *Household Production and Consumption*, ed. by N. Terleckyj. New York: Columbia University Press, 1976.

[9] Moffitt, R.: "Life Cycle Profiles of Fertility: A State-Dependent Multinomial Probit Model," mimeo, Rutgers University, 1980.

[10] Pennington, R.: *Introductory Computer Methods and Numerical Analyses* (second edition). London: The McMillian Company, 1970.

[11] Stroud, A., and D. Secrest: *Gaussian Quadrature Formulas*. Englewood Cliffs: Prentice-Hall, 1966.

Econometrica, Vol. 50, No. 6 (November, 1982)

ERRATUM

IN THE NOTE "A Computationally Efficient Quadrature Procedure for the One-Factor Multinomial Probit Model," by J. S. Butler and Robert Moffitt (*Econometrica*, 50(1982), 761–764) the following corrections should be made: On page 762, second line, prob($y_{i1}, \ldots, Y_{iT}$) should not be printed twice; in the third line, $f(\nu_{i1} \mid \mu_i)$ should be replaced by $\prod_{T=1}^{T} f(\nu_{it} \mid \mu_i)$.

Games, Economic Dynamics, and Time Series Analysis. 1982 ©Physica-Verlag, Wien–Würzburg

A Time Series Model with Qualitative Variables[1])

By *D.M. Grether*, Pasadena[2]) and *G.S. Maddala*

1. Introduction

The literature on time-series analysis has been largely confined to the analysis of time-series data where:

(i) The number of observations is large, and
(ii) the variables are all observed as continuous variables.

There are a large number of problems of practical interest that depend on time-series analysis of a different type of data sets. These data sets, which are being made available through numerous longitudinal surveys, have the following characteristics:

(1) The number of cross-section units is large and the number of time periods is small. We thus have a large number of short time series.
(2) Very often the dependent variable is either a categorical variable or a censored variable.

In the present paper we consider the estimation of a distributed lag model based on panel data where the time series on the dependent variable is observed as a categorical variable. In Section 2 we provide examples of some situations where this type of model is applicable. In later sections we present the estimation method and some empirical results.

Earlier discussions of similar problems can be found in *Chamberlain* [1980] and *Heckman* [1979]. The model considered here is different from the models discussed by these authors. Briefly stated, the main differences are as follows: Chamberlain considers the model

$$y_{it}^* = \eta_i + \sum_{j=0}^{k} \beta_j x_{i,t-j} + u_{it} \qquad \begin{array}{l} i = 1,2,\ldots,N \\ t = 1,2,\ldots,T \end{array} \tag{1.1}$$

where y_{it}^* is the "index" variable that is observed only as a qualitative variable. A major emphasis in his paper is on how to handle the "incidental" parameters η_i. He suggests

[1]) Financial support from the National Science Foundation is gratefully acknowledged. We would like to thank R.P.H. Fishe for the computations done in Section 5; and D.R. Kiewiet and M.P. Fiorina for their many helpful comments. Also we gratefully acknowledge the Sherman Fairchild Distinguished Scholars Program and the Program for the Study of Enterprise and Public Policy.

[2]) *D.M. Grether*, California Institute of Technology, 91125 Pasadena, California, U.S.A.

some conditional maximum likelihood methods for this model (consider the likelihood function conditional on sufficient statistics for the incidental parameters).

The model that Heckman considers is of the form:

$$y_{it}^* = \alpha y_{i,t-1} + \beta x_{it} + u_{it} \tag{1.2}$$

where

$$\begin{aligned} y_{it} &= 1 \qquad \text{if } y_{it}^* > 0 \\ &= 0 \qquad \text{otherwise}. \end{aligned} \tag{1.3}$$

Thus, it is the realized values of the "index" variable in the previous periods that affect the current value of the index variable. In the case where y_{it}^* determines the probability of a person finding employment in period t, the model says that this depends on whether the person was employed or not in the previous period (what Heckman calls "state dependence"). Heckman's model contains more lags than one and there are other complications in the formulations adopted by Heckman, but the essence of his models is that it is the lagged values of the dichotomous realizations that occur as explanatory variables.

The model we consider can be termed a "lagged index" model, as contrasted to a "lagged dummy" model that Heckman considers. It is

$$y_{it}^* = \alpha y_{i,t-1}^* + \beta x_{it} + u_{it} \tag{1.4}$$

where we do not observe y_{it}^* but observe the variable y_{it} as defined in (1.3) (or alternatively a polychotomous variable). In the case where y_{it}^* determines the probability of finding employment in period t, model (1.4) says that this depends on the corresponding index in period $t-1$. The model (1.2), on the other hand, captures previous employment experience through the variables $y_{i,t-j}$. Thus, in the labor supply case the model (1.2) is more reasonable than (1.4), though one can make a case for (1.4) as well (or perhaps a combination of (1.2) and (1.4)).

In the following section we will give some examples of cases where the "lagged index" model makes more sense.

2. Some Examples of the Lagged Index Model

Consider the following model

$$y_{it}^* = \alpha y_{i,t-1}^* + \beta x_{it} + u_{it} \qquad \begin{aligned} i &= 1, \ldots, N \\ t &= 1, \ldots, T \end{aligned}$$

$$\begin{aligned} y_{it} &= 1 \qquad \text{if } y_{it}^* > 0 \\ &= 0 \qquad y_{it}^* \leqslant 0. \end{aligned} \tag{2.1}$$

Thus, this is a standard distributed lag model with the dependent variable observed qualitatively. For example, y_{it}^* might be the posterior log-odds in favor of some hypothesis, $y_{i,t-1}^*$ the prior log-odds, and x_{it} the log likelihood ratio. Suppose that individuals on the basis of certain observed data state which of a pair of hypotheses they believe is correct, and suppose further that they receive a valuable prize if their guess is correct, Then their choice of hypotheses is equivalent to the statement that y_{it}^* is positive or negative. If individuals' decisions follow Bayes' rule, then $\alpha = \beta = 1$. Alternatively, if people use the representativeness heuristic of *Kahneman/Tversky* [1972], they tend to ignore their priors, so according to this theory α is less than β. Of course, if instead people use the anchoring and adjustment heuristic [*Tversky/Kahneman*], one might expect α to be greater than β. The same prediction would follow from the theories of *Howell* [1967, 1971]. Thus, there are a number of alternative theories that bear on this setup. For an example of an experimental design that could be used to generate this type of data see *Grether* [1980].

The study of party affiliation by political scientists provides another example for the application of this model. There is a substantial empirical literature for both the United States and the United Kingdom on the concept of party identification. Party identification has been defined as "the individual's effective orientation to an important group-object in his environment" [*Campbell* et. al.] . One feature of party identification that has been subject to considerable debate is its stability. Based upon a survey Campbell et. al estimated that only 20 percent of the population had (as of the survey) ever changed party identification. According to the traditional approach, people have a long-term orientation towards a political party which is much less volatile than voting intentions. This orientation is more stable than positions on issues [*Converse; Converse/Markus*].

Recently some have questioned the importance of the concept and have challenged its stability as well [*Brody; Dreyer; Fiorina*]. In the United States party identification is a measure of degreee of affiliation with either the Democratic or Republican party. This sense of identification is according to the traditional interpretation supposed to change slowly in response to the performance of the party, performance of the president, general economic conditions, domestic turmoil, personal experience, and so forth. These considerations suggest that a partial adjustment model may be appropriate. Let $\tilde{y}_{it}^* = \beta' x_{it}$ be the desired or long-term equilibrium party identification of voter i at time t. If there were no social or psychological costs in changing political affiliations, then we would have

$$y_{it}^* = \tilde{y}_{it}^* + u_{it}$$

where y_{it}^* is the actual party identification. Since there are possibly some social and psychological costs, we have

$$y_{it}^* - y_{i,t-1}^* = \alpha(\tilde{y}_{it}^* - y_{i,t-1}^*) + u_{it}$$

so that

$$\begin{aligned} y_{it}^* &= (1-\alpha) y_{i,t-1}^* + \alpha \tilde{y}_{it}^* + u_{it} \\ &= (1-\alpha) y_{i,t-1}^* + \alpha\beta' x_{it} + u_{it}. \end{aligned}$$

We further assume that

$$E(u_{it}) = 0$$

$$E(u_{it}^2) = \sigma_u^2 .$$

In practice, of course, y^*_{it} is not observed as a continuous variable; party identification being measured as a polychotomy on a five or a seven point scale [e.g. strong Democratic, independent, to strong Republican).

3. Estimation of the Lagged Index Model

Rewrite the model (2.1) as

$$y^*_{it} = \beta x^*_{it}(\alpha) + \alpha^t \eta_{i0} + w_{it} \tag{3.1}$$

where

$$x^*_{it}(\alpha) = \sum_{j=0}^{t-1} \alpha^j x_{i,t-j}$$

$$w_{it} = \frac{u_{it}}{1 - \alpha L}$$

$$\eta_{i0} = \beta \sum_{j=0}^{\infty} \alpha^i x_{i,-j} = E_i(y^*_{i0}).$$

If y^*_{it} were observed, then one could obtain consistent estimates of the parameters of the model using the method suggested by *Klein* [1958]. For the case at hand the same method works using a logit or probit estimation. The proof of consistency is basically that given by *Lee* [1980] who considers the Tobit estimator and parallels that given by *Amemiya* [1973] for the case of serially independent disturbances. For a proof of the strong consistency and a derivation of the limiting distribution of the Tobit estimator with serial correlation see *Robinson* [1980]. In general, w_{it} are going to be autocorrelated so these estimates will not be efficient. Of course, efficient estimates can be obtained by the method of maximum likelihood. While in principle this is the appropriate estimation method, in practice it is not of much use. The reason is that with serial correlation the evaluation of the likelihood function involves the calculation of the T-fold integrals of the multivariate distributions. This leads to excessive computational problems if T is greater than two. The only other problem would be that if N is large relative to T, then there is an incidental parameter problem. If there is only one observation per individual on the dependent variable (i.e. $T = 1$), then one can treat the initial conditions as being random across individuals which simply adds another component to the disturbance term. The contribution of the component is not identified, but the estimation is otherwise straightforward; (3.1) is estimated using a standard probit program searching over admissible values of α. Those estimates corresponding to the maximum value of the likelihood function are chosen. As there is only one observation over time, there cannot be any serial correlation present so these estimates are efficient and consistent as N goes to infinity provided the x's satisfy appropriate regularity conditions.

Now consider the more common situation in which one has many observations (over time) on the y_{it}'s and on the x_{it}'s. Notice that one cannot use the preceding procedure with all the data and obtain consistent estimates. The reason is that the disturbances in the model

$$w_{it} = \alpha^t \eta_{i0} + \frac{u_{it}}{1-\alpha L} \tag{3.2}$$

are heteroscedastic due to the variation in α^t, and in logit or probit type models heteroscedasticity causes estimates to be inconsistent. One could assume $\eta_{i0} = \eta_0$, but for the application at hand this is equivalent to assuming that, prior to the sample, all voters had identical views of business conditions, of their own financial conditions, of the president's performance, etc. which is surely false. This problem does not arise if one were studying the effect of the state of the economy on party identification, as in this case the x_{it}'s would (for each t) be the same for all individuals. In this case one could simply include α^t as an explanatory variable in the logit or probit estimation. This is not a feasible alternative when studying party identification as the data sources are large but infrequent surveys. Thus, having party ID a function of aggregate measures only would lead to a substantial degrees-of-freedom problem.

Chamberlain [1980] considers the conditional likelihood approach to a similar problem. The model he deals with may be written as

$$y^*_{it} = \beta x_{it} + \eta_i + u_{it}. \tag{3.3}$$

Unfortunately the procedure he uses does not work with dynamic models. To see this, consider the model (3.3) for the case where the observed variable, y_{it}, is a dichotomous variable. For $T = 2$ the conditional likelihood function for individual i for whom the $y^*_{i1} > 0, y^*_{i2} \leqslant 0$ is

$$\frac{\dfrac{e^{\beta x_{1i}+\eta_i}}{1+e^{\beta x_{1i}+\eta_i}}\;\dfrac{1}{1+e^{\beta x_{2i}+\alpha\eta_i}}}{\dfrac{e^{\beta x_{1i}+\eta_i}}{1+e^{\beta x_{1i}+\eta_i}}\;\dfrac{1}{1+e^{\beta x_{2i}+\alpha\eta_i}} + \dfrac{e^{\beta x_{2i}+\alpha\eta_i}}{1+e^{\beta x_{2i}+\alpha\eta_i}}\;\dfrac{1}{1+e^{\beta x_{1i}+\eta_i}}}$$

$$= \frac{e^{\beta x_{1i}+\eta_i}}{e^{\beta x_{1i}+\eta_i} + e^{\beta x_{2i}+\alpha\eta_i}} = \frac{1}{1+e^{\beta(x_{2i}-x_{1i})-(1-\alpha)\eta_i}}$$

Thus the η_i do not drop out and this form of the conditional likelihood approach does not provide the necessary simplification.

The following procedure, on the other hand, should produce consistent estimates of all the parameters (provided $N \to \infty$). First, estimate

$$y^*_{it} = \beta x^*_{it}(\alpha) + w_{it}$$

using a standard logit or probit program using data on the dependent variable for time t

only. Then reestimate the model using data for some other time period. These estimations provide estimates of α and of

$$\frac{\beta}{(\alpha^{2t}\sigma_\eta^2 + \sigma_u^2)^{1/2}}$$

for two different values of t. This allows one to obtain an estimate of σ_η^2/σ_u^2; call it r. Finally, using all the data we can estimate

$$y_{it} = \beta \tilde{x}_{it}^*(\alpha) + \alpha^t \tilde{\eta}_{it} + u_{it}$$

$$= \frac{\beta x_{it}^*(\alpha)}{(\alpha^{2t} r + 1)^{1/2}} + \frac{\alpha^t \bar{\eta}}{(\alpha^{2t} r + 1)^{1/2}} + w_{it}$$

where w_{it} is serially correlated but has equal variances for each observation. Obviously there are a variety of ways that one can pool the estimates from separate cross sections to obtain a final set of estimated parameters.

An obvious alternative procedure would be to try to estimate all the parameters by a two step procedure analogous to two stage least squares. First, one would estimate the reduced form equation to obtain $\hat{y}_{i,t-1}^*$ and then estimate the model (1.4) directly by probit or logit using $\hat{y}_{i,t-1}^*$ as an explanatory variable. The trouble with this procedure is that while it produces consistent estimates of the β's (up to a common scale factor) α is not identified. The reason is that the disturbances in the reduced form and structural equations have different (and unidentified) variances.

If N equals one so that the data are for a single time series y_t^*, then things are much simpler. In this case one simply performs a grid search for α using the maximum likelihood probit method applied directly to

$$y_t^* = \beta x_t^*(\alpha) + \eta z_t^*(\alpha) + w_t \tag{3.1$'$}$$

where

$$z_t^*(\alpha) = \alpha^t.$$

The parameter estimates chosen are those corresponding to the $\hat{\alpha}$ which produces the maximum value of the likelihood function.

4. An Empirical Illustration

The data are from the 1972, 1974, 1976 election panel study administered by the Center for Political Studies at the University of Michigan. The panel consisted of 1320 individuals who were interviewed both before and after the 1972 election and either before or after the 1974 and 1976 elections. The questions used for this example concerned: party identification, civil rights, the performance of the president, the government's economic performance, future expectations concerning the economy, and personal financial conditions. The party ID variable was measured as a seven point scale (strong

Republican, weak Republican, Independent-Republican, Independent-Independent, Independent-Democrat, weak Democrat, strong Democrat), and the presidential performance was dichotomous (approve, disapprove). All other variables were either three point scales or were collapsed to three point scales which we coded as binary variables with the center category as the control. For example, regarding civil rights, the respondents were asked whether they thought that civil rights leaders were pushing too fast, about right, or too slowly. For this question two binary variables (one for too fast and one for too slow) were created.

Table 1 shows the results of estimating the equation for party identification for 1976. Note that over half the sample was lost due to missing data and split-form questionnaires – not all respondents were asked every question for each election. Note also that since only one year's data on the dependent variable are used, the serial correlation problem does not matter so that the standard errors, etc. are consistently estimated (conditionally upon the value of α). It is clear that presidential performance is highly significant, while chi-square tests indicate that the other variables are not statistically significant at conventional levels. The evaluation of the government's economic performance and the pace of

Variable		Coefficient	*t*-ratio [1])
Constant		.05	.3
Presidential performance		.97	10.7
Financial condition – good		.03	.4
– Poor		.02	.3
Government' economic performance	–good	.16	1.4
	– poor	–.04	.4
Economic expectation	– good	–.06	.7
	– poor	–.03	.2
Civil rights – too fast		.03	.4
– too slow		–.19	1.3

α = .4
n = 622
$\ln L$ = –1097.95
$\hat{R}^2$ = .23

Estimated Cutoffs	Standard Errors
0.0	n.a.
.8	.06
1.1	.07
1.4	.07
1.8	.08
2.4	.09

Tab. 1: Probit Estimates Party ID 1976[2])

[1]) Calculated conditional upon α = .4.
[2]) Data for independent variables taken from 1976, 1974 and 1972 surveys.

Variable	Coefficient	t-ratio[1])
Constant	.04	.3
Presidential performance	.91	10.8
Government's economic performace – good	.15	1.4
– poor	–.02	.2
Civil rights – too fast	.03	.4
– too slow	–.17	1.2

α = .4
n = 622
$\ln L$ = –1098.2
$\hat{R}^2$ = .23

Estimated Cutoffs	Standard Errors
0.0	n.a.
.8	.06
1.1	.07
1.4	.07
1.8	.08
2.4	.09

Tab. 2: Probit Estimate Party ID 1976[2])

[1]) Calculated conditional upon $\alpha = .4$.
[2]) Data for independent variables taken from 1976, 1974 and 1972 surveys.

civil rights actions are the only variables that are close to being significant. These results are generally consistent with those of *Fiorina* [1979] who found that presidential performance and a Nixon pardon variable were highly significant in 1976, but that other variables were marginal. Table 2 shows the results when the personal financial condition and economic expectations variables are dropped. Both sets of results are quite similar. In both cases the maximum likelihood estimate of α is .4, which supports the more recent or revisionist arguments and runs counter to the traditional view that party identification changes only very slowly. Hypothesis tests that $\alpha = .8$ or $\alpha = .9$ are rejected ($\chi^2(1) = 10$–14 respectively). From the likelihood ratio statistics one can calculate approximate confidence intervals and estimate the standard deviation of $\hat{\alpha}$. In this case it appears that the standard error of $\hat{\alpha}$ is approximately .14. Notice that in addition to the coefficient estimates being stable the estimated cutoffs are nearly the same, and both sets suggest that the thresholds for the different points on the seven point scale are not evenly spaced (especially towards the ends of the scales). This is of interest as political scientists occasionally code these ordinal variables as interval levels (0, 1, 2, 3, 4, 5, 6) and use the them in regressions, which can have unfortunate consequences [*Grether* 1974, 1976].

The grid search using the 1974 data on party identification (and 1974 and 1972 data on the explanatory variables) did not converge to $\hat{\alpha}$ equal to .4, but produced the boundary solution $\hat{\alpha}$ equal 1.0. As the data for 1976 are richer (three years as opposed to two for the independent variables) we take .4 as the preliminary estimate of α. Table 3

Variable	Coefficient	t-ratio[1]
Constant	.37	2.4
Presidential performance	.55	6.3
Government's economic performance – good	–.22	1.6
– poor	–.08	1.0
Civil rights – too fast	.06	.9
– too slow	–.29	1.9

α = .4
n = 622
$\ln L$ = –1157.64
$\hat{R}^2$ = .10

Estimated Cutoffs	Standard Errors
0.00	n.a.
.57	.05
.89	.06
1.16	.06
1.49	.07
2.06	.08

Tab. 3: Probit Estimates Party ID 1974[2]

[1] Calculated conditional upon $\alpha = .4$.
[2] Data for independent variables taken from 1974, and 1972 surveys.

shows the estimates obtained for the equation eliminating the financial and expectational variables. The correction factor for the heteroscedasticity was obtained from the ratio of the 1976 and 1974 coefficients for presidential performance, and the model reestimated using all 1244 observations. The results are shown in Tables 4 and 5. Note that estimates of α using both data sets is .5. The presidential performance variable is the only substantive variable that is highly significant, though the civil rights variable is nearly so. It is unreasonable to assume that the average initial condition (presample) was zero and the shift variable is included for this reason. The overall constants in 1974 and 1976 respectively are $a + \alpha^t\bar{\eta}$ and $a + \alpha^{t+1}\bar{\eta}$. Thus the constant terms in Table 4 and Table 5 are estimates of $a + \alpha^t\bar{\eta}$ and the coefficients of the shift variables are estimates of $(\alpha^{t+1} - \alpha^t)\,\bar{\eta}$ and are negative and statistically significant. This suggests that prior to sample period individuals on average were inclined toward the Republican end of the scale. As before $\hat{\alpha}$ is significantly different from the extreme values, e.g. .8 or .2 ($\chi^2(1) = 4.18$ and 5.44 respectively). Thus, to the extent that the traditional view can be fairly represented as arguing that α is close to one, then that position is not supported.

Note that though ignoring serial correlation in the residuals and using the usual probit ML method gives us consistent estimates of the regression parameters, there still remains the problem of getting consistent estimates of the standard errors.

Denote by L^* the (pseudo) likelihood function, i.e. the likelihood function one would have by assuming serially independent residuals. Let θ be the set of parameters to be estimated. Then the appropriate covariance matrix for $\hat{\theta}$ obtained by maximizing the

Variable	Coefficient	t-ratio[1])
Constant	.43	3.5
Presidential performance	.82	11.8
Financial condition – good	.01	.2
– poor	.03	.3
Government's economic performance – good	.02	.2
– poor	–.03	.5
Economic expectation – good	–.04	.5
– poor	–.13	1.1
Civil rights – too fast	.04	.8
– too slow	–.21	1.9
Dummy (1976 = 1)	–.42	4.9

$\alpha = .5$
$n = 1244$
$\ln L = -2265.88$
$\hat{R}^2 = .16$

Estimated Cutoffs	Standard Errors
0.0	n.a.
.7	.04
1.0	.04
1.3	.05
1.6	.05
2.2	.06

Tab. 4: Probit Estimates 1974 and 1976 Pooled[2]

[1]) Calculated conditional upon $\alpha = .5$.
[2]) Data for independent variables taken from 1976, 1974, and 1972 surveys.

pseudo likelihood function is given by:

$$\text{Plim}\left(-\frac{\partial^2 \text{Log}\, L^*}{\partial\theta\partial\theta'}\right)^{-1}\left(\frac{\partial \text{Log}\, L^*}{\partial\theta}\frac{\partial \text{Log}\, L^*}{\partial\theta'}\right)\left(-\frac{\partial^2 \text{Log}\, L^*}{\partial\theta\partial\theta'}\right)^{-1}.$$

Though this expression can, in principle, be computed, it is very cumbersome to do so. In the computation of the standard errors we have reported, we have just used the expression

$$\left(-\frac{\partial^2 \text{Log}\, L^*}{\partial\theta\partial\theta'}\right)^{-1}.$$

As noted earlier, this expression is correct in the case of a single cross-section and thus the standard errors in Table 1 are consistently estimated. Since the main qualitative conclusions following from Tables 1 and 4 are the same, it would seem that not much would be gained from the extra computation of the correct expression in the case of the results of the pooled sample presented in Table 4.

Variable	Coefficient	t-ratio[2])
Constant	.34	4.8
Presidential performance	.84	13.2
Civil rights – too fast	.04	.7
– too slow	–.22	2.0
Dummy (1976 = 1)	–.43	6.0

$\alpha = .5$
$n = 622$
$\ln L = -2266.83$
$\hat{R}^2 = .15$

Estimated Cutoffs	Standard Errors
0.0	n.a.
.7	.04
1.0	.04
1.3	.05
1.6	.05
2.2	.06

Tab. 5: Probit Estimates 1974 and 1976 Pooled[2])

[1]) Calculated conditional upon $\alpha = .5$.
[2]) Data for independent variables taken from 1976, 1974, and 1972 surveys.

After Transition

Before Transition: Party ID	0	1	2	3	4	5	6	Total
0	147	51	9	5	3	3	0	218
1	57	149	33	11	14	6	0	270
2	23	32	54	20	9	6	0	144
3	6	8	23	55	19	9	2	122
4	3	12	10	21	64	37	13	160
5	6	6	3	8	31	85	26	165
6	2	1	2	3	9	43	105	165
Total	244	259	134	123	149	189	146	1244

Tab. 6: Party ID Transition 1972–1974 and 1974–1976

An alternative model for political affiliation would be that some people hold strong political opinions and others do not. These transitions are always small for one group while the other will occasionally jump from one extreme to the other. The data in Table 6 suggest that the model is not adequate to describe our data. Note that nearly all transitions are to neighboring cells and there are almost no transitions from one extreme to the other.

5. Some Monte Carlo Evidence

To check the practical usefulness of the estimation procedure we used, we conducted two series of sampling experiments. In each case we generated 100 samples of size 100 each.

In experiment 1, we considered the model:

$$y_t^* = \frac{\beta(1-\alpha)}{1-\alpha L} x_t + u_t \tag{5.1}$$

where L is the lag operator defined as $Lx_t = x_{t-i}$. We set $\beta = 1$ and generated x_t as IN(0,1), and u_t as IN(0, σ_u^2). The variance of u_t was changed for different values of α so that the variance of the systematic part in (5.1) which in this case is $((1-\alpha)/(1+\alpha))$ is four times σ_u^2. The implied theoretical R^2 for equation (5.1) is thus 0.8 in all cases.

The model given in (5.1) was estimated for two cases:

(i) y_i^* observed as a continuous variable

and

(ii) y_t^* observed as a dichotomous variable defined as:

$$y_t = 1 \quad \text{if } y_t^* > 0$$
$$= 0 \quad \text{otherwise.}$$

For estimation purposes we write (5.1) as:

$$y_t^* = \beta x_t^*(\alpha) + \alpha^t \eta + u_t \tag{5.2}$$

where $x_t^*(\alpha) = [\sum_{i=0}^{t-1} \alpha^i x_{t-i}](1-\alpha)$ and $\eta = E(y_0^*)$ is another parameter to be estimated.

In the case where y_t^* is observed as a continuous variable, we estimate (5.2) by searching over α, i.e. estimating (5.2) by OLS for each value of α and choosing the value of α for which the residual sum of squares is minium. In the case y_t^* is observed as a dichotomous variable, we use the same procedure except that equation (5.2) is estimated by the probit ML method. We choose the value of α for which the likelihood is maximum. Note that β is estimable only up to a scale factor. The search was conducted at intervals of .025 over different values of α.

The summary results are presented in Table 7. We used three values of α in the experiments.

In experiment 2, we considered the model:

$$y_t^* = \alpha y_{t-1}^* + \beta x_t + u_t. \tag{5.3}$$

Again we used the same parameter values as in experiment 1 for β and variance of x_t. The only difference is that the variance of u_t was not varied with α. If we rewrite the model in (5.3) as

$$y_t^* = \left(\frac{\beta}{1-\alpha L}\right)x_t + \left(\frac{1}{1-\alpha L}\right)u_t \tag{5.4}$$

the ratio of the variances of the systematic part and the error, with the specifications we made, is constant for different values of α.

For the case where y_t^* is observed as a continuous variable, we estimate equation (5.3) by OLS, since u_t are serially independent. In the case where y_t^* is observed as a dichotomous variable, we estimate equation (5.4) by the probit ML for different values of α, as in the case of experiment 1 but ignoring the serial correlation in the residuals.

The results of these experiments are also presented in Table 7.

The results of experiment 1 shed light on how much information is lost in the fact that y_t^* is observed only as a dichotomous variable rather than a continuous variable. The bias terms are of comparable magnitude and the variances of α when y_t^* is observed as a dicho-

Experiment 1:

Model: $y_t^* = \frac{\beta(1-\alpha)}{1-\alpha L}x_t + u_t$

α	y_t^* Continuous			y_t^* Observed as Discrete		
	Mean	Bias	Variance	Mean	Bias	Variance
.5	.498	−.002	.001526	.502	+.002	.004153
.6	.598	−.002	.001409	.598	−.002	.003727
.7	.698	−.002	.001205	.699	−.001	.003508

Experiment 2:

Model: $y_t^* = \alpha y_{t-1}^* + \beta x_t + u_t$

α	y_t^* Continuous			y_t^* Observed as Discrete		
	Mean	Bias	Variance	Mean	Bias	Variance
.5	.499	−.001	.00146	.502	+.002	.004805
.6	.601	+.001	.00121	.603	+.003	.004458
.7	.699	−.001	.00099	.704	+.004	.003392

Tab. 7: Results of Sampling Experiments

tomous variable are about 2.5–3.0 times the corresponding variances where y_t^* is observed as a continuous variable.

The results of experiment 2 shed light on the consequences of two factors:

(i) y_t^* is observed as a dichotomous variable rather than as a continuous variable.
(ii) The serial correlation in the residuals in (5.4) is ignored in the probit ML estimation of (5.4).

Again, the bias terms are not large. The variances in the case y_t^* is observed as a dichotomous variable are about 2.5–4 times the corresponding variances when y_{it}^* is continuous.

These results suggest that the estimation procedure we used in our empirical work is expected to perform well for the sample sizes we had.

6. Summary and Conclusions

In this paper we have discussed a number of dynamic models with qualitative variables. For one of these models, the lagged index model, we have proposed a method of obtaining consistent estimates of all the parameters. The method was applied to some United States panel data relevant to the issue of the stability of preferences for political parties. The evidence supports the current view that party identification is subject to short-term fluctuations. Monte Carlo calculations suggest that the method should work reasonably well in practice.

References

Amemiya, T.: Regression Analysis When the Dependent Variable Is Truncated Normal. Econometrica **41**, 1973, 997–1016.

Brody, R.: Stability and Change in Party Identification: Presidential to Off-Years. Paper presented at 1977 annual meeting of the American Political Science Association. Momeographed, 1977.

Campbell, A. et al.: The American Voter. New York 1960.

Chamberlain, G.: Analysis of Covariance with Qualitative Data. Review of Economic Studies **47**, 1980, 225–238.

Converse, P.E.: The Nature of Belief Systems in Mass Publics. Ideology and Discontent. Ed. by D.E. Apter. Glenco, Illinois, 1964.

Converse, P.E., and *G.B. Markus*: Plus ça change . . .: The New CPS Election Study Panel. American Political Science Review **73**, 1979, 32–49.

Dreyer, E.: Change and Stability in Party Identification. Journal of Politics **25**, 1973, 712–722.

Fiorina, M.P.: Retrospective Voting in American National Elections. Mimeographed. Pasadena 1979.

Grether, D.M.: Correlations with Ordinal Data. Journal of Econometrics **2**, 1974, 241–246.

–: On the Use of Ordinal Data in Correlation Analysis. American Sociological Review **41**, 1976, 908–912.

–: Bayes Rule as a Descriptive Model: The Representativeness Heuristic. Quarterly Journal of Economics **95**, 1980, 537–557.

Heckman, J.: Statistical Models for Discrete Panel Data. Center for Mathematical Studies in Businiess and Economics Report No. 7902, University of Chicago, 1979.

Howell, W.C.: An Evaluation of Subjective Probability in a Visual Discrimination Task. Journal of Experimental Psychology **75**, 1967, 979–986.

–: Uncertainty from Internal and External Sources: A Clear Case of Overconfidence. Journal of Experimental Psychology **89**, 1971, 240–243.

Kahneman, D., and *A. Tversky*: Subjective Probability: A Judgment of Representativeness. Cognitive Psychology 3, 1972, 430–454.

Klein, L.R.: The Estimation of Distrubted Lags. Econometrica **26**, 1958, 553–565.

Lee, L.-F.: Strong Consistency of the Tobit Estimator in the Presence of Serially Correlated Disturbance. Minneapolis 1980.

Robinson, P.M.: On the Asymptotic Properties of Estimators of Models Containing Limited Dependent Variables. Mimeographed. Vancouver 1980.

Tversky, A., and *D. Kahneman*: Judgment under Uncertainty: Heuristics and Biases. Science **185**, 1974, 1124–1131.

[15]

INTERNATIONAL ECONOMIC REVIEW
Vol. 24, No. 1, February, 1983

MULTIPERIOD PROBIT MODELS AND ORTHOGONALITY CONDITION ESTIMATION*

By Robert B. Avery, Lars Peter Hansen and V. Joseph Hotz[1]

1. INTRODUCTION

The availability of panel data sets on individuals or firms has generated considerable interest in techniques for estimating multiperiod econometric models with limited dependent variables. For instance, such data sets have been used in estimating econometric models of product purchases, labor supply, and consumer expenditures.[2] Application of the method of maximum likelihood (ML) to these models is straightforward when disturbances are appropriately assumed to be independent over time. However, serious computational difficulties arise in implementing ML when disturbances are temporally correlated. Therefore, this paper proposes alternative methods to ML that are computationally tractable and are appropriate for limited dependent variable models of panel data with serially correlated disturbances. Although our methods have more general applicability, in this paper we focus on multiperiod probit models.

The estimators we consider do not require an explicit parameterization of the temporal covariances of the disturbance terms. It turns out that the quasi-maximum likelihood estimator which is formed with an incorrect specification that the disturbance terms are serially uncorrelated is consistent and asymptotically normal.[3] This estimator can be viewed as a member of a class of orthogonality condition (OC) estimators which impose sample analogues of population orthogonality conditions implied by period-by-period probit regressions. The quasi-maximum likelihood estimator exploits only the orthogonality of the disturbances of the probit regressions and functions of the contemporaneous right-hand-side variables. However, under an assumption that these right-hand-side variables are strictly exogenous, the regression disturbances are also orthogonal to functions of the right-hand-side variables from other time periods. When the disturbance

* Manuscript received October 16, 1981; revised September 24, 1982.

[1] We wish to acknowledge the helpful comments of Randall Brown, David Stapleton, Guilherme Sedlacek, and members of the Econometrics Workshop at Carnegie-Mellon University on an earlier version of this paper. We also wish to thank Robert Moffitt and J. S. Butler for providing us with a copy of their equi-correlated disturbance maximum likelihood computer algorithm. The views expressed in this paper are those of the authors and do not necessarily reflect the views of the Federal Reserve Board. This research was supported in part by NSF Grant SES-8007016.

[2] See Heckman [1981] for a general discussion of discrete choice models as well as Heckman and Willis [1975], Heckman and MaCurdy [1980], and Moffitt [1981] for applications of limited dependent variable models using panel data.

[3] Heckman proposes this ML type estimator in a recent paper (see Heckman [1981]).

terms are serially correlated, there are gains in asymptotic efficiency to including these additional orthogonality conditions. Some of the OC estimators which we consider exploit these extra orthogonality conditions.

In conjunction with our proposed estimation strategy, we consider ways of testing two aspects of the model specification. Since the efficiency gains alluded to above rely on a strict exogeneity specification, we propose some convenient procedures for testing strict exogeneity. Also, we consider ways of testing for specific parameterizations of the serial correlation of disturbances, even though our estimation strategy does not require such parameterizations.

The remainder of the paper is organized as follows. In Section 2 we set up the multiperiod probit model. In Section 3 we discuss the potential problems with ML estimation. In Section 4 we motivate and describe a class of OC estimators and propose tests for exogeneity. In Section 5 we illustrate our procedures using a model of a female labor force participation. Our conclusions are in Section 6.

2. MULTIPERIOD PROBIT MODEL

In this section we specify explicitly the multiperiod probit model. It is convenient to break this discussion into two parts. First, we stipulate the parameter vector to be estimated and the variables that are observed by the econometrician. Second, we describe the intertemporal interaction between the disturbance vector and the right-hand-side variables observed by the econometrician.

Suppose one wishes to use panel data to study an econometric model of the form:

$$y^*_{it} = x'_{it}\beta_0 + \delta_{it} \qquad (i=1, 2,\ldots, N), (t=1, 2,\ldots, T). \tag{2.1}$$

In (2.1) the i subscript indexes the individuals of a cross-section and the t subscript indexes the time period in the available panel; x_{it} is a k-dimensional vector of observed right-hand-side variables; δ_{it} is an unobserved disturbance; β_0 is an unknown parameter vector to be estimated; and y^*_{it} is a continuous dependent variable. The econometrician does not observe y^*_{it} directly but instead observes a censored (or limited) form y_{it} where:

$$y_{it} = \begin{cases} 1 & \text{if } \; y^*_{it} \geq 0 \\ 0 & \text{otherwise.} \end{cases}$$

To complete the specification of the model, we stipulate the intertemporal interaction between the x's and the δ's. We assume that

$$E[\delta_{it} \mid x_{it}] = 0 \tag{2.2}$$

or equivalently,

$$E[y^*_{it} \mid x_{it}] = x'_{it}\beta_0$$

For most of our discussion we will make the stronger requirement that:

$$E(\delta_i \mid x_i) = 0, \tag{2.3}$$

where $\delta_i' = (\delta_{i1}, \ldots, \delta_{iT})$ and $x_i' = (x_{i1}', \ldots, x_{iT}')$. This requirement implies that δ_{it} is uncorrelated with functions of current, past, and future x's; thus the x's are strictly exogenous. In the spirit of most cross-sectional analyses, we also rule out crosssectional dependencies by assuming that the random vectors $\{(\delta_i', x_i')\}_{i=1}^N$ are independently and identically distributed.[4] Finally, we also assume that the distribution of each element of δ_i, conditioned on x_i, is normal with a zero mean and a unit variance.[5] The disturbances of a given individual are presumed to be serially correlated; in other words $E(\delta_{it}\delta_{i\tau})$ is not zero even when $t \neq \tau$.

3. MAXIMUM LIKELIHOOD ESTIMATION

While a number of alternative strategies exist for the estimation of β_0 in probit models in the case of a single time period model (see Amemiya [1976, 1981]), the most popular appears to be maximum likelihood (ML) estimation. The advantage of ML is that such estimators are consistent, asymptotically normal, and asymptotically efficient (see Haberman [1974]). Even though the likelihood function for the simple probit model is nonlinear in the parameters, existing iterative algorithms are able to deliver such estimates at relatively low cost.

It is natural, therefore, to consider ML estimators for the panel data version of the probit model. Heckman [1981] has recently discussed a class of models that includes the multiperiod probit model and has investigated the use of ML in estimating the parameters of these models. The specification outlined in Section 2 is equivalent to Heckman's model with general correlation of the errors but no "state dependence" or lagged dependent variables. Given that δ_i, conditioned on x_i, is normally distributed with a constant covariance matrix Σ_0, the sample likelihood can be written as:

$$L(\beta, \Sigma) = \prod_{i=1}^{N} \left[\int_{-\infty}^{a_{i1}(\beta)} \cdots \int_{-\infty}^{a_{iT}(\beta)} \phi(\xi;\, Z_i'\Sigma Z_i)\, d\xi \right] \tag{3.1}$$

where $\phi(\ )$ denotes the T-variate standardized multivariate normal density function (ξ is a $T \times 1$ vector), and $a_{it} = [2y_{it} - 1]x_{it}'\beta$ and Z_i is a $T \times T$ diagonal matrix with typical elements $[2y_{it} - 1]$.

[4] The assumption that the random vectors $\{(\delta_i', x_i')\}_{i=1}^N$ be independent and identically distributed can be relaxed. White [1980a, 1980b, 1982] has shown how to relax the identical distribution assumption in other contexts. We obtain the same rules for statistical inferences as would emerge from White's approach. In time series problems (problems in which T is driven to infinity in obtaining asymptotic approximation), one might wish to relax the independence assumption. Our estimators turn out to be special cases of Hansen's generalized method of moments estimators (see Hansen [1982]) and the asymptotic theory developed for these estimators does not assume independence.

[5] In the single-period probit model, without additional *a priori* restrictions, it is possible to identify only a normalized coefficient vector, $\beta_0 = \beta_0^*/\sigma_0$, where σ_0^2 is the variance of the underlying disturbance. In the multiperiod setting, only one period need be normalized with either σ_0^2 or β_0 varying across periods. However, in this paper we will restrict our attention to models in which β_0 is constant across time periods and all disturbances have a common variance of one.

An immediate problem arises in implementing ML estimation. If $\sum_0$ is unrestricted, computation of the T-variate integrals in (3.1) is problematic, especially for $T>2$. In the general case, computational tractability requires that these integrals be approximated. While Clark [1961] has proposed a tractable approximation, the error associated with his procedure is difficult to control. Thus, the ML estimation of the panel probit model with $\sum_0$ unrestricted is not viable in many applications.

Given this problem, parsimonious parameterizations of $\sum_0$ have been suggested by Heckman and Willis [1975], Moffitt [1981], Heckman [1981], and Butler and Moffitt [1982], among others, to make ML estimation feasible. One proposed parameterization is to assume that all off-diagonal elements of $\sum_0$ are equal so that the disturbances are presumed to be "equi-correlated." The sample likelihood, (3.1), simplifies to be

$$(3.2)\quad L^*(\beta, \rho) = \prod_{i=1}^{N} \int_{-\infty}^{\infty} \prod_{t=1}^{T} F([x'_{it}\beta + \varepsilon\rho^{1/2}][1-\rho^2]^{-1/2}[2y_{it}-1])f(\varepsilon)d\varepsilon,$$

where $F(\ )$ is the standard normal distribution function, $f(\ )$ is the standard normal density function, and $\rho=\sigma_{t\tau}$, $t\neq\tau$. This likelihood function is relatively easy to compute since it involves only one numerical integration of cumulative normal error functions for which algorithms are available on many computer systems.

While ML is computationally feasible under the simple disturbance correlation structure presented above, consistency of the ML estimator of β_0 is not, in general, robust with respect to misspecification of $\sum_0$. For instance, if Σ is incorrectly constrained to have equal off-diagonal elements, then maximizing (3.2) with respect to β and Σ will yield an inconsistent estimator of β_0. (The one exception to this is the case where the off-diagonal elements are constrained to be zero.)

In the next section, we propose a class of estimators applicable to panel data probit models which provide the econometrician with an alternative to ML. These estimators can be constructed to be both computationally feasible and more flexible in the types of auxiliary assumptions that can be made.

4. ORTHOGONALITY CONDITION ESTIMATORS FOR MULTIPERIOD PROBIT MODELS

The objective of this section is to illustrate how to construct estimators for multiperiod probit models that are computationally practical and possess desirable large sample properties. We propose a class of orthogonality condition (OC) estimators which require the evaluation of nothing more complex than period-by-period probit regression functions. None of the estimators we consider are asymptotically as efficient as ML.

Our proposed estimators of multiperiod probit models can be motivated in the following way. The conditional expectation of y_{it} given x_i is

$$(4.1)\quad E[y_{it}\,|\,x_i] = P\{\delta_{it} > -x'_{it}\beta_0\,|\,x_{it}\} = F(x'_{it}\beta_0).$$

This implies the following regression equation:

(4.2) $$y_{it} = F(x'_{it}\beta_0) + d_{it}$$

where d_{it} is a disturbance term orthogonal to functions of x_i. For each individual we can specify a system of T such regressions and thus a vector of T disturbances. Let $y'_i = (y_{it}, \ldots, y_{iT})$ and define the vector:

(4.3) $$H(y_i, x_i, \beta)' = [y_{i1} - F(x'_{i1}\beta), y_{i2} - F(x'_{i2}\beta), \ldots, y_{iT} - F(x'_{iT}\beta)],$$

with a typical element $h(y'_{it}, x_{it}, \beta)$. Then the "true" residuals are:

$$d'_i = (d_{i1}, d_{i2}, \ldots, d_{iT}) = H(y_i, x_i, \beta_0)'.$$

A common approach to estimating a system of regression equations is to minimize a quadratic form in the disturbance vector. For the multiperiod probit model this amounts to minimizing

(4.4) $$\frac{1}{N}\sum_{i=1}^{N} H(y_i, x_i, \beta)' V H(y_i, x_i, \beta)$$

by choice of β, where V is a symmetric positive semidefinite matrix. For instance, in Modified Generalized Least Squares (MGLS) estimation, the matrix in the quadratic form is chosen to be the inverse of the estimated covariance matrix of the disturbance vector. However, the regression disturbance vector d_i in the multiperiod probit model is conditionally heteroskedastic. That is,

(4.5) $$\Omega_i = E(d_i d_i \mid x_i)$$

is individual-specific creating complications. Thus, in place of the constant matrix V in (4.4), one must substitute a person-specific matrix V_i calculated by inverting an estimate of the person-specific covariance matrix, Ω_i. While the use of the person-specific matrix V_i leads to a cost increase in evaluating (4.4), a more serious problem is to obtain a consistent estimator of Ω_i. This requires consistent estimators of both β_0 and $\sum_0$. Consistent estimators of β_0 can be obtained using the methods described below. A consistent estimator of elements in $\sum_0$ can be obtained by maximizing the conditional likelihood function formed for each pair of time periods where β is set equal to some initially consistent estimator of β_0. When there are many time periods, estimation of $\sum_0$ can be quite expensive. The procedures considered below for estimating β_0 do not require an initial consistent estimator of $\sum_0$, but sacrifice asymptotic efficiency instead.[6]

Estimators of β_0 that minimize quadratic forms given by (4.4) have first-order conditions which can be viewed as setting cross products of estimated disturbances and functions of x_i to zero. For instance, if $G(y_i, x_i, \beta)$ is the T^2k-dimensional

[6] In general, the MGLS estimator will not be as asymptotically efficient as ML in cases where $\sum_0$ is not diagonal. This is because there is additional information contained in the orthogonality conditions formed with disturbances from regressions of y_{it} not only on x_{it} but the $y_{i\tau}$'s $(\tau \neq t)$ and noncontemporaneous exogenous variables which are exploited in ML estimation but not in MGLS.

vector containing all possible cross products of elements in the T-dimensional vector $H(y_i, x_i, \beta)$ and the $[T \times k]$ matrix $\partial H(y_i, x_i, \beta)/\partial\beta$, then these first-order conditions can be represented as

$$(4.6) \qquad \frac{1}{N}\sum_{i=1}^{N} A_{Ni}G(y_i, x_i, \beta) = 0.$$

where A_{Ni} is a $k \times (T^2k)$ matrix, which may vary across observations. For the MGLS estimator outlined above, A_{Ni} consists of zeros and elements of Ω_{Ni}^{-1} where Ω_{Ni} is a consistent estimator of Ω_i described above. Although the MGLS estimator is asymptotically optimal within the class of estimators which satisfy (4.6), as we have argued above, it may be difficult to implement in practice.

Given this difficulty, we consider a class estimators of β_0 which satisfy (4.6) when A_{Ni} is constrained to be of the form $A_{Ni} = B_{1N}B_2(x_i, \beta)$ so that (4.6) becomes:

$$(4.7) \qquad B_{1N}\frac{1}{N}\sum_{i=1}^{N} M(y_i, x_i, \beta) = 0$$

where B_{1N} is a consistent estimator of a constant matrix B_1 and $M(y_i, x_i, \beta) = B_2(x_i, \beta)G(y_i, x_i, \beta)$. Later we will suggest a particular choice of $B_2(x_i, \beta)$ to use for multiperiod probit models. For a given choice of vector $M(y_i, x_i, \beta)$, the choice of B_{1N} can be linked explicitly to the choice of the weighting matrix W_N for estimators that minimize the criterion function

$$(4.8) \qquad C(\beta) = O_N(\beta)'W_N O_N(\beta)$$

where

$$O_N(\beta) = \frac{1}{N}\sum_{i=1}^{N} M(x_i, \beta),$$

are termed the "sample orthogonality conditions," and W_N is a consistent estimator of a $q \times q$ symmetric and positive semidefinite matrix W_0 with rank greater than or equal to k. Such estimators, which we denote as orthogonality condition (OC) estimators, are special cases of estimators studied by Hansen [1982] and are of the same form as the Nonlinear Instrumental Variables Estimators of Amemiya [1974, 1977] and Jorgenson and Laffont [1974]. Hansen shows that OC estimators are consistent and asymptotically normal, and he derives both the optimal choice of W_N given $M(y_i, x_i, \beta)$, and expressions for the asymptotic covariance matrix of the estimators. This asymptotic covariance matrix accommodates, without modification, the conditional heteroskedasticity of d_i.[7] What makes this method particularly attractive for multiperiod probit models is that computation of a consistent estimator of the optimal W_N and of coefficient standard errors does not require a consistent estimator of Σ_0.

[7] The asymptotic covariance matrix for estimators of β_0 which use alternative choices of W_N in criterion function (4.8) will have the form:

$$(D_0'W_0D_0)^{-1}(D_0'W_0S_0W_0D_0)(D_0'W_0D_0)^{-1}$$

where W_N converges in probability to W_0. A consistent estimator of this covariance matrix is formed using W_N, D_N and S_N, with the latter defined in (4.11) and (4.12).

In constructing our particular choice of $B_2(x_i, \beta)$ and hence of $M(y_i, x_i, \beta)$ we use the following functions:

$$M_0(y_i, x_i, \beta) = \sum_{t=1}^{T} \frac{f(x'_{it}\beta)x_{it}}{[1-F(x'_{it}\beta)][F(x'_{it}\beta)]} h(y_{it}, x_{it}, \beta),$$

$$M_{+j}(y_i, x_i, \beta) = \sum_{t=1}^{T-j} \frac{f(x'_{it}\beta)x^{1}_{it}}{\sqrt{[1-F(x'_{it}\beta)]F(x'_{it}\beta)}} \frac{h(y_{it+j}, x_{it+j}, \beta)}{\sqrt{[1-F(x'_{it+j}\beta)F(x'_{it+j}\beta)]}},$$

(4.9)

$$M_{-j}(y_i, x_i, \beta) = \sum_{t=1+j}^{T} \frac{f(x'_{it}, \beta)x^{1}_{it}}{\sqrt{[1-F(x'_{it}\beta)]F(x'_{it}\beta)}} \frac{h(y_{it-j}, x_{it-j}, \beta)}{\sqrt{[1-F(x'_{it-j}\beta)]F(x'_{it-j}\beta)}}$$

$$\text{for} \quad j = 1, 2, \ldots, p$$

where x^{1}_{i} is a subvector of x_i with elements that vary over time and where $p \leq T-1$ is the number of leads and lags actually used in estimation. It is convenient for us to separate the cross product terms into two groups, those involving residuals and contemporaneous x's and those involving residuals and lead and lagged x's. Our particular choice of $M(y_i, x_i, \beta)$ is then given by:

$$(4.10) \qquad M(y_i, x_i, \beta) = \begin{bmatrix} M_0(y_i, x_i, \beta) \\ M_{+1}(y_i, x_i, \beta) \\ \vdots \\ M_{+p}(y_i, x_i, \beta) \\ M_{-1}(y_i, x_i, \beta) \\ M_{-2}(y_i, x_i, \beta) \\ \vdots \\ M_{-p}(y_i, x_i, \beta) \end{bmatrix} = \begin{bmatrix} M_0(y_i, x_i, \beta) \\ M_l(y_i, x_i, \beta) \end{bmatrix}$$

where the vector $M(y_i, x_i, \beta)$ has $q = k + k_1(2p)$ elements, k_1 being the dimension of x'_1.

We make a few comments about the choice of $M(y_i, x_i, \beta)$ in (4.10). While our choice of the form of $M(x_i, \beta)$ is ad hoc, to reduce the dimensionality of B_1, we treat the time periods symmetrically in constructing $M(y_i, x_i, \beta)$. Second, the individual specific weights are chosen so that $M_0(y_i, x_i, \beta)$ in (4.9) is the i-th individual component of the first derivative of the likelihood function when $E(\delta_i\delta'_i \mid x_i)$ is specified as the identity matrix. This latter feature implies that the quasi-ML estimator under the incorrect assumption that the δ_i's are serially uncorrelated is a special case of an OC estimator.

Alternative choices of W_N in (4.8) generate alternative OC estimators of β_0. We focus on two choices. The first estimator imposes only the contemporaneous orthogonality conditions given in (4.9). This estimator, $\tilde{b}_N$, is obtained by minimizing (4.8) with W_N given by:

$$\tilde{W}_N = \begin{bmatrix} I_k & 0 \\ 0 & 0 \end{bmatrix}$$

where I_k is a $k \times k$ identity matrix. It can be easily shown that the OC estimator is the quasi-ML estimator under the assumption that $\sum_0 = I$. The second estimator, b_N^*, is obtained by minimizing (4.8) with W_N given by $W_N^* = S_N^{-1}$ where

$$S_N = \frac{1}{N}\sum_{i=1}^{N}\begin{bmatrix} M_0(y_i, x_i, \tilde{b}_N) \\ M_I(y_i, x_i, \tilde{b}_N)\end{bmatrix}[M_0(y_i, x_i, \tilde{b}_N)' M_I(y_i, x_i, \tilde{b}_N)']$$

(4.11)

$$= \begin{bmatrix} s_{11N} & s_{12N} \\ s'_{12N} & s_{22N}\end{bmatrix}$$

The matrix W_N^* is a consistent estimator of $W_0^* = \{E[M(x_i, \beta_0)M(x_i, \beta_0)']\}^{-1}$ and produces an estimator of β_0 that has the smallest asymptotic covariance matrix among the estimators that minimize a criterion function of the form given in (4.8).

Using results in Hansen [1982], a consistent estimator of the asymptotic covariance matrix of $\tilde{b}_N$ is $d_{1N}^{-1} s_{11N} d_{1N}^{-1\prime}$ where

$$\text{(4.12)} \qquad D_N = \frac{1}{N}\sum_{i=1}^{N}\begin{bmatrix} \dfrac{\partial M_0(y_i, x_i, \tilde{b}_N)}{\partial\beta} \\ \dfrac{\partial M_I(y_i, x_i, \tilde{b}_N)}{\partial\beta}\end{bmatrix} = \begin{bmatrix} d_{1N} \\ d_{2N}\end{bmatrix},$$

and a consistent estimator for the asymptotic covariance matrix of b_N^* is $(D_N S_N^{-1} D_N)^{-1}$. Note that the matrix D_N is a consistent estimator of $E[\partial M(y_i, x_i, \beta_0)/\partial\beta)]$. It will always be the case that:

$$(D_N S_N^{-1} D_N')^{-1} \leq d_{1N}^{-1} s_{11N} d_{1N'}^{-1}.$$

Furthermore, note that both of these estimated covariance matrices can be calculated with $\tilde{b}_N$, the computationally simpler of the two estimators considered above. Thus estimated efficiency gains can be determined before deciding whether to calculate the asymptotically more efficient estimators b_N^*.

Since b_N^* employs more orthogonality conditions that $\tilde{b}_N$, it may be of interest to test whether it is appropriate to impose the extra conditions. Such a test can be interpreted as a test of the exogeneity specification of the model. Other authors (e.g., Sims [1972] and Chamberlain [1982]) have noted that strict exogeneity imposes testable restrictions on the data and have proposed exogeneity tests. We propose an orthogonality condition test which is distinct but closely related to such tests.

Under the maintained assumption that $E(\delta_{it} \mid x_{it}) = 0$, it follows that the k orthogonality conditions $E[M_0(y_i, x_i, \beta_0)] = 0$ are valid. Only these orthogonality conditions are used in estimating β_0 by $\tilde{b}_N$. Under the stronger specification of strict exogeneity, i.e., $E(\delta_i \mid x_i) = 0$, the additional orthogonality conditions, namely,

$$\text{(4.13)} \qquad E[M_I(y_i, x_i, \beta_0)] = 0,$$

are also valid. These additional orthogonality conditions are exploited in estimating β_0 by b_N^* but not by $\tilde{b}_N$. Below we investigate two alternative tests of conditions (4.13).

Our first test is based solely on the b_N^* estimator. Under the null hypothesis (4.13), a result in Hansen [1982] can be used to show that $N \cdot O_N(b_N^*)' W_N^* O_N(b_N^*)$ is asymptotically chi-square distributed with $2pk_1$ degrees of freedom. Thus one can test the strict exogeneity specification used in the model by comparing the value of the minimized criterion function using W_N^* with critical values for the chi-square distribution.

Our second test is a Wald-type test and relies solely on the $\tilde{b}_N$ estimator. Under the null hypothesis (4.13), results in Hansen [1982] imply that

$$\sqrt{N} \sum_{n=1}^{N} M_i(y_i, x_i, \tilde{b}_N)$$

is asymptotically normal with mean zero and an asymptotic covariance matrix that is estimated consistently by:

$$s_{22N} - d_{2N} d_{1N}^{-1} s_{12N} - s'_{12N} d_{1N}^{-1\prime} d'_{2N} + d_{2N} d_{1N}^{-1} s_{11N} d_{1N}^{-1\prime} d'_{2N}.$$

In Section 5 we present examples of each of these tests.

5. AN EMPIRICAL EXAMPLE: MARRIED WOMEN'S LABOR FORCE PARTICIPATION

In this section, we consider an application of the estimation and testing procedures discussed in the previous sections. We examine a simple model of married women's annual labor force participation (LFP) decisions using data drawn from the Panel Study of Income Dynamics. Our intent is to illustrate the alternative estimation strategies described in previous sections for multiperiod probit models. We also demonstrate the use of testing procedures in evaluating basic model specifications.

The sample means, standard deviations, and definitions of variables used in the model are presented in Table 1. We have chosen to use a relatively simple set of explanatory variables (the first nine variables in Table 1) to predict women's annual labor force participation (the tenth variable). LFP decisions each year are presumed to be probit functions of a linear combination of the nine explanatory variables.

In Table 2 we present several alternative estimators of β_0 for the labor force participation determinants indicated above.[8] Column (1) contains ML estimates of β_0 under an equi-correlated specification of the disturbance covariance matrix.

[8] All of the estimators, standard errors and test statistics for the multiperiod probit models presented were derived with the program HOTZTRAN, which is available from the authors upon request. This program can also estimate similar models with a tobit specification.

TABLE I
SAMPLE MEANS OF VARIABLES FOR 1974–1978[1]
(Standard Deviations of Variables in Parentheses)
(Cross-Sectional Sample = 500 Observations)

Variable	1974	1975	1976	1977	1978
EDUC (wife's education in number of grades completed)	11.430 (2.659)				
RACE (race of household, 0 = white, 1 = black)	.226 (.418)				
EXPER (wife's work experience equal to age – schooling – 6	24.190 (10.011)				
*EXPER*2 (wife's experience squared)	952.270 (620.442)	1011.650 (640.114)	1073.030 (659.807)	1136.410 (679.519)	1201.790 (699.248)
KIDS < 6 (number of children less than 6 years old)	.286 (.853)	.176 (.479)	.136 (.431)	.126 (.445)	.098 (.375)
LOC UE[1] (unemployment rate of county in which household resides)	10.500 (2.134)	10.326 (1.584)	9.866 (1.575)	9.492 (1.104)	9.624 (1.078)
FAM Y (real family income in 1967 $, excludes wife's earnings)	10291.602 (6443.426)	10132.255 (7218.918)	10306.044 (7270.611)	10406.205 (6873.307)	10447.103 (6629.478)
#*KIDS* (total number of kids currently living with parents)	1.844 (1.892)	1.724 (1.814)	1.542 (1.715)	1.388 (1.612)	.914 (1.171)
HUS UE (annual number of hours husbands unemployed)	45.160 (201.472)	42.132 (162.426)	50.352 (234.175)	52.608 (210.254)	40.288 (184.342)
WORK (wife's labor force status, 0 = did not work during year, 1 = did work during year)	.504 (.500)	.534 (.499)	.550 (.497)	.538 (.499)	.528 (.499)

[1] Data Source: Panel Study of Income Dynamics. A random sample of 500 households (from a total sample of over 5,000) was chosen from those which met following criteria: (1) the husband and wife of the household remained the same from 1974–1978; (2) the wife was between 30 and 65 in 1975; (3) the wife did not report being retired in any of the years 1974–1978; (4) none of the sample variables were missing from 1974–1978.

The estimates reported in column (2) were obtained using quasi-ML which exploits only the contemporaneous orthogonality conditions ($\bar{b}_N$ in Section 4); and column (3) contains OC estimates that were obtained by exploiting additional orthogonality conditions between disturbances and functions of some of the x's in the other time periods (b_N^* in Section 4). In forming these estimates, we set $p=4$ and included only those variables changing significantly over time — *FAM Y*, #*KIDS*, and *HUS UE* — in the vector x_i^j. Thus, the estimates of b_N^* in column (3) exploit contemporaneous, lead, and lag orthogonality conditions and weight them optimally. Standard errors for the first estimator were formed from the estimates of the inverse of the Fisher information matrix while those for the latter two estimators were formed as outlined in Section 4. For the quasi-ML estimator, $\bar{b}_N$, we also report the estimated standard errors in square brackets that are computed assuming the disturbances are serially uncorrelated. These latter

TABLE 2
COEFFICIENT ESTIMATES FOR WOMEN'S LEP MULTIPERIOD PROBIT EXAMPLE
(Standard Errors in Parentheses)

	(1)	(2)	(3)
CONSTANT	−.243 (.273)	.267 (.456) [.283]	.396 (.446)
EDUC	.027 (.017)	.027 (.019) [.011]	.024 (.018)
RACE	.0029 (.100)	.069 (.113) [.067]	.066 (.112)
EXPER	.041 (.010)	.026 (.024) [.013]	.021 (.023)
EXPER2	$-.944\times10^{-3}$ $(.153\times10^{-3})$	$-.846\times10^{-3}$ $(.413\times10^{-3})$ $[.229\times10^{-3}]$	$-.794\times10^{-3}$ $(.404\times10^{-3})$
KIDS<6	−.042 (.019)	−.091 (.061) [.033]	−.128 (.057)
LOC UE	$-.737\times10^{-2}$ $(.976\times10^{-2})$	$-.549\times10^{-2}$ (.015) [.013]	$-.584\times10^{-2}$ (.015)
FAM Y	$-.135\times10^{-4}$ $(.308\times10^{-5})$	$-.241\times10^{-4}$ $(.710\times10^{-5})$ $[.426\times10^{-5}]$	$-.265\times10^{-4}$ $(.581\times10^{-5})$
#KIDS	−.052 (.013)	−.094 (.026) [.017]	−.084 (.024)
HUS UE	$.162\times10^{-4}$ $(.124\times10^{-3})$	$.175\times10^{-3}$ $(.201\times10^{-3})$ $[.151\times10^{-3}]$	$.731\times10^{-4}$ $(.115\times10^{-3})$

Column (1) contains coefficient estimates using ML under an equi-correlated specification of the disturbance covariance structure. Estimate of correlation is found in Table 3.

Column (2) contains coefficient estimates using Orthogonality Condition Estimation, imposing only contemporaneous orthogonality conditions. The first standard errors listed allow for serial correlation. The second standard errors (in square brackets) are computed under the assumption that residuals are not serially correlated and are biased if residuals are serially correlated.

Column (3) contains coefficient estimates using Orthogonality Condition Estimation imposing weighted sum of all 4 lead and lag orthogonality conditions for variables *FAM Y*, *#KIDS*, and *HUS UE*, and of contemporaneous orthogonality conditions for all other variables. Optimal weighting scheme used.

standard error estimates will be biased unless residuals truly are serially uncorrelated.

The estimated standard errors of the ML estimators assuming equi-correlated disturbances are in all cases lower than those of both OC estimators. This may reflect the fact that the OC estimators are not as efficient as ML estimators when the disturbances are, in fact, equi-correlated. If $\sum_0$ does not have equal off-diagonal elements, however, not only will the reported ML standard error estimators be inconsistent, but so will the coefficient estimators. As noted in Section 4, there is an efficiency gain from using b_N^* instead of $\tilde{b}_N$. Unlike the ML estimators, the legitimacy of this latter efficiency gain does not depend upon the correct parameterization of $\sum_0$. Note also that there is a substantial difference between the correct and incorrect standard errors of $\tilde{b}_N$.

Either of the OC estimators, $\tilde{b}_N$ and b_N^*, can be used to compute consistent and asymptotically normal estimates of $\sum_0$. As outlined in Section 4, one can estimate each element of $\sum_0$ separately by maximizing the conditional likelihood function formed by the bivariate probit probabilities of outcomes in each pair of time periods, and utilizing a consistent estimator of β_0. This allows us to test alternative specifications of $\sum_0$. One possible hypothesis is that all off-diagonal elements of $\sum_0$ are zero, in which case $\tilde{b}_N$ will be the ML estimator and hence asymptotically efficient. We can also test the specification underlying the equi-correlated ML estimators as well as the assumption of stationarity of the errors. By stationarity we simply mean that $E(\delta_{it}\delta_{it-\tau})$ depends only on τ.

The unrestricted estimates of $\sum_0$ and corresponding test statistics are presented in Table 3. We also present the ML estimate of the common off-diagonal

TABLE 3

ESTIMATES OF ALTERNATIVE $\sum_0$ SPECIFICATIONS[1]

ML Estimator of $\sum_0$ under Equi-Correlated Specification:

.729
(.023)

Two Step OC Estimator of $\sum_0$ under Unrestricted Covariance Specification:[2]

	1974	1975	1976	1977
1975	.903 (.021)			
1976	.616 (.054)	.737 (.061)		
1977	.557 (.056)	.684 (.056)	.886 (.024)	
1978	.404 (.067)	.427 (.066)	.647 (.056)	.730 (.057)

Test of Equi-Correlated Specification of $\sum_0$:

$x^2 = 87.480$ with nine degrees of freedom (% significance $= 5.21 \times 10^{-11}$)

Test of Stationarity Specification of $\sum_0$:

$x^2 = 16.396$ with six degrees of freedom (% significance $= 1.180$)

[1] Estimated standard errors in parentheses.

[2] The estimates of $\sum_0$ were estimated using $\tilde{b}_N$ as the estimator of β_0.

element of Σ_0 under the equi-correlation specification of column (1) in Table 2. The unrestricted estimators' covariance matrix was used to form chi-square tests of the equi-correlated and stationarity assumptions which are also presented in Table 3. There is a dramatic rejection of equi-correlated specification and a marginal rejection of stationarity which suggests caution in the use of the equi-correlated ML estimators.

While not as asymptotically efficient as b_N^*, the estimator $\tilde{b}_N$ has a number of virtues. First, since $\tilde{b}_N$ is equivalent to the standard probit ML estimator assuming serially uncorrelated errors, it can be computed easily with standard probit programs (although the reported standard errors will be incorrect). Second, $\tilde{b}_N$ can be used to estimate consistently the matrix W_N^* used to compute b_N^* and provide starting values for the numerical search required to calculate b_N^*. Finally, the efficiency gains of the b_N^* estimator can be ascertained using $\tilde{b}_N$ without actually calculating b_N^*.

Since the b_N^* estimator exploits the assumption of strict exogeneity of the x's, it is worthwhile to test the over-identifying restrictions implied by this assumption. As noted in Section 4, one such test is based on the minimized value of the criterion function used to estimate b_N^*. We present this test statistic in Table 4. It is also possible to test the validity of the orthogonality conditions for the lead and lag values of variables in the vector x_i^1. These tests were constructed using $\tilde{b}_N$ and are also presented in Table 4. Results from all of these tests do not contradict the strict exogeneity specification over the period 1974–1979. When these tests were repeated using data from 1970–1979, we did find substantial evidence against strict exogeneity of the x's.[9]

TABLE 4
EXOGENEITY TEST RESULTS

Tests of all noncontemporaneous orthogonality conditions using b_N^* found in column (3) of Table 2.	$\chi^2 = 31.019$ with 24 degrees of freedom (% significance = 15.3).
Test using $\tilde{b}_N$ of all lead orthogonality conditions on elements of x^1.	$\chi^2 = 10.622$ with 12 degrees of freedom (% significance = 56.2).
Tests using $\tilde{b}_N$ of all lag orthogonality conditions on elements of x^1.	$\chi^2 = 15.328$ with 12 degrees of freedom (% significance = 22.4).

6. CONCLUSIONS

We have proposed a class of OC estimators for multiperiod probit models that are consistent, asymptotically normal, and computationally tractable. These

[9] A complete set of estimates and test statistics using the 1970–1979 data is available from the authors upon request.

OC estimators do not require that the error covariance structure be restricted *a priori*. Furthermore, as has been emphasized by Sims [1972b], most estimation strategies which attempt to correct for serial correlation exploit exogeneity specifications in a crucial way. These same comments are pertinent to our b_N^* estimator. A useful by-product of our estimation strategy is a straightforward test of the over-identifying restrictions implied by strict exogeneity. We have demonstrated the tractability of our proposed estimators with a relatively large 500-person, five-time-period model of women's labor force participation. This model would have been extremely expensive to estimate by ML without imposing a parsimonious and possibly incorrect specification of the error covariance structure.

Board of Governors, Federal Reserve System
University of Chicago
Carnegie-Mellon University and Economics Research Center/NORC

REFERENCES

AMEMIYA, T., "The Nonlinear Two-Stage Least Squares Estimator," *Journal of Econometrics*, 2 (1974), pp. 105–110.

———, "The Maximum Likelihood, the Minimum Chi-Square and the Nonlinear Weighted Least-Squares Estimated in the General Qualitative Response Model," *Journal of the American Statistical Association* 71 (June 1976), pp. 347–351.

———, "The Maximum Likelihood and Nonlinear Three-Stage Least Squares Estimator in the General Nonlinear Simultaneous Equations Model," *Econometrica*, 45 (1977), pp. 955–968.

———, "Qualitative Response Models: A Survey," *Journal of Economic Literature*, 19 (December 1981), pp. 1483–1536.

BUTLER, J. S. AND R. MOFFITT, "A Computationally Efficient Quadrature Procedure for the One-Factor Multinomial Probit Model," *Econometrica*, 50 (May 1982), pp. 761–764.

CHAMBERLAIN, G., "Panel Data," DSSRI Discussion Paper No. 8209, University of Wisconsin-Madison (April 1982).

CLARK, C., "The Greatest of a Finite Set of Random Variates," *Operations Research*, 9 (1961).

HABERMAN, S., *Qualitative Data Analysis*. (Chicago: University of Chicago Press, 1974).

HANSEN, L. P., "Large Sample Properties of Generalized Methods of Moments Estimator," *Econometrica* 50 (July 1982), pp. 1029–1054.

HECKMAN, J., "Dummy Endogenous Variables in a Simultaneous Equation System," *Econometrica*, 46 (1978 b), pp. 931–959.

———, "Statistical Models for Discrete Panel Data," in C. Manski and D. McFadden (eds.), *Structural Analysis of Discrete Data with Econometric Applications*. (Cambridge: MIT Press, 1981).

HECKMAN, J., AND T. MACURDY, "A Life-Cycle Model of Female Labour Supply," *Review of Economic Studies* 62 (1980), pp. 47–74.

HECKMAN, J. AND R. WILLIS, "Estimation of a Stochastic Model of Reproduction: An Econometric Approach," in N. E. Terleckyj (ed.), *Household Production and Consumption*. (New York: Columbia University Press, 1975).

JORGENSON, D. AND J. LAFFONT, "Efficient Estimation of Nonlinear Simultaneous Equations with Additive Disturbances," *Annals of Economic and Social Measurement*, 3 (1974), pp. 615–640.

MOFFITT, R., "Life-Cycle Profiles of Fertility, Labor Supply and Wages of Married Women:

A State-Dependent Multinomial Probit Model," unpubl'shed manuscript, Rutgers College, (1981).

SIMS, C. A., "Money, Income and Causality," *American Economic Review*, 62 (1972a), pp. 540-552.

———, "Are There Exogenous Variables in Short-Run Production Relationships?" *Annals of Economic and Social Measurement*, 1 (1972 d), pp. 17-36.

WHITE, H., "Nonlinear Regression on Cross-Section Data," *Econometrica*, 48 (1980a), pp. 721-746.

———, "A Heteroskedasticity-Consistent Covariance Matrix and a Direct Test for Heteroskedasticity," *Econometrica*, 48 (1980b), pp. 817-838.

———, "Instrumental Variables Regression on Cross-Section Data," *Econometrica*, 50 (March 1982), pp. 483-500.

[16]

The Analysis of Panel Data Under a Markov Assumption

J. D. KALBFLEISCH and J. F. LAWLESS*

Methods for the analysis of panel data under a continuous-time Markov model are proposed. We present procedures for obtaining maximum likelihood estimates and associated asymptotic covariance matrices for transition intensity parameters in time homogeneous models, and for other process characteristics such as mean sojourn times and equilibrium distributions. Generalizations to handle covariance analysis and to the fitting of certain nonhomogeneous models are presented, and an example based on a longitudinal study of the smoking habits of school children is discussed. Questions of embeddability and estimation are examined.

KEY WORDS: Markov processes; Maximum likelihood estimation; Regression analysis; Longitudinal data; Embeddability.

1. INTRODUCTION

Continuous-time Markov models have found wide application in the social sciences, especially in the study of data that record life history events (e.g., social mobility studies) for individuals. A recent review of this work is given by Bartholomew (1983); see also, for example, Bartholomew (1982), Singer and Spilerman (1976a,b), and Tuma et al. (1979). In many instances, a full history of the individual processes is not available. In this article we consider "panel data" in which the observations consist of the states occupied by the individuals under study at a sequence of discrete time points; we assume no information to be available about the timing of events between observation times.

Methods for the analysis of panel data under a continuous-time Markov model have been discussed by Bartholomew (1983), Singer and Spilerman (1976a,b), Wasserman (1980), and others. Most of the methodology so far proposed has severe limitations, such as (a) inability to handle observation times that are not equally spaced; (b) inability to produce standard errors, tests, and interval estimates for all model characteristics of interest; and (c) inability to generalize easily to handle covariance analysis. We propose here algorithms for maximum likelihood estimation that overcome these difficulties and that furthermore provide a very efficient way of obtaining maximum likelihood estimates (MLE's).

Section 2 sets notation and reviews a number of results associated with continuous-time Markov processes. Section 3 presents the basic algorithm. Estimates of asymptotic covariance matrices for parameters and estimates of other process characteristics such as equilibrium distributions are also discussed. Some further aspects of maximum likelihood estimation are discussed in Section 4, and Section 5 considers generalizations to covariance analysis and to the fitting of certain nonhomogeneous models. The remainder of the article contains an example based on a longitudinal study of the smoking habits of school children (Section 6), a discussion of the embedding problem for continuous-time Markov processes and its relationships to estimation (Section 7), and some concluding comments.

2. CONTINUOUS-TIME MARKOV PROCESSES

Suppose individuals independently move among k states, denoted by $1, \ldots, k$, according to a continuous-time Markov process. Let $X(t)$ be the state occupied at time t by a randomly chosen individual. For $0 \leq s \leq t$, let $P(s, t)$ be the $k \times k$ transition probability matrix with entries

$$p_{ij}(s, t) = \Pr\{X(t) = j \mid X(s) = i\},$$

for $i, j = 1, \ldots, k$. As is well known (e.g., see Cox and Miller 1965), this process can be specified in terms of the transition intensities,

$$q_{ij}(t) = \lim_{\Delta t \to 0} p_{ij}(t, t + \Delta t)/\Delta t, \qquad i \neq j.$$

For convenience, we also define

$$q_{ii}(t) = -\sum_{j \neq i} q_{ij}(t), \qquad i = 1, \ldots, k,$$

and let $Q(t)$ be the $k \times k$ transition intensity matrix with entries $q_{ij}(t)$.

This article is primarily concerned with time-homogeneous models in which $q_{ij}(t) = q_{ij}$ independent of t. In this case, the process is stationary and we write

$$P(t) = P(s, s + t) = P(0, t)$$

and $Q = (q_{ij})$ to denote the transition intensity matrix. Note that $q_{ij} \geq 0$ for $i \neq j$ and that $\sum_{j=1}^{k} q_{ij} = 0$. It is well known (e.g., see Cox and Miller 1965) that

$$P(t) = e^{Qt} = \sum_{r=0}^{\infty} Q^r t^r / r!.$$

Consider the time-homogeneous model, and suppose that $q_{ij} = q_{ij}(\boldsymbol{\theta})$ depends on b functionally independent parameters $\theta_1, \ldots, \theta_b$, with $\boldsymbol{\theta} = (\theta_1, \ldots, \theta_b)$ for each $i, j = 1, \ldots, k$. As a simple example, consider a Markov model for marital stability discussed by Tuma et al. (1979, p. 824). Here, an individual is in state 1 (not married), state 2 (married), or state 3 (has "emigrated" from the study for some reason);

* J. D. Kalbfleisch and J. F. Lawless are Professors, Department of Statistics and Actuarial Science, University of Waterloo, Waterloo, Ontario N2L 3G1, Canada. Research was supported in part by grants from the Natural Sciences and Engineering Research Council of Canada. The authors thank K. S. Brown for the data on school children in Section 6 and for discussions concerning these data and the methods proposed here. They also thank W. M. Vollmer and E. Kelly for work on the development of the computer algorithms.

Journal of the American Statistical Association
December 1985, Vol. 80, No. 392, Theory and Methods

state 3 is absorbing. The transition intensity matrix has the form

$$Q = \begin{pmatrix} -\lambda_1-\mu_1 & \lambda_1 & \mu_1 \\ \lambda_2 & -\lambda_2-\mu_2 & \mu_2 \\ 0 & 0 & 0 \end{pmatrix}, \tag{2.1}$$

and we have $\boldsymbol{\theta} = (\lambda_1, \mu_1, \lambda_2, \mu_2)$, say. The matrix $P(t)$ is a complicated function of these parameters. For example (see Tuma et al. 1979),

$$p_{11}(t) = \frac{(a_1 + \delta_2)e^{\delta_1 t} - (a_1 + \delta_1)e^{\delta_2 t}}{\delta_2 - \delta_1}, \tag{2.2}$$

where $a_1 = \lambda_1 + \mu_1$, $a_2 = \lambda_2 + \mu_2$, and

$$\delta_1 = -\tfrac{1}{2}(a_1 + a_2) + \tfrac{1}{2}[(a_1 - a_2)^2 + 4\lambda_1\lambda_2]^{1/2}$$
$$\delta_2 = -\tfrac{1}{2}(a_1 + a_2) - \tfrac{1}{2}[(a_1 - a_2)^2 + 4\lambda_1\lambda_2]^{1/2}. \tag{2.3}$$

We comment further on this model below.

3. MAXIMUM LIKELIHOOD ESTIMATION

Suppose for now that each of a random sample of n individuals is observed at times $t_0, t_1, \ldots, t_m$. (We will discuss the possibility of immigration or emigration from the group of individuals observed later.) If n_{ijl} denotes the number of individuals in state i at t_{l-1} and j at t_l, and if we condition on the distribution of individuals among states at t_0, then the likelihood function for $\boldsymbol{\theta}$ is

$$L(\boldsymbol{\theta}) = \prod_{l=1}^{m} \left\{ \prod_{i,j=1}^{k} p_{ij}(t_{l-1}, t_l)^{n_{ijl}} \right\}. \tag{3.1}$$

In the time-homogeneous case with $w_l = t_l - t_{l-1}$, $l = 1, \ldots, m$, (3.1) gives the log-likelihood,

$$\log L(\boldsymbol{\theta}) = \sum_{l=1}^{m} \sum_{i,j=1}^{k} n_{ijl} \log p_{ij}(w_l). \tag{3.2}$$

Throughout, we suppress the dependence of $p_{ij}(w_l; \boldsymbol{\theta})$ on $\boldsymbol{\theta}$.

The MLE $\hat{\boldsymbol{\theta}}$ or, equivalently, the MLE $\hat{Q} = Q(\hat{\boldsymbol{\theta}})$ of Q, is obtained by maximizing (3.2). One approach (see Wasserman 1980) utilizes a numerical algorithm that requires no derivatives of $\log L(\boldsymbol{\theta})$. There are various algorithms that could be used (e.g., see Chambers 1977, chap. 6). We propose here a more efficient quasi-Newton procedure that uses first derivatives of $\log L(\boldsymbol{\theta})$. This leads to faster convergence and an estimate of the asymptotic covariance matrix of $\hat{\boldsymbol{\theta}}$. Our approach is made feasible by the provision of an efficient algorithm for the computation of $P(t; \boldsymbol{\theta})$ and its derivative with respect to $\boldsymbol{\theta}$. This leads to simple computation of $\log L(\boldsymbol{\theta})$ and its derivatives.

To compute $P(t; \boldsymbol{\theta}) = \exp\{Q(\boldsymbol{\theta})t\}$ for a given $\boldsymbol{\theta}$, we use a canonical decomposition: if, for the given $\boldsymbol{\theta}$, $Q(\boldsymbol{\theta})$ has distinct eigenvalues $d_1, \ldots, d_k$ and A is the $k \times k$ matrix whose jth column is a right eigenvector corresponding to d_j, then $Q = ADA^{-1}$, where $D = \operatorname{diag}(d_1, \ldots, d_k)$. Then

$$P(t) = A \operatorname{diag}(e^{d_1 t}, \ldots, e^{d_k t})A^{-1}, \tag{3.3}$$

where the dependence of Q, $P(t)$, A and the d_j's on $\boldsymbol{\theta}$ is suppressed for notational convenience. When Q has repeated eigenvalues, an analogous decomposition of Q to Jordan canonical form is possible (see Cox and Miller 1965). This is rarely necessary, since for most models of interest, $Q(\boldsymbol{\theta})$ has distinct eigenvalues for almost all $\boldsymbol{\theta}$.

Derivatives can be computed in a similar way. In particular, the matrix with entries $\partial p_{ij}(t; \boldsymbol{\theta})/\partial\theta_u$ can be obtained as

$$\partial P(t)/\partial\theta_u = AV_uA^{-1}, \quad u = 1, \ldots, b, \tag{3.4}$$

where V_u is a $k \times k$ matrix with (i, j) entry

$$g_{ij}^{(u)}(e^{d_i t} - e^{d_j t})/(d_i - d_j), \quad i \neq j,$$
$$g_{ii}^{(u)}te^{d_i t}, \quad i = j,$$

and $g_{ij}^{(u)}$ is the (i, j) entry in $G^{(u)} = A^{-1}(\partial Q/\partial\theta_u)A$. A derivation of this result, which also appears in Jennrich and Bright (1976), is given in Appendix A. The derivatives $\partial Q/\partial\theta_u$ are usually very simple, and calculation of (3.4) is easy once A and D are obtained. It is generally the case that $P(t)$ is a complicated function of $\boldsymbol{\theta}$; the above formulas, however, allow us to avoid use of any explicit representation of the elements $p_{ij}(t)$ as functions of $\boldsymbol{\theta}$.

3.1 The Scoring Procedure

The quasi-Newton (or scoring) procedure described below is an efficient and simple method for obtaining the MLE of $\boldsymbol{\theta}$. From (3.2) we find

$$S_u(\boldsymbol{\theta}) = \frac{\partial \log L}{\partial\theta_u} = \sum_{l=1}^{m} \sum_{i,j=1}^{k} n_{ijl} \frac{\partial p_{ij}(w_l)/\partial\theta_u}{p_{ij}(w_l)},$$
$$u = 1, \ldots, b, \tag{3.5}$$

$$\frac{\partial^2 \log L}{\partial\theta_u\partial\theta_v} = \sum_{l=1}^{m} \sum_{i,j=1}^{k} n_{ijl} \times \left\{ \frac{\partial^2 p_{ij}(w_l)/\partial\theta_u\partial\theta_v}{p_{ij}(w_l)} - \frac{\partial p_{ij}(w_l)/\partial\theta_u \partial p_{ij}(w_l)/\partial\theta_v}{p_{ij}^2(w_l)} \right\}.$$

Direct use of a Newton–Raphson algorithm would require the evaluation of both first and second derivatives. We use instead the scoring device in which the second derivatives are replaced by estimates of their expectations. This leads to an algorithm in which only first derivatives are required.

Let $N_i(t_{l-1}) = \sum_{j=1}^{k} n_{ijl}$ represent the number of individuals in state i at time t_{l-1}. By first taking the expectation of n_{ijl} conditional on $N_i(t_{l-1})$ and then using the fact that $\sum_{j=1}^{k} \partial^2 p_{ij}(w_l)/\partial\theta_u\partial\theta_v = 0$, we find that

$$E\left(-\frac{\partial^2 \log L}{\partial\theta_u\partial\theta_v} \right) = \sum_{l=1}^{m} \sum_{i,j=1}^{k} \frac{E\{N_i(t_{l-1})\}}{p_{ij}(w_l)} \frac{\partial p_{ij}(w_l)}{\partial\theta_u} \frac{\partial p_{ij}(w_l)}{\partial\theta_v},$$

which can be estimated by

$$M_{uv}(\boldsymbol{\theta}) = \sum_{l=1}^{m} \sum_{i,j=1}^{k} \frac{N_i(t_{l-1})}{p_{ij}(w_l)} \frac{\partial p_{ij}(w_l)}{\partial\theta_u} \frac{\partial p_{ij}(w_l)}{\partial\theta_v}. \tag{3.6}$$

Computation of (3.5) and (3.6) for any given θ is facilitated by the results (3.3) and (3.4).

The algorithm is now simply described. Let $\boldsymbol{\theta}_0$ be an initial estimate of $\boldsymbol{\theta}$, $S(\boldsymbol{\theta})$ be the $b \times 1$ vector $(S_u(\boldsymbol{\theta}))$, and $M(\boldsymbol{\theta})$ the $b \times b$ matrix $(M_{uv}(\boldsymbol{\theta}))$. Then an updated estimate is obtained as

$$\boldsymbol{\theta}_1 = \boldsymbol{\theta}_0 + M(\boldsymbol{\theta}_0)^{-1}S(\boldsymbol{\theta}_0),$$

where it is assumed that $M(\boldsymbol{\theta}_0)$ is nonsingular. The process is now repeated with $\boldsymbol{\theta}_1$ replacing $\boldsymbol{\theta}_0$. With a good initial estimate $\boldsymbol{\theta}_0$, the algorithm produces $\hat{\boldsymbol{\theta}}$ upon convergence, and

$M(\hat{\boldsymbol\theta})^{-1}$ is an estimate of the asymptotic covariance matrix of $\hat{\boldsymbol\theta}$. If the true value of $\boldsymbol\theta$ is an interior point of the parameter space, $\sqrt{n}(\hat{\boldsymbol\theta} - \boldsymbol\theta)$ has a limiting multivariate normal distribution as the number of individuals (n) under observation approaches infinity.

3.2 Illustration

Consider the model (2.1) with $\boldsymbol\theta = (\lambda_1, \mu_1, \lambda_2, \mu_2)$. To implement the algorithm, we determine the eigenvalues and eigenvectors of $Q(\boldsymbol\theta_0)$, where $\boldsymbol\theta_0$ is the trial value. In this case, the eigenvalues can be obtained algebraically; they are 0, δ_1, and δ_2, where δ_1 and δ_2 are defined in (2.3). The eigenvectors are more complicated functions of $\boldsymbol\theta$. It is important to note, however, that no use is made of these algebraic expressions; for the given $\boldsymbol\theta_0$ the numerical values of the eigenvectors and eigenvalues can be easily obtained with standard software.

Once the canonical decomposition of $Q(\boldsymbol\theta_0)$ is obtained, the matrices $P(w_l; \boldsymbol\theta_0)$ are obtained from (3.3) and the derivatives from (3.4). The matrices $G^{(u)}$ in (3.4) are simply computed; for example,

$$G^{(1)} = A^{-1}\begin{pmatrix} -1 & 1 & 0 \\ 0 & 0 & 0 \\ 0 & 0 & 0 \end{pmatrix} A.$$

The entire procedure is easily programmed and executes quickly on a computer. A listing of a FORTRAN subroutine that implements the general methodology of this article is available from the authors. An example is given in Section 6.

As is remarked further below, there is an advantage here to parameterize in terms of $\boldsymbol\theta = (\log \lambda_1, \log \mu_1, \log \lambda_2, \log \mu_2)$, since the parameter space for $\boldsymbol\theta$ is then unrestricted. This guarantees that the result of an iteration will not fall outside the parameter space. Estimates that lie on the boundary of the parameter space do cause difficulty and are discussed in Section 4.

3.3 Estimates of Derived Quantities

Often, specific characteristics of the model are of interest, such as $-q_{ii}(\boldsymbol\theta)^{-1}$, the mean sojourn time in state i. In general, such quantities are estimated by replacing $\boldsymbol\theta$ with $\hat{\boldsymbol\theta}$, and the asymptotic variance is estimated from the multivariate delta theorem (see Rao 1973, p. 388). For example, the mean sojourn time in state i is estimated by $-q_{ii}(\hat{\boldsymbol\theta})^{-1}$ and its estimated asymptotic variance is $q_{ii}(\hat{\boldsymbol\theta})^{-4}$ times

$$\sum_{u=1}^{b}\sum_{v=1}^{b} \frac{\partial q_{ii}(\boldsymbol\theta)}{\partial\theta_u}\frac{\partial q_{ii}(\boldsymbol\theta)}{\partial\theta_v} M^{uv}(\boldsymbol\theta)\bigg|_{\boldsymbol\theta=\hat{\boldsymbol\theta}},$$

where $M^{uv}(\boldsymbol\theta)$ is the u, v element of $M(\boldsymbol\theta)^{-1}$. In like manner, for example, the transition probabilities $p_{ij}(t; \boldsymbol\theta)$ for fixed i, j, and t can be estimated. The required derivatives are computed using (3.3) and (3.4).

One important characteristic of ergodic models is the equilibrium probability vector $\boldsymbol\pi' = (\pi_1, \ldots, \pi_k)$, specified as the unique solution to the equation $Q'\boldsymbol\pi = \mathbf{0}$ that satisfies $\sum_{i=1}^{k} \pi_i = 1$. In order to determine an asymptotic covariance matrix for $\hat{\boldsymbol\pi}$ via the delta theorem, we require derivatives $\partial\pi_i/\partial\theta_j$. In Appendix B we prove that the following procedure yields an asymptotic covariance matrix for $\hat{\pi}$.

Let $Q_1(\boldsymbol\theta)$ be the $k \times (k-1)$ matrix obtained by deleting the last column of Q, and define the $(k-1) \times (k-1)$ matrix $B(\boldsymbol\theta)$ with (i, j) element

$$B_{ij}(\boldsymbol\theta) = q_{ji}(\boldsymbol\theta) - q_{ki}(\boldsymbol\theta), \qquad i, j = 1, \ldots, k-1.$$

In addition, let $C(\boldsymbol\theta)$ be the $(k-1) \times b$ matrix whose j'th column is given by

$$(\partial Q_1/\partial\theta_j)'\boldsymbol\pi. \tag{3.7}$$

The derivatives of $\pi_1, \ldots, \pi_{k-1}$ with respect to $\theta_1, \ldots, \theta_b$ are contained in the matrix W with (i, j) element $\partial\pi_i/\partial\theta_j$, where

$$W(\boldsymbol\theta) = -B(\boldsymbol\theta)^{-1}C(\boldsymbol\theta). \tag{3.8}$$

An estimate of the asymptotic covariance matrix of $\hat{\boldsymbol\pi}_1' = (\hat{\pi}_1, \ldots, \hat{\pi}_{k-1})$ is

$$V_{\boldsymbol\pi} = W(\hat{\boldsymbol\theta})VW(\hat{\boldsymbol\theta})', \tag{3.9}$$

where $V = M(\hat{\boldsymbol\theta})^{-1}$ is the estimated covariance matrix for $\hat{\boldsymbol\theta}$. It will be noticed that the matrices $B(\hat{\boldsymbol\theta})$ and $C(\hat{\boldsymbol\theta})$ are easily calculated from quantities already computed when obtaining $\hat{\boldsymbol\theta}$.

3.4 Some Simple Extensions

In many studies, some of the individuals are observed only over part of the observation period. If individuals who enter or leave the observation period are like those who stay in the study in all relevant respects (the same transition probabilities apply to both groups), then the methods apply without change. Note, however, that $N_i(t_{l-1})$ of (3.5) is the number of individuals in state i at t_{l-1} for whom the state occupied at t_l is known.

It is similarly unnecessary that all individuals be observed over the same set of time points. The amount of computation, however, increases linearly with the number of distinct time intervals w_l in the sample.

These methods can be extended in a simple way to fit certain nonhomogeneous Markov models. Suppose, for example, that $\{X(t)\}$ is a Markov process with time-dependent intensity matrix $Q(t) = Q_0 \cdot g(t; \lambda)$, where Q_0 is a fixed intensity matrix with unknown entries (q_{ij}), and $g(t; \lambda)$ is a known function of time up to an unspecified parameter λ. In this case, $g(t; \lambda)$ defines, for given λ, an operational time. For given λ, let $s = \int_0^t g(u; \lambda)\, du$ and define $Y(s) = X(t)$. The process $\{Y(s): 0 < s < \infty\}$ is then a homogeneous Markov process with intensity matrix Q_0. Thus for any given λ we replace t_l with $s_l = \int_0^{t_l} g(u; \lambda)\, du$ and w_l with $w_l^* = s_l - s_{l-1}$. The parameters of Q_0 are estimated by the methods outlined above. In addition, the maximized log-likelihood can be obtained for that λ. By varying λ, this additional parameter can be estimated by observing the effect on the maximized log-likelihood. Our approach to variance estimation and confidence intervals is to consider λ as fixed (usually at the value $\hat{\lambda}$, which maximizes the maximized log-likelihood) and then to use the estimated covariance matrix $M(\hat{\boldsymbol\theta})^{-1}$ for the corresponding estimate $\hat{\boldsymbol\theta}$ of $\boldsymbol\theta$. The associate editor has pointed out the similarity between the interpretation and treatment of the λ parameter here and that of the "conditional" approach to the estimation of the transformation parameter λ in the transformation family of Box and Cox (1964); see Hinkley and Runger (1984) for a review and discussion of this topic.

A second type of time-dependent model can also be treated. In this, the transition matrix $Q(t)$ is allowed to change at the observation times but is constant between observation times. Thus, for example, we might consider

$$Q(t) = Q_1, \quad 0 \le t < t_{m_1}$$
$$= Q_2, \quad t_{m_1} \le t < t_m,$$

for some specified m_1 less than m. Estimation of Q_1 and Q_2 proceeds by treating the first m_1 and the second $m_2 - m_1$ time intervals separately.

4. SOME FURTHER ASPECTS OF ESTIMATION

In this section we discuss some points associated with implementing the algorithm for maximum likelihood estimation. Many of these comments have to do with the shape of the likelihood function and the information available about the parameters.

1. An initial estimate $\boldsymbol{\theta}_0$ of $\boldsymbol{\theta}$ can usually be obtained in an ad hoc way by examining the transition counts n_{ijl}; an example is given in Section 6. An alternative approach would involve a preliminary tabulation of the likelihood surface.

2. There is an advantage to parameterizing the model by writing $q_{ij} = \exp(a_{ij})$, $i \neq j$. This is because the parameters a_{ij} can take any real value whereas $q_{ij} \ge 0$. This reparameterization avoids problems that can arise when an iteration results in parameter vectors outside the parameter space. Note also that it is possible to have $q_{ij} = 0$. When this happens, successive iterates of a_{ij} will typically become large and negative. In this situation we have found it useful to set the corresponding $q_{ij} = 0$ and fit the model, against using the a_{ij}'s, with one less parameter. The resulting estimate is then compared with one in which q_{ij} is taken as a small positive value.

3. When the times w_l between successive observations are large, it is clear on intuitive grounds that not all parameters will be well estimated. The result can be a likelihood surface for the q_{ij}'s or a_{ij}'s that has ridges defined by certain parameters that are imprecisely estimated. For example, if the w_l's are very large and the process is ergodic, then $p_{ij}(w_l) \doteq \pi_j$, where $\boldsymbol{\pi}' = (\pi_1, \ldots, \pi_k)$ is the vector of equilibrium probabilities. In this case, a large number of individuals under study will allow precise estimation of $\boldsymbol{\pi}$, but individual q_{ij}'s will be imprecisely estimated.

4. If $w_l = w$ for all l, it may be possible to determine $\hat{\boldsymbol{\theta}}$ in a relatively simple way. The empirical transition matrix $\tilde{P}(w)$ with $\tilde{p}_{ij\cdot}(w) = n_{ij\cdot}/n_{i\cdot\cdot}$, where $n_{ij\cdot} = \sum_{l=1}^{m} n_{ijl}$ and $n_{i\cdot\cdot} = \sum_{j=1}^{k} n_{ij\cdot}$, provides an estimate of $P(w)$. If the equation $\tilde{P}(w) = \exp(Qw)$ admits a solution $\hat{Q} = Q(\hat{\boldsymbol{\theta}})$, then $\hat{\boldsymbol{\theta}}$ is a MLE of $\boldsymbol{\theta}$. The conditions under which this approach can be used are very restrictive. There is a close relationship with the so-called embeddability problem (see Singer and Spilerman 1976a), which is discussed in Section 7.

An Illustrative Example. Consider an ergodic two-state process with

$$Q = \begin{pmatrix} -\alpha & \alpha \\ \beta & -\beta \end{pmatrix},$$

where $\alpha, \beta > 0$. It is easily shown that

$$P(w) = (p_{ij}(w)) = \begin{pmatrix} 1 - \pi + \pi e^{-\psi w} & \pi(1 - e^{-\psi w}) \\ (1 - \pi)(1 - e^{-\psi w}) & \pi + (1 - \pi)e^{-\psi w} \end{pmatrix}, \tag{4.1}$$

where $\pi = \alpha/(\alpha + \beta)$ and $\psi = \alpha + \beta$. Suppose that $w_l = w$ $(l = 1, \ldots, m)$ so that the likelihood (3.1) can be written as

$$L = [1 - p_{12}]^{n_{11\cdot}} p_{12}^{n_{12\cdot}} p_{21}^{n_{21\cdot}} [1 - p_{21}]^{n_{22\cdot}}, \tag{4.2}$$

where $p_{ij} = p_{ij}(w)$. For fixed w, the parameter space $\{(\pi, \psi)$: $0 < \pi < 1, \psi > 0\}$ is mapped one to one by (4.1) onto $A = \{(p_{12}, p_{21})$: $0 < p_{12} < 1, 0 < p_{21} < 1, p_{12} + p_{21} < 1\}$. We can maximize L for $(p_{12}, p_{21}) \in A$ and then use the relationship (4.1) to obtain $\hat{\pi}, \hat{\psi}$.

Let $\tilde{p}_{12} = n_{12\cdot}/n_{1\cdot\cdot}$, $\tilde{p}_{21} = n_{21\cdot}/n_{2\cdot\cdot}$, which is the unconstrained maximum of (4.2). If $(\tilde{p}_{12}, \tilde{p}_{21}) \in A$, (4.1) can be used to show that

$$\hat{\pi} = \frac{\tilde{p}_{12}}{\tilde{p}_{12} + \tilde{p}_{21}}, \qquad \hat{\psi} = -\frac{1}{w}\log[1 - \tilde{p}_{12} - \tilde{p}_{21}].$$

If, however, $\tilde{p}_{12} + \tilde{p}_{21} \ge 1$, the supremum of L in A lies on the boundary $p_{12} + p_{21} = 1$ and we find

$$\hat{p}_{12} = 1 - \hat{p}_{21} = (n_{11\cdot} + n_{21\cdot})/n_{\cdot\cdot\cdot},$$

where $n_{\cdot\cdot\cdot} = \sum_{i,j} n_{ij\cdot}$. Thus $\hat{\pi} = (n_{11\cdot} + n_{21\cdot})/n_{\cdot\cdot\cdot}$ and $\hat{\psi} = \infty$. The parameter π (which incidentally determines the equilibrium distribution) has an admissible MLE, but the likelihood is, for fixed π, bounded but increasing as $\psi \to \infty$.

Note that $p_{12}(w) + p_{21}(w) = 1 - e^{-\psi w}$. If ψw is large, then $p_{12} + p_{21}$ will be close to one, and it is clear that observations for which $\tilde{p}_{12} + \tilde{p}_{21} \ge 1$ will arise much more frequently than when ψw is small. Finally, we remark that for this two-state case there is a close connection with the embeddability problem in that there is no finite MLE of ψ precisely when the empirical transition matrix $\tilde{P}(w)$ is nonembeddable, but this does not appear to be a general phenomenon. We discuss this further in Section 7.

5. THE INCORPORATION OF COVARIATES

In many applications, there are measured covariates on each individual under study, and interest centers on the relationship between these covariates and the intensities q_{ij} in the Markov model. One advantage of the methods in Section 3 is that they generalize in a straightforward way to allow for the regression modeling of Q, though with many distinct covariate values in the sample, computations may be too extensive to be easily implemented directly. Implementation may require that the covariates be grouped.

Suppose that each individual has an associated vector of s covariates, $\mathbf{z}' = (z_1, z_2, \ldots, z_s)$, where $z_1 = 1$. For given $\mathbf{z}$, we suppose that the process is homogeneous Markov with transition intensity matrix

$$Q(\mathbf{z}) = (q_{ij}(\mathbf{z})),$$

where

$$q_{ij}(\mathbf{z}) = \exp(\mathbf{z}'\boldsymbol{\beta}_{ij}), \quad i \neq j, \tag{5.1}$$

and $q_{ii}(\mathbf{z}) = -\sum_{j \neq i} q_{ij}(\mathbf{z})$. In (5.1), $\boldsymbol{\beta}_{ij} = (\beta_{1ij}, \ldots, \beta_{sij})'$ is a vector of s regression parameters relating the instantaneous rate of transitions from state i to state j to the covariates $\mathbf{z}$. In most applications, some of the regression parameters are specified (usually taken to be zero) and only a subset is to be estimated; the relationship between components of $\mathbf{z}$ and a subset of the transition rates would usually be of interest.

The particular parametric form in (5.1), a log-linear model for the Markov rates $q_{ij}(\mathbf{z})$, is chosen primarily for analytical convenience; other parameterizations may be more appropriate in particular applications. This model has, however, the attractive feature of yielding nonnegative transition intensities for any $\mathbf{z}$ and $\boldsymbol{\beta}_{ij}$'s, and it has been suggested by several authors. Tuma and Robins (1980, pp. 1034–1035) provided an example.

The algorithm of Section 3 requires a separate canonical decomposition of $Q(\mathbf{z})$ for each of the r distinct covariate vectors $\mathbf{z}$ in the sample. Let these be denoted by $\mathbf{z}_h = (z_{1h}, \ldots, z_{sh})$ with $z_{1h} = 1$, and let

$$Q_h = Q(\mathbf{z}_h) = (q_{ij}(\mathbf{z}_h)), \qquad h = 1, \ldots, r,$$

as defined in (5.1). Let $n_{ijl}^{(h)}$ be the number of individuals with covariate values $\mathbf{z}_h$ that are in state i at t_{l-1} and state j at t_l. The likelihood is then a product of terms like (3.1), where the hth term arises from data collected on a homogeneous model with intensity matrix Q_h. Thus the log-likelihood is

$$\log L(\boldsymbol{\theta}) = \sum_{h=1}^{r} \sum_{l=1}^{m} \sum_{i,j=1}^{k} n_{ijl}^{(h)} \log p_{ij}(w_l; \mathbf{z}_h),$$

where

$$P_h(t) = \exp(Q_h t) = (p_{ij}(t; \mathbf{z}_h)).$$

The parameter $\boldsymbol{\theta}$ is being used to indicate the vector of parameters in $\boldsymbol{\beta}_{ij}$ $(i \neq j)$ that are to be estimated. The maximum likelihood equations involve the sum of r terms, one for each $\mathbf{z}_h$. Thus the score vector is

$$S(\boldsymbol{\theta}) = \sum_{h=1}^{r} S^{(h)}(\boldsymbol{\theta}),$$

where $S^{(h)}(\boldsymbol{\theta})$ is computed as outlined in Section 3 [see Equation (3.5)]. In like manner, the Fisher scoring matrix $M(\boldsymbol{\theta}) = \sum M^{(h)}(\boldsymbol{\theta})$ is obtained by calculating the scoring matrix $M^{(h)}(\boldsymbol{\theta})$ for each h using (3.6) and formulas (3.3) and (3.4). The algorithm requires the derivatives of $P_h(t)$ with respect to the elements of $\boldsymbol{\theta}$, so a separate diagonalization of each Q_h is required. Note that the computation of $G^{(u)}$ in (3.4) requires calculation of the derivatives of $Q(\mathbf{z}_h)$ with respect to θ_u. Since $\theta_u = \beta_{cij}$ for some c, i, j, these derivatives are easily calculated; we find

$$\partial Q(\mathbf{z}_h)/\partial \beta_{cij} = z_{ch} q_{ij}(\mathbf{z}_h) L,$$

where L is a $k \times k$ matrix with all elements 0 except $L_{ij} = 1$ and $L_{ii} = -1$.

The specification and fitting of models with covariates is discussed further in Section 6.

6. ILLUSTRATIONS

In a study on smoking behavior, children from two Ontario counties (Waterloo and Oxford) who were entering sixth grade at time $t_0 = 0$ were surveyed at times (in years) $t_1 = .15$, $t_2 = .75$, $t_3 = 1.10$, and $t_4 = 1.90$. The study was designed to compare a control group from each county with a treatment group who received educational material on smoking during the first two months of study. A part of the information obtained at each follow-up time was the "smoking status" of each child, which is classified into three states:

State 1—child has never smoked.
State 2—child is currently a smoker.
State 3—child has smoked, but has now quit.

We consider a homogeneous Markov process with intensity matrix

$$Q = \begin{pmatrix} -\theta_1 & \theta_1 & 0 \\ 0 & -\theta_2 & \theta_2 \\ 0 & \theta_3 & -\theta_3 \end{pmatrix},$$

where $\theta_i > 0$ $(i = 1, 2, 3)$ as a model for the underlying continuous-time process for "smoking status." The purpose of our discussion is to illustrate the methodology developed in earlier sections, and not to present a thorough analysis of the data.

Figure 1 presents the transition counts n_{ijl} $(i, j = 1, 2, 3; l$

(t_0, t_1)

	1	2	3	
1	93 (96.0)	3 (1.7)	2 (.3)	98
2	0 (0)	8 (12.9)	10 (5.1)	18
3	0 (0)	1 (.5)	8 (8.5)	9

(t_1, t_2)

	1	2	3	
1	89 (85.7)	2 (4.2)	2 (3.1)	93
2	0 (0)	7 (4.0)	5 (8.0)	12
3	0 (0)	5 (2.8)	15 (17.2)	20

(t_2, t_3)

	1	2	3	
1	83 (84.9)	3 (2.9)	3 (1.2)	89
2	0 (0)	9 (6.8)	5 (7.2)	14
3	0 (0)	2 (2.3)	20 (19.7)	22

(t_3, t_4)

	1	2	3	
1	76 (74.5)	3 (4.3)	4 (4.3)	83
2	0 (0)	6 (3.7)	8 (10.3)	14
3	0 (0)	0 (4.3)	28 (23.7)	28

Figure 1. Transition Counts for Four Time Intervals. Expected transition counts are in parentheses.

	1	2	3	
1	61 (62.4)	1 (1.4)	2 (.2)	64
2	0 (0)	8 (11.5)	8 (4.5)	16
3	0 (0)	1 (.5)	7 (7.5)	8

	1	2	3	
1	59 (57.3)	1 (2.6)	1 (1.2)	61
2	0 (0)	7 (4.7)	3 (5.3)	10
3	0 (0)	3 (1.9)	14 (15.1)	17

	1	2	3	
1	56 (56.1)	2 (2.1)	1 (.8)	59
2	0 (0)	8 (5.9)	3 (5.1)	11
3	0 (0)	2 (1.7)	16 (16.3)	18

	1	2	3	
1	51 (51.2)	2 (2.9)	3 (1.9)	56
2	0 (0)	6 (4.4)	6 (7.6)	12
3	0 (0)	0 (2.6)	20 (17.4)	20

Figure 2. Transition Counts for High-Risk Individuals. Expected transition counts are in parentheses.

$= 1, \ldots, 4$) for the "Oxford treatment" group. From these data, the scoring algorithm of Section 3.1 gives the MLE of Q as

$$\hat{Q} = \begin{pmatrix} -.136 & .136 & 0 \\ 0 & -2.28 & 2.28 \\ 0 & .470 & -.470 \end{pmatrix}.$$

Initial estimates for the algorithm can be obtained in several ways. One possibility is to use a single interval (e.g., t_2, t_3) and to assume that individuals make 0 or 1 transitions in the interval. Thus, for example, we obtain an initial estimate of q_{11} from $\exp(q_{11}(t_3 - t_2)) = 83/89$. The corresponding estimates, .20, 1.26, and .27 for θ_i ($i = 1, 2, 3$) are adequate. The asymptotic covariance matrix for $\hat{\boldsymbol{\theta}}$ can also be obtained from (3.6) and used to give approximate confidence intervals for the θ's.

Questions of fit of the Markov model can, to some extent, be assessed by comparing observed transition frequencies, n_{ijl}, with expected frequencies, $e_{ijl} = n_{i,l}\hat{p}_{ij}(w_l)$, where $n_{i,l} = \sum_{j=1}^{k} n_{ijl}$. A likelihood ratio, or asymptotically equivalent Pearson chi-squared statistic to test the fit of the Markov model is readily obtained by methods similar to those used in Markov chains (e.g., Anderson and Goodman 1957). If none of the $p_{ij}(w_l)$'s is restricted to be zero, the likelihood ratio statistic is

$$\Lambda = 2 \sum_{l=1}^{m} \sum_{i,j=1}^{k} n_{ijl} \log(n_{ijl}/e_{ijl}),$$

which is asymptotically (m fixed, $n \to \infty$) a chi-squared variate on $mk(k - 1) - b$ degrees of freedom. The related Pearson statistic is

$$\chi^2 = \sum_{l=1}^{m} \sum_{i,j=1}^{k} (n_{ijl} - e_{ijl})^2/e_{ijl}.$$

For the example at hand, $p_{21}(w_l) = p_{31}(w_l) = 0$, and the degrees of freedom become $4m - b = 13$. We find that $\Lambda = 33.2$ and $\chi^2 = 19.9$. Although these are based on some small frequencies, it is apparent that there is fairly strong evidence against the Markov model.

It is common to find that time-homogeneous Markov models are not strictly appropriate. Fitting Markov models is, nonetheless, a useful and often necessary first step in developing a suitable model. The time-homogeneous Markov model is a convenient baseline; insight can be obtained by examining the nature of departures from this model.

In the present situation, other models provide a somewhat better fit to the data. The population is very heterogeneous, and one possibility is to examine more homogeneous subgroups. Data were collected on each child, which pertained to the exposure he/she received from relatives and friends that smoked. On this basis, each child was assigned to a "high risk" or a "low risk" group. The observed and expected transition rates from the high risk group are given in Figure 2. We find $\Lambda = 22.4$, and the fit of the Markov model is somewhat better.

Other possibilities also arise. Examination of Figures 1 and 2 shows that the number of transitions from State 2 to State 3 is unusually high in the first interval that immediately follows the treatment program. A Markov model describes much more accurately subsequent transition patterns in these data. Another possibility is to consider time dependence in the transition intensities. One approach is to fit separate models to different time intervals and to compare the estimated transition intensities. Another approach is to fit a parametric time-dependent model. For example, we considered models with

$$q_{ij}(t) = q_{ij}e^{-\lambda t} \quad \text{for} \quad i, j = 2, 3$$

to look for a monotone trend in the propensity of individuals to alter their smoking habits as they get older. This gives no significant improvement in this instance.

Comparisons among the four treatment-county groups are also of interest. These can be done using likelihood ratio tests or by the methods of Section 5, which utilize a regression

Table 1. Simulated Data From Model (6.1)

		(t_0, t_1)			(t_1, t_2)			(t_2, t_3)			(t_3, t_4)			(t_4, t_5)		
z		1	2	3	1	2	3	1	2	3	1	2	3	1	2	3
(0,0)	1	13	2	0	14	1	2	12	2	1	11	0	2	11	1	0
	2	4	8	3	1	9	0	1	6	3	1	7	0	0	6	1
	3	0	0	0	0	0	3	0	0	5	0	0	9	0	0	11
(0,1)	1	14	1	0	16	0	1	19	0	0	17	2	1	16	1	2
	2	3	11	1	3	8	1	1	5	2	2	3	0	3	2	0
	3	0	0	0	0	0	1	0	0	3	0	0	5	0	0	6
(1,0)	1	11	4	0	10	2	2	10	2	3	10	2	2	10	1	0
	2	3	11	1	5	9	1	4	7	0	1	6	2	3	5	0
	3	0	0	0	0	0	1	0	0	4	0	0	7	0	0	11
(1,1)	1	11	3	1	12	1	1	17	1	0	17	0	1	13	1	3
	2	3	11	1	6	6	2	1	5	1	0	6	0	1	5	0
	3	0	0	0	0	0	2	0	0	5	0	0	6	0	0	7

NOTE: Entries are the numbers of transitions over the corresponding time interval.

Table 2. True Values, Maximum Likelihood Estimates, and Estimated Standard Errors for Model (6.1) Fitted to the Data in Table 1

Parameter	True Value	MLE	Estimated Standard Error
a_{12}	−2.30	−2.177	.356
β_1	.50	.700	.406
β_2	−.50	−.772	.406
a_{13}	−2.30	−2.659	.235
a_{21}	−1.90	−1.389	.278
β_3	.50	.284	.307
β_4	.50	.111	.304
a_{23}	−2.30	−2.246	.254

model. The Markov model, however, does not fit the data sufficiently well that one would want to base comparisons solely on it.

To illustrate the methods of Section 5, we consider data simulated from a three-state Markov process with transition matrix

$$\begin{pmatrix} q_{11}(z) & e^{a_{12}+z_1\beta_1+z_2\beta_2} & e^{a_{13}} \\ e^{a_{21}+z_1\beta_3+z_2\beta_4} & q_{22}(z) & e^{a_{23}} \\ 0 & 0 & 0 \end{pmatrix}, \qquad (6.1)$$

which is a natural regression generalization of the marital status example leading to (2.1). For the simulation, the parameters were $a_{12} = a_{13} = a_{23} = -2.30$, $a_{21} = -1.90$, $\beta_1 = \beta_3 = \beta_4 = .50$, and $\beta_2 = -.50$. It was assumed that 15 individuals began in each of States 1 and 2 at time $t_0 = 0$, for each of four groups with regression vectors $(z_1, z_2) = (0, 0), (0, 1), (1, 0), (1, 1)$, respectively. The simulated data are presented in Table 1.

Convergence to the MLE's was rapid, and the region of convergence appeared to be reasonably broad. Convergence occurred from starting values obtained by a method similar to that used in the previous example. The MLE's and their estimated standard errors are given in Table 2. These results allow simple expression of approximate confidence intervals for the parameters. The overall likelihood ratio statistic for testing the fit of the model is $\Lambda = 78.69$ on $80 - 8 = 72$ df, indicating no lack of fit.

7. EMBEDDABILITY AND ESTIMABILITY

Consider again the homogeneous case of Section 2, and suppose that the observation times are equally spaced so that $w_l = w$ $(l = 1, \ldots, m)$. In addition, suppose that the model is saturated so that the elements of $\boldsymbol{\theta}$ are the intensities q_{ij} $(i \neq j)$ and the parameter space is

$$\mathbf{Q} = \{Q = (q_{ij}): q_{ij} \geq 0, q_{ii} = -\sum_{j \neq i} q_{ij}\},$$

the set of admissible intensity matrices. In this case, the likelihood (3.1) can be written as

$$L(\boldsymbol{\theta}) = \prod_{i,j=1}^{k} p_{ij}(w)^{n_{ij.}}, \qquad (7.1)$$

where $n_{ij.} = \sum_{l=1}^{m} n_{ijl}$ is the total number of recorded transitions from i to j. Since, for each i, the likelihood (7.1) is of multinomial form, a natural estimate of $P(w)$ is $\tilde{P}(w) = (\tilde{p}_{ij}(w))$, where

$$\tilde{p}_{ij}(w) = n_{ij.} \Big/ \sum_{j=1}^{k} n_{ij.}, \qquad i, j = 1, \ldots, k.$$

If there exists a matrix $\hat{Q} \in \mathbf{Q}$ such that

$$\tilde{P}(w) = \exp(\hat{Q}w), \qquad (7.2)$$

if follows that $\hat{Q}$ is a maximum likelihood estimate of Q. When applicable, this method gives a simple procedure for maximizing the likelihood (7.1) with respect to $Q \in \mathbf{Q}$.

This approach leads one to consider those conditions on a stochastic matrix P under which the equation

$$\exp(Q) = P \qquad (7.3)$$

admits a solution $Q \in \mathbf{Q}$. This is known as the embeddability problem for homogeneous Markov processes and has been discussed by many authors; for example, see Kingman (1962), Kingman and Williams (1973), Frydman (1980), who extended the problem to include nonhomogeneous processes, and Singer and Spilerman (1976a), who reviewed the area. If $k = 2$, P is embeddable if and only if $\operatorname{tr}(P) > 1$. Simple necessary and sufficient conditions for general k are not known. Equation (7.3) can, however, admit 0, 1 or many solutions in Q for a given P.

Although characterization of embeddability is an interesting and challenging mathematical problem, the implications for the analysis of panel data would seem to be few. There are several reasons for this:

1. If $\tilde{P}(w)$ is nonembeddable, this does not imply that the continuous-time Markov model gives a poor fit to the data, nor that the parameters in that model are poorly estimated. Although $\tilde{P}$ is nonembeddable, there might be stochastic matrices "close" to $\tilde{P}$ that are embeddable (see Example 7.1 below).
2. If $\tilde{P}(w)$ is embeddable, it is quite possible that many of the parameters of the continuous-time model are nonetheless very poorly estimated (see Example 7.2).
3. The approach of estimating Q by solving (7.2) is applicable only if the model is saturated (parameter space is $\mathbf{Q}$) and the observation times are equally spaced. Models and sampling plans used in many applications do not meet these requirements. In addition, this approach allows no possibility of generalization to incorporate covariates.

These observations suggest that considerations of embeddability of $\tilde{P}(w)$ are largely irrelevant with respect to important statistical questions. In addition, even when the approach embodied in (7.2) is possible, it is preferable to consider maximization of (7.1) over the space $\mathbf{Q}$ directly. By so doing, estimates are obtained even if $\tilde{P}$ is nonembeddable and the covariance matrix M^{-1} provides estimates of precision.

We now give three examples that illustrate and extend points already made.

Example 7.1. (See remark 1 above.) Suppose that 100 individuals, beginning in each of $k = 3$ states, are observed over one transition of length $w = 1$, and the observed transition matrix is

$$\tilde{P} = \tilde{P}(1) = \begin{pmatrix} .8 & .2 & .0 \\ .1 & .8 & .1 \\ .2 & .1 & .7 \end{pmatrix}.$$

For any irreducible Markov process with intensity matrix Q, it is clear that all entries of $\exp(Q)$ are nonzero, and since $\tilde{p}_{13} = 0$, it follows that $\tilde{P}$ is nonembeddable. The approach to estimation embodied in (7.2) fails. The algorithm outlined in Section 2, however, converges to

$$\hat{Q} = \begin{pmatrix} -.237 & .237 & 0 \\ .111 & -.231 & .120 \\ .262 & .102 & -.364 \end{pmatrix},$$

which corresponds to

$$\hat{P} = \exp(\hat{Q}) = \begin{pmatrix} .800 & .189 & .011 \\ .100 & .810 & .090 \\ .200 & .100 & .700 \end{pmatrix},$$

in general good agreement with the observed transition rates. In addition, all elements of Q are well estimated. Although $\tilde{P}$ is nonembeddable, there are stochastic matrices "close" to $\tilde{P}$ that are embeddable.

Example 7.2. (See remark 2 above.) Suppose that

$$\tilde{P} = \begin{pmatrix} .51 & .49 \\ .49 & .51 \end{pmatrix}$$

is an estimate based on 100 individuals beginning in each of States 1 and 2 and observed for a single transition over a period of length $w = 1$. Since $\text{tr}(\tilde{P}) > 1$, $\tilde{P}$ is embeddable, and there exists a unique matrix,

$$\hat{Q} = \log \tilde{P} = \begin{pmatrix} -1.956 & 1.956 \\ 1.956 & -1.956 \end{pmatrix},$$

the maximum likelihood estimate of Q. Application of the algorithm in Section 2 leads to this same estimate along with estimates of standard errors. It is easily seen that, although $\hat{Q}$ is unique, only the equilibrium distribution is estimated with precision. In effect, any Q with equilibrium distribution $(\pi_1, \pi_2) = (.5, .5)$ and with large entries will yield a corresponding P that is consistent with the observed transition frequencies.

Example 7.3. There have been many remarks in the literature concerning the possibility that (7.3) may admit multiple solutions $Q \in \mathbf{Q}$. When this occurs, there are multiple maximum likelihood estimates of Q. In this example, we examine conditions under which this can occur, in the case $k = 3$.

Let $Q = (q_{ij})$ be the intensity matrix of a three-state ergodic process, and let $\boldsymbol{\pi} = (\pi_1, \pi_2, \pi_3)'$ be the equilibrium distribution. Since $\boldsymbol{\pi}$ is the left eigenvector of the latent root $\lambda = 0$ of Q, it follows, after some algebra, that

$$Q = \gamma H^{-1} \begin{pmatrix} 0 & 0 & 0 \\ 0 & -1 - b & c \\ 0 & (a - b^2)/c & -1 + b \end{pmatrix} H,$$

where

$$H = \begin{pmatrix} \pi_1 & \pi_2 & \pi_3 \\ 1 & 0 & -1 \\ 0 & 1 & -1 \end{pmatrix} = \begin{pmatrix} 1 & \pi_2 + \pi_3 & -\pi_2 \\ 1 & -\pi_1 & \pi_1 + \pi_3 \\ 1 & -\pi_1 & -\pi_2 \end{pmatrix}^{-1},$$

$$\gamma = -(q_{11} + q_{22} + q_{33})/2,$$

and

$$-1 - b = \frac{q_{11} - q_{31}}{\gamma}, \quad c = \frac{q_{12} - q_{32}}{\gamma}, \quad \frac{a - b^2}{c} = \frac{q_{21} - q_{31}}{\gamma}.$$

If $a < 0$, the remaining two latent roots are complex, and if $a_1^2 = -a$, the relevant 2×2 submatrix is

$$\begin{pmatrix} -1 - b & c \\ (-a_1^2 - b^2)/c & -1 + b \end{pmatrix},$$

with eigenvalues $\lambda = -1 \pm a_1 i$. The left eigenvectors are the rows of

$$K = \begin{pmatrix} \dfrac{-b + a_1 i}{c} & 1 \\ \dfrac{-b - a_1 i}{c} & 1 \end{pmatrix} = c \begin{pmatrix} \dfrac{1}{2a_1 i} & -\dfrac{1}{2a_1 i} \\ \dfrac{b + a_1 i}{2a_1 ci} & \dfrac{-b + a_1 i}{2a_1 ci} \end{pmatrix}^{-1}.$$

For a fixed t, we let $P(t) = \exp(Qt)$ and determine a family of matrices Q_k $(k = 0, 1, 2, \ldots)$, which give rise to the same $P(t) = \exp(Q_k t)$. From the above,

$$Q = \gamma K^{-1} H^{-1} DHK,$$

where $D = \text{diag}(0, -1 + a_1 i, -1 - a_1 i)$ so that

$$P(t) = K^{-1} H^{-1} \exp(\gamma t D) HK.$$

Let k be any integer $(k \neq 0)$ and define $a_1^* = a_1 + 2k\pi/t\gamma$. It can then be seen that $\exp(\gamma t D^*) = \exp(\gamma t D)$, where $D^* = (0, -1 + a_1^* i, -1 - a_1^* i)$. Define also $b^* = ba_1^*/a_1$ and $c^* = ca_1^*/a_1$. In an obvious notation, it follows that $K^* = K$ and the intensity matrix, Q_k say, corresponding to a_1^*, b^*, c^*, H, and γ satisfies

$$\exp(Q_k t) = \exp(Qt).$$

Some additional calculations verify that

$$Q_k = Q + (2k\pi/\gamma a_1 t)(Q + \gamma G),$$

where

$$G = \begin{pmatrix} \pi_2 + \pi_3 & -\pi_2 & -\pi_3 \\ -\pi_1 & \pi_1 + \pi_3 & -\pi_3 \\ -\pi_1 & -\pi_2 & \pi_1 + \pi_2 \end{pmatrix}.$$

If, for example, $\pi_1 = \pi_2 = \pi_3 = \frac{1}{3}$, $a_1 = \frac{1}{4}$, $c = \frac{1}{4}$, $b = 0$, and $\gamma = 1$, then

$$Q = \frac{1}{12} \begin{pmatrix} -9 & 2 & 7 \\ 6 & -7 & 1 \\ 3 & 5 & -8 \end{pmatrix}.$$

Let $P(t) = \exp(Qt)$. For a given t, the matrices

$$Q_k = \frac{1}{12} \begin{pmatrix} -9 & 2 & 7 \\ 6 & -7 & 1 \\ 3 & 5 & -8 \end{pmatrix} + \frac{8k\pi}{12t} \begin{pmatrix} -1 & -2 & 3 \\ 2 & 1 & -3 \\ -1 & 1 & 0 \end{pmatrix}$$

sastisfy $P(t) = \exp(Q_k t)$, $k = \cdots -1, 0, 1, \ldots$. For $Q_k \in \mathbf{Q}$, we require that all entries of Q_k have the proper sign. For fixed $k < 0$ (>0), this happens only if $t > -16k\pi/6$ $(t > 24k\pi)$. Thus, if $k = -1$, $Q_{-1} \in \mathbf{Q}$ only for $t > 16\pi/6 = 8.38$. There are multiple solutions in $\mathbf{Q}$ to $P(t) = e^{Qt}$ only for large t values. For t as large as 8.38, $P(t)$ is observationally indistinguishable from the equilibrium matrix with all rows $(\frac{1}{3}, \frac{1}{3}, \frac{1}{3})$,

$$P(t) = \begin{pmatrix} .33319 & .33324 & .33357 \\ .33350 & .33332 & .33317 \\ .33331 & .33344 & .33326 \end{pmatrix}$$

to five figures.

This and similar examples suggest that multiple roots of (7.2) will not occur in practical applications, at least in the 3×3 case. Equivalently, when $\hat{P}$ is embeddable there will not be multiple maximum likelihood estimates of Q unless $\hat{P}$ is close to the equilibrium matrix. At this time, we have not undertaken a detailed study of higher-dimensioned problems ($k \geq 4$). If, however, multiple MLE's occur, methods similar to those outlined above could be used to determine all of them. Multiple MLE's indicate that the likelihood is badly behaved and point estimates are bound to be misleading.

APPENDIX A: DERIVATION OF (3.4)

Suppose that Q has distinct eigenvalues $d_1, \ldots, d_k$ for all $\boldsymbol{\theta}$ in some open set. The matrix obtained by differentiating each entry in $P(t)$ with respect to θ_u is, from (3.3) and the fact that $Q = ADA^{-1}$,

$$\frac{\partial P(t)}{\partial \theta_u} = \sum_{s=1}^{\infty} \frac{\partial}{\partial \theta_u}\left(\frac{Q^s t^s}{s!}\right)$$

$$= \sum_{s=1}^{\infty} \sum_{l=0}^{s-1} Q^l \frac{\partial Q}{\partial \theta_u} Q^{s-1-l} \frac{t^s}{s!}$$

$$= \sum_{s=1}^{\infty} \sum_{l=0}^{s-1} AD^l G_u D^{s-1-l} A^{-1} \frac{t^s}{s!},$$

where $G_u = A^{-1}(\partial Q/\partial \theta_u)A$. Thus

$$\frac{\partial P(t)}{\partial \theta_u} = A\left(\sum_{s=1}^{\infty} \sum_{l=0}^{s-1} D^l G_u D^{s-1-l} \frac{t^s}{s!}\right) A^{-1}$$

$$= AV_u A^{-1},$$

where V_u is a $k \times k$ matrix with (i, j) element

$$g_{ij}^{(u)} \sum_{s=1}^{\infty} \sum_{l=0}^{s-1} d_i^{s-1-l} d_j^l \frac{t^s}{s!} = g_{ij}^{(u)} \frac{e^{d_i t} - e^{d_j t}}{d_i - d_j}, \quad i \neq j,$$

$$g_{ii}^{(u)} \sum_{s=1}^{\infty} \sum_{l=0}^{s-1} d_i^{s-1} \frac{t^s}{s!} = g_{ii}^{(u)} t e^{d_i t}, \quad i = j,$$

where $g_{ij}^{(u)}$ is the (i, j) element in G_u. This establishes (3.4).

APPENDIX B: DERIVATIONS OF (3.8) AND (3.9)

The $k \times k$ equilibrium probability vector $\boldsymbol{\pi}' = (\pi_1, \ldots, \pi_{k-1}, 1 - \pi_1 - \cdots - \pi_{k-1})$ can be obtained as the unique solution to the system of equations

$$Q_1'\boldsymbol{\pi} = \mathbf{0}, \tag{B.1}$$

where $Q_1 = Q_1(\boldsymbol{\theta})$ is the $k \times (k-1)$ matrix obtained by dropping the last column of $Q(\boldsymbol{\theta})$. Now, $\boldsymbol{\pi}$ is not a particularly simple function of $\boldsymbol{\theta}$ or Q_1, so we will develop derivatives $\partial\pi_i/\partial\theta_j$ by treating $Q_1'\boldsymbol{\pi} = F(\boldsymbol{\theta}, \boldsymbol{\pi})$ as a function defining $\pi_1, \ldots, \pi_{k-1}$ implicitly in terms of $\theta_1, \ldots, \theta_b$.

To obtain derivatives $\partial\pi_i/\partial\theta_j$ $(i = 1, \ldots, k-1)$ for fixed j, we use implicit differentiation of (B.1) with respect to θ_j to obtain the system of equations

$$B(\boldsymbol{\theta}) \begin{pmatrix} \partial\pi_1/\partial\theta_j \\ \vdots \\ \partial\pi_{k-1}/\partial\theta_j \end{pmatrix} + C_j(\boldsymbol{\theta}) = 0, \tag{B.2}$$

where $B(\boldsymbol{\theta})$ is a $(k-1) \times (k-1)$ matrix with (i, j) element

$$\frac{\partial F(\boldsymbol{\theta}, \boldsymbol{\pi})_i}{\partial \pi_j} = \frac{\partial (Q_1'\boldsymbol{\pi})_i}{\partial \pi_j} = q_{ji}(\theta) - q_{ki}(\boldsymbol{\theta}),$$

and where $C_j(\boldsymbol{\theta})$ is the $(k-1) \times 1$ vector given by

$$\frac{\partial F(\boldsymbol{\theta}, \boldsymbol{\pi})}{\partial \theta_j} = \left(\frac{\partial Q_1(\boldsymbol{\theta})}{\partial \theta_j}\right)'\boldsymbol{\pi}.$$

From (B.2), the derivatives $\partial\pi_i/\partial\theta_j$ $(i = 1, \ldots, k-1)$ are given by

$$(\partial\pi_1/\partial\theta_j, \ldots, \partial\pi_{k-1}/\partial\theta_j)' = -B(\boldsymbol{\theta})^{-1}C_j(\boldsymbol{\theta}).$$

The matrix giving all derivatives of $\pi_1, \ldots, \pi_{k-1}$ with respect to each of $\theta_1, \ldots, \theta_b$ is thus

$$W(\boldsymbol{\theta}) = (\partial\pi_i/\partial\theta_j) = -B(\boldsymbol{\theta})^{-1}C(\boldsymbol{\theta}),$$

where $C(\boldsymbol{\theta})$ is the $(k-1) \times b$ matrix with jth column $C_j(\boldsymbol{\theta})$. This establishes formula (3.8).

Formula (3.9) then follows by an application of the multivariate delta theorem (e.g., Rao 1973, p. 388).

[*Received April 1984. Revised June 1985.*]

REFERENCES

Anderson, T. W., and Goodman, L. A. (1957), "Statistical Inference About Markov Chains," *Annals of Mathematical Statistics*, 28, 89–110.

Bartholomew, D. J. (1982), *Stochastic Models for Social Processes* (3rd ed.), London: John Wiley.

——— (1983), "Some Recent Developments in Social Statistics," *International Statistical Review*, 51, 1–9.

Box, G. E. P., and Cox, D. R. (1964), "An Analysis of Transformations" (with discussion), *Journal of the Royal Statistical Society*, Ser. B, 26, 211–252.

Chambers, J. M. (1977), *Computational Methods for Data Analysis*, New York: John Wiley.

Cox, D. R., and Miller, H. D. (1965), *The Theory of Stochastic Processes*, London: Methuen (chap. 4).

Frydman, H. (1980), "The Embedding Problem for Markov Chains With Three States," *Mathematical Proceedings of the Philosophical Society*, 87, 285–294.

Hinkley, David V., and Runger, G. (1984), "The Analysis of Transformed Data," *Journal of the American Statistical Association*, 79, 302–309.

Jennrich, Robert I., and Bright, Peter B. (1976), "Fitting Systems of Linear Differential Equations Using Computer Generated Exact Derivatives," *Technometrics*, 18, 385–392.

Kingman, J. F. C. (1962), "The Imbedding Problem for Finite Markov Chains," *Zeitschrift fur Wahrscheinlichkeitstheorie und Verwandte Gebiete*, 1, 14–24.

Kingman, J. F. C., and Williams, D. (1973), "The Combinatorial Structure of Nonhomogeneous Markov Chains," *Zeitschrift fur Wahrscheinlichkeitstheorie und Verwandte Gebiete*, 26, 77–86.

Rao, C. R. (1973), *Linear Statistical Inference and Its Applications* (2nd ed.), New York: John Wiley.

Singer, B., and Spilerman, S. (1976a), "The Representation of Social Processes by Markov Models," *American Journal of Sociology*, 82, 1–54.

——— (1976b), "Some Methodological Issues in the Analysis of Longitudinal Surveys," *Annals of Economic and Sociological Measurement*, 5, 447–474.

Tuma, N. B., Hannan, M. T., and Groeneveld, L. P. (1979), "Dynamic Analysis of Event Histories," *American Journal of Sociology*, 84, 820–854.

Tuma, N. B., and Robins, P. K. (1980), "A Dynamic Model of Employment Behavior: An Application to the Seattle and Denver Income Maintenance Experiments," *Econometrica*, 48, 1031–1052.

Wasserman, S. (1980), "Analyzing Social Networks as Stochastic Processes," *Journal of the American Statistical Association*, 75, 280–294.

[17]

Econometrica, Vol. 54, No. 6 (November, 1986), 1339–1356

AN ANALYSIS OF THE HEALTH AND RETIREMENT STATUS OF THE ELDERLY[1]

BY ROBIN C. SICKLES AND PAUL TAUBMAN

In this study we use five biennial panels of males in the Retirement History Survey to estimate a model of self assessed health status and retirement status, both of which are categorical dependent variables whose residuals may be correlated. The health variable can take one of four states ranging from better health than others the same age to dead. The retirement variable has two states: working or not working full time. Our maximum likelihood estimator requires ten-way integration of the multivariate normal density function. We outline the Gaussian quadrature formulae used in calculating these multivariate distribution functions. We find many significant variables. Perhaps of most interest is the trade off in retirement between Social Security benefits and wage rates and the sharp decline in retirement before age 62, the earliest date nondisabled men are eligible for benefits. We also find that health is worse for those whose longest occupation is unskilled labor.

KEYWORDS: Health, retirement, panel data, Gaussian quadrature, Social Security benefits.

1. INTRODUCTION

SUBSTANTIAL EMPIRICAL INTEREST has been focused recently on the question of how health and retirement decisions are related. The empirical work to date typically has used a reduced form model and, most recently, nonlinear specifications such as the multinomial logit (Anderson and Burkhauser (1983)) or hazard rate model (Diamond and Hausman (1984), Hausman and Wise (1985)). The aforementioned studies have generally found that health and retirement are not independent and that health and Social Security wealth have significant effects on the retirement decision.

In this paper we focus on the efficient estimation of a structural model of the health and the retirement decisions of the elderly. Our model differs in part from previous work in that we have longitudinal data and random effects that are correlated over time for different individuals. To our knowledge efficient estimates of a structural system of limited dependent variables with random effects have not appeared in the literature. We build our full information maximum likelihood estimator from the univariate results of Butler and Mofitt (1982). With our structural estimates, we can analyze, among other things, the degree to which the endogeneously determined health status affects the probability of retirement and how changes in Social Security benefits and eligibility for transfer payments modify both healthiness and the demand for leisure. The studies cited above addressed these issues in part but either used inefficient estimators or based their

[1] This research was supported by a National Institute of Health grant to the National Bureau of Economic Research. We wish to thank, without implicating, the Editor, C. A. Knox Lovell, G. S. Maddala, Roberto Mariano, Janet Meininger, Janice Shack-Marquez, Peter Schmidt, and an anonymous referee for useful comments. We would also like to thank Alan Mathios for his valuable research assistance. Earlier versions of this paper were presented at the 1985 European Econometric Society meetings in Madrid and the 1985 Joint RSS/ESRC Econometric Study Group Conference at the University of Southampton.

findings on reduced form models. Another study which focused primarily on retirement (Hanoch and Honig (1983)) did not control for random effects. By controlling for heterogeneity we can be more precise and can be more assured of our statistical inferences. Furthermore, we can test whether or not a systems estimator has any empirical appeal by a direct test of the significance of the covariance parameter.

The plan of the paper is as follows. Section 1 discusses the economic model of joint health and retirement status and the variables that enter into it. Section 2 outlines the statistical model. Section 3 discusses the data set used in the analysis and reviews our estimation results. Section 4 concludes.

2. THE ECONOMIC MODEL

Our model contains both a health and a retirement equation. The retirement equation is based on the assumption that an individual maximizes a utility function given by:

$$U = U(C, L, H) \tag{2.1}$$

where C is consumption, L is leisure, and H is health.[2] Health is included to account for pain and suffering and shifts in tastes; e.g., some activities may be less desirable if you have a physically limiting health problem such as arthritis.

Equation (2.1) is maximized subject to a budget constraint and a health production function given in equations (2.2) and (2.3):

$$Y_t = w_t(T - L) + r_t A_t + X_t = P_c C_t + P_H Z_t, \tag{2.2}$$

$$H_t = F(Age_t, Z_t, O_t), \tag{2.3}$$

where w is the hourly wage rate, T is total time (hours) in period t, r is the return on financial investments, A is the amount of financial assets, X is other sources of income including earnings of a spouse, P_c is the price of consumption, P_H is the price of medical care, Z is the amount of medical care, and O is job and personal characteristics.

In principle it is possible to find the first order conditions for a maximum and to obtain demand equations for health, for hours of work and leisure, and for consumption. However, since the theoretical model of retirement is well known and since the information available to us does not allow us to obtain labor supply elasticities, we will merely specify the arguments entering each of the equations.[3]

The standard retirement model asserts that an individual compares the utility generated from working versus that from fully or partially retiring. Utility differs in these situations because working is unpleasant and because income differs. If retired, the individual may be eligible for Social Security benefits and pensions. If he works, he may forfeit all or a part of these benefits and pensions but he

[2] Although our model is a long run static one, some elements of other periods are allowed to enter via discounting future benefits.

[3] See Boskin (1977), Parsons (1980), and Quinn (1977).

receives a wage or salary. Future Social Security and pension payments may also be changed if retirement is postponed. Thus we wish to include in the retirement equation the benefits if retired permanently, the expected change in the benefits if retirement is postponed a year, wage earnings if the person works, and other sources of income.

We define retirement to occur when a person is not working. Based on this definition, people have found that health matters. Within the context of our model, poor health reduces the marginal utility of consumption and of leisure as well as decreasing utility directly.

The general specification of the health equation is based on the work of Anderson and Burkhauser (1983), Grossman (1972), Lee (1982), Taubman and Rosen (1982), and Taubman and Sickles (1984). The unobservable health stock is endogeneously determined and can be augmented by investment in health services or depreciated by the environment of the work place. The health stock differs across individuals and families and is determined in part by: social and demographic factors such as education, longest occupation, race and age; the degree to which an individual is able to gain access to information on available health services which we proxy by marital status, number of children, and education; and ability to pay for health services for which we include income, assets, spouse's income, and pension and social security benefits.

While anecdotal stories exist that suggest retirement per se causes bad health via boredom, we are not aware of any firm evidence that retirement debases health. To the extent that economic decisions are made in a rational fashion, retirement should not directly modify the unobservable health stock. Moreover, Ekerdt (1983) in a detailed study based on medical examinations found retirees' health deteriorated no more than that of a control group of nonretirees. For these reasons, and for reasons of internal model consistency, we specify a triangular model with health affecting retirement but with no feedback from retirement to health.

3. THE STATISTICAL MODEL

Our statistical model is an extension of the single equation limited dependent variable model found in Heckman (1981). The longitudinal nature of the data set is accommodated by using a conventional error components specification (Balestra and Nerlove (1966)) in which heterogeneity among individuals is modeled as a random effect. There are two equations in our system—one which links health status to the retirement decision and one which models changes in the unobservable health stock. Since we argued earlier that these are jointly determined, a systems estimator would be expected to yield more efficient estimates than limited information techniques.[4] In this section we outline both full information (FIML) and limited information maximum likelihood (LIML) estimators.

[4] The potential gains of FIML over two-step estimators in models such as the multivariate error components specification introduced in this study are discussed in Sickles (1985).

The system can be written as

(3.0) $$y_{it}^{*(1)} = x_{it}^{(1)}\beta_1 + \varepsilon_{it}^{(1)},$$

(3.1) $$y_{it}^{*(2)} = \gamma_2 y_{it}^{(1)} + x_{it}^{(2)}\beta_2 + \varepsilon_{it}^{(2)} \qquad (i = 1, \ldots, N;\ t = 1, \ldots, T),$$

where

(3.2) $$\varepsilon_{it}^{(j)} = \mu_i^{(j)} + v_{it}^{(j)} \qquad (j = 1, 2)$$

and where

(3.3) $$E[\varepsilon_{it}^{(j)}\varepsilon_{ks}^{(l)}] = \begin{cases} \sigma_\mu(j) + \sigma_v(j) & \text{for } j = l,\ i = k,\ t = s, \\ \sigma_\mu(j) & \text{for } j = l,\ i = k,\ t \neq s, \\ \sigma_v^{(jl)} & \text{for } j \neq l,\ i = k,\ t = s, \\ 0 & \text{elsewhere.} \end{cases}$$

Here $x_{it}^{(1)}$ and $x_{it}^{(2)}$ are $(1 \times k_1)$ and $(1 \times k_2)$ vectors of exogenous variables, β_1 and β_2 are $(k_1 \times 1)$ and $(k_2 \times 1)$ vectors of structural coefficients, γ_2 is a scalar, $y_{it}^{*(1)}$ and $y_{it}^{*(2)}$ are the unobserved dependent variables for health and retirement, respectively; $y_{it}^{(1)}$ and $y_{it}^{(2)}$ are their observed counterparts; $\varepsilon_{it}^{(1)}$ and $\varepsilon_{it}^{(2)}$ are the structural disturbances which are decomposed by the rule in (3.2). The unobserved are linked to the observed by the following rules:

(3.4) $$y_{it}^{(1)} = j \quad \text{if} \quad A_{j-1}^{(1)} - x_1\beta_1 < \varepsilon_{it}^{(1)} \leq A_j^{(1)} - x_1\beta_1 \qquad (j = 1, \ldots, J_1)$$

with $A_0^{(1)}$, $A_{J_1}^{(1)}$ normalized at $-\infty$, $+\infty$ respectively, and

(3.5) $$y_{it}^{(2)} = j \quad \text{if} \quad A_{j-1}^{(2)} - \gamma_2 y_{it}^{(1)} - x_2\beta_2 < \varepsilon_{it}^{(2)} \leq A_j^{(2)} - \gamma_2 y_{it}^{(1)} - x_2\beta_2 \qquad (j = 1, \ldots, J_2)$$

with $A_0^{(2)}$ and $A_{J_2}^{(2)}$ normalized as $-\infty$, $+\infty$ respectively. The ordered health states recorded in the Retirement History Survey are: health better, the same, and worse than others the same age, and deceased. The retirement states are working full time/not working full time. Thus $J_1 = 4$ and $J_2 = 2$. We use the standard normalization that $\sigma_v(j) = 1$, $j = 1, 2$. Under our maintained assumption that the errors are distributed normally, with joint density $f(\varepsilon_{it}(1), \varepsilon_{is}(2); \sigma_\mu^{(1)}, \sigma_\mu^{(2)}, \sigma_v^{(12)})$, equation (3.4) is the polytomous probit with ordered responses and (3.5) is a binary probit. A computational issue arises when implementing maximum likelihood since calculation of the joint probabilities of observing differing configurations of health-retirement states for the same individual over the T time periods is problematic if the number of time periods is large. Our data set contains five biennial periods. Since the calculation of the joint health-retirement states for an individual at time t requires two dimensional integration, the calculation of the set of health-retirement states for an individual over (at most) five dependent time periods requires ten dimensional integration. Numerical methods for handling such problems are available (Clark (1964)) but are both computationally burdensome and have an approximation error which is difficult to bound.

The evaluation of multi-dimensional integrals for our multivariate error components model, however, is facilitated by the form of the correlation pattern of the disturbances. This point has recently been remade by Butler and Moffitt (1982) who suggest Gaussian quadrature procedures for simpler univariate probit models. For our joint model a similar approach can be taken. Let R_c be the domain of integration for the normal distribution function F corresponding to a particular configuration of health-retirement states for individual i over the T time periods. Then the joint probability of observing these T health-retirement states is

$$\int \underset{R_c}{\cdots} \int dF = \int \underset{R_c}{\cdots} \int f(\varepsilon_{i1}^{(1)}, \ldots, \varepsilon_{iT}^{(1)}, \varepsilon_{i1}^{(2)}, \ldots, \varepsilon_{iT}^{(2)})\, d\varepsilon_{i1}^{(1)}, \ldots, d\varepsilon_{iT}^{(1)}, d\varepsilon_{i1}^{(2)}, \ldots, d\varepsilon_{iT}^{(2)}. \tag{3.6}$$

Let g_1 be the conditional density of $\{v_{i1}^{(1)}, \ldots, v_{iT}^{(1)}, v_{i1}^{(2)}, \ldots, v_{iT}^{(2)}\}$ given $\{\mu_i^{(1)}, \mu_i^{(2)}\}$, g_2 be the conditional density of $\{v_{it}^{(1)}, v_{it}^{(2)}\}$ given $\{\mu_i^{(1)}, \mu_i^{(2)}\}$, h_1 be the marginal density of $\{\mu_i^{(1)}, \mu_i^{(2)}\}$, h_2 be the marginal density of $\mu_i^{(1)}$, and h_3 be the marginal density of $\mu_i^{(2)}$. Because of the assumed error structure $h_1 = h_2 h_3$. Rewrite (3.6) as

$$\begin{aligned}
&\int \underset{R_c}{\cdots} \int dF \\
&= \int \underset{R_c}{\cdots} \int \int_{-\infty}^{\infty} \cdot \int_{-\infty}^{\infty} g_1(v_{i1}^{(1)}, \ldots, v_{iT}^{(1)}, v_{i1}^{(2)}, \ldots, v_{iT}^{(2)}/\mu_i^{(1)}, \mu_i^{(2)}) \\
&\quad h(\mu_i^{(1)}, \mu_i^{(2)})\, d\mu_i^{(1)}\, d\mu_i^{(2)}\, dv_{i1}^{(1)} \cdots dv_{iT}^{(2)} \\
&= \int_{-\infty}^{\infty} h_2(\mu_i^{(1)}) \Bigg\{ \int_{-\infty}^{\infty} h_3(\mu_i^{(2)}) \\
&\quad \Bigg[\int \underset{R_c}{\cdots} \int g_i(v_{i1}^{(1)}, \ldots, v_{iT}^{(1)}, v_{i1}^{(2)}, \ldots, v_{iT}^{(2)}/\mu_i^{(1)}, \mu_i^{(2)}) \\
&\quad dv_{i1}^{(1)} \cdots dv_{i2}^{(2)} \Bigg] d\mu_i^{(2)} \Bigg\}\, d\mu_i^{(1)}.
\end{aligned} \tag{3.7}$$

Since $\{v_{ij}^{(1)}, v_{ik}^{(2)}\}$ $\forall j \neq k$ are independent conditional on $\{\mu_i^{(1)}, \mu_i^{(2)}\}$, expression (3.7) can be written as

$$\begin{aligned}
\int \underset{R_c}{\cdots} \int dF = \int_{-\infty}^{\infty} h_2(\mu_i^{(1)}) \Bigg\{ \int_{-\infty}^{\infty} h_3(\mu_i^{(2)}) \\
\Bigg[\prod_{t=1}^{T} \iint_{R_c} g_2(v_{iT}^{(1)}, v_{iT}^{(2)}/\mu_i^{(1)}, \mu_i^{(2)})\, dv_{it}^{(1)}\, dv_{it}^{(2)} \Bigg] d\mu_i^{(2)} \Bigg\}\, d\mu_i^{(1)}.
\end{aligned} \tag{3.8}$$

The term in brackets can be expressed as

$$\begin{aligned}
&\int_{-\infty}^{\infty} h_3(\mu_i^{(2)}) \Bigg[\prod_{t=1}^{T} \iint_{R_c} g_2(v_{it}^{(1)}, v_{it}^{(2)}/\mu_i^{(1)}, \mu_i^{(2)})\, dv_{it}^{(1)}\, dv_{iT}^{(2)} \Bigg] d\mu_i^{(2)} \\
&= \int_{-\infty}^{\infty} e^{-Z_1^2} \phi_1(Z_1; \mu_i^{(1)})\, dZ_1
\end{aligned} \tag{3.8a}$$

where $Z_1 = \mu_i^{(2)}(2\sigma_\mu^{(2)})^{-1/2}$;

$$\phi_1(Z_1; \mu_i^{(1)}) = \frac{1}{\sqrt{\pi}} \prod_{t=1}^{T} \iint_{R_c} g_2(v_{it}^{(1)}, v_{it}^{(2)}/\mu_i^{(1)}, Z_1(2\sigma_\mu^{(2)})^{1/2})\, dv_{it}^{(1)}\, dv_{it}^{(2)}.$$

The right side of (3.8a) is an expression that can be evaluated exactly with G_1 points by Hermite integration if $\phi_1(Z_1; \mu_i^{(1)})$ is a polynomial of degree $2G_1 - 1$ or less (Stroud and Secrest, 1966, p. 22). In this case, the term in brackets becomes

$$\text{(3.8b)} \qquad \int_{-\infty}^{\infty} \bar{e}^{Z_1^2} \phi_1(Z_i, \mu_i^{(1)})\, dZ_1 = \sum_{g=1}^{G_1} W_{1,g}\phi_1(w_{1,g}; \mu_i^{(1)}) = A(\mu_i^{(1)})$$

and (3.8) can be written as

$$\text{(3.9)} \qquad \int_{R_c} \cdots \int dF = \int_{-\infty}^{\infty} h_2(\mu_i^{(1)}) A(\mu_i^{(1)})\, d\mu_i^{(1)} = \int_{-\infty}^{\infty} e^{-Z_2}\phi_2(Z_2)\, dZ_2$$

where $Z_2 = \mu_i^{(1)}(2\sigma_\mu^{(1)})^{-1/2}$;

$$\phi_2(Z_2) = \frac{1}{\sqrt{\pi}} A(Z_2(2\sigma_\mu^{(1)})^{1/2}).$$

The same argument in (3.8b) can be applied to (3.9) and thus

$$\text{(3.10)} \qquad \int_{R_c} \cdots \int dF = \sum_{g=1}^{G_2} W_{2,g}\phi_2(W_{2,g})$$

where ϕ_2 is assumed to be a polynomial of degree less than or equal to $2G_2 - 1$. Evaluation of (3.10) has been reduced to three nested steps. First, the bivariate distribution function g_2 is evaluated for given $\mu_i^{(1)}$ and $\mu_i^{(2)}$. Next, expression (3.8b) is evaluated for a given $\mu_i^{(1)}$. Finally, the joint probability in (3.9) is calculated. Since $W_{1,g}$, $g = 1, \ldots, G_1$, and $W_{2,g}$, $g = 1, \ldots, G_2$, are known, so are the corresponding Z_1, Z_2 and thus the $\mu_i^{(1)}$ and $\mu_i^{(2)}$ which are involved in the calculation of g_2 and $A(\mu_i^{(1)})$.

Denoting the expression in (3.10) as $P(\theta; y_i^{*(1)}, y_i^{*(2)})$ where

$$\theta = \{\beta_1', \beta_2', \gamma_2, A_1^{(1)}, A_1^{(2)}, A_1^{(3)}, A_2^{(1)}, \sigma_\mu^{(1)}, \sigma_\mu^{(2)}, \sigma_v^{(12)}\},$$

the log likelihood function for the entire sample is

$$\text{(3.11)} \qquad \ln L_N(\theta; y^*) = \sum_{i=1}^{N} \ln P_i(\theta; y_i^{*(1)}, y_i^{*(2)}).$$

We note that attrition occurs in our sample since approximately 80 per cent of the respondents are alive at the end of the sample period. When they die we lose the observation from the sample because respondent information switches to the spouse or is completely lost. No such problem occurs with those who retire and remain alive. They are kept in the sample and almost 15 per cent begin working full-time again in another job and usually with a different employer. Death, however, is an absorption state since the transition probability associated with a movement from death to other health states is zero. Because the joint probability of observing an individual's complete set of sample health-retirement states when he is alive should be unity, there is no need to modify (3.11) after an individual dies and his record is removed from the sample.[5]

Consistent but inefficient estimates of θ can also be generated and used as starting values in the iterative procedure used to maximize (3.11). Since the health equation is a reduced form, limited-information maximum likelihood estimates are gotten by maximizing (3.11) with respect to $(\beta_1, \sigma_\mu^{(1)})$ with $\sigma_\upsilon^{(12)}$ set equal to zero. We consider the LIML estimates of the retirement equation as a special case of FIML where exclusion restrictions from the health equation are not imposed. Write the unrestricted reduced form of (3.0) as

$$(3.12) \qquad y_{it}^{*(1)} = Z_{it}\Pi_1 + \xi_{it}^{(1)}$$

where Z_{it} contains all the predetermined variables of the system and where

$$(3.13) \qquad \xi_{it}^{(1)} = \omega_i^{(1)} + \psi_{it}^{(1)}.$$

The covariance structure of $\xi_{it}^{(1)}$ is

$$E[\xi_{it}^{(1)}\xi_{ks}^{(1)}] = \begin{cases} \sigma_\omega^{(1)} + 1 & \text{for } i = k,\ t = s, \\ \sigma_\omega^{(1)} & \text{for } i = k,\ t \neq s, \\ 0 & \text{otherwise,} \end{cases}$$

and the covariance between $\xi_{it}^{(1)}$ and $\varepsilon_{it}^{(2)}$ is $\sigma_{\psi\upsilon}^{(12)}$. Replace (3.0) with (3.12) and maximize (3.11) with respect to $(\Pi_1', \beta_2', \gamma_2, \sigma_\omega^{(1)}, \sigma_\mu^{(2)}, \sigma_{\psi\upsilon}^{(12)})$. The conditional MLE estimate of $\sigma_\upsilon^{(12)}$ is gotten by concentrating the likelihood function (3.11) with respect to the limited-information estimates of $(\beta_1', \beta_2', \gamma_2, \sigma_\mu^{(1)}, \sigma_\mu^{(2)})$ and maximizing (3.11) with respect to $\sigma_\upsilon^{(12)}$. These consistent estimates of θ could be used in a one-step Newton–Raphson iteration of (3.11) or as starting values in an iterative procedure such as the Berndt–Hall–Hall–Hausman (1974) algorithm which we employ to maximize (3.11).

4. DATA, VARIABLES, AND ESTIMATION RESULTS

The data come from the Retirement History Survey (RHS) which contains five biennial panels taken during the period 1969 through 1977 and individually matched records of Social Security earnings beginning in 1951. The sample contains about 8500 men who were heads of households in 1969.[6] It contains objective health information such as data on death and hospitalization and subjective information such as how one's health compares with others of the same age and how it has changed over time.

Our dependent variable indicator for retirement is constructed in the following fashion. One question asked in the RHS is "are you presently working part time, full time, or are you retired?" We chose to use the working-full-time/not-working-full-time dichotomy instead of either deleting those who are semi-retired or introducing a new category for retirement status. We have examined models in

[5] We thank both Roberto Mariano and Peter Schmidt for contributing to our better understanding of this issue.

[6] Because of potential differences in the way women and men perceive their health, we deleted 2500 women heads of household from our analysis and put off estimating a model with a fully interactive female status dummy.

which we use semi-retired as another category and found comparable results. We rely on either the retired or not retired results for simplicity and comparability with most other studies.

Turning to the health measure, we find a number of empirical studies which conclude that health affects retirement decisions. (See footnote 3.) Many of these studies have used one of two health measures. The first is the answer to a question like "Does your health limit your ability to work or to get about?" For people who retired prior to their 65th birthday, this type of question allows, and perhaps invites, the subject to cite health limitations as a socially acceptable reason. A second health measure frequently used is whether or not a person died within some follow-up time interval. Used alone this is also a far from ideal measure. Deaths from accidents and from diseases which strike swiftly and which would not be preceded by pain, suffering, and loss of ability in earlier years are quite different than those caused by chronic diseases. Long-term debilitating illnesses would not be accurately modeled with the early post-sample death measure while future accidents and the like probably don't affect retirement calculations.

Our study uses a subjective measure of health status which we think is superior to the aforementioned measures. The RHS solicits answers to the question "How does your health compare with that of others of the same age?" The possible responses are better, same, or worse. The public health literature suggests that subjective ratings by the elderly are highly correlated with the arguably more objective physician ratings (Ferraro (1980), Mossey and Shapiro (1982)). Also, in the RHS people who report themselves in worse health are twice as likely to die in a four year span as those in better health (Taubman and Rosen (1982)), and their behavior appears to be consistent with that predicted in the health production function literature (Asher (1982), Taubman and Rosen (1982)). Taubman and Sickles (1984) have used the objective/subjective health variable to analyze the health effects of the Supplemental Security Income (SSI) program with quite reasonable results.

To these subjective rankings we add a fourth category—deceased. While the RHS records a person's death when an interviewer learns of it during an attempted reinterview, interviewers often don't obtain this information. We rely instead on files from Social Security which records this information to stop paying benefits to the decreased, begin paying survivors their benefits, and to justify paying burial allowances. Work by Duleep (1983) indicates that in recent years these files are extremely accurate in obtaining death information. The Social Security data go through 1979. Both year and month of death are given. We have cross-checked the RHS files against Social Security's information up to the 1977 survey date. We found two instances where the RHS lists the person as dead but the other file doesn't. We also found that if Social Security lists an individual as dying between two surveys, the RHS either lists that individual as having no response or the RHS indicates that the respondent is the surviving spouse.

Before turning to the results we should point out that a number of different specifications of the joint health-retirement model were considered. We first examined a model in which the endogenous variables both entered in their unobservable forms as right-hand-side variables. Although we considered only consistent two-step estimators of these models (Mallar (1977)), our results were not at all supportive of this type of fully latent structure. Furthermore, the effect of the unobservable work effort variable on the health stock was negligible and insignificant. Because of the categorical nature of the endogenous variables, structures in which their observed counterparts appear on the right-hand-side are forced to be triangular by the coherency conditions (Gourieroux, Laffont, and Monfort (1980), Heckman (1978)). For our purposes, therefore, only a model in which health affects the mean of retirement or one in which retirement affects the mean of health are empirically relevant and these are nonnested models. We focus on the triangular system in which health determines the mean level of retirement propensity but in which no direct feedback is permitted from retirement to health. Unexplained effects can certainly cause unexplained variations in the two endogenous variables to be correlated and this provides FIML with an efficiency gain over LIML. An examination of the stability of parameter estimates was also carried out at several points in our analysis. Taubman and Sickles (1984) examined the parameter stability of reduced form health models using a larger version of the RHS and found that the thresholds, SSI eligibility, and the sex of the head of household were the most unstable of the significant parameters. In this study we examined only men, had the SSI eligibility variable shifting over time, and allowed for parameter heterogeneity in the thresholds. A formal test of the stability of the other parameters of our system (3.0)-(3.5) was carried out by comparing separate estimates for the first and last time period with estimates when parameters in the first and last time periods were equated. The likelihood ratio test yielded a chi-squared statistic of 19.4 while $\chi^2_{.05,35} \doteq 49$.

The usual rank and order conditions are sufficient for the model to be identified. The particular restrictions we used to achieve identification are the exclusion of the age less than 62 dummy variable and the gain from postponing retirement from the health equation. The excluded variables in the retirement equation are SSI and its interaction with time, and Social Security benefits. Of course, these same benefits are included in the gain from postponing retirement variable, but we restricted the coefficients on all components of this variable to be the same. Such restrictions are equivalent to a zero restriction. We do not see any requirement in economic theory to include the gain variable in the health equation while it properly belongs in the retirement equation.

Due to computational constraints, a random sample of 808 people was selected from the roughly 8500 males in our original sample. The functions ϕ_1 in (3.8a) and ϕ_2 in (3.9) were initially allowed to be polynomials of degree 15 ($G_1 = G_2 = 8$). However, we found very little difference between results based on a polynomial of degree 7 ($G_1 = G_2 = 4$) and the 15 degree polynomial. Because computational expense increases more than linearly with G_1 and G_2, we opted for a $G_1 = G_2 = 4$. The means and standard deviations (calculated from the panel) of the variables used in the analysis are presented in Table I.

Social Security benefits are the benefits one would expect to receive if retirement begins in the respective year. They are computed using covered earnings taken

TABLE I
SAMPLE SUMMARY STATISTICS

Variable	Mean	Standard Deviation
Age	64.3	3.31
Age <62	.215	.411
Black	.0592	.236
Married	.902	.297
Widowed	.0511	.220
Number of Dependents	.229	.713
Receiving SSI	.0275	.164
Years of Education	10.02	3.15
Longest Occupation		
Professional	.218	.409
Clerk	.0893	.285
Skilled Labor	.429	.495
Management	.150	.357
Self-Employed	.104	.305
Social Security Benefits	1716	1642
Income From Assets	1113	3782
Spouse's Earnings	2039	4469
Pension Income	1237	3541
Gain From Postponing Retirement	594	739
Health	1.93	.775
Retirement	1.55	.498

from each person's Social Security record, which is part of the RHS, and then replicating Social Security's rules. Thus we first calculated each person's Average Monthly Earnings (AME). This was accomplished by using the respondent's earnings since 1951, which were truncated at the maximum allowable earnings level. The five lowest years of income are dropped and the sum of the remaining incomes is divided by the number of months worked. The resulting AME is then used to compute the Primary Insurance Amount (PIA) based on the tables in the Social Security Handbook. These account for inflation and therefore change over the 1969–1977 sample period. Once the PIA was computed, the benefits total was determined on the basis of PIA and marital status. By using benefits available rather than those paid to actual retirees, we avoid an obvious selection problem. It should be pointed out that since benefits are increased by 50 per cent if the individual is married, the effect of marital status on both retirement and health will depend in part on the benefits' coefficient.

Income from assets is the sum of yearly income generated from the value of assets: stocks, bonds, life insurance annuities, etc. Pensions are not incorporated in this variable but are included separately.[7] In the U.S. pensions are generally fixed in nominal terms once a person retires; therefore we used the 1975 and 1977 data to calculate the amount of the pension. By 1977 everyone was at least 65 years old. Average income from assets was lower than average Social Security

[7] People drawing pensions retire from a job but can usually return to work at another job with a new employer. Many former government employees work while drawing a government pension. Some nongovernment pensioners also return to work.

benefits but close to average pension income while spouse's earnings were greater than all three.

The gain from postponing retirement is calculated by inflating earnings in 1969 by the percentage increase in the CPI. To this we add the present discounted value of the extra Social Security benefits gained from postponing retirement one additional year where we discounted over the average expected lifetime of the individual. Then we subtracted the Social Security benefits the individual would have received if he had not worked. In these calculations we did not allow for increased annual pensions from working longer since we did not have the data and other studies have indicated wide variation in pension structure across companies including a loss in pension wealth. As noted in Mitchell and Fields (1984), this gain variable may be positively correlated with retirement since the substitution effect (away from leisure) may dominate the income effect (toward leisure).

We included a dummy variable to indicate whether or not the person was eligible in 1975 or 1977 for Supplemental Security Income (SSI), which began in 1974, and interacted this variable with a time trend to identify changes in the health stock over time for SSI eligibles. In an earlier study with a somewhat different model of health (Taubman and Sickles (1984)) it was found that those who were eligible to receive SSI in 1975 or 1977 were in worse health in 1969 than those who would not meet the eligibility criterion, but the differential narrowed over time and became insignificant.

As shown in Table I most of the men are married although widowers make up about 5 per cent of the person-year observations. In our subsample all the men happened to have been married at some point in their life and the omitted category is thus divorced/separated. The most common longest occupation was as a skilled worker with the omitted category of unskilled workers accounting for roughly 25 per cent of the sample.

An interesting problem arises because eligibility for Social Security's old age benefits only occurs at age 62. A 60-year-old could calculate the value of his future Social Security benefit stream and obtain an unsecured loan against it or run down existing assets, but, since (nonhousing) assets are generally small, this may be difficult if capital markets are imperfect. We allow for these difficulties by including in the retirement equation a pre-age-62 dummy variable.[8] We now turn to the estimation results.

The retirement equation, presented in Table II, is familiar to economists although it has a few novel variables as well as some interesting quantitative results. The advantages of not retiring in a particular year are given by the "gain from postponing retirement" variable. It is the most significant of the income variables and its coefficient is an order of magnitude larger than the asset, spouse's earnings, or pension income coefficients. We can easily translate the raw coefficients into marginal probabilities at the sample means by scaling the estimated coefficient by the normal density evaluated at the estimated mean of the

[8] This is not perfectly collinear with a set of time dummies since in 1969 and 1971 some people are not 62.

TABLE II
ESTIMATION RESULTS—RETIREMENT EQUATION

Variable	Coefficient	t Statistic
Age	.192	35.3
Age < 62	−.738	−9.64
Black	.0577	0.36
Married	−.220	−1.74
Widowed	−.176	−1.03
Number of Dependents	−.0271	−0.76
Education	−.0757	−6.44
Professional	.0340	0.25
Clerk	.0404	0.26
Skilled Laborer	.0684	0.57
Management	.0238	0.17
Self-Employed	−0.469	−6.59
Income From Assets	$.161\times10^{-4}$	2.51
Spouse's Earnings	$.179\times10^{-4}$	2.56
Pension Income	$.255\times10^{-4}$	2.15
Gain From Postponing Retirement	$-.206\times10^{-3}$	−6.20
Health	.357	4.45
Threshold 1	11.7	32.2
$\sigma_{\mu}^{(2)}$	.499	11.65

index describing $y^{*(2)}$.[9] If the gain from postponing retirement is increased one standard deviation from its sample mean ($739), then the probability of retiring is reduced by 0.060. Similar increases in income from assets, spouse's earnings, and pension income increase the probability of retirement by about .024, .032, and .036 respectively.

Of the occupation variables, only the self-employed dummy seems to have any significant explanatory power and the effect is quite sizeable: self-employment reduces the probability of retiring by 0.19 relative to the omitted category unskilled labor.

During the 1970's retirement benefits paid by Social Security increased substantially faster than inflation. To some extent benefits grew because of secular growth in wage rates which help determine an individual's PIA and benefits. However, to a large extent, the benefits increased because of two legislated changes. One was the institution of Supplemental Security Income (SSI) to the elderly on welfare.[10] SSI gave money to those on welfare and made them eligible for Medicaid. The other change was the provision of overgenerous protection against changes in the CPI. The indexing provisions were technically deficient because both the benefit schedules and earnings histories, to which the benefit schedules were applied, were shifted with the CPI. Our structural model allows us to examine the consequences of these changes. In preliminary analyses SSI was

[9] The mean index for the retirement equation is 11.86 and the normal density corresponding to $A_1^{(2)}-\bar{X}^{(2)}\beta_2$ is 0.394.

[10] To some extent SSI replaced state based Old Age Assistance but on average it increased benefits substantially.

found to have an insignificant and second order effect in the retirement equation which is why it is excluded in our final results. However, Social Security benefits (embedded in our gain from postponing retirement variable) were quite significant and had a relatively large effect. The first major change in benefits occurred from January 1971 to September 1972 and was about 13 per cent in real terms (Leimer and Lesnoy (1983)). The second major change—basing benefits on wage-indexed earnings—occurred in September 1977. According to figures compiled in Summers (1982), the ratios of primary benefits for an "average-earnings" man retiring at age 65 to earnings in the year before retirement were 34.3, 39.4, 40.7, 43.6, 45.5 for the years 1971, 73, 75, 77, 79. The effect of these Social Security reforms on the probability of retirement seems to be quite small, amounting to only 1.15, .46, 2.60, and 1.71 percentage point increases in the respective years. Although our results do not directly tell us what effect these reforms had on the age of retirement, they indicate that their effect is rather limited and is consistent with the retirement age effects found in Fields and Mitchell (1984) and Hausman and Wise (1983).

Turning to the age variable, we find that it is quite significant and highly correlated with retirement. Based on its coefficient, an individual of 62 is almost 15 per cent less likely to retire than an individual of 64. The dummy for being less than 62 has a highly significant negative coefficient. Finding the effect of age less than 62 is complicated because changing the variable results in an obvious change in age. If we look at the effect of aging one year from 61 to 62, then the probability of retiring increases by almost .37 while aging one year from 60 to 61 increases the probability by almost .075. It would seem that there is evidence for either substantial imperfection in capital markets or a fairly high discount rate for the people in our sample.

Years of schooling have an important bearing on the retirement decision. The better educated retire later in their lives. For example, a college educated male would, at age 64, be almost .12 less likely to retire than a high school graduate. While human capital models often assume that the more educated have the same length of career as the less educated to make the analytics more tractable, there is no necessary reason for this to occur. However, it may well reflect the differential work activities of the more educated which are less affected by aging.

Married and widowed males are both less likely to retire than those who are in the omitted category divorced or separated, although the coefficient for the widowed category is not very significant. The effect of a change in marital status on retirement is confounded by the gain from postponing retirement variable. Since benefits received if one retired are increased by 50 per cent if the individual is married, there is an obvious interaction between the two variables. At average levels of benefits, married males are about 16 per cent less likely to retire than the divorced or separated, with a t statistic of -3.14. The widowed are less likely to retire than the divorced or separated by about .07.

We next focus attention on the health variable which is significant at the 99 per cent level. We find that movement from a poor to a good health status reduces the probability of retirement and thus increases expected average earnings by almost .21. Add to this figure the potential reduction in medical expenditures owing to better health, and there is a substantial real income gain from lower morbidity.

Before moving to the health equation estimates we note that the random effects are sizeable, accounting for almost 50 per cent of the total error variation, and highly significant. Heterogeneity is quite evident in the retirement decision.

We now turn to the health equation, results for which are presented in Table III. Recall that the variable is scaled so that higher numbers indicate worsening health. We present our results as we did with the retirement equation and in general compare states of better health with health same as others the same age.[11]

Focusing first on the economic variables, we see that the only first-order effects come from social security benefits and from pension income. For example, an annual increase in these variables by $10,000 would increase the probability of being in better health by about .14 and .09 respectively.[12] Eligibility for transfer payments from the Supplemental Security Income program are not highly significant although the point estimates provide evidence of the same sort found in

TABLE III

ESTIMATION RESULTS—HEALTH EQUATION

Variable	Coefficient	t Statistic
Age	.0412	6.54
Black	−.137	−1.20
Married	−.0117	−0.11
Widowed	−.164	−1.30
Number of Dependents	.0551	2.11
Education	−.0403	−4.50
Professional	−.342	−3.99
Clerk	−.350	−3.44
Skilled Laborer	−.298	−4.30
Management	−.464	−5.07
Self-Employed	−.0443	−0.67
SSI	3.77	1.22
SSI × Time	−.0506	−1.21
Income From Assets	$-.554 \times 10^{-5}$	−0.92
Social Security Benefits	$-.409 \times 10^{-4}$	−2.90
Pension Income	$-.258 \times 10^{-4}$	−3.91
Spouse's Earnings	$-.201 \times 10^{-5}$	−0.43
Threshold 1	1.29	3.01
Threshold 2	2.82	6.54
Threshold 3	3.79	8.58
$\sigma_\mu^{(1)}$	.379	11.99

[11] Other binary comparisons are easily made by appropriately modifying the thresholds since the only quantitative differences are the $A^{(1)}$'s (and the average value across states for the explanatory variable whose effect we are analyzing). The mean index for the health equation is 1.816 and the normal density associated with the probability of being in better health is 0.347. This will be the scale factor in analyzing the marginal probabilities associated with the raw coefficients.

[12] It is possible that long term ill health has reduced labor market activity and earnings which determine the benefits. Since we do allow for individual specific effects in our equations, we don't think this is the cause of the correlation.

Taubman and Sickles (1984).[13] Those who were eligible for SSI in 1975/77 were in worse health in 1969 than those who would not meet the eligibility criteria but the differential narrowed over time. From 1969–1977 the probability of dying for SSI eligibles vis-a-vis ineligibles fell almost 70 per cent.[14]

The other statistically significant coefficients are on the age, number of dependents, education, and longest occupation variables. Remembering that health is scaled such that poorer health receives a higher number, the age effect is not surprising even if people compare themselves to others of the same age. This means that more older people are dead and/or that people compare themselves to the median rather than the mean person of the same age.

It is generally argued that the more educated are brighter, are better equipped to make decisions, make more informed decisions, and adapt new products more quickly. Thus it is not surprising that the more educated are in better health, ceteris paribus. An increase in completed education from 12 to 16 years would raise the probability of being in better health by about .056.

The omitted longest occupation in our sample is unskilled labor who are in worse health than people in the other occupations. We cannot determine if this occurs because their jobs worsen their health, because less healthy people are more likely to work as unskilled laborers, or because poorer people invest less in health preserving regimes. The probability of being in better health is .16 lower for unskilled laborers than, for example, those who had been in management positions.

An increase from zero to two dependents increases the probability of being in better health by .038 and the effect is significant at the 95 per cent level. There are several possible reasons for this outcome. First, a number of people have argued that larger social networks lead to better health with people exchanging information on health and doctor quality.[15] Second, healthy (unhealthy) parents may beget healthy (unhealthy) children. The unhealthy children may die early. Moreover unhealthy parents may choose to have fewer children because of their low income and energy levels.

We can also examine the direct effect of legislated changes in Social Security benefits on the healthiness of the aged and, through the health and gain from postponing retirement variables, on their propensity to retire. Based on Summers' (1982) figures the total change from 1971–79 in the probability of being in better health due to the reforms was only .0175. The feedback from the health equation would lessen the probability of retiring by only about .0025, reducing the .0592

[13] The t statistic associated with the joint hypothesis that SSI eligibles were in no different health than ineligibles was 1.15 in 1969 and −0.65 by 1977. The difference in significance levels in our two studies may reflect the difference in sample sizes.

[14] One qualification on the SSI results should be noted. Eligibility for SSI in 1975 or 1977 is not completely known for those who died in 1974 or earlier. For those who died prior to 1975 we do have information on whether they were receiving state assistance when the survey starts and they were alive. These people were eligible for SSI. However, it seems that we are still understating the number of eligibles who died prior to 1975. Thus the health of the SSI group between 1969 and 1975 should be worse than our numbers would indicate, meaning that the estimated SSI dummy and the relative improvement over time for the SSI group are probably understated.

[15] See Asher (1982) for a survey on social networks' impact on health and some important evidence.

direct increase in the probability of retiring due to the Social Security reforms of 1971-79 to about .0567.

Heterogeneity is significant and important in the health equation. Although the relative size of the random effects is smaller than with the retirement equation, random effects still contribute almost 27 per cent to the total unexplained variation in the health stock.

A final comment should be made about the use of FIML over LIML estimation. The former is approximately an order of magnitude more cpu intensive than the latter. The estimated correlation between the two equations is −.163 and is highly significant with a t statistic of −3.01. Controlling for heterogeneity in both the retirement and the health equations using direct controls and individual specific random effects seems inadequate in reducing the correlation in unexplained variations to a small and insignificant level. It is clear that the substantial computational investment needed to implement a systems estimator such as FIML is justified on grounds of efficiency.

5. CONCLUSIONS

This study has focused on the structural estimation of a joint health-retirement model in which both sample truncation and error dependencies substantially complicate the implementation of an efficient estimator. We have been able to isolate the effect of perceived health status' on the retirement decision in a structural setting. Furthermore, we have performed several important policy simulations to see how double indexing and increased transfer payments affected the retirement decision both directly and by way of modifications in the health status of the eligible individuals. Our results indicate that retirement decisions are strongly affected by health status, variables that change the shape and position of the income/leisure opportunity set, marital status, self employment status, and education. We also find that those not yet eligible for Social Security are far less likely to retire. This suggests that if part of the solution to the known future financing difficulties of the Social Security system involves raising the normal retirement age to 67 or 68, then a major policy decision is whether to leave 62 as the early retirement age or to raise it to 64 or 65. The latter change would induce more people to work longer and pay more taxes.

Our health equation results indicate that Social Security and pension payments have positive effects on healthiness. The other significant variables are number of dependents and longest occupation being unskilled.

We calculate that the planned and unplanned increases in Social Security benefits in the 1970's raised the probability of retirement by about .057 and increased the probability of being in better health by almost .018.

We also find that random effects are quite important in both equations. Also, due to the rather significant estimated correlation between equations after we control for heterogeneity, efficiency gains from FIML do appear to be worth the computational investment necessary for its implementation.

Department of Economics, Rice University, P.O. Box 1892, Houston, TX 77251, U.S.A.

and

Department of Economics, University of Pennsylvania, Philadelphia, PA 19104-6297, U.S.A.

Manuscript received July, 1984; final revision received March, 1986.

REFERENCES

ANDERSON, K., AND R. BURKHAUSER (1983): "The Effect of Actual Mortality Experience within a Retirement Decision Model," unpublished manuscript, Vanderbilt University, Nashville, TN.

ASHER, C. (1982): "The Impact of Social Support Networks on Adult Health," *Medical Care*, 22, 349-359.

BALESTRA, P., AND M. NERLOVE (1966): "Pooling Cross-Section and Time Series Data in the Estimation of a Dynamic Model: The Demand for Natural Gas," *Econometrica*, 34, 585-612.

BERNDT, E., B. HALL, R. HALL, AND J. HAUSMAN (1974): "Estimation and Inference in Non-linear Structural Models," *Annals of Economic and Social Measurement*, 3, 653-665.

BOSKIN, M. (1977): "Social Security and Retirement Decisions," *Economic Inquiry*, 15, 1-15.

BUTLER, J. S., AND R. MOFFITT (1982): "A Computationally Efficient Quadrature Procedure for the One-Factor Multinomial Probit Model," *Econometrica*, 50, 761-764.

CLARK, C. (1964): "The Greatest of a Finite Set of Random Variables," *Operations Research*, 9, 145-162.

DIAMOND, P., AND J. HAUSMAN (1984): "The Retirement and Unemployment Behavior of Older Men," in *Retirement and Economic Behavior*, ed. by H. Aaron and G. Burtless. Washington, D.C.: Brookings Institution.

DULEEP, H. (1983): "The Socioeconomic Determinants of Mortality: The Role of Income," paper presented at the American Economic Association Winter Meetings, December, 1983.

EKERDT, D., L. BADEN, R. BOSSE, AND E. DIBBS (1983): "The Effects of Retirement on Physical Health," *American Journal of Public Health*, 73, 779-783.

FERRARO, K. (1980): "Self-Ratings of Health Among the Old and the Old-Old," *Journal of Health and Social Behavior*, 21, 377-383.

FIELDS, G., AND O. MITCHELL (1984): "The Effects of Social Security Reforms on Retirement Ages and Retirement Incomes," NBER Working Paper No. 1348, Cambridge, MA.

GOURIEROUX, G., J. J. LAFFONT, AND A. MONFORT (1980): "Coherency Conditions in Simultaneous Linear Equation Models with Endogeneous Switching Regimes," *Econometrica*, 48, 675-696.

GROSSMAN, M. (1972): "On the Concept of Health Capital and the Demand for Health," *Journal of Political Economy*, 80, 223-255.

HANOCH, G., AND M. HONIG (1983): "Retirement, Wages, and the Labor Supply of the Elderly," *Journal of Labor Economics*, 1, 131-151.

HAUSMAN, J., AND D. WISE (1983): "Retirement and Subsequent Work," paper presented at the NBER Conference on Pensions, Labor, and Individual Choice, Dorado Beach, Puerto Rico.

——— (1985): "Social Security, Health Status, and Retirement," in *Pensions, Labor, and Individual Choice*, ed. by D. A. Wise. Chicago: University of Chicago Press.

HECKMAN, J. (1978): "Dummy Endogeneous Variables in a Simultaneous Equation System," *Econometrica*, 46, 931-960.

——— (1981): "Statistical Models for Discrete Panel Data," in *Structural Analysis of Discrete Data with Econometric Applications*, ed. by C. Manski and D. McFadden. Cambridge: MIT Press.

LEE, L. F. (1982): "Health and Wage: A Simultaneous Equations Model with Multiple Discrete Indicators," *International Economic Review*, 23, 199-222.

LEIMER, D., AND S. LESNOY (1983): "Social Security and Private Saving: An Examination of Feldstein's New Evidence," ORS Working Paper Series No. 31, U.S. Department of Health and Human Services, Washington, D.C.

MALLAR, C. D. (1977): "The Estimation of Simultaneous Probability Models," *Econometrica*, 45, 1717-1722.

MITCHELL, O., AND G. FIELDS (1984): "The Economics of Retirement Behavior," *Journal of Labor Economics*, 2, 84-105.

MOSSEY, J., AND E. SHAPIRO (1982): "Self-Rated Health: A Predictor of Mortality Among the Elderly," *American Journal of Public Health*, 72, 800–808.

PARSONS, D. (1980): "The Decline in Male Labor Force Participation," *Journal of Political Economy*, 88, 117–134.

QUINN, J. (1977): "Microeconomic Determinants of Early Retirement: A Cross-Sectional View of White Married Men," *Journal of Human Resources*, 12, 329–346.

SICKLES, R. C. (1985): "An Analysis of Simultaneous Linear Limited Dependent Variable Models and Some Nonstandard Cases," forthcoming in *Advances in Statistical Analaysis and Statistical Computing: Theory and Applications*, Vol. 2, ed. by R. Mariano. Greenwich: JAI Press.

STROUD, A., AND D. SECREST (1966): Gaussian Quadrature Formulas. Englewood Cliffs: Prentice-Hall.

SUMMERS, L. (1982): "Observations on the Indexation of Old Age Pensions," NBER Working Paper No. 1023, Cambridge, MA.

TAUBMAN, P., AND S. ROSEN (1982): "Healthiness, Education and Marital Status," in *Economic Aspects of Health*, ed. by V. Fuchs. Chicago: University of Chicago Press.

TAUBMAN, P., AND R. C. SICKLES (1984): "Supplemental Security Income and the Health of the Poor," NBER Working Paper No. 1062.

[18]

Limited Dependent Variable Models Using Panel Data

G. S. Maddala

ABSTRACT

This paper presents a survey of the methods used in the estimation of limited dependent variable models with panel data. It first reviews some issues in the analysis of panel data when the dependent variables are continuous. The problems of fixed effects vs. random effects and serious correlation vs. state dependence are discussed with reference to continuous data. The paper then discusses these problems with reference to the panel logit, panel probit, and panel tobit models. The paper presents a comparative assessment of these models.

I. Introduction

The present paper reviews some problems that arise in the analysis of panel data when the dependent variables are truncated, censored, or qualitative. The paper discusses panel logit, panel probit, and panel tobit models with fixed and random effects. Hazard rate models and duration models are excluded (for these models, see Amemiya 1985, Chapter 11, and Heckman 1984). The purpose of this paper is to present an overview and comparative assessment of the panel logit, probit, and tobit models which would aid empirical researchers in this area in choosing the appropriate model. For a thorough discussion of particular models, readers can refer to the several papers by Chamberlain, Heckman, and others referred to at the end of the paper.

Before we proceed with our discussion of the limited dependent variable

The author is a professor of economics at the University of Florida. He gratefully acknowledges financial support from the National Science Foundation and thanks James D. Adams for helpful comments. He claims responsibility for any errors.

models, it would be helpful to review some issues in the analysis of panel data when the dependent variables are continuous. This will give us an idea of what problems one needs to address when using the panel data with limited dependent variables.

Since the panel data that we frequently encounter have a large number N of cross-section units but extend over short time periods T, the asymptotic results we would be interested in would be for fixed T and $N \to \infty$.

II. Some Issues in the Analysis of Panel Data with Continuous Variables

A. *Random Effects and Fixed Effects Models*

One of the early uses of panel data in economics was in the context of estimation of production functions where allowance had to be made for unobserved effects specific to each production unit. The model used is now referred to as the "fixed effects" model and is given by

$$(1) \quad y_{it} = \alpha_i + \beta' x_{it} + u_{it} \qquad i = 1, 2, \ldots, N \quad t = 1, 2, \ldots, T$$

where y_{it} is the output and x_{it} the vector of inputs for the ith firm in the tth period, α_i captures the firm specific unobserved inputs assumed to be constant over time, and u_{it} is the error term. We assume $u_{it} \sim IID(0, \sigma^2)$. This model can be estimated by including N intercept dummy variables or by differencing out the α_i's.

The next important step was the model with random effects by Balestra and Nerlove (1966) where α_i in (1) was treated as a random variable just like u_{it}. The model they considered was a dynamic model where $y_{i,t-1}$ is used as an explanatory variable. Since the introduction of $y_{i,t-1}$ creates some problems we discuss later, we will drop it for the present. Denoting $\bar{y}_i = 1/T\,\Sigma_t\, y_{it}$ and $\bar{y} = 1/N\,\Sigma_i\,\bar{y}_i$ we can decompose the total sum of squares $T_{yy} = \Sigma_{i,t}(y_{it} - \bar{y})^2$ into two components as $T_{yy} = \Sigma_{i,t}(y_{it} - \bar{y})^2 = \Sigma_{i,t}(y_{it} - \bar{y}_i)^2 + \Sigma_{i,t}(\bar{y}_i - \bar{y})^2 = W_{yy} + B_{yy}$. W_{yy} measures within group variation and B_{yy} measures between group variation in y. Using a similar decomposition for all the variances and covariances we get the estimator of β from (1) as $\hat{\beta} = W_{xx}^{-1} W_{xy}$ where $W_{xy} = \Sigma_{i,t}(x_{it} - \bar{x}_i)(y_{it} - \bar{y}_i)$. This is known as the "within group estimator." Assuming $\alpha_i \cong IID(0, \sigma_\alpha^2)$ and $u_{it} \cong IID(0, \sigma^2)$ we get the generalized least squares estimator of β in the random effects model as (see Maddala 1971):

$$(2) \quad \hat{\beta}_{GLS} = (W_{xx} + \Theta B_{xx})^{-1}(W_{xy} + \Theta B_{xy})$$

where $\Theta = \frac{\sigma^2}{\sigma^2 + T\sigma_\alpha^2}$

Fuller and Battese (1973) show that this is the same as using the ordinary least squares estimation with the transformed data:

(3) $y_{it} - \lambda\bar{y}_i$ and $x_{it} - \lambda\bar{x}_i$ where $\lambda = 1 - \sqrt{\Theta}$

This transformation is worth noting because:

(i) it puts the model in a form that is easily estimated and

(ii) it collapses to the fixed effects model if $\lambda = 1$.

The arguments for using "random effects" models instead of the fixed effects models are several. If we have a large number of cross-section units, instead of estimating N of the α_i as in the fixed effects models, we estimate only the mean and variance in the random effects models. This saves a lot of degrees of freedom. Another argument is the one in Maddala (1971) that the α_i measures firm specific effects that we are ignorant about just the same way that u_{it} measures effects for the ith cross-section unit in the tth period that we are ignorant about. Thus, if u_{it} is treated as a random variable, then there is no reason why α_i should not also be treated as random. Another argument used in the analysis of variance literature is that if we want to make inferences about only this set of cross-section units, then we should treat α_i as fixed. On the other hand, if we want to make inferences about the population from which these cross-section data came, we should treat α_i as random. In most of the applied work, the latter is the case. Finally, very often we have some time-invariant observations as well, e.g., years of schooling and family background variables in studies of wages. In this case the model is:

(4) $y_{it} = \gamma' z_i + \beta' x_{it} + \alpha_i + u_{it}$

If we use the fixed effects model we cannot estimate the parameters γ, because α_i captures the effect of all the time-invariant variables. In this case one has to use the random effects model.

The choice between the random and the fixed effects formulations should also depend upon the statistical properties of the implied estimators. Later, in our discussion of dynamic models, we will show that with large values of N and small values of T, the fixed effects model gives inconsistent estimates of the parameters. This is because the estimation of the fixed-effects model, which amounts to differencing out the α_i, produces a linear regression model with lagged dependent variables and serially correlated errors. Note that this problem arises with linear regression models, not just the limited dependent variable models discussed later on.

An interesting result occurs if the α_i's are not independent of the x_{it}'s. Mundlak (1978) argues that the dichotomy between fixed effects and random effects models disappears if we assume that α_i depend on the mean values of x_{it}, an assumption he regards as reasonable in many problems. In this case, the random effects and fixed effects models give the same estimator. We have

(5) $\alpha_i = \pi'\bar{x}_i + w_i$

Substituting this in (1), we get

$$y_{it} = \pi'\bar{x}_i + \beta' x_{it} + w_i + u_{it}$$

Using the Fuller and Battese argument, we note that the estimator of β from the random effects model is obtained by the use of ordinary least squares for the equation:

$$\begin{aligned}(6)\quad y_{it} - \lambda\bar{y}_i &= \pi'(\bar{x}_i - \lambda\bar{x}_i) + \beta'(x_{it} - \lambda\bar{x}_i) + v_{it}\\ &= \beta'(x_{it} - \bar{x}_i) + \delta'\bar{x}_i + v_{it}\end{aligned}$$

where $\delta = (\pi + \beta)(1 - \lambda)$ and λ is defined in (3). Since $\bar{x}_i$ is orthogonal to $x_{it} - \bar{x}_i$ and since $\mathrm{Cov}[(x_{it} - \bar{x}_i)(y_{it} - \lambda\bar{y}_i)] = W_{xy}$ we get the result that $\hat{\beta} = W_{xx}^{-1} W_{xy}$, the within-group estimator. Thus, in this particular case the random effects model gives us the same estimator as the fixed effects model.

We can also obtain an estimate of π. We have $\hat{\delta} = (\Sigma\bar{x}_i\,\bar{x}_i')^{-1}\cdot(\Sigma\bar{y}_i\,\bar{x}_i')(1-\lambda)$ and hence we get

$$\hat{\pi} = (\Sigma\bar{x}_i\,\bar{x}_i')^{-1}\,(\Sigma\bar{x}_i\,\bar{y}_i') - \hat{\beta}$$

The fixed effects and random effects models also yield the same behavior if instead of (5) we have

(7) $\alpha_i = \pi'\bar{x}_i + \gamma' z_i + w_i$

because in this case Equation (6) can be written as

$$y_{it} - \lambda\bar{y}_i = \beta'(x_{it} - \bar{x}_i) + \delta'\bar{x}_i + (1-\lambda)\gamma' z_i + v_{it}$$

and since $1/T\ \Sigma_t(x_{it} - \bar{x}_i)z_i = 0$ we again get the estimator of β as the within-group estimator $W_{xx}^{-1} W_{xy}$.

However, we still have the problem that the coefficients of time invariant variables cannot be estimated. Hausman and Taylor (1981) specify a general model like (4) and consider the case where α_i can be correlated with *some* of the z_i and x_{it}. They decompose z_i into two groups of g_1 variables z_{1i} which are *not* correlated with α_i and g_2 variables z_{2i} which are correlated with α_i. Similarly, they decompose the variables x_{it} into two groups of k_1 variables x_{1it} which are *not* correlated with α_i and k_2 variables x_{2it} which are correlated with α_i. We can, therefore, write

$$\alpha_i = \pi_1'\bar{x}_{2i} + \pi_2' z_{2i} + w_i$$

Substituting this in (4) we get (noting that x_{it} and z_i are now being partitioned).

(8) $y_{it} = \beta_1' x_{1it} + \beta_2' x_{2it} + \gamma_1' z_{1i} + \gamma_2' z_{2i} + \pi_1' \bar{x}_{2i} + \pi_2' z_{2i} + w_i + u_{it}$

We then have

(9) $\bar{y}_i = \beta_1' \bar{x}_{1i} + \beta_2' \bar{x}_{2i} + \gamma_1' z_{1i} + \gamma_2' z_{2i} + \pi_1' \bar{x}_{2i} + \pi_2' z_{2i} + w_i + \bar{u}_i$

Subtracting (9) from (8) we see that the within-group estimator $\hat{\beta}_w = W_{xx}^{-1} W_{xy}$ gives us a consistent estimator β. The question is about the estimation of the parameters γ_1 and γ_2. Note that if we use the standard methods of estimation for random effects models with Equation (8) we can get estimates of γ_1 and π_1 but we cannot get separate estimates of γ_2 and π_2. Hausman and Taylor suggest an instrumental variable procedure to get a separate estimate of γ_2. This procedure can be applied if $k_1 \geq g_2$ in which case $\bar{x}_{1i}$ can be used as instruments for the endogenous variables z_{2i}. Thus, the paper by Hausman and Taylor shows that one can estimate random effects models with instrumental variable methods if the random effects are correlated with some of the explanatory variables, provided some conditions are satisfied.

B. Specification Tests

Before undertaking the elaborate analysis of models where $E(\alpha_i | x_{it}, z_i) \neq 0$, we might estimate some simplified models and test the hypothesis $E(\alpha_i | x_{it}, z_i) = 0$. Complicated models can be estimated if this hypothesis is rejected. For this purpose Hausman (1978) suggests the following specification test: if the null hypothesis is correct, then the *GLS* estimator from the random effects model is both consistent and efficient. On the other hand, the within-group estimator $\hat{\beta}_w$ is consistent regardless of whether the null hypothesis is valid, since all time invariant effects cancel. Thus, we can construct the difference $q = \hat{\beta}_w - \hat{\beta}_{GLS}$, with variance $V(q) = V(\hat{\beta}_w) - V(\hat{\beta}_{GLS})$. Hence we can use $m = \hat{q}'[\hat{V}(\hat{q})]^{-1}\hat{q}$ as a χ^2 statistic with k degrees of freedom, where k is the dimensionality of β. The random effects model is rejected in favor of the fixed effects model if m is sufficiently high.

Yet another specification test is to test $\sigma_\alpha^2 = 0$. This is the case where the individual components do not exist and we can use the OLS method. A test for this hypothesis is given in Breusch and Pagan (1980) who show that under the null hypothesis, if we denote the residuals from the least squares regression by $\hat{u}_{it}$, then

$$m = \frac{NT}{2(T-1)} \left| \frac{\sum_{i=1}^{N} \left(\sum_{t=1}^{T} \hat{u}_{it} \right)^2}{\sum_{i=1}^{N} \sum_{t=1}^{T} \hat{u}_{it}^2} - 1 \right|^2$$

has a χ^2-distribution with 1 degree of freedom. Whether this test precedes or follows the Hausman test depends upon the type of testing strategy we follow. If we start with a simple model and then progressively go to more complicated models, we first apply the test $\sigma_\alpha^2 = 0$ and if it is rejected we next test the hypothesis $E(\alpha_i | x_{it} z_i) = 0$. On the other hand, if we start with a general model and then progressively simplify it, we would follow the reverse procedure.

From the computational point of view, it is more convenient to start with a simple model and then progressively go to more complicated models. This is also the modeling strategy suggested by Milton Friedman, T. C. Koopmans, and Karl Popper, who have argued that the usefulness of models depends on our ability to explain complex phenomena in terms of simple models. However, from the statistical point of view, the significance levels for testing any hypotheses are not well known for this type of modeling strategy. On the other hand, the statistical theory of testing is more tractable if we start with a general model and progressively simplify it by introducing a series of restrictions on the parameters. Many empirical researchers prefer the procedure of starting with simple models and progressively complicating them. A common illustration of this procedure is the estimation of a regression model assuming no serial correlation in the errors, and then estimating an equation with serial correlation if the Durbin-Watson test statistic is significant. We will presently discuss the limitations of this procedure [in Equations (10) and (11)] when we discuss dynamic models.

C. Dynamic Models

One final issue we have to discuss is that of dynamic models. In the case of dynamic models with fixed T, the fixed effects model gives inconsistent estimates. It is easy to see this if we consider $T = 2$ as illustrated in Chamberlain (1980, 227). Consider

$$y_{it} = \beta y_{i,t-1} + \alpha_i + u_{it}$$

and condition it on y_{i0}. The fixed effects model in this case amounts to estimating the regression equation:

$$y_{i2} - y_{i1} = \beta(y_{i1} - y_{i0}) + u_{i2} - u_{i1}.$$

Since the error term is correlated with y_{i1} we get the result that the estimator of β is inconsistent.

Regarding the random effects model, Balestra and Nerlove (1966) encountered some problems with maximum likelihood (ML) estimation. Based on the results of a Monte Carlo study, Nerlove (1971) argues against the use of the ML method in dynamic models with error components (i.e., random effects) and discusses alternatives to the ML method. However, the problems he encounters with the ML method are due to using the ML method conditional on y_{i0} and not taking account of the distribution of y_{i0}.[1]

An important issue that arises in dynamic models is that of serial correlation vs. "state dependence," that is, whether any direct effects of the lagged dependent variable exist apart from those generated indirectly by serial correlation of the errors. An alternative terminology for the "serial correlation model" vs. "state dependence model" is models with "error dynamics" and "system dynamics," respectively. This issue is not special to panel data and arises in the usual regression models as well. To clarify this problem, we will drop the subscript i and consider a single cross-section unit. For example, if we consider the regression model with no lagged variables but serially correlated errors:

(10) $y_t = \beta x_t + u_t,\ u_t = \rho u_{t-1} + e_t$

we can write it as

$$y_t = \rho y_{t-1} + \beta x_t - \rho\beta x_{t-1} + e_t$$

This is the same as the dynamic regression equation

(11) $y_t = \gamma y_{t-1} + \beta_0 x_t + \beta_1 x_{t-1} + e_t$

with the restriction $\gamma\beta_0 + \beta_1 = 0$.

The two models thus differ in this restriction. If the restriction $\gamma\beta_0 + \beta_1 = 0$ holds, the apparent effect of y_{t-1} on y_t is due to serial correlation in the errors. On the other hand, if this restriction does not hold then y_{t-1} has an effect on y_t and we have what is known as "state dependence." Thus, an estimation of Equation (11) and a test of the restriction $\gamma\beta_0 + \beta_1 = 0$ will enable us to discriminate between the "serial correlation model" and the "state dependence model."

Note that a common procedure that is adopted is to estimate the regression model

$$y_t = \beta x_t + u_t$$

and to estimate the serial correlation model if the Durbin-Watson statistic is significant. This procedure is wrong because the Durbin-Watson statistic

1. In his Monte Carlo study, Nerlove generated 20 observations and discarded the first ten and used the last ten observations in the estimation using y_{10} as the initial observation and using the ML method assuming y_{10} as known. However, from the way the data are generated in his study, one can write down the probability distribution of y_{10}. When this was incorporated into the likelihood function, I found that there were no more boundary solutions with the ML method, as was found in Nerlove's Monte Carlo study. Thus, what the Nerlove Monte Carlo study shows is that when T is small, one has to be very careful in defining the likelihood function. The result will depend crucially on whether this is taken conditionally on the initial values or whether the distribution of the initial value is taken into account. This point has also been emphasized in the papers by Anderson and Hsiao (1982) and Bhargava and Sargan (1983).

could be significant not because we have serial correlation in the errors but because we have omitted y_{t-1} and x_{t-1} from the explanatory variables. This omission is called "mis-specified dynamics." Thus, what we are doing is ascribing to "error dynamics" what is really "system dynamics." The proper procedure is to first estimate Equation (11) and test for the restriction $\gamma\beta_0 + \beta_1 = 0$. If this is not rejected, then we test for serial correlation by testing $\rho = 0$. Thus, the test for the serial correlation should be undertaken *after* we have determined that what we have is perhaps a serial correlation model. The use of the Durbin-Watson statistic at the beginning is not a correct procedure.

All these comments apply to panel data as well. To simplify the exposition we have considered a single cross-section unit and omitted the subscript i.

Returning to the case of panel data, the serial correlation model and the state dependence model corresponding to Equation (4) are:

(i) The serial correlation model:

$$y_{it} = \gamma' z_i + \beta' x_{it} + \alpha_i + w_{it}$$

$$w_{it} = \rho w_{i,t-1} + u_{it}$$

(ii) The state dependence model

$$y_{it} - \rho y_{i,t-1} = \gamma' z_i + \beta' x_{it} + \alpha_i + u_{it}$$

Anderson and Hsiao (1982) discuss the estimation of these models under eight different assumptions. The most reasonable assumption, however, is what the model itself implies about the distribution of y_{i0}. The estimation of the models under this assumption is discussed in Anderson and Hsiao's paper as well as in Lee (1981) and Bhargava and Sargan (1983).

Thus, in dynamic models the more important issues are those of distinguishing between serial correlation and "state dependence" and the problem of estimating the model under the assumption about y_{i0} that is not ad hoc but is derived by implication from the model itself. Given the complexity of the estimation procedure (which is however, feasible) for models with continuous variables, it is to be expected that it would be almost impossible to implement a similar procedure for the logit, probit, and tobit models.

We have reviewed some issues in the estimation of continuous variable models based on panel data. We will see how many of these results carry through for the logit, probit, and tobit models and what computational complexities arise.

In the remaining sections of this paper we will discuss the following models:

(i) Fixed effects logit and probit models. Here we argue that for large N and small T (which is typically the case) ML estimation of the fixed effects model gives inconsistent estimates of the parameters. However, in the logit model one can obtain consistent estimates using the conditional ML method (conditioning on the fixed effects). Such conditioning is not possible with the probit model. Hence, for the analysis of the fixed effects model, the logit model is the appropriate one.

(ii) Random effects logit and probit models. For the analysis of random effects, the probit model is the appropriate one. The random effects produce correlations among the errors and the multivariate logistic distribution is too restrictive for this purpose (since it implies that all correlations are 0.5). The probit model is based on the multivariate normal distribution which is more flexible. For the analysis of random effects probit models we consider three models suggested by Heckman and Willis (1976), Avery, Hansen, and Hotz (1983), and Chamberlain (1985).

(iii) Fixed effects and random effects tobit models. These are extensions of the previous models. Illustrative examples are in Heckman and MaCurdy (1980) and Hausman and Wise (1979).

(iv) Autoregressive logit and probit models. These are extensions of models in (i) and (ii) to the case where lagged y's are included as explanatory variables. The conditional logit model can be extended to this case but only under some restrictive assumptions. The random effects probit model can be easily extended to this case.

We will now discuss these four categories of models.

III. Fixed Effects Logit and Probit Models

In the case of continuous variables and no autoregressions, the fixed effects model gives consistent estimates of the slope parameters β in Equation (1). This is not the case when the dependent variable y_{it} is observed only as a qualitative variable and there are only a few time-series observations per individual as is usually the case. Andersen (1973) and Chamberlain (1980) demonstrate this for the logit model and suggest a conditional likelihood approach. The idea is to consider the likelihood function conditional on sufficient statistics for the incidental parameters α_i. In the logit model, as in model (1), these sufficient statistics are $\Sigma_t y_{it}$ for α_i. For the logit model the conditional likelihood approach results in a computationally convenient estimator. The conditional ML estimator of β is consistent, provided that the conditional likelihood function satisfies regularity conditions, which impose mild restrictions on the α_i. Chamberlain

(1980) also shows that the standard errors obtained by the usual conditional logit programs can be used as the asymptotic standard errors for the conditional ML estimator of β.

In the use of the conditional logit approach we discard alternative sets for which $\Sigma y_{it} = 0$ or $\Sigma y_{it} = T$ (i.e., persons who never change states) because they contribute zero to the likelihood function. We will illustrate the method for $T = 2$ and 3. Let the logit model be:

$$\text{Prob}(y_{it} = 1) = \frac{\exp(\beta' x_{it} + \alpha_i)}{1 + \exp(\beta' x_{it} + \alpha_i)}$$

Then $$\text{Prob}(0,1) = \frac{1}{1 + \exp(\beta' x_{i1} + \alpha_i)} \cdot \frac{\exp(\beta' x_{i2} + \alpha_i)}{1 + \exp(\beta' x_{i2} + \alpha_i)}$$

and $$\text{Prob}(1,0) = \frac{\exp(\beta' x_{i1} + \alpha_i)}{1 + \exp(\beta' x_{i1} + \alpha_i)} \cdot \frac{1}{1 + \exp(\beta' x_{i2} + \alpha_i)}$$

Thus, since (1,0) and (0,1) are mutually exclusive,

$$\text{Prob}[(1,0) \mid (1,0) \text{ or } (0,1)] = \frac{\text{Prob}(1,0)}{\text{Prob}(1,0) + \text{Prob}(0,1)} = \frac{\exp[\beta'(x_{i1} - x_{i2})}{D}$$

and $$\text{Prob}[(0,1) \mid (1,0) \text{ or } (0,1)] = \frac{1}{D}$$

where $D = 1 + \exp[\beta'(x_{i1} - x_{i2})]$

The α_i's have been eliminated and we have a standard logit model to estimate, in which changes in the x_{it}'s are used to explain changes in the dichotomous dependent variables. Björklund (1985) uses this two-period model to study the relationship between unemployment and mental health in Sweden.

For the case of $T = 3$, we have to consider two different sets: $\Sigma y_{it} = 1$ and $\Sigma y_{it} = 2$. For the set $\Sigma y_{it} = 1$ we get, since $\exp(\alpha_i)$ cancels,

$$\text{Prob}(1,0,0 \mid \Sigma y_{it} = 1) = \exp[\beta'(x_{i1} - x_{i3})]/D_1$$

$$\text{Prob}(0,1,0 \mid \Sigma y_{it} = 1) = \exp[\beta'(x_{i2} - x_{i3})]/D_1$$

and $$\text{Prob}(0,0,1 \mid \Sigma y_{it} = 1) = 1/D_1$$

where $D_1 = 1 + \exp[\beta'(x_{i1} - x_{i3})] + \exp[\beta'(x_{i2} - x_{i3})]$.

For the set $\Sigma y_{it} = 2$, we get, by cancelling $\exp(2\alpha_i)$,

$$\text{Prob}(1,1,0 \mid \Sigma y_{it} = 2) = \exp[\beta'(x_{i2} - x_{i3})]/D_2$$

$$\text{Prob}(0,1,1 \mid \Sigma y_{it} = 2) = \exp[\beta'(x_{i2} - x_{i1})]/D_2$$

$$\text{Prob}(1,0,1 \mid \Sigma y_{it} = 2) = 1/D_2$$

where $D_2 = 1 + \exp[\beta'(x_{i2} - x_{i3})] + \exp[\beta'(x_{i2} - x_{i1})]$.

For general T, we have to consider the sets $\Sigma y_{it} = 1, 2, \ldots, (T - 1)$. Chamberlain (1980, 231) shows that the conditional ML method can be extended to the multinomial logit model as well as the log-linear model.

By contrast, the fixed effects probit model is difficult to implement computationally. The conditional ML method does not produce computational simplifications as in the logit model because the fixed effects do not cancel out. This implies that all N fixed effects must be estimated as part of the estimation procedure. Further, this also implies that, since the estimates of the fixed effects are inconsistent for small T, the fixed effects probit model gives inconsistent estimates for β as well. Thus, in applying the fixed effects models to qualitative dependent variables based on panel data, the logit model and the log-linear models seem to be the only choices. However, in the case of random effects models it is the probit model that is computationally tractable rather than the logit model. We now, therefore, turn to the random effects probit model.

IV. Random Effects Probit Models

We discussed earlier the arguments in favor of random effects models in panel data. With random effects, the composite error term in (1) is correlated across cross-section units even if u_{it} are *IID*. With the logit model, where the errors are assumed to have a logistic distribution, we need to use the multivariate logistic distribution. Whereas, with the probit model we need to use the multivariate normal distribution. The multivariate logistic distribution has the disadvantage that the correlations are all constrained to be 1/2 (see Johnson and Kotz 1972, 293–94). Though some generalizations are possible, the multivariate logistic distribution does not permit much flexibility. Hence, when we consider random effects models we will confine ourselves to random effect probit models.

Two important properties of the random effects probit models are worth mentioning:

(i) Unlike the estimates from the fixed effects probit model, the estimates from the random effects probit model are consistent.

(ii) The random effects probit model is based on the multivariate normal distribution. However, ignoring the correlations among the errors and using a standard probit estimation method with pooled data produces consistent (though inefficient) estimates.

[Robinson (1982) proves this for the tobit model but the result holds for the probit model as well.] These estimates can be used as initial values in any iterative method to compute the ML estimates.

A. The Heckman and Willis Model

The first application of random effects robit model is that of Heckman and Willis (1976). Their model is:

$$y_{it}^* = \beta' x_{it} + \alpha_i + u_{it} \qquad i = 1, 2, \ldots, N$$
$$t = 1, 2, \ldots, T$$

with

$$(12) \quad y_{it} = 1 \qquad \text{if } y_{it}^* > 0$$
$$= 0 \qquad \text{otherwise}$$

$\alpha_i \sim IN(0, \sigma_\alpha^2)$, $u_{it} \sim IN(0, \sigma_u^2)$ and α_i and u_{it} are mutually independent as well as independent of x_{it}. Define $\sigma^2 = \sigma_\alpha^2 + \sigma_u^2$ and $\rho = \sigma_\alpha^2/\sigma^2$.
Also define $v_{it} = u_{it}/\sigma_u$, $q_i = \alpha_i/\sigma_\alpha$ and $\beta^* = \beta/\sigma$

$$y_{it} = 1 \Rightarrow \frac{u_{it}}{\sigma_u} > \frac{-\beta' x_{it} - \sigma_\alpha q_i}{\sigma_u}$$

If we now define

$$a_{it} = \frac{-\beta^{*\prime} x_{it} - \rho^{1/2} q_i}{(1-\rho)^{1/2}}$$

then we can restate the above condition as

$$y_{it} = 1 \Rightarrow v_{it} > a_{it}$$
$$y_{it} = 0 \Rightarrow v_{it} \leq a_{it}$$

Conditional on given values of α_i, y_{it}^* are independent normal. Hence, conditional on given values of α_i, we can easily write down the joint probability density of y_{it}. To get the unconditional probability density, we multiply this density by the density function for α_i and integrate with respect to α_i. Note that β and α_i are estimable only up to a scale factor.

The joint density of the y_{it} is, therefore,

$$\prod_{i=1}^{N} \int_{-\infty}^{\infty} \prod_{t=1}^{T} [1 - F(a_{it})]^{y_{it}} [F(a_{it})]^{1-y_{it}} \frac{1}{2\pi} e^{-q_i^2/2} \, dq_i$$

where $F(a_{it})$ is the common degree of freedom of the standard normal. Thus, the expression is reduced to the evaluation of the expressions $F(a_{it})$ and a single integral for which good approximations are available. Butler and Moffitt (1982) provide an efficient computational algorithm for the evaluation of this integral and thus the ML estimation of the random effects probit model. Their program is much faster than the one used by Heckman and Willis. The use of the probit model with the entire set of *NT* observations ignoring the correlations will give an initial consistent estimate of β.

B. The Avery-Hansen-Hotz (AHH) Model

The random effects model given by (12) assumes that the correlation between successive disturbances for the same individual unit is a constant ρ. This specification is often referred to as the specification of "equicorrelation." If we relax this assumption, then the estimation of the model involves *T*-fold integrals and the simplification suggested by Heckman and Willis does not hold.

Avery, Hansen, and Hotz (1983), henceforth referred to as AHH, suggest using the method of moments (MOM) estimators for this case. To understand what the method of moments is, let us first consider the usual probit model. Thus, we consider a single time period and drop the subscript t.

The model now is,

$$\begin{aligned} y_i^* &= \beta' x_i + u_i \qquad u_i \sim IN(0,1) \\ y_i &= 1 \text{ if } y_i^* \geq 0 \\ &= 0 \text{ otherwise} \end{aligned}$$

We get

$$E(y_i|x_i) = F(\beta' x_i) \text{ and } \operatorname{Var}(y_i|x_i) = F(\beta' x_i)[1 - F(\beta' x_i)]$$

where $F(\cdot)$ is the cumulative distribution function of the standard normal. The error

$$\epsilon_i = y_i - F(\beta' x_i)$$

is orthogonal to functions of the vector x_i. Note that $E(\epsilon_i|x_i) = 0$ and that ϵ_i are heteroskedastic with variance depending on $\beta' x_i$.

Analogous to the least squares method, the method of moments suggests estimating β by solving the equation

$$(13) \quad \sum_{i=1}^{n} [y_i - F(\beta' x_i)] g(x_i, \beta) = 0$$

where $g(\cdot)$ is a suitably chosen function. One can choose $g(x_i, \beta) = x_i$ but this cannot be justified since $F(\beta' x_i)$ is a nonlinear function. Another alternative is

$$\frac{\partial F(\beta' x_i)}{\partial \beta} = f(\beta' x_i) x_i$$

where $f(\cdot)$ is the density function of the standard normal. However, since ϵ_i's are heteroskedastic we have to weight this in inverse proportion to $\mathrm{Var}(\epsilon_i)$. The GLS method implies choosing

$$(14) \quad g(x_i, \beta) = \frac{\partial F(\beta' x_i)}{\partial \beta} \cdot \frac{1}{\mathrm{Var}(y_i | x_i)}$$

$$= \frac{f(\beta' x_i) x_i}{F(\beta' x_i)[1 - F(\beta' x_i)]}$$

With this choice Equation (13) gives the first-order conditions for the ML estimation of the probit model [see Maddala (1983), 26, for the first-order conditions]. We can also consider $g(x_i, \beta)$ as a weighted nonlinear instrumental variable. Thus, the method of moments is related to GLS estimation method and weighted nonlinear instrumental variable methods.

When we come to panel data, the derivations get more complicated. AHH start with the first-order conditions for GLS estimation and proceed from them. They first write the model as:

$$y_{it}^* = \beta' x_{it} + \delta_{it}$$
$$y_{it} = 1 \text{ if } y_{it}^* > 0$$
$$= 0 \text{ otherwise}$$

where δ_{it} is the composite error term $\alpha_i + u_{it}$. They assume a general covariance matrix Σ for the error terms δ_{it} $(i = 1, 2, \ldots, N)$. In the Heckman and Willis model the correlation between δ_{it} and $\delta_{it'}$ $(t \neq t')$ is ρ. In the AHH model it is $\rho_{tt'}$, unrestricted. AHH argue that if Σ is incorrectly constrained to have equal off-diagonal terms, then the ML estimator of β is inconsistent. It will be consistent only if we assume no correlation (i.e., $\rho = 0$). AHH also make the assumption (for most of their discussion),

$$E(\delta_i | x_i) = 0$$

where $\quad \delta_i' = (\delta_{i1}, \delta_{i2}, \ldots, \delta_{iT})$ and $x_i' = (x_{i1}, x_{i2}, \ldots, x_{iT})$.

This implies that δ_{it} is uncorrelated with functions of current, past and future x's or that x's are strictly exogenous. Also, the distribution of each element of δ_i conditional on x_i is assumed to be normal with mean zero and unit variance.

Under these assumptions we have

$$E(y_{it} | x_i) = E(y_{it} | x_{it}) = F(\beta' x_{it})$$

where $F(\cdot)$ is the cumulative distribution function of the standard normal. The forecast error

$$\epsilon_{it} = y_{it} - F(\beta' x_{it})$$

is orthogonal to functions of the entire vector x_i as long as the random vector has a finite second moment. This implies the following regression equation:

$$(15) \quad y_{it} = F(\beta' x_{it}) + d_{it}$$

where d_{it} is a disturbance term orthogonal to functions of x_{it}.

One can think of estimating this equation by nonlinear GLS but the disturbances d_{it} are heteroskedastic with variances involving the parameters β and Σ. A consistent estimator for β can be obtained by estimating a standard probit model with all the NT observations ignoring the correlations. However, obtaining an estimator for Σ would be quite cumbersome. AHH, therefore, propose the method of moments, which is essentially a weighted nonlinear instrumental variable method. This method starts with the first-order conditions implied by the GLS estimation of (15). Using $d_{it} = y_{it} - F(\beta' x_{it})$, define

$$d_i' = (d_{i1}, d_{i2}, \ldots, d_{iT}) = H_i(y_{it}, x_{it}, \beta)'$$

Then GLS estimation of (15) amounts to minimizing the weighted sum of squares of residuals

$$\frac{1}{N} \sum_{i=1}^{N} H_i' \Omega_i^{-1} H_i \text{ where } \Omega_i = E(d_i d_i')$$

If Ω_i is known, the first-order condition

$$(16) \quad \sum_{i=1}^{N} \frac{\partial H_i'}{\partial \beta} \Omega_i^{-1} H_i = 0$$

can be solved. However, in practice Ω_i is not known and it has to be estimated from the residuals which are themselves functions of β. Instead of considering the detailed expressions, AHH note that condition (16) implies a linear weighting of the cross products of sample residuals and their derivatives with respect to β. Thus, condition (16) can be represented as:

$$(17) \quad \frac{1}{N} \sum_{i=1}^{N} A_i G_i(y_i, x_i, \beta) = 0$$

where $G_i(\cdot)$ is a T^2k dimensional vector containing all possible cross products of elements in the T dimensional vector H_i and the $T \times k$ matrix $\partial H_i / \partial \beta$ and A_i is a $k \times T^2k$ matrix consisting of zeroes and elements of Ω_i^{-1}.

Given the difficulty of estimating A_i, AHH suggest some tractable alternatives. In essence, what they use are expressions analogous to those presented for the simple probit model in (14) but taking into account the fact that in the case of panel data the product of $\partial H_i / \partial \beta$ and H_i involves leads and lags. Let us, for the sake of compactness, denote $F(\beta' x_{it})$ by F_{it}. Then with no leads or lags, the weight used is the inverse of $F_{it}(1 - F_{it})$ as in (14). With leads and lags, for two different time periods t and s, the weight used is the inverse of $[F_{it}(1 - F_{it})]^{1/2}[F_{is}(1 - F_{is})]^{1/2}$. The AHH method thus corrects for serial correlation in a linear manner, whereas Equations (16) or (17) involve corrections in a complicated nonlinear way.

The detailed expressions derived by AHH (1983, 27–28) are quite complicated and need not be reproduced here. However, a computer program HOTZTRAN can be obtained to implement their procedure for the probit as well as the tobit models. The above discussion gives a rough idea of the method of moments that they use.

AHH apply their procedure to study labor force participation of married women. They compare their results with those from the specification of equicorrelation and reject the latter.

C. The Chamberlain Model

One major limitation of the preceding models is that we assumed the random effects to be uncorrelated with the explanatory variables x_{it}. This is a serious limitation and needs to be relaxed. Avery, Hansen, and Hotz (1983, 29) test for the exogeneity assumption (13) which can be performed with the HOTZTRAN program. However, a question arises as to what alternative model to consider if we drop this assumption. Earlier, in our discussion of models with continuous variables, we discussed Mundlak's assumptions (5) which led to the within-group estimator for β or the estimator from the fixed effects model. In the case of qualitative variables, this specification does not lead to the estimator from the fixed effects model.

Chamberlain (1980, 1985) considers the specification

$$(18) \quad \alpha_i = \pi' x_i + v_i$$

where $v_i \sim IN(0, \sigma_v^2)$ and $x_i' = (x_{i1}, x_{i2}, \ldots, x_{iT})$

This specification leads to the random effects model

$$(19) \quad y_{it}^* = \beta' x_{it} + \pi' x_i + v_i + u_{it}$$

$$y_{it} = 1 \text{ if } y_{it}^* > 0$$

$$= 0 \text{ otherwise}$$

The correlation structure of the errors in this model is the same as in the Heckman and Willis model (12). However, the addition of $\pi' x_i$ produces some cross-equation restrictions on the coefficients. We can consider probit equations for each t ($t = 1, 2, \ldots, T$) which involves the use of all the leads and lags of x. If we denote the matrix of these multivariate probit coefficients by D, then D has the structure

$$(20) \quad D = \text{diag.} \{\gamma_1, \gamma_2, \ldots, \gamma_T\}[\beta I + 1\pi']$$

where γ_t are the normalization factors given by $\gamma_t = (\sigma_{tt} + \sigma_v^2)^{-1/2}$ and 1 is a

$T \times 1$ vector of ones. Chamberlain suggests the estimation of the probit coefficients D by running the T probit equations separately. Then he proposes (1985, 1252) estimating β and π by imposing the constraints (20), using a minimum distance estimator.

The minimum distance estimator is just a GLS estimator. To see how it is used when there are restrictions on the parameters, consider a simultaneous equations model

$$By_t + Cz_t = u_t$$

where y_t is a vector of endogenous variables and z_t is a vector of exogenous variables. The reduced form is

$$y_t = Az_t + v_t$$

where $A = -B^{-1}C$ and $v_t = B^{-1}u_t$

Let $E(v_t v_t') = \Omega$.

The estimates of B and C can be obtained by minimizing

$$\sum_{t=1}^{T} (y_t - Az_t)'\Omega^{-1}(y_t - Az_t)$$

subject to the restrictions $A = -B^{-1}C$ or $BA + C = 0$. However, Ω is not known. But we can substitute $\hat{\Omega}$ for Ω where $\hat{\Omega}$ is obtained from the residuals from the OLS estimation of the reduced form equations (i.e., ignoring the restrictions $BA + C = 0$). The GLS estimation with $\hat{\Omega}$ substituted for Ω and subject to the restrictions $BA + C = 0$ is called the "minimum distance method" of estimation. It is discussed in Malinvaud (1970, 675–78). Malinvaud shows that the estimators for B and C are consistent and if the errors u_t are normal, they are asymptotically efficient.

Chamberlain (1985) uses a similar minimum distance method to estimate the relationship between labor force participation of married women and the presence of young children, based on the data from the Michigan Panel Study of Income Dynamics. He also estimates the fixed effects conditional logit model with the same data. The results from the two models are, however, conflicting. The random effects probit model with random effects specified as linear functions of x_i suggested that the cross-section estimates overstate the negative effects of young children on the woman's participation probability. The fixed effects conditional logit model, on the other hand, gives the result that the cross-section estimates underestimate the negative effect. Both models control for the unobserved individual effects, the logit model leaving them unspecified, and the probit model using a special specification. It is possible that the special specification for α_i is not the appropriate one or that the fixed effects logit model should include leads and lags of the x's as part of the structural model.

In summary, there are three models that have been suggested for the random effects probit models:

(i) The Heckman and Willis model (Equation 12), for which Butler and Moffitt (1982) have an efficient computer algorithm.
(ii) The Avery-Hansen-Hotz (1983) model, for which there is the HOTZTRAN computer program. Since this model is a generalization of the Heckman-Willis model, one might wonder why we should consider the former. If the equicorrelation hypothesis and the exogeneity hypothesis are not rejected, we might consider the Butler and Moffitt procedure because it is more efficient than the method of moments considered by AHH. The AHH procedure, on the other hand, is also robust against other forms of serial correlations in the errors.
(iii) The Chamberlain model (1985). This allows for the random effects to depend on the current, future and past x's. A computer program to implement this procedure can be obtained from Professor George Jakubson at Cornell University.

All these procedures, however, assume that the slope coefficients β do not change over time. Since the estimation of a probit model is not costly, it is worthwhile estimating probit models for each cross-section and for the pooled sample before any analysis is performed using the above three models. Note that the pooled probit model gives consistent estimators of β even when there is serial correlation in the errors due to the random effects.

When it comes to an extension of the random effects probit model to more complicated situations like simultaneous equations models, the models by Avery, Hansen and Hotz and by Chamberlain are more complicated to implement. A generalization of the Heckman-Willis model to simultaneous equations is in Sickles and Taubman (1986) who employ the Butler and Moffitt (1982) procedure for estimating the model. The model consists of two equations.

$$y_{1ij}^* = \beta_1 x_{1ij} + \epsilon_{1ij}$$

$$y_{2ij}^* = \gamma y_{1ij}^* + \beta_2 x_{2ij} + \epsilon_{2ij}$$

$$\epsilon_{1ij} = \alpha_{1i} + u_{1ij}$$

$$\epsilon_{2ij} = \alpha_{2i} + u_{2ij}$$

For y_{1ij} they have a polytomous probit model with ordered responses and for y_{2ij} they have a binary probit model. The paper by Sickles and Taubman shows that it is feasible to estimate simultaneous equations models with random effects in each equation.

V. Fixed Effects Tobit Model

The fixed effects tobit model can be written as:

$$y_{it}^* = \alpha_i + \beta' x_{it} + u_{it} \qquad u_{it} \sim IN(0,\sigma^2)$$

$$y_{it} = y_{it}^* \text{ if } y_{it}^* > 0$$
$$= 0 \text{ otherwise.}$$

Let $$d_{it} = 1 \text{ if } y_{it}^* > 0$$
$$= 0 \text{ otherwise.}$$

The log-likelihood function is:

$$\text{(21)} \quad \text{Log } L = \sum_{i,t} (1 - d_{it}) \text{Log } \Phi\left(\frac{-\alpha_i - \beta' x_{it}}{\sigma}\right) + \sum_{i,t} d_{it}\left\{-\frac{1}{2}\log \sigma^2 - \frac{1}{2\sigma^2}(y_{it} - \alpha_i - \beta' x_{it})^2\right\}$$

Unlike the case of the linear model, in this model it is not possible to devise estimators of β and σ that are not functions of the fixed effects α_i. Since the number of observations per cross-section unit is fixed (T is fixed and usually small) it is not possible to consistently estimate the fixed effects α_i and this inconsistency carries through to the estimates of β and σ.

Heckman and MaCurdy (1980) estimate this model by iterative methods. They argue that even though the estimates are inconsistent, from the practical point of view this might not be a serious problem if there are no lagged dependent variables (1980, 59). This observation was based on the results of a Monte Carlo study of the multivariate probit model with fixed effects and $T = 8$ done by Heckman. Though no Monte Carlo study was done for the fixed effects tobit model, one can presume that the same results would carry through for the tobit model.

The procedure used by Heckman and MaCurdy is as follows: start with some initial values of β and σ, maximize the likelihood function (21) with respect to α_i, substitute this ML estimate in (21) and maximize it with respect to β and σ to obtain new estimates of β and σ. This procedure is iterated till convergence. Heckman and MaCurdy report that they obtained rapid convergence (1980, 69). If $d_{it} = 1$ for all t, there is no problem in this model because we observe y_{it} but if $d_{it} = 0$ for all t, then the corresponding estimate of α_i is infinite. Thus, these cross-section units have to be discarded. Let I_1 be the subset of the sample with these units discarded. For the ith cross-section unit the probability $d_{it} = 1$ for at least one t is:

$$p_i = 1 - \text{Prob}(d_{it} = 0 \text{ for all } t)$$
$$= 1 - \prod_{i=1}^{T} \Phi\left(\frac{-\alpha_i - \beta' x_{it}}{\sigma}\right)$$

Conditional on the information that $d_{it} = 1$ for at least one t, the logarithm of the likelihood function is now the same as (21) but with the subscript i used only for subset I_1 and with $\Sigma_{I_1} \log p_i$ subtracted. The maximization of this likelihood function again can be done by the same procedure as the maximization of (21).

The model considered by Heckman and MaCurdy is actually a two equation model but the estimation involves fixed effects in only one tobit type equation because of the way the likelihood function is factored. The model they use is a generalization of Heckman's labor supply model to panel data. We start with a shadow wage equation

(22) $S_{it} = \gamma_1 H_{it} + \gamma_2' x_{1it} + v_{1it}$

and a market wage equation

(23) $W_{it} = \beta' x_{2it} + v_{2it}$

where H is hours of work and x_1 and x_2 are sets of exogenous variables. Heckman assumes that hours of work adjust so that $S_{it} = W_{it}$. Hence, we get

(24) $H_{it} = \dfrac{\beta' x_{2it} - \gamma_2' x_{1it}}{\gamma_1} + \dfrac{v_{2it} - v_{1it}}{\gamma_1}$

If $H_{it} > 0$ the person is in the labor force and we observe H_{it} and W_{it}. If $H_{it} \leq 0$ the person is not in the labor force. The likelihood function for this model is, therefore,

(25) $L = \prod_{H_{it}>0} f(W_{it}, H_{it}) \cdot \prod_{H_{it}<0} \Phi(\Delta_{it})$

where $\Delta_{it} = \dfrac{\gamma_2' x_{1it} - \beta' x_{2it}}{\sigma}$ and $\sigma^2 = \text{Var}(v_{2it} - v_{1it})$

and $f(W, H)$ is the joint density of W and H. One can introduce individual specific effects in the two Equations (22) and (23) for shadow wage and market wage and reparametrize these so that we have individual specific effects in the wage and hours worked equations. Heckman and MaCurdy derive the individual specific effects from a model of life-cycle labor supply. Thus, these effects have a specific meaning and are not postulated in an ad hoc fashion. Heckman and MaCurdy argue that since these effects cannot be assumed to be independent of the explanatory variables, the model should be estimated by fixed effects rather than by the random effects model.

Though we start with individual-specific effects in Equations (22) and (23), we can reparametrize and write the model with individual specific effects in (23) and (24), which are the equations relevant for the likelihood function (25). Thus, we will write

$$H_{it} = \alpha_{1i} + \gamma' z_{it} + u_{1it}$$

$$W_{it} = \alpha_{2i} + \beta' x_{it} + u_{2it}$$

Looking at the likelihood function (25) we see that the second expression does not involve α_{2i} since it depends on H_{it} only. As for the first expression in (25), we can factor $f(W, H)$ into $f_1(W|H) \cdot f_2(H)$. Then it is only $f_1(W|H)$ that involves α_{2i}. This conditional density is normal. Maximizing the likelihood function with respect to α_{2i}, Heckman and MaCurdy (1980, 68) obtain the ML estimates which just involve the sample means of the variables (as in the usual linear fixed effects model, except that these means are over the subset of observations for which $H_{it} > 0$). Substituting these estimates of α_{2i} in the likelihood function, Heckman and MaCurdy obtain a concentrated likelihood function that involves α_{1i} only and is similar in structure to that of a single equation tobit model with fixed effects like (21).

Thus, though the model is a two-equation model with fixed effects in the wages and hours worked equation, by factoring $f(W, H)$ into $f_1(W|H)$ and $f_2(H)$, the fixed effects α_{2i} can be eliminated as in the linear model. We are left with only one set of fixed effects α_{1i} and a tobit model.

VI. Random Effects Tobit Models

The three models that we considered under random effects probit models can all be generalized to the case of tobit models. The HOTZTRAN program computes the method of moments estimators for tobit models. The Heckman and Willis model again involves a univariate integral and the Butler and Moffitt program can be suitably modified. Note that the estimation of the tobit model ignoring the serial correlation problem does give consistent estimates for β (see Robinson 1982). These can be used as initial starting values. The Chamberlain model now involves tobit estimation for each cross-section (including the current, future, and past x's). The only difference is that in the probit model the parameters are estimable up to a scale factor only, whereas all parameters are estimable in the tobit model.

There are very few applications of the random effects tobit model with panel data. As mentioned earlier, Heckman and MaCurdy argued against it in their application on the grounds that the α_i were expected to be correlated with the explanatory variables. There is, however, one example of the random effects tobit model, but this is with self-selection and with $T = 2$. Though the computational problems for such models are different and do not illustrate the modifications of the Heckman-Willis, AHH, and Chamberlain models to the tobit case, this example is worth citing in this context.

An example of the use of random effects tobit model with self-selection is the paper by Hausman and Wise (1979). The model is a two-period model of earnings y_{it}.

$$y_{it} = \beta' x_{it} + \epsilon_{it} \qquad i = 1, 2, \ldots, N$$

$$\epsilon_{it} = \alpha_i + u_{it} \qquad t = 1, 2$$

$$\alpha_i \sim IN(0, \sigma_\alpha^2),\ u_{it} \sim IN(0, \sigma_u^2).$$

The problem is that y_{i2} is observed only if an index of attrition $A_i \leq 0$ where A_i is defined by

$$A_i = R_i \delta + \epsilon_{i3}.$$

A common procedure is to discard observations for which y_{i2} is zero. Hausman and Wise argue that this is an incorrect procedure if the probability of observing y_{i2} varies with its value and the value of other variables. The details of the estimation by Hausman and Wise need not be reproduced here because the detailed structure of models with self-selection differs case by case (see Maddala 1983, Chapter 9). The paper by Hausman and Wise which is an example of an estimation of random effects models with self-selection can provide guidance in such models.

VII. Autoregressive Logit Models

An additional problem occurs if there is "state dependence" in which an individual's past state $y_{i,t-1}$ will help in predicting his or her current state y_{it} after allowing for the individual effects α_i. This problem has frequently been posed in connection with the effect of past unemployment on current unemployment (see Corcoran 1982, Corcoran and Hill 1985, Heckman and Borjas 1980). A model due to Cox (1958), analyzed further by Chamberlain (1978, 1985), is the autoregressive logit model:

$$\text{(26)} \quad \text{Prob}(y_{it} = 1 \mid y_{i,t-1}) = \frac{\exp(\alpha_i + \gamma y_{i,t-1})}{1 + \exp(\alpha_i + \gamma y_{i,t-1})}$$

$$i = 1, 2, \ldots, N,\ t = 1, 2, \ldots, T$$

γ is the increase in the log-odds ratio of being in State 1 due to being in State 1 in the preceding period (after allowing for the individual specific effect).

Again, maximizing the joint likelihood function over α_i and γ will not give a consistent estimate of γ as $N \to \infty$ for fixed T. Intuitively the number of parameters to be estimated grows with N. Inconsistency is likely to be particularly serious in the autoregressive case. Chamberlain, therefore, suggests working with the conditional likelihood function. The sufficient statistics for α_i are $\Sigma_t y_{it}$ and y_{iT}. In addition he deals with initial conditions by conditioning on y_{i1}. Then,

$$\text{Prob}(y_{i1}, y_{i2}, \ldots, y_{iT} | y_{i1}, \Sigma_t y_{it}, y_{iT})$$

$$= \frac{\exp\left(\gamma \sum_{t=2}^{T} y_{it} y_{i,t-1}\right)}{\sum_{d \in B_i} \exp\left(\gamma \sum_{t=2}^{T} d_t d_{t-1}\right)}$$

where

$$B_t = [d = (d_1, d_2, \ldots, d_T) | d_t = 1 \text{ or } 0,\ d_1 = y_{i1},$$
$$\sum_t d_t = \sum_t y_{it},\ d_T = y_{iT}].$$

The conditional probability for the individual observation is given by the sum of products of adjacent y's for the individual, divided by the sum of such products for all individuals in that set (with the same y_{i1}, y_{iT} and $\Sigma_t y_{it}$). Some such sets will not involve γ at all and we have to omit them. This model is in the form of a conditional logit model and can be estimated easily since the α_i have been eliminated. It has been used by Chamberlain (1978, 35–36), Corcoran (1982), and Corcoran and Hill (1985), all to study labor force participation.

To apply this method we need to determine the sets that result in probabilities that depend on γ. For instance, consider $T = 5$, $y_1 = 0$, $y_5 = 1$. Then if $\Sigma y_t = 2$ we get 3 cases:

0 1 0 0 1 with $\Sigma y_t y_{t-1} = 0$ and hence $\text{Prob} = e^0/D = 1/D$

0 0 1 0 1 with $\Sigma y_t y_{t-1} = 0$ and hence $\text{Prob} = e^0/D = 1/D$

0 0 0 1 1 with $\Sigma y_t y_{t-1} = 1$ and hence $\text{Prob} = e^{\gamma}/D$

where $D = 1 + 1 + e^{\gamma} = e^{\gamma} + 2$.

If $\Sigma y_t = 3$ we again get 3 cases

0 1 1 0 1 with $\Sigma y_t y_{t-1} = 1$ and hence $\text{Prob} = e^{\gamma} D^*$

0 1 0 1 1 with $\Sigma y_t y_{t-1} = 1$ and hence $\text{Prob} = e^{\gamma}/D^*$

0 0 1 1 1 with $\Sigma y_t y_{t-1} = 2$ and hence $\text{Prob} = e^{2\gamma}/D^*$

where $D^* = e^{\gamma} + e^{\gamma} + e^{2\gamma}$. Cancelling e^{γ} throughout we get the probabilities as $1/D$, $1/D$ and e^{γ}/D where $D = e^{\gamma} + 2$.

Note that $\Sigma y_t = 1$ and $\Sigma y_t = 4$ give only one case each and hence the conditional probabilities do not involve γ. Even with more cases in a set, conditional probabilities need not involve γ. For instance, consider $y_1 = 1$,

$y_5 = 1$, $\Sigma y_t = 4$. There are three cases = 1 1 1 0 1, 1 1 0 1 1, 1 0 1 1 1. However, for each we have $\Sigma y_t y_{t-1} = 2$. Hence, the conditional probabilities are $e^{2\gamma}/3e^{2\gamma} = 1/3$ which does not involve γ. For the case $T = 5$, there are only six sets that result in conditional probabilities that involve γ. These are:

$$y_1 = 0,\ y_5 = 1 \text{ and } \Sigma y_t = 2 \text{ or } \Sigma y_t = 3$$

$$y_1 = 0,\ y_5 = 0 \text{ and } \Sigma y_t = 2$$

$$y_1 = 1,\ y_5 = 1 \text{ and } \Sigma y_t = 3$$

$$y_1 = 1,\ y_5 = 0 \text{ and } \Sigma y_t = 2 \text{ or } \Sigma y_t = 3$$

This conditional approach would usually result in using only a small percentage of the sample observations. In their application Corcoran and Hill used $T = 5$ but from Table A.2 of their paper, we can infer that the proportion of the sample used in estimation was 7.1 percent. With $N =$ 1,251 this means that only 89 observations were used in the estimation. Chamberlain (1978, 34–36) considers a data set with $T = 5$ and $N = 1,583$. He uses more observations than Corcoran and Hill. The percentage of the sample observations used was 17 percent, which implies that about 270 observations were used. Chamberlain gets an estimate $\hat{\gamma} = 1.96$ which implies that the odds that an individual unemployed last year is unemployed this year are $e^{1.96} = 7.1$ times higher than if the individual was employed last year. Corcoran and Hill obtain these odds as 12.1 if the α_i are ignored and equal to 3.6 making allowance for α_i using the Chamberlain technique. Thus, making allowance for the individual specific effects α_i reduces the effect of past unemployment on current unemployment considerably.

There are two major limitations of the autoregressive model (26). The first is that the use of the alternative set and the conditional logit method might involve discarding a large number of sample observations and using a very small portion of the data, as in the paper by Corcoran and Hill (1985). The second problem is that the model does not permit the use of exogenous variables (this is a computational problem with this technique) and thus has limited use for policy analysis. All it tells is whether y_t depends on y_{t-1} or not, after allowing for individual specific effects α_i. Both these problems can be solved by going to the random effects (probit) models. An alternative model, suggested by Chamberlain (1978, 30) that allows for the use of exogenous variables is the following:

$$\text{(26a)} \quad \text{Prob}(y_{it} = 1 \mid x_i, y_{i,t-1}) = \frac{\exp(\alpha_i) + \gamma y_{i,t-1}}{\exp(\alpha_i) + \exp(-\beta' x_{it})}$$

By multiplying through by $\exp(\beta' x_{it})$ it can be seen that if $\gamma = 0$ this reduces to the fixed effects logit model with no "state dependence." For this model, sufficient statistics for α_i are $S_i = \Sigma_{t=1}^T y_{it}$ and $S_{i11} = \Sigma_{t=2}^T y_{it} y_{i,t-1}$. S_{i11} gives the number of times a one is preceded by a one. Conditioning on y_{i1} to deal with initial conditions, we get the alternative set as

$$B_i = \{d = (d_1, d_2, \ldots, d_T) \mid d_t = 0 \text{ or } 1,\ d_1 = y_{i1},$$
$$\sum_t d_t = \sum_t y_{it}, \text{ and } \sum_t d_t d_{t-1} = \sum_t y_{it} y_{i,t-1}\}.$$

Chamberlain shows that the model now reduces to the usual conditional logit model with no α_i. There do not appear to be any empirical applications of model (26a) though Solomon Polachek in his comment on Corcoran (1982) argued that this model be estimated.

Another problem that also arises with model (26a) is that it does not ensure that $\text{Prob}(y_{it} = 1)$ will necessarily lie in the range $(0, 1)$. Also, Chamberlain suggested model (26a) for testing the fixed effects model, rather than as a generalization of (26). His idea was that a test of the hypothesis $\gamma = 0$ would enable us to judge whether the fixed effects model is adequate.

The problem of allowing for the influence of observed heterogeneous time varying explanatory variables x_{it} in dynamic models can be solved by going to random effects probit models. Also, they can be handled in the framework of log-linear models as pointed out by Lee (forthcoming). A discussion of the log-linear model approach by Lee would be too lengthy to be included here. There do not appear to be any empirical applications of this approach as yet.

VIII. Autoregressive Probit Models

With the probit models, the conditioning approach, used with the logit models, is not feasible because the fixed effects do not factor out. Hence, we consider random effects models. We can generalize the random effects probit models that we considered earlier to the case that includes "state dependence" or lagged values of y. The one extra problem involved here is the problem of the initial conditions. As we mentioned earlier in the case of continuous variables, Balestra and Nerlove (1966) encountered problems with the ML estimation treating y_{i0} as fixed and Anderson and Hsiao (1982) and Bhargava and Sargan (1983) showed the importance of specifying the distribution of y_{i0}. The best specification is the one that is directly derived from the model itself. In the case of the autoregressive probit models this involves very complicated expressions. A less preferable but more tractable procedure is to assume that y_{i0}'s are random variables with a probability distribution

$$\text{Prob}(y_{i0} = 1) = F(x'_{i0}\delta)$$

where δ is a set of unknown parameters to be estimated. This is the assumption used in Heckman (1981).

IX. Other Types of Autoregressive Models

Analogous to the autoregressive logit and probit models, we can think of autoregressive tobit models of the following form:

$$(27)\quad y^*_{it} = \alpha_i + \beta' x_{it} + \gamma y_{i,t-1} + u_{it}$$

$$y_{it} = y^*_{it} \text{ if } y^*_{it} > 0$$

$$= 0 \text{ otherwise}$$

The methods of estimation for fixed effects and random effects tobit models carry through for this type of models, though again there is the problem of the initial conditions. It is better to start with a probability distribution for y_{i0} rather than treat them fixed.

One other problem that arises is the issue of lagged index vs. lagged dummy (or censored) variable models. For instance, in models (26) or (27) it is the lagged value of the realized variable y_{it} rather than the latent variable y^*_{it} that occurs. A lagged index model would be to specify

$$(28)\quad y^*_{it} = \alpha_i + \beta' x_{it} + \gamma y^*_{i,t-1} + u_{it}$$

That is, it is the latent variable $y^*_{i,t-1}$ that influences y^*_{it}, not the realized value. In studies of unemployment, this implies that it is the "propensity to be unemployed" in the last period rather than the actual state of employment or unemployment that determines the current probability of unemployment.

An example of the lagged index model is in Grether and Maddala (1982) where a model like (28), without the α_i, has been estimated with data from the 1972, 1974, 1976 election panel study administered by the Center for Political Studies at the University of Michigan. Though the example is from the political science area, there are likely to be several examples in economics where the lagged index model makes sense. Some Monte Carlo evidence is also presented in Grether and Maddala (1982) on the performance of the suggested estimator.

X. Serial Correlation or State Dependence

The issue of serial correlation vs. state dependence discussed with continuous-variable models in Equations (10) and (11) has also been raised in the case of dummy variable models. In the case of continuous variable models this distinction can be made if there are explanatory variables x. In the case of dummy variable models Heckman (1978) argues that this distinction can be made even without any explanatory variables. He uses some tests based on the observed runs of 0 and 1. Chamberlain (1978, 1984) and Lee (forthcoming) point out the limitations of these tests and suggest corrections. It is not possible to review these tests in detail here, but some simple procedures suggested by Chamberlain are as follows:

Consider the two models:

(29) $y_t^* = \alpha + \rho y_{t-1} + e_t$ and

(30) $y_t^* = \alpha + u_t,\ u_t = \rho u_{t-1} + e_t$

In both models, $y_t = 1$ if $y_t^* > 0$, $y_t = 0$ otherwise. Model (29) is a pure state dependence model and model (30) is a serial correlation model with no state dependence. In model (29)

$$\text{Prob}(y_t = 1 \mid \alpha, y_{t-1}, y_{t-2} \ldots) = \text{Prob}(y_t = 1 \mid \alpha, y_{t-1})$$

In model (30), however, this probability depends on the entire history of the process. Thus, model (29) implies a first order Markov chain but model (30) does not, for the discrete sequence it generates. Hence, one could test whether the effect of y_{t-2} on y_t is zero or not. But what if we specify (29) with y_{t-2} included? Now the distinction depends on whether the coefficient of y_{t-3} is zero, and so on. Chamberlain says that basing the test on the order of autoregression in (29) is not attractive. With the availability of data on x_t, one can reformulate the test as asking whether there is a dynamic response to changes in x_t or not. Consider

(31) $y_{it}^* = \beta' x_{it} + \gamma y_{i,t-1} + u_{it}$

If $\gamma = 0$ then

$$\text{Prob}(y_{it} = \mid x_{it}, x_{i,t-1}, \ldots) = \text{Prob}(y_{it} = 1 \mid x_{it})$$

Thus, a test for state dependence is carried out by including lagged x's and testing whether their coefficients are significant or not. Chamberlain suggests using this simple test in practice allowing for individual specific effects.

One problem with serial correlation is that it depends crucially on the sampling interval. The smaller this interval, the higher the serial correlation. Suppose our period of observation is one day. The probability that a person who worked yesterday would work today would be very close to one. Hence, Chamberlain argues that finding a significant coefficient for γ in (31) may say very little about the underlying process. The underlying process is a complete description of the amount of time spent by the individual in each state (say, employment and unemployment). The analysis now depends on whether the sample is generated by point sampling or interval sampling. In point sampling we observe what state the individual is in at each point in time. In interval sampling we ask whether the individual was ever in one of the states during the previous time period (say, year). An example of this is the question, "Did you work last year?"

Chamberlain (1984) calls the tests he derives, tests for "duration dependence" rather than "state dependence." The tests are based on conditional logit models. For point sampling, he suggests estimating γ_2 from the following model and testing $\gamma_2 = 0$. (We will drop the i-subscript, since the model is to be used for each i. We obtain γ_2 for each i and then get a weighted average.)

$$\text{Prob}\left(y_1, y_2, \ldots, y_T \,\middle|\, y_1, y_2, \sum_{t=1}^{T} y_t, \sum_{t=2}^{T} y_t y_{t-1}, y_{T-1}, y_T\right)$$

$$= \exp\left(\gamma_2 \sum_{t=3}^{T} y_t y_{t-2}\right) \Big/ \sum_{d \in B} \exp\left(\gamma_2 \sum_{t=3}^{T} d_t d_{t-2}\right)$$

where $B = \Big\{ d = (d_1, d_2, \ldots, d_T \mid d_t = 0 \text{ or }, d_1 = y_1, d_2 = y_2$

$\sum_t d_t = \sum_t y_t, \sum_t d_t d_{t-1} = \sum_t y_t y_{t-1}, d_{T-1} = y_{T-1}, d_T = y_T \Big\}$

For interval sampling Chamberlain suggests a similar test for γ_2 except that the conditioning set B is different (details are in Chamberlain 1984). The method requires $T \geq 6$ in order to generate any conditional probabilities that depend on γ_2. For the case $T = 6$, there is only one set that produces conditional probabilities that depend on γ_2. This set includes two sequences: $S_1 = (101000)$ and $S_2 = (100100)$. The conditional probabilities are:

$$\text{Prob}(S_1 \mid S_1 \text{ or } S_2) = \frac{\exp(\gamma_2)}{1 + \exp(\gamma_2)}$$

and

$$\text{Prob}(S_2 \mid S_1 \text{ or } S_2) = \frac{1}{1 + \exp(\gamma_2)}$$

An estimate of $\exp(\gamma_2)$ is obtained by dividing the number of individuals with sequence S_1 by the number of individuals with sequence S_2. Corcoran (1982) and Corcoran and Hill (1985) use Chamberlain's model with interval sampling. It is not clear, however, as to how many observations were available for the estimation of γ_2. As with most of the conditional logit models, it appears that only a small portion of the data set can be used.

XI. Summary and Conclusions

We started with a review of some problems arising in the estimation of continuous time models with panel data. We reviewed the issues of fixed effects vs. random effects, the problem of initial conditions in dynamic models, and the issue of serial correlation vs. state dependence.

We next reviewed these issues with qualitative and limited dependent variable models. With qualitative variables, for fixed effects models we use the conditional logit model of Chamberlain. In dynamic models this usually involves discarding a large proportion of the sample data. All in all, estimation of random effects models appears to be more advantageous. They use all the observations and are more flexible. Here the model we consider is the probit model rather than the logit model. We considered three methods for the estimation of random effect probit models: the Heckman-Willis model, the Avery-Hansen-Hotz model, and the Chamberlain model.

With tobit models, one can estimate both the fixed effects and random effects models. Also, there are no extra problems with dynamic models except the problem of how to deal with initial conditions. Here it is desirable to treat the initial variables as random rather than as fixed.

With dynamic models, one should consider whether the lagged index model or the lagged dummy (or censored) variables model is appropriate for the problem at hand. The estimation of the former is more straightforward than the latter.

Since serial correlation is dependent on the interval of observation, one should study "duration dependence." Chamberlain suggests some conditional logit models for this, suitable for point and interval sampling.

Besides the models considered here, there are other types of models based on panel data and using the methods of limited dependent variables. An example of this is the estimation of "frontier production functions" with panel data. Illustrations of this are Pitt and Lee (1981) and Schmidt and Sickles (1984).

One problem that needs further discussion is that of specification testing. Tests for exogeneity are available in the Avery-Hansen-Hotz method (the HOTZTRAN program). Chamberlain's models are concerned with tests for exogeneity as well as omitted variable bias. The Breusch and Pagan test needs to be extended to cover limited dependent variables and the tests discussed in Lee and Maddala (1985) need to be extended to cover panel data.

References

Amemiya, Takeshi. 1985. *Advanced Econometrics*. Cambridge: Harvard University Press.

Andersen, E. B. 1973. *Conditional Inference and Models for Measuring*. Copenhagen: Mentalhygiejnisk Forlag.

Anderson, T. W., and C. Hsiao. 1982. "Formulation and Estimation of Dynamic Models Using Panel Data." *Journal of Econometrics* 18(1):67–82.

Avery, R. B., L. P. Hansen, and V. J. Hotz. 1983. "Multiperiod Probit Models and Orthogonality Condition Estimation." *International Economic Review* 24(1):21–35.

Balestra, P., and M. Nerlove. 1966. "Pooling Cross-Section and Time-Series Data in the Estimation of a Dynamic Model: The Demand for Natural Gas." *Econometrica* 34(4):585–612.

Bhargava, A., and J. D. Sargan. 1983. "Estimating Dynamic Random Effects Models From Panel Data Covering Short Time Periods." *Econometrica* 51(6):1635–59.

Björklund, Anders. 1985. "Unemployment and Mental Health: Some Evidence From Panel Data." *The Journal of Human Resources* 20(4):469–83.

Breusch, T., and A. R. Pagan. 1980. "The Lagrange Multiplier Test and Its Applications to Model Specification in Econometrics." *Review of Economic Studies* 47:239–53.

Butler, J. S., and R. Moffitt. 1982. "A Computationally Efficient Quadrature Procedure for the One-Factor Multinomial Probit Model." *Econometrica* 50(3):761–64.

Chamberlain, Gary. 1978. "On the Use of Panel Data." Manuscript. Harvard University.

———. 1980. "Analysis of Covariance With Qualitative Data." *Review of Economic Studies* 47:225–38.

———. 1982. "Multivariate Regression Models for Panel Data." *Journal of Econometrics* 18:5–46.

———. 1985. "Panel Data." In *Handbook of Econometrics*, ed. Z. Griliches and M. D. Intrilligator, vol. 2, 1248–1318. Amsterdam: North-Holland Publishing Co.

———. 1984. "Heterogeneity, Omitted Variable Bias and Duration Dependence." In *Longitudinal Analyses of Labor Market Data*, ed. J. Heckman and B. Singer. New York: Academic Press.

Corcoran, Mary. 1982. "The Employment, Wage and Fertility Consequences of Teenage Women's Nonemployment." In *The Youth Labor Market Problem: Its Nature, Causes and Consequences*, ed. R. B. Freeman and D. A. Wise. Chicago: University of Chicago Press.

Corcoran, Mary, and Martha S. Hill. 1985. "Reoccurence of Unemployment Among Young Adult Men." *The Journal of Human Resources* 20(2):165–83.

Cox, D. R. 1958. "The Regression Analysis of Binary Sequences" (with Discussion). *Journal of the Royal Statistical Society* Series B, 20:215–42.

Fuller, W. A., and G. E. Battese. 1973. "Transformations for Estimation of Linear Models With Nested Error Structure." *Journal of the American Statistical Association* 68:626–32.

Grether, D. M., and G. S. Maddala. 1982. "A Time Series Model With Qualitative Variables." In *Games, Economic Dynamics and Time Series Analysis*, ed. M. Diestler, E. Furst, and G. Schwodiauer, 291–305. Vienna-Wurzburg: Physica-Verlag.

Hansen, Lars P. 1982. "Large Sample Properties of Generalized Method of Moments Estimators." *Econometrica* 50(4):1029–54.

Hausman, Jerry. 1978. "Specification Tests in Econometrics." *Econometrica* 46:1252–72.

Hausman, Jerry, and William E. Taylor. 1981. "Panel Data and Unobservable Individual Effects." *Econometrica* 49(6):1377–98.

Hausman, Jerry, and David Wise. 1979. "Attrition Bias in Experimental and Panel Data: The Gary Income Maintenance Experiment." *Econometrica* 47(2):455–73.

Heckman, James J. 1978. "Simple Statistical Models for Discrete Panel Data Developed and Applied to Test the Hypothesis of True State Dependence Against the Hypothesis of Spurious State Dependence." Annales de L'INSEE, 30/31 (1978), 227–69.

———. 1981. "Statistical Models for Discrete Panel Data." In *Structural Analysis of Discrete Data With Econometric Applications*, ed. C. F. Manski and D. McFadden, 114–78. Cambridge: MIT Press.

———. 1981. "The Incidental Parameters Problem and the Problem of Initial Conditions in Estimating a Discrete Time Discrete Data Stochastic Process." In *Structural Analysis of Discrete Data With Econometric Applications*, ed. C. F. Manski and D. McFadden, 179–95. Cambridge: MIT Press.

———. 1981. "Heterogeneity and State Dependence." In *Studies in Labor Markets*, ed. S. Rosen, 91–139. Chicago: University of Chicago Press.

———. 1984. "Econometric Duration Analysis." *Journal of Econometrics* 24(1/2):63–132.

Heckman, James J., and George J. Borjas. 1980. "Does Unemployment Cause Future Unemployment? Definitions, Questions and Answers From a Continuous Time Model of Heterogeneity and State Dependence." *Economica* 47(187):247–83.

Heckman, James J., and Thomas E. MaCurdy. 1980. "A Life-Cycle Model of Female Labor Supply." *Review of Economic Studies* 47:47–74.

Heckman, James J., and Robert Willis. 1976. "Estimation of a Stochastic Model of Reproduction: An Econometric Approach." In *Household Production and Consumption*, ed. N. Terleckyj. New York: National Bureau of Economic Research.

Johnson, Norman L., and Samuel Kotz. 1972. *Continuous Multivariate Distributions*. New York: Wiley.

Lee, Lung-fei. 1981. "Efficient Estimation of Dynamic Error Components Models With Panel Data." In *Time-Series Analysis*, ed. O. D. Anderson and M. R. Perryman, 267–85. Amsterdam: North-Holland.

———. Forthcoming. "Analysis of Econometric Models for Discrete Panel Data in the Multivariate Log-Linear Probability Models." Discussion Paper #23, October 1980, Center for Econometrics and Decision Sciences, University of Florida. *Journal of Econometrics*.

Lee, Lung-fei, and G. S. Maddala. 1985. "The Common Structure of Tests for Selectivity Bias, Serial Correlation, Heteroscedasticity and Non-Normality in the Tobit Model." *International Economic Review* 26(1):1–20.

Maddala, G. S. 1971. "The Use of Variance Components Models in Pooling Cross-Section and Time-Series Data." *Econometrica* 39(2):341–58.

———. 1983. *Limited Dependent and Qualitative Variables in Econometrics*. New York: Cambridge University Press.

Malinvaud, E. 1970. *Statistical Methods of Econometrics*. Amsterdam: North-Holland Publishing Co.

Mundlak, Yair. 1978. "On the Pooling of Time-Series and Cross-Section Data." *Econometrica* 46(1):69–85.

Nerlove, Marc. 1971. "Further Evidence on the Estimation of Dynamic Economic Relations From a Time-Series of Cross-Sections." *Econometrica* 39(2):359–82.

Pitt, M. M., and Lung-fei Lee. 1981. "The Measurement of Sources of Technical Inefficiency in the Indonesian Weaving Industry." *Journal of Development Economics* 9(1):43–64.

Robinson, P. M. 1982. "On the Asymptotic Properties of Estimators of Models Containing Limited Dependent Variables." *Econometrica* 50(1):27–41.

Schmidt, Peter, and Robin Sickles. 1984. "Production Frontiers and Panel Data." *Journal of Business and Economic Statistics* 2:367–74.

Sickles, Robin C., and Paul Taubman. 1986. "A Multivariate Error Components Analysis of the Health and Retirement Status of the Elderly." *Econometrica* 54(6):1339–56.

Part IV
Frontier Production Functions

[19]

© Journal of Business & Economic Statistics, Vol. 2, No. 4, October 1984

Production Frontiers and Panel Data

Peter Schmidt
Department of Economics, Michigan State University, East Lansing, MI 48824

Robin C. Sickles
Department of Economics, University of Pennsylvania, Philadelphia, PA 19104

1. INTRODUCTION

This article considers estimation of a *stochastic frontier* production function—the type introduced by Aigner, Lovell, and Schmidt (1977) and Meeusen and van den Broeck (1977). Such a production frontier model consists of a production function of the usual regression type but with an error term equal to the sum of two parts. The first part is typically assumed to be normally distributed and represents the usual statistical noise, such as luck, weather, machine breakdown, and other events beyond the control of the firm. The second part is nonpositive and represents technical inefficiency—that is, failure to produce maximal output, given the set of inputs used. Realized output is bounded from above by a frontier that includes the deterministic part of the regression, plus the part of the error representing noise; so the frontier is stochastic. There also exist so-called *deterministic frontier* models, whose error term contains only the nonpositive component, but we will not consider them here (e.g., see Greene 1980). Frontier models arise naturally in the problem of efficiency measurement, since one needs a bound on output to measure efficiency. A good survey of such production functions and their relationship to the measurement of productive efficiency was given by Førsund, Lovell, and Schmidt (1980).

Previous work on production frontiers, with the exception of Pitt and Lee (1981), has assumed error terms that are independently distributed across observations; this assumption is reasonable only in a (single) cross section. Thus previous empirical implementations of frontier models have used cross-sectional data. There are great potential advantages to modifying existing frontier models to allow the use of panel data. In this article we exploit these advantages using a unique panel data set of U.S. domestic airlines and identify firm-specific productive efficiency.

Stochastic-frontier models currently suffer from three serious difficulties. First, the technical inefficiency of a particular firm (observation) can be estimated but not consistently. We can consistently estimate the (whole) error term for a given observation, but it contains statistical noise as well as technical inefficiency. The variance of the distribution of technical inefficiency, conditional on the whole error term, does not vanish when the sample size increases (see Jondrow et al. 1982 for a discussion of this point). Second, the estimation of the model and the separation of technical inefficiency from statistical noise require specific assumptions about the distribution of technical inefficiency (e.g., half-normal) and statistical noise (e.g., normal). It is not clear how robust one's results are to these assumptions. Another way to emphasize this point is to note that the evidence of technical inefficiency is skewness of the production-function error, and not everyone will agree that skewness should be regarded as evidence of inefficiency. Third, it may be incorrect to assume that inefficiency is independent of the regressors. If a firm knows its level of technical inefficiency, for example, this should affect its input choices.

All three of these problems are potentially avoidable if one has panel data, say T observations on each of N firms. The technical inefficiency of a particular firm can be estimated consistently at $T \rightarrow \infty$; adding more observations on the same firm yields information not attainable by adding more firms. Second, with a panel one need not make such strong distributional assumptions as are necessary with a single cross section. Essentially, evidence of inefficiency can be found in constancy over time as well as in skewness. Finally, estimates of the parameters and of the firms' inefficiency levels can be obtained without assuming that technical inefficiency is uncorrelated with the regressors. Therefore, we will consider a variety of different estimators, depending on what one is willing to assume about the distribution of technical inefficiency and its potential correlation with the regressors.

The model to be analyzed is presented in Section 2 of this article. Section 3 discusses estimation of the model by ordinary least squares. The *within* estimator is presented in Section 4. Section 5 presents the GLS estimator, whereas Section 6 discusses an estimator due to Hausman and Taylor (1981). Section 7 discusses MLE, given a distributional assumption on the effects. Section 8 discusses some tests of the assumptions that lead to the different estimators. Section 9 illustrates these methods using a new and fairly lengthy panel of U.S. domestic airlines, and Section 10 is the conclusion.

2. PRESENTATION OF THE MODEL

We begin with a single-equation production function. (Alternatively, with a change in the sign of the one-sided error, it could be a cost function.) The model to be analyzed is of the form

$$y_{it} = \alpha + X_{it}'\beta + v_{it} - u_i,$$

$$i = 1, \ldots, N, t = 1, \ldots, T. \quad (1)$$

Here i indexes firms and t indexes time periods. The value y_{it} is output (for firm i in time t), whereas X_{it} is a vector of K inputs. The v_{it} are uncorrelated with the regressors X_{it}—for example, by the Zellner, Kmenta, and Dreze (1966) argument. The u_i represent technical inefficiency and, correspondingly, $u_i \geq 0$ for all i. We assume the u_i to be iid with mean μ and variance σ_u^2 and independent of the v_{it}. A particular distribution (e.g., half-normal) may or may not be assumed for the u_i. Furthermore, the u_i may or may not be assumed to be uncorrelated with the regressors (X_{it}); presumably this depends on whether u_i is known to firm i or not.

For $T = 1$ (pure cross section of N firms), the model in (1) is exactly the stochastic frontier of Aigner, Lovell, and Schmidt (1977). For $T > 1$, it is a straightforward generalization of that model, and it fits exactly the usual framework in the panel-data literature, with a *firm effect* but no *time effect*. The only difference from the standard panel-data literature is that our firm effects are one-sided, and we will in some cases assume a (nonnormal) distribution for them.

It may also be profitable to rewrite the model slightly in two ways. First, let $E(u_i) = \mu > 0$ (as before), and define

$$\alpha^* = \alpha - \mu, \; u_i^* = u_i - \mu \quad (2)$$

so that the u_i^* are iid with mean 0. Then in the model

$$y_{it} = \alpha^* + X_{it}'\beta + v_{it} - u_i^*, \quad (3)$$

the error terms v_{it} and u_i^* have zero mean, and most of the results of the panel data literature apply directly, except of course those that hinge on normality. Second, define

$$\alpha_i = \alpha - u_i = \alpha^* - u_i^*, \quad (4)$$

and the model becomes

$$y_{it} = \alpha_i + X_{it}'\beta + v_{it}. \quad (5)$$

This is useful because we will have occasion to refer to the α_i shortly.

3. ESTIMATION BY ORDINARY LEAST SQUARES

Ordinary least squares may be applied to (3), treating $(v_{it} - u_i^*)$ as the disturbance. The resulting estimates of α^* and β will be consistent as $N \to \infty$ (though not as $T \to \infty$ for fixed N) if the individual effects (u_i) are uncorrelated with the regressors (X_{it}). Under these circumstances, however, a better alternative exists (see Section 5), so ordinary least squares estimation is not recommended.

4. DUMMY VARIABLES (WITHIN ESTIMATOR)

The so-called *within* estimator treats the u_i as fixed—that is, it estimates a separate intercept for every firm, as in (5). This can be done by suppressing the constant term and adding a dummy variable for each of the N firms or, equivalently, by keeping the constant term and adding $(N - 1)$ dummies. Another equivalent procedure is to apply the within transformation—that is, to apply OLS after expressing all data in terms of deviations from the firm means (e.g., replace y_{it} by $y_{it} - \bar{y}_i$, etc.). In the latter case, the N intercepts are recovered as the means of the residuals by firm.

The chief advantage of the within estimator is that its consistency does not hinge on uncorrelatedness of the regressors and the individual effects. It also does not depend on the distribution of the effects, since in treating them as fixed it simply proceeds conditionally from whatever their realizations may be. The within estimate of β is consistent as *either* N or $T \to \infty$. Consistency of the individual estimated intercepts (α_i), however, requires $T \to \infty$.

All of this is well known and requires basically no adaptation to the frontier case (e.g., see the usual panel data literature, Mundlak 1978 and Hausman and Taylor 1981). In the frontier case, however, we can use the fact that $u_i \geq 0$ to appropriately normalize the effects (u_i) and the overall constant (α), at least if N is large. If the N estimated intercepts are $\hat{\alpha}_1, \ldots, \hat{\alpha}_N$, simply define

$$\hat{\alpha} = \max(\hat{\alpha}_i) \text{ and}$$

$$\hat{u}_i = \hat{\alpha} - \hat{\alpha}_i, \qquad i = 1, 2, \ldots, N. \quad (6)$$

This definition amounts to counting the most efficient firm in the sample as 100% efficient. Provided only that the density of u is nonzero in some neighborhood $(0, \epsilon)$ for some $\epsilon > 0$, the efficiency of the most efficient firm in the sample will indeed approach 100% as $N \to \infty$. (This is essentially the argument of Greene 1980 in the single cross-section case.) Thus the estimates in (6) are consistent for α and the u_i as N and $T \to \infty$.

To summarize, we can estimate the individual intercepts (one for each firm) consistently as $T \to \infty$. Thus we can compare efficiency across firms. In addition, as $N \to \infty$ we can consistently separate the overall intercept from the one-sided individual effects, which allows us to measure efficiency relative to an absolute standard (100%).

The distributional properties of the estimators defined in (6) are not trivial; that is, if we wish to assign standard errors, compute confidence intervals, and so forth, some unsolved problems arise.

When N is large relative to T, these problems are essentially avoided. In this case, the variability of the $\hat{\alpha}_i$ as estimates of the α_i is large relative to the variability of $\min(u_i)$ as an estimate of zero; that is, we can ignore the variability involved in the "max" operation. Then treating $\hat{\alpha}$ and the $\hat{u}_i$ as simple linear functions of the $\hat{\alpha}_i$, the distribution of $\hat{\alpha}$ and the $\hat{u}_i$ is easily calculated.

When T is large relative to N, we can do the converse and ignore the variability of the $\hat{\alpha}_i$. Then essentially $\hat{\alpha} = \max(\alpha_i) = \alpha - \min(u_i)$, and we have the problem of the distribution of the smallest observation in a random sample of size N from the distribution of u. For moderately large N, and for reasonable distributions of u, $\min(u_i)$ will follow an extreme-value (double-exponential) distribution. Hence standard results apply (e.g., see Galambos 1978). Alternatively, if we assume a particular distribution for the u_i, we can obtain more precise results. For example, if the u_i are iid exponential with parameter Θ, then $\min(u_i)$ is exponential with parameter Θ/N (e.g., see Johnson and Kotz 1970, pp. 211–212). Thus $\hat{\alpha} = \max(\alpha_i) = \alpha - \min(u_i)$ would have a mean equal to $\alpha - \Theta/N$ and a variance equal to Θ^2/N^2. Given that the MLE of Θ, say $\hat{\Theta}$, has a mean equal to $\Theta(N-1)/N$, an unbiased estimator of α is $\hat{\alpha} + \hat{\Theta}/(N-1)$, whereas an unbiased predictor of u_i is $\hat{u}_i + \hat{\Theta}/(N-1)$; furthermore, confidence intervals are easily constructed. (Of course, distributions other than exponential will not give such simple results.)

When we are not satisfied with ignoring either kind of variability, things are more complicated. The estimator $\hat{\alpha}$ in (6) is actually $\hat{\alpha} = \alpha + \max[(\hat{\alpha}_i - \alpha_i) - u_i]$. The terms $[(\hat{\alpha}_i - \alpha_i) - u_i]$ are mixtures of a normal and a one-sided distribution. Worse, they are not independent over i, so standard results do not apply. Just what can be done here remains to be seen.

A considerable disadvantage of the within estimator is that it is impossible to include in the specification regressors that are invariant over time, even though they vary across firms. In this case our estimated firm effects will include the effects of all variables that are fixed within the sample at the firm level, possibly including some (e.g., capital stock) that are not in any sense a representation of inefficiency. To avoid this problem one must make assumptions about uncorrelatedness of effects and regressors and/or about the distribution of the effects.

5. GENERALIZED LEAST SQUARES ESTIMATION

We now treat the effects (u_i) as random, and we make the assumption that they are uncorrelated with the regressors. At this point, however, we still do not make any distributional assumption for the effects. This leads to the generalized least squares estimation of (3), exactly as in the panel-data literature, the covariance of the error $(v_{it} - u_i^*)$ being of the usual form. This covariance matrix depends on σ_v^2 and σ_u^2, and we distinguish the case in which these are known from the (realistic) case in which they are not known and must be estimated with α^* and β.

We begin by summarizing some well-known results from the panel-data literature. With σ_v^2 and σ_u^2 known, the GLS estimator (of α^* and β) is consistent as either N or $T \to \infty$. It is more efficient than the within estimator, but this difference in efficiencies disappears as $T \to \infty$. (It remains as $N \to \infty$ for fixed T, the usual panel case.) When σ_v^2 and σ_u^2 are not known (i.e., the realistic case), GLS is based on their consistent estimates, say $\hat{\sigma}_v^2$ requires $\hat{\sigma}_u^2$. Consistent estimation of σ_u^2 requires $N \to \infty$. Thus the strongest case for GLS is when N is large and T is small; the assumption of uncorrelatedness of effects and regressors buys extra efficiency. If T is large and N is small, GLS is useless (unless σ_u^2 were known a priori). If N and T are both large, GLS is feasible but not more efficient than within.

Given our estimate of β, say $\hat{\beta}$, we can recover estimates of the individual firm intercepts (α_i) from the residuals. If we define the residuals as $\hat{\epsilon}_{it} = y_{it} - X_{it}'\hat{\beta}$, we can estimate α_i by the mean (over time) of the residuals for firm i:

$$\hat{\alpha}_i = \frac{1}{T}\sum_t \hat{\epsilon}_{it}, \qquad i = 1, 2, \ldots, N. \tag{7}$$

These estimates are consistent as $T \to \infty$, provided that $\hat{\beta}$ is consistent (which requires $N \to \infty$ or σ_u^2 known). We can also decompose the $\hat{\alpha}_i$ into estimates of $\hat{\alpha}$ and the $\hat{u}_i$, as in (7), for which consistency requires $N \to \infty$ plus consistency of the $\hat{\alpha}_i$. Thus consistent estimation of technical inefficiency requires both $N \to \infty$ and $T \to \infty$, just as for within. (Another possibility is to use the best linear unbiased predictor (BLUP) of Taub 1979 and Lee and Griffiths 1979. After (3) is estimated, the BLUP of u_i^* is $-\hat{\sigma}_u^2 \sum_t (y_{it} - \hat{\alpha}^* - X_{it}'\hat{\beta})/(T\hat{\sigma}_u^2 + \hat{\sigma}_v^2)$, and the resulting estimate of α_i is $\hat{\alpha}^* - \hat{u}_i^*$. For large T, this is equivalent to (7).)

The important advantage of the GLS estimator relative to the within estimator, in the present context, is not efficiency but rather the ability to include time-invariant regressors. In cases in which time-invariant regressors are relevant, this is important so that their effects do not contaminate measured efficiency.

6. THE HAUSMAN-TAYLOR ESTIMATOR

The GLS estimator hinges on the assumption that the effects and regressors are uncorrelated, whereas the within estimator does not. In a recent paper, Hausman and Taylor (1981) proposed an estimator that is a hybrid of the two, in the sense that one may assume the effects to be uncorrelated with some but not all of the regressors.

This estimator may be motivated in terms of the efficiency gains in imposing such (uncorrelatedness) restrictions. In the present context, however, a more compelling motivation is the potential to include time-invariant regressors. Hausman and Taylor gave an elegant and complete statement of the conditions for the coefficients of time-invariant regressors to be identified. Basically, the number of time-varying regressors that are uncorrelated with the effects must be at least as large as the number of time-invariant regressors that are correlated with the effects.

Individual effects can be estimated consistently from the residuals if T is large and separated from the intercept if N is large, exactly as for GLS.

7. MAXIMUM LIKELIHOOD, GIVEN INDEPENDENCE AND A DISTRIBUTION

In the previous frontier literature, the effects have been assumed independent of regressors, and specific distributional assumptions have been made for v and u (usually normal for v and half-normal for u). As we have seen, these strong assumptions can be avoided when one has panel data. Nevertheless, it is still possible to make these assumptions, in which case a maximum-likelihood estimator is feasible.

We therefore assume that the v_{it} are iid with density $f(v)$, known up to some parameters, that the u_i are iid with density $g(u)$, also known up to some parameters, and that u and v are independent of each other and of the regressors. If we define $\epsilon_{it} = v_{it} - u_i$ and note that these are independent over i, then the likelihood function follows easily from the joint density of $(\epsilon_{i1}, \ldots, \epsilon_{iT})$, which is given by

$$h(\epsilon_{i1}, \ldots, \epsilon_{iT}) = \int_0^\infty g(u) \prod_{t=1}^{T} f(\epsilon_{it} + u)\, du. \quad (8)$$

Given this density, the likelihood function is

$$L = \prod_{i=1}^{N} h(y_{i1} - \alpha - X'_{i1}\beta, \ldots, y_{iT} - \alpha - X'_{iT}\beta). \quad (9)$$

Its maximization yields the MLE's of the parameters (α, β, and the parameters in the densities of u and v).

Pitt and Lee (1981) derived the likelihood function (9) for the case in which the v_{it} are normal and the u_i are half-normal, and they calculated maximum-likelihood estimates for a sample of Indonesian weaving firms.

The asymptotic properties of the MLE's in this model require further work, since they have not yet been worked out carefully. We conjecture that (given suitable regularity conditions) the MLE's are consistent and asymptotically efficient as $N \to \infty$, regardless of T. What happens as $T \to \infty$ for fixed N is less clear. Certainly consistent estimation of the parameters of the distribution of u must require $N \to \infty$, but results for the other parameters are less obvious. As far as efficiency is concerned, we conjecture that the MLE's are generally more efficient (asymptotically) than the estimators previously considered, since they exploit distributional information that the other estimators do not exploit. But it is conceivable that at least for some distributional choices, this information is useless asymptotically. For example, if both v and u are normal, then *within*, GLS, and MLE are all asymptotically equivalent (as both N and $T \to \infty$). Whether *one-sided* distributions of u exist, such that this equivalence occurs, is not yet clear.

The preceding estimator assumes both independence of effects and regressors and specific distributions for v and u. If we relax the distributional assumptions but maintain independence, we are led to GLS, as discussed in Section 5. On the other hand, if we maintain the distributional assumptions but relax independence, things are less clear. As discussed in Section 4, we can estimate by within and then use the distributional assumption in normalizing the effects; but this is not entirely satisfactory, since the distributional assumption may be useful in estimating the parameters. A more promising possibility is to follow Mundlak (1978) and Chamberlain (1980) by modeling the correlation between X and u. When this is done, GLS = within. For nonnormal u, however, GLS may not be the optimal estimator, and the optimal estimator may not equal within.

8. TESTS OF UNCORRELATEDNESS AND DISTRIBUTIONAL FORM

The estimators that have been presented differ in the extent to which they depend on the effects being uncorrelated with the regressors and/or on a distributional assumption for the effects. These assumptions can in turn be tested using Hausman-type (1978) tests, based on the differences between the various estimators.

Testing the null hypothesis that effects and regressors are uncorrelated was discussed in detail by Hausman and Taylor (1981, Sect. 2.2 and 3.3). The test they proposed is a Hausman-type test of the significance of the difference between the within estimator and the GLS estimator (to test the hypothesis that the effects are uncorrelated with *all* regressors) or of the significance of the difference between the within estimator and the Hausman–Taylor estimator (to test the hypothesis that the effects are uncorrelated with a specified subset of the regressors). This requires N to be large, since the GLS and Hausman–Taylor estimators require large N to estimate σ_u^2. Indeed, since only N realizations of u exist in the data, any asymptotic test about u must, of necessity, require $N \to \infty$, so this is not surprising.

Given that the effects are uncorrelated with the regressors, a distributional assumption (e.g., normal v, half-normal u) can be tested by a Hausman test of the difference between the GLS estimator and the MLE. Similarly, the joint hypothesis that the effects are uncorrelated with the regressors and that the distributional assumptions are correct could be based on the difference between the MLE and the within estimator.

Since we have not provided an estimator that exploits a distributional assumption without assuming effects to be independent of regressors, no Hausman-type test is available of the distributional assumptions only. If both N and T are large, however, we could use standard goodness-of-fit tests to see whether the estimated effects from within follow the hypothesized distribution, and this test would not depend on the correlation between effects and regressors. A distributional assumption (e.g., normality) about the error terms v could also be tested by standard methods using within residuals, and such asymptotic tests would require only that either N or T be large.

9. EMPIRICAL ILLUSTRATION

In this section we illustrate the methods outlined before by estimating a production function for the U.S. domestic airline industry. The source of the data was the Civil Aeronautics Board Form 41 data base provided by the Air Transport Association of America and maintained by the Boeing Computer Services, Inc. A detailed description of the accounts in the Form 41 from which expense and quantity indexes were compiled is available on request. The data are by airline by quarter from 1970 I to 1978 III. The airlines used in the study are American, Allegheny, Braniff, Continental, Delta, Eastern, Frontier, North Central, Ozark, Piedmont, United, and Western. Each observation on the calculated Divisia indexes of price and quantity required information on 230 separate accounts. Appendix A contains a discussion of the broad categories of inputs and output and the main contents of these categories. For a lengthier discussion, see Sickles (1983).

The input categories are capital, labor, energy, and materials, and the output is capacity ton miles (CTM). We implicitly assume that any unfilled space is wastage. On the other hand, it is obviously cheaper to fly an airplane from one point to another if it is empty and if it does not make intermediate stops. We therefore controlled for differences in the airlines' networks by including, as arguments in the production function, load factor, average stage length (miles between each takeoff and landing), and their interaction. We also included quarterly seasonal dummy variables. The Divisia indexes were constructed using industry price weights so that the major portion of estimated inefficiencies should be due to inefficient use of inputs instead of being purchased at suboptimal prices. We assume Cobb–Douglas technology and Hicks-neutral technological change. We also abstract from the complications that would be introduced by a more plausible treatment of the dynamics of production (e.g., by allowing for quasi-fixed factors of production or sluggish adjustment to desired production levels).

Appendix B reports the within, GLS, and MLE estimates of the production function. The estimated factor-productivity growth of between 1.5% and 2% per year for each of the models is close to the 2.5% growth rate calculated directly from the data as the difference in the Divisia indexes of output and of the inputs. All three sets of results are close in terms of $\bar{R}^2$, estimated output elasticities, and significance of coefficients.

Given the considerable differences in the sizes of the firms, one might suspect heteroscedasticity to be a problem. We, however, did not find it to be so. Running separate regressions for each airline, estimated error variances were not very different. For example, we have $s^2 = .00015$ for the largest airline in the sample and $s^2 = .00013$ for the smallest; this difference is insignificant.

Table 1 displays the estimated technical efficiency of the 12 airlines and their average output. The efficiencies are close for all three models, and the rankings are almost identical. Two comments about these efficiencies are in order. First, because of the small number of firms in the sample ($N = 12$), the normalization of the most efficient firm as 100% technically efficient is questionable. We have a reasonably long sample ($T = 35$), however, so we can have some faith in the *relative* efficiency rankings. (In other words, we should have more faith in the statement that Delta is 12% more efficient than Eastern than we should in the specific technical efficiencies of 95.2% and 83.2%, respectively.) Second, our efficiency rankings for the period 1970–1978 do not seem to do a good job of predicting post-1978 financial success; some of our most efficient firms are now bankrupt or nearly so. An obvious explanation (which we believe) is that this is simply due to the difference between regulated and unregulated environments. An airline may have been very good at flying

Table 1. Technical Efficiencies

Firm	Average Capacity Output (thousands)	Firm Efficiency (%) Within	GLS	MLE
American	1,138,244	89.2	83.3	85.6
Allegheny	146,727	75.1	78.0	77.8
Braniff	341,447	89.2	87.7	89.6
Continental	332,006	100.0	98.0	99.4
Delta	763,683	95.2	94.0	96.2
Eastern	841,230	83.2	80.4	80.8
Frontier	68,620	95.7	100.0	100.0
North Central	58,267	71.9	77.0	76.8
Ozark	48,116	70.7	75.7	75.6
Piedmont	49,656	70.2	75.1	74.7
United	1,430,228	93.1	87.8	91.0
Western	310,974	98.0	95.9	98.6

from point A to point B but poor at choosing A and B or the fare to change.

Given the similarities in the results, it is not surprising that the null hypothesis of no correlation between effects and regressors is accepted. The Hausman test χ^2_{11} is 3.74. Given the uncorrelatedness of the effects and regressors, the distributional test can be carried out by comparing the GLS estimator with the MLE estimator. For this test the χ^2_{11} is 13.73. The joint hypothesis of uncorrelated regressors *and* correct distribution is tested by comparing the within with the MLE estimates. In this case the χ^2_{11} was 13.64. All of these are well within the acceptance region at the .05 level.

It is also interesting to examine the within inefficiencies directly. They do not look too different from drawings from a half-normal distribution, though of course, with only 12 observations this is hard to tell. If we split their possible range into the three cells $u \leq .10$, $.10 < u \leq .20$, and $.20 < u$, the observed counts are 5, 3, and 4. Treating the inefficiencies as half-normal data, the MLE of σ^2_u is .03208, which leads to expected cell counts of 5.08, 3.17, and 3.75; these are surprisingly close to those observed. Presumably other tests of fit would also fail to reject half-normality, given the small sample size.

10. CONCLUSIONS AND FURTHER DIRECTIONS

In this article we have considered estimation of a stochastic frontier production function model, given panel data. We have provided a variety of estimators, depending on whether or not one is willing to assume that technical inefficiency (the individual effect, in panel-data jargon) is uncorrelated with the regressors and on whether or not one is willing to make specific distributional assumptions for the errors (e.g., normal for the general error term and half-normal for technical inefficiency). We have also indicated how to test these assumptions.

Since we rely here on asymptotics, it is important that either N or T (or both) be large. The most favorable case is naturally when both N and T are large, since we can then estimate the parameters of the model and the technical efficiency of each firm consistently, regardless of which of the preceding sets of assumptions we choose; all of the methods discussed in this article are potentially applicable.

If T is large but N is small, we are restricted to using the within estimator, which exploits neither a distributional assumption nor uncorrelatedness of effects and regressors and which does not allow time-invariant regressors. We can consistently estimate the intercept for each firm, but there is no consistent way of separating the overall intercept from the one-sided effects. Thus we can compare efficiencies across firms but not relative to an absolute standard.

If N is large but T is small, we are closest in spirit to both the usual panel-data literature and the usual frontier literature. We can choose any of the estimators described before, depending on what we are willing to assume, and we can test our assumptions. Although we can estimate the intercept of each firm (or the technical efficiency of each firm, if we use MLE), we cannot do so consistently; consistency of estimated-firm effects inherently requires $T \rightarrow \infty$.

ACKNOWLEDGMENT

The support of National Science Foundation Grants SES-7926716 and SES-8218114 is gratefully acknowledged.

APPENDIX A: DATA

The source of data was the Civil Aeronautics Board Form 41 data base provided to Sickles by the Air Transport Association of America and maintained by the Boeing Computer Services, Inc., from 1970 I to 1978 III. Mergers during this time were handled by combining accounts for the relevant parties at the time of merger. The airlines in the study are American, Allegheny, Braniff, Continental, Delta, Eastern, Frontier, North Central, Ozark, Piedmont, United, and Western. Each observation on the calculated indexes of price and quantity required information on 230 separate accounts.

The labor input was composed of 55 separate labor accounts aggregated into five major employment classes. They are pilots, flight attendants, machinists, passenger/cargo and aircraft handlers, and other personnel. Labor-related expenses such as insurance, pensions, and payroll taxes were allocated to each class on the basis of the expense share of the class. Expense/person quarters in 1972 III were normalized to 1.0 before the Divisia indexes for price and quantity were calculated.

The capital input was developed by constructing four categories of expenses that were directly or indirectly identified with capital. These expense categories were flight equipment purchased and rented, ground equipment purchased, ground equipment rented, and landing fees. Quantity indexes for flight equipment purchased and rented were calculated by imputing to purchased aircraft the rental price of a comparably configured aircraft. This assumes of course that depreciation of the aircraft is negligible. Because of the strict Federal Aviation Administration maintenance requirements, this assumption seems quite reasonable. It is one that was adopted in a previous study by Caves, Christensen, and Tretheway (1981). We adjusted for differing aircraft utilization rates by scaling the capital quantity on the basis of average hours ramp to ramp during the day relative to the maximum average quarterly usage during the period. Ground-equipment rental expenses and the implicit deflator for nonresidential fixed investment were used for the second category. Ground-equipment rental expenses were calculated using the perpetual inventory approach, a 1955 benchmark, and the Jorgensen–Hall user price for capital formula. A 15-year replacement rate and accelerated or straight-line (depending on the firm's current profitability) depreciation schedules were assumed. The fourth capital category is landing fees or the rental cost of the airport facilities. A price deflator for landing fee expenses was cost/capacity ton landed.

The energy input was developed by combining information on aircraft gallons used with expense data per period. Furthermore, we transformed the gallons used into the BTU equivalent using the conversion rate for turbo fuel, the predominant fuel used by the carriers since the mid-1960's.

The fourth input, *materials*, is comprised of many broad classes of materials, which were themselves aggregates of 56 different accounts. These categories included advertising, communications, insurance, outside services, supplies, passenger food, commissions, and other operating and nonoperating expenses.

The capacity ton mile quantity index was generated from data on total capacity ton miles for first class and coach. Price deflators for the three categories were derived from the revenue output accounts. Thus our measure of output is transferred space. We are implicitly assuming that unused space is wastage and is a demand consideration that is outside the scope of this study.

APPENDIX B: ESTIMATION RESULTS

Within: $\bar{R}^2 = .992$ and $\sigma_v^2 = .00142$

$$\begin{aligned}\ln CTM = {} & \underset{(1.25)}{.675\text{AA}} + \underset{(1.05)}{.533\text{AL}} + \underset{(1.30)}{.675\text{BN}} \\ & + \underset{(1.51)}{.783\text{CO}} + \underset{(1.39)}{.734\text{DL}} + \underset{(1.14)}{.615\text{EA}} \\ & + \underset{(1.51)}{.739\text{FR}} + \underset{(1.02)}{.502\text{NC}} + \underset{(1.00)}{.490\text{OZ}} \\ & + \underset{(0.99)}{.485\text{PI}} + \underset{(1.32)}{.714\text{UA}} + \underset{(1.48)}{.763\text{WA}} \\ & + \underset{(8.86)}{.00383t} + \underset{(5.67)}{.147K} + \underset{(7.06)}{.218L} \\ & + \underset{(16.12)}{.605E} + \underset{(5.30)}{.148M} - \underset{(-1.05)}{.00566\ \text{Winter}} \\ & + \underset{(3.33)}{.0179\ \text{Spring}} + \underset{(6.07)}{.0346\ \text{Summer}} \\ & - \underset{(-12.6)}{1.33\ \text{Load F}} - \underset{(-2.64)}{.000418\ \text{STGL}} \\ & + \underset{(7.34)}{.00149\ \text{Load F} * \text{STGL}}.\end{aligned}$$

GLS: $\bar{R}^2 = .986$, $\sigma_v^2 = .00142$, and $\sigma_u^2 = .0259$

$$\begin{aligned}\ln CTM = {} & \underset{(.077)}{.345} + \underset{(9.26)}{.00352t} + \underset{(6.11)}{.154K} \\ & + \underset{(7.45)}{.226L} + \underset{(16.1)}{.597E} + \underset{(5.78)}{.157M} \\ & - \underset{(-1.11)}{.00597\ \text{Winter}} + \underset{(3.35)}{.0180\ \text{Spring}} \\ & + \underset{(6.02)}{.0344\ \text{Summer}} - \underset{(-12.96)}{1.356\ \text{Load F}} \\ & - \underset{(-2.05)}{.000303\ \text{STGL}} \\ & + \underset{(7.50)}{.00151\ \text{Load F} * \text{STGL}}.\end{aligned}$$

MLE: $\bar{R}^2 = .985$, $\sigma_v^2 = .00129$, and $\sigma_u^2 = .1990$

$$\begin{aligned}\ln CTM = {} & \underset{(-2.22)}{-.0957} + \underset{(12.26)}{.00294t} + \underset{(31.8)}{.201K} \\ & + \underset{(13.6)}{.238L} + \underset{(70.4)}{.527E} + \underset{(15.9)}{.215M} \\ & - \underset{(-1.24)}{.00548\ \text{Winter}} + \underset{(3.99)}{.0184\ \text{Spring}} \\ & + \underset{(8.64)}{.0386\ \text{Summer}} \\ & - \underset{(-18.8)}{1.412\ \text{Load F}} - \underset{(-22.3)}{.00345\ \text{STGL}} \\ & + \underset{(11.4)}{.00147\ \text{Load F} * \text{STGL}}.\end{aligned}$$

[*Received September 1983. Revised February 1984.*]

REFERENCES

AIGNER, D. J., LOVELL, C. A. K., and SCHMIDT, P. (1977), "Formulation and Estimation of Stochastic Frontier Production Function Models," *Journal of Econometrics*, 6, 21–37.

CAVES, D. W., CHRISTENSEN, L. R., and TRETHEWAY, M. W. (1981), "U.S. Trunk Air Carriers, 1972–1977: A Multilateral Comparison of Total Factor Productivity," in *Productivity Measurement in Regulated Industries*, eds. Thomas G. Cowing and Rodney E. Stevenson, New York: Academic Press.

CHAMBERLAIN, G. (1980), "Analysis of Covariance With Qualitative Data," *Review of Economic Studies*, 47, 225–238.

FØRSUND, F. R., LOVELL, C. A. K., and SCHMIDT, P. (1980), "A Survey of Frontier Production Functions and of Their Relationship to Efficiency Measurement," *Journal of Econometrics*, 13, 5–25.

GALAMBOS, J. (1978), *The Asymptotic Theory of Extreme Order Statistics*, New York: John Wiley.

GREENE, W. H. (1980), "Maximum Likelihood Estimation of Econometric Frontier Functions," *Journal of Econometrics*, 13, 27–56.

HAUSMAN, J. A. (1978), "Specification Tests in Econometrics," *Econometrica*, 46, 1251–1272.

HAUSMAN, J. A., and TAYLOR, W. E. (1981), "Panel Data and Unobservable Individual Effects," *Econometrica*, 49, 1377–1399.

JOHNSON, N. L., and KOTZ, S. M. (1970), *Distributions in Statistics: Continuous Univariate Distributions—1*, New York: John Wiley.

JONDROW, J., LOVELL, C. A. K., MATEROY, I. S., and

SCHMIDT, P. (1982), "On the Estimation of Technical Inefficiency in the Stochastic Frontier Production Function Model," *Journal of Econometrics*, 19, 233–238.

LEE, L. F., and GRIFFITHS, W. E. (1979), "The Prior Likelihood and Best Linear Unbiased Prediction in Stochastic Coefficient Linear Models," University of New England Working Paper in Econometrics and Applied Statistics, Armidale, Australia.

MEEUSEN, W., and VAN DEN BROECK, J. (1977), "Efficiency Estimation From Cobb–Douglas Production Functions With Composed Error," *International Economic Review*, 18, 435–444.

MUNDLAK, Y. (1978), "On the Pooling of Time-Series and Cross-Section Data," *Econometrica*, 46, 69–86.

PITT, M. M., and LEE, L. F. (1981), "The Measurement and Sources of Technical Inefficiency in the Indonesian Weaving Industry," *Journal of Development Economics*, 9, 43–64.

SICKLES, R. (1983), "A Multivariate Error-Components Analysis of Technology and Specific Factor Productivity Growth With an Application to the U.S. Airlines," University of Pennsylvania Working Paper 410.

TAUB, A. J. (1979), "Prediction in the Context of the Variance-Components Model," *Journal of Econometrics*, 10, 103–108.

ZELLNER, A. S., KMENTA, J., and DRÈZE, J. (1966), "Specification and Estimation of Cobb–Douglas Production Functions," *Econometrica*, 34, 784–795.

Journal of Econometrics 46 (1990) 185–200. North-Holland

PRODUCTION FRONTIERS WITH CROSS-SECTIONAL AND TIME-SERIES VARIATION IN EFFICIENCY LEVELS*

Christopher CORNWELL

University of Georgia, Athens, GA 30601, USA

Peter SCHMIDT

Michigan State University, East Lansing, MI 48823, USA

Robin C. SICKLES

Rice University, Houston, TX 77001, USA

In this paper we consider the efficient instrumental variables estimation of a panel data model with heterogeneity in slopes as well as intercepts. Using a panel of U.S. airlines, we apply our methodology to a frontier production function with cross-sectional and temporal variation in levels of technical efficiency. Our approach allows us to estimate time-varying efficiency levels for individual firms without invoking strong distributional assumptions for technical inefficiency or random noise. We do so by including in the production function a flexible function of time whose parameterization depends on the firm. We also generalize the results of Hausman and Taylor (1981) to exploit assumptions about the uncorrelatedness of certain exogenous variables with the temporal pattern of the firm's technical inefficiency. Our empirical analysis of the airline industry over two periods of regulation yields believable evidence on the pattern of changes in efficiency across regulatory environments.

1. Introduction

In this paper we consider the efficient instrumental variables estimation of a panel data model in which coefficients in addition to the intercept vary over individuals, and we apply the methodology we develop to a model in which there is cross-sectional and temporal variation in productivity levels (or, equivalently, in levels of technical efficiency), using data on U.S. airlines. We

*Earlier versions of this paper were given at the 1986 Winter Meetings of the Econometric Society, the 1987 TIMS/ORSA Meetings, the 1987 American Statistical Association Meetings, and the National Bureau of Economic Research Conference on Productivity in the Service Sector, July 1987. Comments by Robert Gordon, Zvi Griliches, V. Kerry Smith, and M. Ishaq Nadiri strengthened the paper considerably. Schmidt and Sickles are grateful to the National Science Foundation for its support.

therefore extend the current literatures on panel data, productivity measurement, and frontier production functions.

The early literature on stochastic frontier production functions [e.g., Aigner, Lovell, and Schmidt (1977)] assumed the existence of data on a single cross-section of firms, and the separation of technical inefficiency from random noise required strong assumptions about their distributions. More recently, Schmidt and Sickles (1984) considered the case in which panel data are available. In their model only the intercept varied over firms; differences in the intercept were interpreted as differing efficiency levels, with the level of efficiency for each firm assumed to be time-invariant. The Schmidt and Sickles model does not require strong distributional assumptions about technical inefficiency or random noise, nor is the assumption of independence between technical inefficiency and the explanatory variables (inputs) needed. However, the assumption that technical inefficiency is time-invariant is very strong, and depending on the data, may prove unrealistic.

In this paper we seek to relax the assumption that technical inefficiency is time-invariant, but in such a way as to not lose the advantages of panel data. We do so by introducing into the production function a flexible (e.g., quadratic) function of time, with coefficients varying over firms. This function can be thought of as representing productivity growth, at a rate that varies over firms, and it implies that levels of inefficiency for each firm vary over time. This model is similar to the model of Sickles, Good, and Johnson (1986), who considered the measurement of efficiency growth using a profit function which included a flexible function of time, but assumed that efficiency growth was the same for all firms. Our model generalizes their treatment by allowing for cross-sectional variation in productivity growth rates. However, the model still imposes enough structure on the way in which productivity levels change over time that strong distributional assumptions are avoided.

Previous treatments of the linear model with panel data, such as Hausman and Taylor (1981) and Amemiya and MaCurdy (1986), have dealt with the case in which only the intercept varies across individuals (firms). We extend the analysis of Hausman and Taylor to the above model in which there is cross-sectional heterogeneity in slopes as well as (or instead of) intercepts. This case has previously been treated in the random coefficients literature [for example, see Swamy (1971, 1974)], but under the assumption that the variation in coefficients is independent of the regressors; like Hausman and Taylor, we allow some or all of the regressors to be correlated with the cross-sectional variation in coefficients.

The plan of the paper is as follows. Section 2 extends the current panel data literature to a model with heterogeneity in slopes as well as intercept. Section 3 applies our panel data results to the problem of productivity measurement in U.S. airlines, and section 4 gives our empirical results. Section 5 concludes.

2. A panel data model with heterogeneity in slopes and intercept

Our model may be written as

$$y_{it} = X_{it}'\beta + Z_i'\gamma + W_{it}'\delta_i + \varepsilon_{it}, \qquad i = 1,\ldots,N, \quad t = 1,\ldots,T, \tag{2.1}$$

where X_{it} is $K \times 1$, Z_i is $J \times 1$, and W_{it} is $L \times 1$, and the parameter vectors β, γ, and δ_i are dimensioned conformably. For the purpose of discussion we can think of the data set being comprised of N individuals (firms) and T time periods per individual. Note that the variables in X and W vary over time, while the variables in Z do not.

The distinguishing feature of our model is that W has coefficients that depend on i. If W just contains a constant, then (2.1) reduces to the standard panel data model in which only the intercept varies across individuals (firms). Let $\delta_i = \delta_0 + u_i$. Then we can write the model as

$$\begin{aligned} y_{it} &= X_{it}'\beta + Z_i'\gamma + W_{it}'\delta_0 + v_{it}, \\ v_{it} &= W_{it}'u_i + \varepsilon_{it}. \end{aligned} \tag{2.2}$$

The u_i are assumed to be iid zero mean random variables with covariance matrix Δ. The disturbances ε_{it} are taken to be iid with a zero mean and constant variance σ^2, and uncorrelated with regressors and u_i.

It is convenient to work with the matrix form of (2.2). This is given by

$$\begin{aligned} y &= X\beta + Z\gamma + W\delta_0 + v, \\ v &= Qu + \varepsilon, \end{aligned} \tag{2.3}$$

where W is $NT \times L$, $Q = \text{diag}(W_i)$, $i = 1,\ldots,N$, is $NT \times NL$, and u is $NL \times 1$.

We assume $L \leq T$, so that Q is of full column rank. This is not necessary for the identifiability of β. However, it is necessary for estimation of the individual δ_i. Also, if $L > T$, some of the matrices which we must invert would be singular. This is not really a substantive matter, since the projections involved are still well defined, but the algebra would become more complicated. Taking Q to be of full column rank, we denote these projections as follows. Let $P_Q = Q(Q'Q)^{-1}Q'$ be the projection onto the column space of Q and $M_Q = I - P_Q$ be the projection onto the null space of Q.

We derive three different estimators for (2.3), each of which is a straightforward extension of an established procedure for the standard panel data model. The choice between them primarily depends on whether the effects (u_i) are correlated with the explanatory variables $(X_{it}$, Z_i, and $W_{it})$.

The first estimator we consider is a generalization of the within estimator from the analysis of covariance. In the standard model, this amounts to transforming the data into deviations from individual means and performing least squares on the transformed data. Similarly, we can transform (2.3) by M_Q and apply least squares. Note that since $M_Q Z = 0$, γ cannot be estimated. The within estimator of β is given by

$$\hat{\beta}_W = (X'M_Q X)^{-1} X'M_Q y. \tag{2.4}$$

The within estimator is an instrumental variables estimator, with instruments M_Q (or, equivalently, $M_Q X$). Its consistency does not depend on assumptions of uncorrelatedness of (X, Z) and (Qu).[1]

Second, we can estimate (2.3) by generalized least squares (GLS). The GLS estimator of $(\beta, \gamma, \delta_0)$ is

$$[(X,Z,W)'\Omega^{-1}(X,Z,W)]^{-1}(X,Z,W)'\Omega^{-1}y, \tag{2.5}$$

where $\Omega = \text{cov}(v) = \sigma^2 I_{NT} + Q(I_N \otimes \Delta)Q'$. While Ω is a large matrix, it is block-diagonal, with blocks of the form $\sigma^2 I_N + W_i \Delta W_i'$; thus its inversion is practical.

Alternatively, GLS is ordinary least squares (OLS) applied to the transformed equation

$$\Omega^{-1/2}y = \Omega^{-1/2}X\beta + \Omega^{-1/2}Z\gamma + \Omega^{-1/2}W\delta_0 + \Omega^{-1/2}v. \tag{2.6}$$

This transformation was first suggested, for the model with cross-sectional variation only in the intercept, by Fuller and Battese (1973). This expression is not of much actual computational use, however, since $\Omega^{-1/2}$ is harder to calculate than Ω^{-1}; we have

$$\Omega^{-1/2} = \frac{1}{\sigma} M_Q + F, \tag{2.7}$$

where

$$F = Q(Q'Q)^{-1/2}\left[\sigma^2 I_{NL} + (Q'Q)^{1/2}(I_N \otimes \Delta)(Q'Q)^{1/2}\right]^{-1/2} \times (Q'Q)^{-1/2}Q'. \tag{2.8}$$

[This formula follows from a straightforward application of Wansbeek and Kapteyn (1982).]

The consistency of GLS hinges on the uncorrelatedness of (X, Z, W) and Qu. However, GLS allows the estimation of γ, and for fixed T, it is more

[1] More details on the fixed effects treatment of (2.4) can be found in Cornwell (1985).

efficient than the within estimator (2.4). This is exactly the same relationship that exists between GLS and within in the standard model; an explicit proof can be found in Cornwell (1985, sect. 3.3).

Our third estimator is an extension of Hausman and Taylor (1981). Taking an instrumental variables approach, they exploit assumptions about explanatory variables that are uncorrelated with the effects to derive a simple consistent estimator and an asymptotically efficient estimator for the standard panel data model.[2] The extent to which their estimators represent an improvement over the within estimator depends on the number of exogeneity restrictions one is willing to impose. Noting that the within estimator of β always exists and is consistent, Hausman and Taylor use it as a basis of comparison, presenting clear conditions under which their instrumental variables estimators are different.

Following Hausman and Taylor, consider the case in which some of the regressors are correlated with the effects. In particular assume that (X_1, Z_1, W_1) are uncorrelated with the effects, in the sense that $\text{plim}(NT)^{-1}X_1'Qu = 0$, and similarly for Z_1 and W_1, while (X_2, Z_2, W_2) are correlated with the effects. Let the dimensions of X_1, Z_1, W_1, X_2, Z_2, and W_2 be k_1, j_1, l_1, k_2, j_2, and l_2 (with $k_1 + k_2 = K$, $j_1 + j_2 = J$, and $l_1 + l_2 = L$).

A generalization of the Hausman and Taylor simple, consistent estimator is obtained as follows. As in the standard model, we begin with the within estimator, in this case (2.4). The within residuals are

$$(y - X\hat{\beta}_W) = Z\gamma + W\delta_0 + \left[Qu + \varepsilon + X(\beta - \hat{\beta}_W)\right]. \tag{2.9}$$

We transform (2.9) by premultiplying by $\Omega^{-1/2}$:

$$\Omega^{-1/2}(y - X\hat{\beta}_W) = \Omega^{-1/2}Z\gamma + \Omega^{-1/2}W\delta_0$$
$$+ \Omega^{-1/2}\left[Qu + \varepsilon + X(\beta - \hat{\beta}_W)\right]. \tag{2.10}$$

The simple consistent estimator is then defined as instrumental variables of (2.10), using as instruments

$$B^* = \Omega^{-1/2}B = \Omega^{-1/2}(X_1, Z_1, W_1). \tag{2.11}$$

Note that B is transformed by $\Omega^{-1/2}$. Following White (1984, pp. 95–99) the use of untransformed instruments is clearly suboptimal, if we assume 'reduced form' equations for (Z_2, W_2) which are linear in (X_1, Z_1, W_1). This

[2]Amemiya and MaCurdy (1986) introduce an alternative instrumental variables estimator that, under stronger assumptions, is more efficient than the Hausman and Taylor estimator. For a clear exposition of the relationship between the two estimators, see Breusch, Mizon, and Schmidt (1989).

yields the estimator

$$\begin{bmatrix} \hat{\gamma}_W \\ \hat{\delta}_{0W} \end{bmatrix} = \left[(Z,W)'\Omega^{-1/2}P_{B^*}\Omega^{-1/2}(Z,W) \right]^{-1}$$

$$\times (Z,W)'\Omega^{-1/2}P_{B^*}\Omega^{-1/2}(y - X\hat{\beta}_W). \tag{2.12}$$

The estimator will exist if we have enough instruments, i.e., if the order condition $k_1 + j_1 + l_1 \geq J + L$, or equivalently $k_1 \geq j_2 + l_2$, is satisfied. The corresponding rank condition is that the matrix to be inverted in (2.12) be (asymptotically) of full rank. If it holds, the estimator will be consistent.

To define our efficient instrumental variables estimator, we estimate (2.6) by instrumental variables, using as instruments

$$A^* = \Omega^{-1/2}A = \Omega^{-1/2}(M_Q, X_1, Z_1, W_1). \tag{2.13}$$

Letting $G = (X, Z, W)$, this yields

$$\begin{bmatrix} \tilde{\beta}^* \\ \tilde{\gamma}^* \\ \tilde{\delta}_0^* \end{bmatrix} = (G'\Omega^{-1/2}P_{A^*}\Omega^{-1/2}G)^{-1}G'\Omega^{-1/2}P_{A^*}\Omega^{-1/2}y. \tag{2.14}$$

Conditions for the existence of (2.14), as well as the relationship between the efficient estimates (2.14) and the simple consistent estimates (2.12) can be summarized as follows. If $k_1 < j_2 + l_2$, $\tilde{\beta}^* = \hat{\beta}_W$ and $(\tilde{\gamma}^*, \tilde{\delta}_0^*)$ does not exist. If $k_1 = j_2 + l_2$, $\tilde{\beta}^* = \hat{\beta}_W$ and $(\tilde{\gamma}^*, \tilde{\delta}_0^*) = (\hat{\gamma}_W, \hat{\delta}_{0W})$, where $(\hat{\gamma}_W, \hat{\delta}_{0W})$ is defined in (2.12). And, if $k_1 > j_2 + l_2$, $(\tilde{\beta}^*, \tilde{\gamma}^*, \tilde{\delta}_0^*) \neq (\hat{\beta}_W, \hat{\gamma}_W, \hat{\delta}_{0W})$ with the former being more efficient than the latter. These results are directly analogous to the results for the standard model given by Hausman and Taylor. See Cornwell (1985, ch. 4, app. A) for proofs of these results.

A remaining detail is the consistent (as $N \to \infty$) estimation of σ^2 and Δ, the unknown parameters in Ω. If SSE_w is the unexplained sum of squares in the within regression, $\hat{\sigma}^2 = SSE_w/N(T-L)$ is a consistent estimate of σ^2. To estimate Δ, let e_i be the IV residuals for individual i (e.g., from the simple consistent IV estimator) and define

$$\hat{\Delta} = \frac{1}{N}\sum_{i=1}^{N} \left[(W_i'W_i)^{-1}W_i'e_ie_i'W_i(W_i'W_i)^{-1} - \hat{\sigma}^2(W_i'W_i)^{-1} \right]. \tag{2.15}$$

A direct calculation reveals that this estimator is consistent [Cornwell (1985, ch. 4, app. B)].

3. A frontiers model with time-varying inefficiency

Schmidt and Sickles (1984) consider the estimation of a stochastic frontier production function with panel data, using the model

$$y_{it} = \alpha + X_{it}'\beta + v_{it} - u_i, \tag{3.1}$$

where y = output, X = inputs, v = statistical noise, and $u > 0$ is a firm effect representing technical inefficiency. This model can obviously be put in the form

$$y_{it} = \alpha_i + X_{it}'\beta + v_{it}, \tag{3.2}$$

where $\alpha_i = \alpha - u_i$. The model (3.2) is of the standard form found in the panel data literature, and β can be estimated by standard methods such as 'within', GLS, or the Hausman and Taylor instrumental variables estimator. It can also be estimated by MLE, assuming a particular distribution for the one-sided error u_i in (3.1). Schmidt and Sickles apply (3.2) to a panel of airlines for the period 1970.I–1977.IV (the period prior to deregulation), assuming a Cobb–Douglas technology. Results from the use of 'within', GLS, and MLE (assuming a half-normal distribution for the firm effects) are compared, and a Hausman–Wu specification error test is carried out to test the null hypothesis that firm-specific effects are uncorrelated with the regressors.

The great benefit of panel data is that one can choose whether to assume particular distributions of v and u, or whether to assume that technical inefficiency is uncorrelated with the inputs, and that therefore these assumptions are testable. However, these benefits come at the cost of the assumption that the firm effects are constant over time. This is a very strong assumption, and probably would be unrealistic in many potential applications. In terms of the Schmidt and Sickles application, as the airline industry moved into the deregulatory transition and beyond, the potential for unstable productivity patterns (reflected in the firm effects) should be clear. Firms within the industry would be expected to respond differently to the new regulatory environment. Although this issue has been dealt with in part by Sickles, Good, and Johnson (1986), the model introduced therein was highly parameterized and required maximum likelihood on a highly nonlinear model. The model we propose here is more parsimoniously parameterized and can be estimated in straightforward ways.

In order to relax the assumption that the firm effects are time-invariant, but in such a way that the advantages of panel data are preserved, we will replace the firm effect (α_i) in (3.2) by a flexibly parameterized function of time, with parameters that vary over firms. The functional form chosen in this paper is a quadratic:

$$\alpha_{it} = \theta_{i1} + \theta_{i2}t + \theta_{i3}t^2. \tag{3.3}$$

Since (3.3) is linear in the elements of θ_{ij} $(j = 1,2,3)$, we have exactly the type of model considered in section 2.

In terms of the notation of section 2, we have $W_{it}' = [1, t, t^2]$, $\delta_i' = [\theta_{i1}, \theta_{i2}, \theta_{i3}]$, and with this notation the model (3.2) can be written

$$y_{it} = X_{it}'\beta + W_{it}'\delta_i + v_{it}. \tag{3.4}$$

Clearly the specification (3.3) implies that output levels vary both over firms and over time. Efficiency measurement focuses on the cross-sectional variation, and the model allows efficiency levels to vary over time. Conversely, the measurement of productivity growth focuses on the temporal variation, and the model allows the rate of productivity growth to vary over firms.

Time-varying firm productivity and efficiency levels and rates of productivity growth can be derived from the residuals based on the within, GLS, and efficient instrumental variables estimators presented in section 2.[3] In Schmidt and Sickles (1984), using the model (3.1), the residuals $(y_{it} - X_{it}'\hat{\beta})$ are an estimate of $(v_{it} - u_i)$, and the firm effect (for a given firm) is estimated by averaging its residuals over time. Specifically, the estimate of α_i is

$$\hat{\alpha}_i = \bar{y}_i - \bar{x}_i\hat{\beta}. \tag{3.5}$$

This estimate is consistent as $T \to \infty$. The analogous procedure for the present model is to estimate δ_i by regressing the residuals $(y_{it} - X_{it}'\hat{\beta})$ for firm i on W_{it}; that is, on a constant, time and time-squared. The fitted values from this regression provide an estimate of α_{it} in (3.3) that is consistent (for all i and t) as $T \to \infty$. Finally, in Schmidt and Sickles the frontier intercept α and the firm-specific level of inefficiency for firm i are estimated, respectively, as

$$\hat{\alpha} = \max_j(\hat{\alpha}_j) \quad \text{and} \quad \hat{u}_i = \hat{\alpha} - \hat{\alpha}_i. \tag{3.6}$$

The analogous procedure here is to estimate the frontier intercept at time t and the firm-specific level of technical inefficiency of firm i at time t as

[3] For a discussion of maximum-likelihood estimators for stochastic panel frontiers which treat time-varying inefficiency see Kumbhaker (1990).

follows:

$$\hat{\alpha}_t = \max_j (\hat{\alpha}_{jt}) \quad \text{and} \quad \hat{u}_{it} = \alpha_t - \hat{\alpha}_{it}. \tag{3.7}$$

4. Empirical results

Our data are on U.S airlines over the time period 1970.I–1981.IV, so that $T = 48$. The data follow certificated carriers that existed throughout the study period and that accounted for over 80% of domestic air traffic. Information on output and input prices and quantities was obtained from over 250 accounts from the CAB Form-41. These accounts were aggregated into the four broad input measures of capital, labor, energy, and materials; one output measure, available ton miles; and two output attributes, average stage length (thousands of miles) and service quality. Service quality is based on the number of complaints received by the CAB's Office of Consumer Affairs and is normalized by the number of passenger enplanements for that quarter. The output and input quantities and prices are constructed as Tornqvist indices. We examined the following airlines: American, Allegheny, Delta, Eastern, North Central, Ozark, Piedmont, and United so that $N = 8$. We control for seasonal factors with three dummy variables (with fall the omitted category), and condition on two service attributes, average stage length and quality. For a further discussion of data construction see Sickles (1985) and Sickles, Good, and Johnson (1986). The functional form that we use for (3.1) is a special case of the transcendental logarithmic function [Christensen, Jorgenson, and Lau (1973)]. We assume that the average technology is given by a first-order approximation in the logarithms of input quantities and a second-order approximation in the logarithms of output attributes.[4] In addition, we make the assumptions that input quantities and output characteristics are separable in production, that productivity levels and growths are disembodied, and that seasonal factors are neutral. This reduces the possible number of unrestricted parameters from 66 to 15, a manageable number given the time-series nature of our data, the typical collinearity problems associated with data of this sort, and the use of no additional restrictions embodied in the first-order conditions for output maximization, cost mini-

[4] We attempted to include second-order terms for the inputs, but the almost perfect collinearity in the moment matrix prevented us from obtaining unique parameter estimates. Within results using the generalized inverse gave us an F-statistic of 8.75 for the test of the joint insignificance of the second-order effects of the logarithms of input quantities. The joint insignificance of these parameters is thus not rejected at reasonable significance levels. Instead of dealing with the problem by imposing more structure, e.g., adding optimizing assumptions in the form of first-order conditions to increase the degrees of freedom, we decided let the data and its limitations speak. We simply cannot identify second-order input effects using our data set and largely (or completely) the within variation in variables.

Table 1
Summary statistics (48 quarters, 8 airlines).

Variable	Mean	Standard deviation
ln Q	19.04	1.38
ln K	16.84	1.11
ln L	17.54	1.15
ln E	16.10	1.27
ln M	16.91	1.14
ln stage length	−1.08	0.65
ln quality	−3.36	0.55
(ln stage length)^2	1.59	1.45
(ln quality)^2	11.57	3.79
(ln stage length)* ln quality	3.60	2.18

mization, or profit maximization. The average production technology under consideration is therefore:

$$\ln Q = \ln \alpha_0 + \alpha_k \ln K + \alpha_L \ln L + \alpha_E \ln E + \alpha_M \ln M + \sum_i \delta_i \,\text{Season}_i$$
$$+ \sum_i \gamma_i \ln \text{Attribute}_i + \sum\sum_{i \le j} \gamma_{ij} \ln \text{Attribute}_i \ln \text{Attribute}_j, \tag{4.1}$$

where Q is available ton miles, K, L, E, M are capital, labor, energy, and material input quantities, the seasons are indexed from winter through summer, and where the attributes are average stage length and our service quality index. Summary statistics for the variables in (4.1) are given in table 1.

Estimation results are given in tables 2 and 3. Table 2 displays benchmark GLS and within estimates that are comparable to those given in Schmidt and Sickles (1984) in that only the intercept is allowed to vary across firms. Productivity, however, is allowed to vary over the period. The results of GLS and within are comparable, with energy having the largest output elasticity, followed by labor, materials, and capital. Returns to scale are not significantly different from unity for both estimates at the 95% level, and annual productivity growth is about 1.5% in the median period, 1975.I. The $\bar{R}^2$ for both sets of results is above 0.999. Table 3 presents the within, GLS, and efficient instrumental variables estimates given in (2.4), (2.5), and (2.14). Consider first the GLS and within estimates. The output elasticities do change somewhat across estimation procedures (GLS versus within) as well as across specifications (table 2 versus table 3). The within estimated capital elasticity in table 3 is considerably higher than either estimate in table 2, while the within estimated materials elasticity is considerably lower. Returns to scale are still insignificantly different from unity at the 95% level.

Table 2

Heterogeneity in intercept only.

	GLS		Within	
Variable	Estimate	S.E.	Estimate	S.E.
ln K	0.183	0.027	0.169	0.027
ln L	0.242	0.030	0.243	0.030
ln E	0.502	0.025	0.500	0.025
ln M	0.203	0.028	0.203	0.028
Winter	0.00198	0.0064	0.00151	0.0060
Spring	0.0223	0.0066	0.0229	0.0062
Summer	0.0284	0.0066	0.0303	0.0062
ln stage length	0.221	0.054	0.101	0.076
ln quality	0.0073	0.041	0.0122	0.040
(ln stage length)^2	0.0434	0.016	0.0103	0.0213
(ln quality)^2	−0.00370	0.0058	−0.00355	0.0058
ln stage length* ln quality	0.0251	0.0081	0.0261	0.0081
Intercept	0.0205	0.290	—	—
Time	0.000591	0.00084	0.0000743	0.00083
Time^2	0.000065	0.000017	0.0000875	0.00000191
σ_u^2	0.00180		—	
σ^2	0.00166		0.00169	

The consistency of the GLS estimates depends on the effects being uncorrelated with all of the explanatory variables. As explained in Schmidt and Sickles (1984), this assumption can be tested using a Hausman–Wu test based on the significance of the differences between the GLS and within estimates. This test statistic equals 17.2. Its asymptotic distribution is chi-squared with 12 degrees of freedom, and a value of 17.2 is significant only at about the 0.15 level. Thus there is some evidence against the exogeneity assumptions underlying the GLS estimator, but it is not significant at usual confidence levels such as 0.05, although this may reflect the low power of the test against nonlocal alternatives.

Despite the insignificance of the evidence against the GLS estimator's exogeneity assumptions, it is reasonable to ask if there is a subset of the explanatory variables for which uncorrelatedness with the effects is more strongly supported by the data. If so, we can impose these uncorrelatedness assumptions using the efficient instrumental variables estimator of section 2. For this purpose we will assume that the seasonal dummy variables and the intercept and time trend variables are uncorrelated with the effects, while the output attribute variables will be treated as correlated with the effects. Correlation patterns between the effects and the input variables were harder to assign *a priori*, but we decided to treat capital and energy as correlated with the effects, and labor and materials as uncorrelated with the effects. We did this for several reasons. The labor input index is based on headcount

Table 3

Heterogeneity in intercept, time, time^2.

Variable	GLS Estimate	GLS S.E.	Within Estimate	Within S.E.	EffIV Estimate	EffIV S.E.
ln K	0.193	0.0303	0.233	0.0321	0.221	0.0276
ln L	0.317	0.0326	0.300	0.0273	0.300	0.0270
ln E	0.466	0.0286	0.498	0.0259	0.494	0.0245
ln M	0.147	0.0300	0.139	0.0249	0.137	0.0242
Winter	0.00189	0.00613	0.00280	0.00491	0.00218	0.00484
Spring	0.0202	0.00629	0.0207	0.00509	0.0211	0.00495
Summer	0.0264	0.00625	0.0252	0.00515	0.0263	0.00496
ln stage length	0.0780	0.0666	−0.0608	0.0902	−0.102	0.0788
ln quality	−0.0383	0.0429	−0.0237	0.0349	−0.0172	0.0342
(ln stage length)^2	−0.0247	0.0255	−0.0874	0.0365	−0.105	0.0335
(ln quality)^2	−0.00714	0.00628	−0.00464	0.00516	−0.00384	0.00505
ln stage length* ln quality	0.0110	0.00883	0.00941	0.00724	0.00992	0.00705
Intercept	−0.0404	0.396	—	—	−0.407	0.406
Time	0.00104	0.00171	—	—	0.000224	0.000214
Time^2	0.0000464	0.0000314	—	—	0.0000465	0.0000372
	0.00407			0.0179		
Δ	−0.000211	0.0000180		−0.000561	0.0000328	
	0.264×10^{-5}	-0.291×10^{-6}	0.552×10^{-8}	0.448×10^{-5}	-0.474×10^{-6}	0.90×10^{-8}
σ^2	0.00166			0.00100		

data. Since adjustment costs for numbers of employees are typically much higher than for hours (which are not measured in the CAB Form-41), any short-run (quarterly) firm shock will likely result in reduced hours or overtime, not in numbers of employees [Schultze (1985) and Shapiro (1986)]. Furthermore, since union contracts cover approximately 70% of the employees in our sample airlines, rational expectations would suggest that any information available to the contracting parties when the contract was made would have been conditioned on, and therefore any unforeseen firm-specific supply shifts would be orthogonal to employment variation while the contract was in force [Sargent (1978)]. The other input which is assumed to be uncorrelated with firm effects is the materials index. This is a residual category, roughly 70% of which is for professional services contracted outside the firm. These include advertising, charter travel bookings, unplanned maintenance of firm's flight equipment by another carrier, and catering services. These data came to us in expenditure form and a Tornqvist index was constructed using a variety of price deflators such as the McCann Erickson Advertising index, the producer price index for miscellaneous business services, and the producer price index for processed foods. The aggregate price indices would have no correlation with airline-specific productivity changes unless firms had a substantial degree of monopsony power in those markets. There is no evidence that this is the case. Whatever weak correlation might have existed between the materials expenditure data and firm productivity effects would be mitigated by the index construction.

The efficient instrumental variables estimates based on these exogeneity assumptions are given in table 3. The coefficient estimates are fairly similar to the within estimates, and there is a slight improvement in the precision of the estimates. Furthermore, the eight uncorrelatedness assumptions that underly the efficient instrumental variables estimator are testable, and the Hausman–Wu statistic (based on differences between the within and efficient instrumental variables estimates) is only 1.08. Thus there is no evidence in the data to make us doubt these exogeneity assumptions.

Table 4 presents the relative efficiency levels derived from our estimates for the carriers at three points in time: 1970.I, 1975.I, 1981.IV. The efficiencies are calculated using the GLS, within, and efficient instrumental variables estimates. As expected, the within and efficient instrumental variables results are quite similar, while GLS efficiency levels and rankings are quite different from within and efficient instrumental variables. In either case there is evidence of considerable change in the efficiency rankings over time; for example, American and United show large improvements in their efficiency rankings from 1970 to 1980.[5]

[5]Productivity levels (%) derived from the within results of table 2 for American, Alleghany, Delta, Eastern, North Central, Ozark, Piedmont, and United are: 96, 80, 100, 89, 78, 82, 81, and 97. Since parameter heterogeneity is allowed for only the constant term, productivity levels are

Table 4

Efficiency levels (%) for selected time periods (1970.I, 1975.I, 1980.IV).

Carrier	GLS	Within	EffIV
American	81, 95, 93	65, 90, 93	72, 93, 94
Alleghany	92, 88, 83	85, 86, 83	86, 86, 80
Delta	92, 99, 99	78, 91, 94	81, 93, 92
Eastern	74, 92, 92	60, 81, 88	64, 84, 87
North Central	86, 100, 88	85, 100, 84	86, 100, 82
Ozark	100, 96, 65	100, 97, 99	100, 96, 93
Piedmont	88, 93, 97	89, 98, 100	90, 97, 94
United	87, 92, 100	66, 84, 100	72, 88, 100

Table 5

Annual productivity growth rates (%) from 1970.I–1981.IV.

Carrier	GLS	Within	EffIV
American	0.45	2.08	1.13
Alleghany	−0.05	−0.42	−1.27
Delta	−0.62	1.08	2.21
Eastern	0.86	2.08	1.24
North Central	−0.38	−0.33	−1.07
Ozark	−3.55	−0.33	−1.30
Piedmont	0.12	0.64	−0.30
United	1.08	2.55	1.60
Output share weighted average	0.44	1.85	1.22

Growth rates in productivity can be calculated by examining the time derivative of the estimate of (3.2). Although these estimates were quite unstable when evaluated period-by-period, we can compare the average values between the first and last period and calculate simple annualized percent rates of growth in total factor productivity (TFP). These calculations are summarized in table 5. Below the rates of total factor productivity growth are the output share weighted averages, which are comparable to the esti-

constant over the sample period, an assumption which is clearly rejected at any reasonable level of significance (F-statistic = 17.06; 0.05, 14,348 = 1.65). Although the constancy of the inefficiencies is rejected, there is still the possibility that productivity rankings may not be affected a great deal. This is not the case, although there does appear to be more concordance between rankings in the later periods. Spearman rank correlations between the productivities based on the standard model and (2.14) are −0.539, −0.476, and 0.428.

mates from the naive model with heterogeneity in the intercept only. We can see that, although magnitudes are not equal, the estimates based on within and efficient instrumental variables are of the same sign (except for Piedmont which is quite small) and roughly the same magnitude. TFP growth rates calculated from the (probably misspecified) GLS estimates are quite different from the within and efficient instrumental variables TFP growth rates and suggest an industry average growth rate of 0.44, versus the 1.22–1.85 implied by the consistent within and efficient instrumental variables estimates.

It is obvious in table 4 that, on average, the firms in our sample became more efficient over time. The average level of efficiency for our eight firms is roughly 82% in 1970.I and grows to almost 95% in 1980 before dropping slightly in 1981. It is important to stress that this increase in efficiency levels is not just a reflection of the fact that there was productivity growth over the sample period. A firm's efficiency level for a given time period is calculated by comparing the firm's output to the frontier level calculated using the production function of the most efficient firm [the one with the highest intercept u_{it} in eq. (3.2)]; see eq. (3.5). Thus the empirical fact that drives an increase in efficiency levels over time is that the firms' productivity levels are becoming more similar over time. It is easy to conjecture that this is due to increasing competitive pressures in the airline industry over the sample period, although in fact most of the increase in average efficiency levels occurred before the formal passage of the air deregulation act in late 1978.

The temporal pattern of changes in efficiency levels displayed in table 4 is of obvious interest. It indicates exactly the kind of detail available in the present model and not available in the simpler model of Schmidt and Sickles (1984).

6. Conclusions

In this paper we have specified a simple model which, in the presence of panel data, allows us to estimate time-varying efficiency levels for individual firms, without making strong distributional assumptions for technical inefficiency or random noise. We do so by including in the production function a flexible function of time, with parameters that differ across firms. We also generalize the earlier econometric results of Hausman and Taylor (1981) to develop an econometric technique that allows us to choose how many explanatory variables we wish to assume to be uncorrelated with the firm's temporal pattern of productivity growth. We have used this model and these estimators to analyze the U.S. airline industry during two periods of regulation and obtained results that are quite intuitive and reasonable, including believable evidence on the pattern of changes in efficiency across regulatory environments.

References

Aigner, D.J., C.A.K. Lovell, and P. Schmidt, 1977, Formulation and estimation of stochastic frontier production function models, Journal of Econometrics 6, 21–37.

Amemiya, T. and T. MaCurdy, 1986, Instrumental variables estimation of an error components model, Econometrica 54, 869–880.

Breusch, T., G. Mizon, and P. Schmidt, 1989, Efficient estimation using panel data, Econometrica 57, 695–700.

Christensen, L.R., D.W. Jorgenson, and L.J. Lau, 1973, Transcendental logarithmic production frontiers. Review of Economics and Statistics 55, 28–45.

Cornwell, C., 1985, Panel data with cross-sectional variation in slopes as well as intercept, Unpublished doctoral dissertation (Michigan State University, East Lansing, MI).

Fuller, W. and G. Battese, 1973, Transformations for estimation of linear models with nested error structure, Journal of the American Statistical Association 68, 626–632.

Kumbhakar, S.C., 1990, Production frontiers, panel data, and time-variant technical inefficiency, Journal of Econometrics, this issue.

Hausman, J.A. and W. Taylor, 1981, Panel data and unobservable individual effects, Econometrica 49, 1377–1399.

Schmidt, P., 1985, Frontier production functions, Econometric Reviews 4, 289–328.

Schmidt, P. and R.C. Sickles, 1984, Production frontiers and panel data, Journal of Business and Economic Statistics 2, 367–374.

Sargent, T.J., 1978, Estimation of dynamic labor demand schedules under rational expectations, Journal of Political Economy 86, 1009–1044.

Schultze, C., 1986, Microeconomic efficiency and nominal wage stickiness, American Economic Review 75, 1–15.

Shapiro, M.D., 1986, The dynamic demand for capital and labor, Quarterly Journal of Economics 101, 513–542.

Sickles, R.C., 1985, A nonlinear multivariate error-components analysis of technology and specific factor productivity growth with an application to the U.S. airlines, Journal of Econometrics 27, 61–78.

Sickles, R., D. Good, and R. Johnson, 1986, Allocative distortions and the regulatory transition of the airline industry, Journal of Econometrics 33, 143–163.

Swamy, P.A.V.B., 1971, Statistical inference in random coefficient regression models (Springer-Verlag, New York, NY).

Swamy, P.A.V.B., 1974, Linear models with random coefficients, in: P. Zarembka, ed., Frontiers of econometrics (Academic Press, New York, NY).

Wansbeek, T. and A. Kapteyn, 1982, A class of decompositions of the variance–covariance matrix of a general error components model, Econometrica 50, 713–724.

White, H., 1980, A heteroskedasticity-consistent covariance matrix estimator and a direct test for heteroskedasticity, Econometrica 48, 817–838.

White, H., 1984, Asymptotic theory for econometricians (Academic Press, New York, NY).

Part V
Special Problems with Panel Data

[21]

Econometrica, Vol. 47, No. 2 (March, 1979)

ATTRITION BIAS IN EXPERIMENTAL AND PANEL DATA: THE GARY INCOME MAINTENANCE EXPERIMENT[1]

BY JERRY A. HAUSMAN AND DAVID A. WISE

CAREFUL ATTENTION TO SAMPLE DESIGN is an important consideration in both social experimentation and in panel surveys of individuals. Techniques of randomization and response surface design have been highly developed with the aim of obtaining the maximum amount of information from a given experiment or survey. In practice, however, social experimentation and panel data differ in one important respect from classical design assumptions as exemplified in the pioneering analysis of R. A. Fisher [**4**]. This difference arises from the fact that each individual in panel data is his own best control. In a classical experiment, seed might be planted in different plots at random and fertilized at different intensity levels chosen at random. Differences in yield would then be used to assess the effectiveness of the fertilizer. A characteristic of recent[2] social experiments is that individuals are surveyed before the experiment begins, and their pre-experimental behavior is then compared to their behavior after receipt of the experimental "treatment." Information on controls, persons who receive no experimental treatment, is also obtained. However, it has been found that much more information is gained from the change in a given individual's behavior than by comparing differences in the average behavior of experimentals and controls. The reason for this finding is the presence of significant, unobserved individual effects. For instance, in a previous study of the earnings response of white males in the New Jersey negative income tax experiment (Hausman and Wise [**10**]) the authors found that about 85 per cent of the total variance in response was due to the variation in individual specific terms that persisted over time.

It is because of the importance of individual effects that the design of social experiments includes pre-experimental observations of individuals, and corresponding data collection, and then the observation of the same individuals subject to experimental treatment over an extended period of time (ranging from two to fifteen years). But the inclusion of the time factor in the experiment raises a problem which does not exist in classical experiments—attrition. Some individuals decide that keeping the detailed records that the experiments require is not worth the payment, some move, some are inducted into the military. In some experiments, persons with large earnings receive no experimental treatment benefit and thus drop out of the experiment altogether. This attrition may negate

[1] The research reported herein was performed pursuant to Contract Number HEW 100-76-0073 from the Department of Health, Education, and Welfare, Washington, D.C. The opinions and conclusions expressed herein are solely those of the authors and should not be construed as representing the opinions or policy of any agency of the United States government.

This study was part of continuing analysis of the Gary Experiment at MATHEMATICA POLICY RESEARCH. The authors also acknowledge research support of the National Science Foundation. Research assistance was provided by G. Burtless. We thank K. Kehrer, C. Mallar, and Zvi Griliches for their comments. An editor also provided helpful comments on an earlier draft of the paper.

[2] For example, the New Jersey, Gary, and Seattle–Denver income maintenance experiments and the health insurance experiment currently in progress, all sponsored by HEW.

the randomization in the initial experimental design. If the probability of attrition is correlated with experimental response, then traditional statistical techniques will lead to biased and inconsistent estimates of the experimental effect.

Attrition is a problem in any panel survey, not only those conducted in conjunction with social experiments, where individuals are followed over time. Two important bodies of panel data, the Michigan Income Dynamics Survey and the National Longitudinal (Parnes) Surveys, for example, followed people for 5 and 10 years, respectively. While the attrition in these surveys has typically not been as severe as in social experiments, the same problems of potential bias arises, if attrition is not random.

In this paper we propose a method that uses a probability model of attrition, in conjunction with a traditional random effects model of individual response, to correct for attrition bias. The maximum likelihood procedure used provides consistent and asymptotically efficient estimates of the parameters of a structural model, including experimental response; and allows a test of whether or not non-random attrition has occurred. These procedures are closely related to previous models based on non-random samples by Hanoch [**7**], Hausman and Spence [**9**], Hausman and Wise [**11**], Heckman [**14**], Madalla and Nelson [**17**], and Nelsòn [**20**]. All of these models except Hausman and Wise considered the problem of non-random samples in the single period context. We consider the problem in a multi-period framework, due to its importance in both panel data and social experimentation. A modified scoring algorithm, first employed by Berndt, Hall, Hall, and Hausman [**3**], provides estimates at a reasonably small computation cost.

After formal discussion of the problem and statistical specification of our model, the method is used to estimate the earnings response of black males in the Gary Income Maintenance Experiment. Attrition bias is a potentially important problem in this experiment, but the extent of the bias seems to depend crucially on the specification of the model used to evaluate the experimental effect. Empirical results indicate a much greater bias with simple analysis of variance models than with behavioral specifications incorporating more exogenous variables. Attrition bias in a structural model estimating only a single experimental effect was found to be small although statistically significant. No attrition bias was found in a structural specification that allowed estimation of the effects of all four treatments. Simple analysis of variance estimates, however, were substantially affected by attrition.

1. STATISTICAL SPECIFICATION

Two statistical models are commonly used to analyze individual behavior over time. In this paper we will use the random effects specification, although the techniques can be applied in a straightforward manner to the fixed effects specification as well. Initially, we will concentrate on a two-period model. Later we will indicate the appropriate extension for more periods. The "linear regression" model used for individual behavior has the form

$$(1.1)\qquad y_{it} = X_{it}\beta + \varepsilon_{it} \qquad (i = 1, \ldots, N;\ t = 1, 2),$$

where i indexes individuals and t indexes time periods. In a social experiment X_{i1} may differ from X_{i2} because of experimental treatment, along with changes in individual characteristics which occur with the passage of time. Such changes, of course, may also occur in panel survey data. The residual in the specification is then decomposed into two orthogonal components, an individual effect μ_i, which is assumed to be drawn from an iid distribution and to be independent of the X_{it}'s, and a time effect, η_{it}, which is assumed to be a serially uncorrelated random variable drawn from an iid distribution. Thus, the assumptions on ε_{it} are:

$$(1.2)\qquad \begin{array}{l} \varepsilon_{it} = \mu_i + \eta_{it}, \qquad E(\varepsilon_{it}) = 0, \qquad V(\varepsilon_{it}) = \sigma_\mu^2 + \sigma_\eta^2 = \sigma^2, \\ \varepsilon_{it} \sim N(0, \sigma^2). \end{array}$$

The contribution to the variance of the individual component σ_μ^2 is typically greater than σ_η^2 which highlights the importance of letting individuals serve as their own controls. The correlation between ε_{i1} and ε_{i2}, $\rho_{12} = \sigma_\mu^2/(\sigma_\mu^2 + \sigma_\eta^2)$, often ranges from .4 to .9. The correlation coefficient indicates the proportion of total variance explained by the unobserved individual effect.

If attrition occurs in the sample, a common practice is to discard those observations for which y_{i2} is missing. But suppose that the probability of observing y_{i2} varies with its value, as well as the values of other variables. Then the probability of observing y_{i2} will depend on ε_{i2} and least squares will lead to biased estimates of the underlying structural parameters and the experimental response.

To develop a model of attrition, define the indicator variable a_i and let $a_i = 0$ if attrition occurs in period two, so that y_{i2} is not observed, and let $a_i = 1$ if attrition does not occur, so that y_{i2} is observed. Suppose that y_{i2} is observed if $A_i = \alpha y_{i2} + X_{i2}\theta + W_i\gamma + \omega_i \geqslant 0$, where W_i is a vector of variables which do not enter the conditional expectation of y but affect the probability of observing y_{i2}, θ and γ are vectors of parameters, and the ω_i are iid random variables. Substituting for y_{i2} leads to $A_i = X_{i2}(\alpha\beta + \theta) + W_i\gamma + \alpha\varepsilon_{i2} + \omega_i$. But since α and θ enter the specification in an equivalent manner, we combine them to form a "reduced form" specification which is $A_i = X_i\xi + W_i\gamma + \varepsilon_{i3}$. Define the vectors $R_i = [W_i, X_{i2}]$ and $\delta = [\xi, \gamma]'$. We assume that ε_{i2} and ω_i are normally distributed, and normalize by setting the variance σ_{33} of ε_{i3} equal to 1. Then the probabilities of retention and attrition are probit functions given, respectively, by

$$(1.3)\qquad \begin{array}{l} \text{pr}\,(a_i = 1) = \Phi[R_i\delta] \qquad \text{and} \\ \text{pr}\,(a_i = 0) = 1 - \Phi[R_i\delta], \end{array}$$

where $\Phi[\cdot]$ is the unit normal distribution function.[3] We could estimate the parameters of equation (1.3) as it is. However, our primary goal is to correct for the effects of attrition on estimates of the parameters in equation (1.1) by

[3] The specification of A_i and the normalization described in this paragraph were used by Hausman and Spence [9] in modeling non-random missing data. A comparable formulation, using an alternative normalization and specification for A_i, was suggested by Hausman and Wise [11, fn. 8, 9, and 10].

integrating it with the probability of attrition.

Suppose we estimate the model of equation (1.1) using only complete observations. The conditional expectation of y_{i2}, given that it is observed, is,

$$(1.4) \qquad E(y_{i2}|X_{i2}, a_i = 1) = X_{i2}\beta + \rho_{23}\sigma \frac{\phi(R_i\delta)}{\Phi[R_i\delta]},$$

where ρ_{23} is the correlation between ε_2 and ε_3. Thus, this procedure will lead to biased and inconsistent estimates of β unless $\rho_{23} = 0$.[4] Least squares estimates based on complete observations but using first period data only will also be inconsistent, even though attrition occurs only in the second period, if ε_{i1} and ε_{i2} have a common component. For then ε_{i1} and ε_{i3} will also be correlated. The expected value of y_{i1}, given that individual i is in the sample in the second period is given by

$$(1.5) \qquad E(y_{i1}|X_{i1}, a_i = 1) = X_{i1}\beta + \rho_{12}\rho_{23}\sigma \frac{\phi(R_i\delta)}{\Phi[R_i\delta]},$$

where $\rho_{13} = \rho_{12}\rho_{23}$.

The second term in equation (1.5) is smaller than the second term in the conditional expectation of y_{i2} in equation (1.4). But so long as individual effects exist across periods, attrition in one period will affect the estimates of all earlier periods, if only complete observations are used.

To recapitulate, we gather together the following definitions:

$$(1.6) \qquad \begin{aligned} y_{i1} &= X_{i1}\beta + \varepsilon_{i1}, \\ y_{i2} &= X_{i2}\beta + \varepsilon_{i2}, \\ A_i &= R_i\delta + \varepsilon_{i3}. \end{aligned}$$

Attrition occurs if the index $A_i \leq 0$. From the conditional expectations of equations (1.4) and (1.5), we see that the critical parameter in the determination of attrition bias is the correlation ρ_{23} between ε_{i2} and ε_{i3}. We want a method of estimation that will yield asymptotically efficient and consistent estimates of the structural parameters of (1.6) and will allow a convenient test of the hypothesis that $\rho_{23} = 0$. We shall use a maximum likelihood procedure. The joint normal terms, ε_{i1}, ε_{i2}, and ε_{i3} have mean zero and covariance matrix

$$(1.7) \qquad \Sigma = \begin{bmatrix} \sigma^2 & \rho_{12}\sigma^2 & \rho_{12}\rho_{23}\sigma \\ & \sigma^2 & \rho_{23}\sigma \\ & & 1 \end{bmatrix},$$

where $\sigma_{11} = \sigma_{22} = \sigma^2$ and we have normalized by setting $\sigma_{33} = 1$. We need to consider two possibilities: $a_i = 1$ and $a_i = 0$. If $a_i = 1$, both y_{i1} and y_{i2} are observed

[4] A variance components estimator will also be inconsistent.

and the joint density of a_i, y_{i1}, and y_{i2} is given by

$$f(a_i = 1, y_{i1}, y_{i2}) = \text{pr}\,[a_i = 1|y_{i1}, y_{i2}]f(y_{i2}|y_{i1})f(y_{i1})$$

(1.8)
$$= \Phi\left[\frac{R_i\delta + (\rho_{23}/\sigma)(y_{i2} - X_{i2}\beta)}{(1-\rho_{23}^2)^{\frac{1}{2}}}\right]\frac{1}{(\sigma^2(1-\rho_{12}^2))^{\frac{1}{2}}}$$

$$\cdot\,\phi\left(\frac{y_{i2} - \rho_{12}Y_{i1} - (X_{i2} - \rho_{12}X_{i1})\beta}{(\sigma^2(1-\rho_{12}^2))^{\frac{1}{2}}}\right)\frac{1}{\sigma}\,\phi\left(\frac{y_{i1} - X_{i1}\beta}{\sigma}\right),$$

where the first term follows from the fact that the conditional density $f(\varepsilon_{i3}|\varepsilon_{i2})$ is $N((\rho_{23}/\sigma)\varepsilon_{i2}, 1-\rho_{23}^2)$. If $a_i = 0$, y_{i2} is not observed and must be "integrated out." In this instance the fact that $f(\varepsilon_{i3}|\varepsilon_{i1})$ is $N(\rho_{12}\rho_{23}/\sigma)\varepsilon_{i1}, 1-\rho_{12}^2\rho_{23}^2)$ leads to the expression,

$$f(a_1 = 0, y_{i1}) = \text{pr}[a_i = 0|y_{i1}]f(y_{i1})$$

(1.9)
$$= \left\{1 - \Phi\left[\frac{R_i\delta + (\rho_{12}\rho_{23}/\sigma)(y_{i1} - X_{i1}\beta)}{(1-\rho_{12}^2\rho_{23}^2)^{\frac{1}{2}}}\right]\right\}\frac{1}{\sigma}\,\phi\left(\frac{y_{i1} - X_{i1}\beta}{\sigma}\right).$$ [5]

[5] An alternative formulation, suggested previously by Hausman and Wise [**11**], is to let

$$A_i = \alpha y_{i2} + R_i\tilde{\delta} + \omega_i,$$

where $R_i\tilde{\delta} = X_{i2}\theta + W_i\gamma$ and the ω_i are iid normal random variables assumed to be independent of ε_1 and ε_2. If we normalize by setting the variance of ω equal to 1, the covariance matrix of ε_1, ε_2, and ω is given by

$$\Sigma = \begin{bmatrix} \sigma^2 & \rho_{12}\sigma^2 & 0 \\ & \sigma^2 & 0 \\ & & 1 \end{bmatrix}.$$

If we now substitute for y_{i2} in the expression for A_i, we obtain

$$A_i = X_{i2}(\alpha\beta + \theta) + W\gamma + \alpha\varepsilon_{i2} + \omega_i = R_i\delta + \varepsilon_{i3},$$

with the covariance matrix for ε_1, ε_2, and ε_3 given by

$$\Sigma = \begin{bmatrix} \sigma^2 & \rho_{12}\sigma^2 & \rho_{12}\alpha\sigma^2 \\ & \sigma^2 & \alpha\sigma^2 \\ & & \alpha^2\sigma^2 + 1 \end{bmatrix}.$$

Expressions comparable to equations (1.8) and (1.9) are then given by

$$f(a_i = 1, y_{i1}, y_{i2}) = \Phi[R_i\delta + \alpha(y_{i2} - X_{i2}\beta)]\cdot f(y_{i2}|y_{i1})\cdot f(y_{i1})$$

and

$$f(a_i = 0, y_{i1}) = \left\{1 - \Phi\left[\frac{R_i\delta + \alpha\rho_{12}(y_{i1} - X_{i1}\beta)}{(1+\alpha^2\sigma^2(1-\rho_{12}^2))^{\frac{1}{2}}}\right]\right\}\cdot f(y_{i1}),$$

where explicit expressions for $f(y_{i2}|y_{i1})$ and $f(y_{i1})$ are the same as in (1.8) and (1.9).

In this formulation, attrition bias depends on the value of α and is zero only if α equals zero. A test for attrition bias is, of course, straightforward. To see the relationship between α and ρ_{23} in the specification used in the body of the paper, note that $\varepsilon_{i3} = \alpha\varepsilon_{i2} + \omega_i$, where ω and ε_2 are independent, can also be written as $\varepsilon_{i3} = \rho_{23}(\sigma_3/\sigma)\varepsilon_{i2} + \omega_i$, where $\alpha = \rho_{23}(\sigma_3/\sigma)$. Thus, $\alpha = 0$ if and only if $\rho_{23} = 0$. Normalizing by setting $\sigma_3^2 = 1$, instead of $\sigma_\omega^2 = 1$, would make the two specifications the same. In this specification, however, we have explicitly assumed that ω is independent from ε_1 and ε_2. But since we have not in the text specification attempted to identify the covariance between ω and ε_2, the two specifications are equivalent. We have not tried to distinguish correlation between ε_2 and ε_3 due only to the fact that ε_2 shows up in ε_3 from correlation between ω and ε_2.

The log likelihood function follows from equations (1.8) and (1.9). Order the observations so that the first s correspond to $a_i = 1$ and the remaining $T-s$ to $a_i = 0$. Then with k a constant the log likelihood function contains the unknown parameters $\beta, \delta, \sigma^2, \rho_{12}, \rho_{23}$. It is given by

$$l = k + \sum_{i=1}^{s} \Bigg\{ -\tfrac{1}{2}\log\sigma^2 - \frac{1}{2\sigma^2}(y_{i1} - X_{i1}\beta)^2 - \tfrac{1}{2}\log(\sigma^2(1-\rho_{12}^2))$$

$$- \frac{1}{2\sigma^2(1-\rho_{12}^2)}(y_{i2} - \rho_{12}y_{i1} - (X_{i2} - \rho_{12}X_{i1})\beta)^2$$

$$+ \log \Phi\left[\frac{R_i\delta + (\rho_{23}/\sigma)(y_{i2} - X_{i2}\beta)}{(1-\rho_{23}^2)^{\frac{1}{2}}}\right]$$

$$+ \sum_{i=s+1}^{N} \Bigg\{ -\tfrac{1}{2}\log\sigma^2 - \frac{1}{2\sigma^2}(y_{i1} - X_{i1}\beta)^2$$

$$+ \log\left[1 - \Phi\left(\frac{R_i\delta + (\rho_{12}\rho_{23}/\sigma)(y_{i1} - X_{i1}\beta)}{(1-\rho_{12}^2\rho_{23}^2)^{\frac{1}{2}}}\right)\right]\Bigg\}.$$

While it may appear complicated, the likelihood function has a simple structure defined in terms of normal density and distribution functions. It combines the variance components specification of the dependent variable y in equation (1.1) with the probit formulation of equation (1.3). The critical parameter for attrition bias is ρ_{23}; and inspection of the likelihood function demonstrates that if $\rho_{23} = 0$, the likelihood function separates into two parts corresponding to the variance components specification for y and the probit specification for attrition. Thus, if attrition bias is not present, generalized least squares techniques used to estimate equation (1.1) will lead to asymptotically efficient and consistent estimates of the structural parameters of the model, as expected.

We pause for a moment to consider identification of the parameters of A_i. Because of the specification of the equation determining A_i in equation (1.6), $A_i = \alpha y_{i2} + X_{i2}\theta + W_i\gamma + \omega_i$, all variables included in the conditional mean of y_{i2}, the vector X_{i2}, should also be included in R_i, the attrition specification vector. However, for (local) identification it can be shown that no variables "excluded" from X_{i2} need to be included in R_i. That is, the vector W_i need not appear in the specification of A_i. A heuristic argument for identification follows from noting that if the attrition bias parameter, ρ_{23}, is plus one or minus one and $\theta = 0$, then the second period attrition probability is identical to a Tobit specification where W_i does not appear in R_i. On the other hand, if $\rho_{23} = 0$, then the likelihood function factors into two distinct parts, a normal regression model and a probit equation. A consideration of the Hessian of the likelihood function for intermediate values of ρ_{23} establishes nonsingularity and thus local identification. When additional variables are included in W_i, the analysis remains the same.

The specified model of attrition extends in a straightforward manner to more than two periods. An attrition equation is specified for each period; it may include time effects. If once attrition occurs the individual does not return to the sample, then a series of conditional probabilities analogous to equations (1.8) and (1.9) result. The last period for which the individual appears in the sample gives information on which the random term in the attrition equations is conditioned. For periods in which the individual remains in the sample, an equation like (1.8) is used to specify the joint probability of no attrition and the observed values of the left hand side variables.[6]

Maximization of the likelihood function (1.10) yields estimates of β, δ, σ^2, ρ_{12} and ρ_{23}.[7] Numerical estimates based on the Gary experiment are presented in the next section.

2. ATTRITION IN THE GARY INCOME MAINTENANCE EXPERIMENT[8]

The primary goal of the income maintenance, or "negative income tax," experiments is to obtain estimates of potential labor supply and earnings responses to possible income maintenance plans.[9] Individuals in the experiments are surveyed to obtain retrospective data for a pre-experimental ("baseline") period, normally just prior to the beginning of the experimental period. Two groups are distinguished during the experimental period: controls and "experimentals." Controls are not on an experimental treatment plan, but receive nominal payments for completing periodic questionnaires. Experimentals are randomly assigned to one of several income maintenance plans. The Gary (Indiana) experiment had four basic plans defined by an income guarantee and a tax rate. The two guarantee levels were $4,300 and $3,300 for a family of four and were adjusted up for larger and down for smaller families. The two marginal tax rates were .6 and .4. The behavior of experimentals during the experiment can be compared to their own pre-experimental behavior and to that of the control group to obtain estimates of the effect of the treatment plans.

Persons received payments under the experimental plans according to a moving average scheme that took into account income in the previous six months in the determination of payments for a given month. This was to insure that payments did not vary widely with fluctuation in monthly income so long as average monthly income remained stable.[10]

[6] A similar model can be used for analysis of panel data in which missing an interview does not result in terminal attrition. A probability model similar to equation (1.3) is specified for each period. State dependence can be introduced in the probability model by conditioning on status in the previous period. Missing observations are then "integrated out" by the same procedure used to derive equation (1.9).

[7] We have used an algorithm proposed by Berndt, Hall, Hall, and Hausman [**3**]. It uses only first derivatives. It is similar to the method of scoring discussed by Anderson [**1**]. Nelson [**20**] reported difficulty in using second derivative methods (Newton-Raphson) in a similar problem. We began with least squares estimates of the parameters and our algorithm always converged to the global optimum. This procedure is computationally easier than using initial consistent estimates that could be obtained, for example, using methods discussed by Heckman [**15**].

[8] In addition to attrition, a potential problem is created because the sample is stratified according to our endogenous variable. We have found, however, that this problem does not lead to significant bias in parameter estimates. A paper on this topic, Hausman and Wise [**13**], or an appendix to this paper that considers the subject will be provided to the reader upon request to the authors.

[9] This summary of NIT experiments is only a brief outline. More detail is contained in Watts and Rees [**23**] and McDonald, Moffitt, and Kehrer [**18**]. For a discussion of the econometric theory of the response to a NIT, both Hall [**6**] and Hausman and Wise [**10**] are relevant.

[10] For a more detailed discussion of this procedure, see Kehrer, et al. [**16**].

Two broad groups of families were studied in the Gary experiment: black, female-headed households and black, male-headed households. There was little attrition among the first group, but the attrition rate among male-headed families was substantial. (See Moffitt [**19**].) Of our sample[11] of 585 black males for whom we had baseline data, 206, or 35.2 per cent, did not complete the experiment.[12] Among the 334 experimentals, the attrition rate was 31.1 per cent, while 40.6 per cent of the 251 controls failed to complete the experiment. This difference in attrition rates is not surprising since the experiment is much more beneficial to experimentals than to controls. Other characteristics of individuals may also affect attrition. The effect of these characteristics will be estimated using the model specified in Section 1.

We emphasize again that non-random attrition does not necessarily lead to biased estimates of a structural model of the type presented in equations (1.1) and (1.2). Attrition which is related only to the exogenous variables in a structural model does not lead to biased estimates, since these variables are controlled for in the statistical analysis. However, if attrition is related to endogenous variables, biased estimates result.

Attrition related to endogenous variables is easy to imagine. Beyond a "breakeven" point, "experimentals" receive no benefits from the experimental treatment. The breakeven point occurs when the guarantee minus taxes paid on earnings is zero. Thus, individuals with high earnings receive no treatment payment and may be much like controls vis á vis their incentive to remain in the experiment. But since high earnings are caused in part by the unobserved random term of the structural equation (1.1), attrition may well be related to it. In particular, attrition may be related to the random term in the earnings function for period 2, leading to correlation between ε_2 and ε_3 in equation (1.6).

We will present our empirical analysis in stages beginning with a simple analysis of variance model and proceeding to more elaborately parameterized structural models. To estimate the effect on earnings, say, of the treatment plans, it would appear that a straightforward and simple method is all that is necessary. We need only estimate experimental effects by comparing the mean responses of experimentals and controls; or, equivalently, by estimating the parameters in a simple analysis of variance model. There are, however, several reasons for using a more elaborate specification with more exogenous variables. If assignment to treatment groups is not in practice completely random, then we may want to control for other variables that affect earnings in order to obtain unbiased estimates of treatment effects. In addition, we may want to "parameterize" the experimental treatments in terms of income and wage effects in order to be able to predict the effect of plans not included among the treatment ones. (This, of course, may not make much sense with only two income guarantees and two tax rates.) Finally, we may want to

[11] The sample was put together for us by Mathematica Policy Research, who have primary reponsibility for analysis of the Gary experiment. Additional information on data availability can be obtained from Mathematica.

[12] While this attrition rate is high, attrition of black males in the New Jersey negative income tax experiment was so high that analysis of the experimental data for blacks was highly suspect. See Peck in Watts and Rees [**23**, Vol. 2, Part 6, Ch. 1].

use the experimental data just like any other survey data to estimate traditional earnings functions. We will see as we proceed that the possibility of attrition adds another dimension to consider in choosing a method of analysis.

We begin with a straightforward analysis of variance model because under usual assumptions underlying randomized controlled experiments it would be the most natural and appropriate method to obtain estimates of experimental effects. Controlled experiments are in fact designed to permit this method of analysis; they presumably obviate the necessity of controlling for individual characteristics other than experimental treatments.[13] We will see, however, that it may not be the most appropriate method of analysis when non-random attrition occurs.

A. *A Simple Analysis of Variance Model*

A simple analysis of variance specification is of the form:

$$E_{it} = \alpha + \delta_2 + \xi + \varepsilon_{it} \qquad (i = 1, \ldots, N; t = 1, 2) \tag{3.1}$$

where E is the logarithm of monthly earnings, α is the average of E over the pre-experimental period, δ_2 is a time (inflation) effect for period 2, ξ is the experimental effect, ε is a random term with zero mean for each i and each t, i indexes individuals, and t indexes time. The parameters of this model may be estimated by comparison of mean values of E for controls and experimentals for the two time periods.

The relevant information and parameter estimates are presented in Table I. Two important simplifications have been made for purposes of estimation. First, since only three observations are available during the experiment, each for a one month period, their average has been used to obtain a monthly earnings figure for the experimental period.[14] Second, the four experimental treatment groups have been treated as one. They will be distinguished in subsequent analysis. The average of the logarithms of earnings of controls increased by .1108 between the baseline and the experimental periods, while the increase for experimentals was only .0492. The time effect, δ_2, has been estimated by the difference between the average for controls in period 2 and the average over both controls and experimentals in period 1. The estimate is .1180 with a standard error of .1673. The

[13] A good treatment of analysis of variance estimation within the context of a social experiment is presented by Hall [**6**]. The analysis of variance models we have used closely parallel those suggested by Hall in analyzing the effect on white males of treatments in the New Jersey NIT experiment. Attrition among white males in that experiment was much less severe than among black males in this one (and in the New Jersey experiment, as well). We have argued verbally ourselves that simple analysis of variance models should be the preferred method of analyzing data from social experiments, at least to estimate initial experimental effects, because this method does take advantage of basic experimental design. Many of the efforts to obtain labor supply effects based on the New Jersey experiment, for example, seemed to fail largely because, in addition to ignoring truncation in sample selection, they also were overparameterized to control for many individual characteristics or as a concomitant of parameterization of experimental treatments. This more structural approach in many ways runs counter to the spirit and raison d'etre of elaborate social experiments.

[14] This averaging severely attenuates the unobserved individual effect in equation (3.2) below due to the high variance (transitory effect) in weekly observations. Average annual observations are much preferred, but were not available from the experiment.

TABLE I

AVERAGE EARNING FOR EXPERIMENTALS AND CONTROLS, AND ESTIMATES OF PARAMETERS IN THE MODEL: $E_{it}=\alpha+\delta_2+\xi+\varepsilon_{it}$

Average earnings		
	Period 1	Period 2
Experimentals	6.2584	6.3176
Controls	6.2710	6.3818
Parameter	Estimates	(standard errors)
Pre-experimental average, α	6.2638	(0.4517)
Time effect, δ_2	0.1180	(0.1673)
Experimental effect, ξ	−.0642	(0.0826)

experimental effect is estimated by the difference in the average for controls and experimentals in period 2. It is −.0642 with a standard error of .0826. Thus, the estimates do indicate a negative effect of the experimental treatments on labor earnings, but this method yields rather imprecise estimates. We also found, as in the New Jersey experiment, that hourly wages of experimentals and controls did not differ. Thus −.0642 per cent is a reasonable indicator of the effect of the experimental treatment on hours worked.

This method of estimation uses information for all persons in our sample of 585 by including data for those who dropped out to obtain the baseline means. (About one-third of the sample dropped out between periods 1 and 2.) But the experimental effect is calculated using only period 2 data; individual specific effects are not allowed.

B. *An Analysis of Variance Model with Individual Specific Terms*

An alternative analysis of variance specification is of the form:

$$E_{it}=\alpha+\delta_2+\xi+\mu_i+\eta_{it}, \tag{3.2}$$

where the μ_i are random individual specific terms, and the η_{it} are independent and identically distributed with mean zero and a common variance. This formulation takes advantage of the correlation between the "random" component, $\mu_i+\eta_{it}$, of earnings in the two time periods. It essentially allows each individual to serve as his own control. But this advantage is gained at the expense of calculating the time effect δ_2 using only data for persons who did not drop out of the experiment—379 of the original 585 observations. It leads, however to a more precise estimate of the experimental effect ξ, the parameter of primary interest. Both methods yield unbiased estimates if the assumptions of equations (3.1) and (3.2) are correct.

An asymptotically efficient generalized least squares method has been used to estimate the parameters of equation (3.2).[15] The results are shown in Table II. The

[15] This estimator is the mixed estimator of combined variance components and fixed effects models. See Scheffé [**22**, Ch. 8].

standard error of the experimental effect is only about one-half as large as that obtained in the specification that ignores individual specific terms. The proportion of the total variance explained by the individual effects is .2212; it serves as an indicator of their importance. The estimate of the experimental effect remains about the same—a reduction in earnings of just over 6 per cent.[16] But it is still not significantly different from zero by conventional standards.

TABLE II

ESTIMATES OF PARAMETERS IN THE RANDOM INDIVIDUAL EFFECTS MODEL: $E_{it} = \alpha + \delta_2 + \xi + \mu_i + \eta_{it}$

Parameter	Estimates	(standard errors)
Pre-experimental average, α	6.2947	(0.0214)
Time effect, δ_2	0.0860	(0.0361)
Experimental effect, ξ	−.0621	(0.0419)

C. *Analysis of Variance Model Corrected for Attrition*

Although analysis of variance is the classical statistical method for analyzing the results of an experiment, the results may be biased by attrition. From the calculations in Section 1, we can see that attrition will lead to bias if either μ_i or η_i is correlated with the probability of attrition. We argued above that experimentals with higher than average income might be expected to have a higher attrition rate since they receive little or no benefit from the experiment. To check for possible attrition bias, the analysis of variance model of equation (3.2) was combined with the probability of attrition specification of model (1.3). Since analysis of variance has a straightforward regression interpretation, the likelihood function of equation (1.9) is maximized using the technique discussed in Section 2 with "dummy variables" associated with the analysis of variance effects. The attrition specification allows attrition to depend on variables that enter the structural model of earnings (discussed below) as well as other variables. They are:

Constant.

Experimental Effect: One for experimentals and zero for controls.

Education: Years of education.

Experience: Years of experience since starting work.

Income: Log of non-labor family income. It includes foodstamps, AFDC payments, public assistance, and earnings of other family members.

Union: A dummy variable that is one for union members and zero otherwise.

Poor Health: A dummy variable that is one if the individual said that his health was poor in relation to "others" and it limited the amount of work he did; otherwise the variable is zero.

The results are shown in Table III. The experimental effect is now estimated to be about 11 per cent and is significantly different from zero at conventional levels of significance. We found in Section 1 that attrition bias would be zero only if ρ_{23}

[16] The alternative fixed effects estimator, which takes μ_i to be a non-stochastic individual constant, yields an estimate of the experimental effect of −.0568 and a time effect of .0828.

TABLE III

PARAMETER ESTIMATES FOR THE ANALYSIS OF VARIANCE SPECIFICATION COMBINED WITH THE ATTRITION MODEL

Analysis of variance		Attrition	
Parameters	Estimates (standard errors)	Variables	Estimates (standard errors)
Pre-experimental average, α	6.2636 (0.0265)	Constant	-.9210 (.2608)
Time effect, δ_2	.1064 (.0408)	Experimental Effect	.2361 (.1131)
Experimental effect, ξ	.1098 (.0453)	Education	.0172 (.0195)
		Experience	-.0002 (.0050)
		Income	.0934 (.0290)
		Union	1.2018 (0.1100)
		Poor Health	.2715 (.1013)
Attrition bias parameter ρ_{23}	-.8213 (.0449)	Earnings correlation ρ_{12}	.1697 (.0350)
Likelihood value	36.24	Earnings variance σ_η^2	.2147 (.0006)

were zero. Here we find a very precisely measured estimate of $-.8213$.[17] That is, persons with higher earnings, given other measured characteristics, are more likely to drop out of the experiment. Another method to test for attrition bias is to compare differences in estimates of α, δ_2, and ξ when a "correction" is made for attrition with estimates under the hypothesis that there is no attrition bias. Since under the null hypothesis that $\rho_{23}=0$ the analysis of variance estimates for equation (3.1) are asymptotically efficient, the lemma of Hausman [**8**] can be applied to perform a specification test. The lemma states that the variance of the difference of the estimates is the difference of the respective variances. Concentrating on the experimental effect estimates, we see that the difference between the analysis of variance and maximum likelihood estimates is $-.0477$, with a standard error of .0171. The χ^2 statistic relative to the hypothesis of no difference has a value of 7.75. The hypothesis of no difference is rejected at any reasonable level of significance. Analysis of variance techniques which do not account for possible attrition bias lead to parameter estimates that differ substantially from the maximum likelihood estimates that take account of such bias. Furthermore, the maximum likelihood estimate of the experimental effect is significantly different from zero at usual levels of significance.

Finally, we note that experimentals appear to have a lower probability of attrition than controls. Higher non-labor income, poor health, and union membership are also associated with lower attrition rates, and the relevant

[17] The null hypothesis of $\rho_{23}=0$ is rejected using a (Wald) χ^2 test. The χ^2 statistic with one degree of freedom is 334.6.

estimates are rather precisely measured. More education is estimated to be associated with less attrition and more work experience with more, but neither effect is measured with much precision.

We also estimated an analysis of variance model with a slightly more complex attrition specification. The estimates in Table III imply a probability of attrition for experimentals that is .047 less than for controls, if the probabilities are evaluated at the mean values of the other variables. To permit more general differences in the attrition behavior of experimentals and controls, we estimated a model with separate experimental and control coefficients on each of the attrition variables. That is, we allowed complete interaction between all variables and experimental status. However, none of the interactions was found to have a noticeable effect on attrition. None of the interaction terms was greater than one-fourth the size of the corresponding main effect. The attrition bias term ρ_{23} was estimated to be −.8147, nearly identical to the estimate of −.8213 found for the less complex specification, while the estimated experimental effect, −.1098, was identical to the one in the previous model. The maximum likelihood value of 36.62 barely exceeds the value of 36.24 found in Table III. The appropriate χ^2 likelihood ratio statistic (with five degrees of freedom) provides no evidence that the more complicated specification adds to our ability to predict attrition.

We have to this point been referring loosely to the difference between estimates that are corrected for attrition and those that are not as resulting from "attrition bias." This seems to be a correct interpretation since without attrition the analysis of variance model would presumably give an unbiased estimate of the experimental effect. We will see below, however, that the experimental effect estimated from a structural model is not altered much when a correction is made for attrition. Thus, it might be more appropriate to say that analysis of variance estimates of the experimental effect are less robust with respect to attrition than structural model estimates. Why this result might be expected is explained below.

D. *A Structural Model of Earnings Corrected for Attrition*

Structural models have been widely used in the analysis of income maintenance experiments. Such models permit estimation of the income and substitution effects which are needed to predict the response to plans which have not been included in the experimental design. However, to estimate a simple experimental response, it might be argued that only analysis of variance models are needed, given appropriate randomization in the original experimental design. If, in fact, allocation to treatment groups is completely random so that variables indicating treatment group are orthogonal to other exogenous variables that might influence earnings, addition of these variables will affect neither the experimental effect estimates nor their standard errors. If, however, treatment group assignment is not orthogonal to other exogenous variables, we cannot predict a priori whether estimates of the treatment effect from the structural model will be more or less precise than the simple analysis of variance estimates. On the one hand, the variance σ_η^2 is reduced by controlling for other determinants of earnings such as education and experience. On the other hand, additional variables use up degrees of freedom, thereby tending to increase the variance of parameter estimates.

We have, however, already found strong evidence of attrition bias within the context of the analysis of variance model, and are led to consider an alternative approach. Recall that the bias results from correlation between attrition and earnings in the second period. It may, in turn, be thought of as resulting from correlation between the error in the second period earnings equation and the probability of attrition. If exogenous variables that affect earnings, as well as attrition, are left out of the earnings equation, the correlation between attrition and the error in the earnings equation is magnified. Thus, if attrition is primarily related to exogenous variables in the structural model which are included in the stochastic term in the analysis of variance model, the structural model may be much less affected by attrition than the analysis of variance model.

We have estimated a variance components specification of the structural model $E_{it} = X_{it}\beta + \varepsilon_{it}$, with $\varepsilon_{it} = \mu_i + \eta_{it}$, as discussed in Section 1. Estimates are presented in Table IV. For comparison, generalized least squares estimates of the structural parameters (that are not corrected for attrition) have been included

TABLE IV[a]

PARAMETER ESTIMATES OF THE EARNINGS FUNCTION STRUCTURAL MODEL WITH AND WITHOUT A CORRECTION FOR ATTRITION

Variables	With attrition correction: maximum likelihood estimates (standard errors) Earnings function parameters	With attrition correction: maximum likelihood estimates (standard errors) Attrition parameters	Without attrition correction: generalized least squares estimates (standard errors) Earnings function parameters
Constant	5.8539	−.6347	5.8911
	(0.0903)	(.3351)	(.0829)
Experimental effect	−.0822	.2414	−.0793
	(.0402)	(.1211)	(.0390)
Time effect	.0940	—	.0841
	(.0520)	—	(.0358)
Education	.0209	−.0204	.0136
	(.0052)	(.0244)	(.0050)
Experience	.0037	−.0038	.0020
	(.0013)	(.0061)	(.0013)
Income	−.0131	.1752	−.0115
	(.0050)	(.0470)	(.0044)
Union	.2159	1.4290	.2853
	(.0362)	(0.1252)	(.0330)
Poor health	−.0601	.2480	−.0578
	(.0330)	(.1237)	(.0326)
	$\hat{\sigma}_\eta^2 = .1832$	$l^* = 64.35$	$\hat{\sigma}_\eta^2 = .1236$
	(.0057)		
	$\hat{\rho}_{12} = .2596$	$\rho_{23} = -.1089$	$\hat{\rho}_{12} = .2003$
	(.0391)	(1.0429)	

[a] As an indication of computational costs for our sample of 585 observations, the GLS estimation which does not take account of attrition costs about $4.50 using TSP on the MIT 370–168 computer. The cost of maximum likelihood estimation of the attrition model ranged between $7 and $13 dollars, depending on the initial guesses of the parameters.

together with the maximum likelihood estimates that incorporate the effects of attrition. From the last column of the table, we see that the random effects model yields an estimated negative experimental effect of about 7.9 per cent.[18] The individual specific terms account for only 20 per cent of the total variance of the error term, as indicated by the estimated value of ρ_{12} in this model. As mentioned previously, this relatively low value probably results from using the average of only three monthly observations to calculate earnings. Annual figures would presumably include much less random noise. The coefficients on the right-hand side variables all have the expected sign and are measured rather precisely. In fact, the results agree closely with the estimates of Hausman-Wise [**10**, p. 429] based on data from the New Jersey experiment, where a primary consideration in estimation was correction for truncation bias introduced by the sample design.

Estimates of the parameters in the attrition model of equations (1.6) and (1.7) are presented in the first two columns of Table IV. The attrition bias parameter ρ_{23} is estimated to be $-.1089$. It indicates a small but statistically significant correlation between earnings and the probability of attrition. Although the estimate of the experimental effect is very close to the generalized least squares estimate, some of the other estimates differ substantially from the least squares values. The effect of income on earnings decreases by 23 per cent, while the effect of another year of education increases by 43 per cent. The experimental effect increases in magnitude from $-.079$ to $-.082$, an increase of 3.6 per cent.[19] Thus, within the context of a structural model, some attrition bias seems to be present, but not enough to substantially alter the estimate of the experimental effect. This is in marked contrast with the analysis of variance case, where attrition seems to affect the estimates significantly.[20]

Finally, we observe that non-labor income, poor health, and union membership are statistically significant and are estimated to reduce the probability of attrition. Experimentals are less likely to drop out than controls. The relevant estimates are not, however, precisely measured. Education and years of work experience are estimated to have small and statistically insignificant negative influences on retention in the sample. Recall that these are "reduced form" estimates in that the direct effect of these variables on attrition cannot be distinguished from their indirect effects through earnings.

Within the context of this structural model we also estimated a more complicated model of attrition, the same one used within the analysis of variance context.

[18] The experimental effect using a fixed effects model was estimated to be minus 6.4 per cent.

[19] Using the lemma of Hausman [**8**], the difference of .003 has an estimated standard error of .0097. Thus, the difference in the two experimental effect estimates is not statistically different from zero.

[20] Comparison with the analysis of variance model yields a likelihood ration of 56.22 with 5 degrees of freedom, which is significant at all reasonable test sizes. Note, however, that if it were not for attrition, unbiased estimates of the experimental effect would result from an analysis of variance if a correct experimental design were used. In fact, the experimental effect is just as precisely estimated in Table III as in Table IV, which indicates that while the coefficients of the additional variables are significant they do not help to obtain a more precise estimate of the experimental effect.

It allows for full interaction between the determinants of earnings and experimental status. Instead of allowing merely for an experimental effect as indicated by the estimates in Table IV, separate coefficients for experimentals and controls were distinguished for education, years of experience, non-labor family income, health, and union membership. As with the analysis of variance model, no significant differences in these coefficient estimates were found. None of the estimated interaction terms exceeded one-fourth the magnitude of the main effect terms.[21] The estimate of the attrition parameter ρ_{23}, however, decreased to only $-.040$. The experimental effect was estimated to be $-.0790$, almost identical to the generalized least squares estimate of Table IV.

E. *A Structural Model of Earnings with Treatment Groups Distinguished*

Because the more complicated model of attrition does not add much to the explanation of attrition, we returned to the non-interaction specification to estimate a final structural model. Instead of specifying a simple experimental effect, we allowed separate effects for each of the four experimental plans. The results are presented in Table V. The likelihood value increased to 71.59 as compared with a value of 64.35 in Table IV. The relevant likelihood ratio statistic, distributed as χ^2 with 6 degrees of freedom, has a value of 14.48. It is significant at the 2.5 per cent level. Although the individual experimental effects are not estimated precisely, their magnitudes are of interest. For convenience, the relevant estimates from the table have been reproduced in the tabulation below. Keep in mind that these estimates are rather imprecise.

		Tax Rate	
		High	Low
Guarantee	High	−.115	−.093
	Low	−.001	−.083

The effect of the guarantee seems to be large relative to the effect of the tax rate. For the high guarantee level, increasing the tax rate does not alter earnings substantially. For the low guarantee level, in fact, persons with a high tax rate are estimated to earn more than persons on the low tax rate plan.

Although it is normally assumed that the effect of an increase in the guarantee should be to reduce labor supply and thus earnings, the *average* effect to be expected from a decrease in the tax rate is not clear. While for an individual already receiving experimental payments (those "on" the experiment), the effect of a decrease in the tax rate may be to increase labor supply, it also brings onto the experiment some persons who were not receiving payments before—some of those above the initial breakeven point. These persons are likely to work less. The

[21] The maximizing value of the likelihood function increased to only 66.32 relative to the value of 64.35 without these interactions. The two values yield a likelihood ratio statistic of 3.94. This statistic under the null hypothesis of no interactions is distributed as χ^2 with 5 degrees of freedom, and has an expected value of 5.0. Thus, no significant interaction is found.

TABLE V

PARAMETER ESTIMATES FOR STRUCTURAL MODEL WITH FOUR TREATMENT EFFECTS AND CORRECTION FOR ATTRITION

Variables	Earnings function parameters (standard errors)	Attrition parameters (standard errors)
Constant	5.8503	−.6692
	(0.0702)	(.3417)
High guarantee–High tax	−.1148	.5042
	(.0720)	(.2167)
High guarantee–Low tax	−.0930	.3990
	(.0610)	(.1774)
Low guarantee-High tax	.0009	.1255
	(.1027)	(.1601)
Low guarantee-Low tax	−.0831	.1843
	(.0746)	(.1483)
Time effect	.0831	—
	(.0533)	
Education	.0209	−.0212
	(.0052)	(.0248)
Experience	.0083	−.0050
	(.0013)	(.0062)
Income	−.0129	.1785
	(.0056)	(.0488)
Union	.2186	1.4277
	(.0363)	(0.1273)
Poor Health	−.0606	.2843
	(.0335)	(.2483)
	$\hat{\rho}_{12} = .2614$	$\hat{\rho}_{23} = -.0562$
	(.0396)	(.0487)
	$\hat{\sigma}^2_\eta = .1821$	$l^* = 71.59$
	(.0003)	

number brought onto the experiment by a decrease in the tax rate may be larger when the guarantee is low than when it is high.

As might be expected, the experimental treatments have different effects on the probability of attrition. Individuals with high guarantees are estimated to have a substantially lower probability of attrition than persons with low guarantees. Persons with high guarantees, of course, receive greater benefits from the experiment.

To recapitulate a bit: We have used a model incorporating the probability of attrition to estimate the treatment effect of the Gary income maintenance experiment. First, we found a significant negative experimental effect on earnings of about 8 per cent. This effect is due almost entirely to a decrease in hours worked. We also found weak evidence that the guarantee level had a greater effect on earnings than the tax level. (To estimate income and substitution effects, the treatment plans would have to be parameterized in terms of implied net wage rates and non-labor income and incorporated into a structural model of hours and wages.) Second, while significant attrition bias is found in both the analysis of variance and the structural models, it is much more serious in the analysis of variance case. The analysis of variance estimate of experimental effect changes substantially when a correction is made for attrition. However, when a structural model is used, the experimental effect estimated by generalized least squares is found to be very close to the maximum likelihood estimates that incorporate the probability of attrition. Thus, the structural model seems more robust with respect to attrition bias.

3. CONCLUSION

We have specified a model of attrition and have proposed a maximum likelihood method of estimating its parameters. The model yields efficient estimates of structural parameters in the presence of attrition, as well as an estimate of a parameter that indicates the presence or absence of attrition bias. While the method was demonstrated using data from the Gary income maintenance experiment, it is applicable to any panel data. For instance, in the initial years of the National Longitudinal (Parnes) Survey, about 15 per cent of the young males "dropped out" of the survey. The majority of the dropouts entered the military either by the draft or through enlistment. It might well be the case, for example, that the random term in a model of earnings for these young men would be correlated with the dropout probability. Possibly persons with unusually low earnings are more likely to enlist in the armed forces than those with high earnings. This would lead to attrition bias if least squares estimators were used. Because attrition occurs from almost all samples of individuals who are followed through time, techniques which test for possible bias and correct for it when it is present should find many applications in the analysis of panel data, whether collected by traditional survey methods or in conjunction with social experiments.

Massachusetts Institute of Technology
and
Harvard University

Manuscript received June, 1977; final revision received January, 1978.

REFERENCES

[1] ANDERSON, T. W.: "Some Scaling Models and Estimation Procedures in the Latent Class Model," in *Probability and Statistics: The Harold Cramer Volume*, edited by O. Grenander. New York: 1959.

[2] AMEMIYA, T.: "Regression Analysis when the Dependent Variable is Truncated Normal," *Econometrica*, 41 (1973), 997–1016.

[3] BERNDT, E., B. HALL, R. HALL, AND J. HAUSMAN: "Estimation and Inference in Nonlinear Structural Models," *Annals of Economic and Social Measurement*, 3 (1974), 653–665.

[4] FISHER, R. A.: *The Design of Experiments*. Edinburgh: Oliver and Boyd, 1935.

[5] GOLDFELD, S. M., AND R. E. QUANDT: "The Estimation of Structural Shifts by Switching Regressions," *Annals of Economic and Social Measurement*, 2 (1973), 475–485.

[6] HALL, R. E.: "The Effects of the Experimental Negative Income Tax on Labor Supply," in *Work Incentives and Income Guarantees: The New Jersey Negative Income Tax Experiment*, edited by J. A. Pechman and P. M. Timpane. Washington: The Brookings Institution, 1975.

[7] HANOCH, G.: "A Multivariate Model of Labor Supply: Methodology for Estimation," September, 1976, mimeograph.

[8] HAUSMAN, J. A.: "Specification Tests in Econometrics," forthcoming in *Econometrica*, 46 (1978), 1251–1273.

[9] HAUSMAN, J. A., AND A. M. SPENCE: "Non-Random Missing Data," mimeograph, 1977.

[10] HAUSMAN, J. A., AND D. A. WISE: "The Evaluation of Results from Truncated Samples: The New Jersey Negative Income Tax Experiment," *Annals of Economic and Social Measurement*, 5 (1976), 421–445.

[11] ———: "Attrition and Sample Selection in the Gary Income Maintenance Experiment," mimeograph, 1976.

[12] ———: "Social Experimentation, Truncated Distributions, and Efficient Estimation," *Econometrica*, 45 (1977), 319–339.

[13] ———: "Stratification on Endogenous Variables and Estimation: The Gary Income Maintenance Experiment," mimeograph, 1977.

[14] HECKMAN, J.: "Shadow Prices, Market Wage, and Labor Supply," *Econometrica*, 42 (1974), 679–694.

[15] ———: "The Common Structure of Statistical Models of Truncation, Sample Selection, and Limited Dependent Variables and a Simple Estimator for Such Models," *Annals of Economic and Social Measurement*, 5 (1976), 475–492.

[16] KEHRER, K. C., E. K. BRUML, G. T. BURTLESS, AND D. N. RICHARDSON: "The Gary Income Maintenance Experiment: Design, Administration, and Data Files," mimeograph, 1975.

[17] MADDALA, G. S., AND F. D. NELSON: "Switching Regression Models with Exogenous and Endogenous Switching," *Proceedings of the Business and Economics Statistics Section, American Statistical Association*, 70 (1975), 423–426.

[18] MCDONALD, J. F., R. A. MOFFITT, AND K. C. KEHRER: "The Negative Income Tax and Labor Supply: Methodological Issues and Analytic Strategy," mimeograph, 1976.

[19] MOFFITT, R. A.: "Selection Bias in the Analysis of Experimental Data: Empirical Results in the Gary Negative Income Maintenance Experiment," mimeograph, 1976.

[20] NELSON, F. D.: "Censored Regression Models with Unobserved, Stochastic Censoring Thresholds," mimeograph, 1976.

[21] QUANDT, R. E.: "The Estimation of the Parameters of a Linear Regression System Obeying Two Separate Regimes," *Journal of the American Statistical Association*, 53 (1958), 878–880.

[22] SCHEFFÉ, H.: *The Analysis of Variance*. New York: John Wiley and Sons, Inc., 1959.

[23] WATTS, H. W., AND A. REES (EDS.): *Final Report of the New Jersey Graduated Work Incentives Experiment*. Madison, Wis.: Institute for Research on Poverty, University of Wisconsin, Madison, 1974.

[22]

Econometrica, Vol. 52, No. 4 (July, 1984)

ECONOMETRIC MODELS FOR COUNT DATA WITH AN APPLICATION TO THE PATENTS-R & D RELATIONSHIP

BY JERRY HAUSMAN, BRONWYN H. HALL, AND ZVI GRILICHES[1]

This paper focuses on developing and adapting statistical models of counts (nonnegative integers) in the context of panel data and using them to analyze the relationship between patents and R & D expenditures. Since a variety of other economic data come in the form of repeated counts of some individual actions or events, the methodology should have wide applications.

The statistical models we develop are applications and generalizations of the Poisson distribution. Two important issues are (i) Given the panel nature of our data, how can we allow for separate persistent individual (fixed or random) effects? (ii) How does one introduce the equivalent of disturbances-in-the-equation into the analysis of Poisson and other discrete probability functions?

The first problem is solved by conditioning on the total sum of outcomes over the observed years, while the second problem is solved by introducing an additional source of randomness, allowing the Poisson parameter to be itself randomly distributed, and compounding the two distributions. Lastly, we develop a test statistic for the presence of serial correlation when fixed effects estimators are used in nonlinear conditional models.

INTRODUCTION

THIS PAPER AROSE out of the analysis of a specific substantive problem: the relationship between the research and development (R & D) expenditures of firms and the number of patents applied for and received by them. There are two salient aspects of the data we wish to analyze. (i) Our dependent variable is a *count* of the total number of patents applied for by a particular firm in a given year. It varies from zero to several or even many, for some firms. (ii) We have repeated observations for the same firms. That is, our data form a combined time-series cross-section *panel*. In this paper, we focus, therefore, on developing and adapting statistical models of counts (nonnegative integers) in the context of panel data and using them to analyze the relationship between patents and R & D expenditures. This is not, however, the only possible application for the methods discussed in this paper. A variety of other economic data come in the form of repeated counts of some individual actions or events. The number of spells of sickness in a year, the number of records purchased per month, the number of cars owned, or the number of jobs held during a year, all have nonnegligible probabilities of zero and are nonnegative integers.

The statistical models we develop are applications and generalizations of the Poisson distribution. After rewriting the Poisson distribution as a function of a number of independent variables we have to deal with two additional issues. (i) Given the panel nature of our data, how can we allow for separate persistent individual (fixed or random) effects? (ii) How does one introduce the equivalent

[1] We are indebted to NSF Grants SES79-24108, SOC78-04279, and PRA79-13740 for financial support of this work. Whitney Newey provided research assistance. A referee provided helpful comments.

of disturbance-in-the-equation into the analysis of Poisson and other discrete probability functions?

The first problem is solved by conditioning on the total sum of outcomes over the observed years, while the second problem is solved by introducing an additional source of randomness, allowing the Poisson parameter to be itself randomly distributed, and compounding the two distributions. The relevant likelihood functions and the associated computational methods are described in the body of the paper.

The substantive application continues the work of Pakes and Griliches [**25**]. In that work patent data for 8 years (1968–1975) and 121 U.S. companies were analyzed as a function of their current and lagged R & D expenditures. A log-log functional form was used and the "zero value" problem was "solved" by (a) choosing companies so as to minimize this problem (only 8 per cent of the observations were zero in any one year) and (b) setting zeroes equal to one and adding a dummy variable to allow the equation to choose implicitly another value between zero and one. The questions of interest were (a) the strength (fit) of the relationship between patents and R & D, (b) the elasticity of patents with respect to R & D expenditures, (c) the shape of the distributed lag of R & D effects, and (d) the presence and sign of a trend in this relationship. The major findings were: A high fit ($R^2 \cong .9$) cross-sectionally and a lower ($R^2 \cong .3$) though still statistically significant fit in the "within" time series dimension of the data. The estimated elasticity was around 1.0 in the cross-sectional dimension, dropping to about .5 in the within, shorter-run time dimension. The shape of the distributed lag was not well defined, with some indication of lag-truncation bias (the possible influence of pre-sample unmeasured R & D expenditures) which could not, however, be well distinguished from a fixed firm effect.[2] A negative time trend was found in most of the examined data subsets.

In this paper we wish to reexamine the earlier findings using a more appropriate model for such data, a model that reflects explicitly its integer nature. We do not expect the results to change much since the "zero" problem is relatively minor in this sample (8 per cent). We are interested, however, in developing this methodology because the sample is being expanded to encompass many more smaller firms with a concomitant increase in the importance of such issues. We use a sample of 128 firms for the 7 years 1968–1974. The patent data were tabulated for us by the Office of Technology Assessment and Forecasting of the U.S. Patent Office and the R & D data were taken from the Compustat tape and other sources (see Pakes and Griliches [**25**] for more detail on sample derivation and construction), and deflated by an approximate R & D cost deflator.

The rest of the paper is organized as follows: Section 1 presents the simple Poisson regression model and applies it to our data. Section 2 develops a generalization which allows each firm to have its own average propensity to

[2] It is difficult to distinguish in a short series between a left-out pre-sample cumulated R & D value whose effect is dying out slowly and a "permanent fixed" individual firm effect. See Griliches and Pakes [**15**] for further discussion of these issues.

patent by conditioning separately the count distribution of each firm on the sum of its patents for the whole period. Section 3 allows for the "over-dispersion" in the data by letting each firm's Poisson parameter have a random distribution of its own, leading to the estimation of a negative-binomial model for these data. Section 4 explores in our nonlinear context the parallels to the "within"–"between" dichotomy in linear models. Section 5 summarizes the major methodological and substantive results and discusses some possible future lines of work.

1. THE POISSON MODEL AND APPLICATION

The Poisson distribution is often a reasonable description for events which occur both "randomly and independently" in time.[3] It seems a natural first assumption for many counting problems in econometrics. Let us denote the Poisson parameter as λ, and consider specifications of the form $\log \lambda = X\beta$ where X is a vector of regressors which describe the characteristics of an observation unit in a given time period. Denote n_{it} as the observed event count for unit i during the time period t. The advantages of the Poisson specification are: (i) In many ways it is analogous to the familiar econometric regression specification. In particular, $E(n_{it} \mid X_{it}) = \lambda_{it}$. Furthermore, estimation of unknown parameters is straightforward and is done either by an iterative weighted least squares technique or by a maximum likelihood algorithm. The log likelihood function is globally concave so that maximization routines converge rapidly. (ii) The "zero problem," $n_{it} = 0$, is a natural outcome of the Poisson specification. In contrast to the usual logarithmic regression specification we need not truncate an arbitrary continuous distribution. Likewise, the integer property of the outcomes n_{it} is handled directly. For large n_{it} a continuous approximation often suffices. But for small n_{it}, a specification which models the counting properties of the data (both large and small) seems in order. (iii) The Poisson specification allows for convenient time aggregation so long as its basic assumption of time independence holds true. Thus, if the counting process is Poisson over time $t = 1, T$ with parameter λ_{it}, then the aggregate data over period one to T are also Poisson with parameter $\lambda_i = \sum_{t=1}^{T} \lambda_{it}$. This property permits the convenient generalization of the Poisson model to be developed below. The time independence property is also a potential weakness of our specification given the often noted serial correlation of residuals in econometric specifications. We will attempt to distinguish carefully between true time independence versus apparent dependence due to unobserved heterogeneity of the individual units.

Our basic Poisson probability specification is

$$(1.1) \qquad \operatorname{pr}(n_{it}) = f(n_{it}) = \frac{e^{-\lambda_{it}} \lambda_{it}^{n_{it}}}{n_{it}!}.$$

[3] It has a long history in the analysis of accident data with perhaps the most famous example being von Bortkiewicz's 1898 study of accidental death by mule kick in the German army. The Poisson and subsequent models that we consider might also usefully be analyzed as members of the "generalized linear model" class of Nelder and Wedderburn [22]. See also Johnson and Kotz [19]. Gilbert [12] has applied the Poisson model to economic data.

In our application, i indexes firms and t indexes years and we specify $\log\lambda_{it} = X_{it}\beta$. Note that λ_{it} is a deterministic function of X_{it}, and the randomness in the model comes from the Poisson specification for the n_{it}. The moment generating function of the Poisson distribution is $m(t) = e^{-\lambda}e^{\lambda e^t}$ so that the first two moments are $E(n_{it}) = \lambda_{it}$ and $V(n_{it}) = \lambda_{it}$. The regression property of this specification arises from $E(n_{it}) = \lambda_{it}$, but it is not uncommon to find that the variance of n_{it} is larger than the mean empirically, implying "overdispersion" in the data. After an initial exploration of the Poisson model, we shall consider the possibility of such overdispersion.

The log likelihood of a sample of N firms over T time periods for this Poisson specification is

$$(1.2) \qquad L(\beta) = \sum_{i=1}^{N} \sum_{t=1}^{T} \left[n_{it}! - e^{X_{it}\beta} + n_{it} X_{it}\beta \right].$$

The gradient and Hessian take the forms

$$(1.3) \qquad \begin{aligned} \frac{\partial L}{\partial \beta} &= \sum \sum \left[X_{it}'(n_{it} - e^{X_{it}\beta}) \right], \\ \frac{\partial^2 L}{\partial \beta \partial \beta'} &= \sum \sum \left[-(X_{it}'X_{it}) e^{X_{it}\beta} \right]. \end{aligned}$$

The first order conditions indicate that β can be estimated either by an iterative nonlinear weighted least squares program with $n_{it} - \lambda_{it}$ as the "residual" or by a maximum likelihood (ML) program. The Hessian demonstrates that the likelihood function is globally concave as long as X is of full column rank and $e^{X_{it}\beta}$ does not go to zero for all X_{it}. With a globally concave likelihood function, a wide choice of ML algorithms can be used. In our applications convergence to the global maximum was always rapid. The variance matrix of the asymptotic distribution $V(\beta)$ is calculated from the Hessian matrix evaluated at $\hat{\beta}$.

We fit our initial Poisson specification to a model with current R&D and five lagged values of R&D, and a time trend. The results are found in Table I. We also present the corresponding estimates of a least squares regression of $\log(n_{it}) = X_{it}\beta + \epsilon_{it}$ where $\log(n_{it})$ is set to zero and a dummy variable used when $n_{it} = 0$. The results of the Poisson model are broadly similar to OLS although note that the estimated standard errors of the Poisson estimates are approximately three times smaller. The coefficient of current R&D is higher but the sum of the lag coefficients are quite similar. We note an exogeneous decrease in patents of 6 per cent per year. Lastly, we have the somewhat disturbing pattern of a U-shaped distributed lag which may well indicate a substantial truncation effect. This pattern disappears, however, when we allow for firm specific effects below.

We now consider alternative specifications of the basic Poisson model. In column 4 of Table I we include only contemporaneous R&D since we find later in the paper that when firm specific effects are added the lagged effects become quite small and difficult to identify. Note that the coefficient of current R&D is very close to the sum of the coefficients in our initial specification. The ex-

TABLE I

ESTIMATES OF THE PATENTS MODEL—TOTALS[1]

Variable	Mean	Coefficients				
		Poisson	OLS[2]	Poisson	OLS	Poisson
$\log R_0$	2.17 (1.64)	.36 (.03)	.21 (.12)	.87 (.004)	.81 (.02)	.65 (.01)
$\log R_{-1}$	2.15 (1.62)	.13 (.05)	.12 (.17)			
$\log R_{-2}$	2.12 (1.61)	.09 (.05)	− .05 (.18)			
$\log R_{-3}$	2.08 (1.62)	− .13 (.06)	− .08 (.18)			
$\log R_{-4}$	2.03 (1.63)	.11 (.07)	.01 (.19)			
$\log R_{-5}$	1.96 (1.64)	.53 (.05)	.64 (.15)			
time		− .06 (.002)	− .06 (.02)	− .04 (.002)	− .009 (0.15)	.04 (.01)
time × $\log R_0$						− .02 (.008)
dummy[3] (scientific sector)	0.52					.37 (.01)
log book value[4]	5.36 (2.00)					.24 (.004)
intercept		1.68 (0.20)	1.58 (.08)	1.55 (.018)	1.32 (.08)	.39 (.04)
dummy ($n_{it} = 0$)	0.08		1.37 (.12)		1.41 (.12)	
sum of log R coefficients		.88	.84	.87	.81	.57[5]
standard error of residuals			.869		.914	
log likelihood		− 10,621.1		− 11,198.4		− 9,077.5

[1] The sample is 128 firms, annual data from 1968 to 1974. In column 1, standard deviations are in parentheses.
[2] For the OLS estimates, the dependent variable is log of patents, with a dummy for observations with zero patents.
[3] The scientific sector dummy is for firms in the drug, computer, scientific instrument, chemical, and electric component industries.
[4] The log book variable is the natural logarithm of the inflation adjusted book value of the firms in 1971.
[5] Sum evaluated at midpoint of the period, 1971.

ogeneous time effect has now decreased in magnitude to 4 per cent per year. In column 5 we find very similar though slightly lower results in the OLS regression. As a first-step in accounting for differences in propensity to patent across these firms which are drawn from all manufacturing sectors, we add a dummy variable for the scientific sector which includes firms in the drug, computer, scientific instruments, chemical, and electrical equipment industries, and a proxy for firm size, the inflation adjusted book value of the firm in 1971. Both variables have strong positive effects on the expected number of patents. In addition, we interact R&D with time to attempt to sort out a pure exogenous effect of time from a decrease in the effectiveness of R&D over time. The estimates indicate that the effect of R&D seems to be decreasing since the estimated coefficient is $-.02$ while the time coefficient has now switched sign to $+.04$. Both effects are precisely estimated and they tend to persist as we move to more elaborately specified models.

To evaluate the adequacy of the Poisson specification we now turn to an investigation of the residuals. Starting with the Poisson residual $u_{it} = n_{it} - \lambda_{it}$ we define the standardized residual as u_{it} divided by its estimated standard deviation: $\epsilon_{it} = (n_{it} - \lambda_{ig})/\sqrt{\lambda_{it}}$. We use these residuals to test our model specification in two ways.[4] First, the independence assumption can be tested by forming the 7×7 covariance matrix $\Sigma = (1/N)\sum_{i=1}^{N}(\epsilon_i \epsilon_i')$ where ϵ_i is a vector of residuals for firm i. The estimated correlation matrix has off diagonal element which equal .8 approximately. Significant correlation exists which casts serious doubts on the adequacy of our Poisson specification. Next we consider the variance property. Given the Poisson specification the variance of the ϵ_{it}'s should be unity. In Figure 1 we show a log-log plot of $\sigma_i^2 = (1/(T-1))\sum_t (u_{it} - \bar{u}_i)^2$ for $\bar{u}_i = (1/T)\sum_t \epsilon_{it}$ against $\bar{\lambda}_i = (1/T)\sum_t \lambda_{it}$. We do not find the expected one-to-one relationship at all. The variance increases considerably more rapidly than does the mean. A simple regression of $\log \sigma_i^2$ on $\log \bar{\lambda}_i$ takes the form, $\log \sigma_i^2 = -.68 + 1.42 \log \bar{\lambda}_i$. Thus, we need also to attend to this failure of our initial specification.

2. FIRM SPECIFIC EFFECTS

Investigation of the standardized residuals from the Poisson estimation clearly indicates the presence of serial correlation. Such a finding is not uncommon in panel data of the type we are using. If unobserved firm specific effects exist, the residuals for a given firm might all be of the same sign indicating the way in which the firm deviates from the "average firm." We know from the analysis of linear panel data models that there are two methods which can be used for this type of problem: random effects and fixed effects. We explore first the random effects specification. In the regression model this implies an equicorrelated

[4] One potential problem arises here. Since a common β is used to form u, under the null hypothesis of zero covariance of the true u_{it}'s, induced covariance of order $(1/NT)$ exists among the u_{it}'s. But since $NT = 896$ in our sample, this problem and the associated Cox–Snell [11] corrections are quite small.

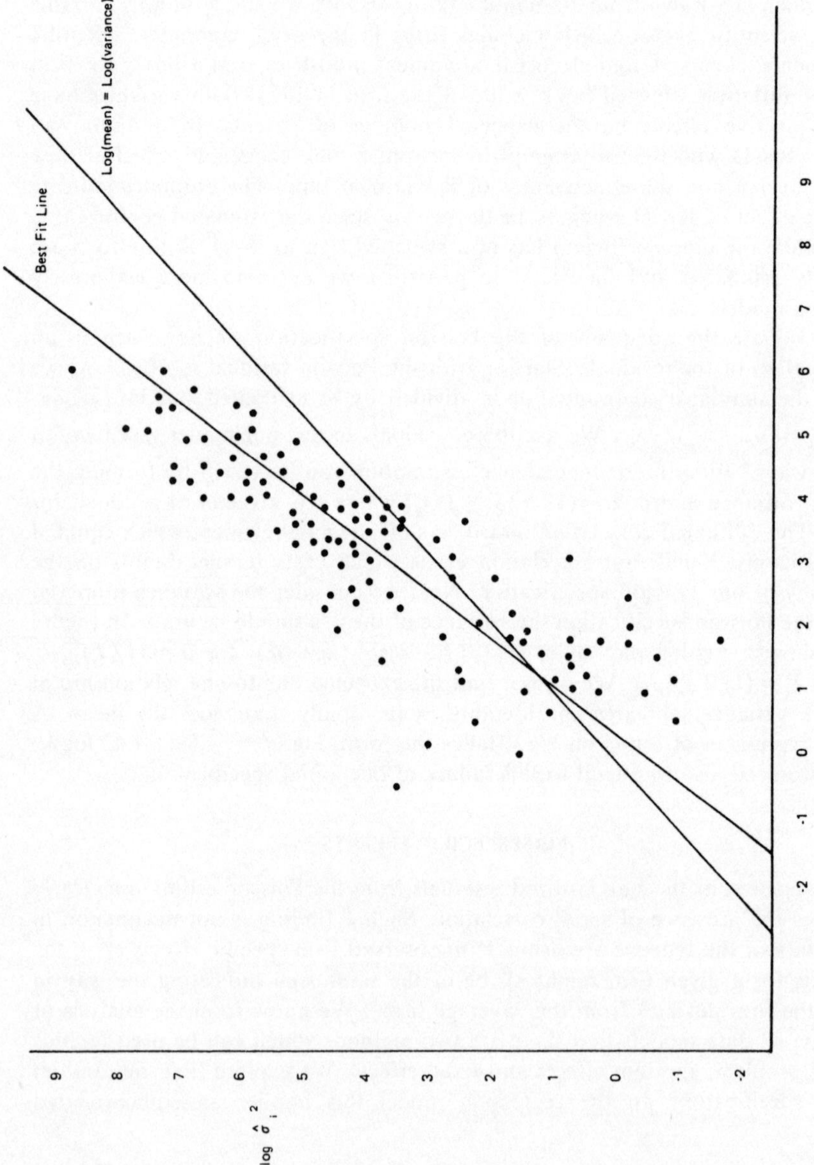

FIGURE 1—Within firm residual variance versus average lambda.

covariance matrix and is sometimes sufficient to explain the apparent serial correlation. In our Poisson specification the random effect has somewhat similar implications. We specify $\tilde{\lambda}_{it} = \lambda_{it}\tilde{\alpha}_i$ where $\tilde{\alpha}_i$ is a random firm specific effect. The Poisson parameter $\tilde{\lambda}_{it}$ is now also a random variable rather than a deterministic function of X_{it}. Correlation of $\tilde{\lambda}_{it}$ and $\tilde{\lambda}_{it'}$ $(t \neq t')$ arises from the $\tilde{\alpha}_i$ while $\tilde{\lambda}_{it}$ and $\tilde{\lambda}_{jt}$ are uncorrelated by the assumption of independent $\tilde{\alpha}_i$.

The other approach to firm specific effects is to condition on the $\tilde{\alpha}_i$ and apply conditional maximum likelihood techniques of Anderson [**1, 2**]. We then have a fixed effects specification. While asymptotic efficiency is sacrificed by the conditioning, no distribution need be specified for the $\tilde{\alpha}_i$. Perhaps more important while we might specify the $\tilde{\alpha}_i$ to be random, conditional on the X_{it} they may no longer be randomly distributed or exchangeable, in the sense of diFinetti. For example, firms which are better at producing patents for unobserved reasons may invest more in R&D because they obtain a higher return to the expenditures. The random effects specification is then no longer valid.[5] We use Hausman's [**17**] test to decide whether there exists a significant nonrandom correlation between the X_{it} and the $\tilde{\alpha}_i$'s.

We first consider the random effects specification. Because $\tilde{\lambda}_{it}$ needs to be positive, we write it in the form

$$\tilde{\lambda}_{it} = \lambda_{it}\alpha_i = e^{X_{it}\beta + \mu_0 + u_i}$$

where μ_i is the firm specific effect and μ_0 is the overall intercept. We include μ_0 in λ_{it} so that $Ee^{\mu_i} = 1$. The Poisson probability specification then becomes

$$\text{(2.1)} \qquad \text{pr}(n_{it} \mid X_{it}, \mu_i) = \frac{e^{-\lambda_{it}e^{\mu_i}}(\lambda_{it}e^{\mu_i})^{n_{it}}}{n_{it}!}.$$

The joint density of $(n_{i1}, \ldots, n_{iT})$ and μ_i takes the form

$$\begin{aligned} \text{(2.2)} \qquad & \text{pr}(n_{i1}, \ldots, n_{iT}, \mu_i \mid X_{i1}, \ldots, X_{iT}) \\ &= \text{pr}(n_{i1}, \ldots, n_{iT} \mid X_{i1}, \ldots, X_{iT}, \mu_i)\, g(\mu_i) \\ &= \prod_t \frac{\lambda_{it}^{n_{it}}}{n_{it}!} e^{-e^{\mu_i}\Sigma_t\lambda_{it}} e^{\mu_i\Sigma_t n_{it}} g(\mu_i), \end{aligned}$$

where $g(\mu_i)$ is the probability density function of μ. In equation (2.2) we have made the important assumption that the conditional density of μ_i given X_{it} equals the unconditional density of μ_i. Thus, the μ's are assumed to be randomly distributed across firms. Since μ_i is an unobservable random variable we now integrate it out from equation (2.2). To do so, we assume that $\alpha_i = e^{\mu_i}$ is distributed as a gamma random variable with parameters (δ, δ), so that $E\alpha_i = 1$

[5] This problem has been recently discussed by Mundlak [**21**], Hausman [**17**], Chamberlain [7], and Hausman–Taylor [**18**]. Gourieroux et al. [**13**] emphasize problems which may arise if a particular distribution is chosen for the α_i.

and $V\alpha_i = 1/\delta$. As long as λ_{it} contains an intercept this normalization involves no loss of generality. We integrate by parts to find[6]

$$\text{(2.3)} \quad \operatorname{pr}(n_{i1}, \ldots, n_{iT} \mid X_{i1}, \ldots, X_{iT})$$

$$= \int_0^{\infty} \prod_t \left[\frac{\lambda_{it}^{n_{it}}}{n_{it}!} \right] e^{-\alpha_i \sum_t \lambda_{it}} \alpha_i^{\sum_t n_{it}} f(\alpha_i)\, d\alpha_i$$

$$= \prod_t \left[\frac{X_{it}^{n_{it}}}{n_{it}!} \right] \left[\frac{\delta}{\sum \lambda_{it} + \delta} \right]^{\delta} \left(\sum \lambda_{it} + \delta \right)^{-\sum n_{it}} \frac{\Gamma(\sum n_{it} + \delta)}{\Gamma(\delta)}$$

where $\Gamma(\cdot)$ is the gamma function, $\Gamma(z) = t^{z-1}e^{-t}$ for $z > 0$. For this model the expectation of n_{it} is λ_{it} and the variance is $\lambda_{it}(\lambda_{it} + \delta)/\delta$. Therefore, the ratio of the variance to the mean is now $1 + \lambda_{it}/\delta$ so that the ratio grows with λ_{it}, which is what we observed in the residuals in Figure 1 although the observed relationship is not exactly quadratic as would be implied by the above formula. Maximum likelihood estimation of the parameters of the model in equation (2.3) is straightforward although we can no longer prove global concavity due to the addition of the δ parameter. Evaluation of the log gamma function and its derivative (the digamma function) is akin to calculation of a logarithm on a computer. Starting values are provided by the initial Poisson estimates and guesses of the delta parameter using $V(\alpha) = 1/\delta$.

Results for the random effects Poisson specification are given in columns 1 through 3 of Table II. We see that the U-shaped lag structure of R&D is somewhat attenuated from that in Table I, but there is still a significant positive coefficient on the last lag. The total R&D effect is lower than that in our basic model in Table I although the exogenous time effect and the decline in the R&D coefficient over time remain about the same. The implied variance to mean ratio for patents at the means of the variables is about 20 and it grows with the estimated λ_{it}.

We emphasized in our derivation of the random effects specification of equation (2.3) the requirement that the unconditional and conditional density of μ_i given X_{it} was identical. This requirement can be dropped when a conditional maximum likelihood approach is used to develop a fixed effects specification. But we cannot simply estimate separate μ_i parameters in equation (2.1) because for T held fixed and N large we have the incidental parameter problem and maximum likelihood need not be consistent (see Neymann and Scott **[24]**, Andersen **[3]**, and Haberman **[16]**). Instead, we use the conditional maximum likelihood approach of Andersen **[1, 2]** and condition on the sum of patents $\sum_t n_{it}$. Since the Poisson distribution is a member of the exponential family, a

[6] Note that this specification is close to the classic Greenwood–Yule **[14]** specification which leads to a negative binomial specification. A similar probability specification was derived by Bates and Neyman **[6]** for a somewhat different model of accident proneness from that of Greenwood and Yule. Bates and Neyman named the distribution the multivariate negative binomial distribution. It is also referred to as the negative multinomial distribution.

TABLE II

ESTIMATES OF THE POISSON MODEL WITH FIRM EFFECTS

	Random Effects[a]			Fixed Effects[b]		
	1	2	3	4	5	6
log R_0	.36 (.02)	.45 (.01)	.482 (.012)	.31 (.04)	.35 (.03)	.481 (.034)
log R_{-1}	.03 (.04)			.02 (.05)		
log R_{-2}	.06 (.05)			.04 (.06)		
log R_{-3}	.08 (.05)			.07 (.06)		
log R_{-4}	− .07 (.05)			− .07 (.07)		
log R_{-5}	.13 (.03)			.07 (.05)		
time	− .04 (.01)	− .03 (.0005)	.0368 (.0025)	− .03 (.003)	− .027 (.002)	.0369 (.0079)
time · log R_0			− .0170 (.0006)			− .0171 (.0020)
log book value			.32 (.04)			
dummy (scientific sector)			.18 (.16)			
intercept	2.30 (.16)	2.65 (.011)	0.49 (.17)			
δ	1.20 (.15)	.98 (.12)	1.40 (.15)			
sum of log R coefficients	.59	.45	.414[c]	.43	.35	.413[c]
log likelihood	− 3827.5	− 3846.18	− 3779.6	− 3009.4	− 3014.4	− 2979.0
Tests for correlated firm effects				15.2	13.7	.01

[a] Random effects $\alpha_i = e^{\mu_i}$, α_i distributed independently as a gamma random variable with parameters (δ, δ).

[b] Fixed effects: Estimates conditional on the sum of patents over all T years.

[c] "Sum" evaluated at the midpoint of the period, 1971.

sufficient statistic exists for $T\tilde{\lambda}_i = \sum \tilde{\lambda}_{it}$ and it is $\sum n_{it}$. Since $\sum_t n_{it}$ is distributed as Poisson with parameter $\sum_t \tilde{\lambda}_{it} = \alpha_i \sum \lambda_{it}$, conditional maximum likelihood follows in a straightforward manner. Furthermore, it is known in the literature, e.g. Rao **[26]**, that the distribution of n_{it} conditional on $\sum_t n_{it}$ gives a multinomial distribution

$$\text{(2.4)} \quad \text{pr}\left(n_{i1}, \ldots, n_{iT} \mid \sum n_{it}\right)$$

$$= \text{pr}\left(n_{i1}, \ldots, n_{i,T-1}, \sum_{t=1}^{T} n_{it} - \sum_{t=1}^{T-1} n_{it}\right) \Big/ \text{pr}\left(\sum n_{it}\right)$$

$$= \frac{\dfrac{e^{-\sum_t \tilde{\lambda}_{it}} \prod_t \tilde{\lambda}_{it}^{n_{it}}}{\prod_t (n_{it}!)}}{\dfrac{e^{-\sum_t \tilde{\lambda}_{it}} \left(\sum_t \tilde{\lambda}_{it}\right)^{\sum_t n_{it}}}{\left(\sum_t n_{it}\right)!}} = \frac{\left(\sum_t n_{it}\right)!}{\prod_t (n_{it}!)} \prod_t \left[\frac{\tilde{\lambda}_{it}}{\sum_t \lambda_{it}}\right]^{n_{it}}.$$

Set $p_{it} = \tilde{\lambda}_{it}/(\sum_t \tilde{\lambda}_{it})$ and we have the multinomial distribution since $\sum p_{it} = 1$. Furthermore, for our particular specification we have

$$p_{it} = e^{X_{it}\beta + \mu_i} \Big/ \left(\sum_t e^{x_{it}\beta + \mu_i}\right) = e^{X_{it}\beta} \Big/ \sum_t e^{X_{it}\beta}$$

which is the so-called multinomial logit specification used by McFadden **[20]** in the discrete choice problem.[7] Define the share of patents for firm i in a given year by $s_{it} = n_{it}/\sum_i n_{it}$. The logit model then explains the share of total patents in each year given the firms' total number of patents in T years.

The log likelihood function takes the form

$$\text{(2.5)} \quad L(\beta) = \sum_{i=1}^{N} \sum_{t=1}^{T} \Gamma(n_{it} + 1) - \sum_{i=1}^{N} \sum_{t=1}^{T} n_{it} \log \sum_{s=1}^{T} e^{-(X_{it} - X_{is})\beta}.$$

Equation (2.5) differs from the discrete choice likelihood function because here in general all the s_{it}'s are nonzero instead of only one nonzero value for the choice which is made. The gradient and Hessian for this likelihood are similar to those for the usual multinomial log specification: in particular, the Hessian can be shown to be globally concave by the Cauchy inequality provided the parameters are bounded, and hence its computations should and did converge rapidly.

The results for the conditional Poisson are given in columns 4 through 6 of Table II. The lag coefficients of R & D are now all small and insignificant with a $\chi_5^2 = 10$ for the test that they are jointly equal to zero. The U-shape of the

[7] Chamberlain [7] also derives a multinomial logit in his generalization of Cox's [10] fixed effects binomial logit model.

distributed lag no longer appears. The firm specific effect, α_i now represents both the accumulated stock of knowledge from past R&D in the firm[8] and unobserved permanent differences across the firms which affect their propensity to patent. Conditioning on permanent differences in the firms' levels of R&D expenditures has reduced the sum of the lag coefficients from .88 in the pooled model and .59 in the random effects model to .43.[9]

In Column 5 we estimate the model which contains only current R&D and find a coefficient of .35 which is 20 per cent below the sum of the coefficients in the previous specification. The time coefficient remains at -3 per cent per year. In column 6 we redo the specification with a time and R&D interaction. This specification corresponds to that of column 3 where the scientific sector dummy and book value variables have been absorbed into the fixed effect. The coefficient of current R&D now rises to .48 while our earlier findings about the declining potency of R&D are repeated. Time itself has a positive coefficient of 4 per cent per year while the interaction with R&D has a coefficient of $-.02$.

To test whether our firm specific effects are correlated with the X in the model, we compare the random effects estimates to the fixed effects estimates using Hausman's [17] test. For the specification in columns 1 and 4, this test is distributed as χ^2_7 under the null hypothesis. Our statistic equals 15.2 which leads to a rejection of the random effects model. However, when we test column 3 against column 6 we accept the null hypothesis that the firm specific effects remaining after inclusion of the scientific sector dummy and the firm size variable are independent of the X_{it}'s. The value of the statistic is .01, distributed as χ^2_3 under the null.

Lastly, we consider diagnostic tests. We can no longer disregard the induced correlation in the conditional model since $\sum_t \hat{u}_{it} = 0$ which follows from the fixed effects assumption and the definition $\lambda_{it} = s_{it}\sum n_{it}$. Thus, under the null hypothesis of no serial correlation among the n_{it}, we have serial correlation of order $(-1/T)$ among the $\hat{u}_{it}$.

We form an asymptotic test as N becomes large by seeing whether the estimated covariance matrix from the residuals of the multinomial model of equations (2.4) and (2.5) has the form it would take under the null hypothesis of no serial correlation. Using the predicted probabilities

$$\hat{p}_{it} = e^{X_{it}\hat{\beta}} \Big/ \sum_{t=1}^{7} e^{X_{it}\hat{\beta}}$$

[8]With more years of data we might well want to let this initial stock of knowledge decay over time. However, we did not find evidence of such a decay process in our residuals.

[9]It may be interesting to report also the comparable original OLS estimates for this model. Without the time interaction and firm specific variables the estimated coefficient of log R is .81, .77, .29, and .39 for the total, between, within, and variance-components specifications respectively. With the additional variables they are .49, .54, .29, and .29. The variance-components results are close to the within because most of our variance is between (95 per cent for log Patents and 97 per cent for log R) which is downweighted in this specification. These results are mirrored in the random-effects specification results reported in the text. Note, however, that the comparable results are somewhat higher for the Poisson than the OLS specification.

we form the vector of each firm's predicted probabilities $\hat{p}_1 = (\hat{p}_{i1}, \ldots, \hat{p}_{i7})$ and compute the multinomial covariance matrix:

$$\tilde{\Omega}_i = \text{diag}(\hat{p}_i) - \hat{p}_i'\hat{p}_i . \tag{2.6}$$

Since $\tilde{\Omega}_i$ is singular by construction, we delete the first row and column to form a 6×6 matrix Ω_i. Likewise, we take the estimated residuals

$$\hat{u}_{it} = \left(n_{it} - \hat{p}_{it}\left(\sum_{t=1}^{7} n_{it} \right) \right) \Big/ \left(\sum_{t=1}^{7} n_{it} \right)^{1/2} \qquad (t = 1, \ldots, 7) \tag{2.7}$$

and compute the covariance matrix $\tilde{S}_{i.} = \hat{u}_i\hat{u}_i'$. We delete the first row and column to form S_i. We then calculate the statistic

$$R_i = \Omega_i^{-1/2} S_i \Omega_i^{-1/2'} \tag{2.8}$$

which should be close to the identity matrix if serial correlation is not present. To test for serial correlation we use the test statistic developed in Appendix B:

$$Q = \frac{1}{N}\left(\sum_{i=1}^{N} m_i(\hat{\beta}) \right)' \hat{V}_m^{-1} \left(\sum_{i=1}^{N} m_i(\hat{\beta}) \right) \tag{2.9}$$

where $m_i(\beta)$ is the 15 element column vector composed of the unique nondiagonal elements of R_i in equation (2.8) and $\hat{V}_m$ is its asymptotic variance matrix which is calculated in Appendix B. The test statistic is computed to be 39.6. Under the null hypothesis this statistic is distributed as central χ^2_{15}. Having rejected the null hypothesis of independence we turn, in the next section, to the consideration of a more general model which allows for another source of within stochastic variation and which may be able to account for this apparent nonindependence.

3. NEGATIVE BINOMIAL MODELS

Even with the fixed effects Poisson model we still have the restriction that the variance and mean are equal, $En_{it} = V(n_{it}) = \lambda_{it}$. On the other hand, the random effects Poisson has a variance to mean ratio of $1 + \lambda_{it}/\delta$ which increases with λ_{it} as our data indicates holds true. Speaking somewhat loosely, we would like to combine the two models to permit the variance to grow with the mean while at the same time we want to have a conditional fixed effect α_i which could be correlated with the right hand side variables, especially R & D. To develop such a model, we begin with the famous negative binomial specification of Greenwood and Yule [**14**]. We then develop a fixed effects version of the negative binomial specification.

Greenwood and Yule in their model of accident proneness assumed that the number of accidents in a year for a given worker followed a Poisson distribution. They further assumed that the (unconditional) parameter λ_i was distributed in the population randomly and followed a gamma distribution. Our situation differs in two respects from that of Greenwood and Yule. First, we want to specify a conditional model for λ_{it} to ascertain the importance of research and development to the distribution of patents. Also, we have panel data rather than a single cross-section so that we can allow for both the possibility of permanent unobserved firm effects as well as the possibility that these firm effects are correlated with the R&D and other explanatory variables. To start, we return to the situation of Section 1 and consider the yearly patents model. We assume that the Poisson parameter λ_{it} follows a gamma distribution with parameters (γ, δ) and specify $\gamma = e^{X_{it}\beta}$ with δ common both across firms and across time.[10] The mean and variance of λ_{it} are then $E\lambda_{it} = e^{X_{it}\beta}/\delta$ and $V(\lambda_{it}) = e^{X_{it}\beta}/\delta^2$. Note that even if X_{it} remains constant for a firm over time λ_{it} can still vary. This situation should be distinguished from the random effects specification of Section 1 where $\tilde{\lambda}_{it} = \tilde{\alpha}_i e^{X_{it}\beta}$ so that $\tilde{\lambda}_{it}$ was constant for a given firm if the X_{it}'s remained constant. On the other hand, in keeping with the models of Section 2, we have not allowed for firm specific effects. Thus, the λ_{it}'s are independent for a given firm over time.

We now take the gamma distribution for the λ_{it} and integrate by parts to find

$$\text{(3.1)} \quad \text{pr}(n_{it}) = \int_0^\infty \frac{1}{n_{it}!} e^{-\lambda_{it}} \lambda_{it}^{n_{it}} f(\lambda_{it})\, d\lambda_{it}$$

$$= \frac{\Gamma(\gamma_{it} + n_{it})}{\Gamma(\gamma_{it})\Gamma(n_{it} + 1)} \left(\frac{\delta}{1+\delta} \right)^{\gamma_{it}} (1+\delta)^{-n_{it}}$$

which is the negative binomial distribution with parameters (γ_{it}, δ). Computation of maximum likelihood estimates proceeds as for equation (2.3) with the use of partial fraction expansions of the gamma and digamma functions permitting rapid evaluation. The moments of n_{it} have the form $En_{it} = e^{X_{it}\beta}/\delta$ and $V(n_{it}) = e^{X_{it}\beta}(1+\delta)/\delta^2$. Therefore, the variance to mean ratio $V(n_{it})/E(n_{it}) = (1+\delta)/\delta > 1$. Thus, the negative binomial specification allows for overdispersion with the original Poisson a limiting case as $\delta \to \infty$. We estimate a δ of about .05, implying a variance to mean ratio of 21 which is roughly consistent with the Poisson random effects model presented earlier.

Both estimates are higher than would be suggested by Figure 1 because the models we have used impose a constant variance to mean ratio across firms while the data suggest that the ratio grows with the number of patents. Another potential shortcoming of the negative binomial specification is that it does not allow for firm specific effects so that serial correlation of the residuals (i.e.,

[10] The parameter δ is different from its use in the last section.

nonindependence of the counts) may be a problem. We will return to this question later after we look at the results.

The estimates from the negative binomial specification are given in Table III. In the first two columns we consider specifications with and without lagged R&D. The total coefficient of R&D is about .75 for either specification, which is a decrease of 15 per cent from the corresponding model of Table I. We still find a large positive coefficient on the last lag of R&D. In column 3 we add the time and R&D interaction along with the scientific sector dummy variable and book value for the firm. Taking into account the time-R&D interaction, the estimated coefficient of current R&D falls from .55 in 1968 to .48 in 1974; the level is slightly lower and the decline slightly smaller than in the corresponding Poisson model. But as we suspected might happen, when we compute standardized residuals the problem of serial correlation reappears. Thus, we turn again to a model with firm specific effects to take account of this problem.

In order to add firm specific effects to the negative binomial model we consider a random effects specification as we did in Section 2 for the Poisson model. It is more convenient in this case, however, first to describe the fixed effects version of our model and then add the random (no correlation with the X's) interpretation to it. To do so we need to find a convenient distribution for the sum of the patents for a given firm ($\sum_t n_{it}$) which we will condition on as we did in the Poisson specification of equation (2.4). There once we conditioned on the firm specific effect α_i we returned to a deterministic specification of the λ_{it}. The situation differs here because of the stochastic nature of the λ_{it} even after conditioning. The derivation of the fixed effects negative binomial model is given in the Appendix. The resulting joint probability of a firm's patents conditional on

TABLE III

ESTIMATES OF THE NEGATIVE BINOMIAL MODEL

	Totals		
$\log R_0$	.43 (.08)	.75 (.02)	.56 (.03)
$\log R_{-1}$	− .04 (.14)		
$\log R_{-2}$	.16 (.14)		
$\log R_{-3}$	− .12 (.13)		
$\log R_{-4}$	− .07 (.15)		
$\log R_{-5}$	.41 (.10)		
time	− .05 (.01)	− .03 (.01)	.017 (.025)
time · $\log R_0$			− .012 (.006)
dummy (scientific sector)			.40 (.04)
log book value			.24 (.02)
intercept	− 1.10 (.07)	− 1.27 (.07)	− 2.20 (.13)
δ	.14 (.002)	.04 (.002)	.057 (.003)
sum of $\log R$ coefficients	.76	.75	.51[a]
log likelihood	− 3,820.8	− 3,845.3	− 3,747.4

[a] Sum evaluated at the midpoint of the period, 1971.

the seven year total is

$$\text{(3.2)} \quad \mathrm{pr}\left(n_{i1}, \ldots, n_{iT} \mid \sum n_{it}\right)$$

$$= \left(\prod_t \frac{\Gamma(\gamma_{it} + n_{it})}{\Gamma(\gamma_{it})\Gamma(n_{it}) + 1} \right) \left[\frac{\Gamma\left(\sum_t \gamma_{it}\right)\Gamma\left(\sum_t n_{it} + 1\right)}{\Gamma\left(\sum_t \gamma_{it} + \sum_t n_{it}\right)} \right].$$

The log likelihood of the sample follows once we specify γ_{it}. We let the parameters of the underlying model be

$$(\gamma_{it}, \delta_i) = (e^{X_{it}\beta}, \phi_i / e^{\mu_i})$$

where both ϕ_i and μ_i are allowed to vary across firms. The mean is

$$\tilde{\lambda}_{it} = (e^{X_{it}\beta + \mu_i})/\phi_i$$

while the variance is

$$V(\tilde{\lambda}_{it}) = (e^{X_{it}\beta + 2\mu_i})/\phi_i^2 .$$

Therefore, we have multiplied the mean by e^{μ_i} as we did for the deterministic Poisson parameter in the fixed effects case. Likewise, the standard deviation has been multiplied by the same amount. Considering the corresponding unconditional negative binomial model we calculate

$$En_{it} = (e^{X_{it}\beta + \mu_i})/\phi_i$$

with

$$V(n_{it}) = (e^{X_{it}\beta + \mu_i}/\phi_i)(1 + e_i^{\mu_i/\phi_i})$$

so that the variance to mean ratio is $(e^{\mu_i} + \phi_i)/\phi_i$. Thus we allow for both overdispersion, which the fixed effects Poisson specification did not, as well as a firm specific variance to mean ratio, which the original negative binomial specification did not.

Estimates for the fixed effects negative binomial model are given in the last three columns of Table IV. The coefficient of R & D is about one-half as large as the original negative binomial specification and is quite close to the conditional Poisson estimate. However, the standard errors on lagged R & D are much larger, reflecting the increased "noise" in the negative binomial specification. When we

TABLE IV

ESTIMATES OF THE NEGATIVE BINOMIAL MODEL WITH FIRM EFFECTS

	Random Effects			Fixed Effects		
log R_0	.45 (.06)	.52 (.025)	.49 (.04)	.41 (.06)	.37 (.03)	.39 (.04)
log R_{-1}	− .12 (.10)			− .15 (.10)		
log R_{-2}	.13 (.15)			.14 (.16)		
log R_{-3}	.01 (.19)			− .03 (.19)		
log R_{-4}	− .06 (.18)			− .07 (.17)		
log R_{-5}	.19 (.11)			.08 (.11)		
time	− .03 (.003)	− .02 (.003)	.01 (.01)	− .02 (.004)	− .02 (.003)	− .006 (.010)
time · log R_0			− .010 (.003)			− .004 (.003)
dummy (scientific sector)			.17 (.11)			
log book 71			.13 (.04)			
intercept	1.33 (.10)	1.47 (.10)	.64 (.22)	1.84 (.13)	1.86 (.11)	1.80 (.13)
a	2.56 (.36)	2.15 (.30)	2.56 (.35)			
b	1.72 (.34)	1.56 (.31)	1.74 (.37)			
sum of log R coefficients	.60	.52	.45[a]	.38	.37	.38[a]
log likelihood	− 3,303.1	− 3,310.6	− 3,304.9	− 2,467.3	− 2,468.9	− 2,468.5
Tests for correlated firm effects				580.	65.0	127.0

[a]Sum evaluated at the midpoint of the period, 1971.

interact time and R&D in column 6 we find important differences from the Poisson fixed effects model. First, the estimate of the coefficient of current R&D is .39, which is somewhat lower than the Poisson model estimate of .48. Next the pure time effect continues to be negative, although insignificantly so, while in all previous models it becomes positive when the interaction term was added. Correspondingly, the interaction term has a much smaller estimated magnitude. This last set of results continues to indicate the decline in effectiveness of R&D in producing patents. But since the negative binomial specification allows for an additional source of variance, the estimated standard errors are all larger, and the conclusions, while similar to the previous ones, are much less precise.

We again form a test for serial correlation. Define

$$\hat{f}_{it} = e^{X_{it}\hat{\beta}} \Big/ \sum_{t=1}^{7} e^{X_{it}\hat{\beta}}.$$

An extra term arises from the negative binomial (Dirichlet) assumption

$$\hat{g}_i = \left(\sum_{t=1}^{7} n_{it} + \sum_{t=1}^{7} e^{X_{it}\beta} \right) \Big/ \left(1 + \sum_{t=1}^{7} e^{X_{it}\beta} \right). \tag{3.3}$$

Then we compute

$$\tilde{\Omega}_i = \hat{g}_i \left[\operatorname{diag}(\hat{f}_i) - \hat{f}_i' \hat{f}_i \right]. \tag{3.4}$$

We again drop the first row and column to form Ω_i and use the residuals $\hat{u}_i$ to form $\tilde{S}_i$. The test statistic of equations (2.8) and (2.9) is used again. It is calculated to be 64.7 so that significant nonindependence is still present. It is interesting to note, however, that if we divide the sample on assets of \$100 million, the test statistic equals 19.2 for the 44 small firms which is not significant for a χ^2_{15} random variable. But for the 84 larger firms the test statistic equals 58.5. The model is satisfactory for the small firms which created the "zero patent" problem, but trends in patents for a few quite large firms leave us with some serial correlation which is not explained by the model. While statistically significant, the serial correlation is not large with the r^2 between adjacent residuals of about .15 and its sign changing from positive to negative as the distance between observations increases.

We lastly consider the random effects version of the negative binomial specification. In the fixed effects specification we set the parameters of the underlying model as

$$(\gamma_{it}, \delta_i) = (e^{X_{it}\beta}, \phi_i / e^{\mu_i})$$

so that both ϕ_i and μ_i vary across firms. Upon conditioning on the total number of patents in equation (3.2), the ϕ_i and μ_i parameters are eliminated and only $\gamma_{it} = e^{X_{it}\beta}$ appears. Analogously to the Poisson random effects specification, we now assume that ϕ_i / e^{μ_i} is randomly distributed across firms, independent of the X_{it}'s. An interesting difference exists between the Poisson random effects specification and the negative binomial random effects specification. In the Poisson case, $\tilde{\lambda}_{it} = \lambda_{it}\tilde{a}_i$ where $\tilde{a}_i$ is a random firm specific effect. Note that for constant λ_{it}, $\tilde{\lambda}_{it}$ is also constant, which would occur if the X_{it}'s are constant. However, in the negative binomial specification λ_{it} varies randomly across years even if the X_{it}'s are constant because it is a realization from a gamma probability distribution each year. Thus, we have randomness both across firms and across time, which corresponds to the usual specification in the linear case where we have the variance components decomposition for the stochastic disturbance $\epsilon_{it} = \alpha_i + \eta_{it}$.

We choose a distribution for $\delta_i = \phi_i / e^{\mu_i}$ which will allow us to integrate δ_i out of the marginal probability statement

$$\text{(3.4)}\qquad \operatorname{pr}(n_{i1}, \ldots, n_{iT} \mid X_{i1}, \ldots, X_{iT}) = \operatorname{pr}(n_{i1}, \ldots, n_{iT} \mid X_{i1}, \ldots, X_{iT}, \delta_i)\, g(\delta_i)$$

where $g(\cdot)$ is the probability density of the incidental parameters. Because of the variance components, we need a two parameter distribution for δ_i and for ease of integration we take the ratio

$$\delta_i/(1+\delta_i) = 1/(1 + e^{\mu_i}/\phi_i)$$

to be distributed as a beta random variable with parameters (a, b). Therefore, $\delta_i/(1+\delta_i)$ has a density function

$$f(z) = \left[B(a,b)\right]^{-1} z^{a-1}(1-z)^{b-1}$$

where $B(\cdot)$ is the beta function. The ratio $\delta_i/(1+\delta_i)$ takes values on the unit interval which implies $\delta_i > 0$, which is appropriate for the scale parameter. The mean is

$$E(\delta_i/(1+\delta_i)) = a/(a+b)$$

with variance

$$V(\delta_i/(1+\delta_i)) = ab/(a+b+1)(a+b).^{11}$$

We integrate using the beta density to find

$$\text{(3.5)}\qquad \operatorname{pr}(n_{i1}, \ldots, n_{iT} \mid X_{i1}, \ldots, X_{iT})$$

$$= \int_0^1 \prod_{i=1}^{T} \left[\frac{\Gamma(\gamma_{it} + n_{it})}{\Gamma(\gamma_{it})\Gamma(n_{it}+1)} z_i^{\gamma_{it}}(1-z_i)^{n_{it}} \right] f(z_i)\, dz_i$$

$$= \frac{\Gamma(a+b)\Gamma(a + \sum \gamma_{it})\Gamma(b + \sum n_{it})}{\Gamma(a)\Gamma(b)\Gamma(a + b + \sum \gamma_{it} + \sum n_{it})} \prod_t \frac{\Gamma(\gamma_{it} + n_{it})}{\Gamma(\gamma_{it})\Gamma(n_{it}+1)}$$

[11]Note that the scale parameter δ is not identified here. We set $\delta = 1$. This result is to be expected for the conditional model given the results of equation (3.3).

where $z_i = \delta_i/(1+\delta_i)$. Note that the last term in equation (3.5) corresponds exactly to a term in the fixed effects model of equation (3.3). But we now estimate additional parameters a and b from the beta distribution which describe the distribution of the δ_i across firms.[12]

Estimates of the random effects negative binomial specification are shown in columns 1 to 4 of Table IV. They fall in between the estimates from the totals model and the estimates from the fixed effects model. In the second column of Table IV, where only R&D and time are used in the specification of γ_{it}, the coefficient of R&D is estimated to be .52, compared to .75 for the totals model and .37 for the fixed effects model. With all five lags on R&D present, the estimates differ significantly from the fixed effects and totals estimates only in the last lag, which is where any firm effect due to presample R&D (truncation bias) will appear. The estimate of the time coefficients is negative and the same as the fixed effects estimate. The parameters of the beta distribution are estimated quite precisely along with a large increase in the likelihood function compared to the totals model. The variance to mean ratio of the effects is now estimated to be about 1.7 which is somewhat higher than the corresponding Poisson random effects estimate of about one. But now this ratio is being allowed to vary across firms rather than taking on a constant value as it does in the negative binomial totals or Poisson random effects models. A Hausman test of the random versus fixed effects specification yields 580 and 65 respectively for the first two specifications which leads to a rejection of the hypothesis of no correlation between the δ_i and R&D. This result was to be expected, given the evidence in Figure 1 that the unexplained variance rises more than proportionately with predicted patents and hence with R&D.

In column 3 of Table IV we now include the R&D-time interaction term and the two firm specific variables, book value and scientific sector. The results differ markedly from the Poisson case where this specification gave almost identical results for the random effects and fixed effects models. Here the estimates of the coefficients of R&D and book value differ significantly in the two cases. The Hausman test statistic equals 127.0, which clearly rejects the no correlation hypothesis, although the estimated coefficients are quite similar.

4. BETWEEN FIRM MODELS

Within the context of the linear panel data models it is often useful to separate the total sample variability into between firm and within firm variability. That is, given the model $y_{it} = X_{it}\beta + \alpha_i + \eta_{it}$, $i = 1, N$ and $t = 1, T$, the between model takes the form $y_{i.} = X_{i.}\beta + \alpha_i + \eta_{i.}$ where the dot notation signifies averages over time, for example $y_{i.} = (1/T)\sum y_{it}$. The corresponding within model is given by $(y_{it} - y_{i.}) = (X_{it} - X_{i.})\beta + \eta_{it} - \eta_{i.}$. This decomposition is unique and the resulting samples are orthogonal. But our conditional models differ from the

[12]Since these are unobservable random variables, the scale parameter merely serves as a normalization.

linear model because we no longer can use linear projections which separate the variables uniquely into $X_{i\cdot}$ and $X_{it} - X_{i\cdot}$ components. We explore the parallel definition of "between" models in this section. Our first conditional model, the fixed effects Poisson specification, separates the original total sample into a conditional multinomial probability times a marginal Poisson probability

$$\text{(4.1)}\quad \operatorname{pr}(n_{i1}, \ldots, n_{iT} \mid X_{i1}, \ldots, X_{iT}) = \operatorname{pr}\Big(n_{i1}, \ldots, n_{iT} \mid X_{i1}, \ldots, X_{iT}, \sum_t n_{it}, \alpha_i\Big) \times \operatorname{pr}\Big(\sum_t n_{it}, \alpha_i \mid X_{i1}, \ldots, X_{iT}\Big).$$

The first probability of the right hand side of equation (4.1) was derived in equation (2.5) to be a multinomial distribution. The marginal probability follows from taking the product of the moment generating function of the Poisson distribution

$$\prod_{s=1}^{T} m_s(t) = \prod_s e^{-\Sigma_s \lambda_s} e^{\Sigma_s \lambda_s e^t}$$

so that the sum $\sum_t n_{it}$ is distributed as Poisson with parameter $\Lambda_i = \sum_s \lambda_{is} = T\lambda_{i\cdot}$. We need to integrate out the unobservable random firm effect α_i from the marginal probability for $\sum_t n_{it}$ in equation (4.1). Therefore as we did in equation (2.3) we assume that $\alpha_i = e^{\mu_i}$ is distributed as a gamma random variable with parameters (δ, δ). We use the results of equation (2.3) on the sum of the patents $\sum_t n_{it}$ to derive the marginal probability

$$\text{(4.2)}\quad \operatorname{pr}\Big(\sum_t n_{it} \mid X_{i1}, \ldots, X_{iT}\Big) = \Big(\sum_t e^{X_{it}\beta}\Big)^{\Sigma_t n_{it}} \left[\frac{\delta}{\sum_t e^{X_{it}\beta} + \delta}\right]^{\delta} \times \left[\Big(\sum_t e^{X_{it}\beta} + \delta\Big)\right]^{-\Sigma_t n_{it}} \frac{\Gamma\Big(\delta + \sum_t n_{it}\Big)}{\Gamma(\delta)\Gamma(\sum n_{it} + 1)}.$$

Note that as with the linear between specification, the between Poisson model suffers from the same problem as the random effects Poisson specification—it assumes that the firm specific effects are uncorrelated with the explanatory variables, including R & D. Note also that *all* the X_{it} enter the between model in equation (4.2) instead of just $X_{i\cdot}$ appearing. Thus the between model does not depend on $X_{i\cdot}$ (or $TX_{i\cdot}$) like the linear between model but instead depends on the within period variation via $\sum_t e^{X_{it}\beta}$, because of the nonlinearity introduced by the exponential functions. Still, a close relationship to the linear case exists. Rather than partitioning the sums of squares into a between and within component, we partition the likelihood of the original sample into two components, conditional and marginal, so that the log likelihoods add up: $L(\beta, n_{i1}, \ldots, n_{iT}) = L_C(\beta, n_{i1}, \ldots, n_{iT} | \sum_t n_{it}) + L_M(\beta, \sum_t n_{it})$ for a common parameter vector β. The log likelihood function on the left hand side of the equation is given by equation (1.2) while the conditional log likelihood $L_C(\cdot)$ corresponds to the density in equation (2.4) and the marginal log likelihood L_M is the between model of equation (4.2). Similarly, the Fisher information regarding the parameters adds up, $J_T = J_C + J_M$ for $J_T = -\lim E(\partial^2 L/\partial\beta\partial\beta')$ with the variance matrices for the estimates β following by matrix inversion. Although the interpretation is not as neat in the Poisson case as in the linear case where no within sample variation enters the between model, the idea of partitioning the information in the data into two additive components still goes through.

In the first two columns of Table V we give the estimates of the between Poisson specification. The coefficient of current R&D expenditures is somewhat less than that of the original Poisson model. The estimate of δ implies a variance to mean ratio for the seven year sum of patents of about 20 at the firm means, which is the same as the estimate we obtained for the random effects model on individual years of data. When we add the firm variables, however, this ratio is cut in half, in contrast to the results from individual years of data. The size of the coefficient on time interacted with R&D suggests that the earlier R&D expenditures are substantially more important than the later expenditures for the overall level of patents.

For the negative binomial model the partitioning of the likelihood into conditional and marginal pieces is not as neat, however, since the form of the gamma functions allows us to identify the coefficients of variables which do not change over time from the conditional model. To see this, observe that if we include any variables which are constant over time in γ_{it} in equation (3.2), they will not necessarily cancel from the likelihood function and therefore their coefficients will be estimable. If we look at the Dirichlet derivation of the model, however, these variables do not really belong in γ_{it} since this derivation starts with the vector of patent shares in each year and treats them as random variables

TABLE V

ESTIMATES OF MARGINAL ("BETWEEN") FIRM MODELS

	Poisson		Negative Binomial	
$\log R_0$	.75 (.04)	1.18 (.15)	1.02 (.06)	1.29 (.15)
time − $\log R_0$		− .26 (.04)		− .27 (.04)
dummy (scientific sector)		0.20 (.18)		0.26 (.18)
log book value		0.29 (.10)		0.32 (.10)
intercept	1.72 (.08)	0.58 (.16)		
δ	1.29 (.15)	1.55 (.17)		
a			4.24 (.63)	2.82 (.49)
b			2.32 (.28)	3.17 (.69)
log likelihood	− 806.5	− 792.9	− 802.4	− 797.6

which are based on the underlying random variables λ_{it}, $t = 1, \ldots, T$. The λ_{it} may be freely rescaled by any factor which is constant over time leaving the shares unchanged. Therefore, the estimability of such coefficients is a kind of specification test of the model; failure of the test implies that the variance pattern in our data is not that implied by the Dirichlet or negative multivariate hypergeometric distribution.[13] A similar problem exists when we derive the between specification of the negative binomial model; because of the functional form of the gamma, we have identification of the coefficient of the time variable even though all we observe is the sum of patents over the seven years.

We now make the same assumptions on δ_i as we did for the derivation of the random effects negative binomial model of equation (3.3) to derive the between firm negative binomial model. We take the negative binomial distribution with parameters $(\sum_t \gamma_{it}, \delta_i)$ and specify $\delta_i/(1+\delta_i)$ to be distributed as a beta random variable so that the between firm specification takes a generalized hypergeometric form,

$$\text{(4.3)} \quad \operatorname{pr}\left(\sum n_{it} \mid X_{i1}, \ldots, X_{iT}\right) = \frac{\Gamma(\sum \gamma_{it} + \sum n_{it})\Gamma(a+b)\Gamma(a+\sum \gamma_{it})\Gamma(b+\sum n_{it})}{\Gamma(\sum \gamma_{it})\Gamma(\sum n_{it}+1)\Gamma(a)\Gamma(b)\Gamma(a+b+\sum \gamma_{it}+\sum n_{it})}$$

where a and b are the parameters of the underlying beta distribution. The log likelihood function for equation (4.3) follows directly. It is interesting to note that in equation (4.3) the leading terms in the numerator and denominator arise from the combinatorial term in the negative binomial distribution of equation (2.3) while the remaining terms arise from the ratio of two beta functions.

In columns 3 and 4 of Table V we give the results of the between negative binomial model of equation (4.3). By analogy to the between estimates for a variance components model, we can estimate only the overall variance of the model and not the decomposition into within firm and between firm variances. We accomplish this by dropping the intercept from γ_{it} and using the beta distribution to estimate the mean firm effect and its variance. The only difference between this model and the random effects Poisson model of columns 1 and 2 is the underlying distributional assumption on which each was based: the Poisson model variance arises only from the firm effect, whereas the negative binomial variance is a compounding of two effects which cannot be separated. The maxima of the likelihood functions for the two models are correspondingly close; in fact, for the second model the Poisson likelihood is higher. The coefficient estimates themselves are quite similar.

[13] We included the scientific sector and firm size variables in the model of column 6, Table IV and found that they were insignificant with a χ^2 of 2.2 with 2 degrees of freedom. The coefficients of interest ($\log R_0$: .42 (.05), time: $-.005$ (.010), time $\log R_0$: $-.004$ (.003)) do not change very much and we conclude that this form of misspecification is not a serious problem in our model.

5. SUMMARY

Our various models can be thought of as differing along two conceptual dimensions: (i) where and to what extent do they allow for "disturbances in the equation," for variability not explicitly accounted for either by the X's or by the assumed underlying Poisson process, and (ii) are the relevant coefficients (β's) different when estimated in the conditional ("within") rather than in the marginal ("between") dimension of the data. That is, do we get different answers when we focus on the shorter term time-series aspects of the data than when we sum or average over a longer time period and use primarily the cross-sectional aspect of the data. In Mundlak's **[21]** language, are the individual "effects" *correlated* with the X's?

Table VI attempts to organize and summarize all of our different models. We start with the "total" Poisson: It assumes no disturbances in the equation and maintains the equality of coefficients across all dimensions of the data. It can be partitioned into two components: conditional ("within") and a marginal ("between"). If the two yielded the same estimated coefficients, their log likelihoods would sum to the earlier total. The actual sum is higher, implying that the coefficients do differ (as can also be seen in column 3), that there is a correlation between individual firm effects and their R & D expenditures.

All the other models represent different ways of adding randomness. The Poisson "random effects" model adds a pure firm disturbance with no within (year to year) variablility. Note the large increase in the log likelihood (from $-9{,}078$ to $-3{,}780$). The negative binomial "total" allows the Poisson parameter λ_{it} to be distributed randomly, across firms and time, according to a Gamma distribution. Adding such a disturbance again increases the likelihood greatly (from $-9{,}078$ to $-3{,}747$). The random effects negative binomial, which is in effect a Beta distribution (as described in the previous section), allows the

TABLE VI

SUMMARY OF RESULTS

Model	Log Likelihood: Poisson	Log Likelihood: Negative Binomial	Total R & D Coefficients[2]: Poisson	Total R & D Coefficients[2]: Negative Binomial
1. Totals (no firm effects)	− 9,077.5	− 3,747.4	.57 (.006)	.51 (.02)
2. Marginal (no firm effects)	− 6,065.2	− 776.1	.56 (.008)	.66 (.19)
3. Conditional	− 2,979.0	− 2,468.5	.41 (.03)	.37 (.04)
Sum of 2 and 3	− 9,044.2	− 3,244.6		
Tests of 2 and 3[1] against 1	$\chi^2_2 = 66.6$	$\chi^2_6 = 1006.$		
4. Totals (random effects)	− 3,779.6	− 3,304.9	.41 (.01)	.45 (.04)
5. Marginal (random effects)	− 792.9	− 797.6	.14 (.13)	.21 (.19)
Sum of 5 and 3	− 3,771.9	− 3,266.1		
Test of 5 and 3[1] against 4	$\chi^2_2 = 15.4$	$\chi^2_6 = 77.6$		

[1] These tests are likelihood ratio tests for the equality of the coefficients in the marginal and conditional models.
[2] This coefficient is computed as the total effect of log R & D in 1971, $\beta_R + 4 \cdot \beta_{t \cdot R}$.

variance of the effects to differ in the within and between dimensions. It is essentially a "variance components" version of the negative binomial. It is clear from the results reported in Table V that the data want *both* a disturbance in the conditional within dimension (compare the conditionals for the negative binomial and Poisson) and a different one, with a different variance, in the marginal (between) dimension. The big changes in fit come from the introduction of such variability and from allowing it to differ across these two dimensions of the data. Most of this variability is in the between dimension (compare the log likelihoods for the two Poisson marginals, one without and the other with firm effects), but there is also variability in the time dimension. The estimated coefficients differ in two dimensions, but much less so (the likelihood rises only from $-3{,}305$ to $-3{,}245$).

Substantively, our results differ from those of Pakes and Griliches **[25]** primarily because of the introduction of additional firm specific variables (log book value and scientific industry dummy) and the log R-time interaction. Adding the firm specific variables reduces the coefficient of log R from about .8 to .6 and brings the "between" and "within" estimates closer to each other. While there is still some (positive) correlation left between the individual firm propensity to patent and its R & D intensity, it is now much smaller. In fact, it would not be a bad approximation to assume that controlling for industry and size, the remaining firm effects are largely random.

Another way of summarizing our results is to look at our estimates of the elasticity of patenting with respect to R & D. They differ along two somewhat separate dimensions: (1) the implicit weighting of the individual observations—especially the random effects models versus the rest—with the former downweighting the larger observations (since they allow the variance to increase as the square of λ) and the differential treatment of zero values; and (2) what variables are included in the equation (none vs. 5 lagged R & D terms, size variables and sector dummies) and whether we allow for a correlation between firm effects (or past R & D) and the included R & D terms. With the implied error variance proportional to λ (Poisson) we start with a total elasticity of about .9 which is reduced to .4 when all the various adjustments are made. It is still higher than the .3 OLS-within estimates because it makes a more proper allowance for the observed zero values. The difference between .4 and .9 can be decomposed roughly as follows: size and sector effects about .3; lagged R & D effects during the first five years about .07; effects of pre-sample R & D correlated within sample R & D, about .08. In other words, while the current R & D component of the overall R & D elasticity of patents is .38, the overall sum is at least .55 (which is close to the Pakes and Griliches **[25]** estimates). It could be significantly higher, however, since we can only estimate that contribution of past R & D which is correlated with the included recent R & D terms.

The random effects model downweights the larger firms and starts out with a lower estimate of the total R & D coefficient (about .6), and reduces very much the influence of the size variables in the rest of the analysis. In this it is consistent with the results reported by Bound et al. **[5]** who showed for a larger cross-sectional sample, that the estimated patents-R & D elasticity is quite sensitive to the weighting scheme used (or equivalently, that it is not really a constant elasticity relationship).

The rest of the conclusions are quite similar, however. The "pure" current R & D coefficient is around .38, time lagged R & D terms add another .08, while allowing for correlated effects of pre-sample R & D adds another .07 or so, yielding .53 as a lower bound on the total effect of R & D on subsequent patenting.[14] Of course, if one were willing to interpret observed size difference as the result of earlier R & D investments, then one could get an overall elasticity closer to unity (c.f. the marginal results reported in Table IV).

The major new substantive finding is that the negative trend in the patent data has a strong interactive component. That is, rather than the propensity to patent just declining exogenously over time, firms are getting less patents from their more recent R & D investments, implying a decline in the "effectiveness" or productivity of R & D.

Methodologically, we have shown how a panel of count data can be analyzed consistently. We described and illustrated the theoretical and empirical necessity to generalize the Poisson model to allow for both "individual" effects and for "overdispersion" in the data and derived models which allowed us to do so. More work needs to be done, however, on the analysis of residuals from such models. Also, it would be interesting to introduce firm effects which could decay over time. This would allow us to consider the effects of lag truncation in such models (along the lines of the Griliches–Pakes work for linear distributed lag models). But even without such refinements, this type of model has many potential uses in econometric data analysis which we expect to pursue further in the future.

Massachusetts Institute of Technology,
National Bureau of Economic Research, Palo Alto, California,
and
Harvard University

Manuscript received December, 1981; final revision received June, 1983.

APPENDIX A

To derive the fixed effects negative binomial model, we first find the moment generating function for the negative binomial distribution to be

$$m(t) = \left(\frac{1 + \delta - e^t}{\delta} \right)^{-\gamma}.$$

[14]These interpretations are based on using the observed evidence for truncation of the lag structure to attribute the correlation with firm effects to correlation with previous R & D whose effects decay very slowly.

Since the moment generating function of a sum of independent random variables equals the product of their moment generating functions we see that if δ is common for two independent negative binomial random variables w_1 and w_2, then $w_1 + w_2 = z$ is distributed as a negative binomial with parameters $(\gamma_1 + \gamma_2, \delta)$. We first derive the distribution, conditioned on z, for the two observation case

$$\text{(A.1)} \qquad \mathrm{pr}(w_1 \mid z = w_1 + w_2) = \frac{\mathrm{pr}(w_1)\mathrm{pr}(z - w_1)}{\mathrm{pr}(z)}$$

$$= \frac{\dfrac{\Gamma(\gamma_1 + w_1)}{\Gamma(\gamma_1)\Gamma(w_1 + 1)}(1+\delta)^{-(w_1+w_2)}\left(\dfrac{\delta}{1+\delta}\right)^{\gamma_1+\gamma_2} \cdot \dfrac{\Gamma(\gamma_2 + w_2)}{\Gamma(\gamma_2)\Gamma(w_2 + 1)}}{\dfrac{\Gamma(\gamma_1 + \gamma_2 + z)}{\Gamma(\gamma_1 + \gamma_2)\Gamma(z + 1)}(1+\delta)^{-z}\left(\dfrac{\delta}{1+\delta}\right)^{\gamma_1+\gamma_2}}$$

$$= \frac{\Gamma(\gamma_1 + w_1)\Gamma(\gamma_2 + w_2)\Gamma(\gamma_1 + \gamma_2)\Gamma(w_1 + w_2 + 1)}{\Gamma(\gamma_1 + \gamma_2 + z)\Gamma(\gamma_1)\Gamma(\gamma_2)\Gamma(w_1 + 1)\Gamma(w_2 + 1)}.$$

Note that in equation (A.1) we are left with the ratio of gamma functions which depend only on the parameter γ, not on the parameter δ. Thus, each firm, in effect, can have its own δ so long as it does not vary over time. The parameter δ has been eliminated by the conditioning arguments.

More generally we consider the joint probability of a given firm's patents conditional on the seven year total

$$\text{(A.2)} \qquad \mathrm{pr}\left(n_{i1}, \ldots, n_{i7} \mid \sum n_{it}\right) = \left(\prod_t \frac{\Gamma(\gamma_{it} + n_{it})}{\Gamma(\gamma_{it})\Gamma(n_{it} + 1)}\right)\left[\frac{\Gamma\left(\sum_t \gamma_{it}\right)\Gamma\left(\sum_t n_{it} + 1\right)}{\Gamma\left(\sum_t \gamma_{it} + \sum_t n_{it}\right)}\right].$$

The marginal distribution of a given n_{it} conditional on $\sum n_{it}$ is a negative hypergeometric distribution (for integer values of the γ_{it}'s) so equation (A.2) is sometimes called a negative multivariate hypergeometric distribution for integer γ_{it}, e.g. Cheng Ping **[8]** and Johnson and Kotz **[19]**.

We can also derive this distribution from the conditional Poisson model of the previous section, i.e., the multinomial distribution of equation (2.4). In that model the multinomial parameters

$$p_{it} = \lambda_{it} \Big/ \sum_t \lambda_{it} = e^{X_{it}\beta} \Big/ \sum_t e^{X_{it}\beta}$$

arose from the Poisson distribution. The natural mixing distribution for these parameters is the Dirichlet distribution which takes the p_{it}'s as random variables on the unit interval and enforces the adding up condition. We then integrate over equation (2.4)

$$\text{(A.3)} \qquad \mathrm{pr}\left(n_{i1}, \ldots, n_{iT} \mid \sum n_{it}\right) = \frac{\left(\sum n_{it}\right)!}{\prod_t n_{it}!} E\left(\prod_t p_{it}^{n_{it}}\right)$$

$$= \frac{\Gamma\left(\sum_t n_{it} + 1\right)\Gamma\left(\sum_t \gamma_{it}\right)}{\Gamma\left(\sum_t \gamma_{it} + \sum_t n_{it}\right)} \prod_t \frac{\Gamma(\gamma_{it} + n_{it})}{\Gamma(\gamma_{it})\Gamma(n_{it} + 1)}$$

where $\gamma_{i1}, \ldots, \gamma_{iT}$ are the parameters of the Dirichlet density. Note that equations (A.2) and (A.3) are identical as expected. The mean of equation (A.2) is $E(n_{it}/\sum_t n_{it}) = \gamma_{it}\sum_s n_{is}/\sum_s \gamma_{is}$ which is the same as $s_{it}\sum_s n_{is}$ from the multinomial distribution. The variance takes the form of the variance of a multinomial variate times a ratio which arises from the Dirichlet parameters,

$$V(n_{it}) = \left(\sum_t n_{it}\gamma_{it} \Big/ \sum \gamma_{it}\right)\left(1 - \gamma_{it} \Big/ \sum \gamma_{it}\right)\left(\sum n_{it} + \sum \gamma_{it}\right) \Big/ \left(1 + \sum \gamma_{it}\right).$$

We have again increased the variance over the multinomial case and made it grow with the expected number of patents to allow for overdispersion. The Dirichlet distribution occurs because each λ_{it} is distributed as a gamma random variable with parameters (γ_{it}, δ_i). It can be shown that the random variable $\lambda_{i1}/(\lambda_{i1} + \lambda_{i2})$ is distributed as a Beta random variable with parameters $(\gamma_{i1}, \gamma_{i2})$ for any δ_i which is the same across all t. The Dirichlet distribution is the multivariate generalization of the Beta distribution. The random vector $(\lambda_{i1}/\sum_t \lambda_{it}, \ldots, \lambda_{iT}/\sum_t \lambda_{it})$ is distributed as a Dirichlet random vector with parameters γ_{it}, $t = 1, \ldots, T$. Thus we have derived the conditional negative binomial model in two ways: The first finds the conditional model for the negative binomial specification. Equivalently, one can begin with the conditional Poisson model and let the p_{it}'s be random variables. Both derivations yield interesting insights into the basic model.

APPENDIX B: BY JERRY HAUSMAN AND WHITNEY NEWEY[15]

To obtain a test for serial correlations in the fixed effects model, we use the fact that

$$E(u_{it}u_{is}) = \begin{cases} (1 - p_{it})p_{it}, & s = t, \\ -p_{it}p_{is}, & s \neq t, \end{cases}$$

where

$$p_{it} = e^{X_{it}\beta} \Big/ \sum_{t=1}^{7} e^{X_{it}\beta} \quad \text{and}$$

$$u_{it} = \left(n_{it} - p_{it}\left(\sum_{t=1}^{7} n_{it}\right)\right) \Big/ \left(\sum_{t=1}^{7} n_{it}\right)^{1/2}$$

Then for $p_i = (p_{i1}, \ldots, p_{i6})$ and $u_i = (u_{it}, \ldots, u_{i6})$, we have

(B.1) $$E(u_i'u_i) = \operatorname{diag}(p_i) - p_i'p_i = \Omega_i,$$

where the last equality defines Ω_i. We have deleted the last observation in forming p_i and u_i due to the fact that $\sum_{t=1}^{7} u_{it} = 0$. Equation (B.1) implies that

(B.2) $$E(\Omega_i^{-1/2}u_i'u_i\Omega_i^{-1/2}) = I_6$$

where I_6 is a six-dimensional identity matrix. A test for serial correlation can now be based on the sample counterpart of the off-diagonal elements of the 6×6 matrix $\Omega_i^{-1/2}u_i'u_i\Omega_i^{-1/2}$. Considering this matrix as a function β, let $m_i(\beta)$ be a 15 element column vector made up of the unique off-diagonal elements of this matrix. Then if the fixed effects model is correct, equation (B.3) will imply under the null hypothesis of no serial correlation that

(B.3) $$q = \left(\sum_{i=1}^{N} m_i(\hat\beta)/\sqrt{N}\right)'[\hat V_m]^{-1}\left(\sum_{i=1}^{N} m_i(\hat\beta)/\sqrt{N}\right) \xrightarrow{d} \chi^2(15)$$

as N gets larger for fixed T where $\hat V_m$ is a consistent estimator of the asymptotic covariance matrix of $\sum_{i=1}^{N} m_i(\hat\beta)/\sqrt{N}$. Note that a first-order Taylor's expansion around the population value β_0 gives

(B.4) $$\sum_{i=1}^{N} m_i(\hat\beta)/\sqrt{N} = \sum_{i=1}^{N} m_i(\beta_0)\sqrt{N} + \left[\frac{1}{N}\sum_{i=1}^{N} \frac{\partial m_i}{\partial \beta}(\tilde\beta)\right]\sqrt{N}(\hat\beta - \beta_0).$$

[15] For a general treatment of this type of specification test, see Newey [23].

where $\tilde{\beta}$ lies between β_0 and $\hat{\beta}$. A central limit theorem and uniform convergence yields asymptotic normality of the statistic in equation (B.4) which leads to the χ^2 distribution of equation (B.3).

To estimate $\hat{V}_m$ let $l_i(\beta)$ the log of the likelihood for observation i, and $U_i(\beta) = \partial l_i(\beta)/\partial\beta$ be the score vector for observation i. The relationship of the test statistic and the score vector follows from

$$\text{(B.5)} \qquad E[\partial m_i(\beta_0)/\partial\beta] = -E[m_i(\beta_0)U_i(\beta_0)'].$$

Due to the presence of $\Omega_i^{-1/2}(\beta)$ in the definition of $m_i(\beta)$, $E[\partial m_i(\beta_0)/\partial\beta]$ will not be zero in general. However using equation (B.5) and an outer product estimator of the information matrix, a consistent estimation of $\hat{V}_m$ is

$$\text{(B.6)} \qquad \hat{V}_m = \frac{1}{N}\sum_{i=1}^{N} m_i(\hat{\beta})m_i(\hat{\beta})'$$

$$-\frac{1}{N}\sum_{i=1}^{N} m_i(\hat{\beta})U_i(\hat{\beta})'\left[\sum_{i=1}^{N} U_i(\hat{\beta})U_i(\hat{\beta})'\right]^{-1}\sum_{i=1}^{N} U_i(\hat{\beta})m_i(\hat{\beta})'.$$

It follows that the test statistic of equation (B.3) is analogous to a Lagrange multiplier test and can be computed via a regression.

REFERENCES

[1] ANDERSEN, E. B.: "Asymptotic Properties of Conditional Maximum Likelihood Estimators," *Journal of the Royal Statistical Society*, B, 32(1970), 283–301.

[2] ———: "The Numerical Solution of a Set of Conditional Estimation Equations," *Journal of the Royal Statistical Society*, B, 34(1972), 42–54.

[3] ———: *Conditional Inference and Models for Measuring*. Copenhagen: Mentalhygiejnisk Forlag, 1973.

[4] ANDERSON, T.: *Multivariate Statistical Analysis*. New York, 1958.

[5] BOUND, J., C. CUMMINS, Z. GRILICHES, B. H. HALL, AND A. JAFFE: "Who Does R & D and Who Patents?" NBER Working Paper #908, Cambridge, 1982.

[6] BATES, G. E., AND J. NEYMAN: "Contributions to the Theory of Accident Proneness," *University of California Publications in Statistics*, 1. Berkeley: University of California Press, 1952, 215–253.

[7] CHAMBERLAIN, G.: "Analysis of Variance with Qualitative Data," *Review of Economic Studies*, 47(1980), 225–238.

[8] CHENG PING: "Minimax Estimates of Parameters of Distributions Belonging to the Exponential Family," *Acta Mathematica Sinica*, 5(1964), 277–299.

[9] CHERNOFF, H., AND E. LEHMANN: "The Use of the Maximum Likelihood Estimates in χ^2 Tests for Goodness of Fit," *Annals of Mathematical Statistics*, 25(1954), 579–586.

[10] COX, D. R.: *Analysis of Binary Data*. London: Methuen, 1970.

[11] COX, D. R., AND E. J. SNELL: "A General Definition of Residuals," *Journal of the Royal Statistical Society*, B, 30(1968), 248–275.

[12] GILBERT, G. C.: "Econometric Models for Discrete Economic Processes," paper given at the European Meetings of the Econometric Society, Athens, 1979.

[13] GOURIEROUX, C., A. MONFORT, AND A. TROGNON: "Pseudo Maximum Likelihood Methods: Application to Poisson Models," INSEE mimeo, Paris, 1981.

[14] GREENWOOD, M., AND G. U. YULE: "An Inquiry into the Nature of Frequency Distribution of Multiple Happenings," *Journal of the Royal Statistical Society*, A, 83(1920), 255–279.

[15] GRILICHES, Z., AND A. PAKES: "Estimation of Distributed Lags in Short Panels," NBER Working Paper #4, Cambridge, 1980.

[16] HABERMAN, S.: "Maximum Relationship Estimates in Experimental Response Models," *Annals of Statistics*, 5 (1977), 815–841.

[17] HAUSMAN, J. A.: "Specification Tests in Econometrics," *Econometrica*, 46 (1978), 1251–1272.

[18] HAUSMAN, J. A., AND W. E. TAYLOR: "Panel Data and Unobservable Individual Effects," *Econometrica*, 49(1981), 1377–1398.

[19] JOHNSON, NORMAN L., AND SAMUEL KOTZ: *Discrete Distributions*. New York: John Wiley, 1969.

[20] McFadden, D.: "Conditional Logit Analysis of Qualitative Choice Behavior," in P. Zarembka, ed., *Frontiers of Econometrics*. New York: Academic Press, 1974.

[21] Mundlak, Y.: "On the Pooling of Time Series and Cross Section Data," *Econometrica*, 46(1978), 69–86.

[22] Nelder, J., and R. Wedderburn: "Generalized Linear Models," *Journal of the Royal Statistical Society*, 135(1972), 370–384.

[23] Newey, W. K.: "Maximum Likelihood Specification Testing and Instrumented Score Tests," unpublished M.I.T. Ph.D. thesis, Cambridge, Mass., 1983.

[24] Neyman, J., and E. L. Scott: "Consistent Estimates Based on Partially Consistent Observations," *Econometrica*, 16(1948), 1–32.

[25] Pakes, A., and Z. Griliches: "Patents and R&D at the Firm Level: A First Look," *Economic Letters*, 5(1980), 377–381.

[26] Rao, C. R.: *Advanced Statistical Methods in Biometric Research*. New York: John Wiley, 1952.

[23]

Journal of Econometrics 30 (1985) 239–267. North-Holland

ALTERNATIVE METHODS FOR EVALUATING THE IMPACT OF INTERVENTIONS

An Overview

James J. HECKMAN and Richard ROBB, Jr.*

University of Chicago, Chicago, IL 60637, USA

This paper presents methods for estimating the impact of training on earnings when non-random selection characterizes the enrollment of persons into training. We explore the benefits of cross-section, repeated cross-section and longitudinal data for addressing this problem by considering the assumptions required to use a variety of new and conventional estimators given access to various commonly encountered types of data. We investigate the plausibility of assumptions needed to justify econometric procedures when viewed in the light of prototypical decision rules determining enrollment into training. We examine the robustness of the estimators to choice-based sampling and contamination bias.

1. Introduction

This paper considers the problem of estimating the effect of training on earnings when enrollment into training is the outcome of a non-random selection process. The analysis of training presented here serves as a prototype for the analysis of the closely related problems of deriving selection bias free estimates of the impacts of unionism, migration, job turnover, unemployment and affirmative action programs on earnings.

Our previous study [Heckman and Robb (1985)] investigates the prior restrictions needed to be imposed to secure consistent estimators of the selection bias free impact of training on earnings when the analyst has access to different types of data. We consider the plausibility of these restrictions in the light of economic theory.

Here we report the key findings from our previous paper. Occasionally, the reader is referred to that paper for precise statements of technical conditions or proofs that do not provide essential insights for understanding the main points.

*We thank Ricardo Barros for helpful comments. This research was supported by NSF Grants SES-8107963 and SES-8411242 and NIH Grant R01-HD-19226 to the Quantitative Methods Center at NORC.

0304-4076/85/$3.30

We present assumptions required to use three types of widely available data to solve the problem of estimating the impact of training on earnings free of selection bias: (1) a single cross-section of post-training earnings, (2) a temporal sequence of cross-sections of unrelated people (repeated cross-section data), and (3) longitudinal data in which the same individuals are followed over time. These three types of data are listed in order of their availability and in inverse order of their cost of acquisition. Assuming random sampling techniques are applied to collect all three types of data, the three sources form a hierarchy: longitudinal data can be used to generate a single cross-section or a set of temporal cross-sections in which the identities of individuals are ignored, and repeated cross-sections can be used as single cross-sections.

Our conclusions are rather startling. Although longitudinal data are widely regarded as a panacea for selection and simultaneity problems, there is no need to use longitudinal data to identify the impact of training on earnings if conventional fixed effect specifications of earnings functions are adopted. Estimators based on repeated cross-section data for unrelated persons identify the same parameter. An analogous statement holds for virtually all longitudinal estimators.

However, we question the plausibility of conventional specifications. They are not motivated by economic theory, and when examined in that light they seem implausible. We propose richer longitudinal specifications of the earnings process and enrollment decision derived from economic theory. In addition, we propose a variety of new estimators. A few of these estimators require longitudinal data, but for most, longitudinal data are not required. A major conclusion of our paper is that the relative benefits of longitudinal data have been overstated, because the potential benefits of cross-section and repeated cross-section data have been understated.

We also question recent claims that cross-section approaches to estimating the impact of training on earnings are strongly dependent on arbitrary assumptions about distributions of unobservables and about the nature of exclusion restrictions. While some widely-used cross-section estimators suffer from this defect, such commonly invoked assumptions are not an essential feature of the cross-sectional approach. However, we demonstrate that unless explicit distributional assumptions are invoked all cross-section estimators require the presence of at least one regressor variable in the decision rule determining training. This requirement may seem innocuous, but it rules out a completely non-parametric cross-section approach. Without prior information, it is not possible to cross-classify observations on the basis of values assumed by explanatory variables in the earnings function and do 'regressor free' estimation of the impact of training on earnings that is free of selection bias. A regressor is required in the enrollment rule. For most cross-section estimators this requires precise specification of the decision rule. Longitudinal and repeated cross-section estimators do not require this.

In analyzing the assumptions required to use various data sources to consistently estimate the impact of training on earnings free of selection bias, we discuss the following topics:

(1) How much prior information about the earnings function must be assumed?
(2) How much prior information about the decision rule governing participation must be assumed?
(3) How robust are the proposed methods to the following commonly encountered features of data on training:
   (a) non-randomness of available samples and especially oversampling of trainees (the choice based sample problem)?
   (b) time inhomogeneity in the environment ('non-stationarity')?
   (c) the absence of a control group of non-trainees or the contamination of the control group so that the training status of individuals is not known for the control sample?

Notably absent from this list of questions is any mention of the efficiency of estimators for cross-section, repeated cross-section and longitudinal data. A discussion of efficiency makes sense only within the context of a fully specified model. The focus in this paper is on the tradeoffs in assumptions that must be imposed in order to estimate a single coefficient when the analyst has access to different types of data. Since different assumptions about the underlying model are invoked in order to justify the validity of alternative estimators, an efficiency comparison is often meaningless. Under the assumptions about an underlying model that justify one estimator, properties of another estimator may not be defined. Only by postulating a common assumption set that is unnecessarily large for any single estimator is it possible to make efficiency comparisons. For the topic of this paper – model identification – the efficiency issue is a red herring.

Even if a common set of assumptions about the underlying model is invoked to justify efficiency comparisons for a class of estimators, for two reasons conventional efficiency comparisons are often meaningless. First, the frequently stated claim that longitudinal estimators are more efficient than cross-section estimators is superficial. It ignores the relative sizes of the *available* cross-section and longitudinal samples. Because of the substantially greater cost of collecting longitudinal data free of attrition bias, the number of persons followed in longitudinal studies rarely exceeds 500 in most economic analyses. In contrast, the *available* cross-section and repeated cross-section samples have thousands of observations. Given the relative sizes of the available cross-section and longitudinal samples, 'inefficient' cross-section and repeated cross-section estimators may have a much smaller sampling variance than 'efficient' longitudinal estimators fit on much smaller samples. In this sense, our proposed cross-section and repeated cross-section estimators may be *feasibly efficient* given the relative sizes of the samples for the two types of data sources.

Second, many of the cross-section and repeated cross-section estimators proposed in this paper require only sample means of variables. They are thus very simple to compute and are also robust to mean zero measurement error in all of the variables.

This paper is organized as follows. Section 2 describes the notation and an economic model for enrollment of individuals into training. Sections 3–9 each begin by listing a set of findings from our earlier paper. The findings are discussed and illustrated via simple examples. The paper concludes with a brief summary.

2. Notation and a model of program participation

2.1. *Earnings functions*

To focus on essential aspects of the problem, we assume that individuals experience only one opportunity to participate in training. This opportunity occurs in period k. Training takes a single period for participants to complete. During training, participants earn no labor income.

Denote earnings of individual i in period t by Y_{it}. Earnings depend on a vector of observed characteristics, X_{it}. Post-program earnings ($t > k$) also depend on a dummy variable, d_i, which equals one if the ith individual participates and is zero if he does not. Let U_{it} represent the error term in the earnings equation and assume that $\mathrm{E}[U_{it}] = 0$. Adopting a linear specification,

$$\begin{aligned} Y_{it} &= X_{it}\beta + d_i\alpha + U_{it}, \qquad t > k, \\ &= X_{it}\beta + U_{it}, \qquad t \leq k, \end{aligned} \tag{1}$$

where β and α are parameters.

Throughout this paper we assume that X_{it} is uncorrelated with U_{it}. When X_{it} contains lagged values of Y_{it}, we assume that (1) can be solved for a reduced form expression of exogenous variables, and we use that expression in place of (1). In some cases, independence between X_{it} and lagged, current or future values of U_{it} will be required as well.

Eq. (1) assumes that training has the same effect on everyone. In the next section we consider issues that arise when α varies among individuals. Throughout most of this paper we ignore effects of training which grow or decay over time. [See Heckman and Robb (1985) for a discussion of this topic.]

We now turn to the stochastic relationship between d_i and U_{it} in (1). For this purpose, we develop a more detailed notation which describes the enrollment rules that select individuals into training.

2.2. *Enrollment rules*

The decision to participate in training may be determined by a prospective trainee, by a program administrator or both. Whatever the specific content of the rule, it can be described in terms of an index function framework. Let IN_i be an index of benefits to the appropriate decision-makers from taking training. It is a function of observed (Z_i) and unobserved (V_i) variables. Thus

$$IN_i = Z_i\gamma + V_i. \tag{2}$$

In terms of this function,

$$d_i = 1 \quad \text{iff} \quad IN_i > 0$$
$$= 0 \quad \text{otherwise.}$$

The distribution function of V_i is denoted as $F(\mathrm{v}_i) = \Pr(V_i < \mathrm{v}_i)$. V_i is assumed to be independently and identically distributed across persons. Let $p = \mathrm{E}[d_i] = \Pr[d_i = 1]$ and assume $1 > p > 0$.

The central problem considered in this paper arises when the decision to take training is not random with respect to the disturbance in the earnings function. More precisely, the problem of selection bias arises when

$$\mathrm{E}[U_{it}d_i] \neq 0.$$

This may occur because of stochastic dependence between U_{it} and the unobservable V_i in (2) (selection on the unobservables) or because of stochastic dependence between U_{it} and Z_i in (2) (selection on the observables).

To interpret various specifications of eq. (2), we need to specify an economic model. A natural starting point is a model of trainee self-selection based on a comparison of the expected value of earnings with and without training. The earnings function is assumed to be (1). For simplicity, we assume that training programs accept all applicants. Our previous paper considers more general models.

All prospective trainees are assumed to discount earnings streams by a common discount factor $1/(1+r)$. From (1) training raises trainee earnings by α per period. While in training, individual i receives a subsidy S_i, which may be negative (so there may be direct costs of program participation). Trainees forego income in training period k. To simplify the expressions, we assume that people live forever.

As of period k, the present value of earnings for a person who does not receive training is

$$PV_i(0) = \mathrm{E}_{k-1}\left(\sum_{j=0}^{\infty}\left(\frac{1}{1+r}\right)^j Y_{i,k+j}\right).$$

E_{k-1} means that the expectation is taken with respect to information available to the prospective trainee in period $k-1$. The expected present value of earnings for a trainee is

$$PV_i(1) = \mathrm{E}_{k-1}\left(S_i + \sum_{j=1}^{\infty}\left(\frac{1}{1+r}\right)^j Y_{i,k+j} + \sum_{j=1}^{\infty}\frac{\alpha}{(1+r)^j}\right).$$

The risk-neutral wealth-maximizing decision rule is to enroll in the program if $PV_i(1) > PV_i(0)$ or, letting IN_i denote the index function in decision rule (2),

$$IN_i = PV_i(1) - PV_i(0) = \mathrm{E}_{k-1}[S_i - Y_{ik} + \alpha/r], \tag{3}$$

so the decision to train is characterized by the rule

$$\begin{aligned} d_i &= 1 \quad \text{iff} \quad \mathrm{E}_{k-1}[S_i - Y_{ik} + \alpha/r] > 0, \\ &= 0 \quad \text{otherwise.} \end{aligned} \tag{4}$$

Let W_i be the part of the subsidy which the econometrician observes (with associated coefficient ϕ) and let τ_i be the part which he does not observe:

$$S_i = W_i\phi + \tau_i.$$

A special case of this model arises when agents possess perfect foresight so that $\mathrm{E}_{k-1}[S_i] = S_i$, $\mathrm{E}_{k-1}[Y_{ik}] = Y_{ik}$ and $\mathrm{E}_{k-1}[\alpha/r] = \alpha/r$. Collecting terms,

$$\begin{aligned} d_i &= 1 \quad \text{iff} \quad S_i - Y_{ik} + \alpha/r = W_i\phi + \alpha/r - X_{ik}\beta + \tau_i - U_{ik} > 0, \\ &= 0 \quad \text{otherwise.} \end{aligned} \tag{5}$$

Then $(\tau_i - U_{ik}) = V_i$ in (2) and (W_i, X_{ik}) corresponds to Z_i in (2). Assuming that (W_i, X_{ik}) is distributed independently of V_i makes (5) a standard discrete choice model.

Suppose decision rule (5) determines enrollment. If the costs of program participation are independent of U_{it} for all t (so both W_i and τ_i are independent of U_{it}), then $\mathrm{E}[U_{it}d_i] = 0$ only if the unobservables in period t are (mean) independent of the unobservables in period k or

$$\mathrm{E}[U_{it}|U_{ik}] = 0 \quad \text{for} \quad t > k.$$

Whether or not U_{it} and d_i are uncorrelated hinges on the serial dependence properties of U_{it}. If U_{it} is a moving average of order m so

$$U_{it} = \sum_{j=1}^{m} a_j \varepsilon_{i,t-j},$$

where the $\varepsilon_{i,t-j}$ are iid, then for $t - k > m$, $\mathrm{E}[U_{it} d_i] = 0$. On the other hand, if U_{it} follows a first-order autoregressive scheme, then $\mathrm{E}[U_{it}|U_{ik}] \neq 0$ for all finite t and k.

3. Random coefficients and the structural parameter of interest

We identify two different definitions associated with the notion of a selection bias free estimate of the impact of training on earnings. The first notion defines the structural parameter of interest as the impact of training on earnings if people are randomly assigned to training programs. The second notion defines the structural parameter of interest in terms of the difference between the post-program earnings of the trained and what the earnings in post-program years for these same individuals would have been in the absence of training. The two notions come to the same thing only when training has an equal impact on everyone or else assignment to training is random and attention centers on estimating the mean response to training. The second notion is frequently the most useful one for forecasting future program impacts when the same enrollment rules that have been used in available samples characterize future enrollment.

In seeking to determine the impact of training on earnings in the presence of non-random assignment of persons to training, it is useful to distinguish two questions that are frequently confused in the literature:

Q1: 'What would be the mean impact of training on earnings if people were randomly assigned to training?'

Q2: 'How do the post-program mean earnings of the trained compare to what they would have been in the absence of training?'

The second question makes a hypothetical contrast between the post-program earnings of the trained in the presence and in the absence of training programs. This hypothetical contrast eliminates factors that would make the earnings of trainees different from those of non-trainees even in the absence of any training program. The two questions have the same answer if eq. (1) generates earnings so that training has the same impact on everyone. The two questions also have the same answer if there is random assignment to training and attention centers on estimating the *population* mean response to training.

In the presence of non-random assignment and variation in the impact of training among persons, the two questions have different answers. Question 2 is the appropriate one to ask if interest centers on forecasting the change in the mean of the post-training earnings of trainees when the same selection rule pertains to past and future trainees. It is important to note that the answer to this question is all that is required to estimate the future program impact if future selection criteria are like past criteria.

To clarify these issues, we consider a random coefficient version of (1) in which α varies in the population. In this model, the impact of training may differ across persons and may even be negative for some people. We write in place of (1)

$$Y_{it} = X_{it}\beta + d_i\alpha_i + U_{it}, \qquad t > k.$$

Define $\mathrm{E}[\alpha_i] = \bar{\alpha}$ and $\varepsilon_i = \alpha_i - \bar{\alpha}$ where $\mathrm{E}[\varepsilon_i] = 0$. With this notation, we can rewrite the equation above as

$$Y_{it} = X_{it}\beta + d_i\bar{\alpha} + \{U_{it} + d_i\varepsilon_i\}. \tag{6}$$

An alternative way to derive this equation is to express it as a two-sector switching model following Roy (1951), Heckman and Neumann (1977) and Lee (1978). Let

$$Y_{1it} = X_{it}\beta_1 + U_{1it}$$

be the wage of individual i in sector 1 in period t. Let

$$Y_{0it} = X_{it}\beta_0 + U_{0it}$$

be the wage of individual i in sector 0. Letting $d_i = 1$ if a person is in sector 1 and letting $d_i = 0$ otherwise, we may write the observed wage as

$$\begin{aligned} Y_{it} &= d_i Y_{1it} + (1 - d_i) Y_{0it} \\ &= X_{it}\beta_0 + \mathrm{E}[X_{it}|d_i = 1](\beta_1 - \beta_0)\, d_i \\ &\quad + [(X_{it} - \mathrm{E}[X_{it}|d_i = 1])(\beta_1 - \beta_0) + U_{1it} - U_{0it}]\, d_i + U_{0it}. \end{aligned}$$

Letting $\bar{\alpha} = \mathrm{E}[X_{it}|d_i = 1](\beta_1 - \beta_0)$, $\varepsilon_i = (X_{it} - \mathrm{E}[X_{it}|d_i = 1])(\beta_1 - \beta_0) + U_{1it} - U_{0it}$, $\beta_0 = \beta$ and $U_{0it} = U_{it}$, produces eq. (6).

In this model there is a fundamental non-identification result when no regressors appear in the decision rule (2). Without a regressor in (2) and in the absence of any further distributional assumptions it is not possible to identify $\bar{\alpha}$ unless $\mathrm{E}[\varepsilon_i|d_i=1, Z_i]=0$ or some other known constant.

To see this, note that

$$\mathrm{E}[Y_{it}|d_i=1, Z_i, X_{it}] = X_{it}\beta + \bar{\alpha} + \mathrm{E}[\varepsilon_i|d_i=1, Z_i, X_{it}] + \mathrm{E}[U_{it}|d_i=1, Z_i, X_{it}],$$

$$\mathrm{E}[Y_{it}|d_i=0, Z_i, X_{it}] = X_{it}\beta + E[U_{it}|d_i=0, Z_i, X_{it}].$$

Unless $\mathrm{E}[\varepsilon_i|d_i=1, Z_i, X_{it}]$ is known, without invoking distributional assumptions it is impossible to decompose $\bar{\alpha} + \mathrm{E}[\varepsilon_i|d_i=1, Z_i, X_{it}]$ into its constituent components unless there is independent variation in $\mathrm{E}[\varepsilon_i|d_i=1, Z_i, X_{it}]$ across observations [i.e., a regressor appears in (2)]. Without a regressor, $\mathrm{E}[\varepsilon_i|d_i=1, Z_i, X_{it}]$ is a constant which cannot be distinguished from $\bar{\alpha}$.

This means that in models without regressors in the decision rule we might as well work with the redefined model

$$Y_{it} = X_{it}\beta + d_i\alpha^* + \{U_{it} + d_i(\varepsilon_i - \mathrm{E}[\varepsilon_i|d_i=1])\}, \tag{7}$$

where

$$\alpha^* = \bar{\alpha} + \mathrm{E}[\varepsilon_i|d_i=1],$$

and content ourselves with the estimation of α^*. If everywhere we replace α with α^*, the fixed coefficient analysis of eq. (1) applies to (7).

The parameter α^* answers Q2. It addresses the question of determining the effect of training on the people selected as trainees. This parameter is useful in making forecasts when the same selection rule operates in the future as has operated in the past. In the presence of non-random selection into training it does not answer Q1. Indeed, without regressors in decision rule (2), this question cannot be answered unless specific distributional assumptions are invoked.

Random assignment of persons to training does not usually represent a relevant policy option. For this reason, we will focus attention on question two. Hence, if the training impact varies among individuals, we will seek to estimate α^* in (7). Since eq. (7) may be reparametrized in the form of eq. (1), we work exclusively with the fixed coefficient earnings function. Our earlier paper gives precise statements of conditions under which $\bar{\alpha}$ is identified in a random coefficient model.

4. Cross-sectional procedures

Standard cross-sectional procedures invoke unnecessarily strong assumptions. All that is required to identify α in a cross-section is access to a regressor in (2). In *the absence of a regressor, assumptions about the marginal distribution of U_{it} can produce consistent estimators of the training impact.*

4.1. *Without distributional assumptions a regressor is needed*

Let $\bar{Y}_t^{(1)}$ denote the sample mean of trainee earnings and let $\bar{Y}_t^{(0)}$ denote the sample mean of non-trainee earnings:

$$\bar{Y}_t^{(1)} = \sum d_i Y_{it} \Big/ \sum d_i, \qquad \bar{Y}_t^{(0)} = \sum (1-d_i) Y_{it} \Big/ \sum (1-d_i),$$

for $0 < \sum d_i < I$, where I is the number of observations. We retain the assumption that the data are generated by a random sampling scheme. If no regressors appear in (1) then $X_{it}\beta = \beta_t$ and

$$\operatorname{plim} \bar{Y}_t^{(1)} = \beta_t + \alpha + \mathrm{E}[U_{it}|d_i = 1],$$

$$\operatorname{plim} \bar{Y}_t^{(0)} = \beta_t + \mathrm{E}[U_{it}|d_i = 0].$$

Thus

$$\operatorname{plim}\left(\bar{Y}_t^{(1)} - \bar{Y}_t^{(0)}\right) = \alpha + \mathrm{E}[U_{it}|d_i = 1]/(1-p),$$

since $p\mathrm{E}[U_{it}|d_i = 1] + (1-p)\mathrm{E}[U_{it}|d_i = 0] = 0$. Even if p were known, α cannot be separated from $\mathrm{E}[U_{it}|d_i = 1]$ using cross-sectional data on sample means. Sample variances do not aid in securing identification unless $\mathrm{E}[U_{it}^2|d_i = 0]$ or $\mathrm{E}[U_{it}^2|d_i = 1]$ is known *a priori*. Similar remarks apply to the information from higher moments.

4.2. *Overview of cross-sectional procedures which use regressors*

If, however, $\mathrm{E}[U_{it}|d_i = 1, Z_i]$ is a non-constant function of Z_i, it is possible (with additional assumptions) to solve this identification problem. Securing identification in this fashion explicitly precludes a fully non-parametric strategy in which both the earnings function (1) and decision rule (2) are estimated in each (X_{it}, Z_i) stratum. For within each stratum, $\mathrm{E}[U_{it}|d_i = 1, Z_i]$ is a constant function of Z_i and α is not identified from cross-section data. Restrictions across strata are required.

If $\mathrm{E}[U_{it}|d_i = 1, Z_i]$ is a non-constant function of Z_i it is possible to exploit this information in a variety of ways depending on what else is assumed about the model. Here we simply sketch alternative strategies. In our earlier paper, we present a systematic discussion of each approach.

(a) Suppose Z_i or a subset of Z_i is exogenous with respect to U_{it}. Under conditions specified more fully below, the exogenous subset may be used to construct an instrumental variable for d_i in eq. (1), and α can be consistently estimated by instrumental variables methods. No distributional assumptions about U_{it} or V_i are required [Heckman (1978)].

(b) Suppose that Z_i is distributed independently of V_i and the functional form of the distribution of V_i is known. Under standard conditions, γ in (2) can be consistently estimated by conventional methods in discrete choice analysis [Amemiya (1981)]. If Z_i is distributed independently of U_{it}, $F(-Z_i\hat{\gamma})$ can be used as an instrument for d_i in eq. (1) [Heckman (1978)].

(c) Under the same conditions as specified in (b),

$$\mathrm{E}[Y_{it}|X_{it}, Z_i] = X_{it}\beta + \alpha(1 - F(-Z_i\gamma)).$$

γ and α can be consistently estimated using $F(-Z_i\hat{\gamma})$ in place of $F(-Z_i\gamma)$ in the preceding equation [Heckman (1976, 1978)] or else the preceding equation can be estimated by non-linear least squares, estimating β, α and γ jointly (given the functional form of F) [Barnow, Cain and Goldberger (1980)].

(d) If the functional forms of $\mathrm{E}[U_{it}|d_i = 1, Z_i]$ and $\mathrm{E}[U_{it}|d_i = 0, Z_i]$ as functions of Z_i are known up to a finite set of parameters, it is sometimes possible to consistently estimate β, α and the parameters of the conditional means from the (non-linear) regression function

$$\mathrm{E}[Y_{it}|d_i, Z_i] = X_{it}\beta + d_i\alpha + d_i\mathrm{E}[U_{it}|d_i = 1, Z_i] + (1 - d_i)\mathrm{E}[U_{it}|d_i = 0, Z_i]. \quad (8)$$

One way to acquire information about the functional form of $\mathrm{E}[U_{it}|d_i = 1, Z_i]$ is to assume knowledge of the functional form of the joint distribution of (U_{it}, V_i) (e.g., that it is bivariate normal), but this is not required. Note further that this procedure does not require that Z_i be distributed independently of V_i in (2) [Barnow, Cain and Goldberger (1980)].

(e) Instead of (d), it is possible to use a two-stage estimation procedure if the joint density of (U_{it}, V_i) is assumed known up to a finite set of parameters. In stage one $\mathrm{E}[U_{it}|d_i = 1, Z_i]$ and $\mathrm{E}[U_{it}|d_i = 0, Z_i]$ are determined up to some unknown parameters by conventional discrete choice analysis. Then regression (8) is run using estimated E values in place of population E values on the right-hand side of the equation.

(f) Under the assumptions of (e), use maximum likelihood to consistently estimate α [Heckman (1978)]. Note that a separate value of α may be estimated for each cross-section so that depending on the number of cross-sections it is possible to estimate growth and decay effects in training (e.g., α_t can be estimated for each cross-section).

Conventional selection bias approaches (d)–(f) as well as (b)–(c) rely on strong distributional assumptions but in fact these are not required. Given that a regressor appears in decision rule (2), if it is uncorrelated with U_{it}, the regressor is an instrumental variable for d_i. It is not necessary to invoke strong distributional assumptions, but if they are invoked, Z_i need not be uncorrelated with U_{it}. In practice, however, Z_i and U_{it} are usually assumed to be independent. We next discuss the instrumental variables procedure in greater detail.

4.3. The instrumental variable estimator

This estimator is the least demanding in the *a priori* conditions that must be satisfied for its use. It requires the following assumptions:

> There is at least one variable in Z_i, Z_i^e, with a non-zero γ coefficient in (2), such that for some known transformation of Z_i^e, $g(Z_i^e)$, $E[U_{it}g(Z_i^e)]=0$. (9a)

> Array X_{it} and d_i into a vector $J_{1it}=(X_{it}, d_i)$. Array X_{it} and $g(Z_i^e)$ into a vector $J_{2it}=(X_{it}, g(Z_i^e))$. In this notation, it is assumed that
>
> $$E\left[\sum_{i=1}^{I_t}(J'_{2it}J_{1it}/I_t)\right]$$
>
> has full column rank uniformly in I_t for I_t sufficiently large, where I_t denotes the number of individuals in period t. (9b)

With these assumptions, the I.V. estimator,

$$\begin{pmatrix}\hat{\beta}\\ \hat{\alpha}\end{pmatrix}_{\mathrm{IV}}=\left(\sum_{i=1}^{I_t}(J'_{2it}J_{1it}/I_t)\right)^{-1}\sum_{i=1}^{I_t}(J'_{2it}Y_{it}/I_t),$$

is consistent for (β, α) regardless of any covariance between U_{it} and d_i.

It is important to notice how weak these conditions are. The functional form of the distribution of V_i need not be known. Z_i need not be distributed independently of V_i. Moreover, $g(Z_i^e)$ may be a non-linear function of variables appearing in X_{it} as long as (9) is satisfied.

The instrumental variable, $g(Z_i^e)$, may also be a lagged value of time-varying variables appearing in X_{it}, provided the analyst has access to longitudinal data. The rank condition (9b) will generally be satisfied in this case as long as X_{it} exhibits serial dependence. Thus longitudinal data (on exogenous characteristics) may provide a source of instrumental variables.

4.4. Identification through distributional assumptions about the marginal distribution of U_{it}

If no regressor appears in decision rule (2), the estimators presented so far in this section cannot be used to estimate α consistently unless additional restrictions are imposed. Heckman (1978) demonstrates that if (U_{it}, V_i) are jointly normally distributed, α is identified even if there is no regressor in enrollment rule (2). His conditions are overly strong.

If U_{it} has zero third and fifth central moments, α is identified even if no regressor appears in the enrollment rule. This assumption about U_{it} is implied by normality or symmetry of the density of U_{it} but it is weaker than either provided that the required moments are finite. The fact that α can be identified by invoking distributional assumptions about U_{it} illustrates the more general point that there is a tradeoff between assumptions about regressors and assumptions about the distribution of U_{it} that must be invoked to identify α.

We have established that under the following assumptions, α in (1) is identified:

$$\mathrm{E}\left[U_{it}^3\right] = 0, \tag{10a}$$

$$\mathrm{E}\left[U_{it}^5\right] = 0, \tag{10b}$$

$$\{U_{it}, V_i\} \text{ is iid.} \tag{10c}$$

A consistent method of moments estimator can be devised that exploits these assumptions. [See Heckman and Robb (1985).] Find $\hat{\alpha}$ that sets a weighted average of the sample analogues of $\mathrm{E}[U_{it}^3]$ and $\mathrm{E}[U_{it}^5]$ as close to zero as possible.

To simplify the exposition, suppose that there are no regressors in the earnings function (1), so $X_{it}\beta = \beta_t$. The proposed estimator finds the value of $\hat{\alpha}$ that sets

$$(1/I_t)\sum_{i=1}^{I_t}\left[(Y_{it} - \bar{Y}) - \hat{\alpha}(d_i - \bar{d})\right]^3 \tag{11a}$$

and

$$(1/I_t)\sum_{i=1}^{I_t}\left[(Y_{it} - \bar{Y}) - \hat{\alpha}(d_i - \bar{d})\right]^5 \tag{11b}$$

as close to zero as possible in a suitably chosen metric where, as before, the overbar denotes sample mean. In our earlier paper, we establish the existence of a unique consistent root that sets (11a) and (11b) to zero in large samples.

5. Repeated cross-section methods for the case when training identity of individuals is unknown

In a time homogeneous environment, estimates of the population mean earnings formed in two or more cross-sections of unrelated persons can be used to obtain selection bias free estimates of the training effect even if the training status of each person is unknown (but the population proportion of trainees is known or can be consistently estimated). With more data, the time homogeneity assumption can be partially relaxed.

Assuming a time homogeneous environment and access to repeated cross-section data and random sampling, it is possible to identify α (a) without any regressor in the decision rule, (b) without need to specify the joint distribution of U_{it} and V_i, and (c) without any need to know which individuals in the sample enrolled in training (but the proportion of trainees must be known or consistently estimable).

To see why this claim is true, suppose that no regressors appear in the earnings function.[1] In the notation of eq. (1), $X_{it}\beta = \beta_t$. Then, assuming a random sampling scheme generates the data,

$$\operatorname{plim} \bar{Y}_t = \operatorname{plim} \sum Y_{it}/I_t = \mathrm{E}[\beta_t + \alpha d_i + U_{it}] = \beta_t + \alpha p, \quad t > k,$$

$$\operatorname{plim} \bar{Y}_{t'} = \operatorname{plim} \sum Y_{it'}/I_{t'} = \mathrm{E}[\beta_{t'} + U_{it'}] = \beta_{t'}, \quad t' < k.$$

In a time homogeneous environment, $\beta_t = \beta_{t'}$ and

$$\operatorname{plim}(\bar{Y}_t - \bar{Y}_{t'})/\hat{p} = \alpha,$$

where $\hat{p}$ is a consistent estimator of $p = \mathrm{E}[d_i]$.

With more than two years of repeated cross-section data, one can apply the same principles to identify α while relaxing the time homogeneity assumption. For instance, suppose that population mean earnings lie on a polynomial of order $L - 2$:

$$\beta_t = \pi_0 + \pi_1 t + \cdots + \pi_{L-2} t^{L-2}.$$

From L temporally distinct cross-sections, it is possible to estimate consistently the $L - 1$ π-parameters and α provided that the number of observations in each cross-section becomes large, and there is at least one pre-program and one post-program cross-section.

If the effect of training differs across periods, it is still possible to identify α_t, provided that the environment changes in a 'sufficiently regular' way. For

[1] If regressors appear in the earnings function, the following procedure can be used. Rewrite (1) as $Y_{it} = \beta_t + X_{it}\pi + d_i\alpha + U_{it}$. It is possible to estimate π from pre-program data. Replace Y_{it} by $Y_{it} - X_{it}\hat{\pi}$ and the analysis in the text goes through. Note that we are assuming that no X_{it} variables become non-constant after period k.

example, suppose

$$\beta_t = \pi_0 + \pi_1 t \qquad \text{for} \quad t > k,$$

$$\alpha_t = \phi_0(\phi_1)^{t-k} \quad \text{for} \quad t > k.$$

In this case, $\pi_0, \pi_1, \phi_0, \phi_1$ are identified from the means of four cross-sections, so long as at least one of these means comes from a pre-program period.

In Heckman and Robb (1985) we rigorously state the conditions required to consistently estimate α using repeated cross-section data that does not record the training identity of individuals. Section 9 examines the sensitivity of this class of estimators to violations of the random sampling assumption.

6. Longitudinal procedures

Most longitudinal procedures require knowledge of certain moments of the joint distribution of unobservables in the earnings and enrollment equations. We present several illustrations of this claim, as well as a counterexample. The counterexample identifies α by assuming only that the error term in the earnings equation is covariance stationary.

We now consider three examples of estimators which use longitudinal data.

6.1. The fixed effects method

This method was developed by Mundlak (1961, 1978) and refined by Chamberlain (1982). It is based on the following assumption:

$$\mathrm{E}[U_{it} - U_{it'} | d_i, X_{it} - X_{it'}] = 0 \quad \text{for all } t, t', \quad t > k > t'. \tag{12}$$

As a consequence of this assumption, we may write a difference regression as

$$\mathrm{E}[Y_{it} - Y_{it'} | d_i, X_{it} - X_{it'}] = (X_{it} - X_{it'})\beta + d_i \alpha, \qquad t > k > t'.$$

Suppose that (12) holds and the analyst has access to one year of preprogram and one year of post-program earnings. Regressing the difference between post-program earnings in any year and earnings in any pre-program year on the change in regressors between those years and a dummy variable for training status produces a consistent estimator of α.

Some decision rules and error processes for earnings produce (12). For example, consider a certainty environment in which the earnings residual has a permanent-transitory structure:

$$U_{it} = \phi_i + \varepsilon_{it}, \tag{13}$$

where ε_{it} is a mean zero random variable independent of all other values of $\varepsilon_{it'}$

and is distributed independently of ϕ_i, a mean zero person-specific time-invariant random variable. Assuming that S_i in decision rule (5) is distributed independently of all ε_{it} except possibly for ε_{ik}, then (12) will be satisfied.

Eq. (12) may also be satisfied in an environment of uncertainty. Suppose eq. (13) governs the error structure in (1) and

$$E_{k-1}[\varepsilon_{ik}] = 0,$$

but

$$E_{k-1}[\phi_i] = \phi_i,$$

so that agents cannot forecast innovations in their earnings, but they know their own permanent component. Provided that S_i is distributed independently of all ε_{it} except possible for ε_{ik}, this model also produces (12).

We investigate the plausibility of (12) with respect to more general decision rules and error processes in section 8.

6.2. U_{it} follows a first-order autoregressive process

Suppose next that U_{it} follows a first-order autoregression:

$$U_{it} = \rho U_{i,t-1} + \nu_{it}, \tag{14}$$

where $E[\nu_{it}] = 0$ and the ν_{it} are mutually independently (not necessarily identically) distributed random variables with $\rho \neq 1$. Substitution using (1) and (14) to solve for $U_{it'}$ yields

$$Y_{it} = [X_{it} - X_{it'}\rho^{t-t'}]\beta + (1 - \rho^{t-t'})d_i\alpha$$

$$+ \rho^{t-t'}Y_{it'} + \left\{ \sum_{j=0}^{t-(t'+1)} \rho^j \nu_{i,t-j} \right\}, \qquad t > t' > k. \tag{15}$$

Assume further that the perfect foresight rule (5) determines enrollment, and the ν_{ij} are distributed independently of S_i and X_{ik} in (5). Heckman and Wolpin (1976) invoke similar assumptions in their analysis of affirmative action programs. As a consequence of these assumptions,

$$E[Y_{it}|X_{it}, X_{it'}, d_i, Y_{it'}] = (X_{it} - X_{it'}\rho^{t-t'})\beta$$

$$+ (1 - \rho^{t-t'})d_i\alpha + \rho^{t-t'}Y_{it'}, \tag{16}$$

so that (linear or non-linear) least squares applied to (16) consistently estimates

α as the number of observations becomes large. (The appropriate non-linear regression increases efficiency by imposing the cross-coefficient restrictions.)

6.3. U_{it} is covariance-stationary

The next procedure invokes an assumption implicitly used in many papers on training [*e.g.*, Ashenfelter (1978), Bassi (1983), and others] but exploits the assumption in a novel way. We assume

U_{it} is covariance stationary so $\mathrm{E}[U_{it}U_{i,t-j}] = \mathrm{E}[U_{it'}U_{i,t'-j}] = \sigma_j$ for $j \geq 0$ for all t, t', (17a)

Access to at least two observations on pre-program earnings in t' and $t'-j$ as well as one period of post-program earnings in t where $t - t' = j$, (17b)

$$p\mathrm{E}[U_{it'}|d_i = 1] \neq 0. \tag{17c}$$

Unlike the two previous examples, we make no assumptions here about the appropriate enrollment rule or about the stochastic relationship between U_{it} and the cost of enrollment S_i.

By the argument of footnote 1, we lose no generality by suppressing the effect of regressors in (1). Thus let

$$Y_{it} = \beta_t + d_i\alpha + U_{it}, \qquad t > k,$$

$$Y_{it'} = \beta_{t'} + U_{it'}, \qquad t' < k,$$

where β_t and $\beta_{t'}$ are period-specific shifters.

From a random sample of pre-program earnings from periods t' and $t'-j$, σ_j can be consistently estimated from the sample covariances between $Y_{it'}$ and $Y_{i,t'-j}$:

$$m_1 = \left(\sum(Y_{it'} - \bar{Y}_{t'})(Y_{i,t'-j} - \bar{Y}_{t'-j})\right)/I, \qquad \operatorname{plim} m_1 = \sigma_j.$$

If $t > k$ and $t - t' = j$ so that the post-program earnings data are as far removed in time from t' as t' is removed from $t'-j$, form the sample covariance between Y_{it} and $Y_{it'}$:

$$m_2 = \left(\sum(Y_{it} - \bar{Y}_t)(Y_{it'} - \bar{Y}_{t'})\right)/I,$$

which has the probability limit

$$\text{plim}\, m_2 = \sigma_j + \alpha p \mathrm{E}[U_{it'}|d_i = 1], \qquad t > k > t'.$$

Form the sample covariance between d_i and $Y_{it'}$,

$$m_3 = \left(\sum (Y_{it'} - \bar{Y}_{t'}) d_i\right)/I,$$

with probability limit

$$\text{plim}\, m_3 = p\mathrm{E}[U_{it'}|d_i = 1], \qquad t' < k.$$

Combining this information and assuming $p\mathrm{E}[U_{it'}|d_i = 1] \neq 0$ for $t' < k$,

$$\text{plim}\, \hat{\alpha} = \text{plim}((m_2 - m_1)/m_3) = \alpha.$$

7. Repeated cross-section analogues of longitudinal procedures

Most longitudinal procedures can be fit on repeated cross-section data. Repeated cross-section data are cheaper to collect and they do not suffer from problems of non-random attrition which plague panel data.

The previous section presented longitudinal estimators of α. In each case, however, α can actually be identified with repeated cross-section data. Here we establish this claim. Our earlier paper gives additional examples of longitudinal estimators which can be implemented on repeated cross-section data.[2]

7.1. *The fixed effect model*

As in section 6.1, assume that (12) holds so

$$\mathrm{E}[U_{it}|d_i = 1] = \mathrm{E}[U_{it'}|d_i = 1],$$

$$\mathrm{E}[U_{it}|d_i = 0] = \mathrm{E}[U_{it'}|d_i = 0],$$

for all $t > k > t'$. Let $X_{it}\beta = \beta_t$ and define, in terms of the notation of section 4.1,

$$\hat{\alpha} = \left[\bar{Y}_t^{(1)} - \bar{Y}_t^{(0)}\right] - \left[\bar{Y}_{t'}^{(1)} - \bar{Y}_{t'}^{(0)}\right].$$

[2] We also produce one example of a longitudinal procedure which has no repeated cross-section analogue.

Assuming random sampling, consistency of $\hat{\alpha}$ follows immediately from (12):

$$\begin{aligned}\operatorname{plim}\hat{\alpha} &= \left[\alpha + \beta_t - \beta_t + \mathrm{E}[U_{it}|d_i = 1] - \mathrm{E}[U_{it}|d_i = 0]\right] \\ &\quad - \left[\beta_{t'} - \beta_{t'} + \mathrm{E}[U_{it'}|d_i = 1] - \mathrm{E}[U_{it'}|d_i = 0]\right] \\ &= \alpha .\end{aligned}$$

7.2. U_{it} follows a first-order autoregressive process

In one respect the preceding example is contrived. It assumes that in pre-program cross-sections we know the identity of future trainees. Such data might exist (*e.g.*, individuals in the training period k might be asked about their pre-period k earnings to see if they qualify for admission), but this seems unlikely. One advantage of longitudinal data for estimating α in the fixed effect model is that if the survey extends before period k, the identity of future trainees is known.

The need for pre-program earnings to identify α is, however, only an artifact of the fixed effect assumption (13). Suppose instead that U_{it} follows a first-order autoregressive process given by (14) and that

$$\mathrm{E}[\nu_{it}|d_i] = 0, \qquad t > k, \tag{18}$$

as in section 6.2. With three successive post-program cross-sections in which the identity of trainees is known, it is possible to identify α.

To establish this result, let the three post-program periods be t, $t+1$ and $t+2$. Assuming, as before, that no regressor appears in (1),

$$\operatorname{plim}\bar{Y}_j^{(1)} = \beta_j + \alpha + \mathrm{E}\left[U_{ij}|d_i = 1\right],$$

$$\operatorname{plim}\bar{Y}_j^{(0)} = \beta_j + \mathrm{E}\left[U_{ij}|d_i = 0\right].$$

From (18),

$$\mathrm{E}[U_{i,t+1}|d_i = 1] = \rho\mathrm{E}[U_{it}|d_i = 1],$$

$$\mathrm{E}[U_{i,t+1}|d_i = 0] = \rho\mathrm{E}[U_{it}|d_i = 0],$$

$$\mathrm{E}[U_{i,t+2}|d_i = 1] = \rho^2\mathrm{E}[U_{it}|d_i = 1],$$

$$\mathrm{E}[U_{i,t+2}|d_i = 0] = \rho^2\mathrm{E}[U_{it}|d_i = 0].$$

Using these formulae, it is straightforward to verify that $\hat{\rho}$, defined by

$$\hat{\rho} = \frac{\left(\bar{Y}_{t+2}^{(1)} - \bar{Y}_{t+2}^{(0)}\right) - \left(\bar{Y}_{t+1}^{(1)} - \bar{Y}_{t+1}^{(0)}\right)}{\left(\bar{Y}_{t+1}^{(1)} - \bar{Y}_{t+1}^{(0)}\right) - \left(\bar{Y}_{t}^{(1)} - \bar{Y}_{t}^{(0)}\right)},$$

is consistent for ρ, and that $\hat{\alpha}$ defined by

$$\hat{\alpha} = \frac{\left(\bar{Y}_{t+2}^{(1)} - \bar{Y}_{t+2}^{(0)}\right) - \hat{\rho}\left(\bar{Y}_{t+1}^{(1)} - \bar{Y}_{t+1}^{(0)}\right)}{1 - \hat{\rho}},$$

is consistent for α.

For this model, the advantage of longitudinal data is clear. Only two time periods of longitudinal data are required to identify α, but three periods of repeated cross-section data are required to estimate the same parameter. However, if Y_{it} is subject to measurement error, the apparent advantages of longitudinal data become less clear. Repeated cross-section estimators are robust to mean zero measurement error in the variables. The longitudinal regression estimator discussed in section 6.2 does not identify α unless the analyst observes earnings without error. Given three years of longitudinal data and assuming that measurement error is serially uncorrelated, one could instrument (15) using earnings in the earliest year as an instrument. Thus one advantage of the longitudinal estimator disappears in the presence of measurement error.

7.3. *Covariance stationarity*

For simplicity we suppress regressors in the earnings equation and let $X_{it}\beta = \beta_t$. Assume that conditions (17) are satisfied. Before presenting the repeated cross-section estimator, it is helpful to record the following facts:

$$\operatorname{var}(Y_{it}) = \alpha^2(1-p)p + 2\alpha \mathrm{E}[U_{it}|d_i = 1]\,p + \sigma_u^2, \qquad t > k, \tag{19a}$$

$$\operatorname{var}(Y_{it'}) = \sigma_u^2, \qquad t' < k, \tag{19b}$$

$$\operatorname{cov}(Y_{it}, d_i) = \alpha p(1-p) + p\mathrm{E}[U_{it}|d_i = 1]. \tag{19c}$$

Note that $E[U_{it}^2] = E[U_{it'}^2]$ by virtue of assumption (17a). Then

$$\hat{\alpha} = (p(1-p))^{-1}\left(\frac{\sum(Y_{it} - \bar{Y}_t)d_i}{I_t} - \sqrt{\left(\frac{\sum(Y_{it} - \bar{Y}_t)d_i}{I_t}\right)^2 - p(1-p)\left(\frac{\sum(Y_{it} - \bar{Y}_t)^2}{I_t} - \frac{\sum(Y_{it'} - \bar{Y}_{t'})^2}{I_{t'}}\right)}\right) \tag{20}$$

is consistent for α.

This expression arises by subtracting (19b) from (19a). Then use (19c) to get an expression for $E[U_{it}|d_i = 1]$ which can be substituted into the expression for the difference between (19a) and (19b). Replacing population moments by sample counterparts produces a quadratic equation in $\hat{\alpha}$, with the negative root given by (20). The positive root is inconsistent for α.

Notice that the estimators of sections 6.3 and 7.3 exploit different features of the covariance stationarity assumptions. The longitudinal procedure only requires that $E[U_{it}U_{i,t-j}] = E[U_{it'}U_{it'-j}]$ for $j > 0$; variances need not be equal across periods. The repeated cross-section analogue presented above only requires that $E[U_{it}U_{i,t-j}] = E[U_{it'}U_{i,t'-j}]$ for $j = 0$; covariances may differ among equispaced pairs of the U_{it}.

8. First difference methods

Plausible economic models do not justify first difference methods. Lessons drawn from these models are misleading.

8.1. Models which justify condition (12)

Whenever condition (12) holds, α can be estimated consistently from the difference regression method described in section 6.1. Section 6.1 presents a model which satisfies condition (12): the earnings residual has a permanent-transitory structure, decision rule (4) or (5) determines enrollment, and S_i is distributed independently of the transitory component of U_{it}.

However, this model is rather special. It is very easy to produce plausible models that do not satisfy (12). For example, even if (13) characterizes U_{it}, if S_i in (5) does not have same joint (bivariate) distribution with respect to all ε_{it}, except for ε_{ik}, (12) may be violated.

Even if S_i in (5) is distributed independently of U_{it} for all t, it is still not the case that (12) is satisfied in a general model. For example, suppose X_{it} is distributed independently of all U_{it} and let

$$U_{it} = \rho U_{i,t-1} + \nu_{it},$$

where ν_{it} is a mean-zero, iid random variable and $|\rho| < 1$. If $\rho \neq 0$ and the perfect foresight decision rule characterizes enrollment, (12) is not satisfied for $t > k > t'$ because

$$\begin{aligned} \mathrm{E}[U_{it}|d_i = 1] &= \mathrm{E}[U_{it}|U_{ik} + X_{ik}\beta - \alpha/r < S_i] = \rho^{t-k}\mathrm{E}[U_{ik}|d_i = 1] \\ &\neq \mathrm{E}[U_{it'}|d_i = 1] = \mathrm{E}[U_{it'}|U_{ik} + X_{ik}\beta - \alpha/r < S_i], \end{aligned}$$

unless the conditional expectations are linear (in U_{ik}) for all t and $k - t' = t - k$. In that case

$$\mathrm{E}[U_{it}|d_i = 1] = \rho^{k-t'}\mathrm{E}[U_{ik}|d_i = 1],$$

so $\mathrm{E}[U_{it} - U_{it'}|d_i = 1] = 0$ only for t, t' such that $k - t' = t - k$. Thus (12) is not satisfied for all $t > k > t'$.

For more general specifications of U_{it} and stochastic dependence between S_i and U_{it}, (12) will not be satisfied.

8.2. *More general first difference estimators*

Instead of (12), assume that

$$\begin{aligned} &\mathrm{E}[(U_{it} - U_{it'})(X_{it} - X_{it'})] = 0 \quad \text{for some} \quad t, t', \quad t > k > t', \\ &\mathrm{E}[(U_{it} - U_{it'})d_i] = 0 \quad \text{for some} \quad t > k > t'. \end{aligned} \tag{21}$$

Two new ideas are embodied in this assumption. In place of the assumption that $U_{it} - U_{it'}$ be conditionally independent of $X_{it} - X_{it'}$ and d_i, we only require uncorrelatedness. Also, rather than assume that $\mathrm{E}[U_{it} - U_{it'}|d_i, X_{it} - X_{it'}] = 0$ for all $t > k > t'$, the correlation needs to be zero only for some $t > k > t'$. For the appropriate values of t and t', least squares applied to the differenced data consistently estimates α.

Our earlier paper presents three examples of models that satisfy (21) but not (12). Here we discuss one of them. Suppose that

U_{it} is covariance stationary, (22a)

U_{it} has a linear regression on U_{ik} for all t (i.e., $\mathrm{E}[U_{it}|U_{ik}] = \beta_{tk}U_{ik}$), (22b)

U_{it} is mutually independent of (X_{ik}, S_i) for all t, (22c)

α is common to all individuals (so the model is of the fixed coefficient form), (22d)

The environment is one of perfect foresight where decision rule (5) determines participation. (22e)

Under these assumptions, condition (21) characterizes the data.

To see this note that (22a) and (22b) imply there exists a δ such that

$$U_{it} = U_{i,k+j} = \delta U_{ik} + \omega_{it}, \quad j > 0, \quad t > k,$$

$$U_{it'} = U_{i,k-j} = \delta U_{ik} + \omega_{it'}, \quad j > 0,$$

and

$$\mathrm{E}[\omega_{it} | U_{ik}] = \mathrm{E}[\omega_{it'} | U_{ik}] = 0.$$

Now observe that

$$\mathrm{E}[U_{it} | d_i = 1] = \delta \mathrm{E}[U_{ik} | d_i = 1] + \mathrm{E}[\omega_{it} | d_i = 1].$$

But, as a consequence of (22c),

$$\mathrm{E}[\omega_{it} | d_i = 1] = 0,$$

since $\mathrm{E}[\omega_{it}] = 0$ and because (22c) guarantees that the mean of ω_{it} does not depend on X_{ik} and S_i. Similarly,

$$\mathrm{E}[\omega_{it'} | d_i = 1] = 0,$$

and thus (21) holds.

Linearity of the regression does not imply that the U_{it} are normally distributed (although if the U_{it} are joint normal the regression is linear). The multivariate t density is just one example of many examples of densities with linear regressions.

8.3. *Anomalous features of first difference estimators*

Nearly all of the estimators require a control group (i.e., a sample of non-trainees). The only exception is the fixed effect estimator in a time homogeneous environment. In this case, if condition (12) or (21) holds, if we let $X_{it}\beta = \beta_t$ to simplify the exposition, and if the environment is time homogeneous so $\beta_t = \beta_{t'}$, then

$$\hat{\alpha} = \bar{Y}_t^{(1)} - \bar{Y}_{t'}^{(1)}$$

consistently estimates α. The frequently stated claim that 'if the environment is stationary, you don't need a control group' [see, e.g., Bassi (1983)] is false except for the special conditions which justify use of the fixed effect estimator.

Most of the procedures considered here can be implemented using only post-program data. The covariance stationary estimators of sections 6.3 and

7.3, certain repeated cross-section estimators and first difference methods constitute an exception to this rule. In this sense, these estimators are anomalous.

Fixed effect estimators are also robust to departures from the random sampling assumption. For instance, suppose condition (12) or (21) is satisfied, but that the available data oversample or undersample trainees (i.e., the proportion of sample trainees does not converge to $p = E[d_i]$). Suppose further that the analyst does not know the true value of p. Nevertheless, a first difference regression continues to identify α. Most other procedures do not share this property.

9. Non-random sampling plans

Virtually all methods can be readily adjusted to account for choice based sampling or measurement error in training status. Some methods require no modification at all.

The data available for analyzing the impact of training on earnings are often non-random samples. Frequently they consist of pooled data from two sources: (a) a sample of trainees selected from program records and (b) a sample of non-trainees selected from some national sample. Typically, such samples overrepresent trainees relative to their proportion in the population. This creates the problem of choice based sampling analyzed by Manski and Lerman (1977) and Manski and McFadden (1981).

A second problem, contamination bias, arises when the training status of certain individuals is recorded with error. Many control samples such as the Current Population Survey or Social Security Work History File do not reveal whether or not persons have received training.

Both of these sampling situations combine the following types of data:

(A) Earnings, earnings characteristics, and enrollment characteristics (Y_{it}, X_{it} and Z_i) for a sample of trainees ($d_i = 1$),

(B) Earnings, earnings characteristics, and enrollment characteristics for a sample of non-trainees ($d_i = 0$),

(C) Earnings, earnings characteristics, and enrollment characteristics for a national 'control' sample of the population (e.g., CPS or Social Security Records) where the training status of persons is not known.

If type (A) and (B) data are combined and the sample proportion of trainees does not converge to the population proportion of trainees, the combined sample is a choice based sample. If type (A) and (C) data are combined with or without type (B) data, there is contamination bias because the training status of some persons is not known.

Most procedures developed in the context of random sampling can be modified to consistently estimate α using choice based samples or contaminated control groups (i.e., groups in which training status is not known for individuals). In some cases, a consistent estimator of the population proportion of trainees is required. We illustrate these claims by showing how to modify the instrumental variables estimator to address both sampling schemes. Our earlier paper gives explicit case by case treatment of these issues for each estimator developed there.

9.1. The I.V. estimator: Choice-based sampling

If condition (9a) is strengthened to read

$$\mathrm{E}\left[X_{it}'U_{it}|d_i\right]=0, \qquad \mathrm{E}\left[g(Z_i^e)U_{it}|d_i\right]=0, \tag{23}$$

and (9b) is also met, the I.V. estimator is consistent for α in choice-based samples.

To see why this is so, write the normal equations for the I.V. estimator in the following form:

$$\begin{pmatrix} \frac{\sum X_{it}'X_{it}}{I_t} & \frac{\sum X_{it}'d_i}{I_t} \\ \frac{\sum g(Z_i^e)X_{it}}{I_t} & \frac{\sum g(Z_i^e)d_i}{I_t} \end{pmatrix}\begin{pmatrix}\hat{\beta}\\ \hat{\alpha}\end{pmatrix}=\begin{pmatrix} \frac{\sum X_{it}'Y_{it}}{I_t} \\ \frac{\sum g(Z_i^e)Y_{it}}{I_t} \end{pmatrix}$$

$$=\begin{pmatrix} \frac{\sum X_{it}'X_{it}}{I_t} & \frac{\sum X_{it}'d_i}{I_t} \\ \frac{\sum g(Z_i^e)X_{it}}{I_t} & \frac{\sum g(Z_i^e)d_i}{I_t} \end{pmatrix}\begin{pmatrix}\beta\\ \alpha\end{pmatrix}+\begin{pmatrix} \frac{\sum X_{it}'U_{it}}{I_t} \\ \frac{\sum g(Z_i^e)U_{it}}{I_t} \end{pmatrix}. \tag{24}$$

Since (23) guarantees that

$$\operatorname*{plim}_{I_t\to\infty}\frac{\sum X_{it}'U_{it}}{I_t}=0 \quad\text{and}\quad \operatorname*{plim}_{I_t\to\infty}\frac{\sum g(Z_i^e)U_{it}}{I_t}=0, \tag{25}$$

and the rank condition (9b) holds, the I.V. estimator is consistent.

In a choice based sample, let the probability that an individual has enrolled in training be p^*. Even if (9a) and (9b) are satisfied, there is no guarantee that condition (25) will be met without invoking (23). This is so because

$$\operatorname*{plim}_{I_t \to \infty} \frac{\sum X_{it}' U_{it}}{I_t} = \mathrm{E}\left[X_{it}' U_{it} | d_i = 1 \right] p^* + \mathrm{E}\left[X_{it}' U_{it} | d_i = 0 \right] (1 - p^*),$$

$$\operatorname*{plim}_{I_t \to \infty} \frac{\sum g(Z_i^e) U_{it}}{I_t} = \mathrm{E}\left[g(Z_i^e) U_{it} | d_i = 1 \right] p^*$$

$$+ \mathrm{E}\left[g(Z_i^e) U_{it} | d_i = 0 \right] (1 - p^*).$$

These expressions are not generally zero, so the I.V. estimator is generally inconsistent.

In the case of random sampling, $p^* = \Pr[d_i = 1] = p$ and the above expressions are identically zero. They are also zero if (23) is satisfied. However, it is not necessary to invoke (23). Provided p is known, it is possible to reweight the data to secure consistent estimators under the assumptions of section 4. Multiplying eq. (1) by the weight

$$\omega_i = d_i \frac{p}{p^*} + (1 - d_i) \left(\frac{1 - p}{1 - p^*} \right),$$

and applying I.V. to the transformed equation produces an estimator that satisfies (25). It is straightforward to check that weighting the sample at hand back to random sample proportions causes the I.V. method to consistently estimate α and β. [See Heckman and Robb (1985).]

9.2. *The I.V. estimator: Contamination bias*

For data of type (C), d_i is not observed. Applying the I.V. estimator to pooled samples (A) and (C), assuming that observations in (C) have $d_i = 0$, produces an inconsistent estimator.

In terms of the I.V. eq. (24), from sample (C) it is possible to generate the cross-products

$$\frac{\sum X_{it}' X_{it}}{I_C}, \quad \frac{\sum g(Z_i^e) X_{it}}{I_C}, \quad \frac{\sum X_{it}' Y_{it}}{I_C}, \quad \frac{\sum g(Z_i^e) Y_{it}}{I_C},$$

which converge to the desired population counterparts where I_C denotes the number of observations in sample (C). Missing is information on the cross-products

$$\frac{\sum X_{it}' d_i}{I_C}, \quad \frac{\sum g(Z_i^e) d_i}{I_C}.$$

Notice that if d_i were measured accurately in sample (C),

$$\underset{I_C \to \infty}{\text{plim}} \frac{\sum X_{it}' d_i}{I_C} = p\mathrm{E}\left[X_{it}' | d_i = 1 \right],$$

$$\underset{I_C \to \infty}{\text{plim}} \frac{\sum g(Z_i^e) d_i}{I_c} = p\mathrm{E}\left[g(Z_i^e) | d_i = 1 \right].$$

But the means of X_{it} and $g(Z_i^e)$ in sample (A) converge to

$$\mathrm{E}[X_{it} | d_i = 1] \quad \text{and} \quad \mathrm{E}\left[g(Z_i^e) | d_i = 1 \right],$$

respectively. Hence, inserting the sample (A) means of X_{it} and $g(Z_i^e)$ multiplied by p in the second column of the matrix I.V. eq. (24) produces a consistent I.V. estimator provided that in the limit the size of samples (A) and (C) both approach infinity at the same rate.

9.3. *Repeated cross-section methods with unknown training status and choice-based sampling*

The repeated cross-section estimators discussed in section 5 are inconsistent when applied to choice-based samples unless additional conditions are assumed. For example, when the environment is time-homogeneous and (12) also holds, $(\bar{Y}_t - \bar{Y}_{t'})/p$ remains a consistent estimator of α in choice-based samples as long as the same proportion of trainees are sampled in periods t' and t. If a condition such as (12) is not met, it is necessary to know the identity of trainees in order to weight the sample back to the proportion of trainees that would be produced by a random sample in order to obtain consistent estimators. Hence the class of estimators that does not require knowledge of individual training status is not robust to choice-based sampling.

9.4. *Control function estimators*

A subset of cross-sectional and longitudinal procedures is robust to choice-based sampling. Those procedures construct a control function, K_{it}, with the following properties:

K_{it} depends on variables $\ldots, Y_{i,t+1}, Y_{it}, Y_{i,t-1}, \ldots, X_{i,t+1}, X_{it}, X_{i,t-1}, \ldots, d_i$ and parameters ψ, and

$$\mathrm{E}[U_{it} - K_{it} | d_i, X_{it}, K_{it}, \psi] = 0, \tag{26a}$$

$$\psi \text{ is identified.} \tag{26b}$$

When inserted into the earnings function (1), K_{it} purges the equation of dependence between U_{it} and d_i. Rewriting (1) to incorporate K_{it},

$$Y_{it} = X_{it}\beta + d_i\alpha + K_{it} + \{U_{it} - K_{it}\}. \tag{27}$$

The purged disturbance $\{U_{it} - K_{it}\}$ is orthogonal to the right-hand-side variables in the new equation. Thus (possibly non-linear) regression applied to (27) consistently estimates the parameters (α, β, ψ). Moreover, (26) implies that $\{U_{it} - K_{it}\}$ is orthogonal to the right-hand-side variables conditional on d_i, X_{it} and K_{it}:

$$\mathrm{E}[Y_{it} | X_{it}, d_i, K_{it}] = X_{it}\beta + d_i\alpha + K_{it}.$$

Thus if type (A) and (B) data are combined in *any* proportion, least squares performed on (27) produces consistent estimates of (α, β, ψ) provided the number of trainees and non-trainees in the sample both approach infinity. The class of control function estimators which satisfy (26) can be implemented without modification in choice-based samples.

We encountered a control function in section 6. For the model satisfying (14) and (18),

$$K_{it} = \rho(Y_{i,t-1} - X_{i,t-1}\beta - d_i\alpha), \qquad t > k+1,$$

so $\psi = (\rho, \beta, \alpha)$. The sample selection bias methods (d)-(e) described in section 4.2 exploit the control function principle. Our longer paper gives further examples of control function estimators.

10. Conclusion

This paper presents alternative methods for estimating the impact of training on earnings when non-random selection characterizes the enrollment of persons into training. We have explored the benefits of cross-section, repeated cross-section and longitudinal data for addressing this problem by considering the assumptions required to use a variety of new and conventional estimators given access to various commonly encountered types of data. We also investigate the plausibility of assumptions needed to justify econometric procedures when viewed in the light of prototypical decision rules determining enrollment into training. Because many of the available samples are choice-based samples and because the problem of measurement error in training status is pervasive in many available control samples, we examine the robustness of the estimators to choice-based sampling and contamination bias.

A key conclusion of our analysis is that the benefits of longitudinal data have been overstated in the recent econometric literature on training because a false comparison has been made. A cross-section selection bias estimator does not require the elaborate and unjustified assumptions about functional forms often invoked in cross-sectional studies. Repeated cross-section data can often be used to identify the same parameters as longitudinal data. The uniquely longitudinal estimators require assumptions that are different from and often no more plausible than the assumptions required for cross-section or repeated cross-section estimators.

References

Amemiya, T., 1981, Qualitative response models: A survey, Journal of Economic Literature 19, 1483–1536.

Ashenfelter, O., 1978, Estimating the effect of training programs on earnings, Review of Economics and Statistics 60, 47–57.

Barnow, B., G. Cain and A. Goldberger, 1980, Issues in the analysis of selectivity bias, in: E. Stromsdorfer and G. Farkas, eds., Evaluation studies, Vol. 5 (Sage Publications, Beverly Hills, CA).

Bassi, L., 1983, Estimating the effect of training programs with nonrandom selection, Ph.D. dissertation (Princeton University, Princeton, NJ).

Chamberlain, G., 1982, Multivariate regression models for panel data, Journal of Econometrics 18, 1–46.

Heckman, J., 1976, Simultaneous equations models with continuous and discrete endogenous variables and structural shifts, in: S. Goldfeld and R. Quandt, eds., Studies in nonlinear estimation (Ballinger, Cambridge, MA).

Heckman, J., 1978, Dummy endogenous variables in a simultaneous equations system. Econometrica 46, 931–961.

Heckman, J., 1979, Sample selection bias as a specification error, Econometrica 47, 153–161.

Heckman, J. and G. Neumann, 1977, Union wage differentials and the decision to join unions, Unpublished manuscript (University of Chicago, Chicago, IL).

Heckman, J. and R. Robb, 1985, Alternative methods for evaluating the impact of interventions, in: J. Heckman and B. Singer, eds., Longitudinal analysis of labor market data, Econometric Society monograph series (Cambridge University Press, New York).

Heckman, J. and K. Wolpin, 1976, Does the contract compliance program work? An analysis of Chicago data, Industrial and Labor Relations Review, 554–564.

Lee, L.F., 1978, Unionism and wage rates: A simultaneous equations model with qualitative and limited dependent variables, International Economic Review 19, 415–433.

Manski, C. and S. Lerman, 1977, The estimation of choice probabilities from choice-based samples, Econometrica 45, 1977–1988.

Manski, C. and D. McFadden, 1981, Alternative estimators and sample designs for discrete choice analysis, in: C. Manski and D. McFadden, eds., Structural analysis of discrete data with econometric applications (MIT Press, Cambridge, MA).

Mundlak, Y., 1961, Empirical production functions free of management bias, Journal of Farm Economics 43, 45–56.

Mundlak, Y., 1978, On the pooling of time series and cross section data, Econometrica 46, 69–85.

Roy, A., 1951, Some thoughts on the distribution of earnings, Oxford Economic Papers 3, 135–146.

Journal of Business & Economic Statistics, July 1986, Vol. 4, No. 3

On Cross-Lagged Panel Models With Serially Correlated Errors

Lawrence S. Mayer
Department of Decision and Information Systems, Arizona State University, Tempe, AZ 85287

Cross-lagged panel studies are studies in which two or more variables are measured for a large number of subjects at each of several points in time. The variables divide naturally into two sets, and the purpose of the analysis is to estimate and test the cross-effects between the two sets. One approach to this analysis is to treat the cross-effects as parameters in regression equations. This study contributes to this approach by extending the regression model to a multivariate model that captures the correlation among the variables and allows the errors in the model to be correlated over time.

KEY WORDS: Panel analysis; Serial correlation; Regression; Autoregressive error; Path analysis.

1. INTRODUCTION

Cross-lagged panel studies are statistical studies in which two or more variables are measured for a large number of subjects at each of several waves or points in time. The variables divide naturally into two sets and the primary purpose of the analysis is to estimate and test the strength of the relationship between the two sets. Usually the sets represent components of an empirical theory of the process under study, and a major issue is the direction and strength of the relationship between those components. Such studies are found in the mainstreams of social, behavioral, and business research, particularly in areas in which empirical theory is too weak to allow formal development of a model of the behavior of the components over time. One approach to analysis in such studies is to adopt a simple vector-valued autoregressive model of the variables at wave t and to assume that the parameters of this model reflect the relationship between the two sets of variables. This study contributes to this approach by considering the problems of estimation and hypothesis testing for the cross-lagged panel model in which serial correlation is present in the error structure.

The assumption that the observed process is autoregressive is often an acceptable first-order approximation to the true but unknown temporal behavior. Such cross-lagged panel models have been used to assess the direction and strength of the relationships between policy inputs to a city or firm and the behavior of that city or firm, for which theory or experience suggests that the observed variables are somewhat linearly related but there is no well-developed theory of the behavior of the variables over time. To be more concrete and to set the context for the results here, I mention a few examples.

Cross-lagged panel models were used to assess the relationship between financial variables and performance variables for local governments. For example, policy analysts have studied the temporal relationship between police expenditures and level of crime for major cities. The primary issue in this example, and in most examples of cross-lagged panel analyses, is one of causal priority. To be more specific, is there evidence that the expenditures influence the crime rate, as suggested by some theories of local politics, or does the evidence indicate that the expenditures respond to the crime rate, as suggested by other theories? From a theoretic point of view, the issue is whether cities deal with social problems by diagnosing the severity and then allocating resources or by allocating resources according to political realities and then hoping that the problems will respond to these allocations.

These models have been used in marketing research to shed light on competing theories of the relationship between brand retention and brand preference. Does retention of ads for a particular brand lead to preference for that brand, or is the effect reversed, with preference for a brand dictating retention of the ads? Or are the two variables reciprocally related or, perhaps, unrelated? The nature of this relationship is central to understanding and thus developing a tenable theory of consumer behavior, a major issue in current marketing research.

A third example of the use of the cross-lagged models is from educational research. In the study of the role of primary schools in the socialization of children the issue of the relationship between participation and performance is critical. Do students that participate readily learn to become good performers, or do good performers learn to participate? Or do both effects exist in a feedback system? Are participation and performance unrelated? Clearly, different answers tend to support different educational theories and also lead to different suggestions regarding improving the performance of our primary school systems. This issue has been explored by cross-lagged panel studies, and in fact, cross-lagged panel methods have become a major tool in analyzing the relationships among measurements made over time on school children.

The final example is from psychiatry and is one on which I have worked. There has been considerable controversy in the medical community over whether psychotherapy is like other areas of clinical medicine in that approval of treatment is increased if the patient improves under the treatment. On the other hand, psychiatry is thought by some to be unique in that the relationship is reversed, with approval being the driving force in determining the degree of improvement. Such a conclusion, if supported by data, is thought to damage the case that psychiatry is on par, scientifically, with other specialties, such as surgery, since the patient need not approve of ulcer removal to have an ulcer successfully removed. Cross-lagged panel studies have been used to assess the relationship between approval and improvement in psychiatry.

To see more on the use of cross-lagged panel models in testing social theory, including analysis of the first three examples above, the reader should consult Crano, Kenny, and Campbell (1972), Greenberg, Kessler, and Logan (1979), Eaton (1978), Polachek and McCutcheon (1983), and Frey (1984).

Methods of analysis for cross-lagged panel studies have evolved over the last 20 years [Kessler and Greenberg (1981) provided an excellent review of this development]. Early methods concentrated on correlational statistics and were stimulated and motivated by the work of Campbell (1963), which in turn, was motivated, to some degree, by the seminal work of Lazarsfeld (1948) on the analysis of panel studies involving discrete variables. Probably the most significant advancement in the methodology of cross-lagged panel analysis was the development of a regression, as opposed to correlation, approach. This approach assesses the effect of each set of variables on the other by operationalizing these effects as regression parameters and then estimating and testing these parameters. For examples of this approach see Pelz and Andrews (1964), Duncan (1969), Heise (1970), Hannan and Young (1977), and Rogosa (1980). Recently, I (Mayer 1985) extended the regression approach by formulating a multivariate regression model that captures the cotemporal relationships among the variables being modeled. I proceeded to develop estimators and tests for the parameters of the model.

Although the cross-lagged panel study models variables over time, for the most part it has been assumed that the errors of the model are independent across waves. In this article I extend the applicability of these results by extending the regression approach to a cross-lagged panel model in which the errors display serial correlation over time.

The problem of serially correlated errors in a cross-lagged panel model was considered briefly by Kessler and Greenberg (1981) and Markus (1979). They assumed that the error structure is first-order autoregressive, then estimated the parameters by transforming the model to generalized differences and applying ordinary least squares or instrumental variables. I extend their work by considering three issues. First, how can the presence of serially correlated errors be detected? Second, if serially correlated errors are present, what are reasonable estimators of the regression coefficients? And finally, how can the presence of effects and cross-effects be tested if serially correlated errors are present?

In the next section the multivariate regression form of the cross-lagged panel model with serially correlated errors is introduced and notation is set. Results are presented in Section 3 and then, in Section 4, are applied to a panel data set on enrolled patients' attitudes toward health maintenance organizations. In the final section the implications and current direction of this research are discussed.

2. THE MULTIVARIATE CROSS-LAGGED PANEL MODEL

Let $\mathbf{z}_{it} = (\mathbf{x}_{it}'; \mathbf{y}_{it}')$ be k variables measured on the ith replication (or subject) at the tth wave ($i = 1, \ldots, n$; $t = 0, \ldots, T$), where $\mathbf{x}_{it}$ and $\mathbf{y}_{it}$ are vectors of p and q variables, respectively. Let $\mathbf{Z}_t = (\mathbf{X}_t; \mathbf{Y}_t)$ be the $n \times k$ matrix with $\mathbf{z}_{it}$ as the ith row. The regression structure is

$$\mathbf{Z}_t = \mathbf{Z}_{t-1}\mathbf{B} + \mathbf{E}_t, \qquad t = 1, \ldots, T, \tag{2.1}$$

where $\mathbf{E}_t = (\mathbf{F}_t; \mathbf{G}_t)$ is an unobserved random error matrix with ith row $\mathbf{e}_{it}$ and $\mathbf{B}$ is a $k \times k$ unknown parameter matrix of regression coefficients. The error matrix $\mathbf{E}_t$ has autoregressive structure

$$\mathbf{E}_t = \mathbf{E}_{t-1}\mathbf{A} + \mathbf{H}_t, \tag{2.2}$$

where $\mathbf{H}_t = (\mathbf{K}_t; \mathbf{L}_t)$ is an unobserved pure error matrix with ith row $\mathbf{h}_{it}$; $(\mathbf{h}_{1t}, \ldots, \mathbf{h}_{nt})$ are independent Gaussian vectors with common mean $\mathbf{0}$ and covariance matrix $\mathbf{\Lambda}$, and $\mathbf{A}$ is a $k \times k$ unknown parameter matrix of autoregressive coefficients.

Model specification is completed by specifying the behavior of the process at wave 0. We assume the rows of $\mathbf{Z}_0$, the observed matrix at wave 0, are independent Gaussian vectors with common mean $\mathbf{0}$ and common covariance matrix $\mathbf{\Theta}_0$, and the rows of $\mathbf{E}_0$, the error matrix at wave 0, are independent Gaussian vectors with common mean $\mathbf{0}$ and common covariance matrix $\mathbf{\Sigma}_0$.

Expression (2.2) yields that $\{\mathbf{e}_{1t}, \ldots, \mathbf{e}_{nt}\}$, the rows of $\mathbf{E}_t$, are independent Gaussian vectors with common mean $\mathbf{0}$ and common covariance matrix $\mathbf{\Sigma}_t$, where

$$\mathbf{\Sigma}_t = \mathbf{A}'\mathbf{\Sigma}_{t-1}\mathbf{A} + \mathbf{\Lambda}, \qquad t = 1, \ldots, T. \tag{2.3}$$

Similarly, the rows of $\mathbf{Z}_t$ are independent Gaussian vectors with common mean **0** and common covariance matrix $\boldsymbol{\Theta}_t$, where

$$\boldsymbol{\Theta}_t = \mathbf{B}'\boldsymbol{\Theta}_{t-1}\mathbf{B} + \boldsymbol{\Sigma}_t$$
$$= \mathbf{B}'\boldsymbol{\Theta}_{t-1}\mathbf{B} + \mathbf{A}'\boldsymbol{\Sigma}_{t-1}\mathbf{A} + \boldsymbol{\Lambda}, \qquad t = 1, \ldots, T. \tag{2.4}$$

Combining expressions (2.1) and (2.2) yields a second-order autoregressive representation for the cross-lagged panel model, as follows:

$$\mathbf{Z}_t = \mathbf{Z}_{t-1}(\mathbf{B} + \mathbf{A}) - \mathbf{Z}_{t-2}\mathbf{BA} + \mathbf{H}_t, \qquad t = 2, \ldots, T. \tag{2.5}$$

This expression represents the process in a form that has independent errors, but it does not represent the first two waves.

The matrices **B** and $\boldsymbol{\Sigma}_t$, if partitioned to conform with $\mathbf{Z}_t$, are

$$\mathbf{B} = \begin{bmatrix} \mathbf{B}_{11} & \mathbf{B}_{12} \\ \mathbf{B}_{21} & \mathbf{B}_{22} \end{bmatrix} \quad \text{and} \quad \boldsymbol{\Sigma}_t = \begin{bmatrix} \boldsymbol{\Sigma}_t(11) & \boldsymbol{\Sigma}_t(12) \\ \boldsymbol{\Sigma}_t(21) & \boldsymbol{\Sigma}_t(22) \end{bmatrix}.$$

The matrices **A** and $\boldsymbol{\Lambda}$ can be partitioned similarly.

In time series analysis proofs and calculations are often simplified by assuming that the matrices $\boldsymbol{\Theta}_0$ and $\boldsymbol{\Sigma}_0$ satisfy

$$\boldsymbol{\Theta}_0 = \mathbf{B}'\boldsymbol{\Theta}_0\mathbf{B} + \boldsymbol{\Sigma}_0 = \boldsymbol{\Theta}_t, \qquad t = 1, \ldots, T,$$
$$\boldsymbol{\Sigma}_0 = \mathbf{A}'\boldsymbol{\Sigma}_0\mathbf{A} + \boldsymbol{\Lambda} = \boldsymbol{\Sigma}_t, \qquad t = 1, \ldots, T,$$

in which case the model is said to be stationary. For cross-lagged panel analysis these assumptions do simplify proofs but may not obtain in practice, particularly since the number of waves is usually fixed and very small. In addition, these assumptions make some calculations very difficult (see Anderson 1978). Consequently, I choose not to assume stationarity. This choice prohibits me from making inferences that are asymptotic in T.

3. PARAMETER ESTIMATION AND HYPOTHESIS TESTING

The primary estimation problems in cross-lagged panel studies are to estimate the matrix of regression coefficients, the matrix of autoregressive coefficients, and the covariance matrices. The primary testing problems are to test for the presence of temporal effects and to test for the presence of temporal cross-effects.

3.1 The Effects of Serial Correlation

Analysis of the problem of estimating the matrix of regression coefficients in the cross-lagged panel model begins by showing that the pooled least squares estimator, which is maximum likelihood if the errors are independent across waves (Anderson 1978), may perform poorly even if the number of replications is large. This observation is made precise in Theorem 1.

Theorem 1. For the $T + 1$ wave cross-lagged panel model with serially correlated errors the pooled least squares estimator of **B** is not consistent as the number of replications becomes large.

Proof. The proof begins by defining

$$\mathbf{C}_t(j) = n^{-1}\sum_{i=1}^{n} \mathbf{z}_{i,t-j}\mathbf{z}'_{i,t}, \qquad j = 0, 1,$$

$$\mathbf{C}(0) = T^{-1}\sum_{t=0}^{T-1} \mathbf{C}_t(0),$$

$$\mathbf{C}(1) = T^{-1}\sum_{t=1}^{T} \mathbf{C}_t(1),$$

$$\overline{\boldsymbol{\Theta}}_{T-1} = T^{-1}\sum_{t=0}^{T-1} \boldsymbol{\Theta}_t,$$

and

$$\overline{\boldsymbol{\Sigma}}_{T-1} = T^{-1}\sum_{t=0}^{T-1} \boldsymbol{\Sigma}_t.$$

In this notation the pooled least squares estimator is

$$\mathbf{B}_{LS} = [\mathbf{C}(0)]^{-1}\mathbf{C}(1). \tag{3.1}$$

The behavior of $\mathbf{B}_{LS}$ follows from the asymptotic behaviors of $\mathbf{C}(1)$ and $\mathbf{C}(0)$.

Noting that

$$\operatorname*{plim}_{n\to\infty} \mathbf{C}_t(0) = \boldsymbol{\Theta}_t,$$

we have

$$\operatorname*{plim}_{n\to\infty} \mathbf{C}(0) = T^{-1}\sum_{t=0}^{T-1} \operatorname*{plim}_{n\to\infty} \mathbf{C}_t(0)$$
$$= T^{-1}\sum_{t=0}^{T-1} \boldsymbol{\Theta}_t = \overline{\boldsymbol{\Theta}}_{T-1}.$$

Applying the weak law of large numbers,

$$\operatorname*{plim}_{n\to\infty} \mathbf{C}_t(1) = \operatorname*{plim}_{n\to\infty} n^{-1}\mathbf{Z}'_{t-1}\mathbf{Z}_t$$
$$= \operatorname*{plim}_{n\to\infty} n^{-1}[\mathbf{Z}'_{t-1}\mathbf{Z}_{t-1}\mathbf{B} + \mathbf{Z}'_{t-1}\mathbf{E}_t]$$
$$= \boldsymbol{\Theta}_{t-1}\mathbf{B} + \boldsymbol{\Sigma}_t\mathbf{A},$$

and consequently

$$\operatorname*{plim}_{n\to\infty} \mathbf{C}(1) = T^{-1}\sum_{t=1}^{T} \operatorname*{plim}_{n\to\infty} \mathbf{C}_t(1)$$
$$= T^{-1}\sum_{t=1}^{T} [\boldsymbol{\Theta}_{t-1}\mathbf{B} + \boldsymbol{\Sigma}_t\mathbf{A}]$$
$$= \overline{\boldsymbol{\Theta}}_{T-1}\mathbf{B} + \overline{\boldsymbol{\Sigma}}_{T-1}\mathbf{A}.$$

Applying the basic principle of weak covergence to combine the two limits,

$$\operatorname*{plim}_{n\to\infty} \mathbf{B}_{LS} = \operatorname*{plim}_{n\to\infty} [\mathbf{C}(0)]^{-1}[\mathbf{C}(1)]$$

$$= [\operatorname*{plim}_{n\to\infty} \mathbf{C}(0)]^{-1} \operatorname*{plim}_{n\to\infty} \mathbf{C}(1)$$

$$= \mathbf{B} + \overline{\mathbf{\Theta}}_{T-1}^{-1} \ddagger \mathbf{A},$$

which is not, in general, equal to $\mathbf{B}$; and thus the pooled least squares estimator, $\mathbf{B}_{LS}$, is not a consistent estimator of $\mathbf{B}$.

Theorem 1 is analogous to the result in econometrics that for a regression model of a single time series the ordinary least squares estimator is inconsistent—in the number of waves—if the model has serially correlated errors (e.g., Johnston 1972; Malinvaud 1980); but Theorem 1 is a result about growth in n and not in T.

3.2 Detecting Serial Correlation in the Cross-Lagged Panel Model

Having shown that the serial correlation in the error structure cannot, in general, be ignored, I consider the problem of detecting the degree to which it is present in a given panel study.

The most common methods of detecting correlation in the errors, those of the Durbin–Watson lineage, are not recommended for use with the cross-lagged panel model for several reasons. First, they do not apply to models that have multiple responses or to models that have only lagged endogenous predictors (e.g., Johnston 1972; Judge, Griffiths, Hill, and Lee 1980; Malinvaud 1980). Second, these methods are accurate asymptotically in the number of *waves*. To be most useful with cross-lagged panel studies a procedure must be accurate asymptotically in the number of *replications*.

The first method of detecting the presence of serial correlation in the errors is to estimate the matrix $\mathbf{A}$ from the residual matrices obtained from $\mathbf{B}_{LS}$, the pooled least squares estimator defined in expression (3.1). The residual matrix $\tilde{\mathbf{E}}_t$ is defined by

$$\tilde{\mathbf{E}}_t = \mathbf{Z}_t - \mathbf{Z}_{t-1}\mathbf{B}_{LS}, \qquad t = 1, \ldots, T,$$

and the matrix $\mathbf{A}$ of autoregressive coefficients is estimated by

$$\tilde{\mathbf{A}} = \left(T^{-1} \sum_{t=1}^{T} \tilde{\mathbf{E}}_t'\tilde{\mathbf{E}}_t\right)^{-1}\left[(T-1)^{-1} \sum_{t=2}^{T} \tilde{\mathbf{E}}_{t-1}'\tilde{\mathbf{E}}_t\right].$$

This estimator is easy to compute and gives a rough indication of the size of $\mathbf{A}$. It is not a good estimator of $\mathbf{A}$ even if the number of replications is large, as shown by Theorem 2.

Theorem 2. For the $T + 1$ wave cross-lagged panel model with serially correlated errors the estimator $\tilde{\mathbf{A}}$ of $\mathbf{A}$ is not consistent in the number of replications.

Proof. To prove that $\tilde{\mathbf{A}}$ is not, in general, consistent, it suffices to show that $\tilde{\mathbf{A}}$ is not consistent for a particular model. Consider the model that happens to be stationary and let

$$\mathbf{B}_{\text{lim}} = \operatorname*{plim}_{n\to\infty} \mathbf{B}_{LS}.$$

Consider the behavior of the components of $\tilde{\mathbf{A}}$. First

$$(nT)^{-1} \sum_{t=1}^{T} \tilde{\mathbf{E}}_t'\tilde{\mathbf{E}}_t$$

$$= (nT)^{-1} \sum_{t=1}^{T} (\mathbf{Z}_t'\mathbf{Z}_t - \mathbf{B}_{LS}'\mathbf{Z}_{t-1}'\mathbf{Z}_{t-1}\mathbf{B}_{LS}). \quad (3.2)$$

Taking the limit in probability and applying the principle of weak convergence yields

$$\operatorname*{plim}_{n\to\infty} (nT)^{-1} \sum_{t=1}^{T} \tilde{\mathbf{E}}_t'\tilde{\mathbf{E}}_t = \mathbf{\Theta} - \mathbf{B}_{\text{lim}}'\mathbf{\Theta}\mathbf{B}_{\text{lim}}. \quad (3.3)$$

Second,

$$[n(T-1)]^{-1} \sum_{t=2}^{T} \tilde{\mathbf{E}}_{t-1}'\tilde{\mathbf{E}}_t = [n(T-1)]^{-1}$$

$$\times \left[\sum_{t=2}^{T} \mathbf{B}_{LS}'\mathbf{Z}_{t-2}'\mathbf{Z}_{t-1}\mathbf{B}_{LS} - \mathbf{B}_{LS}'\mathbf{Z}_{t-2}'\mathbf{Z}_t\right]. \quad (3.4)$$

Premultiplying the expression for $\mathbf{Z}_t$ in (2.3) by $\mathbf{Z}_{t-2}'$ summing over t and subtracting

$$[n(T-1)]^{-1} \sum_{t=2}^{T} \mathbf{Z}_{t-2}'\mathbf{Z}_{t-1}\mathbf{B}_{LS}$$

gives

$$[n(T-1)]^{-1}\left[\sum_{t=2}^{T} \mathbf{Z}_{t-2}'\mathbf{Z}_t - \sum_{t=2}^{T} \mathbf{Z}_{t-2}'\mathbf{Z}_{t-1}\mathbf{B}\right]$$

$$= n(T-1)^{-1} \sum_{t=2}^{T} [\mathbf{Z}_{t-2}'\mathbf{Z}_{t-1}(\mathbf{B} + \mathbf{A})$$

$$- \mathbf{Z}_{t-2}'\mathbf{Z}_{t-2}\mathbf{B}\mathbf{A} - \mathbf{Z}_{t-2}'\mathbf{Z}_{t-1}\mathbf{B}_{LS} + \mathbf{Z}_{t-2}'\mathbf{F}_t]. \quad (3.5)$$

Substituting (3.5) into (3.4) yields

$$[n(T-1)]^{-1} \sum_{t=2}^{T} \mathbf{E}_{t-1}'\mathbf{E}_t$$

$$= \mathbf{B}_{LS}'\left[n(T-1)^{-1} \sum_{t=2}^{T} (\mathbf{Z}_{t-2}'\mathbf{Z}_{t-1})(\mathbf{B} + \mathbf{A})\right.$$

$$\left. - \mathbf{Z}_{t-2}'\mathbf{Z}_{t-2}[\text{cf3BA} - \mathbf{Z}_{t-2}'\mathbf{Z}_{t-1}\mathbf{B}_{LS} + \mathbf{Z}_{t-2}'\mathbf{F}_t\right]$$

$$= \mathbf{B}_{LS}'[n(T-1)]^{-1}\left[\sum_{t=1}^{T} \mathbf{Z}_{t-2}'\mathbf{Z}_{t-2}\right][\mathbf{B}_{LS}(\mathbf{B} + \mathbf{A})$$

$$- \mathbf{B}\mathbf{A} + \mathbf{B}_{LS}\mathbf{B}_{LS} + (\mathbf{Z}_{t-2}'\mathbf{Z}_{t-2})^{-1}\mathbf{Z}_{t-2}'\mathbf{F}_t].$$

Taking limits in probability yields

$$\operatorname*{plim}_{n\to\infty}[n(T-1)]^{-1}\mathbf{E}_{t-1}'\mathbf{E}_t$$

$$= \mathbf{B}_{\text{lim}}\mathbf{\Theta}_T[\mathbf{B}_{\text{lim}}(\mathbf{B} + \mathbf{A} - \mathbf{B}_{\text{lim}}) - \mathbf{B}\mathbf{A}], \quad (3.6)$$

since

$$\operatorname*{plim}_{n\to\infty} n^{-1}\mathbf{Z}'_{t-2}\mathbf{F}_t = 0.$$

Combining (3.3) and (3.6) and appealing to weak convergence yields

$$\operatorname{plim} \tilde{\mathbf{A}} = [\mathbf{\Theta}_T - \mathbf{B}_{\text{lim}}\mathbf{\Theta}_T\mathbf{B}_{\text{lim}}]^{-1}$$
$$\times [\mathbf{B}_{\text{lim}}\mathbf{\Theta}_T(\mathbf{A} + \mathbf{B} - \mathbf{B}_{\text{lim}}) - \mathbf{BA}].$$

To show that this expression does not, in general, reduce to $\mathbf{A}$ it suffices to consider the case $k = 1$, in which

$$\operatorname*{plim}_{n\to\infty} \tilde{a} = (1 + ab)^{-1}ab(b + a) \neq a,$$

where $\tilde{a}$, a, and b are the one-dimensional versions of $\tilde{\mathbf{A}}$, $\mathbf{A}$, and $\mathbf{B}$. I conclude that $\tilde{\mathbf{A}}$ is not consistent.

The second simple method of assessing the size of the autoregressive coefficients applies only to the case $p = q$. It assumes that the off-diagonal blocks $\mathbf{A}_{12}$ and $\mathbf{A}_{21}$ of $\mathbf{A}$ are zero and estimates the diagonal blocks. It begins with the marginal model of $\mathbf{X}_t$, obtained from expression (2.5), which is

$$\mathbf{X}_t = \mathbf{X}_{t-1}\mathbf{B}_{11} + \mathbf{Y}_{t-1}\mathbf{B}_{21} + \mathbf{F}_t \quad \text{and}$$
$$\mathbf{F}_t = \mathbf{F}_{t-1}\mathbf{A}_{11} + \mathbf{H}_t. \quad (3.7)$$

To estimate the matrix of autoregressive coefficients let $\mathbf{X}_{t-1}$ be expressed as in (3.7), postmultiply that expression by $\mathbf{A}_{11}$, and then subtract the result from $\mathbf{X}_t$. This exercise gives

$$\mathbf{X}_t = \mathbf{X}_{t-1}(\mathbf{B}_{11} + \mathbf{A}_{11}) - \mathbf{X}_{t-1}\mathbf{B}_{11}\mathbf{A}_{11}$$
$$+ \mathbf{Y}_{t-1}\mathbf{B}_{21} - \mathbf{Y}_{t-2}\mathbf{B}_{21}\mathbf{A}_{11} + \mathbf{H}_t.$$

To apply the principle of maximum likelihood to this representation, we reexpress it as

$$\mathbf{X}_t = \mathbf{R}_{t-1}\mathbf{P} + \mathbf{S}_t,$$

where

$$\mathbf{R}_{t-1} = (\mathbf{X}_{t-1}; \mathbf{X}_{t-2}; \mathbf{Y}_{t-1}; \mathbf{Y}_{t-2})$$

and

$$\mathbf{P} = [\mathbf{A}'_{11} + \mathbf{B}'_{11}; (\mathbf{B}_{11}\mathbf{A}_{11})'; \mathbf{B}'_{21}; (\mathbf{B}_{21}\mathbf{A}_{11})']'.$$

The marginal conditional likelihood function given $\mathbf{Z}_0$ and $\mathbf{Z}_1$ is

$$(2\pi)^{-n(T-1)/2}|\mathbf{\Lambda}^{(11)}|^{-n(T-1)/2}\exp\Big\{-\tfrac{1}{2}\sum_{t=2}^{T}$$
$$\times \operatorname{tr}(\mathbf{X}_t - \mathbf{R}_{t-1}\mathbf{P})'\mathbf{\Lambda}^{(11)-1}(\mathbf{X}_t - \mathbf{R}_{t-1}\mathbf{P})\Big\}.$$

Setting the derivative of the likelihood function to zero and solving yields

$$\hat{\mathbf{P}} = \left[\sum_{t=2}^{T} \mathbf{R}'_{t-1}\mathbf{R}_{t-1}\right]^{-1} \sum_{t=1}^{T} \mathbf{R}_{t-1}\mathbf{X}_t$$

as the maximum likelihood estimator of $\mathbf{P}$. If $\mathbf{B}^*_{21}$ and $(\mathbf{B}_{21}\mathbf{A}_{11})^*$ are the blocks of $\hat{\mathbf{P}}$ corresponding to the blocks $\mathbf{B}_{21}$ and $(\mathbf{B}_{21} + \mathbf{A}_{11})$ of $\mathbf{P}$, then by the invariance property of maximum likelihood, $\mathbf{A}^*_{11} = (\mathbf{B}^*_{21})^{-1}(\mathbf{B}_{21}\mathbf{A}_{11})^*$ is a (marginal) maximum likelihood estimator of $\mathbf{A}_{11}$.

A similar calculation using $\mathbf{Y}_t$ in place of $\mathbf{X}_t$ yields a marginal maximum likelihood estimator $\mathbf{A}^*_{22}$ of $\mathbf{A}_{22}$. Finally, $\mathbf{A}^*_{11}$ and $\mathbf{A}^*_{22}$ are used to assess the size of the diagonal blocks of $\mathbf{A}$. If they are nonnegligible, then I suspect that serial correlation is present in the error structure of the model and proceed to test its presence more formally.

3.3 Estimating the Parameters With Serial Correlation in the Error Structure

Once it is determined that serial correlation may be present in the error structure, attention turns to estimating the parameters of the cross-lagged panel model.

The first method of estimation is to use the maximum likelihood estimator derived from the joint likelihood of all $T + 1$ waves.

From the expression in (2.5) the conditional density function $f(\mathbf{Z}_t \mid \mathbf{Z}_{t-1}, \ldots, \mathbf{Z}_0)$ of $\mathbf{Z}_t$ given $\mathbf{Z}_{t-1}, \ldots, \mathbf{Z}_0$ is

$$(2\pi)^{-nk/2}|\mathbf{\Lambda}|^{-n/2}\exp\{-\tfrac{1}{2}\operatorname{tr}[\mathbf{Z}_t - \mathbf{Z}_{t-1}(\mathbf{B} + \mathbf{A})$$
$$+ \mathbf{Z}_{t-2}\mathbf{BA}]'\mathbf{\Lambda}^{-1}[\mathbf{Z}_t - \mathbf{Z}_{t-1}(\mathbf{B} + \mathbf{A}) + \mathbf{Z}_{t-2}\mathbf{BA}]\},$$
$$t = 2, \ldots, T. \quad (3.8)$$

Since $\mathbf{Z}_0$ has independent Gaussian rows with common mean $\mathbf{0}$ and covariance matrix $\mathbf{\Theta}_0$ and $\mathbf{E}_0$ has independent Gaussian rows with mean $\mathbf{0}$ and covariance matrix $\mathbf{\Sigma}_0$, the conditional density of $\mathbf{Z}_1$ given $\mathbf{Z}_0$ is

$$f(\mathbf{Z}_1 \mid \mathbf{Z}_0) = c|\mathbf{\Delta}'\mathbf{\Sigma}_0\mathbf{\Delta} + \mathbf{\Lambda}|^{-n/2}\exp\{-\tfrac{1}{2}\operatorname{tr}(\mathbf{Z}_1 - \mathbf{Z}_0\mathbf{B})'$$
$$\times (\mathbf{\Delta}'\mathbf{\Sigma}_0\mathbf{\Delta} + \mathbf{\Lambda})^{-1}(\mathbf{Z}_1 - \mathbf{Z}_0\mathbf{B})\} \quad (3.9)$$

and the density of $\mathbf{Z}_0$ is

$$f(\mathbf{Z}_0) = C|\mathbf{\Theta}_0|^{-n/2}\exp\{-\tfrac{1}{2}\operatorname{tr}\mathbf{Z}'_0\mathbf{\Theta}_0^{-1}\mathbf{Z}_0\}, \quad (3.10)$$

where c and C are known constants.

The likelihood function $L(\mathbf{B}, \mathbf{A}, \mathbf{\Lambda}, \mathbf{\Sigma}_0, \mathbf{\Theta}_0)$ is the product of the density functions in (3.8), (3.9), and (3.10). Formally,

$$L(\mathbf{B}, \mathbf{A}, \mathbf{\Lambda}, \mathbf{\Sigma}_0, \mathbf{\Theta}_0)$$
$$= \prod_{t=2}^{T} f(\mathbf{Z}_t \mid \mathbf{Z}_0, \ldots, \mathbf{Z}_{t-1})f(\mathbf{Z}_1 \mid \mathbf{Z}_0)f(\mathbf{Z}_0). \quad (3.11)$$

Unconditional maximum likelihood estimators are obtained by maximization of this function. No closed-form expressions are obtained. Furthermore, the numerical maximization is quite difficult, since the structure of $\mathbf{\Sigma}_t$ involves the regression parameter matrix $\mathbf{B}$ in a nonlinear fashion. I have been unable to use any standard statistical routines to evaluate these estimators.

The second method of estimation maximizes a conditional likelihood function. It allows the model of $\mathbf{Z}_1$ to have a different regression parameter matrix, $\mathbf{B}_0$, and maximizes the joint likelihood function of $\mathbf{Z}_1, \ldots, \mathbf{Z}_T$. This method is far simpler than the unconditional likelihood method. It does not yield closed-form expressions but can be done with a standard maximum likelihood program such as the LISREL program contained in SPSS-X.

For this method the conditional density of $\mathbf{Z}_1$ given $\mathbf{Z}_0$, $f_0(\mathbf{Z}_1 \mid \mathbf{Z}_0)$, is obtained from $f(\mathbf{Z}_1 \mid \mathbf{Z}_0)$ in (3.9) by replacing $\mathbf{B}$ by $\mathbf{B}_0$; the likelihood function becomes

$$L(\mathbf{B} + \mathbf{A}, \mathbf{BA}, \boldsymbol{\Lambda}, \mathbf{B}_0, \boldsymbol{\Sigma}_0 \mid \mathbf{Z}_0)$$

$$= f_0(\mathbf{Z}_1 \mid \mathbf{Z}_0) \prod_{t=2}^{T} f(\mathbf{Z}_t \mid \mathbf{Z}_0, \ldots, \mathbf{Z}_{t-1}). \quad (3.12)$$

Maximization of this function yields conditional maximum likelihood estimates given $\mathbf{Z}_0$.

The third method of estimation, also a conditional likelihood method, is far more tractable than the first two. It uses the conditional likelihood function given $\mathbf{Z}_0$ and $\mathbf{Z}_1$. Formally, the likelihood is

$$L(\mathbf{A} + \mathbf{B}, \mathbf{BA}, \boldsymbol{\Lambda} \mid \mathbf{Z}_0, \mathbf{Z}_1)$$

$$= \prod_{t=2}^{T} f(\mathbf{Z}_t \mid \mathbf{Z}_0, \ldots, \mathbf{Z}_{t-1}), \quad (3.13)$$

which arises from the model as expressed in (2.5). With a slight change in notation the model becomes

$$\mathbf{Z}_t = \mathbf{M}_{t-1}\mathbf{Q} + \mathbf{H}_t, \qquad t = 2, \ldots, T,$$

where $\mathbf{M}_{t-1} = (\mathbf{Z}_{t-1}; \mathbf{Z}_{t-2})$ and

$$\mathbf{Q}' = (\mathbf{Q}_1'; \mathbf{Q}_2') = [(\mathbf{B} + \mathbf{A})'; (-\mathbf{BA})'].$$

Treating the first two waves, $\mathbf{Z}_0$ and $\mathbf{Z}_1$, as fixed and applying a result of Anderson (1978, p. 373) on estimating the parameters of higher-order vector-valued autoregressive processes yields that the estimators

$$\hat{\mathbf{Q}} = \begin{bmatrix} \hat{\mathbf{Q}}_1 \\ \hat{\mathbf{Q}}_2 \end{bmatrix} = \begin{bmatrix} \mathbf{K}(1,1) & \mathbf{K}(1,2) \\ \mathbf{K}(2,1) & \mathbf{K}(2,2) \end{bmatrix}^{-1} \begin{bmatrix} \mathbf{K}(1,0) \\ \mathbf{K}(2,0) \end{bmatrix},$$

$$\hat{\boldsymbol{\Lambda}} = [n(T-1)]^{-1} \sum_{t=1}^{T} (\mathbf{Z}_t - \mathbf{H}_{t-1}\hat{\mathbf{Q}})'(\mathbf{Z}_t - \mathbf{H}_{t-1}\hat{\mathbf{Q}})$$

$$(3.14)$$

are maximum likelihood estimators of $\mathbf{Q}$ and $\boldsymbol{\Lambda}$, where

$$\mathbf{K}(i,j) = (Tn)^{-1} \sum_{t=1}^{T} \mathbf{Z}_{t-i}'\mathbf{Z}_{t-j}, \qquad i, j = 0, 1, 2.$$

Note that this method, like the second, yields maximum likelihood estimators of $\mathbf{Q}_1 = \mathbf{A} + \mathbf{B}$ and $\mathbf{Q}_2 = -\mathbf{BA}$ but does not yield estimates of $\mathbf{A}$ and $\mathbf{B}$. Fortunately, the parameters $\mathbf{Q}_1$ and $\mathbf{Q}_2$ can be interpreted in terms of the second-order process diaplayed in (2.5).

The major disadvantage of this third method is that it makes no use of the $2nk$ observations of the first two waves. Probably 80% of the panel studies that I have seen have no more than three waves (in fact, a sizable minority have only two waves); in these studies at least two-thirds of the df would not be used.

3.4 Testing for the Presence of Effects and Cross-Effects

The central methodological issue in most cross-lagged panel studies is testing for the presence of temporal effects and cross-effects.

The hypothesis of no temporal effects is the standard hypothesis that both $\mathbf{B}$ and $\mathbf{A}$ are null. Methods of testing follow from Anderson (1978) and need no elaboration. Instead, I turn to the test for the presence of temporal cross-effects. Three methods of testing for the presence of cross-effects arise from applying the likelihood ratio principle to each of the likelihood functions considered in estimating the parameters of the model.

Note that the asymptotic distribution of all of these tests is considered as n, the number of independent replications, becomes large but $T + 1$, the number of waves, remains fixed. Growth in n, but not in T, reflects the sampling situation in most cross-lagged panel studies. Additional independent replications are easily obtained, but additional waves are rarely possible. Since I have not assumed stationarity, large sample behavior of these tests as T, or T and n, becomes large does not follow from direct application of the asymptotic theory of likelihood ratio tests. Dickey, Hasza, and Fuller (1984) and others have considered the large sample behavior in T for tests developed for similar nonstationary models.

The conditional likelihood test is based on the statistic

$$t_1 = 2 \log(L_1^* / L_1^{(0)}),$$

where L_1^* is the maximum of the unconditional likelihood function $L(\mathbf{B}, \mathbf{A}, \boldsymbol{\Lambda}, \boldsymbol{\Sigma}_0, \boldsymbol{\Theta}_0)$ given in (3.11) and $L_1^{(0)}$ is the maximum of the same function under the null hypothesis H_0 that $\mathbf{B}$ and $\mathbf{A}$ are block diagonal. Applying the asymptotic theory of likelihood ratio tests yields that the test statistic t_1 is asymptotically chi-squared with $2pq$ df and has the usual optimal large-sample properties associated with such tests (Cox and Hinkley 1974).

This test requires two maximizations of the unconditional likelihood function under nonlinear constraints on the parameter matrices, a calculation I find quite difficult and on which I comment in the next section.

The second test is a conditional likelihood ratio test based on the statistic

$$t_2 = 2 \log(L_2^* / L_2^{(0)}),$$

where L_2^* is the maximum of the conditional likelihood function $L(\mathbf{B} + \mathbf{A}, \mathbf{BA}, \boldsymbol{\Lambda}, \mathbf{B}_0, \boldsymbol{\Sigma}_0 \mid \mathbf{Z}_0)$ given in (3.12) and $L_2^{(0)}$ is the maximum of the same function under the constraint that $\mathbf{B} + \mathbf{A}$, $\mathbf{BA}$, and $\mathbf{B}_0$ are block diagonal. This test, unlike the first, can be computed on a standard maximum likelihood routine such as LISREL by doing the optimization with, and then without, the constraints imposed by H_0.

Again applying the theory of likelihood ratio tests yields that the statistic t_2 is asymptotically chi-squared with $8pq$ df and that the test has the standard large-sample optimality properties among all tests derived from the conditional likelihood function.

The third test, like the associated estimators, is more tractable than the first two. It arises from consideration of the conditional likelihood function $L(\mathbf{B} + \mathbf{A}, \mathbf{BA}, \Lambda \mid \mathbf{Z}_0, \mathbf{Z}_1)$ given in (3.13). Let

$$t_3 = 2 \log[L_3^* / L_3^{(0)}],$$

where L_3^* is the likelihood function evaluated at the estimators of $\mathbf{Q}_1 = \mathbf{B} + \mathbf{A}$, $\mathbf{Q}_2 = \mathbf{BA}$, and Λ given in (3.14) and $L_3^{(0)}$ is the maximum of the same function under the constraint that $\mathbf{B} + \mathbf{A}$ and $\mathbf{BA}$ are block diagonal.

A strategy for obtaining the maximum of the conditional likelihood function is outlined: under the null hypothesis the model in (2.5) can be expressed as

$$\mathbf{X}_t = \mathbf{X}_{t-1}(\mathbf{B}_{11} + \mathbf{A}_{11}) - \mathbf{X}_{t-2}\mathbf{B}_{11}\mathbf{A}_{11} + \mathbf{K}_t,$$

$$\mathbf{Y}_t = \mathbf{Y}_{t-1}(\mathbf{B}_{22} + \mathbf{A}_{22}) - \mathbf{Y}_{t-2}\mathbf{B}_{22}\mathbf{A}_{22} + \mathbf{L}_t, \quad (3.15)$$

which can be summarized in vector form as

$$\mathbf{n}_t = \mathbf{S}_t\mathbf{q} + \mathbf{f}_t, \quad (3.16)$$

where $\mathbf{n}_t$ and $\mathbf{f}_t$ are $kn \times 1$ vectors, $\mathbf{S}_t$ is $kn \times 2pq$, and $\mathbf{q}$ is a $2pq$ vector. This representation is obtained by unraveling the matrices in (3.15) in a method that preserves the regression structure. The vector $\mathbf{q}$ contains the elements of $\mathbf{B}_{11} + \mathbf{A}_{11}$ followed by the elements of $\mathbf{B}_{22} + \mathbf{A}_{22}$, $\mathbf{B}_{11}\mathbf{A}_{11}$, and $\mathbf{B}_{22}\mathbf{A}_{22}$. Let $\mathbf{\Pi}$ be the $kn \times kn$ covariance matrix of the error matrix $\mathbf{f}_t$. The covariance structure arises from the covariance matrix Λ of the error matrix $\mathbf{F}_t$ of the original model. The model in (3.16) is a multivariate version of the seemingly unrelated regressions model of econometrics (Zellner 1962; Schmidt 1976).

If $\mathbf{\Pi}$ were known the maximum estimator of $\mathbf{q}$ would be

$$\hat{\mathbf{q}} = \left(\sum_{t=2}^{T} \mathbf{S}_t\mathbf{\Pi}^{-1}\mathbf{S}_t\right)^{-1} \sum_{t=2}^{T} \mathbf{\Pi}^{-1}n_t, \quad (3.17)$$

where $\mathbf{\Pi}$ is the $kn \times kn$ covariance matrix of $\mathbf{f}_t$. To estimate $\mathbf{\Pi}$ let

$$\mathbf{q}_{LS} = \left(\sum_{t=2}^{T} \mathbf{S}_t'\mathbf{S}_t\right)^{-1} \sum_{t=2}^{T} \mathbf{S}_t'\mathbf{n}_t \quad (3.18)$$

be the least squares estimator of $\mathbf{q}$.

Define an estimator $\mathbf{Q}_{LS}$ of $\mathbf{Q}$ by letting $\mathbf{Q}_{LS}^{(1)}$ be the ^{2} elements of q_{LS} put into a $p \times p$ matrix corresponding to $\mathbf{Q}^{(1)}$. Define $\mathbf{Q}_{LS}^{(2)}$, $\mathbf{Q}_{LS}^{(3)}$, $\mathbf{Q}_{LS}^{(4)}$ similarly. Let

$$\mathbf{Q}_1^{LS} = \begin{bmatrix} \mathbf{Q}_{LS}^{(1)} & \mathbf{Q} \\ \mathbf{Q} & \mathbf{Q}_{LS}^{(2)} \end{bmatrix}, \qquad \mathbf{Q}_2^{LS} = \begin{bmatrix} \mathbf{Q}_{LS}^{(3)} & \mathbf{Q} \\ \mathbf{Q} & \mathbf{Q}_{LS}^{(4)} \end{bmatrix},$$

and $\mathbf{Q}^{LS} = (\mathbf{Q}_1^{LS}, \mathbf{Q}_2^{LS})$. Define the least squares estimator of Λ by

$$\Lambda_{LS} = (T-1)^{-1}n^{-1}\sum_{t=2}^{T} \times (\mathbf{Z}_t - \mathbf{S}_{t-1}\mathbf{Q}_{LS})'(\mathbf{Z} - \mathbf{S}_{t-1}\mathbf{Q}_{LS}) \quad (3.19)$$

in the notation of display (3.16).

The least squares estimator was used to obtain estimators that approximate the maximum likelihood estimator $\hat{\mathbf{q}}$. Let $\mathbf{\Pi}_{LS}$ be the covariance matrix obtained from Λ_{LS} as $\mathbf{\Pi}$ was from Λ. Let $\tilde{\mathbf{q}}$ be the estimator obtained by substituting $\mathbf{\Pi}_{LS}$ for $\mathbf{\Pi}$ in the expression (3.17) for $\hat{\mathbf{q}}$. Then let $\tilde{\mathbf{Q}}$ be the estimator of $\mathbf{Q}$ obtained as $\mathbf{Q}_{LS}$ was obtained but substituting $\tilde{q}$ for $\mathbf{q}_{LS}$. Finally, define $\tilde{\Lambda}$ by expression (3.19), with $\mathbf{Q}_{LS}$ replaced by $\tilde{\mathbf{Q}}$.

Applying the theory of seemingly unrelated regressions yields that the estimators $\tilde{\mathbf{Q}}$ and $\tilde{\Lambda}$ are asymptotically equivalent to the maximum likelihood estimators under the null hypothesis of no cross-effects and thus the maximum of likelihood function $L_3^{(0)}$ is approximated by the function evaluated at the estimators $\tilde{\mathbf{Q}}$ and $\tilde{\Lambda}$.

The test based on t_3 is asymptotically chi-squared with $2pq$ df and has the large-sample optimality properties among all tests generated from the conditional likelihood function given $\mathbf{Z}_0$ and $\mathbf{Z}_1$.

4. APPLICATION OF METHODS TO A PANEL STUDY

The upper management of a consortium of health maintenance organizations wants to know if there is significant correlation between patients' attitudes toward health maintenance organizations (HMO's) and their perceptions of the quality of care they are receiving from the HMO in which they are enrolled. If so, they would like to know if over time there appears to be a "causal priority" between such attitudes and perceptions. Does the patient's attitudes toward HMO's precede or "drive" his or her perceptions of the quality of the care being received? If yes, then management might want to invest resources in a campaign to improve the attitudes of the general public toward HMO's. On the other hand, if the effect over time is reversed, with the perceptions of the quality of care preceding or "driving" the attitude toward HMO's, then management may want to invest those same resources in a more focused campaign to improve the patient's perceptions of the care received.

To obtain a preliminary insight into the issue, management conducted a survey of randomly selected patients enrolled in their member HMO's. For a variety of reasons, including minimizing cost and disruption, a panel design was used. Patients were interviewed upon completion of each self-initiated visit to the HMO, the visits being considered waves. To demonstrate my methods I analyzed a subsample of 50 patients over three waves. This subsample was chosen randomly, but for the sake of simplicity patients with incomplete data or unusual health-care status (e.g., the terminally ill) were not considered for the subsample.

Two indicators of attitudes toward HMO's are used in this analysis. The first, X_1, indicates the patient's attitude toward the specific HMO in which he or she is enrolled. The second, X_2, indicates the patient's attitude toward the concept of "socialized medicine," meaning the government providing the general public a low-cost alternative to fee-for-service health-care. These variables were thought to capture two closely related dimensions in the overall attitude toward HMO's. Both variables are rescaled, in part to mask propriety data, to have mean 10 and a standard deviation of about 3, with a higher value indicating a more positive attitude.

Two perceptions of quality of health care received are included. The first, Y_1, indicates the perception of the quality of care received in the visit just concluded, and the second, Y_2, indicates the perception of the quality of care received since initial enrollment. The two variables, although related, were thought to capture different issues of quality of care. Again the variables were scaled to have mean of 10 and standard deviation of about 3, with a higher value indicating a more positive perception.

The results begin with some evidence that for the example at hand the three methods of inference—unconditional, conditioned on the first wave, and conditioned on the first two waves—produce very similar results. In Appendix A are the results obtained by applying the 3 methods to a simple 2-variable submodel that included 20 patients and the 2 variables X_1 and Y_1.

I chose a submodel and a subsample because for the unconditional likelihood function the computations for the full 4-variable model with 50 observations exceeded the limited capacity to do numerical optimization. The estimates of the sum $\mathbf{B} + \mathbf{A}$ of the matrix of regression coefficients and the matrix of autoregressive parameters are presented, as are the tests for the presence of the cross-effects. Noting that the methods produce similar results, I chose to use the two conditional methods for the full analysis and to report the results of only one method in cases for which the two produced similar results.

Appendix B displays some correlations for the raw data. The correlation matrix shows that there is some relationship between the two indicators of the attitude toward HMO's ($r = .38$) but little marginal relationship between the two pairs of measurements. The multiple correlations indicate that the attitudes and perceptions of time t are well predicted by the attitudes and perceptions at time $t - 1$. The comparison between the multiple correlation and serial correlations indicates that the majority of this predictability can be attributed to the relationship between a measurement at time $t - 1$ and the same measurement at time t. For each variable the serial correlation is within .02 of the multiple correlation. Along with these summary statistics the usual data descriptive methods (histograms, box plots, stem and leaf plots, and others) were used to examine the shapes of the distributions of the measurements. All were quite symmetric and fairly Gaussian, with no significant outliers.

Appendix C gives estimates of the autoregressive parameter matrices derived from the two informal methods described in Section 3. The maximum likelihood estimates of the standard errors of the estimates are given for the second method. The estimated autoregressive coefficients for each variable and the ratio of these coefficients to their estimated standard errors are large enough to convince us that serial correlation in the errors cannot be ignored. For the sake of completeness I computed the likelihood ratio test for the hypothesis of no serial correlation developed by Mayer and Carroll (1986) and got a value of 58.63 for a statistic that is asymptotically chi-squared with 26 df (the .01 level critical value is 45.64). I conclude that serial correlation is present in the error structure.

Appendix D displays estimates of $\mathbf{B} + \mathbf{A}$ and $\mathbf{BA}$ obtained from the conditional likelihood function (given $\mathbf{Z}_0$ and $\mathbf{Z}_1$). The ratios of the estimated coefficients to their estimated standard errors are also given. Noting that marginally these ratios are approximately t random variables, there is strong evidence that the attitudes and perceptions are fairly stable over time. For the off-diagonal coefficients the only ratio larger than 2 in absolute value is within the set of indicators of attitude toward HMO's. It suggests that over time a patient's attitude toward socialized medicine is significantly related to his or her attitude toward the HMO in which he is enrolled. But this within-pairs cross-effect is not an indicator of the temporal relationship between the attitudes and the perceptions. The other ratios suggest that there may be no significant feedback between attitudes toward HMO's and the perceptions of quality of care received. To explore the issues of cross-effects more fully, the standardized coefficients from the conditional analysis are also displayed. These coefficients, which indicate the change in standardized units of the dependent variable given a one-standardized-unit change in the predictor variable, also suggest that the cross-effects are quite small.

Appendix D also displays estimates of the covariance matrices $\mathbf{\Lambda}$ and $\mathbf{\Sigma}_0$. Note the drastic difference between the two. This difference is expected since the initial wave is modeled in terms of only a mean and covariance matrix and thus without regression structure. This difference is the critical factor in the decision to shy away from automatically assuming stationarity.

Appendix E presents the tests for the presence of effects and cross-effects. The first test shows that the model does have temporal structure. The likelihood ratio test statistic, which is asymptotically chi-squared with

32 df, has a value of 756, quite strong evidence against the hypothesis of independence of the measurements across waves.

The issue is whether this structure across waves is in part due to the cross-effects between the attitudes and perceptions. The likelihood ratio statistic for the hypothesis of no cross-effects suggests not. It is asymptotically chi-squared with 16 df and issues a value of 20.22.

I conclude that the attitudes and perceptions have very strong temporal effects in both the measurements and in the errors but that these effects are primarily attributable to the stability of these attitudes and perceptions. For the most part they are not attributable to the cross-effects between the attitudes and the perceptions. Simply stated, there is little evidence that either pair of variables affects the other.

Appendix F displays the estimators and tests that are obtained if the serial correlation in the model is ignored and the independent error model is fit to the data and used for hypothesis testing. Note that the estimate of **B** is analogous to the estimate of **B** + **A** in the model with serially correlated errors. The estimates of cross-effects are somewhat smaller than they were with serially correlated errors. The likelihood ratio test statistic for the presence of cross-effects in the model with independent errors is (nominally) asymptotically chi-squared with 8 df and has a value of 45.30, fairly strong evidence that cross-effects are present. Thus by ignoring the serial correlation in the model the estimates of the cross-effects are made smaller but the alleged evidence in support of the presence of cross-effects is increased significantly. This increase in evidence is in part due to the fact that the cross-effects are capturing some of the effect that would be attributed to the autoregressive parameters if such parameters were included.

5. DISCUSSION

The use of the cross-lagged panel model in social and business research is increased and the results are enhanced by the incorporation of realistic assumptions about the behavior of variables over time, including the behavior of the errors. The assumption that the errors for a single replication or sampling unit are independent over waves, an assumption required for the use of the classical multiple regression methods, is not likely to hold for most social and economic variables. For example, if a voter at a given time has more liberal political attitudes than would be predicted from his or her income, then he or she is likely to have the same liberal bias and the same income a week or month later. In general, very few social variables, measured or unmeasured, have a random pattern over time. Dependence of measurements and residuals seem particularly likely if attitudes, perceptions, or social or economic behaviors are being observed. A large part of modern econometrics deals with removing the assumption of independent errors from models of economic behavior over time.

The results presented are intended to help develop cross-lagged panel models beyond the independent error formulation. They are products of an ongoing project that concentrates on incorporating more realistic assumptions into the cross-lagged panel model. They are both extensions of the work of social methodologists on the analysis of continuous variable panel data and an application of results in multivariate statistics to a common modeling problem of applied social and business research.

The autoregressive error structure presented is only one structure capable of modeling temporal dependence in the errors of a linear model. A second method of allowing dependence in the error structure was formulated by econometricians for the univariate continuous variable panel model (e.g., Balestra and Nerlove 1966; Maddala 1971; Wallace and Hussain 1969). In this formulation the error for a given observation can be decomposed into the sum of a pure error and a replication effect. The replication effect captures the tendency for sampling units (subjects) that are above the regression line at the first wave to stay above the regression line across waves. My work with business data has convinced me that this error structure is often more realistic than the independent error structure and is a viable competitor to the serial correlated structure.

Anderson and Tsiao (1981; 1982) studied the problem of estimating the parameters of the univariate panel model with this decomposable error. I am currently extending their results to the multivariate model and considering the problem of distinguishing between errors that are serially correlated and errors that are decomposable.

ACKNOWLEDGMENTS

I gratefully acknowledge the help of colleagues and students. Discussions with T. W. Anderson, D. R. Rogosa, and S. S. Carroll and correspondence with D. Dickey were particularly fruitful. I also acknowledge the comments of the editor and referees, which contributed significantly to this revision of an earlier draft.

APPENDIX A: HMO EXAMPLE—INFERENCES FOR THE TWO-VARIABLE SUBMODEL (X_1, Y_1)

A.1 Estimates of Q_1 = B + A

Unconditional estimate: .87, −.11, −.11, .59

Conditional (on Z_0) estimate: .81, −.10, −.11, .58

Conditional (on Z_0 and Z_1) estimate: .80, −.10, −.11, .59

A.2 Hypothesis Tests for Presence of Cross-Effects (H_0: $B_{12} = B_{21} = 0$)

Unconditional: t_1 = 9.39, asymptotically chi-squared, df = 2

Conditional on $\mathbf{Z}_0$: t_2 = 10.40, asymptotically chi-squared, df = 4

Conditional on $\mathbf{Z}_1$, $\mathbf{Z}_2$: t_3 = 6.85, asymptotically chi-squared, df = 2

APPENDIX B: HMO EXAMPLE—CORRELATION STATISTICS FOR THE RAW DATA

B.1 Correlation Matrix for Raw Data

$$\begin{bmatrix} 1.00 & .38 & .20 & .20 \\ & 1.00 & .12 & .05 \\ & & 1.00 & .38 \\ & & & 1.00 \end{bmatrix}$$

B.2 Multiple Correlations

X_1: .96, X_2: .88, Y_1: .95, Y_2: .72

B.3 Serial Correlations

X_1: .94, X_2: .87, Y_1: .93, Y_2: .70

APPENDIX C: HMO EXAMPLE—ESTIMATES OF THE AUTOREGRESSIVE PARAMETERS

C.1 Estimates From Pooled Least Squares Residuals

A: .33, .20, .00, .06, .21, .42, .03, .10, .01, .11, .41, .14, .07, .10, .26, .36

C.2 Diagonal Blocks Estimated From Partitioned Model

$\mathbf{A}_{11}$: .36, .21, .19, .43
$\mathbf{A}_{22}$: .39, .11, .10, .35

Estimated standard errors.
$\mathbf{A}_{11}$: .07, .08, .08, .09
$\mathbf{A}_{22}$: .14, .06, .07, .12

C.3 Likelihood Ratio Test for Serial Correlation

t = 58.63, asymptotically chi-squared, df = 26

APPENDIX D: HMO EXAMPLE—ESTIMATES OF THE REGRESSION PARAMETER MATRICES

D.1 Estimates of the Parameter Matrices

B + **A**: 1.57, .34, .03, −.11, −.16, .66, .19, .11, −.09, −.06, .99, .13, .04, .00, .01, .79

BA: .62, .42, .03, −.07, .06, .18, −.13, −.15, −.13, −.19, .19, .19, −.06, .00, −.03, .08

(From the conditional analysis given $\mathbf{Z}_0$ and $\mathbf{Z}_1$.)

D.2 Ratio of Estimates to the Estimated Standard Errors

B + **A**: 9.46, 2.37, .26, −1.10, −.64, 3.06, 1.01, .78, −.69, −.55, 9.46, 1.58, .10, .02, −.02, 3.84

BA: 4.59, 3.08, .33, −.79, .32, .87, −1.01, −1.06, −1.15, −1.05, 2.63, .14, −.21, .00, .14, .39

(From the conditional analysis given $\mathbf{Z}_0$ and $\mathbf{Z}_1$.)

D.3 Estimates of the Covariance Matrices

Λ: .62, −.24, −.22, −.21, .79, .15, .15, .94, −.15, 1.6

$\mathbf{\Sigma}_0$: 21.47, 6.73, 8.39, 4.13, 1.81, 13.71, 4.20, .82, 3.80, 5.96

(From the conditional analysis given $\mathbf{Z}_0$.)

D.4 Standardized Regression Coefficients

B + **A**: 1.97, −.25, −.18, .06, .30, .72, −.08, −.01, .03, .20, 1.24, −.01, −.08 .10, .13, .74

BA: .96, −.13, −.29, −.12, .40, −.22, −.17, 0, .30, .20, .33, .04, −.06, .15, .23, .08

(From the conditional analysis given $\mathbf{Z}_0$.)

APPENDIX E: HMO EXAMPLE—TESTING FOR THE PRESENCE OF CROSS-EFFECTS

E.1 Likelihood Ratio Rest for Presence of Any Temporal Effects (H_0: B = A = 0)

t = 756.10, asymptotic chi-squared, df = 32

E.2 Maximum Likelihood Estimates Under the Hypothesis of No Cross-Effects

B + **A**: 1.50, .30, 0, 0, −.16, .72, 0, 0, 0, 0, .99, .05, 0, 0, −.05, .76

BA: .56, .37, 0, 0, −.05, .12, 0, 0, 0, 0, .17, −.09, 0, 0, .03, .02

E.3 Likelihood Ratio Test for Presence of Cross-Effects

t_3 = 20.22, asymptotic chi-squared, df = 16

APPENDIX F: HMO EXAMPLE—INFERENCES IF SERIAL CORRELATION IGNORED

F.1 Estimates of Parameter Matrix

B: .79, −.04, −.03, −.03, −.06, .87, 0, .02, .03, 0, .65, .03, .01, .01, .01, .72

F.2 Ratio of Estimates to Estimated Standard Errors

B: 31.32, −1.06, −1.05, −.56, −1.97, 20.00, .12, −.34, 1.20, .15, 20.59, .67, .19, .11, .13, 9.71

F.3 Likelihood Ratio Test of Presence of Effects

t = 1870, asymptotic chi-squared, df = 16

F.4 Likelihood Ratio Test of Presence of Cross-Effects

t = 45.30, asymptotic chi-squared, df = 8

[*Received January 1985. Revised January 1986.*]

REFERENCES

Anderson, T. W. (1978), "Repeated Measures on Autoregressive Processes," *Journal of the American Statistical Association*, 73, 371–378.

Anderson, T. W., and Tsiao, C. (1981), "Estimation of Dynamic Models With Error Components," *Journal of the American Statistical Association*, 76, 598–606.

——— (1982), "Formulation and Estimation of Dynamic Models Using Panel Data," *Journal of Econometrics*, 18, 47–82.

Balestra, P., and Nerlove, M. (1966), "Pooling Cross-Section and Time Series Data in the Estimation of a Dynamic Model: The Demand for Natural Gas," *Econometrica*, 34, 585–612.

Campbell, D. T. (1963), "From Description to Experimentation: Interpreting Trends as Quasi-experiments," in *Problems in the Measurement of Change*, ed. C. W. Harris, Madison: University of Wisconsin Press, pp. 212–254.

Cox, D. R., and Hinkley, D. V. (1974), *Theoretical Statistics*, London: Chapman & Hall.

Crano, W. D., Kenny, D. A., and Campbell, D. T. (1972), "Does Intelligence Cause Achievement: A Cross-Lagged Panel Analysis," *Journal of Educational Psychology*, 63, 258–275.

Dickey, D. A., Hasza, D. P., and Fuller, W. A. (1984), "Testing for Unit Roots in Seasonal Time Series," *Journal of the American Statistical Association*, 79, 355–367.

Duncan, O. D. (1969), "Some Linear Models for Two-Wave, Two-Variable Panel Analysis," *Psychological Bulletin*, 72, 177–182.

Eaton, W. (1978), "Life Events, Social Supports, and Psychiatric Symptoms," *Journal of Health and Social Behavior*, 19, 230–234.

Frey, R. (1984), "Does *n*-Achievement Cause Economic Development? A Cross-Lagged Analysis of the McClelland Thesis," *Journal of Social Psychology*, 122, 67–70.

Greenberg, D. F., Kessler, R. C., and Logan, C. H. (1979), "A Panel Model of Crime Rates and Arrest Rates," *American Sociological Review*, 44, 843–850.

Hannan, M. T., and Young, A. A. (1977), "Estimation in Panel Models: Results on Pooling Cross-Sections and Time Series," in *Sociological Methodology, 1977*, ed. D. Heise, San Francisco: Jossey-Bass, pp. 52–83.

Heise, D. (1970), "Causal Inference From Panel Data," in *Sociological Methodology, 1970*, eds. E. Borgatta and G. Bohrnstedt, San Francisco: Jossey-Bass, pp. 3–27.

Johnston, J. (1972), *Econometric Methods* (2nd ed.), New York: McGraw-Hill.

Judge, G., Griffiths, W., Hill, A., Lee, T. (1980), *The Theory and Practice of Econometrics*, New York: John Wiley.

Kessler, R. C., and Greenberg, D. F. (1981), *Linear Panel Analysis: Models of Quantitative Change*, New York: Academic Press.

Lazarsfeld, P. F. (1948), "The Use of Panels in Social Research," in *Continuities in the Language of Social Research*, ed. P. F. Lazarsfeld, New York: Free Press, pp. 330–337.

Maddala, G. S. (1971), "The Use of Variance Components Models in Pooling Cross-Section and Time Series Data," *Econometrica*, 39, 341–358.

Malinvaud, E. (1980), *Statistical Methods of Econometrics*, Amsterdam: North-Holland.

Markus, G. (1979), *Analyzing Panel Data*, Beverly Hills, CA: Sage Publications.

Mayer, L. S. (1985), "Statistical Inferences in Cross-Lagged Panel Studies," technical report, Stanford University, Dept. of Statistics.

Mayer, L. S., and Carroll, S. S. (1986), "Detecting Serial Correlation in the Error Structure of a Cross-Lagged Panel Model," *Communications in Statistics*, 15, 345–366.

Pelz, D. C., and Andrews, F. M. (1964), "Detecting Causal Priorities in Panel Study Data," *American Sociological Review*, 29, 836–848.

Polachek, S., and McCutcheon, E. (1983), "Union Effects on Employment Stability: A Comparison of Panel Versus Cross-Sectional Data," *Journal of Labor*, 4, 273–285.

Rogosa, D. R. (1980), "A Critique of Cross-Lagged Correlation," *Psychological Bulletin*, 88, 245–258.

Schmidt, P. (1976), *Econometrics*, New York: Marcel Dekker.

Wallace, T., and Hussain, A. (1969), "The Use of Error Components Models in Combining Cross Section With Time Series Data," *Econometrica*, 37, 55–72.

Zellner, A. (1962), "An Efficient Method of Estimating Seemingly Unrelated Regressions and Tests for Aggregation Bias," *Journal of the American Statistical Association*, 57, 348–368.

[25]

Panel Data and Labor Market Studies
J. Hartog, G. Ridder and J. Theeuwes (eds.)

TIME-SERIES AND CROSS-SECTIONAL ESTIMATES ON PANEL DATA : WHY ARE THEY DIFFERENT AND WHY SHOULD THEY BE EQUAL ?

Jacques MAIRESSE

ENSAE et EHESS
Paris, France

1. INTRODUCTION

One of the oldest problem in econometrics is the appearance of important differences between cross-sectional and time-series estimates. However, in the past, these two types of estimates were not usually found in the same studies and they were not based on the same data sources. Typically the cross-sectional estimates were performed on individual observations from household or firm surveys, and the time-series estimates were obtained from the aggregate numbers in the national accounts. The discrepancies that these estimates revealed could, therefore, be accounted for reasons related to the particular features of the models, aggregation issues, the definition and measurement of the variables, or the characteristics of the samples.

With the advent of panel data econometrics, the problem has become much more acute. One cannot explain away so easily the disparities between estimates computed from the cross-sectional and time-series dimensions of the data, such as the estimates respectively known as the "between" and "within" estimates (more precisely, between-individuals and within-individual estimates). These estimates arise now from the same body of data within the framework of the same study. If one makes the basic assumptions about the exogeneity of the explanatory variables in standard regression models (i.e. that they are independent of or uncorrelated with the numerous unobserved or unknown factors, which are summarized by the error terms in the equations), the between and the within estimates, as well as the straightforward "total" ordinary least-squares estimates combining them, should all be consistent, and one would expect that their differences would be statistically insignificant.

In this note, I shall briefly review some of the reasons why these differences are often very significant, and suggest that there is no general nor clear support for the preference usually given to the time-series type estimates relatively to the cross-sectional ones. I shall also reconsider why econometricians think it is important after all that the two types of estimates should be equal. In order to be more specific and motivate some of these reflections, I present various Cobb-Douglas production functions estimates based on three samples of large manufacturing firms in France, Japan and the United States over the period 1967-79. The definition of some of the most common and simple estimators in panel data econometrics is relegated in Appendix 1. An idea of the biases which may arise in these estimators from random errors in variables is given in Appendix 2.

2. A PRODUCTION FUNCTION ILLUSTRATION

The disparities that can occur between cross-sectional and time-series estimates are illustrated in Table I. This table presents the estimates which we obtain for the elasticity of capital α, assuming a simple Cobb-Douglas production function with and without constant returns to scale, and using our three comparable panels of French, Japanese and American firms. In the case of the non constant returns to scale specification, it gives also the corresponding estimates of the elasticity of scale μ (μ=1 under constant returns to scale). We can compare the six types of estimates mentioned in Appendix 1 : total, between and within both in levels and in differences. The discrepancies between these estimates are indeed striking, and particularly so when we do not impose constant returns to scale.

In fact the estimates go roughly two by two, and we can distinguish three groups. First of all, the total and between estimates in levels (TL and BL) indicate constant returns to scale (or slightly decreasing returns) and an elasticity of capital on the order of 0.30 for France, 0.45 for Japan and 0.20 for the United States. Next, the within estimates in levels and the between estimates in differences (WL and BD) are on the order of 0.15 to 0.20 for the elasticity of capital in France and in the United States, of 0.20 to 0.35 in Japan, and show decreasing returns of -0.10 to -0.15 for the first two countries and of -0.25 to -0.30

TABLE I : ALTERNATIVE ESTIMATES OF PRODUCTION FUNCTION ELASTICITIES

REGRESSIONS		LEVELS			DIFFERENCES		
		Total TL	Between BL	Within WL	Total TD	Between BD	Within WD
FRANCE 1967-79	$\hat{\alpha}$	0,303 (0,009)	0,313 (0,031)	0,196 (0,011)	0,260 (0,014)	0,163 (0,039)	0,266 (0,014)
N = 441 T = 13	$\hat{\sigma}$	0,362	0,338	0,133	0,122	0,024	0,119
	R^2	0,174	0,192	0,052	0,064	0,038	0,066
	$\hat{\alpha}$	0,304 (0,009)	0,315 (0,031)	0,146 (0,012)	0,061 (0,018)	0,147 (0,039)	0,010 (0,019)
	$\hat{\mu}$-1	-0,018 (0,004)	-0,017 (0,014)	-0,152 (0,011)	-0,386 (0,023)	-0,118 (0,033)	-0,474 (0,026)
	$\hat{\sigma}$	0,362	0,337	0,131	0,118	0,024	0,115
	R^2	0,117	0,195	0,080	0,113	0,065	0,122
JAPAN 1967-79	$\hat{\alpha}$	0,452 (0,007)	0,469 (0,023)	0,278 (0,009)	0,183 (0,010)	0,359 (0,029)	0,170 (0,010)
N = 845 T = 13	$\hat{\sigma}$	0,375	0,343	0,148	0,118	0,026	0,115
	R^2	0,292	0,326	0,082	0,031	0,151	0,026
	$\hat{\alpha}$	0,453 (0,007)	0,469 (0,025)	0,204 (0,009)	0,011 (0,012)	0,322 (0,028)	-0,043 (0,012)
	$\hat{\mu}$-1	-0,002 (0,003)	0,000 (0,012)	-0,280 (0,009)	-0,437 (0,017)	-0,237 (0,026)	-0,519 (0,018)
	$\hat{\sigma}$	0,375	0,343	0,142	0,114	0,025	0,111
	R^2	0,292	0,326	0,154	0,094	0,230	0,096
UNITED STATES 1967-79	$\hat{\alpha}$	0,221 (0,007)	0,222 (0,024)	0,213 (0,008)	0,289 (0,009)	0,178 (0,030)	0,294 (0,009)
	$\hat{\sigma}$	0,286	0,266	0,106	0,099	0,019	0,097
N = 462 T = 13	R^2	0,154	0,163	0,096	0,149	0,073	0,153
	$\hat{\alpha}$	0,238 (0,007)	0,242 (0,023)	0,162 (0,009)	0,090 (0,012)	0,150 (0,030)	0,049 (0,013)
	$\hat{\mu}$-1	-0,043 (0,003)	-0,042 (0,009)	-0,112 (0,008)	-0,360 (0,015)	-0,093 (0,023)	-0,435 (0,017)
	$\hat{\sigma}$	0,280	0,261	0,104	0,094	0,019	0,091
	R^2	0,190	0,202	0,124	0,226	0,105	0,243

for the last. Finally, the total and within estimates in differences (TD and WD) give elasticities of capital of about 0.20 to 0.30, if we impose constant returns to scale ; however, if we do not, they indicate very weak or almost null elasticities of capital (smaller than 0.10) with strongly decreasing returns to scale (-0.35 to -0.50). The fact that the total and between estimates in levels are extremely close, results from the much larger share of the between variability in the total variability when we consider levels (or the logarithms of levels). Conversely the closeness of the total and within estimates in differences results from the much larger share of the within variability in the total variability when taking first differences (or annual rates of growth). There is no simple explanation, however, for the proximity of the within estimates in levels and the between ones in differences.

Figure 1 displays the six types of estimates from Table 1 for the non constant returns specification (taking the estimated capital and scale elasticities α and μ as the y and x variables respectively). It shows clearly that the disparities between the various estimates (for a given country) can be in fact larger than the differences between countries (for a given type of estimate). It shows also most clearly that these disparities follow a quite comparable pattern for the three country samples, which strongly suggests that they may arise from the same systematic biases. One would have first to elucidate the nature of such biases in order to assess the true magnitudes of the parameters and to be sure that the estimated differences between countries are real.

3. POSSIBLE REASONS FOR THE OBSERVED DISPARITIES

In fact, when confronted with disparities such as the ones we have just seen, econometricians have most often taken the view that the within estimator (or covariance estimator) was the proper one for the error components regression model, considering that the between estimator was largely biased [1]. The individual error term u_i in the regression is thought to represent specific factors that are possibly correlated with the explanatory variables. Such correlations will result in a bias of the between estimate in levels, but will not affect the within estimate in levels as well as the estimates in first differences (since u_i cancels out in the expression of these estimates). In the

FIGURE 1

ALTERNATIVE ESTIMATES OF THE ELASTICITY OF CAPITAL $\hat{\alpha}$
AND THE ELASTICITY OF SCALE $\hat{\mu}$
FOR THE FRENCH, JAPANESE AND AMERICAN SAMPLES

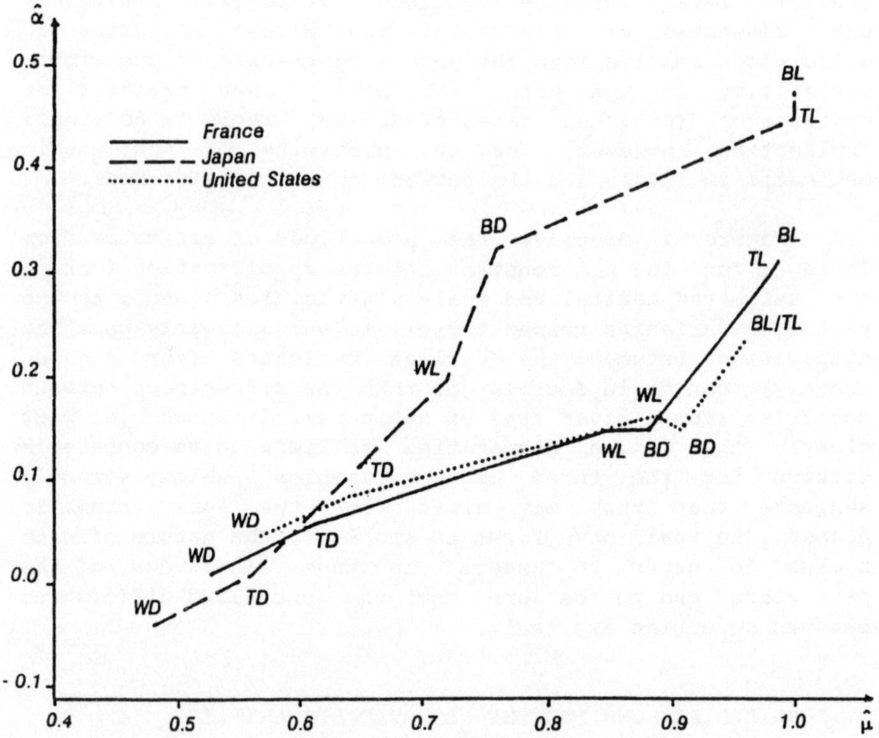

From the upper left to the bottom right of the graph, the estimates are the following :

BL. Between in levels : $(y_{i.})$
TL. Total in levels : (y_{it})
BD. Between in differences : $(\Delta y_{i.})$
WL. Within in levels : $(y_{it} - y_{i.})$
TD. Total in differences : (Δy_{it})
WD. Within in differences : $(\Delta y_{it} - \Delta y_{i.})$

context of the production function, u_i corresponds to differences in the quality of management of firms and in the characteristics of their environment. One would expect that these factors matter in their investment and employment decisions and that they would be positively correlated with their capital-labor ratios, thus accounting for an upward bias in the between and total estimates in levels of capital elasticity.

However, there exist also good reasons why the individual time-varying error term ε_{it} should be correlated with the explanatory variables in the regression, and hence why the within estimate in levels and the estimates in differences should be biased [2]. The between estimate in levels will be much less affected by these correlations (since ε_{it} is averaged in the between regression and is practically wiped out for large enough T). In the case of the production function, ε_{it} corresponds in particular to short-term changes in the hours of work (and work effort) and in the utilization rates of equipment. Such changes are not taken into account by our measures of labor and capital (i.e. the total number of employees and gross book values respectively), and they are not fully reflected in the industry year dummies included in our regressions (to the extent they are unsynchronized across firms). Under certain conditions, this would result in a downward bias of the within estimate in levels and of the estimates in differences of capital elasticity. Other specification errors related to the form of the production function (for example, the omission of intermediate goods) or to the simultaneity of production and factor demand decisions, are also likely to lead to a reduction of these same estimates (and of the corresponding estimates of scale elasticity).

Such explanations should encourage us to improve our models of the production function and of the firm behavior ; however, they are not perhaps the most relevant. Measurement errors in variables seem to provide a rather simple and plausible cause for the observed disparities. If these errors are not systematic but more or less random (and not serially correlated) from one year to another, the transformation of the data in "between" (i.e. in terms of individual means) tend to minimize their importance and thus to reduce the corresponding downward biases in the estimated parameters. On the contrary, going "within" (i.e. considering the deviations of the data to the individual means), or even more so taking first differences, tend to magnify the variability of random errors (relatively to that of the variables) and thus to increase the parameters underestimation. Errors in the measurement of the capital-labor ratio variable might thus roughly account for the pattern of the disparities that we find for the estimates of capital elasticity. Details about this line of interpretation are given in Appendix 2.

Finally, the a priori expectations that one has on the true values of the estimated parameters are important, independently of the plausibility that one can attach to the various possible specification biases. In our analysis of the production function (but this is true also for other econometric studies in differents contexts), the within estimates in levels and the estimates in differences that we obtain for the capital and scale elasticities appear more or less unlikely, or even incredible ; on the contrary the between estimates seem relatively reasonable.

4. WHY DO WE WANT TIME-SERIES AND CROSS-SECTIONAL ESTIMATES TO BE EQUAL ?

One may think in a more fundamental way about the reasons why econometricians hope or wish that the estimates of their models would be equal in the time-series and cross-sectional dimensions of their data. Three connected reasons (or three aspects of a more general underlying reason) can be provided.

The first reason proceeds directly from the need of forecasting and the aim of understanding, which are the two main concerns of econometric modeling. From what one learns in comparing different situations at a given time, it is tempting to infer what have been or will be (or could have been or could be) the evolutions over time of these situations. Such method is usual in many scientific fields besides economics. Its interest remains with the availability of panel data. To ignore the cross-sectional dimension of panel data and to consider only the time-series dimension would in fact be tantamount to neglecting an important, frequently even predominant, part of the available information. The number of years (or number of periods) in panel data sets may be quite small, and in general the number of individual units (firms or households) is much larger. Furthermore, the dispersion of the changes over time in the (level) variables is usually very small in comparison with the dispersion of differences across individuals.

The second reason deepens the first. It follows from the necessity for the econometrician to rely, with very few exceptions, on non-experimental data, when he wants to validate the models suggested by theories and prior knowledge and to assess the values of their important parameters. For that he must be able to admit that the error terms entering the models, which subsume their inevitable approximations or imperfections (true disturbances, unknown or neglected variables, measurement and modeling errors), can be viewed as being random, and he must be able to suppose that some of the explanatory variables that he explicitly takes into account (but cannot control) are exogenous (i.e uncorrelated with the error terms, or in practice weakly correlated with them). These assumptions legitimate the application of statistical methods, and they allow, in particular, the construction of unbiased or consistent estimators of the parameters of interest. Thus it is in order to comply with the basic requirements of econometric inference, that one has to find an agreement between the necessary hypotheses and the available data, whether these data are cross-sections or time-series. It seems also rather "natural", when studying panel data, that one would want to reach such an agreement in both of these dimensions. In other words, one will consider that in a well specified model the explanatory variables (or some of them) may be exogenous in both the cross-sectional and time-series dimensions, these two dimensions providing the "equivalent" of two different "designs of experiments". Contrary to some intuition, when one thinks carefully about it, the conditions for "experimental equivalence" do not seem to be satisfied more readily in analyses of changes over time than in analyses of individual differences. One must question these conditions for each specific model and for each body of data, without really having any general clue about their validity.

The third reason derives from the second, and is of a heuristic nature. Finding that the cross-sectional and time-series estimates of a model are close enough can be considered as an important evidence of a good specification of a model. Conversely, finding significant disparities between the two types of estimates is an indication of the existence of one or several errors of specification. It is thus an inducement to investigate what may be these errors of specification and to improve the initial model. More generally, in recent years, the theory of specification tests has developed on the basis of the comparison of estimators which should be consistent if the assumptions of the model are satisfied (and different if some of them are not). When one has some knowledge about the errors of specification involved or (and) if one is ready to make additional hypotheses about them, it becomes possible to go one step further and to check whether they can actually account for the sign and order of magnitude of the observed discrepancies between estimators. If this is the case, one may retrieve some more information about these errors of specification, and in the end enrich the model [3].

Such approach is attractive in principle ; it is, however, difficult in practice. The possible errors of specification may be numerous and in general one knows very little about them. Futhermore, they may not be very interesting in themselves (measurement errors, for example), although they can greatly affect the estimates of the parameters of interest. That is why the actual attitude of econometricians is rather diverse and more or less ambitious. They may consider only the time-series estimates and ignore the cross-sectional ones, looking for reasons to prefer the former and to discard the latter (rather than trying to reconcile them). They may give largely intuitive economic interpretations to the different estimates, for example in terms of "permanent effects" for the cross-sectional estimates and of "transitory effects" for the time-series ones [4]. They may also investigate in various ways the robustness of the different estimates and try to find out what would be the orders of magnitude of their possible biases under more or less plausible assumptions. Finally, the view that the estimates should be equal appears as an ideal requirement, one which may be difficult to meet, but one which is nonetheless fruitful to pursue.

APPENDIX 1 : VARIOUS USUAL ESTIMATORS IN PANEL DATA ECONOMETRICS

The random effects or error components regression model, frequently used in panel data econometrics, can be written as

(1 TL) $$y_{it} = \alpha x_{it} + a + (u_i + \varepsilon_{it})$$

in the simplest case of only one independent variable x explaining the dependent variable y, with i=1 to N and t=1 to T, where i denotes the ith individual and t the tth year. α is the parameter of interest and a the overall constant. The special feature of this regression is that the total disturbance is made up of two components : a random effect u_i specific to the individual and a general individual time-varying error ε_{it}, such that $E(u_i) = E(\varepsilon_{it}) = 0$ and $E(u_i \varepsilon_{it}) = 0$. The basic standard assumption is that of exogeneity : $E(u_i x_{it}) = E(\varepsilon_{it} x_{it}) = 0$.

In the production function example given in the text, this simple regression corresponds to the Cobb-Douglas specification with constant returns to scale in log linear form, y being the logarithm of labor productivity (measured by deflated sales per person) and x being the logarithm of the capital-labor ratio (measured by gross book values adjusted for inflation per person). α is the output elasticity of capital. The specification with non constant returns is obtained by adding another term $(\mu-1)z_{it}$ in the equation, where z is the logarithm of the labor variable (measured by the total number of employees) and μ is the elasticity of scale parameter. Actually the variables have been first centered relatively to their industry year means, which is equivalent to including industry year dummies in the regressions.

Besides the regression (1) or "total" regression based on the untransformed observations, it is interesting to consider the "within" and "between" regressions which can be regarded intuitively as being performed in the cross-sectional and the time-series dimensions of the data. These two regressions can be written respectively :

(1 BL) $$y_{i.} = \alpha x_{i.} + a + (u_i + \varepsilon_{i.})$$

(1 WL) $y_{it} - y_{i.} = \alpha(x_{it} - x_{i.}) + (\varepsilon_{it} - \varepsilon_{i.})$

where $y_{i.} = 1/T \sum_{t=1}^{T} y_{it}$ are the individual means (and $y_{..} = 1/N \sum_{i=1}^{N} y_{i.}$ is the general mean).

The between regression is performed on the average cross-section (i.e. on $y_{i.}$ and $x_{i.}$, i=1 to N) and the within regression can be interpreted as an average of the N regressions (i=1 to N) made on the individual time-series (i.e. on $(y_{it} - y_{i.})$ and $(x_{it} - x_{i.})$, t = 1 to T). The between regression is based only on the interindividual differences of the variables, while the within regression bears only on the intraindividual changes of the variables.

Under the assumption of exogeneity for both error components, the least squares estimates performed on all three regressions are consistent and should not exhibit significant disparities :

(2 TL) $\hat{\alpha}_{TL} = \sum_{i=1}^{N} \sum_{t=1}^{T} (y_{it}-y_{..})(x_{it}-x_{..}) \;/\; \sum_{i=1}^{N} \sum_{t=1}^{T} (x_{it}-x_{..})^2$

(2 BL) $\hat{\alpha}_{BL} = \sum_{i=1}^{N} (y_{i.}-y_{..})(x_{i.}-x_{..}) \;/\; \sum_{i=1}^{N} (x_{i.}-x_{..})^2$

(2 WL) $\hat{\alpha}_{WL} = \sum_{i=1}^{N} \sum_{t=1}^{T} (y_{it}-y_{i.})(x_{it}-x_{i.}) \;/\; \sum_{i=1}^{N} \sum_{t=1}^{T} (x_{it}-x_{i.})^2$

and $\text{plim}\ \hat{\alpha}_{TL} = \text{plim}\ \hat{\alpha}_{BL} = \text{plim}\ \hat{\alpha}_{WL} = \alpha$ when $N \longrightarrow \infty$.

Although this attracts perhaps less attention, one frequently finds discrepancies of a comparable nature to the between and within disparities when one compares estimates obtained from variables normally in levels to those performed on their first differences. The total regression (1TL) (supposedly expressed in the levels of the variables) can also be written in first differences :

(3 TD) $y_{it} - y_{it-1} = \alpha\ (x_{it} - x_{it-1}) + \varepsilon_{it} - \varepsilon_{it-1}$

and the least squares estimates based on this new regression (total regression in differences) should also be consistent :

$$(4\ \text{TD})\quad \hat{\alpha}_{TD} = \sum_{i=1}^{N}\sum_{t=1}^{T}(y_{it}-y_{it-1})(x_{it}-x_{it-1}) / \sum_{i=1}^{N}\sum_{t=1}^{T}(x_{it}-x_{it-1})^2$$

and $\text{plim}\ \hat{\alpha}_{TD} = \alpha$ when $N \to \infty$.

It is interesting to combine the first difference transformation, and the between and within ones, leading to two other regressions and two new estimates, which are also consistent in principle. The between regression in differences (BD) is performed on the individual mean differences (or equivalently on the "long differences").The within regression in differences (WD) is based on the deviations of the year differences from these mean differences.

If the levels variables are in logarithms, as in the case of our production function example, the first differences correspond to the (log) annual rates of growth. Hence the between regression in differences is performed on the individual average growth rates and the within one on the deviations of the annual growth rates from the average growth rates.

APPENDIX 2 : ERRORS IN VARIABLES BIASES AND USUAL ESTIMATORS IN PANEL DATA ECONOMETRICS

If we consider that the explanatory variable x in the simple error components regression model is affected by a random error of measurement, it is easy to show that the six types of estimates presented in Appendix 1 : total, within and between in levels and first differences, are biased in different proportions. More precisely if the error e_{it} in the observed (value of the) variable x_{it} is random and independent of the true (value of the) variable x^*_{it} ($x_{it} = x^*_{it} + e_{it}$), and if it is also independent of the error in the model ($u_i + \varepsilon_{it}$), it is known (and straightforward to see) that the (total) least squares estimates $\hat{\alpha}_{TL}$ is biased downward in proportion to the ratio of the variance of the measurement error to the variance of the observed variable : $\lambda_{TL} = \sigma^2_{eTL}/\sigma^2_{xTL}$. It can be seen likewise that the between and within estimates in levels and the estimates in first differences are biased downward in the corresponding proportions λ_{BL}, λ_{WL}, λ_{TD}, λ_{BD}, λ_{WD}. These proportions can be derived from the first one λ_{TL} under the additional hypothesis that the measurement error e_{it} is serially uncorrelated. With this hypothesis one can show that :

$$\sigma^2_{eBL} = (1/T)\sigma^2_{eTL} \qquad \sigma^2_{eWL} = (1-1/T)\sigma^2_{eTL} \qquad \sigma^2_{eBL} = 2\sigma^2_{eTL}$$

$$\sigma^2_{eBD} = (2/(T-1))\sigma^2_{eTL} \qquad \sigma^2_{eWD} = 2(1-1/(T-1))\sigma^2_{eTL}$$

while the corresponding variances σ^2_{xBL}, ..., σ^2_{xWD} are observed. Since the variable x_{it} is in general positively (and strongly) autocorrelated, it is the case that λ_{WL} and λ_{TD} will be much larger than λ_{TL}, and λ_{BL} much smaller.

If we consider our estimates of the capital elasticity in the production function, it appears that for our three samples λ_{TD} and λ_{WD} should be about 50 times (at least) λ_{TL}, λ_{WT} about 10 times and λ_{BD} about 4 times, while λ_{BT} should be only of the order of 0.08 λ_{TL}. If we suppose that the measurement errors in the capital-labor ratio variable are such that $\lambda_{TL} = 0.03$ and if we take 0.30 as the true value of α, we would expect that $\hat{\alpha}_{BL} \sim 0.30$; $\hat{\alpha}_{TL} \sim 0.29$; $\hat{\alpha}_{BD} \sim 0.26$; $\hat{\alpha}_{WL} \sim 0.21$; $\hat{\alpha}_{TD}$ and $\hat{\alpha}_{WD}$ pratically nil. This corresponds indeed, at least approximately, to the actual pattern of our different estimates.

Rather than assuming the true values of α and λ_{TL}, it is also possible to estimate these values consistently (under all the hypotheses made for the measurement error and the regression model), by comparing any two of our estimates. Thus we find for the French sample : $\lambda_{TL} \sim 0.035$ and $\alpha \sim 0.31$ (only very slightly different from α_{TL}) by comparing the total and within estimates in levels ; or $\lambda_{TL} \sim 0.015$ and $\alpha \sim 0.30$ by comparing the total estimates in levels and in first differences ; or $\lambda_{TL} \sim 0.14$ and $\alpha \sim 0.35$ by comparing the total estimates in levels and the between estimates in differences ("long differences"). Though the estimated α are quite stable in these three computations, unfortunately the estimated shares of the measurement error variance λ_{TL} do vary a lot. Such differences of estimation are likely to be significant, pointing out the existence of further errors of specification (which probably concern our hypotheses about the measurement error as well as other aspects of the model).

ACKNOWLEDGEMENTS

This note corresponds to the last section of a longer paper published in French : "The laws of production are not what they were : an introduction to the econometrics of panel data" (Mairesse 1988). It has its origin in research pursued in collaboration with Zvi Griliches, to whom I am particularly grateful. I thank Jean-Marie Chanut for his excellent collaboration, and Annie and Bronwyn Hall for their first draft translation of the paper in English.

NOTES

1 - On the reasons why the between estimates may be biased and why the within estimates should be prefered, see the early works of Mundlak (1961) and Hoch (1962) in the context of the production function, and more recently Mundlak (1978).
2 - On the reasons why the within estimates of the production function may be biased and the reasons to prefer the between estimates, see Mairesse (1978) and Griliches-Mairesse (1984).
3 - Appendix 2 gives an illustration of this type of approach. See also Griliches-Hausman (1986).
4 - For such an interpretation in the context of the estimation of labor and investment demand equations on firm panel data, see Mairesse-Dormont (1985) ; see also Eisner (1978). In the context of our production function example, the within estimates (and the estimates in differences) of the elasticities of capital and scale might be interpreted as "short term" elasticities and the between estimates as "long term" elasticities. Thus one would intuitively expect that the former would be smaller than the latter.

REFERENCES

Eisner, R. (1978) : "Factors in Business Investment", National Bureau of Economic Research and Ballinger, Cambridge, USA.

Griliches, Z. and J. Hausman (1986) : "Errors in Variables in Panel data", Journal of Econometrics 31, pp. 93-118.

Griliches, Z. and J. Mairesse (1984) : "Productivity and R&D at the Firm Level", In Z. Griliches, ed., R & D, Patentsand Productivity, pp. 339-74. Chicago, University of Chicago Press.

Hoch, I. (1962) : "Estimation of Production Function Parameters Combining Time-Series and Cross-Section Data", Econometrica 30, pp. 34-53.

Mairesse, J. (1978) : "New Estimates of Embodied and Disembodied Technical Progress", Annales de l'INSEE 30-31, pp. 681-719.

Mairesse, J. and B. Dormont (1985) : "Labor and Investment Demand at the Firm level : A Comparison of French, German, and U.S. Manufacturing, 1970-79", European Economic Review 28 (1-2), pp. 201-31.

Mairesse, J. (1988) : "Les lois de la production ne sont plus ce qu'elles étaient : une introduction à l'économétrie des panels", La Revue Economique, 39, pp. 225-271.

Mairesse, J. et Z. Griliches (1988) : "Hétérogénéité et panels : y-a-t-il des fonctions de production stables ?", Essais en l'honneur de Edmond MALINVAUD, pp. 1010-1054, Paris, Economica et Editions EHESS.

Mundlak, Y. (1961) : "Empirical Production Function Free of Management Bias", Journal of Farm Economics 43, pp. 44-56.

Mundlak, Y. (1978) : "On the Pooling of Time-Series and Cross-Section Data", Econometrica 46, pp. 49-85.

Name Index